Praise for *Aging and Older Adulthood*

"The second edition of this textbook builds on the solid foundation of its predecessor and incorporates new research and developments in a user-friendly way. It is easy to tell that the author is passionate about teaching adult development and aging courses. In particular, I liked how Erber did not sacrifice historically important theories and studies in her book. Thus, I highly recommend this textbook as it represents an excellent introduction to a topic with increasing societal and global importance."

Manfred Diehl, Colorado State University

"Erber's *Aging and Older Adulthood* incorporates the latest research findings along with a compassionate, humanistic perspective. The new material on research applications to everyday problems of older adults, such as driving, shopping, and medical decision-making, will be of interest to those planning careers in aging as well as those planning on growing old."

Susan Kemper, University of Kansas

"This text has a number of features that will appeal to both instructors and students. For example, the author weaves a genuine attention to issues of diversity through each and every chapter. The author also includes realistic examples that demonstrate the significance of concepts to readers' own work with older adults, their own families, and even themselves, no matter their age. Most importantly, this text integrates three approaches that are essential to understanding aging: a biopsychosocial focus that spans key domains relevant to aging, a lifespan developmental perspective that views aging as a process rather than an event, and an empirical approach that recognizes the importance of theory and research in understanding and improving the experience of late life.

In sum, this text is a vibrantly written, comprehensive, and current introduction to aging and older adulthood, ideal for students from many disciplines who need to be prepared for their own aging and the aging of others around them."

Brian D. Carpenter, Washington University

To Lauren, Isaac, Megan, Rebecca, and Eli,
the future generation

Aging and Older Adulthood

SECOND EDITION

Joan T. Erber

Florida International University

⟨W⟩WILEY-BLACKWELL

A John Wiley & Sons, Ltd., Publication

This second edition first published 2010
© 2010 Joan T. Erber

Edition history: Thomson Wadsworth (1e, 2005)

Blackwell Publishing was acquired by John Wiley & Sons in February 2007. Blackwell's publishing program has been merged with Wiley's global Scientific, Technical, and Medical business to form Wiley-Blackwell.

Registered Office
John Wiley & Sons Ltd, The Atrium, Southern Gate, Chichester, West Sussex, PO19 8SQ, United Kingdom

Editorial Offices
350 Main Street, Malden, MA 02148-5020, USA
9600 Garsington Road, Oxford, OX4 2DQ, UK
The Atrium, Southern Gate, Chichester, West Sussex, PO19 8SQ, UK

For details of our global editorial offices, for customer services, and for information about how to apply for permission to reuse the copyright material in this book please see our website at www.wiley.com/wiley-blackwell.

The right of Joan T. Erber to be identified as the author of this work has been asserted in accordance with the UK Copyright, Designs and Patents Act 1988.

Library of Congress Cataloging-in-Publication Data

Erber, Joan T.
   Aging and older adulthood / Joan T. Erber. – 2nd ed.
      p.   cm.
   Includes bibliographical references and index.
   ISBN 978-1-4051-7005-5 (pbk. : alk. paper) 1.   Aging–Research. 2.   Older people–Research.
3.   Gerontology. I.   Title.
   HQ1061.E73 2010
   305.26–dc22

                                                      2009008321

A catalogue record for this book is available from the British Library.

Set in 11.5/13.5pt Bembo by SPi Publisher Services, Pondicherry, India
Printed in Singapore

1   2010

About the Author

Joan T. Erber received her PhD in Psychology from Saint Louis University, after which she completed a Post-Doctoral Fellowship in Aging and Development at Washington University in St. Louis. She is Professor of Psychology at Florida International University, where she was a recipient of a State University System Professorial Excellence Program (PEP) Award. Dr. Erber has extensive experience teaching undergraduate and graduate courses in adult development and aging and conducting research on the processes of aging. Her numerous publications focus on aging and memory and how age stereotypes influence our perceptions and evaluations of older adults. Her research findings, some of which were funded by grants from the National Institute on Aging, are published in scientific journals such as *Psychology and Aging, Journal of Gerontology: Psychological Sciences*, and *Experimental Aging Research*. Dr. Erber has served on editorial boards of journals that publish research on aging. She is a Fellow of the Gerontological Society of America (GSA), the Association for Psychological Science (APS), and the American Psychological Association (APA). She is a past president of the APA Division 20 (Adult Development and Aging).

Brief Contents

Contents

2   Theory and Method in Studying Aging and Older Adulthood   33

3   Biological Aging and Health   63

Integrated Themes in Aging and Older Adulthood

Integrated Examples of the Diversity Theme

Integrated Examples of the Environmental Influences on Aging Theme

Integrated Examples of the Applications to Everyday Life Theme

Preface and Acknowledgments

Thanks in large part to advances in medical science and technology, we are living in a society that is rapidly aging, and many of us will live well into the older adult years. With the baby boom generation entering older adulthood, the ranks of the older adult age group will swell all the more. It is no wonder that developmental researchers and practitioners are turning their attention to this important period of the adult life span.

My interest in aging and older adulthood began some time ago when, as an undergraduate psychology major at Washington University in St. Louis, I enrolled in a course on the psychology of aging taught by the late Dr. Robert Kleemeier. After earning my PhD degree in Psychology at Saint Louis University, I had the opportunity to return to Washington University as a postdoctoral fellow in the longstanding Aging and Development Program headed at that time by Dr. Jack Botwinick. This was the beginning of my career in the field of aging.

During my years at Washington University, including two as a postdoctoral fellow and additional time as a research associate, I conducted studies on aging and taught upper-division undergraduate courses in the psychology of aging and social gerontology. When I joined the psychology faculty of Florida International University, I continued teaching an undergraduate psychology of aging course as well as a graduate proseminar on adult development and aging.

As I was teaching these courses, the thought of writing a book on aging and older adulthood was always in the back of my mind and gradually my ideas began to take shape. The book I envisioned would focus on up-to-date theories and research on issues central to aging and older adulthood. Research findings are the basis for what we know and are the guiding force for what still needs investigating.

My book explains how research studies attempt to answer questions of both theoretical and practical importance as they relate to aging and older adulthood. I explain the hypotheses and findings of the studies I included in a manner that is not oversimplified but at the same time should be comprehensible to readers who may have limited experience in conducting research themselves. In some instances, I describe studies that report conflicting findings, and I offer suggestions to explain why the results of these studies may have differed. Such is the nature of science and my goal is to raise students' awareness of this. At the same time, I make every effort to tie together the research themes and findings so that they tell a coherent story.

What's New in This Edition?

Research on aging and older adulthood is an ongoing endeavor that is constantly leading to new ideas and fresh insights. The research I cite in this edition is substantially updated. New to this edition are:

- Updated content and references that reflect the latest research in the study of aging, such as neurological findings on brain structure and functioning as well as factors that influence cognitive functioning, health-care decision making, and social relationships.
- *Applying Research* boxes offer examples of current research findings that can be applied to the everyday lives of older adults.
- *Understanding Aging* boxes highlight phenomena such as "sundown syndrome" and "end-of-life desires," which provide a deeper insight into the aging process.
- *Questions to Consider* at the end of each chapter stimulate readers to think about how the information in the chapter relates to them personally.
- Finally, this edition introduces an end-of-book glossary with definitions of key terms from all 13 chapters.

Theoretical Models

An important goal I had in writing this book was to present a theoretical framework that would lend cohesion to the material covered. The Selective Optimization with Compensation Model and the Ecological Model are described in detail in the initial chapter. These two theoretical models are able to subsume research findings that indicate people experience changes as they age. At the same time, both models allow that aging can be a positive process with great potential for being successful. At the end of each chapter, I revisit these models, discussing how they relate to the topics covered. I do this to demonstrate that theoretical models are an effective mechanism for gaining a deeper understanding of what is known as well as what we still need to learn about aging and older adulthood.

Integrated Themes: Diversity, Environment, and Applications

I feel it is important to integrate themes into the text. This book provides integrated coverage of the following themes: diversity, environmental influences on aging, and applications to everyday life. These themes are outlined on the pages following the table of contents, with specific examples of where information occurs throughout the text.

Layout of the Book

Aging and Older Adulthood, second edition, has 13 chapters. This edition is slightly condensed, so the length is ideal for a textbook in one-semester undergraduate courses or for basic reading in a graduate proseminar. Although it is not essential, I suggest that for maximum clarity the chapters be covered in order.

Chapter 1 introduces the topic of aging and older adulthood and gives a brief history of how the study of aging got started and how age is defined. In addition, it includes basic updated information on the characteristics of the older adult population and the influences that are assumed to play a role in the aging process. At the end of this chapter, I introduce the two theoretical models, which will be revisited in the final section of each subsequent chapter.

Chapter 2 lays the groundwork for approaches taken in the study of aging and older adulthood as well as the advantages and disadvantages of the research designs that can be used. It also touches upon topics related to measurement, sampling, and ethics. Overall, this chapter contains basic information that is important for understanding and evaluating the research findings in substantive areas that are covered in the chapters that follow.

Chapter 3 includes topics of interest to both biologists and psychologists. How long can we expect to live, to what extent is biological aging under our control, and what can we do to insure a high quality of life in older adulthood? What kinds of changes in body systems can we expect with normal aging and how can we compensate for any changes that occur? In this edition, there is expanded coverage of age-related changes in the brain.

Chapter 4 focuses on recent theories and research on sensory, perceptual, and attentional processes. There is detailed information on vision and hearing with regard to changes that often occur with increasing age. Such information is basic to the understanding of age-related changes in memory, problem solving, and social processes, which are covered in subsequent chapters. Chapter 4 has been reorganized to achieve better flow and greater clarity.

Chapter 5 is devoted to memory, a subject of great interest not only to aging researchers but also to individuals who are aging. An entire book could be written about memory and aging, but this chapter touches upon theories about how memory works, what is characteristic of older adults' memory, and what people believe to be true about memory and aging.

Chapter 6, on intellectual functioning, includes scientific views of intelligence and how level of intelligence is determined. It describes which intellectual abilities decline and which are maintained with increasing age. In addition to psychometric approaches, the concept of intelligence is applied to older adults' competence in various aspects of their everyday lives.

Chapter 7 has an applied focus and explores thinking and problem solving in the everyday world. For example, how do older adults use their cognitive capabilities in dealing with real-world situations such as solving social, moral, and interpersonal dilemmas or giving advice to others who are facing such dilemmas? How do older adults go about making decisions about their own health care or perhaps about more mundane consumer purchases?

Chapter 8 covers theories about personality and coping. It also discusses how lay people (nonscientists) view the personality traits of older adults. In addition, it covers topics related to self-concept and personal control, including strategies people use that can affect their quality of life in older adulthood.

Chapter 9 examines social interaction and social ties in older adulthood. It describes prominent theories and discusses specific relationships (marital, intergenerational, grandparenthood, siblings, and friendship). Included in this chapter is the topic of elder abuse, a social problem that in recent years has been gaining the attention it deserves.

Chapter 10 highlights aspects of life planning that hold great significance for older adults: employment, retirement, and living arrangements. What is typical for the work life and exit from the workforce for today's older adults and what changes can we expect in the future? Also, what options do older adults have for living environments, and what are the advantages and disadvantages of each?

Chapter 11 discusses mental health services for older adults, the kinds of psychopathology that occur most frequently in the older adult population, and the types of therapy that are most effective in treating problems that older adults experience.

Chapter 12 covers topics related to death, dying, and loss, which are critical episodes within the experience of living, and which may be quite different for older adults in the future.

Chapter 13, new to this edition, is a final, brief statement that speculates on aging and older adulthood in the not too distant future. This chapter is intended to stimulate young adults to think about what the older years may be like when they enter that stage of life. It includes a section that describes views on the meaning of positive aging.

Student Learning Aids

Each chapter opens with a vignette that touches upon concepts that will be covered. Throughout the chapter, the reader is referred back to this vignette to demonstrate its connection to specific facts or theories. In addition, there are *Questions to Consider* at the end of the chapter that encourage readers to think about the meaning of the material. *Key Terms* in each chapter are printed in bold and listed at the end of each chapter. All key terms appear in the glossary at the end of the book. At the end of each chapter is a list of *Key Points* for review.

Instructor Materials

Aging and Older Adulthood, second edition, comes with an Instructor Manual written by the author, which is available at the book's website. For each chapter, the Instructor Manual summarizes the main ideas. In addition, there are suggested websites that instructors can consult to find up-to-date information on the subject matter covered in each chapter. There is also a test bank with questions listed in the order in which the information occurs in the chapter. The test bank is followed by a set of short answer questions, with suggested responses.

Acknowledgments

I wish to acknowledge those who played a role in my career in the field of aging and the integration of my knowledge and experience in the form of this book. My initial course with Dr. Kleemeier at Washington University whetted my interest in this field of study. Subsequently, I was privileged to conduct research and teach in the Aging and Development Program of Washington University in St. Louis with Dr. Martha Storandt and the now late Dr. Jack Botwinick. My years at Washington University were highly influential in my thinking and motivation for writing this book. More recently, the suggestions and encouragement I received from my former PhD adviser, the now late Dr. Donald H. Kausler, were invaluable. Writing a textbook is a major undertaking, and his early encouragement played an important role in my bringing the project to fruition. Also, I acknowledge my students, who provided me with their views of the aging process and for whom I hope this book will open the door to continued interest and pursuit of careers in the field.

On a more personal level, I am grateful to my late parents, who took a keen interest in my career and over the years willingly shared their insights on their own aging experiences. And I am indebted to Dr. Martha Storandt and the late Dr. Jack Botwinick, who allowed me the necessary flexibility during my time at Washington University so that I could pursue my career while raising my children.

I wish to express my gratitude to the following individuals, who reviewed the manuscript and whose constructive criticism and excellent feedback contributed to the quality of this book: Douglas Friedrich, University of West Florida; Louise Phillips, University of Aberdeen, UK; Helga Walz, University of Baltimore; Celia Wolk Gershenson, University of Minnesota.

Finally, I thank Christine Cardone, Editor at Wiley-Blackwell who encouraged me to produce the second edition of *Aging and Older Adulthood* and provided excellent professional guidance along the way.

1 Introduction to Aging and Older Adulthood

Chapter Overview

Close-ups on Adulthood and Aging

At age 65, Marge feels more energetic than she did when she was in her 30s. At her last routine medical checkup, her doctor told her that her blood pressure is close to that of the average 35-year-old and that she is in excellent physical shape for someone her age. Marge just retired from the office where she worked for more than 30 years. But rather than relaxing and occasionally playing cards with her friends, and instead of moving to a retirement community as many of her age peers plan to do, Marge has decided to complete the undergraduate degree she was on her way to earning 45 years ago. She just received her acceptance from the same college she attended decades earlier. Because it is in another state, she will live in the dormitory while she attends classes full-time. She intends to take full advantage of cultural events offered on campus and to make use of a new student recreation facility that just opened. Marge plans to learn a foreign language and to satisfy her wanderlust by spending her junior year abroad. She is a little concerned that the undergraduates might consider her an old lady, especially with her head of gray curls that she has no intention of altering. However, Marge is eager to mingle with these young adults and learn more about their generation.

The Study of Aging and Older Adulthood

What is aging and when does older adulthood begin? Later, we will look at ways of defining age and determining when older adulthood starts. However, from the beginning of time, people have wondered about aging, and there have been numerous myths about how to slow down the aging process and prolong life (Birren, 1996; Birren & Schroots, 2001). One such myth involved speculation about the miraculous healing powers of various substances in certain parts of the world. The Spanish explorer Ponce de Leon (1460–1521) discovered Florida while searching for a fountain of youth that supposedly would rejuvenate anyone who drank or bathed in its waters. People believed that waters or other magical substances would not only restore youth but perhaps guarantee immortality as well. Birren (1996) contends that the modern equivalent of the search for rejuvenation is evident in the pilgrimages people make to health spas and their willingness to follow dietary regimens touted as having special potency for insuring long and healthy lives. Being able to combat aging and extend life seems to have universal appeal, and many entrepreneurs have amassed great wealth by selling anti-aging products of questionable value to naive consumers (Olshansky, Hayflick, & Carnes, 2002).

History of the Scientific Study of Aging

Although interest in aging goes back centuries, the scientific study of aging and older adulthood is more recent. Several well-known researchers (Birren, 1996; Birren & Schroots, 2001; Schroots, 1996) portray how the scientific study of aging got started, and in the following paragraphs are some of the highlights they recount.

In 1835, Belgian mathematician and astronomer Adolphe Quetelet published a book describing the physical and behavioral characteristics of people at various stages of life. In 1884, Francis Galton, an Englishman trained in medicine and mathematics, sponsored a health exhibition in London, where he measured the physical and mental functions of more than 9,000 people ranging from 5 to 80 years of age. Subsequently, Galton's data were analyzed by several scientists. In 1922, G. S. Hall published a book entitled *Senescence: The Second Half of Life*, which summarized what was known about aging in fields such as physiology, medicine, anatomy, and philosophy. This book touched upon psychology as well.

In the latter part of the 19th century and early part of the 20th century, developmental psychologists focused mainly on children, perhaps because of the practical necessities of training teachers and providing child rearing advice to parents (Birren & Schroots, 2001). However, in 1933, Charlotte Buhler published a book on biological and psychological processes throughout the entire course of human development. Written in German, Buhler's book is considered by many to be the foundation of life-span developmental psychology.

The year 1927 saw the establishment of a scientific laboratory designed to study the psychology of aging systematically (Birren, 1996; Birren & Schroots, 2001; Schroots, 1996). This laboratory, based in the psychology department of Stanford University, was headed by Walter R. Miles, who initiated the Stanford Later Maturity Study. According to Birren's (1996) account, the main reason for establishing this laboratory was that men in California were having difficulty finding work because they were considered too old (Chapter 10 discusses the older worker). For more than five years, Miles conducted research on age and psychomotor functioning.

In 1939, E. V. Cowdry, a cytologist at Washington University in St. Louis, edited a classic volume entitled *Problems of Aging,* which went beyond the biomedical aspects of aging to include social, psychological, and psychiatric information. In 1941, the United States Public Health Service organized a conference on mental health and aging. That same year, the Surgeon General of the United States Public Health Service recruited Dr. Nathan W. Shock to head the newly established Section on Aging within the National Institutes of Health (NIH), which is an agency of the United States government.

In sum, by the late 1930s and early 1940s, the scientific study of aging was beginning to take shape in the United States, although research efforts were temporarily halted when the United Stated entered World War II. But when the war ended, interest in aging research was revived and several professional societies for the study of aging were established. In 1945, the Gerontological Society (subsequently renamed the Gerontological Society of America) was founded. The Gerontological Society and the newly established American Geriatric Society began publishing scientific journals on aging. The International Association of Gerontology, founded at about the same time, began to organize national and international conferences on the scientific study of aging.

In 1945, a small group of psychologists petitioned the American Psychological Association (APA) to approve a new division devoted to the study of development in the later years. Dr. Sidney L. Pressey of Ohio State University argued that a division on adulthood and later maturity would "be a natural complement to the present division on childhood and adolescence" and would "recognize that human development and change continue throughout the adult years and old age" (Pressey, 1945, as quoted by Birren & Stine-Morrow, 1999). The first reference to this new APA division (Division 20) appeared in the minutes of an initial organizational meeting held during the 1946 APA convention. Dr. Pressey was the first president of Division 20, initially named "The Division on Maturity and Old Age." At various times over the years Division 20 has been called "The Division on Maturity and Old Age," "The Division of Psychology of Adulthood and Old Age," and "The Division of Psychology of Adulthood and Later Maturity." In 1973, Division 20 was officially designated in the bylaws as the "Division of Adulthood and Aging," which remains its title to this day. Today, Division 20 has well over 1,000 members and plays an influential role in the American Psychological Association.

The NIH (mentioned earlier) is a federal agency that conducts in-house (intramural) research and also funds extramural research that is carried out at various colleges and universities. The NIH is composed of a number of institutes, and in 1974, the National Institute on Aging (NIA) was established with Dr. Robert Butler as its first director. As with the other institutes, the NIA oversees its own intramural research program and also funds research on aging and older adulthood conducted by scientists throughout the nation.

As the quantity of aging research has grown over the past 35 years, so has its quality. Today's researchers are increasingly aware of the complexities of studying aging. Methods for studying aging and older adulthood are covered in Chapter 2.

Geriatrics and Gerontology

Geriatrics and **gerontology** both refer to fields of study related to aging and older adulthood. Geriatrics is the branch of medicine specializing in the medical care and treatment of the diseases and health problems of older adults. Gerontology is the study of the biological, behavioral, and social phenomena from the point of maturity to old age.

Geriatrics and gerontology each have their own definitions, but sometimes it is difficult to make a clear distinction between research studies that fall into one category or the other. The term *geriatrics* is loosely applied to the study of the disease-related aspects of aging, while *gerontology* refers to the study of healthy older adults. Studies of older adults who have been diagnosed with a disease or live in nursing homes usually fall into the category of geriatric research, while studies of healthy community-living older adults fall into the category of gerontology research. However, as described in Chapter 3, most older adults, even those who live independently in the community, are not completely disease-free. Also, not all research conducted in institutional settings is geriatric. For example, studies on social processes among nursing home residents could fall into the category of gerontology.

Why Was the Study of Aging Neglected?

Why did the theories and scientific study of the psychology of aging and older adulthood lag behind those of child psychology? One likely reason was the common belief that development takes place primarily during childhood and adolescence. People assumed that by the time adulthood is reached, personality is formed and no further developmental change occurs.

Until relatively recently, a *two stages of life* viewpoint was prevalent in developmental psychology (Schroots, 1996). According to this perspective, both physical and psychological functions develop up to the point of maturity, after which there is a transition to aging that is characterized by a decline in functioning. From this perspective, there was little reason to study aging and older adulthood because development reaches a peak in young adulthood, only to be followed by a gradual and predictable downhill progression.

More recently, the assumption of uniform decline in functioning beyond young adulthood has been called into question. The view that universal decrement characterizes all functions as age increases is considered overly simplistic by contemporary researchers. Recognition that development is a complex process even at the older end of the age continuum has spurred greater interest in the study of aging and older adulthood. The life-span developmental perspective, which Chapter 2 describes in greater detail, postulates that development is an ongoing process in which the organism and the environment influence one another throughout life.

Another reason for the belated interest in the scientific study of aging and older adulthood is that, in earlier times, both the number and proportion of older adults was relatively small. Historically, old age was not unknown; even in early societies, some individuals lived into advanced old age. However, the number of such individuals was small and made up a tiny segment of the population. The phenomenal increase in the number of older adults during the 20th and into the 21st centuries in developed countries such as the United States is due to improvements in sanitation and nutrition, as well as to astounding medical advances. Chapter 3 discusses factors contributing to the expanding older adult population.

Reasons for Studying Aging and Older Adulthood

Interest in the study of aging and older adulthood has arisen from concerns of a scientific nature, but it also stems from those of a personal and/or practical nature (Woodruff-Pak, 1988).

Scientific reasons

Until recently, our knowledge about adult development has been based mainly on tests, observations, and interviews with young adults. From a scientific point of view, it is important to determine whether the findings of studies on these young adult samples apply to older adults. If the findings obtained with young adults do not generalize to older adults, then their scientific value may be limited. From a developmental standpoint, however, different findings for young versus older adults can have significant theoretical implications for the scientific understanding of basic developmental processes. For example, if young adults have better memory for recent events and older adults recall events that happened long ago better, it is possible that the two age groups differ in how they think.

Personal reasons

From a personal standpoint, knowledge about aging and older adulthood can give us insight into the changes that we are experiencing or can expect to experience. Such insight can be helpful when we plan specific events such as our own retirement or make decisions about how and where we want to live in our older adult years.

Interest in aging and older adulthood may also stem from our concern about others. Information on aging and older adulthood is useful when we cope with dilemmas involving older friends and family members. Perhaps you have noticed an older friend or relative seems to have difficulty hearing or understanding conversations. On the basis of information about age-related changes in hearing (see Chapter 4), what might be done to improve communication? Perhaps an older relative or friend is becoming forgetful. Is this a cause for concern? Chapter 5 covers age-related changes in memory, and Chapter 11 covers the cognitive symptoms of dementia that may be relevant to this concern. Perhaps an older friend or relative seems less outgoing than he or she was at an earlier time. Is this a cause for concern? Chapters 8, 9, and 10 include information on personality, social processes, and lifestyle that is relevant to such concerns.

Practical reasons

Information on aging and older adulthood is valuable from a practical standpoint because older adults are a rapidly growing segment of the population. Health service workers can anticipate increased contact with older adults. Physicians, nurses, psychologists, social workers, physical therapists, occupational therapists, speech therapists, paramedics, and medical support staff are likely to find much of their time spent serving older adults. Educators will have more older adult students in their college and university classes, so providing optimal conditions for older adult learning will be a greater concern in planning university communities. Those who work in business settings will also benefit from knowledge about the aging process because employees will probably remain in the paid labor force until later in life (see Chapter 10 for further discussion of work and retirement), and managers would do well to understand the needs and abilities of older workers. Those who work in housing management, real estate, and banking will have older adult clients. Furthermore, older adults will become ever more important as consumers of manufactured products, so more items will be designed for the older adult market. Those employed in architectural planning will profit from knowledge about aging when they design living environments for older adults.

Up to this point, we referred to *aging* and *older adulthood* without being specific about the meaning of these terms. First, we will look at several ways of defining age. Then we will turn to the question of when older adulthood actually begins and what we can expect when it does.

Defining Age and Older Adulthood

Aging begins at birth and continues throughout life. However, in this book the emphasis is on aging that takes place from the point of maturity (once adulthood is attained) and continues into the later years. Our main focus will be on older adulthood. However, in many instances, we obtain information about older adults by comparing them with individuals from young or middle-aged adult groups. Another way to study older adults is to follow the same individuals over time, observing how their patterns of behavior change as the years go by. Chapter 2 describes the advantages and disadvantages of each approach. Meanwhile, let's turn our attention to how age is defined.

Definitions of Age

Most of us think about age in terms of the number of birthdays we have celebrated.

Chronological age

Chronological age is measured in units of time (months or years) that have elapsed since birth. Marge, who was described at the beginning of the chapter, is 65 years old. Although merely an index of time, chronological age is the most common measure of age and we will return to it later. However, age can also be defined biologically, functionally, psychologically, and socially. Chronological age does not always accurately predict where a particular individual falls along each of these dimensions.

In serving as President of the United States in his 70s, Ronald Reagan would be considered functionally younger than most of his chronological age peers.

Biological age

Biological age has to do with where people stand relative to the number of years that they will live (that is, their longevity). One individual might live to the chronological age of 70, in which case he or she might be considered biologically old at the age of 65. Another might live to the age of 90, so he or she would probably not be considered biologically old at the age of 65 because another 25 years of life remain. Because we cannot usually predict the exact length of a particular individual's life with great accuracy, this way of conceptualizing biological age is speculative.

Another way to define biological age is in terms of the body's organ systems and physical appearance. With regard to these measures, how does one individual compare with others in the same chronological age group (that is, age peers)? Even within the same individual, different aspects of biological functioning and physical appearance must be evaluated separately because they can vary. For example, Marge is biologically younger than her age peers in terms of blood pressure and most likely cardiovascular functioning. However, her gray curls are a sign of physical aging that places her squarely with others in her chronological age group. Chapter 3 looks further at biological aging.

Functional age

Functional age has to do with a person's competence in carrying out specific tasks. As with biological age, functional age involves comparison with chronological age peers. An individual might be considered functionally young when his or her competence in some aspect of functioning compares favorably with that of chronological age peers. For example, an 85-year-old man who drives at night would be considered functionally younger than his chronological age peers who have given up driving at night. (As described in Chapter 4, visual changes that occur with increasing age can make nighttime driving difficult.) Keep in mind that functional capabilities, and thus functional age, can vary within the same individual (Siegler, 1995). For example, the 85-year-old man who drives at night may have severe arthritis that prevents him from walking around the block. Also, functional age is often evaluated in relation to a specific context. In many sports, an athlete might be considered functionally old at the age of 35. However, a 60-year-old chief operating officer of a large corporation or a 60-year-old President of the United States would not be considered functionally old.

Psychological age

Psychological age generally refers to how well a person adapts to changing conditions. To what extent can a person use cognitive, personal, or social skills to adjust to new circumstances or attempt new activities or experiences? Individuals who can adapt to changing conditions are considered psychologically younger than those who have difficulty doing so and prefer to do the same things over and over again. In short, we associate the ability to remain flexible with being psychologically young. Marge's desire to return to college and study abroad would make her psychologically younger than someone who continues to live in the same environment and has no desire to visit new places. Chapters 4 to 7 cover topics related to adaptation in the realm of perceptual, intellectual, and cognitive skills. Topics related to adaptation in the realm of personality, social skills, work, and mental health are covered in Chapters 8 to 11.

Social age

Social age has to do with the views held by most members of a society regarding what individuals in a particular chronological age group should do and how they should behave. For example, people may be expected to complete their education by their early 20s, marry by their late 20s or early 30s, have children by their early or mid 30s, and be established in a career by the age of 40. The individual who does not marry until age 40 and lives with his or her parents up to that time would be considered socially younger than the individual who leaves his or her parents' home at age 22 and marries at age 25. An individual who does not become a parent until age 42 would be considered socially younger than one who becomes a parent at age 28. Someone working in an entry-level job at age 40 would be considered socially younger than someone promoted to a middle-management level at age 40. Marge might be considered socially young because she plans to return to college and live in a dorm with students younger than she is.

Krueger, Heckhausen, and Hundertmark (1995) found that men and women ranging from 25 to 80 years of age had an especially positive view of a 45-year-old woman who conformed to their social expectations for middle adulthood: She had been married for 20 years, had two children aged 19 and 17, and worked as a department manager in a bank. In contrast, they had a negative view of a 45-year-old woman who had been married for only 5 years, had one young child, and worked at a low-level job in a bank with the hope of getting promoted. This woman had not accomplished what was expected by middle adulthood and she would probably be considered socially young for her chronological age and stage in life.

Each society has its own expectations about roles to play and goals to attain in young, middle, and older adulthood. Krueger et al.'s study was conducted in Berlin, Germany, and it remains to be seen whether the results would be the same if a similar study were to be conducted in the United States. Neugarten (1977) contended that people use a social clock to evaluate whether their own progress or the progress of others is "on-time" or "off-time." Later on, however, Neugarten placed less emphasis on a social clock. She argued that in the United States age was becoming increasingly irrelevant as a predictor of needs, lifestyle, and accomplishments (Binstock, 2002).

What Is Older Adulthood?

Although there are numerous ways to define age, we usually fall back on chronological markers when we judge whether someone has entered older adulthood or even middle age. When does middle age end and older adulthood begin?

Subjective age

The chronological age people select to mark the onset of middle and older adulthood seems to be colored by their own age or stage of adulthood. Individuals in their 20s often think middle age starts in the 30s and that older adulthood starts in the 50s but certainly no later than the 60s. In contrast, individuals in their 60s consider themselves to be middle-aged. As adults become older chronologically, the gap between their chronological age and their subjective age becomes wider (Goldsmith & Heiens, 1992) – they feel younger than they are. Furthermore, the gap between subjective age and actual age is wider for middle-aged and older adult women than it is for middle-aged and older adult men (Montepare & Lachman, 1989).

The magic age of 65

There is no set rule about when an individual is considered to be an older adult. Nonetheless, the age of 65 has come to signify the official age of entry into older adulthood. The association of age 65 with the start of older adulthood can be traced to the Social Security system that the U.S. government established in 1935. Among other functions, Social Security (discussed in more detail in Chapter 10) was intended to provide economic security in the form of a monthly pension to older adults when they retired from the paid workforce. Social Security in the United States was modeled after the German retirement system, which had designated 65 as the age when citizens were eligible for pension benefits upon retirement. Similarly, workers in the United States became eligible for Social Security pension benefits once they reached 65, so 65 became an arbitrary marker of older adulthood. However, as one step to insure the Social Security system remains financially solvent, the government is gradually raising the age at which workers become eligible to draw full pension benefits from 65 to 67. Time will tell whether the chronological age associated with entry into older adulthood will be pushed up as the age of eligibility for Social Security benefits increases.

Categories of older adulthood

A great deal of information in this book is about older adults as a group, and many references are made to averages. General statements about older adults are one way of organizing what we know. At the same time, keep in mind that averages do not describe every individual in the group.

(a)   (b)

There are great individual differences among older adults in many aspects of functioning. Some are physically active and others have physical limitations.

It would be a mistake to assume that once a person reaches age 65, he or she becomes a member of a homogeneous group. People in any age group are diverse – they have what psychologists call individual differences, or *interindividual variability*. Among people aged 65 and older (65+) there is interindividual variability on almost every possible measure. Some 65-year-olds are fully retired from the paid labor force, while others work full-time. Some 75-year-olds suffer from incapacitating health problems, while others lead active lives, traveling or participating in walking groups or marathon races. Some 80-year-olds have difficulty with hearing or with memory, while others can hear a pin drop and never forget a name. Study after study has shown that individual differences are even greater in the older age group than they are in young adult or middle-aged groups.

One way to acknowledge the variability in individuals who are aged 65 and over (65+) is to segment older adulthood into categories based on chronological age: **young-old** (ages 65–74), **old-old** (ages 75–84), and **oldest-old** (ages 85+). Compared with individuals in the old-old and oldest-old categories, those in the young-old category have greater physical vigor and are less likely to suffer from significant sensory or cognitive decline. In fact, many young-old adults differ very little from adults in late middle age. In general, old-old adults experience more of what are considered to be age-related changes in sensory, perceptual, and cognitive functioning. Compared with individuals in the young-old and old-old groups, individuals in the oldest-old group have the highest rate of health problems and the greatest need for services.

Many researchers (for example, see Hooyman & Kiyak, 2008; Quadagno, 2008) use this three-tier categorization of older adulthood, and we will refer to it throughout this book. Even so, keep in mind that there are individual differences within each category. For example, some people in the oldest-old group are healthier and more active than people in the young-old group.

The three-tier categorization of chronological age is useful for some purposes, but the fact is that chronological age is an **organismic variable**. As Chapter 2 describes further, an organismic variable cannot be manipulated or controlled. We may find that adults who fall into a certain chronological age range tend to behave in particular ways, solve problems using a certain type of strategy, or express certain opinions. Even so, we cannot conclude that chronological age causes them to behave, solve problems, or think as they do. Age is mixed up, or confounded, with other variables, such as educational exposure and life experiences. Either separately or in combination with age, these variables could be the basis for the behavior, problem-solving strategies, or opinions held by individual members of a particular age group.

Terms for the 65+ age group

A number of terms refer to individuals who are age 65 and older. The term *older adults* has already been used in this chapter. *Old* and *elderly* are used more often to refer to individuals in the old-old and oldest-old groups. Although there is no firm rule, *elderly* often refers to older adults who are in frail health or reside in institutional settings such as nursing homes. The terms *retired* and *retired Americans* are often used but they are not always appropriate because some individuals in the 65+ age group work part- or even full-time. Other terms include *the aged*, *golden-agers*, *older Americans*, and *senior citizens*. Some gerontology researchers jokingly refer to older adults as *chronologically challenged*, *chronologically gifted*, and *chronologically advantaged*.

Older adults are sensitive to the terms people use to describe their age group. Many of them feel that some terms are less favorable than others. For example, a label such as *the aged* might be considered less favorable than *senior citizens*, which would be regarded as less favorable than *older adults* (Kite and Wagner, 2002). In general, older adults prefer that unfavorable terms be avoided because they fear they will become victims of ageism.

Ageism

Ageism refers to a set of ideas and beliefs that are associated with discriminatory attitudes directed toward older adults (Quadagno, 2008). It implies negative beliefs, or stereotypes, about older adults as a group. Ageism can manifest itself in low expectations about an older adult's cognitive capabilities or in negative beliefs about an older adult's personal or social capabilities. According to Palmore (2001), ageism is the third greatest "ism" in American society, following racism and sexism. Unlike racism and sexism, however, all of us could become targets of ageism if we live long enough.

Although ageism connotes discriminatory attitudes, people's views of older adults are not uniformly negative. Hummert (1990) found that young adult college students hold multiple stereotypes about older adults, some negative (for example, "set in ways" and "old-fashioned") but others positive (for example, "generous" and "loving"). Also, many people recognize the diversity among older adults with regard to personal characteristics (Hummert, Garstka, Shaner, & Strahm, 1994). In some instances, people credit older adults with a higher degree of desirable traits such as being responsible, understanding, and cheerful (Erber & Szuchman, 2002). However, people often stereotype older adults as warm but incompetent, and the view that older people are sweet but feeble has been found not only in the United States, but also in Belgium, Costa Rica, Hong Kong, Japan, Israel, and South Korea (Cuddy, Norton, & Fiske, 2005). Thus, evidence of ageism is not confined to Western countries. Relatedly, a subtle form of ageism is evident in *compassionate stereotypes*, which foster a view of older adults as helpless and in need of advocacy (Revenson, 1989). Quadagno (2008) refers to the *new ageism*, which is an overly solicitous attitude toward older adults, including an assumption that important life-changing decisions that affect their lives should be made without consulting them.

Because of the negative effect it can have, ageism should be carefully monitored. Perhaps ageism will decline as the older population continues to grow in size. Discussion of topics related to attitudes toward older adults can be found throughout this book (see Chapters 5 to 8 and 10).

Demographic Profile of Older Americans

Demography is the scientific study of populations that focuses on broad groups within a specific population or sometimes across different populations. Demographers study past and present population trends and characteristics, including size, growth, and migration patterns. They also study population characteristics such as age, gender, marital status, living arrangements, health, educational level, economic status, and geographical distribution. Demographic descriptions are usually expressed in terms of statistical measures such as the mean (average), the median (50% of the population is above and the other 50% below the median), or the percentage of a specific group or subgroup in the population that possesses a particular characteristic. These measures provide an overall picture of a population.

Global Considerations and Demographic Transition

At present, there is a larger proportion of older adults (65+) in the more developed regions of the world and a smaller proportion in the less developed regions. Table 1.1 shows the proportion of the older population in Africa, North America, Latin America and the Caribbean, Asia, Europe, and Oceania.

Demographers have described several distinct stages of transition in the aging of populations (Myers, 1990; Myers & Eggers, 1996). Populations in agriculturally based preindustrialized societies are characterized by a high birthrate and a high death rate. The high birthrate is due mainly to low use or availability of

Table 1.1   *Percentage of population aged 65+ by continent*

Continent	% of population aged 65+
Africa	3
North America	12
Latin America and Caribbean	6
Asia	6
Europe	16
Oceania	10

Source: Population Reference Bureau, 2007.

birth control methods. The high death rate stems largely from poor sanitary conditions, poor nutrition, and lack of medical technology. Such societies consist of a large proportion of younger members and a small proportion of older ones. As societies become more industrialized and technologically advanced, they enter a second stage of transition in which the death rate declines due to better control of infectious and parasitic diseases, but the birthrate remains high. The size of the population grows but younger members still predominate. For societies in the third stage of demographic transition, the rate of growth is slower because the birthrate declines, which results in an increased proportion of older persons. Societies in the fourth and final stage of transition are characterized by extremely low birthrates and death rates, at least into advanced old age. Population growth is minimal, and the proportion of people in the various age categories is similar. Few babies are born, but those who are will have a good chance of living into old age.

The increase in the older population in developed countries such as the United States has been a major force in the expansion of interest in the study of aging and older adulthood. Demographic information is crucial because it can assist us in recognizing the needs of the older age group. For example, as the age distribution of a population shifts, changes in the types of living environments that are available may be necessary. As described in Chapter 10, there may be an increased need for housing that offers services such as meals on the premises and van transportation. Also, information about demographic characteristics of the older adult population is useful when investigators want to recruit a sample of research participants who are representative of the older adult population. Further discussion of sampling strategies appears in Chapter 2.

Demographic information is essential for understanding past and present population characteristics, but it can also be used to project future trends in the size and growth of a particular segment of the population. The projections that demographers make may not be exact, but they offer guidelines about what the likely size and characteristics of the population will be in the future. The population of primary concern for those who study aging and older adulthood is the group age 65 and over.

Number and Proportion of Older Adults

The high birthrate in the **baby boom years** (1946–1964) and advances in medical care in the United States have long been expected to lead to an increased number of people in the 65+ age category. This projection is fast becoming a reality. The first wave of baby boomers celebrated their 60th birthday in 2006, and they will enter the 65+ age category in 2011. The baby boom generation will continue to swell the ranks of the 65+ age group through the year 2030. The United States is undergoing a silent revolution: the aging of its population.

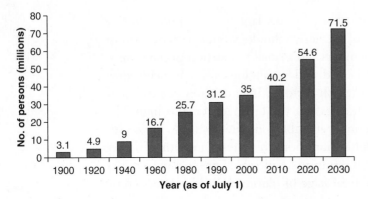

Figure 1.1 *Number of persons aged 65+ in the United States, 1900–2030.*
Source: A Profile of Older Americans (2007).

Figure 1.1 shows how many older adults aged 65+ lived in the United States at several different points in time. Note that, in 1900, the number was a relatively small 3.1 million. By 2000, the number had increased more than tenfold to 35 million. In 2010, there will be 40.2 million, and projected estimates for the future are for 54.6 million older adults (65+) by 2020 and 71.5 million older adults (65+) by 2030 (*A Profile of Older Americans*, 2007).

To further illustrate the growth of the older adult population: In 2006, more than 2.2 million Americans celebrated their 65th birthday; in the same year, approximately 1.8 million persons 65+ died. Census estimates showed an annual net increase of more than 500,000 persons 65+ (*A Profile of Older Americans*, 2007).

Not only is the number of older adults growing, but so is their proportion of the U.S. population. In 1900, older adults (65+) made up 4.1%, but as of 2006 they made up 12.4% of the population (one in every eight Americans). By 2030, the proportion of older adults (65+) is expected to surge to 20% of the United States population (*A Profile of Older Americans*, 2007).

The projection that older adults will make up approximately 20% of the U.S. population by the year 2030 is based on several trends. First, the entire baby boom generation (born between 1946 and 1964) will have entered older adulthood by 2030 and this will swell the sheer number of people in that age group. Second, with the decline in birthrate after 1964, fewer additions were made to the younger segment of the population. A low birthrate contributes to the general aging of the population because there are fewer babies to offset the large number of people entering the older adult age category. If the birthrate were to increase significantly in the future, the number of older adults in the U.S. population would be more balanced by the youngest members. This would reduce the proportion of the population in the older adult age category.

Population pyramid
A **population pyramid** is a bar graph that illustrates how a population is distributed in terms of both age and gender.

The population pyramids in Figure 1.2 show the proportion, or percentage, of the total U.S. population falling into five-year age categories in 1900, 1970, 1995, and 2030. The youngest age group (<5) is at the base of the pyramid, with increasingly older five-year ages in the segments above. The group at the top of each pyramid includes those in the 85+ age category. Population pyramids

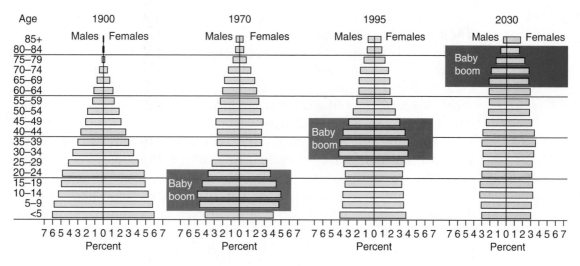

Figure 1.2 *Population pyramids for the United States in 1900, 1970, 1995, and 2030 (projected).* *Source*: U.S. Census Bureau (2002).

represent proportions of a population not only by age but also by gender. The left side of each population pyramid represents the proportion of males in each age cohort, and the right side represents the proportion of females.

The shape of the graph in 1900 suggests why the term *population pyramid* came into use. Note that, in 1900, each five-year category is slightly smaller in proportion than the one immediately beneath it, and the proportion of males and females in each age category is almost identical. The resulting shape is a pyramid.

By 1970, the graph bears much less resemblance to a pyramid, but its shape reflects several important features of the U.S. population. First, a smaller base is due to the decline in birthrate. Also, a low birthrate between the years 1925 and 1940 (possibly in response to the social and economic conditions of the Great Depression and the beginning of World War II) gives the graph a constricted middle, indicating that the proportion of the population between the ages of 30 and 45 is relatively small. Third, compared to 1900, a larger proportion of the population now falls into groups aged 65 and over. In 1995, the shape of the graph is even less like a pyramid than it was in 1970. The birthrate remains steady, and the older (65+) age groups are gaining in proportion.

The shape of the population pyramid projected for the year 2030 is based on a number of assumptions, one of which is birthrate. The youngest five-year segments of the graph are all similar in proportion, which indicates a projected age structure with a constant birthrate that is slightly lower than it was in 1995. At the same time, there is a dramatic increase in the population aged 65+ because by 2030 the baby boomers have all entered their older adult years. The most notable increase in proportion is for the oldest-old (85+) age category. Overall, the graph projected for the U.S. population in 2030 resembles a beanpole rather than a pyramid.

The aging of the older adult population

In developed countries, the older population is itself showing signs of aging. In the U.S., a 43% increase is projected for the oldest-old (85+) age group: In the year 2000 there were 4.2 million but by 2010 there will be 6.1 million people aged 85 and older, attributable in large part to aging baby boomers (Stone, 2006). An additional figure of interest is that, in 2006, there were 73,674 persons aged 100 or more (0.19% of the population). This represents a 97% increase from the 1990 figure of 37,306 (*A Profile of Older Americans*, 2007).

There is little question that in the United States, and most likely in other developed countries, older adults will be an even more important force than they are today. Now that we have covered present and future trends in the older population, let's take a closer look at some characteristics of this growing segment of the U.S. population.

A Snapshot of the Older Population

Populations can be described in terms of characteristics such as gender, marital status, living arrangements, health, level of education, economic status, and geographical distribution. What can be said about the older adult (65+) population in the United States with regard to these dimensions?

Gender

The population pyramids in Figure 1.2 show the proportion of males in each age group on the left and the proportion of females on the right. The symmetrical shape of the population pyramid in 1900 indicates a balanced proportion of males and females in all age categories. In the pyramid projected for 2030, note that there is a greater proportion of females than males in the groups aged 65 and older.

Not surprisingly, the proportion of men and women in the older-adult age group is reflected in their numbers. In the United States in 2006, there were 21.6 million women but only 15.7 million men aged 65 and older, with a ratio of 138 women for every 100 men. This gender gap widens from the young-old to the oldest-old age groups – there were 114 women for every 100 men in the 65–69 group, but 213 women for every 100 men in the 85+ age group (*A Profile of Older Americans*, 2007).

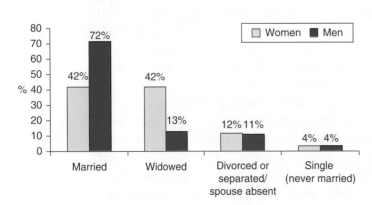

Figure 1.3 *Marital status of older (65+) men and women.*
Source: *A Profile of Older Americans* (2007).

Marital status

In 2006, 72% of older men but only 42% of older women aged 65+ were married. Why are older men more likely than older women to be married?

Men usually marry women younger than themselves. Also, as Chapter 3 describes, women tend to live longer than men. As a result, married women lose their spouses more often than married men do. Another reason more older men are married is that men who lose their spouses are more likely to remarry than are women who lose their

Men usually marry women younger than themselves. As a result, married women lose their spouses more often than married men do.

spouses. In 2006, 42% of older (65+) women were widows (that is, they had lost their spouses and not remarried), whereas only 13% of older men were widowers. There were more than four times as many older widows (8.6 million) as there were older widowers (2.0 million) (*A Profile of Older Americans*, 2007).

In 2006, only 4% of older (65+) men and 4% of older (65+) women fell into the never-married category. However, 12% of older (65+) women and 11% of older (65+) men (a combined total of 23% of persons 65+) were divorced or separated. This figure is substantially higher than the 5.3% of the older population that was divorced or separated in 1980 (*A Profile of Older Americans*, 2007).

Living arrangements

The larger proportion of women in the older age group, combined with gender differences in marital status, has implications for living arrangements. In 2006, more than half (54.8%) of older (65+) noninstitutionalized adults were living with a spouse. However, 72% of 65+ men (10.9 million) but only 42% of 65+ women (8.5 million) lived with a spouse (*A Profile of Older Americans*, 2007). Note also that 40% of older women but only 19% of older men were living alone (*A Profile of Older Americans*, 2007).

The proportion of older (65+) adults who reside in nursing homes and other institutional settings at any given point in time has been a relatively stable 4–5% over a number of years. In 1980, approximately 4.8% of older (65+) adults lived in nursing homes, and in 1990 this figure was approximately 5% (*A Profile of Older Americans*, 1996). In 2006, 4.4% of Americans aged 65+ lived in institutional settings, but this figure increases dramatically with age – 1.3% of people aged 65–74, 4.4% of people 75–84, and 15.4% of people aged 85+ live in institutional settings (*A Profile of Older Americans*, 2007). Approximately 35% of nursing home residents are aged 75–84 and another 37% are 85+ (Mitty, 2006). Given the anticipated

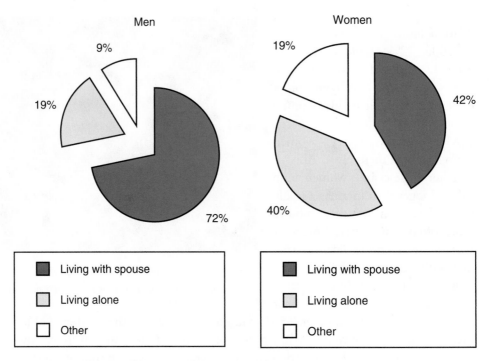

Figure 1.4 *Living arrangements of older (65+) adults.*
Source: A Profile of Older Americans (2007).

increase in the number of people living into the old-old (75–84) and especially the oldest-old (85+) age categories, it is not surprising that the nursing home and assisted-living industry has been growing. With regard to gender, approximately 62% of nursing home residents are women and the majority (86%) are European American (Mitty, 2006). Nursing homes and assisted-living facilities will probably play a needed role as more people live into the old-old and oldest-old age categories, especially for older adults who have been living alone in the community.

Racial and ethnic composition
In 2006, approximately 19% of persons aged 65+ were members of minority groups as follows: 8.3% African Americans; 6.4% of Hispanic origin; 3.1% Asian or Pacific Islanders; less than 1% Native Americans or Native Alaskans; approximately 0.6% of persons 65+ identified themselves as being of two or more races (*A Profile of Older Americans*, 2007).

Health
Many older adults are in good health. In 2006, 39% of noninstitutionalized older adults (65+) assessed their health as excellent or very good (compared to 65% for people aged 18–64). However, the percentage of older adults in minority groups who rated themselves as being in excellent or very good health was lower than the percentage of European American older adults who did so (*A Profile of Older Americans*, 2007).

Even so, most older adults have at least one chronic health condition and health becomes a greater concern as people progress from their young-old to old-old to oldest-old years. Limitations on activities because of chronic health conditions increase with age. Figure 1.5 shows the percentage of young-old, old-old, and oldest-old persons with limitations in activities of daily living (ADL) (*A Profile of Older Americans*, 2007). (More detailed discussion of daily functioning and health appears in Chapter 3.)

As a group, the old-old and oldest-old are more in need of

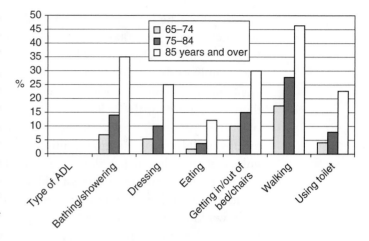

Figure 1.5 *Percentage of persons with limitations in activities of daily living (ADL) by age group.*
Source: *A Profile of Older Americans* (2007).

help compared with the young-old. With regard to gender, older men tend to be better off than older women in terms of physical health (Perls, 2004b). While women live longer than men do on average, older women are more frequently afflicted with chronic health problems, such as arthritis and osteoporosis (thinning of the bones), that restrict their mobility. Furthermore, older women are more likely than older men to live alone, so older women are apt to experience greater difficulty if they do suffer from limitations in functioning.

Education

Older adults of today have achieved higher levels of education compared to older adults in the past. Between 1970 and 2006, the proportion of older adults who completed high school increased from 28% to 77.5%. However, the percentage of older adults who completed high school varies by race and ethnic background as follows: European Americans (80.4%); Asian and Pacific Islanders (70.1%); African Americans (55.1%); and Hispanic Americans (39.7%). As of 2006, approximately 19.5% of adults aged 65+ had a bachelor's degree or more (*A Profile of Older Americans*, 2007). In the future, older adults will have even more formal education than they do today.

Economic status

People once assumed that older adults in the United States were poor. In fact, however, the economic status of older adults has improved, in part due to the Social Security system established by the federal government in 1935 that was designed to provide a base level of economic security for retired older Americans. (Social Security is discussed further in Chapter 10.) The rate of poverty among older adults dropped from 35% in 1959 to 9.4% (3.4 million people aged 65+) in 2006 (*A Profile of Older Americans*, 2007), which declined from the 10.1% poverty rate in 2005. The majority of older adults do not live in poverty and some are affluent. However, in 2006, 3.4 million older adults were below the poverty level (in 2006, guidelines for poverty level were $9,800 for a family of one and $13,200 for a family of two), and an additional 2.2 million older adults were classified as "near-poor" (income between poverty level and 125% of this level). However, there is a gender gap: In 2006, older women had a poverty rate of 11.5%, whereas older men's poverty rate was only 6.6% (*A Profile of Older Americans*, 2007). Certain groups of older adults (widows, minorities, and the very old) remain especially vulnerable to falling below the poverty level (Clark, 2006).

The future economic status of older adults holds much uncertainty. Older adults will be more educated, so their incomes will probably be higher during their working years. However, if young and middle-aged adults do not make financial plans for retirement, they may have to work to older ages than today's older adult generation did. As described in Chapter 10, working to older ages is not unreasonable because older people are healthier now than they were in the past and many jobs are less physically demanding today than they were in the past.

Geographical distribution

In 2006, about half (51.4%) of Americans aged 65+ lived in nine states (*A Profile of Older Americans*, 2007): California (3.9 million); Florida (3.0 million); New York (2.5 million); Texas (2.3 million); Pennsylvania (1.9 million); Illinois, Ohio, Michigan, and New Jersey each had more than 1 million.

Another way to view the geographical distribution of older adults in the United States is to calculate their proportion by dividing the number of older adults (65+) by the total number of people in the state. In 2006 (*A Profile of Older Americans*, 2007), the population of eight states consisted of 14% or more older adults: Florida (16.8%); West Virginia (15.3%); Pennsylvania (15.2%); North Dakota (14.6%); Iowa (14.6%); Maine (14.6%); South Dakota (14.2%); Rhode Island (13.9%).

Relocation

There is a popular belief that once they retire, older adults pack up and move to warmer climates. In general, however, older adults are less likely than other age groups to change residences. From 2005 to 2006, only 4.1% of older adults moved compared to 15.1% of the population under the age of 65. Most older movers (55.3%) stayed in the same county and 82.5% remained in the same state. Only 17.5% of older movers relocated out of state (*A Profile of Older Americans*, 2007). Many older out-of-state movers migrate to locales with warmer climates such as Arizona, Florida, and North Carolina, but some movement is related to a desire for less congestion and more attractive physical environments (Longino, 2003). Retired older adults who relocate are generally "sixty-something," enjoy relatively good health and are able, both physically and financially, to enjoy the recreational and social amenities in their new communities. As described more fully in Chapter 10, however, some of these retirees return to their states of origin when they enter the old-old category (75–84) and begin to experience economic and physical dependency.

At that point, they want to be closer to the family members they left behind when they moved to distant retirement communities in their young-old years.

In sum, the older population in the United States is growing, and this growth is most concentrated in the oldest-old (85+) age group. Older adults are healthier, more educated, and economically better off now than in the past, but those in the oldest-old (85+) age group will probably need some extra services. Many older adults continue to live in the same location even after they retire, but a minority relocate, often to warmer climates. However, some return to their home states when they become widowed or need help from family members. As the characteristics of the older population change, demographers will undoubtedly need to reevaluate the description of this age group.

Developmental Influences and Issues

Many factors influence us over our lifetimes, and developmental investigators have divided these into three categories: **normative age-graded influences**, **normative history-graded influences**, and **nonnormative life events**. Also, two issues have been prominent in the study of development. One is the relative influence of nature versus nurture, and the other is the question of whether developmental change is quantitative or qualitative.

Influences on Development

As we develop, all of us are influenced by events that happen to almost all people at a certain age or stage of life. We are also influenced by events or the environmental climate that surrounds us. Finally, our development may be influenced by events that are unexpected and do not happen to everyone.

Normative age-graded influences

Normative age-graded influences are biological or environmental events and occurrences that are associated with chronological age. Examples of normative age-graded influences that are closely related to biology are puberty and menopause in women. Under the usual circumstances, puberty and menopause occur within certain age ranges during the course of development.

Normative age-graded influences can also be specific to the society in which people live. Many such influences have to do with socialization practices within a particular culture. Examples are the ages when most people go to school, marry, and retire from their jobs. In American society, schooling is normative for people between the ages of 5 and 18 and is becoming normative for people aged 18–22 (college) as well. First-time marriage is normative in the 20s or 30s, and retirement is normative in the 60s.

Social age, described earlier in this chapter, is tied to the expectations a society has for its members, as is the idea of being "on time" in development. In contemporary

American culture, there is greater flexibility in the age at which certain events are expected to occur. Schooling from ages 5 to 18 remains a normative age-graded influence, but it is becoming more common for adults of all ages to seek opportunities for higher education. Thus, the chronological age of college students is broader than it was in previous decades. Also, while it may still be normative for people to marry in their 20s or early 30s, more people are postponing marriage as well as childbearing to their later 30s and 40s. Retirement in the 60s (especially at the age of 65) has been a normative age-graded event, but in recent years, more people are retiring at younger or older ages.

Normative history-graded influences

Normative history-graded influences also play a role in development. These influences can result from an event, or they can represent a more gradual evolution of societal structure. Examples of normative history-graded influences include epidemics, wars, and the state of the economy such as depression, recession, or prosperity.

Also included in the normative history-graded category are sociocultural influences such as child-rearing philosophy and practices, educational philosophy and practices, gender-role expectations, and attitudes toward sexuality and sexual behavior. Changes in these influences can be the triggered by historical events such as war, disease, or the introduction of new technology. In the1940s when men were fighting in World War II, it became more acceptable for women to join the paid labor force. In the mid to late 1980s, the AIDS epidemic led to increased conservatism in attitudes toward sexual behavior. In the 1990s, the computer revolution changed the way people communicate and obtain information. Instead of visiting the local library or shopping mall, people simply log onto a personal computer. Cell phones have made it possible to be mobile but remain in touch.

A history-graded influence of great importance for older adults is the increased availability of health care, which is largely attributable to the federal health insurance program for older adults (Medicare) initiated by the U.S. government in 1965 (see Chapter 3). In 2005, the introduction of Medicare Part D offered new insurance benefits for prescription medication (see http://www.medicare.gov).

Nonnormative life events

Development can also be influenced by nonnormative life events, which do not affect all or even most members of society. The influence of nonnormative life events is not necessarily associated with chronological age or with historical time, but nonetheless such events can play an important role in the development of an individual (Baltes & Smith, 1995). Examples of nonnormative life events include being diagnosed with a rare illness, being involved in an accident, winning the lottery, becoming divorced from one's spouse, and being either downsized or promoted at work.

Normative age-graded influences, normative history-graded influences, and nonnormative life events have been described separately but they do not exist in a vacuum. In reality, they can affect one another. Thus, history-graded influences may interact with a person's age and stage of development. For example, the history-graded influence of the Vietnam War had quite a different effect on young Americans of draftable age than it did on middle-aged and older Americans who were not sent off to fight. The normative history-graded influence of the stock market crash of 1929 and the economic depression that followed had a direct impact on those responsible for supporting their families. It had a lasting effect on many young adolescents who were forced to drop out of school and get jobs to help support their families. For many, future work careers were shaped by this historical economic event. The computer revolution and resulting dependence of our present-day society on computer use has impacted people of various ages differently. Computers are an integral part of our modern educational system, so children and young adults of today are highly computer-literate and at ease with using computers to obtain information. In contrast, today's older adults did not use computers in school and many did not use computers at their jobs. The majority of today's older adults kept their financial records in a notebook. They were accustomed to receiving passbooks for savings accounts at their banks, they consulted a card catalogue to find books at the library, and they made purchases in small neighborhood stores that offered personal service. As described in Chapter 10, older adults can adapt to computers, but unlike younger adults, they remember a time when everything was done without them.

Nonnormative life events are not, by definition, associated with age. Even so, their influence on development may depend upon the age when they occur. Winning the lottery at age 20 could have quite a different influence on development compared with winning the lottery at age 60. Divorce, which would probably be considered a nonnormative life event despite its increasing occurrence, is likely to have a very different effect if it occurs at age 25 than if it occurs at age 65.

Even though American society is more flexible today than it was in the past, it is still probable that an event considered a normative age-graded influence at one stage of life would be considered nonnormative if it occurred at a time of life when it is unexpected or uncommon. Thus, retirement from the paid labor force is a normative age-graded influence at age 65 but a nonnormative life event if it occurs at age 35. Becoming a first-time father is a normative age-graded influence at age 30, but it might be considered a nonnormative life event if it occurs at age 70.

In sum, all three types of influence play a role in development both separately and together. Because of their complexity, a complete understanding of how they affect us would actually require the cooperative efforts of psychologists, sociologists, biologists, and social historians (Baltes & Smith, 1995).

Issues in the Study of Aging

Two issues have been important themes in developmental psychology and each holds special meaning for the study of aging and older adulthood. One is the relative influence of **nature and nurture** in the aging process. Another is whether any differences that exist between people of various ages can be characterized as **quantitative or qualitative differences**.

Nature and nurture

In the study of development, there is often concern with the relative influence of nature (that is, hereditary, genetic, and biological factors) and nurture (that is, environmental factors and life experience). Early controversies revolved around the question of whether human development is attributable to nature or to nurture. Most contemporary views emphasize the interaction between nature and nurture and the difficulty inherent in attributing a developmental outcome to either one or the other. In the case of older adults, nature and nurture have interacted over an extended period of time, which makes it especially difficult to disentangle the relative importance of these two sources of influence on development. The topics of longevity, biological aging, and health (covered in Chapter 3) are closely linked with the issue of nature and nurture.

As mentioned earlier, a principle that applies to almost every aspect of aging is the extensive individual variability. Why do some people remain healthy, active, and cognitively intact well into their later years, while others succumb to physical disabilities or psychological impairment relatively early in the aging process? To what extent do physical and mental disabilities have a genetic basis (nature), and to what extent are they shaped by environmental influences, lifestyle, and life experiences (nurture)?

The science of behavioral genetics is "the study of genetic and environmental factors that create behavioral differences among individuals" (Bergeman & Ong, 2007, p. 149). Developmental behavioral geneticists often compare genetically related individuals such as twins or siblings at various times to determine which aspects of their development are similar and which are different. Are there similarities between identical twins or even siblings, especially those who have spent a large part of their lives in different environments, with regard to cognitive behavior, personality, incidence of psychopathology, physical health, and longevity? To what extent is behavior in older adulthood based solely on individual differences in biological constitution regardless of environment or lifestyle habits? These fascinating questions have no easy answers.

Quantitative and qualitative indexes

When evaluating how people in two or more age groups perform or behave, or how the same people perform or behave if they are followed over time, researchers may use measures that are either quantitative or qualitative. For example, to compare how young and older adults go about solving a problem, one researcher might use a quantitative index such as the amount of time it takes each age group to solve the problem. In contrast, another researcher might use a qualitative index, such as noting the strategy young and older adults use to solve the problem. Sometimes there is a relationship between quantitative and qualitative indexes. For example, one strategy for solving a problem might take more time than another. However, researchers who focus on quantitative measures may not include qualitative measures; similarly, researchers with a qualitative focus may not use quantitative measures.

In sum, the role of both biological and environmental influences on development, and particularly the interaction between the two, continues to be of

Understanding Aging Box 1.1: A New Outlook on Old Age

Consider three general perspectives on the aging process. The earliest is that of *normative aging*, which focuses on behavioral functioning that would be considered normal, or average, as individuals approach or reach older adulthood. Then the idea of *successful aging* (Rowe & Kahn, 1998) was introduced, which emphasizes that, as individuals grow older, a distinction can be made between an average outcome and an ideal outcome. Thus, aging can be differentiated into what is "usual" and what is "possible" (Baltes & Baltes, 1990; Schulz & Heckhausen, 1996). According to the newest perspective, *positive aging*, derived in part from the positive psychology movement (Seligman & Csikszentmihalyi, 2000), a person can experience happiness and well-being even in the face of objective adversity. Robert Hill (2005) proposes that a positive state of mind affords people strength and resources that buffer them from the physical and psychological challenges they encounter as they grow older. He contends that the idea of positive aging is more comprehensive and potentially more inclusive than that of successful aging because it allows for the possibility a person can find meaning and experience quality of life even when there are physical and psychological limitations.

concern to developmental investigators. Also, whether performance or behavior at various stages of development differs in quantity or in quality is of great interest to investigators of aging and older adulthood. The question of quantitative versus qualitative indexes has been a particularly prominent theme in the study of intelligence and problem solving (see Chapters 6 and 7).

Theoretical Models

Theoretical models are valuable for organizing data on aging and older adulthood. They allow us to make sense of what might otherwise be an overwhelming mass of information. Theoretical models also guide the further study of aging and older adulthood by giving us a platform for framing questions that are important to investigate.

Two theoretical models will be revisited throughout this book: the **Selective Optimization with Compensation (SOC) Model of Aging** and the **Ecological Model of Aging**. Each model offers a framework for understanding what we know about aging and older adulthood, and each can help us identify things we still need to learn. The SOC Model focuses on the strategies aging individuals can use, whereas the Ecological Model places more emphasis on the characteristics of the environment. However, these two models complement one another in conceptualizing aging as a process of adaptation. The SOC and Ecological Models both encompass optimistic views of the aging process, although they differ in the details of how to achieve successful/positive aging.

The Selective Optimization with Compensation Model of Aging

The Selective Optimization with Compensation (SOC) Model (Baltes & Baltes, 1990) is founded on the basic assumption that individuals engage in adaptation throughout their lives. They are capable of learning and changing and calling upon extra (reserve) capacity that they might not need to use under ordinary circumstances.

Another assumption of the SOC Model is that throughout development, individuals experience both gains and losses. However, as older adulthood is approached, the losses may outnumber the gains. In addition, with increasing age there may be a reduction in both general reserve capacity and in reserve capacity in specific domains of functioning. When losses predominate in a particular domain, it may become increasingly difficult to function at a high level.

Despite the greater proportion of losses and a reduction in reserve capacity with increasing age, all is not lost. According to the SOC Model, certain strategies can be called into play to maximize the chances for successful aging. One strategy for adapting to loss is to concentrate efforts on domains in which a high level of functioning can be maintained. These domains can vary depending on the individual.

Selection is a strategy of concentrating efforts on domains in which effective functioning is most likely to remain high. However, it might also be necessary to revise one's expectations of functioning in some domains. Optimization is a strategy of focusing on behaviors that maximize not only the quantity but also the quality of life. Compensation refers to substituting new strategies when losses occur. For example, if memory falters, a person might compensate by keeping a list of things to remember. If visual or hearing is less sharp, a person might compensate by using glasses or a hearing aid.

The SOC Model stems from the life-span developmental perspective that Chapter 2 describes in greater detail, and it is well suited for conceptualizing how people deal with age-related changes in the sensory, perceptual, cognitive, personal, and social domains. If individuals are able to select, optimize, and compensate as they experience age-related losses in any of these domains, they have a good chance of achieving both successful and positive aging (see Baltes, 2005).

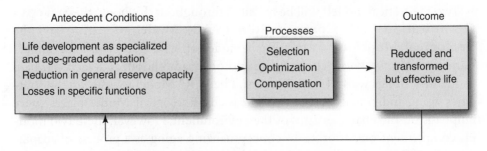

Figure 1.6 *The Ongoing Dynamics of Selective Optimization with Compensation.*
Source: Baltes & Baltes (1990).

The Ecological Model of Aging

The Ecological Model (Lawton & Nahemow, 1973) is based on the premise that the interaction between a person and his or her environment results in some level of adaptation, which is measured in terms of a person's emotional (affective) well-being and behavior.

As Figure 1.7 shows, a person can be characterized in terms of competence, which can be measured by that person's physical, sensory, cognitive, and social capabilities. An environment can be defined in terms of challenge, or press, which can be measured in terms of its physical demands, as well as the level of sensory, intellectual, or social stimulation that is available. To enjoy a positive outcome (adaptation), a person's level of competence must be appropriately matched with the press of the environment in which he or she must function.

In Figure 1.7, the dotted line bisecting the blue adaptation zone represents the ideal level of adaptation, while the blue areas on either side of the dotted line represent an acceptable range of positive adaptation. White areas to the left and right of the blue zone represent zones of negative adaptation (negative affect or maladaptive behavior), which can result when environmental press is either too low or excessive.

Note that the blue zone of positive adaptation is a function of both the person's level of competence and the degree of press in the environment. A person who is low in competence will adapt well in a narrow band of environments that are low in press, but many environments would be too challenging. At the same time, a small band of extremely low press environments would not offer sufficient stimulation even for the individual who is low in competence.

As a person's level of competence increases, a higher level of environmental press is needed for positive adaptation. Also, the blue area broadens as a person's competence increases, illustrating that someone high in competence will adapt positively to a wider range of environmental press compared to someone low in competence. At the same time,

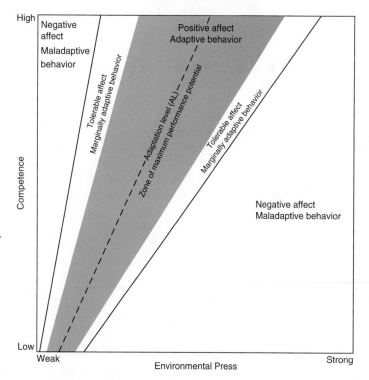

Figure 1.7 *The Ecological Model.*
Source: Lawton & Nahemow (1973).

the person high in competence would adapt poorly in a broad range of environments that offer too little press.

In the original Ecological Model (Lawton & Nahemow, 1973), the older adult was viewed as a recipient of the press exerted by the environment. Later, Lawton (1989, 1999) emphasized the transactional nature of the person–environment interaction. Thus, rather than considering the older adult as a passive responder to the environment, the older adult is viewed as capable of initiating interactions with the environment. An individual who is high in competence will be able to identify and shape resources that are potentially available in the environment. Furthermore, an individual who is low in physical competence may have sufficient cognitive and/or social competence to take advantage of environmental resources compared to the individual who is not competent cognitively or socially.

As with the SOC Model, the Ecological Model is a framework for considering successful/positive aging in many domains – physical, sensory, perceptual, cognitive, personal, and social. At the end of each chapter, we will return to the SOC and Ecological Models for a brief discussion of how they relate to the content covered.

? Questions to Consider

1. When do you think a person enters the older adult age group?
2. Describe an older adult whom you would consider to be socially young. How would this individual differ from one whose social age and chronological age are similar?
3. The SOC Model can apply to people at all ages and stages of life. Can you think of a situation in which you selected some domain of functioning and used it to compensate for another?

Key Points

- People have always been interested in how to slow down the aging process and extend life, but the scientific study of aging and older adulthood is more recent.
- Today there are more older adults and greater recognition that development occurs throughout the adult life span into the older adult years.
- Geriatrics is the branch of medicine specializing in the medical care and treatment of the diseases and health problems of older adults. Gerontology

is the study of the biological, behavioral, and social aspects of aging from maturity to old age.

- Age can be defined chronologically (number of time units since birth), but it can also be defined biologically, functionally, psychologically, and socially.

- As adults get older, the gap between their chronological age and their subjective feelings about age widens. Middle-aged and older adults, especially women, often say they feel younger than their chronological age.

- In the United States, 65 is a common chronological marker of entry into older adulthood, but in the future this number may rise.

- Older adulthood is often segmented into three categories based on chronological age: young-old (ages 65–74), old-old (ages 75–84), and oldest-old (ages 85+). In the United States, the fastest-growing group is the oldest-old (85+) age category.

- Ageism refers to discriminatory attitudes directed toward older adults. Further investigation is needed to determine when and how ageism affects this age group.

- In the United States, baby boomers will swell the ranks of the 65+ age group through the year 2030. At present, the largest proportion of the 65+ group is European American and there are more women than men. Older adults are healthier, more educated, and economically better off today than they were in the past.

- In the United States, the majority of older adults remain in the same geographic location even after they retire, but a small percentage relocate. Some return to their home states later if they experience loss of a spouse or health difficulties.

- Over the life span, development is affected by normative age-graded influences, normative history-graded influences, and nonnormative life events.

- Two prominent themes in the study of development are the relative influence of nature and nurture, and the question of whether developmental change is quantitative or qualitative.

- The Selective Optimization with Compensation (SOC) and Ecological Models are theoretical frameworks that will be used in this book to view what is known about aging and older adulthood. Both suggest how people can adapt to the aging process to achieve an older adulthood that is successful and positive.

Key Terms

ageism   13

baby boom years   15

biological age   8

chronological age   8

demography   14

Ecological Model of Aging   27

functional age   9

geriatrics   5

gerontology   5

nature and nurture   25

nonnormative life events   23

normative age-graded influences   23

normative history-graded influences   23

old-old   12

oldest-old   12

organismic variable   12

population pyramid   16

psychological age   9

quantitative or qualitative
    differences   25

Selective Optimization with Compensation
    (SOC) Model of Aging   27

social age   9

young-old   12

2 Theory and Method in Studying Aging and Older Adulthood

Chapter Overview

Close-ups on Adulthood and Aging

In a few months Julie will graduate from the local university, and at age 21, she is applying for her first full-time job. On a recent visit to her 78-year-old grandmother, Julie confided that she was about to purchase a brand new car, for which she would make monthly payments for the next five years. Her grandmother was shocked that Julie would buy a new car before she had the money to pay for it outright. She said that when she was Julie's age, she used to walk or take the bus to school and work. Long after she married Julie's grandfather they finally saved enough money to buy a used car. Julie's grandmother also said that she used to visit the neighborhood grocery store every day to buy the fresh ingredients she needed to cook dinner. Julie cannot imagine waiting until she can save enough money to pay in full for a car. She cannot conceive of life without credit cards that allow minimum monthly payments for all of her purchases, nor can she picture herself making a daily trip to a neighborhood grocery store. Every two or three weeks, Julie travels 10 miles to a superstore, where she uses her credit card to stock up on frozen dinners she can heat up in the microwave in just a minute or two.

Metatheoretical Approaches to the Study of Aging

Investigators, including those who study adult development and aging, usually have a particular viewpoint about the nature of the universe in general and about developmental phenomena in particular. Such a viewpoint is a metatheoretical orientation, or metamodel, and it guides researchers' beliefs about which aspects of development are worthy of study (Elias, Elias, & Elias, 1977). Metamodels provide a framework for the theories researchers propose, for the hypotheses they generate, for how they design their research, for the samples of participants they include in their studies, and for the method they use to analyze the data they collect. The fact that individual researchers subscribe to different metamodels may explain, at least in part, why their findings may conflict. In some sense, scientific research is never completely objective because it is always driven by a viewpoint. Table 2.1 lists the characteristics of three metamodels that we will now describe.

The Mechanistic Metamodel

Researchers with a **mechanistic metamodel** use a machine metaphor to study development. This is not to say that they believe that people are like machines.

Table 2.1 *Characteristics of the mechanistic, organismic, and contextual metamodels*

Metamodel	Characteristics
Mechanistic	Emphasizes nurture Passive organism reacts to the environment Quantitative differences at different ages Studying larger phenomena by breaking them down into simpler units Development has no particular endpoint
Organismic	Emphasizes nature Active organism creates environment Organisms are qualitatively different at various stages of development Development has a goal, or end point Development is complex and constantly changing
Contextual	Emphasizes both nature and nurture and the bidirectional transactions between organism and environment Both quantitative and qualitative phenomena

Rather, the machine metaphor guides their study of developmental processes. Researchers with a mechanistic metamodel tend to view external environmental forces as input and the organism's behavior as output. Thus, their research tends to focus on the organism's reaction to external forces rather than on the role the organism may play in constructing the environment. If environmental forces are considered to be the main reason people age in less than ideal ways, then attempts might be made to prevent or minimize any negative aspects of aging through control of the environment.

Researchers with a mechanistic orientation view a whole phenomenon as equal to the sum of its parts. Therefore, their approach to the study of development is to break down a complex phenomenon into parts and then to study each one separately. Behavior is viewed as the product of many lawful associations between simple events, possibly the result of numerous stimulus–response sequences.

Researchers with a mechanistic orientation study quantitative differences between young and older adults. They might ask the following questions: Compared with young adults, do older adults display a greater or a lesser degree of a particular behavior? Do older adults demonstrate a higher or lower level of performance on an ability test compared to young adults?

The Organismic Metamodel

Researchers with an **organismic metamodel** use a biological metaphor to study development. They believe development originates from within the organism and that the developing organism acts upon, rather than reacting to, the environment. The environment is not ignored, but it is not the main focus.

According to the organismic metamodel, development is directed toward some goal, or end point. Development occurs in a series of stages in which new and different structures emerge. Organismic researchers focus on patterns of abilities or other characteristics as well as on the nature of the structures underlying such patterns.

In the organismic metamodel, the whole is greater than the sum of its parts. Therefore, researchers would have little interest in studying individual behaviors in isolation. Rather, they would emphasize the importance of complex and constantly changing developmental phenomena that occur within a larger framework.

The organismic metamodel emphasizes qualitative changes in development. The main focus is on variation in the structures, or pattern, of characteristics at different points of the adult life span. Older organisms are not viewed as having either a lesser or a greater quantity of a characteristic or ability. Rather, characteristics and abilities are assumed to be qualitatively different at different stages of life. For example, young and older adults might use different strategies when they approach or solve a problem.

The Contextual Metamodel

Researchers with a **contextual metamodel** view the organism and the environment as being in continual interaction. Thus, development is thought to consist of bidirectional transactions between the organism and the environment. This is a dialectical process, meaning that a constantly changing organism develops within a constantly changing environment. There is no particular direction of movement toward any single end point, or goal. Rather, there are multiple patterns of development, both quantitative and qualitative. These cannot be broken down into simple parts to be studied in isolation.

Developmental researchers with a contextual metamodel often look beyond the age variable. Thus, if they are studying how young versus older adults perform on a memory test, there is special concern with variables such as years of education, prior experience, present lifestyle, socioeconomic status, and cultural (ethnic) background. Also, they would consider it particularly important for tests of intellectual ability to consist of items that relate to the everyday world.

The Life-Span Developmental Perspective

The **life-span developmental perspective** (Baltes, 1987) draws on all three metamodels just described, but it bears the greatest similarity to the contextual metamodel. The life-span developmental perspective considers development to be a multifaceted, ongoing process. A changing organism acts upon, and changes, the environment. At the same time, a dynamically changing environment acts upon, and changes, the organism. Thus, behavior is a product of the organism as well as of the environment.

Because the life-span model assumes that each individual develops in his or her own way, researchers would consider it especially important to follow the same people over time to assess *intraindividual change* (that is, change within the individual). The life-span perspective can be applied to any aspect of development – cognitive, social, or biological – but frequently it is applied to the study of intellectual abilities. Chapter 6, which covers intellectual functioning, revisits the life-span perspective, but the key propositions are listed in Table 2.2.

One proposition of the life-span perspective is that developmental processes can show both gains and losses over the life span. However, the proportion of gains to losses changes as people grow older.

Figure 2.1 shows that the proportion of gains is greater than the proportion of losses in early life through young adulthood. In middle age, the proportion of gains and losses is equivalent, but in older adulthood the proportion of losses outstrips the proportion of gains. Despite the greater proportion of losses in older adulthood, Baltes (1987) proposed that gains may be used to offset any losses that occur. This is one of the main propositions in the Selective Optimization with Compensation (SOC) Model introduced in Chapter 1.

Table 2.2   *Key theoretical propositions of the life-span developmental perspective*

Development occurs over the entire life span

Development occurs throughout life. No one age or stage is dominant with regard to development.

At all points, from birth to death, developmental processes can be both continuous (cumulative) and discontinuous (innovative).

Development is embedded in a historical context

Development varies depending on when it occurs and the sociocultural conditions at that time.

Development is multidimensional, multidirectional, and multicausal

Development can bring change along many dimensions (physical, cognitive, social, and so on).

Such change can occur in multiple directions (increases, decreases).

Changes can vary with regard to timing (onset, duration).

Multiple factors cause development.

The field of development is multidisciplinary

The study of development is greatly enhanced with information from disciplines such as biology, anthropology, psychology, and sociology.

Development includes both gains and losses

At all points of the life span, developmental processes can show both growth (gain) and decline (loss).

There may be gains in some aspects of development and losses in others.

Development is plastic

Plasticity refers to intraindividual (within-person) variability and the modifiability of development. This means that individuals can change and learn during the course of development.

Developmental Research

Psychological research deals with variables. Variables can refer to personal characteristics (for example, age, gender, ethnicity, socioeconomic status, level of education, group membership), environmental characteristics, observed behaviors, test performance scores, responses to questionnaires, type of test instructions that are given prior to administering a test, and so on. Variables can be categorical (that is, broken down into more than one level, each having specific boundaries) or in some cases they can be continuous (that is, having no specified boundaries). Now we will take a closer look at the age variable, which is fundamental to developmental research.

The Age Variable

In developmental research, chronological age is frequently treated as a categorical variable. Thus, when conducting a study, a researcher may include participants from two or more adult age categories, or age groups. When age is a categorical variable, there is no definite rule as to the boundaries, or span, for the separate age categories. The lower boundary for the young adult category could be set at age 18 and the upper boundary might be set at 22, 25, 30, 35, or even 40. Thus, the age span for a young adult group might be as narrow as four years (18–22), or as broad as 22 years (18–40).

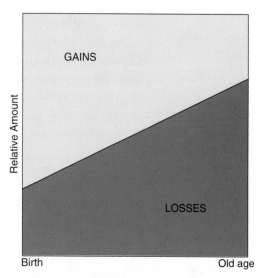

Figure 2.1 *Proportion of gains and losses over the life span*
From Baltes (1987).

In many studies, the lower boundary for the older adult age group is 65, but the upper boundary varies widely across studies. In some studies, the age span that defines the older group is relatively narrow, such as 65–75. In other studies, the age span is extremely broad, such as 65 and over (65+). Studies that use a broad category such as 65+ most likely include individuals from the young-old (65–74), old-old (75–84), and oldest-old (85+) subcategories. As Chapter 1 states, individuals in the young-old, old-old, and oldest-old subcategories tend to differ on a number of dimensions, including health as well as sensory, perceptual, and cognitive capabilities. Depending on which variables are of interest in a particular research study, the possible heterogeneity of a broad 65+ group may not be ideal. Also, comparing the results of two studies that differ greatly in the upper boundary of the older age category can be questionable.

Research studies in which age is a categorical variable often include a young group and an older group. This so-called "extreme age groups design" (Hertzog, 1990) is used to ascertain whether older adults have less, or perhaps more, of certain abilities or characteristics compared to young adults. If the older group were to earn lower scores than a young group on an ability test, it would not be possible to determine whether there is a simple gradual decrease with age or whether the relationship between age and performance is more complex. Including a middle-aged group makes it possible to estimate whether the decrease in average scores from young to older adulthood is gradual or abrupt.

Rather than treating age as a categorical variable, some studies treat age as a continuous variable. For example, a study might include individuals who are 18 years of age and older with no upper limit. If the age variable is continuous, there are no arbitrary cut-offs that classify participants into age categories (such as young and older).

Regardless of whether it is categorical or continuous, age is an organismic variable. As with variables such as gender, ethnicity, and socioeconomic status, age is inherent within the individual. As discussed further under the topic of quasi-experimental approaches to research, a researcher cannot control or manipulate organismic variables.

Factors in Aging Research

Three basic factors must be considered when conducting developmental research on aging (Schaie, 1965):

- age: chronological age, or maturational level, of the research participants;
- cohort: cohort membership, or generation, of the research participants;
- time of measurement: when the research measures are made or the data are collected.

Chronological age

Chronological age, or maturational level, refers to the number of time units that have elapsed since birth. Usually, the chronological age factor is simply called *age*.

Cohort

Cohort refers to a generation of individuals who were born at about the same time, either in a particular year, or within a circumscribed time such as 5 years. Members of a cohort often have certain common experiences during the course of their development. For example, the lives of people in a particular cohort are influenced by the state of medical knowledge available when they were infants, young children, adolescents, and even adults. Today's older adults, for instance, were vulnerable to whooping cough and polio in their childhood years, whereas present-day children are vaccinated against these illnesses.

The early education of cohort members was influenced by the teaching philosophies and technologies available during their years of schooling. Today's older adults did not use computers when they were in school, nor were they likely to have used computers in the workplace in their young- or middle-adult years. Also, today's older adults had fewer opportunities for higher education than today's young adults. In addition, many of today's older adults, like Julie's grandmother described at the beginning of the chapter, are accustomed to saving money to purchase items rather than buying them on credit.

The professional opportunities available to members of a particular cohort depend on the prevailing state of the general economy and the level of technological advancement when they enter the labor force and progress through their work careers. Also, changing societal views mean that today's young women and members of ethnic minority groups have more opportunities to obtain training in the skills needed for productive careers than did women and members of minority groups in the past.

In sum, cohort members are likely to have a common set of experiences as they travel through life. Furthermore, the influence of such experiences occurs at a common stage of development. For example, wars affect every member of a society in some way. However, the effects of a war can vary considerably for different age groups. Particularly when war is waged on foreign soil, it may have a more direct impact on young adults who serve in the military than it does on middle-aged and older adults who are not serving in the military during the war. But when individuals live within a battle zone, all age groups are likely to feel the effects of war.

Cohort is important to consider, but keep in mind that the fact that individuals were born in approximately the same year is no guarantee that they all had exactly the same exposure to specific opportunities and experiences during the course of their development. Even within the same country, individuals in any given cohort may differ in educational and job opportunities as well as access to health care and dietary nutrition. Some individuals grew up in cities and others in rural environments. Some were more economically advantaged than others. Cohort members vary in religious beliefs as well as ethnic backgrounds (European American, African American, Hispanic American, Asian American, Native American), both of which can be associated with diverse views on child rearing and expectations about the role and importance of family.

Time of measurement

Time of measurement refers to conditions that prevail when the research is conducted. When individuals participate in a research study, they are in a particular state of general health. They have a certain work status (for example, being employed full-time) and family status (for example, being married). If a researcher were to retest these same individuals on a subsequent occasion, some of them may have experienced changes in health and work status (being promoted, downsized, or retired). Some may have experienced changes in family status (becoming separated, divorced, widowed, or perhaps remarrying, becoming parents, grandparents, or great-grandparents). All of these factors could have some bearing on their questionnaire responses or their performance on test batteries used in the study.

Not only do individual members of a research sample undergo changes over time, but there may be changes in the tests and methods available for studying the phenomena of interest. For example, a test used 5 years earlier may have been revised and updated. The method for presenting a visual display may be more refined today than it was 5 years earlier. In addition, the personnel working on a research project could change over time. Finally, general societal attitudes and philosophies can change. For example, attitudes toward sexual behavior may

Table 2.3 *"X" indicates factors confounded in cross-sectional, longitudinal, and time-lag research designs*

	Factor		
Type of research design	**Age**	**Cohort**	**Time of measurement**
Cross-sectional	X	X	
Longitudinal	X		X
Time-lag		X	X

have changed from the 1960s to the 1990s, partly in response to the AIDS epidemic, so time of measurement would be an important factor in studies on attitudes toward sexual behavior.

Research Design

When adults from two or more age groups are studied, researchers generally use cross-sectional or longitudinal research designs. In some instances, however, the concern may be exclusively with individuals who fall into one age group, in which case researchers may use a time-lag design.

Depending upon the research design, some factors are *confounded* (see Table 2.3), which means that the effects of two or more factors may be difficult or impossible to separate, or isolate, from one another (Schaie, 1965). This will become clear as we take a closer look at the cross-sectional, longitudinal, and time-lag designs.

The cross-sectional design

When individuals from two or more age groups are studied, the **cross-sectional research design** is the one most commonly used. In a cross-sectional study, a group of young adults (for example, 20–30 years of age) and a group of older adults (for example, 65–75 years of age) might be asked to complete a series of tests or questionnaires. If the young and older groups show differences in their level of performance or in the answers they give on the questionnaires, then we refer to age differences, or more appropriately to *age-related differences*.

Figure 2.2 shows two examples of the cross-sectional design (see columns). For the sake of simplicity, cohorts are defined by a specific age rather than an age range. In one cross-sectional example, data are collected in the year 1990. In a second cross-sectional example, data are collected in 2000. In both examples, the youngest cohort is age 40, the middle cohort is age 50, and the oldest cohort is age 60. Note that data are collected at only one time (either 1990 or 2000), so time of measurement is not a confounding factor. Thus, there is no need for concern about changes that may take place in study participants' health, changes in test instruments, technology or research personnel, and so on. Moreover, participant drop-out (attrition) is minimal in cross-sectional studies because participants are tested only once.

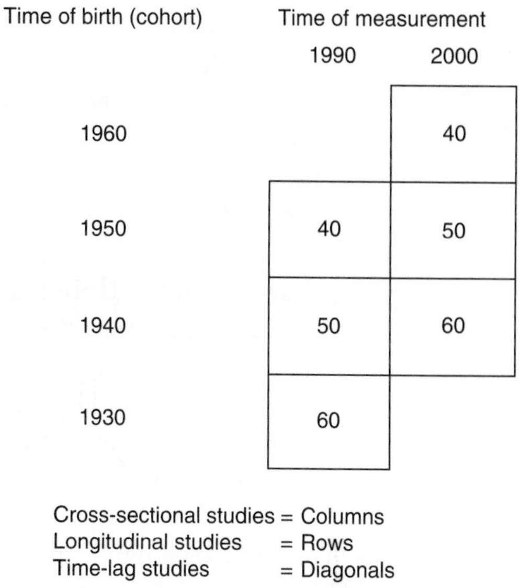

However, the factors of age and cohort are confounded in cross-sectional research. If age-related differences are found, we won't know whether those differences can be attributed to age or to cohort membership. People who are aged 40 in the year 1990 were children in the 1950s and reached young adulthood in the late 1960s. People who are aged 50 in 1990 were children in the 1940s and reached young adulthood in the late 1950s. People who are aged 60 in 1990 were children in the 1930s and reached young adulthood in the late 1940s. Undoubtedly, these three cohort groups were exposed to different influences and experiences throughout the course of their development. In a cross-sectional study, it would be difficult to tell whether any differences found in the responses of 40-, 50-, and 60-year-olds are due to chronological age or to cohort.

Cross-sectional studies are efficient because they are completed within a circumscribed period of time. Such efficiency is the reason that many aging researchers use this design. The results of cross-sectional studies allow researchers to make descriptive statements about the particular age/cohort groups that were included in the study. However, the findings of a cross-sectional study conducted in 1990 on 40-, 50-, and 60-year-olds may not be the same as the findings of a study conducted in the year 2000 on 40-, 50-, and 60-year-olds.

In sum, the cross-sectional design is appropriate when the purpose of a research study is to delineate the current status of young, middle-aged, and older adults. If age-related differences are indeed found between two or more age groups in a cross-sectional study, then those age groups could be targeted for more time-consuming and costly longitudinal studies, which will now be described.

Figure 2.2 *Cross-sectional, longitudinal, and time-lag research designs.*

The longitudinal design

With the **longitudinal research design**, the same individuals are followed over time and tested on two or more occasions. The rows in Figure 2.2 show examples of studies having a longitudinal design. A researcher sets out in the year 1990 to interview, or test, a group of 40-year-olds, who were born in 1950. In 2000, these same individuals are located and retested, at which time they will be aged 50. While it is not shown in Figure 2.2, these individuals could be tested for a third time in 2010 when they reach age 60. If these research participants respond differently in 2000 than they did in 1990, we would refer to age changes, or more appropriately to *age-related changes*.

With the longitudinal research design, age and cohort are not confounded because all participants are members of the same cohort. However, the factors of age and time of measurement are confounded. If age-related changes occur between two times of testing, it will not be possible to determine whether those changes can be attributed to participants' chronological age or to time of measurement. Also, since the longitudinal design calls for repeated testing of the same individuals, there may be practice effects. However, the further apart the points of testing, the less likely practice effects will influence the findings.

A different source of confounding in longitudinal studies comes from participant drop-out, or attrition. In longitudinal studies, the same individuals are tested at least twice, and possibly even more times. Even with conscientious efforts on the part of longitudinal researchers to maintain the interest and motivation of study participants, it is rare that every individual from the original sample tested initially at Time 1 will be available for retesting at subsequent times. Attrition during the course of the study would not present any particular problem if it was random.

Unfortunately, attrition is often selective. This point was illustrated clearly in an excellent study by Siegler and Botwinick (1979), who inspected data from longitudinal research being conducted at Duke University in which tests of intellectual ability were administered every 6 years. Over time, some participants dropped out while others returned for retesting. Time 1 scores were available for everyone who initially participated in the study, so Siegler and Botwinick were able to compare Time 1 scores of participants who subsequently dropped out of the study with Time 1 scores of participants who remained in the study. Time 1 scores of individuals who dropped out were lower than Time 1 scores of those who returned for further testing. Thus, not only was the sample shrinking over time, but because of **selective attrition**, it was becoming more and more positively selective – the higher performers were returning but the lower performers were not. The sample tested at Time 1 may have been adequately representative of the population of interest, but later on the sample may have become less representative of the population.

Longitudinal research is time-consuming and costly. Study participants must be located for retesting and their interest maintained between testing dates to insure that they continue to take part in the study. However, a longitudinal design can provide interesting and important information about whether individuals change over time (that is, whether there is *intraindividual change*, or *intraindividual variability*). For this reason, the longitudinal method is an excellent approach for studying multidirectionality (Hoyer & Rybash, 1996), one of the key propositions in the life-span perspective described earlier in this chapter. The term *multidirectionality* refers to the possibility that some aspects of development involve growth (gain), some involve stability (no change), and some involve

(a) (b)

Grandmothers today and grandmothers ca. 1950 may differ not only in attitudes and opinions, but also in physical appearance.

decline (loss). As Chapter 6 describes in more detail, some abilities increase with age, while others decline. If a longitudinal study examines a range of abilities or characteristics, then it can delineate which ones increase, which ones remain stable, and which ones show age-related decline.

The time-lag design

Strictly speaking, the **time-lag research design** is not developmental because all of the study participants are members of the same age group. With this design, individuals of a particular chronological age are tested at two different times, usually years or decades apart. Individuals of the same chronological age who are tested at different times are members of different cohorts because they were born at different times. The three diagonals in Figure 2.2 represent examples of the time-lag design. Each diagonal is a separate time-lag study in which all participants are aged 40, 50, or 60. In each time-lag study, the factors of cohort and time of measurement are confounded. Thus, the 40-year-olds tested in 1990 were born in 1950, whereas the 40-year-olds tested in 2000 were born in 1960. The 50-year-olds tested in 1990 were born in 1940, whereas the 50-year-olds tested in 2000 were born in 1950. The 60-year-olds tested in 1990 were born in 1930, whereas the 60-year-olds tested in 2000 were born in 1940.

As an illustration, let's suppose that an investigator conducts a study on the characteristics of 60-year-olds of today compared to the characteristics of 60-year-olds several decades ago. It is likely that today's 60-year-olds are healthier and more active than 60-year-olds of earlier decades because of medical advances and greater opportunities to maintain physical fitness. Also, 60-year-olds of today are more likely than 60-year-olds of earlier decades to have plans for launching new careers, furthering their education, and traveling to distant destinations. In this investigation, all participants are the same age, but they are members of different cohorts and they were also tested at different times. Thus, it is difficult to determine whether any differences between these two groups of 60-year-olds are attributable to differing opportunities available to the two cohorts throughout the course of their lives or to more immediate time-of-measurement effects. Julie and her grandmother (described at the beginning of the chapter) illustrate a time–lag comparison. The two women were born into different cohorts, and during their young adult years, each is influenced by what is common in mainstream society at the time. As a young adult, Julie's grandmother walked and used public transportation, paid for things in cash, and shopped daily at a neighborhood grocery store for fresh ingredients. Julie, on the other hand, is purchasing a new car on credit and shops only every few weeks for frozen dinners at a distant superstore.

Sequential designs

In all three research designs described thus far, two factors are confounded. Schaie (1965) proposed that **sequential research designs** could disentangle the effects of all three factors: age, cohort, and time of measurement. As illustrated in Figure 2.3, each of three sequential designs involves some combination of the cross-sectional, longitudinal, or time–lag comparisons.

The cohort-sequential design (Figure 2.3(a)) calls for simultaneous cross-sectional and longitudinal studies. Note that two longitudinal studies are conducted on two different cohorts. This design separates, or isolates, age and cohort effects. However, time-of-measurement effects cannot be isolated, so this design is best when a researcher expects that time-of-measurement effects will be trivial (Elias et al., 1977).

The time-sequential design (Figure 2.3(b)) calls for two or more cross-sectional comparisons at two or more times of measurement. This design isolates

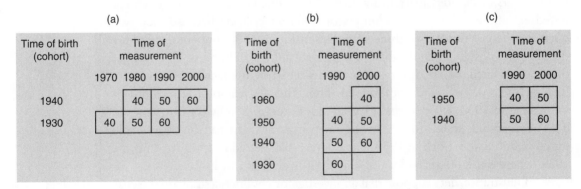

Figure 2.3   *Three sequential designs: (a) A cohort-sequential design (age and cohort effects isolated) (b) A time-sequential design (age and time-of-measurement effects isolated) (c) A cross-sequential design (cohort and time-of-measurement effects isolated).*

the effects of age and time of measurement, but cohort effects cannot be isolated. This design is useful if the main concern is separating the effects of age and time of measurement and a researcher can assume that cohort effects will be trivial (Elias et al., 1977).

The cross-sequential design (Figure 2.3(c)) consists of two or more cross-sectional and longitudinal comparisons. The effects of cohort and time of measurement are isolated but the effect of age is not. Note that the cross-sectional part of this design confounds age and cohort, while the longitudinal part confounds age and time of measurement. This design is useful if the main concern is separating the effects of cohort and time of measurement (Elias et al., 1977).

Sequential designs require a great deal of time and effort. Furthermore, it is not clear that sequential strategies guarantee an unequivocal interpretation of the factors in aging research. However, Schaie (1965) was successful in bringing the importance of confounded factors to the attention of research investigators.

Measurement

In research studies on adult development and aging, data are gathered to measure the variables of interest. The type of data collected may include the responses that study participants make on instruments such as self-report questionnaires, the scores that participants earn on tests of ability, the responses participants make on tests of personality, or the ratings that others make of study participants' behavior in naturalistic or more structured laboratory settings. Regardless of the specific variables of interest or the manner in which they are measured, it is essential that the measurement instruments be both reliable and valid.

Reliability

Reliability has to do with the dependability, or consistency, of the instruments used to measure variables of interest. The test–retest reliability of an instrument is related to whether the responses that research participants make on a test instrument (such as a questionnaire or a test of intellectual ability) are identical, or at least very similar, on separate occasions. When the responses of research participants are potentially ambiguous, then it is important to demonstrate inter-rater reliability by making sure that two or more independent raters, or observers, make similar evaluations of participants' responses or make similar ratings of participants' behavior.

Of special concern to developmental researchers who study adult development is that the reliability of a particular instrument may have been established with young adults. The same instrument may now be applied to older adults with little information on whether it is reliable for that age group. Keep in mind that the reliability of a measurement instrument must be established for all age groups regardless of whether a research study is cross-sectional or longitudinal.

For cross-sectional research, the possibility of age-related differences can be entertained only if it has been demonstrated that the measures are reliable for all age groups included in the study. For longitudinal research, the possibility of age-related change within individuals over time can be entertained only if the measures are reliable for all ages/stages of adulthood.

The concept of reliability applies not only to specific test instruments but also to the findings of research studies. If an investigator conducts a study and obtains certain results, then he or she should obtain consistent results if the study is conducted a second time, assuming that procedure in the second study is the same as it was in the first one.

Validity

Once reliability is established, attention must turn to **validity**. There are several types of validity, but all have to do with whether we are measuring what we think we are measuring. Only if this is the case do we stand a good chance of drawing appropriate conclusions from our data. The concept of validity applies both to specific measurement instruments and to the findings of research studies.

Internal validity

Internal validity refers to the accurate identification and interpretation of the factor(s), or effect(s), responsible for an observation. One way to illustrate what internal validity means in research studies on adult development and aging is to describe situations that threaten it. For example, consider a cross-sectional study in which participants from young and older adult age groups take a memory test. On average, the scores of the young group are higher than those of the older group. Can we conclude that age is the reason for this difference in memory scores? The young and older participants differ in chronological age, but they also differ in cohort membership. The educational background and experience of a particular cohort could certainly influence scores on a memory test. If we conclude that the older group's lower memory scores are attributable solely to chronological age without acknowledging that cohort could also be important, then there is a threat to the internal validity of the study. As mentioned earlier in this chapter, age is an organismic variable, which means that age is inherent in a person and cannot be controlled. For this reason, we refer to age-related differences in a cross-sectional study rather than stating that age is causing the difference in memory scores. Discussion of experimental versus quasi-experimental approaches later on in this chapter should clarify this concept further.

External validity

External validity refers to whether findings obtained from a sample of study participants can be generalized to the population of interest. The internal and external validity of a research study are not totally independent. Any threat to

Applying Research Box 2.1: Focus on Measurement

Investigators who study adult development must be able to measure the extent to which people of different ages possess certain characteristics. The question is: Do the behavioral manifestations of an underlying characteristic differ depending upon the age of the individuals being measured? According to Daniel Mroczek and his colleagues (Mroczek, Hurt, & Berman, 1999), **heterotypic continuity** refers to whether a measure used to assess an underlying characteristic has the same degree of internal validity for different age groups in a cross-sectional study, or for the same people as they are followed over time in a longitudinal study. For example, an underlying mental disorder could be stable and enduring over the adult life span, but the behavioral symptoms of that disorder could fluctuate over time. A self-report questionnaire that taps a narrow set of behaviors that are assumed to be symptomatic of a particular diagnosis could be more valid for one age group than for another. Many depression questionnaires include items about physical functioning such as loss of appetite, loss of interest in sex, or sleep disturbances. These symptoms may be indicative of depression in young adults, but in older adults they may simply be hallmarks of aging. We could be in error if we were to interpret a high score on such a questionnaire as a valid indicator of depression in older adults.

internal validity could, in turn, represent a threat to external validity. If the memory study just described were repeated 10 years hence, young and older research participants would be members of different cohorts. If the basis for the difference between the young and older groups in the original study was actually cohort membership rather than age, then the results of that study would not be repeated (replicated) in the more recent one. This means that the findings of the initial memory study would not generalize to samples of young and older adults who are tested in the future.

Ecological validity

Ecological validity is a type of external validity that has been of great interest to contemporary researchers. Ecological validity refers to whether the results obtained with a particular test instrument reflect real-world functioning or real-world behavior. Scores on an intelligence test might be highly reliable for young and older adults. But do these scores inform us about the level of competence each age group is likely to demonstrate when dealing with real-world situations?

Of particular concern to developmental psychologists is whether a specific test is ecologically valid for both young adults and older adults. For example, some intelligence test items tap skills that are taught in school and needed for successful functioning in academic settings. Perhaps it is not surprising that scores on such tests are related to academic performance. The everyday lives of many young adults involve full-time or part-time engagement in academic pursuits, and their scores on such tests may be valid measures of competence in the everyday life of a student. However, the majority of older adults are not students, so their scores on such tests may have less value (be less ecologically valid) as a measure of their everyday competence. Chapter 6 discusses this issue further.

Sampling

How many individuals should be included in a research study? Research using a case study method usually consists of in-depth investigation of one person, or perhaps a small number of individuals. Open-ended interviews often yield a rich array of descriptive information. In some instances, the information obtained from in-depth case studies can be used to test hypotheses about development in larger samples of individuals.

Most studies on adult development recruit a sample of individuals from the population about whom a particular research question is being investigated (Schaie, 1995). However, obtaining a random sample can be challenging, particularly if participants are required to travel to a research laboratory or complete a lengthy series of tests or questionnaires (Collins, 1996).

The way a sample is selected can affect both the internal and external validity of a research study. If selection factors vary for the different age groups in a developmental study, then the samples may not be equally representative of the population in their respective age groups. To illustrate, consider a study in which an investigator administers a memory test to a sample of young adults and a sample of older adults. The young sample is recruited from the population of undergraduate students enrolled in psychology courses. The older sample is recruited from a nearby nursing home. The investigator finds out that the memory scores of the older group are lower than the memory scores of the young group. If the investigator attributes the older group's lower memory scores solely to age, this would represent a threat to the internal validity of the study. The reason for this threat is that not only do the young and older study participants differ in cohort membership, but they almost certainly differ in health and lifestyle. Individuals in the young sample are probably healthy and, as students, they are actively engaged in a memory-demanding lifestyle. In contrast, individuals in the older sample are likely to be in poor physical health or they would not be living in a nursing home. In addition, a sizable proportion of nursing home residents suffer from cognitive impairment (dementia is discussed further in Chapter 11), which will definitely have a negative influence on their memory scores.

The likely threat to internal validity in this study will compromise its external validity. To illustrate, an investigator administers the same memory test to a sample of young adult college students and a sample of older adults who live independently in the community and actively participate in continuing education programs. This investigator may well find that memory scores are no different for young and older adults. The failure of the second investigator to replicate the findings of the first one means that the results of the first study were not generalizable and therefore lack external validity. Inconsistent findings across studies can often be traced to inconsistency in sampling procedures for the age groups included (Hertzog, 1990). Investigators may fail to recognize, or to acknowledge, that a sample in a particular study may have unique characteristics.

Threats to internal validity are not always as glaring as they were in the example just described. Let's suppose that another investigator conducts a study on memory. In this study, the young adult sample consists of university undergraduates who have volunteered to participate to earn extra credit in their psychology courses. The older adult sample has been recruited from the community with newspaper advertisements targeted to older people who feel that they have problems with their memory. Note that the young sample has not been self-selected for poor memory whereas the older sample has. If the purpose of the study is to compare the memory of young and older adults, and if the investigator is not explicit about the strategy used to recruit samples of young and older adults, then the study may lack internal validity. Another investigator may conduct a similar study, this time comparing the memory of young college students and older adults who pride themselves on their good memory. The findings of this study may not replicate those of the study in which the older sample was recruited on the basis of memory problems. Therefore, the first study lacks external validity as well as internal validity.

To increase the likelihood that any differences between young and older adults in cross-sectional studies are indeed associated with chronological age, some researchers attempt to equate samples from the two age groups on various dimensions. For example, an investigator may try to control for the influence of health factors by screening study participants for health problems. However, this strategy could skew the sampling in different ways for the young and older adults. The incidence of health problems increases with age, so screening older study participants for health problems could result in greater positive bias in the older adult sample than it would in the young adult sample (Salthouse, 1982).

There are no simple solutions to sampling in developmental research. Rather, there are trade-offs. Attempts to equate young and older adult participants on variables other than age may increase a study's internal validity. But this may limit the external validity, or whether the findings can be generalized to broader segments of the young and older adult population.

Approaches to Conducting Aging Research

Researchers who study adult development and aging must have a clear idea about the questions their studies are intended to answer. These questions serve to guide which variables are of interest and the approach that will be taken to collect and analyze the research data. Studies may use an experimental, quasi-experimental, or descriptive approach.

The Experimental Approach

In studies with an **experimental approach**, variables are considered to be independent or dependent. The researcher manipulates the independent variable that has at least two (but sometimes more) categories, or levels. The hallmark of the experimental method is random assignment of research participants to the various levels of the independent variable (often called a *factor*). In a true experiment, in which participants are indeed randomly assigned to the various levels of the independent variable, it is possible to make cause-and-effect statements regarding the influence of the independent variable on the outcome as measured by the dependent variable.

As an example of the experimental approach, let's suppose there is reason to believe that older adults who are instructed to use visual imagery when studying a list of 25 words will remember more of those words at a later time compared with older adults who are given no explicit instructions to use visual imagery but are just told to study the words. In an experiment to test this hypothesis, type of memory instructions is a two-level independent variable. As older adult research participants arrive at the laboratory, they are randomly assigned to one of the two levels: visual imagery instructions or study instructions. Again, those randomly assigned to the visual-imagery instruction condition are told to form visual imagery (and perhaps given an example of how to do so) when shown the list of words. Those randomly assigned to the study instruction condition are just told to study the list with no mention of visual imagery. After viewing the list of 25 words for two minutes, all participants are asked to recall as many as they can.

In this experiment, the dependent measure is the score on the memory test, or how many of the 25 words participants can recall. If those assigned to the visual-imagery condition recall more words than those assigned to the study condition, then we can infer that visual-imagery instructions caused a higher level of memory performance.

In this study, the researcher manipulated the levels of the independent variable, randomly assigned the older adult research participants to either the visual-imagery condition or the study condition, and later found that those in the visual-imagery condition recalled more words. Because research participants were randomly assigned to the two levels of the instruction variable, it is proper to assume that the only difference between the two groups was type of instruction received. Therefore, we can conclude that visual imagery instructions caused the higher recall scores. Note that a statement about cause and effect is appropriate only if research participants were randomly assigned to the two levels of instruction because random assignment insures that all extraneous variables are evenly distributed across both levels of the independent variable. With a sufficiently large sample, it is likely that the memory ability of the participants randomly assigned to the two different instruction conditions will be equivalent at the outset of the study. With a smaller participant sample, the researcher might decide to take a baseline memory measure of participants in each of the two instruction groups to demonstrate that the memory ability of the two groups is equivalent at the outset.

The Quasi-Experimental Approach

Sometimes a study has the same form as a true experiment, but if research participants are not randomly assigned to levels of a categorical factor, then the study actually uses a **quasi-experimental approach**. For example, suppose that a group of young adults and a group of older adults are each instructed to study a list of words and remember as many as they can. On a subsequent memory test, the scores of the older group are lower than the scores of the young group.

The design of this study appears similar to that of the true experiment just described in that age group is a categorical variable with two levels (young and older) and members of each age group have a score on a memory test. However, research participants cannot be randomly assigned to the two age levels as was the case with the two levels of the memory instruction factor in the true experiment. Therefore, in this study, cause-and-effect statements cannot be made. Any difference between the memory performance of the young and older groups could be caused by biological, psychological, or social factors associated with having lived more years or being born into a particular cohort. If the performance of the older group is lower than the performance of the young group, it cannot be concluded that age caused a decrement in memory performance. However, it would be appropriate to state that age is *associated with* a decrement in memory performance.

In sum, age as well as gender, ethnicity, socioeconomic status, educational level, and religious belief are all organismic variables (that is, part of the person). When variables are organismic, studies are quasi-experimental. They may take the form of experiments, but they are not true experiments because participants cannot be randomly assigned to levels of an organismic variable.

Sometimes researchers want to study individuals who fall into naturally occurring groups. Research participants are not randomly assigned to these groups, so these studies are also quasi-experimental. To illustrate, suppose an investigator is interested in studying the level of life satisfaction reported by older adults who live in various housing environments. The investigator learns that the construction of two different apartment buildings is nearing completion, and managers of both buildings are accepting applications from tenants. One building will be age-integrated, meaning that residents can be any age and no special services will be provided for them. The other building will be age-segregated (specifically for adults over the age of 62) and services such as transportation and planned activities will be offered to the tenants.

The investigator thinks that studying older adults who move into these two buildings will be an excellent opportunity to find out whether older adults are happier and more satisfied when they live in an age-integrated setting with no special services as opposed to an age-segregated setting in which special services are provided. The investigator waits until three months after older adults have moved into each of the two buildings to allow time for them to get unpacked and settled. Then the investigator asks the older residents in each building to complete a life satisfaction questionnaire (on which scores can range from 0 for low life satisfaction to 30 for high life satisfaction).

Older adults in the age-integrated and age-segregated buildings are similar in age, socioeconomic status, and ethnic composition. However, there was no random assignment of the older adults to the age-integrated and age-segregated apartment buildings. Therefore, the two groups of residents could differ along dimensions that have not been measured and may not be clearly apparent. Any such differences could actually be the basis for the type of building they selected as well as the degree of happiness and life satisfaction they report. If the investigator finds that older adults in the age-segregated building have higher life satisfaction scores than older adults in the age-integrated building, then we can conclude that there is an association between type of apartment building and older adults' degree of happiness and satisfaction. However, it would not be appropriate to conclude that age-segregated apartments cause happiness and life satisfaction. In sum, when research participants cannot be randomly assigned to levels of a categorical variable, the study has a quasi-experimental design and the findings must be interpreted accordingly, with no reference to cause and effect.

Multifactor Designs

With a **multifactor research design**, there is more than one categorical variable. In some cases, multifactor research designs include both quasi-experimental and experimental variables (or factors). Many multifactor studies on adult development and aging include age, which is a quasi-experimental factor, as well as an experimental factor with two or more levels. Research participants within each age group are randomly assigned to levels of the experimental factor, which is an independent variable. To illustrate, we can elaborate on the memory study described earlier in which instruction was a two-level independent variable (visual-imagery instructions or study instructions) and older participants were randomly assigned to visual-imagery or to study instruction conditions. This study had a **single-factor research design** – type of instructions was the only independent variable.

Researchers with developmental interests often want to ascertain whether age has anything to do with the effectiveness of a treatment. Do visual-imagery instructions have the same positive effect on young adults' memory scores as they do on older adults' scores, or is the positive effect of imagery instructions limited to the older adults? To make this determination, we could add a second categorical variable to the design: age group. Participants from each of two adult age groups (young and older) could be randomly assigned to either a visual-imagery instruction condition or a study instruction condition. As in the

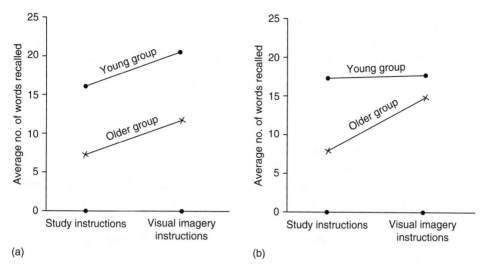

Figure 2.4 *Nonsignificant and significant Age × Memory Instructions interactions: (a) No significant interaction between age and memory instructions (b) Significant interaction between age and memory instructions.*

earlier study, after viewing a list of 25 words, participants are asked to recall as many as they can. Note that the instructions variable is manipulated and therefore it is independent; but the age variable is not manipulated and therefore it is organismic.

With this multifactor design, there are several possible outcomes. One is that, overall, the young group obtains higher memory scores compared with the older group. This would indicate a significant main effect for age. In addition, let's assume that both age groups benefit from visual–imagery instructions, and that the visual–imagery instructions have a comparable positive effect on the young and older groups. This would mean there is also a significant main effect for type of instructions, but the Age × Memory Instructions interaction effect would not be significant (see Figure 2.4(a)). In this case, age is irrelevant with regard to the effectiveness of visual–imagery instructions – the positive effect applies similarly to both age groups. This pattern of results has some value on a practical level, but it would not be interesting from a developmental standpoint.

Another possible outcome is that visual–imagery instructions have a positive effect on one age group but not the other (see Figure 2.4(b)). Overall, the memory scores of the young group may be higher than those of the older group. However, type of memory instructions may have no significant effect on the young group, whose memory scores are the same regardless of which instructions they receive. In contrast, older adults who are randomly assigned to the visual–imagery instruction condition may have higher memory scores than older adults who received the study instructions. This pattern would indicate what psychologists refer to as "a significant Age × Memory Instructions interaction." This simply means that the older adults' memory performance is sensitive to instructions whereas young adults' memory performance is not. Such an interaction would be of considerable interest to aging researchers. They might decide to conduct additional studies to test hypotheses about why visual-imagery instructions have a positive effect only on the older age group.

The Descriptive Approach

With the **descriptive approach**, the researcher does not attempt to manipulate any variables, so variables are neither independent nor dependent. Rather, data are collected on the variables of interest and the relationship between them is studied. In some instances, descriptive research is conducted only on older adults. In other instances, age may be one of many variables included. If age is a categorical variable (for example, young, middle-aged, and older groups), there may be interest in determining whether the relationship between the other variables follows the same pattern or a different pattern for the separate age groups. If age is a continuous variable, then there may be an interest in determining whether the other variables increase, decrease, or remain the same with increasing age.

Correlation is a statistical technique used to compute the extent of the relationship between two variables. (Complex correlation techniques can measure the relationship among many variables.) Correlation coefficients can range from −1.0 to +1.0. Both −1.0 and +1.0 indicate a perfect relationship between two variables. Perfect relationships between variables are rare in psychology. However, the closer a correlation is to −1.0 or +1.0, the stronger the relationship. With a strong **positive correlation** (for example, +.84), a high value on one variable is associated with a high value on the other variable. With a strong **negative correlation** (for example, −.84), a high value on one variable is associated with a low value on the other variable. The accuracy with which the value of one variable can be predicted based on knowledge about the value of the other variable is the same whether the correlation between the two variables is positive or negative.

A correlation of 0 indicates there is no relationship between the two variables. This means that information about one variable tells us nothing about the other variable. The closer the correlation coefficient is to 0, the less accurate the prediction we can make about the value of one variable when we have information about the value of the other variable. Figure 2.5 illustrates a strong positive correlation between two variables, a strong negative correlation between two variables, and no correlation between two variables.

Although a strong correlation (either positive or negative) makes it possible to predict the value of one variable with information about the other, it does not allow any statement about cause and effect. Even if two variables are highly correlated, it is not possible to determine whether one causes the other. To illustrate, suppose that we know there is a strong positive correlation between older adults' activity level and their satisfaction with life. Specifically, older adults with high scores on an activity questionnaire also have high scores on a life satisfaction

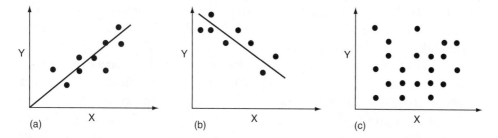

Figure 2.5 *Strong positive, strong negative, and zero correlation between two variables: (a) Strong positive correlation (.84) (b) Strong negative correlation (−.84) (c) Correlation = 0.*

questionnaire. Because these two variables are correlated, knowing the value of the activity score helps us to predict the value of the life satisfaction score. However, we cannot conclude that high activity causes high life satisfaction, nor can we say that high life satisfaction causes a high level of activity. It is entirely possible that a third variable, such as health, plays a role in determining both activity level and life satisfaction.

Ethics in Research on Human Aging

In 1932, the U.S. Public Health Service (USPHS) initiated the Tuskegee Syphilis Study. The Tuskegee Institute, an African American university in Alabama, agreed to let the USPHS use its medical facilities for the purpose of this study, which was essentially to follow the natural course of the disease. Approximately 399 African American sharecroppers, all in the early stages of syphilis, were recruited to participate in the study. Most were illiterate and underprivileged, and instead of being informed of their diagnosis, they were told they would be treated for "bad blood." Study participants were given free meals, free medical examinations, and burial insurance, but they were deliberately denied medication for the disease, even when it was discovered in the 1940s that penicillin could cure it. The health of these men was allowed to deteriorate to the point where they suffered from heart disease, blindness, and insanity. Over the next 40 years, many of these men died, many had infected their wives, and some of their children were born with syphilis. In 1972, journalists exposed the Tuskegee Study as the "longest nontherapeutic experiment on human beings in medical history" (see Jones, 1993). In 1997, President Clinton issued a formal apology, but this study left a harmful legacy – African Americans' distrust of the government and the medical profession.

Conducting research with living organisms entails considerations about ethics, and fortunately more safeguards are in place now compared to when the Tuskegee experiment was conducted. Colleges, universities, and research institutes require that any research on living organisms be submitted to an Institutional Review

Board (IRB). The IRB conducts a careful review of the purpose of the research project and the procedures researchers plan to follow. The IRB only approves research that meets ethics criteria.

In most cases, human research participants are required to sign a consent form before taking part in a study. The consent form must briefly describe the general nature and requirements of the study. For example, participants are informed that they will be asked to complete questionnaires, take timed tests, and so on. The consent form must disclose approximately how long the research session will last, whether participants are expected to return for more than one session, and what compensation or benefit they can anticipate from participating in the study.

In addition, the consent form assures participants that their responses will remain confidential, and it describes exactly how such confidentiality will be guaranteed. For example, names will not be placed on test protocols; test protocols will be coded with a number and stored separately from the consent form the participant has signed; consent forms will be kept in a locked cabinet that is accessible only to the research investigator. The consent form also gives participants an estimate of how many other individuals will be participating in the study because the number of participants could affect the level of confidentiality. A small number of participants may mean less anonymity. Finally, the consent form indicates that participants are free to discontinue at any time.

When presenting proposals to the IRB, researchers must explain both the nature of and reason for any "deception" that may be involved in a study. If there is deception, researchers must describe when and how research participants will be debriefed, or told about the actual purpose of the study. Also, there must be some assurance that deception will have no long-term negative effects on the research participants. If any short-term negative effects are anticipated, these must be justified. The researcher must make a convincing argument that the overall benefits of the findings are expected to outweigh any temporary discomfort participants could experience because of the deception.

Informed consent is necessary for all human research, but special issues may arise with older adult populations. For example, an investigator might want to study older adults who have been diagnosed with dementia. As Chapter 11 describes further, dementia is associated with compromised cognitive abilities, so individuals suffering from dementia may not be fully capable of giving informed consent. Under these circumstances, the investigator must obtain informed consent from participants' next of kin and/or from individuals who are in charge of participants' day-to-day needs and have their well-being in mind.

Revisiting the Selective Optimization with Compensation and Ecological Models

How do theory and method relate to the two theoretical frameworks introduced in the first chapter of this book? The Selective Optimization with Compensation

(SOC) Model (Baltes & Baltes, 1990) and the Ecological Model (Lawton, 1989; Lawton & Nahemow, 1973) have the closest fit with the contextual metamodel in that both conceptualize development as a series of bidirectional transactions and adjustments between the organism and the environment. However, these models can also be used to conceptualize development from mechanistic or organismic points of view, and they fit well with the propositions of the life-span developmental perspective.

The SOC and Ecological Models would both acknowledge the importance of age, cohort, and time of measurement when adult development is studied. In developmental studies, multifactor cross-sectional comparisons of two (or more) adult age groups could be used to investigate which strategies young and older adults would select to optimize their level of functioning in any number of domains. One age group might have more losses than the other, but effective use of compensation strategies could close any gap that may exist between the functioning of the two groups.

With regard to the Ecological Model, a cross-sectional design could be used to evaluate how well young and older adults adapt to living environments that present different levels of challenge, or press. When practicable, longitudinal studies that follow the same individuals over time could ascertain whether there are any changes in the strategies people use to maintain their level of functioning over the adult life span. Investigators could determine whether losses in some domains of functioning are compensated for by gains in other domains at various points in adult life. The longitudinal method would also be useful in determining which level of environmental press is most likely to insure the highest possible level of adaptation at various stages of adulthood.

The time-lag method could be used to determine whether older adults from different cohorts select the same strategies to compensate for age-related losses and thereby optimize their functioning. By testing several cohorts of older adults at different points in time, we could evaluate what kinds of losses are experienced and what types of compensatory strategies older adults use today as opposed to strategies older adults used in the past. The time-lag method could be used to investigate whether today's cohort of older adults is similar to or different from older cohorts in previous years or decades in adapting to environments with varying degrees of press.

Questions to Consider

1. If you have ever attended a high school or college reunion, have you noticed whether the classmates who attended were individuals that you remember as being very friendly and outgoing?
2. When you and your age peers reach older adulthood, do you think your generation will be the same as or different to those who are older adults today?
3. How would you obtain a sample of young adults and a sample of older adults if you wanted to compare the reading speed and reading comprehension of individuals in these two age groups?

Key Points

- Developmental researchers differ in their metatheoretical orientations. These orientations, or metamodels (mechanistic, organismic, or contextual), guide their beliefs about which aspects of development are most important and which theories best explain developmental phenomena.
- The life-span developmental perspective is most closely related to the contextual metamodel.
- Developmental researchers who conduct studies on aging and older adulthood must be concerned with three factors: chronological age, cohort (generation), and time of measurement.
- Developmental researchers use cross-sectional, longitudinal, time-lag, and sequential research designs.
- Cross-sectional designs are the most efficient, but the factors of age and cohort are confounded (that is, they cannot be disentangled).
- Longitudinal designs follow individuals over time. They can detect age-related change within individual members of a cohort (intraindividual change). However, the factors of age and time of measurement are confounded, and there may be selective attrition during the course of the study.
- In time-lag designs, all research participants are the same chronological age but are tested at different points in time. This design confounds the factors of cohort and time of measurement.
- Several complex sequential designs have been proposed as a means of disentangling the factors of age, cohort, and time of measurement.

- Measures used in research studies must be reliable, or consistent.
- Measures must also be valid, or measure what we think they measure.
- Internal validity refers to the accurate identification and interpretation of the factor that is responsible for an observation.
- External validity refers to whether findings from a sample of research participants can be generalized to the population of interest.
- Research on aging and older adulthood can use an experimental, quasi-experimental, or descriptive approach. Only the experimental approach allows conclusions to be drawn about cause and effect.
- Some research studies have multifactor designs in which at least one factor is quasi-experimental and the other is experimental.
- With the descriptive approach, an investigator studies two or more variables and determines the extent to which they are related to one another.
- Guidelines for ethics in human research protect study participants from harm, including invasion of privacy and coercion. Participants must be informed as to the nature and purpose of the study and must be debriefed if any deception is involved.

Key Terms

cohort   40

contextual metamodel   37

cross-sectional research design   42

descriptive approach   56

ecological validity   49

experimental approach   52

external validity   48

heterotypic continuity   49

internal validity   48

life-span developmental perspective   37

longitudinal research design   43

mechanistic metamodel   35

multifactor research design   54

negative correlation   56

organismic metamodel   36

positive correlation   56

quasi-experimental approach   53

reliability   47

selective attrition   44

sequential research designs   46

single-factor research design   54

time-lag research design   45

time of measurement   41

validity   48

3 Biological Aging and Health

Chapter Overview

Close-ups on Adulthood and Aging

Carlos just celebrated his 70th birthday and he definitely adheres to the philosophy that "70 is the new 50." Although Carlos often feels stiff when he wakes up in the morning, a brisk walk before breakfast helps work out the kinks. To keep limber, he rides his exercise bike and takes a class in tai chi. Carlos' mother lived to age 90, and until the last few months of her life she managed on her own with very little help. But even though his family background is in his favor for living a long life, Carlos is not counting on his genetic makeup to carry him through. He eats plenty of fruits and vegetables, limits his intake of alcohol, indulges in rich desserts only on special occasions, and makes sure to take the daily medication the doctor prescribed to control his high blood pressure. Carlos enjoys frequent get-togethers with his cronies to play poker and a good foursome of golf when the weather permits. In addition, his social life includes attending church and visiting with close family members. Carlos is convinced that an active and balanced lifestyle is the key to a long and healthy life.

The Meaning of Longevity

Why does aging occur and what determines how long people will live? In this chapter, we'll explore the biological aspects of aging. Unlike psychological aging, which includes both increments (gains) and decrements (losses), biological aging generally involves "decremental physical changes (both structural and functional) that develop with the passage of time and eventually end with death" (Busse, 1995, p. 754). Even so, these changes do not usually prevent people from leading productive and enjoyable lives.

Biological aging is gradual and cumulative. Biological functioning usually reaches a peak in early adulthood, after which it declines, but the rate of decline is not the same for everyone. Some people experience noticeable physical changes in their mid-60s or earlier, while others (like Carlos, who was described earlier) have the same physical capabilities as the average middle-aged adult into their 70s or later. Frequently we hear reports in the popular media about individuals in their 80s or even 90s who climb mountains, run marathon races, or work in demanding full-time jobs. Such older adults are not in the majority. Even so, most older adults are neither helpless nor dependent.

Some scientists think biological changes are a consequence of the aging process rather than the result of disease (Hayflick, 1995). However, aging in the absence of any disease process is rare because the likelihood of certain diseases increases with age (Masoro, 2006a). Also, although scientists have debated as to whether some diseases are an integral part of aging, it seems likely that aging can affect the consequences of disease when it does occur (Masoro, 2006a).

People who study biological processes in large populations use the terms **morbidity** and **mortality**. Morbidity refers to illness and disease, and mortality refers to death. These two terms are related because illness and disease can result in death, and death is often preceded by illness and disease. However, morbidity does not necessarily result in mortality – people with chronic illnesses can live for a long time with the proper treatment. **Longevity** refers to the length and duration of life. Two aspects of longevity are **life expectancy** and **life span**. As we will see shortly, life expectancy and life span are related but they are not one and the same.

Life Expectancy

Life expectancy is the average number of years people in a particular cohort are expected to live. Life expectancy figures indicate what is anticipated, on average, for large numbers of people but they cannot forecast how many years an individual cohort member will live.

Life expectancy at birth

Life expectancy at birth is the average number of years people born in a specific year (that is, a birth cohort) are expected to live. It is affected by factors such as

Table 3.1 *Life expectancy at birth in the United States*

Year of birth	Both sexes	Males	Females
1900	47.3	46.3	48.3
1970	70.8	67.1	74.7
1980	73.7	70.0	77.4
1990	75.4	71.8	78.8
2000	77.0	74.3	79.7
2005	77.8	75.2	80.4

Source: National Center for Health Statistics (2007).

level of nutrition, sanitary conditions, and medical care, including antibiotics and immunizations that are available to the population of a particular country.

Table 3.1 shows that infants born in the United States in 1900 had an average life expectancy of 47.3 years of age, but by 1970 the average life expectancy was 70.8 years. This dramatic increase is attributable chiefly to medical advances that reduced infant mortality, mortality from childhood diseases, and maternal mortality. Since 1970, life expectancy in the United States has continued to climb gradually, no doubt due to improvements in public health that further reduced mortality from infectious diseases. In addition, medical advances that prevent or treat cardiovascular diseases and cancer have helped boost life expectancy.

With regard to gender, the gap between female and male infants born in 1900 was only two years, but by 1970, it had widened to 7.6 years. By 2005, the gender gap in life expectancy was a somewhat narrower 5.2 years. Table 3.2 shows life expectancy figures by race and sex. Note that the figures for African American infants are lower overall, but the same gender gap exists for African Americans and European Americans. Only time will tell whether this gap will remain stable or whether it will shrink over time.

In the United States, life expectancy at birth could continue to rise gradually with further medical advances, especially as more effective treatments become available for diseases that occur in the middle and older adult years. However, there is some speculation that life expectancy could actually decrease because of a surge in the rate of obesity (National Institutes of Health [NIH], 2005). It is estimated that almost 25% of Americans aged 60+ are obese (*A Profile of Older Americans*, 2007). However, the life-shortening effect of obesity could be moderated by efforts to engage in exercise and adhere to diets that insure long-term weight control.

Table 3.2 *Life expectancy at birth by race and sex in the United States*

Year	European American			African American		
	Both sexes	Males	Females	Both sexes	Males	Females
1970	71.7	68.0	75.6	64.1	60.0	68.3
1980	74.4	70.7	78.1	68.1	63.8	72.5
1990	76.1	72.7	79.4	69.1	64.5	73.6
2000	77.6	74.9	80.1	71.9	68.3	75.2
2005	78.3	75.7	80.8	73.2	69.5	76.5

Source: National Center for Health Statistics (2007).

Understanding Aging Box 3.1: Health and Survival: The Hispanic Paradox

Social scientists have noted what appears to be a differential mortality advantage among older Hispanics who live in the United States. In a government survey of 130,000 individuals conducted between 1985 and 1994, there was no difference in mortality rate between non-Hispanic whites and Hispanics born in Puerto Rico or Cuba. However, other foreign-born Hispanics (Mexicans, Central Americans, and South Americans) who migrated to the United States died later on average and did not get sick as often (Palloni & Arias, 2004). Are those who choose to migrate to the United States hardier than those who were born there? In general, people higher in socioeconomic status (SES) tend to be healthier and to have greater longevity than those lower in SES. However, Turra and Goldman (2007) linked government data collected on 500,000 individuals between 1989 and 1994 with mortality data through 1997. Among Hispanics, especially those of Mexican origin, SES disparities were smaller than they were among non-Hispanic whites. On closer inspection, the mortality advantage for Hispanics was concentrated at lower levels of SES. Further study is planned to determine the basis for this phenomenon.

Global considerations

Not surprisingly, life expectancy at birth varies from country to country (see Figure 3.1). In developed countries (for example, Japan, United Kingdom, and Sweden), life expectancy at birth is about the same or slightly higher than that in the United States. Life expectancy at birth is much lower in less developed countries (for example, Afghanistan, Uganda, and Rwanda), no doubt because of less available medical care, poor nutrition, and less sanitary public health conditions.

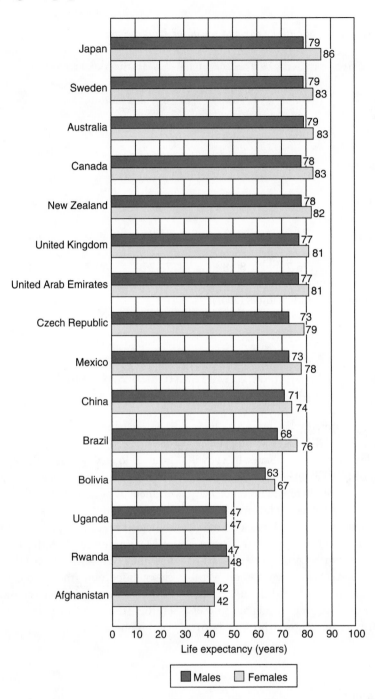

Figure 3.1 *Male and female life expectancies at birth in selected countries.*
Source: Population Reference Bureau (2007).

Table 3.3 *Life expectancy at ages 65 and 75 by race and sex in the United States, 2005*

	European American			African American		
Age	Both sexes	Males	Females	Both sexes	Males	Females
65	18.8	17.2	20.0	17.2	15.2	18.7
75	11.9	10.7	12.8	11.4	10.0	12.3

Source: National Center for Health Statistics (2007).

Life expectancy at ages 65 and 75

Once people celebrate their 65th birthday, how much longer will they live? In the United States, those who reach 65 represent a select group that has survived obstacles that ended the lives of some fellow cohort members, and those reaching age 75 are even more select. Table 3.3 shows life expectancy figures for European Americans and African Americans who reach age 65 and age 75. Note that, on average, men who reach age 65 and age 75 have fewer years left than women do. Also note that at age 75, the gap in life expectancy between European Americans and African Americans is small.

Life Span

Life span is the maximum longevity, or extreme upper limit of time, that members of a species can live. What is that figure for humans?

In the 1970s, there were reports of villagers in isolated mountainous regions of Russia, Turkey, and Ecuador who claimed to be **centenarians** (living to the age of 100). In fact, some gave ages up to 160 (Beller & Palmore, 1974; Kyucharyants, 1974; Medvedev, 1974). Scientists flocked to these remote areas only to discover that these phenomenally old ages were exaggerated. The confusion was due partly to inaccurate birth records but also to the common practice of duplicating names across several generations.

Until recently, the oldest person with a documented birth record was a woman named Jeanne Calment of Arles, France, who was born in 1875 and died in August 1997, at the age of 122 (Weiss, 1997). This record has been challenged by a Brazilian woman, Maria Olivia da Silva, who was born in 1880 and celebrated her 125th birthday in 2005. However, this claim, which appeared on the Wikipedia website in 2007, has not been firmly established.

Rectangular survival curve

Although human life expectancy has increased dramatically over the past century in the United States and other developed countries, the human life span has remained relatively constant over time and across cultures. Today, however, the chances of approaching maximum human longevity are higher, especially in developed countries, so more and more people are living closer to the maximum human life span.

As hygienic conditions improve, as disease-related causes of death are prevented or delayed, and as more people adopt healthy lifestyles, life expectancy should continue to increase gradually and more people will approach the maximum human life span. The term **compression of mortality** (Fries, 1995, 1997) refers to a phenomenon whereby a greater proportion of deaths will occur during a very narrow time period toward the upper limit of the human life span. In other words, more and more people will live closer to the maximum human life span, with the resultant **rectangular survival curve** shown in Figure 3.2.

Quality of life

If people live a long time, will their final years be characterized by disability, dependency, and disease, or will they enjoy independence and robust health (Fries, 1997; Schneider, 1997)? In other words, will compression of mortality be accompanied by a corresponding **compression of morbidity**? Compression of morbidity means that illness or extreme disability will occur only during a narrow period of time immediately prior to death. To the extent that onset of disease and disability can be delayed until a short interval of time late in life, quality of life should remain high until very close to its end.

In summary, human life expectancy has been increasing, but human life span has changed very little over time. The rectangular survival curve illustrates that a larger proportion of people are approaching maximum life span, so more individuals could become centenarians. However, life span is not likely to change until the key to aging is discovered (Hayflick, 1994; Olshansky et al., 2002). Meanwhile, a more realistic goal is to maximize the quality of the years that we have left.

The Biological Aging Process

What is biological aging? Will it happen no matter where or how a person lives, and does it occur earlier under some circumstances than others? According to some theories, biological aging occurs within

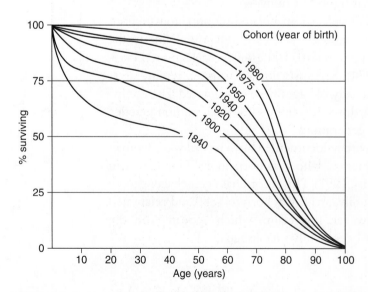

Figure 3.2 *The rectangular survival curve.*
Source: Adapted from Katchadourian (1987).

the organism regardless of outside forces. Other theories contend that biological aging is influenced by our environment and daily habits and also by the way we cope with life's challenges (VonDras & Blumenthal, 2000).

Primary and Secondary Aging

Some researchers distinguish between two categories of biological aging: **primary aging** and **secondary aging**. Primary aging refers to the unavoidable (inevitable) biological processes that are universal, meaning that all members of a species are affected. Its effects may not become apparent for many years, but primary aging is set in motion early in life and progresses gradually over time. However, there are individual differences in the rate at which it occurs. In addition to being inevitable and universal, primary aging is intrinsic, meaning it is determined by factors within the organism. Some scientists use the term *senescence* to mean primary aging (Busse, 1995).

Secondary aging refers to processes experienced by most, but not necessarily all, members of a species. Thus, it is neither inevitable nor universal. Unlike primary aging, secondary aging is associated with defects in biological functioning resulting from hostile environmental influences (Busse, 1995). In short, secondary aging is attributed to disease, disuse, and abuse. Diseases can accelerate aging, as can disuse from lack of exercise, as well as abuse from habits such as smoking, excessive consumption of alcohol, poor nutrition, or overexposure to sun or loud noise. Note that Carlos, who was described earlier, tries to avoid sources of disuse and abuse.

The distinction between primary and secondary aging is not accepted by everyone, nor is it always possible to differentiate the effects of aging from the symptoms of diseases that occur frequently in the later years (Masoro, 2006a). Also, primary aging may render us more vulnerable to disease and other sources of damage usually associated with secondary aging. However, a conceptual distinction can heighten our awareness of aspects of our lives over which we may exert some control.

Theories of biological aging are often grouped into two general categories: programmed and stochastic (Cristofalo, Tresini, Francis, & Volker, 1999). Table 3.4 lists several prominent theories identified with each category, but not every theory falls strictly into one category or the other.

Programmed Theories of Biological Aging

Programmed theories of biological aging consider aging to be under the control of a genetically based blueprint (Hayflick, 1994). As such, these theories are closely related to primary aging.

Cellular aging

Time clock theory was based on Hayflick's early research on cells that were removed from tissues of various organisms and grown in culture. Cells taken from a human

Table 3.4 *Theories of biological aging*

Programmed theories	Stochastic theories
Time clock theory	Error theory
Immune theory	Wear and tear theory
Evolutionary theory	Rate of living theory
	Stress theory
	Cross-linking theory
	Free radical theory

infant doubled approximately 50 times, whereas cells from a mouse (maximum life span of only 3 years) doubled only 10–15 times. This suggested that the life span of a species was controlled by a genetically determined time clock operating at the cellular level.

Even within the human species, cells from infants and young children divided more times than cells from older adults, which presumably had already used up part of their program. Also, cells from children with Down syndrome (a genetic abnormality associated with shorter than average life expectancy) and children with progeria (a rare genetic abnormality characterized by premature aging and extremely reduced life expectancy) divided fewer times than did cells from genetically normal individuals of the same age (Hayflick, 1995). Even so, it was not clear exactly what determined the number of times cells would divide. Furthermore, Cristofalo et al. (1999) contend that the number of cell divisions may be more related to health than to age. Nonetheless, Hayflick's research opened the door to programmed theories of aging.

Recently, researchers have focused on **telomeres**, the protective caps at the tail ends of the chromosomes located in each cell. Each time a cell divides, telomeres lose some length and, when they become too short, cell division is no longer possible and cells become senescent (Cristofalo et al., 1999). Thus, the length of the telomeres may determine cell longevity

Children with a rare genetic disorder, progeria, experience premature aging and reduced life expectancy.

and perhaps, indirectly, the longevity of the organism. Researchers are trying to determine whether supplying cells with an enzyme called telomerase can lengthen or maintain the telomeres, making it possible for cells to continue dividing and avoid becoming senescent. However, there may be a trade-off between stimulating telomerase activity to prevent cell senescence and promoting abnormal cell division typically seen in diseases such as cancer (Harley, 2006).

The immune system

The immune system defends the body against invasion of foreign substances by producing antibodies that circulate and deactivate substances not recognized as self. According to *immune theory*, the immune system is programmed to maintain its efficiency for a certain amount of time, after which it starts to decline. A compromised immune system may not produce sufficient antibodies to protect against foreign invaders. Furthermore, it may produce inferior antibodies, which mistakenly attack and destroy normal cells. Weakened immune system functioning has been linked to age-related diseases such as cancer (Effros, 2006). However, it is premature to conclude that immune system decline is the cause rather than the result of normal aging (Hayflick, 1994).

Evolution

According to the *evolutionary theory* of biological aging, members of a species are genetically programmed to bear and rear their young. Once they reproduce and raise their offspring to independence, they have fulfilled their service in perpetuating the species. Researchers have found that fruit flies forced to delay reproduction to later ages live longer than fruit flies that reproduced early (Phelan, 2006). Nonetheless, even after reproduction, organisms may have sufficient energy to coast along for some period of time. Once excess energy is used up, however, susceptibility to disease increases. Hayflick (1994) likens the years beyond reproduction and raising offspring to the ticking of a watch after the warranty period is over. He suggests that instead of asking, "Why do we age?" we should ask, "How do we manage to live as long as we do?"

Stochastic Theories of Biological Aging

Stochastic theories of biological aging focus on random damage to our vital systems that occurs with the process of living, so these theories are closely related to secondary aging. As damage accumulates, we cease to function efficiently and eventually life becomes impossible to sustain. Support for stochastic theories comes from the fact that aging occurs at different rates even among identical twins who have exactly the same genetic makeup but rarely live exactly the same amount of time. Also, certain environmental factors are associated with accelerated aging and shortened longevity (Cristofalo et al., 1999).

Errors

Error theory postulates that errors occur at the cellular level, resulting in the production of faulty molecules. Errors can result from the organism's metabolic processes or exposure to environmental factors such as radiation. Cells have protective mechanisms that repair errors, but these may not keep up with the damage created by faulty molecules. Over time, unrepaired damage builds up, eventually resulting in metabolic failure and ultimately death (Turker, 1996). We have much to learn about what causes errors and exactly how they are repaired, but this theory is a promising approach to understanding biological aging (Hayflick, 1994).

Wear and tear

Not surprisingly, damage to the body can build up during the course of living. The *rate of living theory*, which is a variant of the *wear and tear theory*, postulates that we begin life with a fixed amount of physiological energy. If we expend it quickly, aging begins early and proceeds rapidly. However, we can retard aging by conserving energy. Appealing as this sounds, there is little direct evidence that taking it easy will retard aging. For example, people who work in physically strenuous jobs do not show signs of aging any earlier than those who work in less physically demanding jobs (Hayflick, 1994, 1995).

Stress

Life can be demanding in ways that are not physical, and according to the *stress theory* of aging, the biological system sustains damage from prolonged exposure to stress. The body has two regulatory systems for responding to stress – the sympathetic nervous system (SNS) and the neuroendocrine hypothalamic-pituitary-adrenal (HPA) axis (Finch & Seeman, 1999). Stress triggers physiological activation that results in secretion of stress-related hormones called glucocorticoids (GC). In young organisms, the HPA axis quickly returns to a normal level following exposure to stress. In older organisms, the HPA axis takes longer to return to a normal level, which means that older organisms have prolonged exposure to GC hormones that have been secreted in response to stress. Prolonged exposure to GC increases the risk of high blood pressure (hypertension) and cardiovascular disease. Ultimately, stress-related damage to the biological system can accelerate the aging process (Nichols, 2006).

Finch and Seeman (1999) describe a study that used a driving simulation test to assess reactions to stress. Young (aged 30–39) and older (aged 70–79) adults responded to potentially dangerous situations similar to those encountered in real-world driving. GC levels were measured prior to the simulated driving test (baseline) and several times later on, up to two hours after the test was completed. GC levels of the younger adults returned to baseline levels well before two hours had elapsed, evidence for greater resiliency. In contrast, GC levels of the older adults remained elevated after two hours, indicating less resiliency. However, the GC level of the less healthy older adults, many of whom suffered from diabetes (discussed later on) and high blood pressure, remained elevated for longer than the GC level of the healthier older adults. Uchino, Berg, Smith, Pearce, and Skinner (2006) studied cardiovascular reactivity in younger and older adults as they confronted daily life stress. Older adults showed greater reactivity (increase in blood pressure) than younger adults did even though older adults' heightened physiological responsiveness was not coupled with an increase in self-reported negative affect.

Exercise and dietary regulation seem to have a protective effect on older adults' neuroendocrine and cardiovascular functioning. For example, regular exercise and restricted diets often result in lowered blood glucose, which could offset the negative effects of exposure to stress-related hormones. In addition, being part of a social network is beneficial for feelings of psychological well-being, which in turn has been associated with less exaggerated responses to stress. In older adults, feelings of loneliness are associated with higher blood pressure (Hawkley & Cacioppo, 2007). At present, we cannot make cause-and-effect statements, but longitudinal studies could help clarify the picture.

Build-up of damaging substances

Some biological theories of aging focus on damaging substances or waste products that could disrupt physiological functioning. *Lipofuscin*, a substance that accumulates in the brain and in heart muscle cells, increases with age, although it has not been established whether, or even how, it interferes with functioning.

Collagen is a common protein that surrounds and supports tendons, ligaments, bone, cartilage, and skin. It consists of parallel molecules held together by ladder-like rungs, or cross-links. When neighboring molecules are joined by a small number of cross-links, they remain pliable. As the number of cross-links increases, the ladders become less pliable. Age-related changes in the skin are a visible example of cross-linking. In young adults, the skin is soft and pliable, but with increasing age and more cross-links, it becomes less so. According to the *cross-linking theory* of aging, cross-linking affects metabolic functioning because it obstructs the passage of nutrients and waste products into and out of cells. As with lipofuscin, cross-linking increases with age, but it is still not clear whether cross-linking is a cause, or simply a by-product, of the aging process (Hayflick, 1994).

Free radical theory focuses on unstable molecular fragments (free radicals), which are formed as a by-product of the body's normal metabolic processes. Because of their instability, free radicals unite with molecules that happen their way, thereby preventing those molecules from functioning normally. Free radicals can damage proteins, fats, and lipids, and they have been implicated in the production of cross-links. They have also been associated with changes in the brain and with cardiovascular disease, cancer, and even the formation of cataracts on the lens of the older eye (Rowe & Kahn, 1998).

There is evidence that antioxidants (including vitamins E and C and beta-carotene) serve to chemically inhibit the formation of free radicals, or at least compromise their ability to unite with susceptible molecules (Rowe & Kahn, 1998). Consumption of antioxidants has been associated with lowered incidence of cardiovascular disease and cancer, both age-related diseases. There are some reports that animals fed antioxidants live longer on average compared to control animals not fed extra antioxidants. However, it has yet to be shown that antioxidants actually increase the maximum longevity (life span) of a species (Hayflick, 1994).

In sum, lipofuscin, collagen, cross-linking, and free radicals accumulate as we age, but do these substances actually cause aging? Olshansky et al. (2002) question the claim made by the anti-aging industry that antioxidant supplements can slow down aging. Antioxidants occur naturally in the body and in fruits and vegetables, but supplements could be harmful because we need some free radicals for certain necessary steps in internal biochemical reactions.

Caloric Restriction and Longevity

The role of diet in aging and longevity has intrigued researchers for decades. In an early study, McCay, Crowell, and Maynard (1935) demonstrated that rats fed a severely reduced number of calories lived longer than rats allowed normal caloric intake. Recent studies have shown that as long as they have nutritionally sound diets, rats that consume 50% fewer calories and weigh 50% less than normally fed control rats have a lower incidence of cancer, increased longevity, and the sleeker appearance of younger rats. Vasselli et al. (2005) reported that rats restricted throughout life had the greatest longevity, whereas those obese throughout life had the shortest longevity. The longevity of rats that had been obese but then lost weight did not differ from that of rats that were nonobese throughout life, which indicates that dietary changes can have a positive effect on longevity.

There are several hypotheses about why caloric restriction has a positive effect on rodents (Weindruch, 1996). Caloric restriction may slow the rate of cell division, thereby reducing the chances of the uncontrolled cell division characteristic of late-life cancers. Also, caloric restriction is associated with lower blood glucose level, which reduces the chances of damage from the build-up of sugar on proteins. Additionally, caloric restriction may limit the formation of free radicals. At present, there is no one answer as to why caloric restriction increases average longevity in rodents. It may slow down the aging program or perhaps it simply delays the onset of disease.

It remains to be seen whether caloric restriction is beneficial for humans. There is evidence that people living on the Japanese island of Okinawa, whose diets are low in calories but high in nutrients, enjoy greater than average longevity. Also, people with reduced caloric intake have a lower incidence of some forms of cancer. Weindruch (1996) recommends a diet that reduces the level of blood glucose and cholesterol, and he suggests that people strive to weigh 10 to 25% less than their natural "set point." Clearly, obesity is a risk factor that can shorten life, but questions remain about the benefits of caloric restriction for normal-weight humans.

In summary, there are numerous theories about why biological aging occurs, but no one that has proved definitive. As yet, no single fundamental mechanism has been identified as holding the key to the process of aging (Martin, 2007). Also, theories of biological aging are often categorized as programmed or stochastic, but keep in mind that genetic programming could render organisms either more or less vulnerable to damage from internal and external sources

Individual Differences in Longevity

The upper limit of the human life span is approximately 120 years, but why do some people live closer to that limit than others? Studying individuals who live a long time is one way to explore this question.

In the United States, the Georgia Centenarian Study has been following people 60 to 100 years of age to determine the relationships between family longevity, social and environmental support, personality characteristics, adaptational skills, satisfaction with life, loneliness, nutrition and dietary patterns, and health (Fees, Martin, & Poon, 1999; Poon, Sweaney, Clayton, & Merriam, 1992). So far, continued follow-up of these individuals indicates that those who control the stress in their lives, engage in regular physical activity, and maintain a good level of nutrition are less likely to show an increase in fatigue over time (Martin, Bishop, Poon, & Johnson, 2006). Harvard Medical School researcher Thomas Perls and his colleagues have studied 150 centenarians. Based on their findings, they developed a quiz people can take to determine their chances of living to 100 (see Table 3.5).

Nature and Nurture

Who among us will have the good fortune to remain healthy and vigorous into the ninth decade or later? To answer this question, scientists are investigating factors related to both nature and nurture.

Nature

Nature refers to heredity, or genetic makeup. The number of genes that underlie the aging process is not known (Turker, 1996), although heredity does seem to be a factor in longevity. Most people who live beyond age 70 have at least one parent or grandparent who lived into the 70s. Those who live into their 90s are likely to have at least one very long-lived parent, though the age of the mother's death seems to be a better predictor of a person's longevity than the age of the father's death (Hayflick, 1994).

Identical twins have exactly the same genetic makeup and are more similar in longevity compared to fraternal twins, who are no more genetically related than other siblings. Even so, identical twins do not always age in a completely parallel fashion, nor do they live exactly the same amount of time (Hayflick, 1994). Thus, nature cannot fully account for the rate at which people age and how long they live.

Table 3.5 *Will you live to be 100?*
After completing a study of 150 centenarians, Harvard Medical School researchers
Thomas Perls, MD, and Margery Hutter Silver, EdD, developed a quiz to help you calculate your
estimated life expectancy.

	Score

1. Do you smoke or chew tobacco, or are you around a lot of secondhand smoke? Yes (−20) No (0)
2. Do you cook your fish, poultry, or meat until it is charred? Yes (−2) No (0)
3. Do you avoid butter, cream, pastries, and other saturated fats as well as fried foods (e.g., French fries)? Yes (+3) No (−7)
4. Do you minimize meat in your diet, preferably making a point to eat plenty of fruits, vegetables, and bran instead? Yes (+5) No (−4)
5. Do you consume more than two drinks of beer, wine and/or liquor a day? (A standard drink is one 12-ounce bottle of beer, one wine cooler, one five-ounce glass of wine, or one and a half ounces of 80-proof distilled spirits.) Yes (−10) No (0)
6. Do you drink beer, wine, and/or liquor in moderate amounts (one or two drinks/day)? Yes (+3) No (0)
7. Do air pollution warnings occur where you live? Yes (−4) No (+1)
8. (a) Do you drink more than 16 ounces of coffee a day? Yes (−3) No (0) (b) Do you drink tea daily? Yes (+3) No (0)
9. Do you take an aspirin a day? Yes (+4) No (0)
10. Do you floss your teeth every day? Yes (+2) No (−4)
11. Do you have a bowel movement less than once every two days? Yes (−4) No (0)
12. Have you had a stroke or heart attack? Yes (−10) No (0)
13. Do you try to get a sun tan? Yes (−4) No (+3)
14. Are you more than 20 pounds overweight? Yes (−10) No (0)
15. Do you live near enough to other family members (other than your spouse and dependent children) that you can and want to drop by spontaneously? Yes (+5) No (−4)
16. Which statement is applicable to you? (a) "Stress eats away at me. I can't seem to shake it off." Yes (−7) (b) "I can shed stress." This might be by praying, exercising, meditating, finding humor in everyday life, or other means. Yes (+7)
17. Did both of your parents either die before age 75 of nonaccidental causes or require daily assistance by the time they reached age 75? Yes (−10) No (0) Don't know (0)
18. Did more than one of the following relatives live to at least age 90 in excellent health: parents, aunts/uncles, grandparents? Yes (+24) No (0) Don't know (0)
19. (a) Are you a couch potato (do no regular aerobic or resistance exercise)? Yes (−7) (b) Do you exercise at least three times a week? Yes (+7)
20. Do you take vitamin E (400−800 IU) and selenium (100−200 mcg) every day? Yes (+5) No (−3)

STEP 1: Add the negative and positive scores together. Example: −45 plus +30 = −15. Divide the preceding score by 5 (−15 divided by 5 = −3).

STEP 2: Add the negative or positive number to age 84 if you are a man or age 88 if you are a woman (example: −3 + 88 = 85) to get your estimated life span.

Table 3.5 *(cont'd)*

The Science Behind the Quiz

Question 1: Cigarette smoke contains toxins that directly damage DNA, causing cancer and other diseases and accelerating aging.

Question 2: Charring food changes its proteins and amino acids into heterocyclic amines, which are potent mutagens that can alter your DNA.

Questions 3,4: A high-fat diet and especially a high-fat, high-protein diet, may increase your risk of cancer of the breast, uterus, prostate, colon, pancreas, and kidney. A diet rich in fruits and vegetables may lower the risk of heart disease and cancer.

Questions 5,6: Executive alcohol consumption can damage the liver and other organs, leading to accelerated aging and increased susceptibility to disease. Moderate consumption may lower the risk of heart disease.

Question 7: Certain air pollutants may cause cancer; many also contain oxidants that accelerate aging.

Question 8: Too much coffee predisposes the stomach to ulcers and chronic inflammation, which in turn raise the risk of heart disease. High coffee consumption may also indicate and exacerbate stress. Tea, on the other hand, is noted for its significant antioxidant content.

Question 9: Taking 81 milligrams of aspirin a day (the amount in one baby aspirin) has been shown to decrease the risk of heart disease, possibly because of its anticlotting effects.

Question 10: Research now shows that chronic gum disease can lead to the release of bacteria into the bloodstream, contributing to heart disease.

Question 11: Scientists believe that having at least one bowel movement every 20 hours decreases the incidence of colon cancer.

Question 12: A previous history of stroke and heart attack makes you more susceptible to future attacks.

Question 13: The ultraviolet in sunlight directly damages DNA, causing wrinkles and increasing the risk of skin cancer.

Question 14: Being obese increases the risk of various cancers, heart disease, and diabetes. The more overweight you are, the higher your risk of disease and death.

Questions 15,16: People who do not belong to cohesive families have fewer coping resources and therefore have increased levels of social and psychological stress. Stress is associated with heart disease and some cancers.

Questions 17,18: Studies show that genetics play a significant role in the ability to reach extreme old age.

Question 19: Exercise leads to more efficient energy production in the cells and, overall, less oxygen radical formation. Oxygen (or free) radicals are highly reactive molecules or atoms that damage cells and DNA, ultimately leading to aging.

Quesiton 20: Vitamin E is a powerful antioxidant and has been shown to retard the progression of Alzheimer's, heart disease, and stroke. Selenium may prevent some types of cancer.

Source: Perls & Silver (1999).

Understanding Aging Box 3.2: Gender Crossover in Late Older Adulthood

In his investigation of older adulthood, Thomas Perls (2004b) reports that starting in the 8th decade but more so in the 9th decade, men are often better off mentally and physically than women. In terms of absolute numbers, more women than men are still alive at age 95. At this very late stage of life, however, a larger proportion of men than women enjoy a high level of mental and physical fitness that allows them to lead lives of relative independence with few major health problems and little need for special care. For reasons we do not yet fully understand, men who survive into their 90s seem to be spared from some of the health problems experienced by many women their age.

Nurture

Nurture refers to environmental influences such as the quality of air a person breathes, diet and exercise habits, educational and work history, level of stress in the environment, and health care. It can also include factors such as marital status and social relationships. Rowe and Kahn (1998) contend that as we grow older, genetics become less important, but where and how we live become more important. Carlos, described at the beginning of the chapter, is not counting on genetics to insure a long and healthy life.

The Nun Study

The Nun Study, a longitudinal research program under the direction of University of Kentucky epidemiologist Dr. David Snowdon, has been following over 500 School Sisters of Notre Dame who reside in religious communities across the United States (Snowdon, 1997). In 1997, when they agreed to take periodic test batteries and to donate their brains to science after their death, these Sisters ranged from 75 to 102 years of age. All of the Sisters have similar educational backgrounds, they all worked throughout their adult lives in teaching and service careers, and they lived for decades in religious communities and had similar dietary and exercise habits. They never married or had children, nor did they indulge in habits such as smoking or drinking alcoholic beverages. In short, for these Sisters, the influence of nurture has been similar from early adulthood when they entered the religious order. Nonetheless, the variability among them is striking. Some have remained healthy and active, both physically and cognitively, well beyond their ninth decade. Others are confined to wheelchairs or suffer from cognitive impairments due to strokes or dementia. Such individual differences suggest that nature, or more likely the interaction between nature and nurture, plays a role in health and longevity. However, the influences of nurture could have varied prior to the Sisters' joining the religious order, so we cannot rule out early environmental influences as a reason for their late-life variability in health and longevity.

Marital status

Marital status has been investigated with regard to both health and longevity. Schone and Weinick (1998) inspected the self-reported health habits of 4,443 community-living men and women aged 65 and older who participated in the U.S. National Medical Expenditure Survey (NMES) administered in 1987. Marital status was clearly associated with preventive health behaviors. Those who were married were more likely to have healthy habits such as physical activity, eating breakfast, wearing seatbelts, and abstaining from smoking. However, the association between marriage and engaging in healthy habits was stronger for older men than it was for older women. Schone and Weinick speculate that women value health more than men do, so they may take the lead in monitoring or encouraging husbands to engage in healthy behaviors. Also, those who were African American, lower in economic status, or had fewer years of education were less likely to engage in healthy behaviors. In addition, older adults with fewer social contacts were less likely to have healthy habits than those with more social contacts. Widowed women have more social contacts than widowed men. For women, healthy behaviors may be associated more with social contacts than with marital status.

Tucker, Wingard, Friedman, and Schwartz (1996) studied marital status and longevity by examining data from 1,077 men and women from the Terman Life-Cycle Longitudinal Study that was initiated in 1921. Terman study participants were a select group of intelligent, educated, middle-class, primarily European American children born in 1910. Tucker et al. categorized the Terman study participants according to their marital status as of midlife (in 1950) as follows: (1) consistently married (married with no prior marital breakups); (2) inconsistently married (married, but with a prior marital breakup); (3) separated or divorced; (4) single. When the mortality of these individuals was checked in 1991, those married as of 1950 were found to have lived longer than those separated or divorced as of 1950. This suggests that when it comes to longevity, marriage is indeed a protective factor.

However, several additional findings serve to remind us that we need to exercise caution before concluding that marriage has a uniformly positive effect on longevity. First, in this select sample, individuals who were single as of midlife (1950) had no greater mortality risk than did those married as of 1950. Second, particularly for men, those individuals who were married at midlife but had already experienced a marital breakup (inconsistently married) had a higher mortality risk than those who were consistently married. Tucker et al. speculate that marital breakup may have long-term negative effects that are not completely reduced by remarriage. However, marital inconsistency could also be associated with lower conscientiousness about health. These findings may not generalize to samples with greater diversity or from different birth cohorts, but they should increase our awareness that when it comes to longevity, marital history rather than marital status may serve as a protective factor.

In sum, investigators have tried to study the role of nature and nurture in longevity. However, longevity is most likely based on a complex mix and interaction of genetic and environmental factors.

Can Social Scientists Predict Longevity?

With such wide variation in human longevity, it is no wonder that social scientists are interested in predicting who will live a long time and who will not. Accurate prediction is a first step toward possible control through interventions that could enable more people to live closer to maximum human longevity.

Tests of cognitive ability, and in some cases self-report measures of health and well-being, have been used to detect whether the end of life is near. In an early study, Kleemeier (1962) administered the Wechsler Adult Intelligence Scale (discussed in more detail in Chapter 6) to 13 elderly men on four occasions over 12 years. During the 12-year interval, the men's scores declined, but the decline was much steeper for the 4 men who were deceased at the end of the 12-year period than it was for the 9 men who survived. Kleemeier's finding of a steeper decline in the deceased individuals became known as **terminal drop** and has been the subject of many subsequent research studies that aim to determine what variables predict mortality.

Deary and Der (2005) tested 898 men and women on several measures in 1988, when they were in their mid-50s. Fourteen years later, 185 people (99 men and 86 women) had died. Reaction time (discussed in Chapter 4) was a strong predictor of mortality – those who were quicker in their 50s were more likely to be alive 14 years later than those who were slower.

Maier and Smith (1999) inspected scores on tests of intellectual functioning administered to 516 individuals (ages 70–103) as part of the Berlin Aging Study in Germany. Each individual was tested only once between 1990 and 1993. By 1996 (3 to 6 years later), 50% of these individuals were deceased, and low test scores were strongly associated with high risk of mortality. To a lesser but still significant extent, subjective feelings of dissatisfaction with aging were also associated with elevated mortality risk. Thus, predictors of mortality were not limited to cognitive functioning, but also included self-evaluations of personal well-being.

Similar findings were reported by Menec, Chipperfield, and Perry (1999) when they inspected data from 1,406 older (ages 65–85+) residents of Manitoba who participated in a longitudinal survey conducted by the Canadian government. Older adults who rated their health as "bad" were more than twice as likely to die within the following 3-year period compared to older adults who rated their health as "excellent." The association between self-perceived health and mortality risk was significant even when information about the number of physician visits, hospitalizations, and disease diagnoses was taken into account. Clearly, we need to learn more about what factors underlie the relationship between self-perceived health and mortality.

Findings from the Nun Study described earlier indicate it may be possible to predict longevity on the basis of cognitive and emotional measures made much earlier in life. Approximately 180 Sisters who entered convents between 1931 and 1943 at age 22 were required to write an autobiography, which was preserved in the archives of the convent. These authenticated handwritten autobiographies were made available to the Nun Study investigators, who analyzed them for grammatical structure and content. By 1991, the Sisters who had written autobiographies as young adults ranged in age from 75 to 95. By the year 2000, 104 Sisters (58%) were still living but 76 Sisters (42%) were deceased. Not only was the level of linguistic ability evident in autobiographies written six decades earlier positively related to survival, but so was emotional content (Danner, Snowdon, & Friesen, 2001). Sisters whose autobiographies contained positive emotional expressions (happiness, interest, hope, gratefulness, contentment, amusement) were more likely to have survived compared to Sisters whose autobiographies expressed negative emotional expressions (sadness, fear, confusion, hopelessness, anger, disgust). Possibly, the autobiographical content reflects a lifelong pattern of emotional response to life events. That positive feelings may predict survival was also suggested by Gruenewald, Karlamangla, Greendale, Singer, and Seeman (2007), who followed a sample of older adults (ages 70–79) from the MacArthur Study of Successful Aging over a 7-year period. Those who reported at the outset that they felt useful to others were more likely to have survived than those who said they did not feel useful to others.

The studies just described are retrospective. Participants were tested and, later on, investigators looked back to assess whether cognitive test scores, self-reported health ratings, or indices of emotional well-being and feelings of usefulness differed for those who survived and those who did not. Hopefully, the findings of such studies will allow us to determine whether a low score on a cognitive test or a self-reported health or emotional scale signals impending mortality. The goal would be to predict which individuals are at risk and then intervene to delay mortality.

Maximizing Longevity

From the beginning of time, people have searched for ways to retard the aging process. In the 20th century, affluent people traveled to Romania for special vitamin injections, to Switzerland for injections of cells from a lamb fetus, and to London for injections of genetic material and enzymes from fetal cells. Many who sought these treatments reported that the effort and expense were worthwhile, but there is little scientific evidence that such treatments restored youth or extended life (Woodruff-Pak, 1988). Furthermore, there is little empirical evidence to support recent claims made by the anti-aging industry that some products currently on the market can reverse aging (Olshansky et al., 2004; Perls, 2004a).

Even so, certain lifestyle practices hold promise for maximizing longevity. First, abstention from smoking decreases the risk of cancer and heart disease.

Individuals who give this habit up enjoy an immediate benefit of reducing the risk of heart disease and a long-term benefit of reducing the risk of cancer and other lung diseases (Rowe & Kahn, 1998).

Modifications in diet such as cutting down the intake of fat and sugar can reduce the risk of heart disease and some forms of cancer. Obesity and sedentary living have become a public health issue, and proper diet and daily physical activity reduce health risks in older adulthood. Both physical activity and positive feelings about physical capability are associated with a reduced likelihood of functional limitations (McAuley et al., 2007). Also, exercise can minimize the effects of circulatory diseases and contribute to the maintenance of bone density in middle-aged and older adults. Carlos, described at the beginning of this chapter, tries to lead his life accordingly. But some older adults shy away from physical activity because they are fearful that muscle strength and flexibility exercises will do them harm (Cousins, 2000). Clearly, we need to customize exercise programs to the needs of individual older adults, who should be given encouragement and positive feedback on their progress.

In addition to adequate medical care and sufficient physical and intellectual stimulation, social factors are important. Health and vitality tend to be preserved when individuals are emotionally engaged and socially integrated, as with Carlos, who was described earlier. Rowe and Kahn (1998) emphasize the importance of close relationships and regular activities that make life meaningful and exciting. Note that the Longevity Quiz in Table 3.5 includes items that tap lifestyle habits and social factors.

Physical Changes and Disease

Physical changes take place over the course of adulthood, although there is considerable variation in the rate at which they occur. Within the same individual, changes may be more noticeable in some parts of the body than in others. Also, as mentioned earlier, a distinction is often made between aging and disease, although certain diseases become more frequent as age increases (Masoro, 2006a). Some diseases are associated with pain, disability, or limitations in functioning even in the early stages. Other diseases have no noticeable symptoms until they are advanced, at which point they can be difficult to treat. Now we will look at some of the age-related physical changes and diseases often encountered in older adulthood.

Body Systems

Some physical changes hold considerable meaning for how aging individuals feel about themselves as well as how people view them. Others are important because they affect how older adults function, especially under demanding and stressful conditions.

Skin and hair

Visible signs of aging in the texture and appearance of the skin and hair are among the first to be noticed. With increasing age, the skin becomes drier and begins to sag and show wrinkles. Thinning and graying of hair (and for men, loss of hair) become more prevalent.

In a classic article, Sontag (1972) argued that Americans have a *double standard of aging* – visible signs of aging are viewed more negatively in women than they are in men. For example, facial wrinkles and gray hair are to be avoided at all costs by women, whereas men's wrinkles are a sign of "character" and their gray hair is a sign of distinction. Furthermore, men are especially harsh in judging signs of aging (Kogan & Mills, 1992).

Two decades after Sontag's article was published, Harris (1994) investigated attitudes toward visible signs of aging by asking people (ages 18 to 80) to read a scenario in which a male or female protagonist (target) was described as having gray hair, sagging skin, and facial wrinkles. The target in the scenario either uses age concealment techniques (such as coloring hair, getting a facelift, or using wrinkle cream) or refuses to use age concealment techniques. Survey participants thought the target's physical signs of aging were unattractive with one exception: The male protagonist's facial wrinkles were not viewed negatively. Apparently, Sontag's double standard of aging is alive and well. Surprisingly, however, participants did not have a favorable view of targets that used age concealment techniques. They especially disapproved of male targets who attempted to conceal their wrinkles and gray hair. In addition, Harris found another type of double standard: Even though survey participants did not approve of the target's attempts to combat the signs of aging, they felt that it would be acceptable if they themselves used age concealment techniques.

The musculoskeletal system

Muscle mass and strength gradually decrease with age, and older adults often take longer than young adults do to recover from exertion (Tonna, 1995). In the musculoskeletal as well as other organ systems, there is an age-related decrease in **reserve capacity** – under ordinary conditions, older adults may function just as well as young and middle-aged adults, but age-related differences become apparent when situations require more than the normal capacity.

With increasing age, joints show degenerative changes. Arthritis, a condition caused by degeneration of the joints, can cause pain and often loss of movement. *Osteoarthritis* (OA) is the most common form of degenerative joint disease, and risk factors include increasing age, obesity, heredity, low socioeconomic status, and female gender (Walji & Badley, 2007). Typically, OA is confined to weight-bearing joints such as the knees, hips, and spine, but it can also affect fingers, wrists, elbows, and neck. OA can result from injury but usually it is due to degeneration from wear and tear over time. If untreated, OA can limit mobility and, in extreme cases, it can lead to loss of physical independence. It is rarely

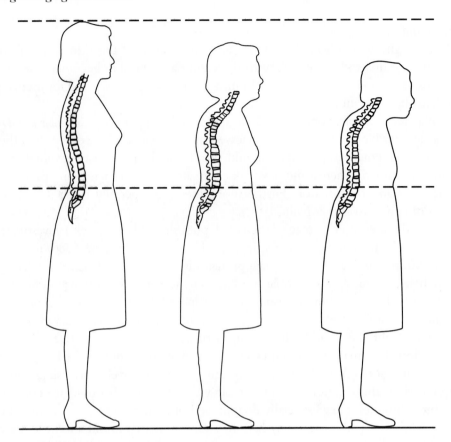

Figure 3.3 *Loss of bone density and cartilage can result in compression of the spine. As a result, older adults lose some height and many develop a rounded, stooped posture.*
Source: Ebersole & Hess (1998).

fatal (Solomon, 1999), but it can reduce the quality of life. Fortunately, advances in surgical techniques, including hip and other joint replacement, as well as appropriate use of medication, physical therapy, and exercise, make it possible for older adults with OA to lead relatively pain-free and active lives (Rowe & Kahn, 1998). Carlos, described at the start of the chapter, handles his early morning stiffness by taking a walk, and he keeps limber with a regular exercise routine.

Loss of bone density in the vertebrae can lead to decreased physical stature. Between ages 55 and 75, men can lose up to an inch and women up to two inches in height (Kausler, Kausler, & Krupshaw, 2007). Along with shortened stature, there can be a rounding of the back and stooped posture, especially in older women.

Osteoporosis is a skeletal disease characterized by extreme loss of bone mass and deterioration of bone tissue, resulting in bone fragility and susceptibility to fracture (Gueldner, Grabo, Britton, Pierce, & Lombardi, 2007). Risk factors include increasing age, female gender (especially small-framed northern

Understanding Aging Box 3.3: Health and the Distribution of Body Fat

The proportion of body fat increases from young adulthood through late middle age. On average, sedentary men have a body fat content of 17% in their 20s, which increases to 29% in their 60s. For active men, these figures are 10% and 17%, respectively, for the 20s and 60s. Sedentary women have a body fat content of 24% in their 20s and 38% in their 60s. For active women, these figures are 17% and 25%, respectively, for the 20s and 50s, but beyond age 60, women's body fat declines (Masoro, 2006b). However, regional distribution of fat (specifically, greater abdominal fat) seems to be more important than absolute amount of body fat in predicting diseases such as Type II adult-onset diabetes mellitus, coronary heart disease, and stroke (Masoro, 2006b). The symptoms of these diseases are not always obvious in the early stages, but medical screening can detect risk factors and steps can be taken to prevent or control them. A large proportion of American men and women are overweight. However, women tend to carry weight on their hips and thighs ("pear shape"), whereas men carry it on their waistlines ("apple shape"). Although the reasons for this gender difference are not clear, abdominal obesity in men is riskier than lower-body obesity in women (Simon, 2004).

European and Asian women), family history of osteoporosis, cigarette smoking, low lifetime calcium and vitamin D intake, and inactive lifestyle. The extensive loss of bone density can result in fractures of the vertebrae, hips, wrists, and ankles when there is slight or no apparent trauma. These fractures can be painful and can result in long periods of immobility. In its earliest asymptomatic stages, osteoporosis can be detected with scan technology for bone density, and medications can control the bone loss. In addition, intake of calcium and vitamin D together with a well-managed regular exercise program and abstention from smoking are important for the maintenance of bone density.

Respiratory and cardiovascular functioning

The respiratory and cardiovascular systems become less efficient with advancing age but, again, the concept of reserve capacity applies. Older adults are most likely to notice changes in functioning when conditions are stressful (Rowe & Kahn, 1998). A decrease in lung elasticity results in smaller lung volume (Cherniack & Cherniack, 2007), and the smaller

Engaging in exercise has many benefits, one of which is maintaining respiratory capacity.

reserve capacity from this reduced volume may limit lengthy participation in strenuous exercise. However, normal age-related changes in lung capacity do not prevent older adults from engaging in exercise, which can help them maintain respiratory capacity.

The cardiovascular system consists of the heart and blood vessels throughout the body (Sullivan, 1995). Arteries are the thick-walled tubes that carry blood away from the heart to a branching network of vessels that distribute blood to tissues throughout the body. Arteries terminate in small thin-walled vessels called capillaries, which transfer nutrients and waste products between the blood and surrounding tissues. Eventually, the capillaries join together and meet in veins, which are the larger vessels that collect blood and return it to the heart. Over time, the walls of the arteries become less elastic and blood pressure often increases. Despite some loss in reserve capacity, however, the cardiovascular system can continue to perform very well in older adulthood.

Even so, cardiovascular disease becomes more frequent with age and it affects approximately one-third of the U.S. population aged 65 and over (Rowe & Kahn, 1998). *Atherosclerosis* is a build-up of a substance called *plaque* that causes a narrowing of the arterial walls and leads to restriction in blood flow. Early on there may be no noticeable symptoms, but later, symptoms appear under stressful conditions and eventually even at rest. *Hypertension* is the term used when blood pressure is elevated to a danger zone, beyond what is typical with increasing age. Over time, hypertension can damage arterial walls and increase the risk of heart attacks, aneurysms, and strokes. *Aneurysms* are weaknesses in the arterial walls that lead to bulging and possible rupture. *Strokes* are disruptions in blood flow to the brain, resulting in temporary or permanent damage depending upon which part of the brain is affected.

Another disease that can affect the vascular system is *diabetes mellitus*, a chronic condition caused by the body's inability to create or effectively use its own insulin. Insulin is a hormone that converts food into glucose, which the body needs for energy. Without sufficient insulin, the level of glucose in the blood is not adequately controlled and this may lead to permanent damage of blood vessels, with complications such as blindness and arterial disease in the heart and peripheral vessels (National Academy on an Aging Society, 2000). Type I (insulin-dependent) diabetes is usually diagnosed in childhood, but Type II (noninsulin-dependent) diabetes is often diagnosed in middle age or older adulthood. To some extent, Type II diabetes is hereditary, but losing excess weight and increasing exercise can reduce the risk. Once diagnosed, Type II diabetes can sometimes be controlled through changes in diet and physical activity, although oral medication and in some cases insulin therapy may become necessary. Type II diabetes is a major health problem (McNamara, 2006). It is costly to manage but, left untreated, complications can result in disability and death. If individuals with this disease follow the necessary diet, exercise, and medication regimen, they are usually able to lead active lives.

The brain

Much of our information about the aging brain has been obtained through autopsy of young and older brains, but post mortem studies have included only limited sample sizes. In recent years, scientists have learned more using **neuroimaging** techniques that visualize the structure and function of the living brain (in vivo assessments). Brain structure can be assessed using CT (*computerized tomography*) scans, which take multiple X-rays of the brain from many angles. MRI (*magnetic resonance imaging*) scans use magnetic fields to map out brain structure. A related technique, fMRI (*functional magnetic resonance imaging*), monitors changes in brain activity using magnetic resonance signals that vary with changing levels of blood oxygenation that signal brain activation as individuals engage in cognitive tasks. PET (*positron emission tomography*) scans are also used to study ongoing neural functioning in different areas of the brain by introducing radioactive chemicals that mark blood flow and metabolic activity (see Kramer, Fabiani, & Colcombe, 2006).

What changes occur in the human brain as people grow older? The weight of the brain reaches a peak between ages 20 and 30, but weight can decrease by 10% by the 10th decade (Bondareff, 2007; Brody, 2006). Also, there is shrinkage in brain volume, which is seen in imaging as an increase in the fluid between the brain and the skull, especially in men. With increasing age, there are more fluid-filled spaces in the brain itself. The shrinkage in brain volume seems to begin in the 40s and to increase after age 60. However, it has not been highly correlated with any abrupt decline in cognitive functioning (Greenwood, 2007).

The brain contains 10 to 20 billion nerve cells (*neurons*). Each neuron has a *cell body*, an *axon* that transmits messages, and *dendrites* that branch out to receive messages from the axons of other neurons. The *synapse* is the gap between the axon of one neuron and the dendrites of another. Nerve impulses must cross the synapse for neurons to communicate with one another, and *neurotransmitters* are the chemical messengers at the synapses that facilitate the transfer of information between neurons. Some studies have found a reduction in the number of neurotransmitters in various areas of the brain, which could account for difficulties many older adults experience with sleep, with processing sensory information, with motor movements and slowing, as well as with memory (Bondareff, 2007; Kausler et al., 2007).

After age 30, neurons die or become less functional, possibly due to a build-up of lipofuscin (mentioned earlier). Also, aging brains accumulate neurofibrillary tangles (filaments of abnormal protein wrapped around the neuron cell body and axon) and senile plaques (consisting partly of beta-amyloid protein fragments), which could interfere with the functioning of normal neurons. Tangles and plaques occur with normal aging but the build-up is more extensive when there is disease. Recent research on rodents conducted at Harvard University has identified different forms of beta-amyloid protein – only certain forms are associated with disease symptoms characteristic of Alzheimer's disease (WCCO, 2008).

In addition to the build-up of tangles and plaques, the dendrites of a neuron can atrophy, which results in fewer connections with other neurons. Clearly,

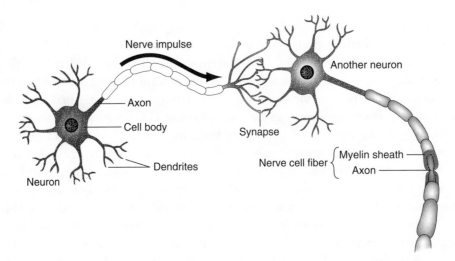

Figure 3.4 *Axons and dendrites allow neurons to communicate over synapses. Neurons in the brains of rats housed in stimulating and complex environments show more dendritic branching than do neurons in the brains of rats housed in unstimulating environments.*
Source: Sternberg (2004).

strokes can damage or destroy neurons, and diseases such as Alzheimer's and Parkinson's (discussed in Chapter 11) are associated with extensive neuronal damage and loss, often with accompanying difficulties in physical and/or cognitive functioning. However, neuron loss during the course of normal aging is less likely to have an appreciable effect on brain functioning.

Various parts of the brain serve different functions, and individual structures of the brain are affected differentially by normal aging (Kausler et al., 2007). The brain stem (hindbrain) appears as a cap on the spinal cord, and its function is to process and integrate sensory information and outgoing motor instructions. The *cerebellum* controls posture, eye movements, and auditory and vestibular functions. Dysfunction of the cerebellum can result in unsteadiness of gait, difficulty performing rapid movements, and tremors. Dizziness, which is a common complaint of people aged 75 and over, can be a symptom of neuronal dysfunction of the cerebellum but could also result from problems in other parts of the brain (Brody, 2006).

The symmetrical left and right cerebral hemispheres, which are connected by bundle of nerve fibers (*corpus callosum*), are situated above the cerebellum and lie within a bony structure called the *cranium*. The cerebral hemispheres are surrounded by several protective membranes (*meninges*) as well as a layer of *cerebrospinal fluid* (CSF). The structures of the cerebral hemispheres are covered by a thin surface called the *cerebral cortex*. Each cerebral hemisphere is divided into four lobes (*frontal, parietal, occipital, and temporal*), and the surface of each lobe is folded into convolutions (gyri) that are separated from each other by grooves (sulci).

On the basis of CT and MRI imaging, the brain occupies 90% of the cranial cavity between ages 20 and 50 but thereafter occupies progressively less space,

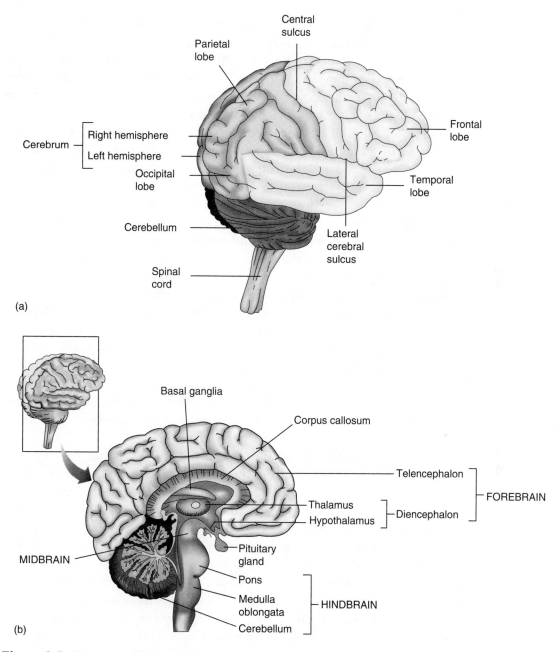

Figure 3.5 *Two views of the human brain.*
Adapted from Tobin (2003, Fig. 42.5, p. 867).

with a concomitant increase in the volume of CSF and widening of the sulci. However, brain volume shrinkage and neuron atrophy have been noted mainly in the frontal lobe and temporal lobe (and the hippocampus, which is the bundle of neurons located in the deeper region of the temporal lobe) as well as in the corpus callosum. Such changes are associated with dementia but are found to a lesser degree with normal aging in individuals who show no significant cognitive impairment (Bondareff, 2007).

Each of the four lobes has specific functions, but the frontal and temporal lobes (as well as the hippocampus) seem to be most affected by the aging process as indicated by the disproportionate number of tangles and plaques and greater widening of the sulci. Frontal lobe functions affected include reasoning, decision making, and control of impulses (see Chapter 4 for a discussion of the frontal lobe model of attention). With regard to the temporal lobes and hippocampus, the processing of auditory information (see Chapter 4) and some types of memory are affected. The parietal and occipital lobes, which process somatic and visual information, respectively, show a lesser degree of age-related changes.

Neuropsychology is the study of brain–behavior relationships. Neuropsychologists use psychological tests and cognitive tasks to evaluate how impairments in various areas of the brain affect cognitive functioning, including memory. On the basis of neuroimaging studies, some of which have tested individuals with known brain lesions, there is evidence that the frontal and temporal areas of the cerebral cortex play a role in conscious memory. The frontal area seems to be the primary center for working memory, whereas the temporal lobe area (including the hippocampus) is the primary center for long-term episodic memory (West, 1996; Woodruff-Pak & Papka, 1999). Chapter 5 describes these types of memory in greater detail. Structural and functional changes in different areas of the aging brain may be related to specific types of memory decrement, even in older adults who are free of dementia or other pathological conditions (West, 1996).

Using neuroimaging techniques such as fMRI and PET, neuroscientists have discovered age-related differences in the pattern and in some cases the extent of brain activation when young and older adults perform various cognitive tasks (Reuter-Lorenz & Cappell, 2008). According to Kramer et al. (2006), some studies have found a lower level of activation in older brains, possibly due to loss of neural resources or to inadequate recruitment of neural resources. In other studies, the brains of older adults show activation in different areas or broader areas, compared to that found with young adults, whose brains show more selective activation. For example, performing a cognitive task may be associated with cortical activity confined to one hemisphere in the young brain, whereas it may result in bilateral activity in the older brain. One hypothesis for the less specialized cortical activation pattern in the older brain is that the older brain is compensating for loss in a specific area. The less specialized activation in the older brain could reflect adaptation to loss and thus be a sign of brain plasticity (Greenwood, 2007). However, bilateral recruitment (or activation of more, or different, brain regions in older compared to younger brains) could also indicate that older brains are reaching their resource limits sooner than young brains (Kramer et al., 2006). Interestingly, Greenwood reports neuroimaging findings that show increased brain activation in areas of the cortex adjacent to those with the most significant age-related atrophy and shrinkage. Further research is needed before we can make definitive statements about the relationship between a specific type of brain atrophy and either the generality or the extent of activation (Raz, 2007; Salthouse, 2007a). However, these findings hold some promise that the brain is capable of adopting compensatory strategies to offset age-related decline (Kramer et al., 2006).

How does the environment affect brain functioning? Studies comparing the brains of old rats housed in complex toy-filled group environments with the brains of old rats housed in standard minimally stimulating cages have found (on autopsy) that rats in the complex environments have more extensive dendritic branching of neurons in several areas of the brain. This suggests that density of dendrites is fostered by environmental stimulation. Dendritic connections between neurons are an important factor in brain functioning that could compensate for whatever neuron loss may occur in old age (Black, Greenough, Anderson, & Isaacs, 1987).

There is some evidence for neuronal plasticity, with new synapses replacing those that are lost (Bondareff, 2007). However, it is difficult to conduct well-controlled research on how environmental stimulation affects the human brain. Even so, there is reason to believe that maintaining good health, as well as mental and physical exercise, fosters maintenance of dendritic density. Engaging in physically and intellectually challenging activities beginning in early adulthood and continuing into middle age and later may protect brain functioning in older adulthood (e.g., Kausler et al., 2007). Controlling stress levels can also be beneficial for brain functioning (Raz & Rodrigue, 2006).

In general, keep in mind that it is difficult to know whether age-related differences found with in vivo studies of the brain are due to aging or whether they result from disease or accumulated effects of substances such as medications and alcohol (Bondareff, 2007). Most in vivo studies of the brain are cross-sectional and wide individual variation can make it difficult to determine whether any differences found are actually a function of age. Raz and Rodrigue (2006) contend that when the brains of super-healthy older adults are compared with the brains of young adults of average health, age effects may be underestimated. Alternatively, older adults who appear healthy may actually have preclinical forms of conditions that inflate estimates of age effects. Measurement of the extent and nature of age-related differences in the brain are likely to be more accurate with longitudinal studies as opposed to the more typically conducted cross-sectional studies.

Urinary and bowel functioning

Age-related changes in urinary and bowel functioning are not uncommon, and in mild forms they do not affect everyday functioning to a large extent. Sometimes symptoms are relieved through changes in dietary and exercise habits. The incidence of urinary incontinence (characterized by loss of bladder control) is higher among older women than older men, but it may affect 30% of community-living older adults and 50% of nursing home residents. Bowel incontinence is less common but more socially disruptive and more likely to lead to institutional living (Engel, 1995). Urinary and bowel incontinence can stem from a number of physical reasons, but in some cases cognitive impairments can interfere with toileting habits. Care can include the use of diapers, medications, and in some instances surgical intervention. Some cases of incontinence have been treated successfully with behavioral intervention techniques such as prompting individuals to use toilet facilities at regular intervals (Burgio & Burgio, 1991).

Sexual functioning

There is a common myth that sexuality is of no interest to older adults, and that older adults who show interest in sexual activity are either silly or sinful (Kausler et al., 2007). In actuality, we have limited information because early surveys on sexual behavior by Kinsey and others did not include many people over age 60, and many older adults are hesitant to discuss sexuality (Starr, 2006). However, recent years have seen a "growing acceptance among health professionals, educators, and older people themselves that sexual interest, capacities, pleasures, and libido remain throughout the life span into the ninth and perhaps the tenth decades" (Weg, 1996, p. 479). Indeed, as baby boomers enter older adulthood, attitudes toward sexuality may be changing (Starr, 2006). Evidence for this is the extensive media exposure of Viagra and similar drugs that treat male erectile dysfunction.

Several factors play a role in older adults' sexual functioning (Starr, 2006). First, earlier interest and enjoyment of sexual activity seem to be reliable predictors for later life. Second, moderately good physical and psychological health is usually needed for continuing sexual interest and expression. Heart disease, strokes, diabetes, pelvic disorders, arthritis, and enlargement of the prostate gland may interfere with the desire and ability to participate in sexual activity (Weg, 1996). Medications, both prescription and over the counter, that are sometimes used to treat chronic conditions can affect older adults' sexual desire and capabilities. Finally, availability of a partner is important. Lack of a partner (especially for older women, who are less likely to remarry when they become widowed) may be a limiting factor. Men's sexual partners are typically similar in age or younger, whereas women's partners are similar in age or older (Stones & Stones, 2007). Since older women greatly outnumber older men (see Chapter 1), they have fewer sexual opportunities.

Normal age-related physical changes mean that the nature of sexual activity may vary from young to middle to older adulthood. The time it takes to become sexually aroused may increase with age, especially for older men. Furthermore, the refractory period prior to physiological readiness for sexual activity may be longer. For some but not all older women, hormonal changes can affect comfort with sexual activity, but these can often be treated. Again, the main barrier to intimate sexual relations in older adulthood is usually lack of a partner.

There is relatively limited information on sexuality in gay, lesbian, and bisexual older adults (Stones & Stones, 2007). But older gay partners tend to maintain longer relationships than young gay partners (Weg, 1996). The absence of legal marriage may limit opportunities that are readily available to heterosexual married couples, and gay older adults may be hesitant to discuss medical issues with their physicians (Kimmel, 2006). Further study is needed regarding the social supports available to these older adults.

In sum, physical changes occur as people grow older, but these do not necessarily interfere with adequate functioning. Some older adults are more prone than others to specific chronic diseases, and proper screening for risk factors can lead to early diagnosis and hopefully to control with medication, surgery, and changes in diet and exercise routines. Older adults with chronic diseases can often function with little or no disability if they receive proper medical care and follow a recommended regimen of diet and exercise.

Leading Causes of Mortality

In the United States, heart disease and cancer are the two leading causes of mortality in individuals age 65+ (see Table 3.6) regardless of race and sex. However, there is some variation among these groups with regard to the next five most frequent causes of mortality. For example, Alzheimer's disease is a more frequent cause of death for European American and Hispanic American women than it is for the other groups (see Table 3.7). Also, diabetes is a more frequent cause of death for African Americans and Hispanic Americans than it is for European Americans. This may reflect the fact that for socioeconomic reasons, medical care is less available to these groups than it is to European Americans. The symptoms of diabetes mellitus are not always obvious in the early stages, but managing the disease at later stages is costly.

Olshansky, Carnes, and Grahn (1998) contend that modern medicine has been successful in preventing or treating health problems that, in earlier times, caused

Table 3.6 *Leading causes of death at age 65+ in the United States for all races and both sexes*

Rank	Cause	% of total deaths
1	Heart disease	30.4
2	Malignant neoplasms (cancer)	22.0
3	Cerebrovascular disease (stroke)	7.4
4	Chronic lower respiratory diseases	6.0
5	Alzheimer's disease	3.7
6	Diabetes mellitus	3.1
7	Influenza and pneumonia	3.0

Source: National Center for Health Statistics (2007).

Table 3.7   *The seven leading causes of death at age 65+ in the United States by race and sex*

Rank	European American males	European American females	African American males	African American females	Hispanic American males	Hispanic American females
1	Heart disease	Heart disease	Heart disease	Heart disease	Heart disease	Heart disease
2	Malignant neoplasms	Malignant neoplasms	Malignant neoplasms	Malignant neoplasms	Malignant neoplasms	Malignant neoplasms
3	Chronic lung disease	Cerebrovascular disease	Cerebrovascular disease	Cerebrovascular disease	Cerebrovascular disease	Cerebrovascular disease
4	Cerebrovascular disease	Chronic lung disease	Diabetes mellitus	Diabetes mellitus	Diabetes mellitus	Diabetes mellitus
5	Influenza and pneumonia	Alzheimer's disease	Chronic lung disease	Nephritis (kidney disease)	Chronic lung disease	Alzheimer's disease
6	Diabetes mellitus	Influenza and pneumonia	Nephritis (kidney disease)	Alzheimer's disease	Influenza and pneumonia	Influenza and pneumonia
7	Alzheimer's disease	Diabetes mellitus	Influenza and pneumonia	Chronic lung disease	Nephritis (kidney disease)	Chronic lung disease

Source: National Center for Health Statistics (2007).

death well before old age. For example, screening for heart disease and treating it through diet, medication, or surgery means that individuals who may have suffered from fatal heart attacks and strokes in their 50s and 60s can now live into late old age. Cancer treatments are more effective as well. Older adults of today and tomorrow have a better chance of enjoying productive, independent lives than their parents or grandparents did.

Everyday Functioning and Health Care

How do changes that occur more frequently with increasing age affect older adults' everyday functioning? What kinds of support should older adults seek to insure that their lives have the highest possible quality?

Activities of Daily Living and Instrumental Activities of Daily Living

Activities of daily living (ADL) is a term that refers to basic self-maintenance tasks, including eating, dressing, bathing, toileting, transferring into and out of a bed or chair, and getting around the house (Fillenbaum, 1995). Ability to perform all or most of these functions is necessary if older adults are to live independently in the community. ADL assessments are often used to determine disability and possible need for health-care services. Among community-living older adults, the percentage with ADL limitations is higher among those aged 85+ than it is among those aged 65 to 84 (*A Profile of Older Americans*, 2007).

Instrumental activities of daily living (IADL) is a term that refers to the more complex activities required for carrying out the business of daily life, including preparing meals, shopping, managing money, doing housework, using the telephone, and taking medications (Lawton & Brody, 1969). Some older adults can continue to live in private homes or apartments if they have help with such activities.

In sum, many older adults (but especially those 85+) have some trouble performing ADLs or IADLs. Approximately 40% of community-living older adults experience difficulty that limits their activities (*A Profile of Older Americans*, 2007).

Medication

It is not uncommon for older adults to have at least one chronic disease but, fortunately, many diseases can be controlled with medication. Today, many drugs are available and physicians are prescribing them. Hypertension, a frequent condition in older adulthood, can usually be managed successfully by strict adherence to a prescribed medication regimen (as with Carlos, described at the beginning of the chapter). However, many older adults do not take their medications exactly as directed. Morrell, Park, Kidder, and Martin (1997) recorded whether older adults adhered to antihypertensive medication regimens over a two-month period of time. Those in the old–old age category (75–84) did not adhere as strictly as did those in the young–old (65–74) age category. Many older adults take several prescription medications for more than one chronic condition, so they would likely benefit from the assistance of charts and containers for keeping track of what pills to take at various times of day (see Chapter 5 for a discussion of memory mnemonics). Liu and Park (2004) followed older adults over a period of three weeks to check how closely they followed instructions on when to carry out home glucose tests. Those who adhered best to the monitoring schedule had a specific plan for when and where they would carry out the glucose tests and they visualized themselves doing so.

With so many effective medications to control chronic health conditions, older adults can live with less pain and greater independence than was possible in the past. Furthermore, medications often enable older adults to avoid hospitalization. For people aged 65+, the average number and average length of hospital stays have decreased significantly since 1980 (*A Profile of Older Americans*, 2007).

Medicare

Most older Americans (65+) qualify for **Medicare**, which is the federal health insurance program initiated in 1965. If they have worked for the required number of quarters (3-month periods) in most jobs, Americans aged 65+ are eligible for Medicare Part A without paying any premium. Medicare Part A covers hospital costs and brief stays in a skilled nursing home or home health care for a limited period of time following a hospital stay. Medicare Part B, for which older adults can elect to pay a premium, covers a portion of physicians' fees, laboratory tests, services such as physical therapy, and some medical equipment. The recently enacted Medicare Part D, for which older adults can elect to pay a monthly premium, covers certain costs of prescription drugs.

Medicare does not cover the costs of all health care – there are deductibles and co-payments even for covered services. Medicare pays for short stays in a nursing home if needed immediately following a hospital stay of at least three days, but older adults who need nursing home care beyond that period of time must pay their own expenses, which can be very costly.

Private insurance companies offer *Medi-gap* policies to cover deductibles and co-payments, but not all older adults can afford such policies. Furthermore, understanding exactly what Medi-gap insurance policies cover can be a daunting task. Many unsuspecting older adults have become victims of scams related to the purchase of Medi-gap policies that do not deliver the benefits they thought were covered. Private insurance companies also offer long-term care (LTC) policies that cover the cost of extended nursing home stays and home health care. However, such policies are expensive, especially if purchased late in life. Understanding which services are covered by a particular LTC policy can be confusing, and older consumers must determine the coverage that they think will best suit their circumstances and needs (see Chapter 7 for discussion of decision making with regard to LTC policies).

Medicaid

Health coverage is available to older Americans through **Medicaid**, a federal program administered by individual states, each of which sets its own rules for eligibility. Unlike Medicare, Medicaid is *means tested* – to qualify for coverage, individuals must fall below a certain income level and own only limited assets (savings and personal property). As mentioned earlier, short nursing home stays are sometimes covered by Medicare, but beyond that, older adults must pay for it themselves. If they "spend down" sufficiently to deplete their assets, they qualify for Medicaid coverage for continued nursing home care. This may not take long, given the high monthly cost of nursing home care.

Revisiting the Selective Optimization with Compensation and Ecological Models

The Selective Optimization with Compensation (SOC) (Baltes & Baltes, 1990) and Ecological (Lawton, 1989; Lawton & Nahemow, 1973) Models can be readily applied to biological aging and health. With increasing age, biological functions generally progress in the decremental direction, but this does not usually deter older adults from leading lives that are active and satisfying.

According to the SOC Model, an effective strategy for maintaining optimal functioning is to focus on the aspects of living that are most important. If functioning declines in some areas, older adults can compensate by putting more effort into areas that can be maintained or improved. The trick is to capitalize on one's physical strengths, taking whatever actions are necessary to control lifestyle habits of diet, exercise, and exposure to stress. The earlier in life this is done, the better the chances of deriving long-term benefits.

With regard to the Ecological Model, decline in biological reserve capacity means that more attention must be paid to the environmental conditions in which older adults live, and a proper match between biological competence and environmental press becomes more important with increasing age. Conditions that are too challenging may accelerate the biological aging process and cause difficulties in adaptation. On the other hand, conditions with too few demands may not be sufficiently challenging and could also result in poor adaptation. An environment with the appropriate level of challenge for the individual older adult is most likely to allow him or her to achieve the highest possible level of adaptation.

? Questions to Consider

1. In the future, do you think that the gender gap in life expectancy will get even larger (favoring females) or that it will shrink?
2. Do you know anybody who is over the age of 100 (centenarian)? If so, what is that person's lifestyle?
3. What kinds of things do you do in your everyday life that could either promote or delay secondary aging?

Key Points

- Life expectancy is the average number of years individuals in a particular birth cohort can be expected to live on the basis of current information that affects mortality.
- Life span is the maximum longevity, or extreme upper limit of time, members of a species can live. As life expectancy approaches life span, the survival curve takes on a more rectangular shape.
- *Morbidity* refers to illness and disease, and *mortality* refers to death. These two terms are related but they are not the same.
- Primary aging refers to unavoidable (inevitable), intrinsic biological processes that affect all members of a species. Secondary aging refers to biological processes due to disease, disuse, and abuse.

- Biological theories of aging can be categorized as programmed or stochastic. Programmed theories focus on genetic blueprints of various species. Stochastic theories focus on random events that occur as a function of living.

- Scientists have studied the influence of nature and nurture on longevity and have tried to determine whether cognitive test scores, health self-ratings, marital status, and emotional outlook can predict how long an individual will live.

- With increasing age, physical changes occur and reserve capacity decreases, but within the same person, changes may be more noticeable in some parts of the body than in others.

- Neuroimaging studies have found changes in the structure and functioning of the aging brain, but there is promise that the brain is capable of compensating for any age-related decline.

- Certain chronic diseases occur more frequently in older adulthood. However, these can often be treated and controlled and older adults can usually lead active and independent lives.

- Older adults often take prescription drugs for chronic health conditions. However, many do not take their medications exactly as directed.

- Activities of daily living (ADL) include basic personal care tasks required for self-maintenance; instrumental activities of daily living (IADL) include more complex activities required for carrying out the business of daily life. Limitations in either or both occur more frequently in the 85+ age group.

- Medicare is a federal health insurance program for most Americans aged 65+. Medicaid is a state/federal program that covers medical expenses for Americans who fall below a certain income level and own limited assets.

Key Terms

activities of daily living (ADL)   96
centenarians   69
compression of morbidity   70
compression of mortality   70
instrumental activities of daily living
   (IADL)   97
life expectancy   65
life span   65
longevity   65
Medicaid   98
Medicare   97
morbidity   65

mortality   65
neuroimaging   89
neuropsychology   92
primary aging   71
programmed theories of biological
   aging   71
rectangular survival curve   70
reserve capacity   85
secondary aging   71
stochastic theories of biological aging   73
telomeres   72
terminal drop   82

4 Sensation, Perception, and Attention

Chapter Overview

Sensory Processes

Threshold and Sensitivity
Absolute Threshold
Signal Detection

Speed of Response

Reaction Time
Applying Research Box 4.1:
Reaction Time and Driving
Age–Complexity Hypothesis
Stimulus Persistence Theory
Moderating Age-Related Slowing

The Senses: A Closer Look

Smell and Taste
Touch, Proprioception, and Pain
Understanding Aging Box 4.1: Older Adults
and Falls

Vision
Hearing
Applying Research Box 4.2: Useful Field
of View

Attention

Theoretical Models
Attention Tasks

Revisiting the Selective Optimization with Compensation and Ecological Models

Questions to Consider

Key Points

Key Terms

Close-ups on Adulthood and Aging

Bernie just celebrated his 67th birthday and lately he has noticed that the local newspaper is becoming difficult to read comfortably. He must hold it at arm's length to decipher the print. He thinks he will cancel his subscription and just read the news on-line or tune in to the cable news channels. Also, for the past two years, he and his wife have been meeting with a group of retired friends for weekly lunches at a local diner. Bernie finds these get-togethers are not as enjoyable as they could be because his friends mumble and he must strain to hear what they are saying, especially when several of them talk at once. Between the clatter of dishes, the piped-in music, and the background chatter at surrounding tables, it is a challenge to keep up with, let alone stay involved in, meaningful conversation. Bernie is going to suggest to his wife that they get together with one or two friends at a time, perhaps in each other's homes, where there will be less noise and fewer distractions.

Sensory Processes

To adapt to and interact with the environment we must be able to take in, or register, what is going on around us. For this purpose we depend upon our eyes, ears, nose, and other sensory organs, through which we experience our initial contact with stimulus events and objects in our environment. Our senses include taste, smell, touch, vision, and hearing. Researchers who study aging have noted the importance of sensory processes; according to the **common cause hypothesis**, the link between sensory processes and cognitive functioning becomes stronger in older adulthood than it was earlier in life (Baltes & Lindenberger, 1997).

Although age-related differences in cognitive functioning may not be fully explained by sensory declines (Anstey, Luszcz, & Sanchez, 2001; Lindenberger, Scherer, & Baltes, 2001), there is little question that having good sensory capabilities is related to good memory and verbal abilities (Schneider & Pichora-Fuller, 2000; Wingfield, Tun, & McCoy, 2005). Also, having good sensory capabilities, particularly vision and hearing, is associated with the ability to perform self-care activities (for example, bathing, dressing, and grooming), to do household chores and go shopping (Marsiske, Klumb, & Baltes, 1997), and to take part in social activities.

Once the sensory organs register it, information can be passed along to the central nervous system for higher-level, perceptual processing, which entails interpreting what the information means and making decisions about how to respond. Often, there is more information in our environment than we can possibly register, let alone process, at any given time. Attention has to do with exactly what information we will process from the large array of stimuli that impinge upon our senses.

Threshold and Sensitivity

Sensory organs need a certain intensity of stimulation before they register the presence of a signal, or stimulus. The term **threshold** refers to the minimum amount of stimulation a sensory organ must receive before the presence of a particular stimulus is registered. For example, a burst of sound must have sufficient intensity for the ear to register that it occurred. The term **sensitivity** refers to the capability of the biological system to respond to stimulation. Sensitivity is the inverse of threshold – the greater the sensitivity to a particular type of stimulation, the lower the threshold will be. Individuals with a high level of sensitivity have a low threshold because they need only a low intensity of stimulation before they register its presence. In contrast, individuals with a low level of sensitivity have a high threshold because the intensity of the stimulation will have to be stronger before they register its presence.

Absolute Threshold

Absolute threshold refers to the intensity of stimulation needed in order for a stimulus to be detected 50% of the time when it is present. To illustrate, let's suppose that an individual is fitted with headphones, seated in a soundproof booth, and instructed to press a key each time a particular tone is heard. The tone is presented numerous times at varying levels of loudness, or intensity. At low levels of intensity, the individual will not hear the tone and thus will not press the key. As the decibels (dB, which is a measure of the intensity of an auditory stimulus) of the tone gradually increase, eventually the individual will register its presence by pressing the key. Absolute threshold is the specific level of intensity the tone must reach before the individual registers its presence (by pressing the key) on half of the occasions when it is presented. If the tone is presented 10 times at the same level of intensity, the individual will register its presence on five occasions.

For auditory thresholds, qualities other than intensity can influence an individual's threshold. For example, threshold can vary depending upon the frequency, or pitch, of the tone (high or low). For older adults, thresholds are often lower for low-pitched tones than they are for high-pitched tones. In the case of visual stimuli, color can affect threshold. An individual may be able to identify one color more readily than another. Older adults are more sensitive to (have lower thresholds for) red, orange, and yellow than they are to blue, green, and purple. Similarly, thresholds can vary for specific odors and tastes and for specific kinds of tactile stimulation.

Signal Detection

Determining thresholds does not take into account decisional processes that enter into an individual's success or failure to register the presence of a stimulus. Assume for a moment that two individuals, Paul and Juan, are instructed to press a key when they hear a tone. Paul presses the key when he has even a slight suspicion the tone has been sounded. Juan is more cautious – he will press the key only when he is certain the tone has been sounded.

The **signal detection model** of determining threshold takes into account not only sensitivity but also decisional response criteria (Green & Swets, 1966). Paul, the less cautious decision maker, will have more *hits* (saying "yes" when the tone is actually present) than Juan will. However, Paul will also have a considerable number of *false alarms* (saying "yes" when the tone is not present). Juan, the more cautious, conservative decision maker, will have fewer hits, but he will also have fewer false alarms.

The signal detection model is important in the study of aging because older adults tend to be more cautious than young adults (Botwinick, 1984). In general, older adults have fewer false alarms (saying "yes" when a stimulus is not present) compared with young adults. By the same token, the more cautious older adults will have more *misses* (saying "no" when the stimulus is indeed present) compared with young adults. Older adults' higher decisional criteria could result in an underestimate of their actual sensitivity.

In sum, older adults' cautiousness can inflate estimates of age-related differences in sensory processes. However, even when age-related differences in decisional criteria are taken into account, some age-related increase in sensory thresholds remains.

Speed of Response

Sensation is related to the sensory organ's initial registration of physical stimulation. Perception refers to the subsequent interpretation of stimuli at the central level (in the brain). Depending on how stimuli are interpreted, decisions will be made about how to respond. Usually responses are visible, but it is difficult to observe what takes place in the brain between the onset of a stimulus and the initiation of a response.

Reaction Time

Reaction time is the interval that elapses between the onset of a stimulus and the completion of a response (Cerella, 1995; Salthouse, 2007b). In a controlled laboratory setting, we can measure reaction time by presenting a visual stimulus such as a light, or an auditory stimulus such as a tone. We can instruct individuals to make a motor response such as pressing a key as soon as they see the light or hear the tone. Or we could instruct individuals to give a vocal response (such as "yes") to register the presence of a stimulus.

Reaction time tasks fall into several categories: simple, choice, and complex. In a simple reaction time task, there is only one stimulus and one possible response. In a laboratory situation, individuals might be instructed to look for the appearance of a cursor on a monitor and as soon as they see it, to make a motor response by pressing a key.

In a choice reaction time task in the laboratory, individuals are on the lookout for two different signals, or stimuli, each requiring a different response. They might be told to press the key on the left when they see a red light and the key on the right when they see a green light. Or they might be instructed to press the key on the left when they hear a high tone and the key on the right when they hear a low tone. Usually, there is greater age-related slowing on choice reaction time tasks than there is on simple reaction time tasks.

Complex reaction time tasks are extensions of choice reaction time tasks because there are more than two stimuli and each one requires a different response or combination of responses. In the laboratory, one of three different shapes (a square, a circle, or a triangle) might be displayed on a screen. Each shape calls for a different response, such as pressing a key on the top, middle, or bottom row of a keyboard, respectively.

Reaction time has two components: premotor time (PMT) and motor time (MT) (Botwinick, 1984). PMT is the time elapsing between the onset of a stimulus and the initiation of a motor response. MT is the time elapsing from the initiation to the completion of the motor response. If we instruct an individual to listen for a tone and press a key as soon as it is heard, PMT would be the time elapsing between the onset of the tone and the initiation of a muscle response in the forearm. PMT is difficult to observe directly because it consists mainly of the time taken for the brain to process information. MT (the time that elapses between the initial muscle activation and the actual lifting of the finger to press the key) can be measured using electromyographic recordings of muscle-action potentials (Kausler, 1991). Approximately 84% of total reaction time is attributable to PMT, while the remaining 16% is attributable to MT (Botwinick, 1984). The relatively large proportion of time devoted to PMT suggests that reaction time is largely a function of central processing in the brain.

Slower reaction time seems to be an inevitable consequence of normal aging (Kausler et al., 2007), but why is it important to study age-related differences in reaction time? From a theoretical point of view, reaction time can assess the organization and efficiency of the central nervous system (Cerella, 1995). Speed of response, even on simple reaction time tasks, can be an indicator of brain functioning (Salthouse, 2007b). From a practical point of view, slowing is important for many aspects of everyday functioning, especially when it comes to safety. The older adult who is slow to enter a revolving door at the entrance to a public building is at risk for sustaining physical injury. The older pedestrian who is slow to respond to a "Walk" sign at an intersection may not make it across a busy street before the sign turns to "Don't Walk." Fatal injuries have resulted when impatient drivers do not realize that older pedestrians need extra time, and car accidents often occur when a driver does not react quickly enough to avoid a dangerous situation.

Applying Research Box 4.1: Reaction Time and Driving

Driving calls for simple, choice, and complex reaction time. *Simple reaction time*: A driver spots a pedestrian in a crosswalk and responds by stepping on the brake; a driver hears an ambulance siren and responds by pulling over to the curb. *Choice reaction time*: A driver approaches a fork in the road and must decide whether to go left or right. *Complex reaction time*: A driver spots an object in the distance that appears to be road debris but he/she must evaluate its spatial placement and composition (metal or cardboard). When deciding how to respond (step on the brake, swerve to the left or to the right, or drive right over the debris), the driver must also consider surrounding traffic conditions. In a tragic case in California in 2003, an 86-year-old driver sped into a crowded farmers' market, killing 10 and injuring more than 70 people. The true cause of this devastating incident will never be known for sure, but the driver's defense attorney argued that he was the victim of "pedal error," mistaking the accelerator for the brake. Following this incident there was national debate over whether to require old drivers to take road tests to renew their licenses.

Age–Complexity Hypothesis

The complexity of a task affects how quickly people respond – the more complex the task, the slower the responses will be. Task complexity can also affect how much slower older adults will be compared to young adults. However, older adults are more variable than young adults are in how quickly they perform reaction time tasks (Verhaeghen, 2006).

According to the **age–complexity hypothesis** (Salthouse, 1991), older adults will be at a greater disadvantage relative to young adults as task complexity increases. As Figure 4.1 illustrates, the gap between young and older

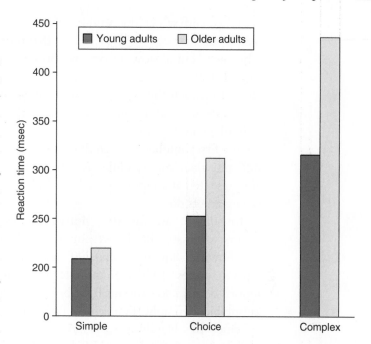

Figure 4.1 *Hypothetical comparison of young and older adults' speed of response on simple, choice, and complex reaction time tasks.*

adults' speed of response becomes larger as tasks go from simple to choice to complex. Compared with simple reaction time tasks, choice and especially complex reaction time tasks require more extensive central (brain) processing (Cerella, 1995). Thus, some investigators think that age-related differences in reaction time are related to age-related decline in the brain's speed of processing information.

Some researchers contend that older adults' decline in speed on reaction time tasks can be attributed to one factor – a generalized slowing in cognitive processing. Other researchers postulate that slowing is one of many factors that play a role in the age-related differences found on various cognitive tasks (Cerella, 1994; Fisk & Fisher, 1994; McDowd & Shaw, 2000). Whether slowing is a common factor that can completely explain age-related differences on all cognitive tasks (reaction time, perceptual processing, memory, and so on) has been a subject of considerable debate (Salthouse, 1996; Salthouse, 2007b; Schulz, 1994; Verhaeghen, 2006; Verhaeghen, Cerella, & Basak, 2006). In addition, there is some debate about the specific origins of age-related slowing – among the suggestions for why central slowing occurs have been loss of neurons, reductions in dendritic branching, and lower quantities of neurotransmitters (Salthouse, 2007b). Chapter 3 discusses age-related changes in the brain.

Stimulus Persistence Theory

In an early article published in the *American Psychologist*, Birren (1974) proposed that the tendency toward slowness with advancing age reflects a basic change in the speed with which the central nervous system processes information. **Stimulus persistence theory** (SPT) is one theoretical model that attempts to explain why such central slowing occurs (Botwinick, 1984; Gilmore, 1996). According to SPT, a stimulus registered by a sensory organ takes longer to be processed and cleared through the nervous system of an older adult than it does through the nervous system of a young adult. If a second stimulus were to follow quickly, then older adults will be less efficient at processing it because they are still clearing the first stimulus through the system. For this reason, older adults have greater difficulty than young adults do when they must process a series of stimuli that are presented at a rapid rate. Older adults need more time between stimuli than young adults do.

To build a case for SPT, Botwinick (1984) described a phenomenon that occurs when stimuli are presented one right after the other: When individuals are shown a sequential series of light pulses at a low rate, they report seeing separate pulses of light. As the rate of the light pulses increases, they eventually report seeing a continuous light because individual pulses of light are perceived as one blended light. The critical flicker fusion (CFF) threshold is the pulse rate at which this blending occurs. A number of studies have reported age-related decline in the CFF threshold (Kline & Scialfa, 1997), so at a relatively high pulsing rate, young adults are still able to distinguish separate pulses of a flickering light, whereas older adults see one continuous light. According to SPT, there is a backup in older adults' central nervous system processing, with the result that sequential stimuli blend together and older adults perceive them as one.

The stimulus persistence model is an intriguing way to conceptualize age-related differences in perceptual processing. Unfortunately, it cannot account for all the research findings on age and perceptual processing (see Botwinick, 1984). Also, the specific mechanism that mediates the slower processing has yet to be specified clearly. Even so, studies that have tested this model demonstrate that older adults will surely benefit when information is not presented too quickly.

Moderating Age-Related Slowing

In general, older adults do not respond as quickly as young adults do, but are there ways to moderate age-related slowing? First, older adults who exercise regularly react more quickly compared to older adults who are not physically active. In fact, some older exercisers have reaction times as fast as many young adults (Kausler et al., 2007). However, the findings for short-term exercise are mixed. Hawkins, Kramer, and Capaldi (1992) found older adults improved their speed of performance after participating in a 10-week aerobic exercise program. However, others (Blumenthal & Madden, 1988; Madden, Blumenthal, Allen, & Emery, 1989) do not find that short-term exercise results in faster responding. Extended periods of training, long-term habits of physical activity, and general physical fitness seem to be the most effective means of increasing older adults' speed of processing.

Second, older adults can increase their speed of responding when they have opportunities to practice (Kausler, 1991). However, young adults also get faster with practice, so the difference between young and older adults' speed of responding cannot be attributed wholly to older adults' lack of practice on a particular task. Age-related differences in speed of responding are not likely to disappear when young and older adults are both allowed to practice, especially when tasks are complex. Still, practice is important for older adults' real-world functioning.

The Senses: A Closer Look

Changes in sensory capabilities usually occur gradually from middle adulthood on. Although there are individual differences, older adults are often less sensitive than young adults are when it comes to registering sensory information. Changes also occur at the perceptual level, which refers to the higher-order central processing that takes place in the brain.

Smell and Taste

The majority of older adults experience some loss in smell and taste sensitivity, which often becomes apparent at around age 60 and tends to progress with increasing age. Loss of sensitivity to odors can stem from anatomical and physiological changes in the olfactory system that are associated with normal aging, but losses could also be caused by smoking, diseases, and use of some medications (Schiffman, 1996). Schiffman contends that the sense of smell can serve as a warning signal, so loss in smell sensitivity could represent a risk that smoke, gas leaks, or food spoilage will not be readily detected. Loss of taste sensitivity is associated more with medications and medical conditions than it is with anatomical and biological losses that occur with normal aging. When older adults have no diseases and take no medications, there are only minimal increases in their thresholds for salty, sweet, sour, and bitter tastes. However, when changes in smell and taste sensitivity do occur, they can affect older adults' appetite because food loses its appeal. Nutritional deficiencies resulting from poor eating habits can have a negative effect on older adults' general health and psychological well-being.

Touch, Proprioception, and Pain

The sense of touch includes tactile sensations related to pressure and temperature, whereas the sense of proprioception refers to an awareness of the position and movement of the body and limbs in space. Both touch and proprioception are mediated by sensory structures as well as higher-order perceptual processes, both of which are susceptible to the effects of aging (Weisenberger, 2007). Older adults have higher thresholds than young adults for detecting vibration and thermal

Understanding Aging Box 4.1: Older Adults and Falls

With increasing age, there is a greater risk of falls from loss of balance, perhaps more so for women than for men. In any given year, more than one-third of people over age 65 experience a fall, and the incidence is even higher among the very old. Falls can result in hip fractures that necessitate hospitalization and rehabilitative services. Older adults' mobility and independence are compromised when they experience falls (Vercruyssen, 1997), so fall prevention programs that include muscle strength and balance training (SBT) are a public health priority. Yardley et al. (2006) interviewed community-living older adults in six countries (Denmark, Germany, Greece, Switzerland, the Netherlands, and the United Kingdom) about their attitude toward fall prevention programs. Older adults in all these countries tended to deny they were at risk of falling, although many claimed they would be interested if such programs would benefit their general health and well-being. Also, many older adults said they would be more positive if given a personal invitation from a health professional and encouragement from family and friends as well as opportunities to participate in home-based programs. In a subsequent survey in the United Kingdom (Yardley, Donovan-Hall, Francis, & Todd, 2007), older adults were more motivated to undertake SBT when they perceived its potential benefit in terms of enjoyment and improvement in general health than they were when they viewed SBT as something that would prevent the threat and consequences of falling.

(hot, cold) stimulation. In addition, older adults have a higher threshold for detecting limb movements and changes in position, especially for the lower extremities such as knees, hips, and ankles. Weisenberger points out that older adults do not seem to differ from young adults in their ability to maintain balance under normal conditions because they compensate for proprioceptive losses by using cues from other sensory sources. However, limitations in cues from other senses, particularly vision, can result in difficulty with balance (Weisenberger, 2007).

With regard to pain, measuring responsiveness is complex, as individuals vary not only in their sensitivity but also in their willingness to report it (Weisenberger, 2007). Harkins and Scott (1996) point to the special difficulties in assessing pain in older adults. First, older adults may be suffering from health problems associated with chronic pain (for example, osteoarthritis, osteoporosis, or diabetes). Such chronic pain could interact with pain stemming from acute conditions. Second, older adults who experience pain from a chronic condition may have less reserve capacity for coping with additional pain from acute sources compared with young adults who are otherwise in relatively good health. Third, it can be difficult to assess pain in older adults with dementia, who are limited in their ability to report the nature and extent of any pain they are experiencing. (See Chapter 11 for further discussion of dementia.) Finally, older adults may have a different criterion from young adults for reporting the point at which they feel pain.

Vision and hearing have received the most extensive and detailed attention from researchers in aging. The following sections describe the age-related

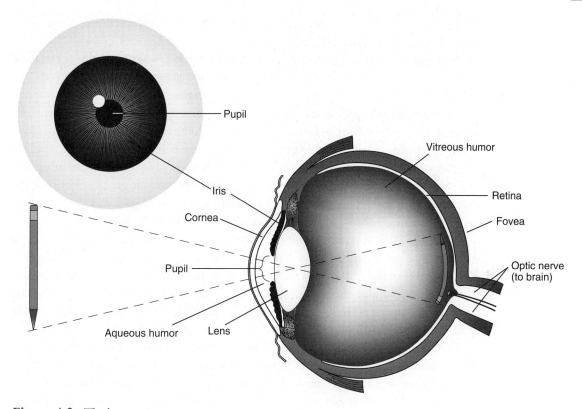

Figure 4.2 *The human eye.*
Source: Sigelman & Rider (2003, Fig. 6.6, p. 156).

differences/changes that occur in the anatomical structures of the eye and ear, as well as those that seem to take place in visual and auditory perception.

Vision

In general, there are changes in visual capability, often beginning in the 30s, but these are gradual. Beginning in their 40s, many people (like Bernie, described earlier) notice that newspaper print seems light and faded and that numbers in the telephone book appear to be very small and difficult to decipher. Furthermore, driving at night is often more effortful.

Structure of the eye

Some visual changes that occur with aging can be traced to changes in the anatomical structures of the eye (see Figure 4.2).

The cornea, the refractive surface that also serves a protective function, undergoes a slight age-related decrease in sensitivity to mechanical stimulation, which means that older adults are not as ready as young adults to detect the presence of a foreign body in the eye. In addition, the luster, thickness, and curvature of the cornea can change, which creates the need for new corrective lenses. In most cases, these changes are not large enough to have a substantial effect on visual functioning (Kline & Scialfa, 1996).

The aqueous humor, the fluid-filled chamber that lies between the cornea and the lens, is the conduit through which nutrients are carried into the lens and metabolic waste products are carried out. Blockages can create increases in pressure. **Glaucoma** is a disease characterized by elevated pressure in the aqueous humor. The onset of age-related glaucoma is often gradual. Initially, it may affect peripheral (side) vision, but over time, central vision may be affected as well. In its early stages, glaucoma can be treated with medication but more advanced cases require surgery (Roberts, 1995). Regular ophthalmologic checkups are the best means of early detection. If left untreated, the prolonged elevation in pressure can cause irreversible damage to the nerve cells in the retina.

The pupil, the opening of the eye surrounded by the iris, controls the amount of light that enters the eye and ultimately reaches the retina. With increasing age, the diameter of the pupil decreases (Kline & Scialfa, 1997), admitting less light into the older eye. Under the identical level of illumination, there is a linear decrease from age 20 to age 60 in the amount of light reaching the retina (Botwinick, 1984). This means that with increasing age higher levels of illumination will be needed.

In addition to a smaller diameter, the pupil becomes less able to adjust its size in response to changing levels of light. Especially at low levels of illumination, the older eye is not as sensitive as the young eye and this undoubtedly contributes to the difficulties older adults experience with nighttime driving. In older adulthood, pupillary adjustment takes longer after exposure to glare from the bright headlights of passing cars. During this prolonged period of adjustment, visual sensitivity is reduced.

The lens of the eye transmits light. It also changes in shape and thus refractive power. Changes in refractive power (accommodation) allow the eye to focus on both near and far objects. With increasing age, the lens increases in size and thickness and decreases in flexibility (Kline & Scialfa, 1996). These changes make it difficult for the older eye to focus on near objects, resulting in far-sightedness that is termed **presbyopia**. Bernie, who was described earlier, is experiencing such a change. Presbyopia differs from myopia (near-sightedness), where the eye cannot focus on objects that are far away. Beginning in middle age, many individuals who never wore glasses before find they need them for reading. Those who

With age-related changes in vision, older adults begin to have difficulty reading small print that is up close, so they often compensate by holding reading materials at a slight distance.

already wear corrective lenses for distance vision often need bifocal lenses that correct for both distance and close-up vision.

In addition to becoming larger and less flexible, the lens tends to yellow with age. Less light can pass through a yellowed lens than through a clear lens, which is one more reason a room that might seem bright enough to the young eye can seem dim to the older eye. Furthermore, the yellowing of the lens results in a modest decline in the ability to discriminate between colors with short wavelengths (Kline & Scialfa, 1997), so older adults have difficulty discriminating between various shades of blue, violet, and green. However, the ability to discriminate shades of red and yellow is usually maintained.

With increasing age, the formation of **senile cataracts** becomes more prevalent. Cataracts are areas of cloudiness or opacity in the lens. Not all older adults develop cataracts, but they are common. Risk factors for cataracts include sunlight, steroid use, and smoking (Kline, 2006). By age 75, approximately 50% of adults in the United States have the early stages of cataracts. By age 80, 70% have clinically significant cataracts. Cataracts reduce visual acuity and also scatter light, which causes increased susceptibility to glare. Although older adults require higher levels of illumination, indirect lighting is preferable for limiting glare. Surgery for cataracts involves replacing the natural lens with a synthetic one and has a high rate of success. However, many older adults must cope with the milder effects of cataracts until such time as they become candidates for surgery.

Ultimately, images are focused on the retina. With age, the number of retinal ganglion cell axons declines (Kline & Scialfa, 1997), and changes in blood vessels that nourish the retina can result in retinal damage. **Macular degeneration** is a disease associated with irreversible loss of nerve cells in the central area of the retina. The macula is located near the fovea and consists of a high concentration of receptor cells that are susceptible to circulatory insufficiencies that may increase with age (Roberts, 1995). Degeneration of these receptor cells affects vision for fine detail, resulting in difficulties with activities such as reading and driving. Several new and very costly drugs show some evidence of slowing the progression of macular degeneration in 25% to 50% of those afflicted. Also, there are some reports that a daily glass of red or white wine and a diet that includes vitamins C and E, zinc, and beta-carotene may reduce the risk of this disease (Kausler et al., 2007).

Diabetic retinopathy is a disease resulting from complications of long-term diabetes (described in Chapter 3), whereby changes in the structure and function of blood vessels cause damage to receptor cells in the retina (Kline & Scialfa, 1996). Often, the extent of damage can be controlled through proper monitoring of blood sugar levels. Macular degeneration and diabetic retinopathy are not inevitable with increasing age, but they do become more prevalent, and the consequences of both are serious.

Visual perception

Not all changes in vision can be traced to changes in the structure of the eye. Vision is also a function of central processing in the brain.

Motion perception is most likely related to central processing, and older adults have decreased ability to respond to moving objects, lower sensitivity to differences in velocity, and greater difficultly processing quickly changing visual stimuli (Gilmore, 1996; Kline & Scialfa, 1997). Motion perception is a critical skill in driving, and older drivers tend to overestimate the velocity of slow-moving vehicles, which means they anticipate slow-moving vehicles will arrive more quickly than they actually do. This is one reason older drivers wait before turning into traffic while impatient young drivers honk their horns because they think there is plenty of time to make the turn. Overestimating the speed of moving vehicles is more characteristic of older women than it is of older men.

Depth perception requires the use of visual cues to determine which objects in the environment are closest and which are farthest away. Decline in depth perception becomes apparent in the 50s, with further modest decline through the 70s. With regard to driving, poor depth perception can make parallel parking difficult because the driver must judge the distance between the car he or she is trying to park and the adjacent cars (Kausler et al., 2007).

Hearing

Hearing consists of peripheral and central systems. Sounds are registered by the peripheral system (the outer, middle, and inner ear) and carried by the auditory nerve to the central nervous system, where they are processed and interpreted (see Figure 4.3).

Hearing loss is among the most common conditions affecting older adults. Approximately 30% of adults over age 65 have noticeable hearing impairment (Kausler et al., 2007), and older adults are more likely than young adults to report problems with everyday tasks that involve hearing. Hearing difficulties are

---

Applying Research Box 4.2: Useful Field of View

Useful field of view (UFOV), an index of visual functioning identified by some researchers who study aging, is the visual area over which stimuli can be recognized and localized without a person's having to make eye or head movements (Kline & Scialfa, 1996). Thus, UFOV measures the amount of information that can be processed during a brief glance (Rogers, 1997), and it can be affected by factors such as number of competing attentional demands and distinctness of the visual stimuli (Ball & Owsley, 1991). In general, UFOV is more restricted in older adults than it is in young adults, but it can increase with training and practice (Ball, Beard, Roenker, Miller, & Griggs, 1988; Kline & Scialfa, 1997). Among older drivers, UFOV scores are a significant predictor of road test performance and crash frequency (Ball & Rebok, 1994), perhaps more so than measures of reaction time and visual acuity (Carr, Jackson, Madden, & Cohen, 1992). Older drivers with low UFOV scores are more likely than those with high UFOV scores to report that they purposely avoid difficult driving situations (Ball et al., 1988), such as when there is rain or heavy traffic.

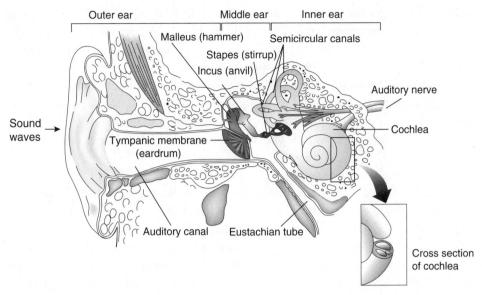

Figure 4.3 *The human ear.*
Source: Adapted from Tobin (2003, Fig. 42.7, p. 872).

associated with poor physical health and reduced levels of psychosocial function-ing (Strawbridge, Wallhagen, Shema, & Kaplan, 2000).

Structure of the ear

Auditory stimuli must be sufficiently loud, or intense, to be registered by the peripheral system. Impairments of a mechanical nature can impede the passing of sound waves through the outer or middle ear and thus can contribute to age-related hearing loss. Changes in the auditory canal, including the presence of impacted wax, can cause *conductive* hearing loss. With increasing age the ear drum becomes stiffer, thinner, and less elastic and thus less easily displaced as a function of sound intensity (Kline & Scialfa, 1997).

In the middle ear, three tiny bones, or *ossicles* (hammer, anvil, and stirrup), transmit acoustic energy to the inner ear by creating mechanical vibrations at the entrance to the fluid-filled inner ear, or cochlea. Over time, calcification of the ossicles decreases their mobility, which results in conductive hearing loss. Conductive loss from age-related changes in the outer and middle ear usually affects all frequencies (high- and low-pitched) to a similar degree.

The inner ear consists of two structures. The semicircular canals control the sense of balance and the cochlea is associated with hearing. The cochlea is a fluid-filled chamber with a membrane (basilar membrane) running down the center. Mechanical vibrations created by the ossicles of the middle ear set the cochlear fluid in motion, which bends the hair cells on the basilar membrane. Bending of the hair cells converts sound waves into neural energy by stimulating the release of neurotransmitter substances at their base, thus initiating nerve impulses that will be transmitted to the brain (Gordon-Salant, 1996). Any damage to the delicate hair cells on the basilar membrane results in *sensorineural* hearing loss. Such damage can be caused by exposure to loud noise or illness, but some degeneration of the hair cells could occur simply with aging. The hair cells in the basal region of the basilar membrane are resonant to high-frequency tones, and it is in this region that hair cells show the most pronounced degeneration in older adults. Accordingly, older adults become less sensitive to high-frequency sounds such as high-pitched door-bells and smoke alarms, birds' chirping, cats' meowing, the sizzle of frying bacon, and the high notes on a piano keyboard (Slawinski, Hartel, & Kline, 1993).

Auditory perception

Signals from the cochlea are transmitted via the auditory nerve to the brain stem and ultimately to the cortex. Neurons in the auditory nerve undergo some degree of age-related degeneration, which could distort auditory signals (Gordon-Salant, 1996). The central auditory system consists of neurons in the brain stem, mid-brain, and temporal lobe, where complex acoustic information is translated into meaningful signals (Figure 3.5 shows these brain structures). Although there is considerable individual variability, there is evidence for age-related decline in the ability to process auditory information at the *central* level.

Presbycusis

Presbycusis is a pattern of hearing loss associated with aging and characterized by an increased threshold for high-frequency tones. Diminished sensitivity to high-frequency tones can begin in the 30s but usually does not become notice-able until the 40s, 50s, or later. As high-frequency loss progresses, it affects speech sounds that fall into the high-frequency range. Thus, older adults have increased thresholds for high-frequency consonants (for example, k, s, sh, f, t, th). With regard to speech perception, older adults have difficulty discriminating between words with high-frequency consonants (for example, "fit" and "sit").

For reasons not completely understood, presbycusis begins earlier and progresses more rapidly in men than it does in women. Also, European Americans are more likely than African Americans to experience presbycusis, and the gap between these two groups widens with increasing age (National Academy on an Aging Society, 1999).

Difficulty with speech perception can be attributed in part to older adults' decreased sensitivity to high-frequency speech sounds. However, older adults often comment, "I hear it but I cannot understand it," a phenomenon known as **phonemic regression**. Older adults' understanding of speech or other complex signals is poorer than it should be based solely on their sensitivity to pure tones (Tun & Wingfield, 1997). Some increase in loudness, or intensity, can be helpful for older adults who experience difficulty with speech perception. However, increased intensity does not usually eliminate difficulty in understanding speech. In fact, speaking too loudly could actually be detrimental. Rather than a speak-er's raising his or her voice in an attempt to help the older listener, it is usually preferable to speak somewhat more slowly and to substitute key words that have fewer high-frequency consonants

Older adults with presbycusis have special difficulty understanding speech in noisy conditions, as with Bernie who was described earlier. Older adults experience greater difficulty than young adults do with understanding speech against a background of noise or "babble" from one or numerous other talkers (Schneider & Pichora-Fuller, 2000; Tun & Wingfield, 1997, 1999). This difficulty is compounded when they are trying to understand rapid (time-compressed) speech (Tun, 1998; Wingfield, 1996).

In summary, presbycusis is associated with sensorineural loss in the inner ear as well as difficulty in processing complex auditory information (such as speech) at the central level. Age-related changes in attentional capacity (discussed later in this chapter), as well as in memory (discussed in more detail in Chapter 5), could also contribute to difficulties in processing auditory information. Older adults benefit greatly if given sufficient time to process auditory information.

Causes of presbycusis

Even though presbycusis is a commonly reported problem among older adults, not all older adults suffer from hearing difficulties. What causes presbycusis? One hypothesis is that presbycusis results from the accumulated effects of exposure to environmental noise from traffic or disturbances in the workplace. In cross-cultural comparisons, age-related hearing loss is less prevalent in relatively noise-free nonindustrialized societies (for example, the Maaban tribe in Africa) compared to noisy industrialized countries such as the United States (Gordon-Salant, 1996). Within the United States, the rate of occurrence is higher among those who worked in occupations such as farming, machine operations, and transportation as opposed to occupations with less noise exposure (National Academy on an Aging Society, 1999). If noise exposure is indeed the source of presbycusis, future cohorts of older adults may have a high incidence because of having attended rock concerts in their younger years.

Although noise probably contributes to presbycusis, there is no proof that presbycusis is attributable solely to noise exposure. Other factors being investigated include diet, medications, alcohol consumption, smoking, hypertension, and genetic influences. As yet, cause-and-effect relationships between presbycusis and these factors have not been clearly established. Presbycusis may be attributable, at least in part, to intrinsic, age-related deterioration of the auditory system. It has even been suggested that presbycusis renders older adults more vulnerable to noise-induced hearing loss. If so, then avoiding exposure to noise is especially important for older listeners (Kline & Scialfa, 1997).

Hearing aids

Hearing aids can be fitted to one ear (monaural) or both ears (binaural) to increase, or amplify, sound. The degree of sound amplification must be sufficient so that auditory signals will cross the individual's threshold. At the same time, the intensity of the signals should not be so great as to be uncomfortably loud. A hearing aid must be tailored to the individual user's profile of hearing loss. For example, someone with a hearing loss in the high-frequency range should wear a hearing aid that amplifies high-frequency but not low-frequency signals.

Among people in the United States with hearing loss, those aged 65 and over are more likely than young and middle-aged adults to wear hearing aids. Even so, two out of three older (65+) individuals with hearing loss do not use a hearing aid (National Academy on an Aging Society, 1999), and only about a quarter of older adults who might benefit from a hearing aid actually own one (Schneider & Pichora-Fuller, 2000).

What are the barriers to hearing aid use? In a survey of 2,300 hearing-impaired individuals over age 50 (National Academy of an Aging Society, 1999), the reason more than half of the respondents gave was cost. In addition, some did not think their hearing was poor enough to necessitate the use of a hearing aid. Indeed, hearing loss can have such a gradual onset that older adults are not aware of it. But approximately 20% reported concerns related to vanity and the belief that a hearing aid carries a social stigma. Some older adults fear that wearing a hearing aid signifies that they are not competent, and they consider a decline in hearing acuity to be a threat to their self-image (Ryan, Hummert, & Anas, 1997). However, reluctance to deal with hearing difficulties often creates more problems than it solves. As the baby boom generation moves into older adulthood and a larger proportion of the population experiences age-related hearing loss, there may be less hesitancy to acknowledge hearing difficulties and more attempts to do whatever is necessary to maximize auditory functioning. Perhaps the recent popularity of Bluetooth technology will make it more difficult to distinguish between hearing aid users and those who want to talk on a hands-free phone!

Although hearing aids amplify sound, they do not address difficulties with auditory processing at the central level (Wingfield et al., 2005). Also, hearing aids have limited usefulness in helping older adults to understand speech when there is background noise (Schneider & Pichora-Fuller, 2000). Newer digital hearing aids have circuitry that selectively reduces the amplification of noise (Gordon-Salant, 1996), but digital hearing aids are costly and far from perfect. Even so, many older adults could derive some benefit from them even if their hearing difficulties are not completely alleviated.

Visual cues

Visual cues, which a listener can derive from reading a speaker's lips or observing a speaker's facial expressions or body language, provide additional information about a speaker's communication. Older adult listeners can use visual cues to compensate for degraded auditory signals, so speakers should make every effort to face older adult listeners so they can take advantage of such cues.

Visual alerting signals can be attached to safety devices designed for individuals with hearing difficulties. Some smoke alarm systems set off flashing lights in addition to auditory signals. Strobe lights that flash when telephones or doorbells ring can be installed. Many movies and television programs have a captioning option for the benefit of individuals with hearing difficulties.

Bottom-up and top-down strategies in language processing

Listeners use a combination of **bottom-up and top-down strategies in language processing** (Tun & Wingfield, 1997; Wingfield, Prentice, Koh, & Little, 2000). A bottom-up strategy calls for registering and processing the details of the sensory-perceptual input. A top-down strategy uses contextual information about the semantic (word meaning) and syntactic (grammatical) structure of language as well as its prosodic features (intonation, stress, and timing). Older adults with presbycusis lose some efficiency in bottom-up strategies, particularly when auditory signals fall into the high-frequency range. However, they can compensate for such limitations by relying more heavily on top-down strategies derived from their knowledge of the language. Top-down strategies are based on the excess information (redundancy) in spoken language, and listeners can use contextual cues to fill in the details of a speaker's message. For example, if the speaker says, "I want to … down," the English-speaking older adult with presbycusis may not be able to distinguish whether the missed word is "sit" or "fit" purely on the basis of bottom-up processing. However, an older listener familiar with language probabilities can make an educated guess that the missed word is "sit" rather than "fit." Listeners can use top-down processing more readily when speakers (a) talk at a normal rate, (b) use sentences that are not too long or too grammatically complex, and (c) use normal prosodic features (intonation, stress, and timing) in their speech (Wingfield & Stine-Morrow, 2000).

Communicating with older adults

Elderspeak refers to a particular style of speaking people tend to use when communicating with older adults. Kemper (1994) demonstrated that service providers and caregivers are more likely to reduce the length and grammatical complexity of what they say, to use simpler words and more repetitions, and to speak more slowly when addressing a group of older adults than they do when addressing a group of young adults.

Elderspeak is characterized not only by shortened sentences, simplified grammar, and slower speech, but often by exaggerated pitch and intonation (exaggerated prosody) as well. But which components of elderspeak are beneficial for older adults and which ones are not helpful? Kemper and Harden (1999) had older adults watch a videotape in which a speaker described a route that was also traced on a map. The older adults reported that the instructions were easier to follow when the speaker reduced the grammatical complexity (that is, minimized the number of subordinated and embedded clauses) and used semantic elaboration (that is, repeated and expanded upon what was said). Simpler grammar and semantic elaboration also helped older adults improve their accuracy when they had to reproduce the same route on a map of their own. In contrast, shortening the length of the speaker's utterances into two- and five-word sentences did not improve the older adults' comprehension of the instructions, nor did it improve their performance when they traced a map of their own. Also, the older listeners did not find that an extremely slow rate of speaking with many pauses or exaggerated prosody were helpful. Apparently, being spoken to in a slower than normal speed and in short phrases with exaggerated pitch and intonation does nothing to enhance older adults' ability to comprehend speech.

The communication predicament of aging model

When people hold stereotyped expectations that older adults cannot hear and are dependent and cognitively incompetent, they often modify their speech patterns to fit these assumptions. People who assume older adults are not competent tend to use patronizing communication in their conversations. Features of patronizing communication include the overly simple grammar and short sentences found in elderspeak. In addition, patronizing communication often entails speaking at a louder than normal level of intensity and using exaggerated prosody and exaggerated nonverbal gestures and terms of endearment such as "honey" and "dear." This form of communication can result in the **communication predicament of aging model** (Ryan, Hummert, & Boich, 1995), whereby the speaker's patronizing manner of communication imposes unnecessary constraints on interactions with an older adult, with the result that both the speaker and the older listener find the exchange to be unsatisfactory. The unfortunate outcome is that both speaker and listener tend to avoid communicating with one another on future occasions.

Ryan, Bourhis, and Knops (1991) and Ryan, Hamilton, and Kwong See (1994) had people read written scripts or listen to tape-recordings of a nurse communicating with an older nursing home resident. People formed an unfavorable impression of a nurse who communicated in a patronizing manner ("I'm here to give you your pills. Be a good girl and take them right now." "There you are, Maggie. Come on, Sweetie. It's time to go to the dining room for supper, remember?"). People thought more highly of the nurse who communicated in a neutral manner ("It is time to take your pills. Here's your glass of water, but take your time." "Mrs. Fields, I've been searching everywhere for you. It's time to go to the dining room for supper."). Not only did people view the patronizing nurse herself as less competent, less respectful, and less benevolent than the neutral nurse, but they also thought that the nursing home resident spoken to by the patronizing nurse was more helpless than the resident spoken to by the neutral nurse. Clearly, the manner in which the nurse communicated made a difference to people's impressions of both the nurse and the older nursing home resident.

Patronizing communication is not limited to conversations between nursing home staff members and nursing home residents. Ryan, Anas, and Gruneir (2006) had young adults read a script of a conversation in which an older male customer asks a female salesperson for help while shopping in a department store. The young adults thought more highly of the salesperson, and they thought that the customer would be more satisfied, when the salesperson addressed the customer in a professional manner. They were less positive when the salesperson showed an overhelping style, using exaggerated intonation and offering too much direction and too strong an opinion about what the older shopper should purchase.

But do older adults always view patronizing communication as negative and insulting? O'Connor and Rigby (1996) recruited older adults from both a senior citizen activity center and a nursing home and told them to imagine they were attending an entertainment event and that, during the intermission, another person comes over and asks if they would like some refreshments. In the neutral scenario, the person says, "I came over to see whether you are enjoying the show and to ask whether you would like some dessert." In the patronizing scenario, the person says, "I've brought some COFFEE and a plate of GOODIES for you, dear. I hope you're COMFY and ENJOYING the SHOW." The nursing home participants, who were chronologically older and lower in self-reported functional health than the activity center participants, did not react as negatively to the patronizing scenario as the activity center participants did. Furthermore, the older adults who expressed a high need for love and reassurance (that is, they endorsed questionnaire statements such as, "I like to be with protective and sympathetic people") felt that the patronizing communication was warm. Also, the older adults with high self-esteem (that is, they endorsed statements such as, "I feel I am a person of worth") reacted less negatively to the patronizing communication than did those with low self-esteem. These findings suggest that older adults' reactions to communications that we might consider to be patronizing are associated with their individual needs and feelings of self-worth (or possibly with cultural differences).

Attention

Our senses are bombarded by many more stimuli than we can register, let alone process in a meaningful way. Fortunately, attention allows us to direct our efforts to processing some portion of the stimulation we receive. But do older adults have the same amount of attentional resources, or attentional capacity, as young adults? How many stimuli can young and older adults process at the same time? How do young and older adults deal with stimuli that are unimportant (irrelevant) and possibly distracting when they are trying to process stimuli that are important (relevant) to the task at hand?

Theoretical Models

First we will examine three theoretical models related to age and attention. Then three types of attention will be described along with some general findings about the capabilities of young versus older adults.

The reduced attentional resources/capacity model

The **reduced attentional resources/capacity model** postulates that the quantity of processing resources (or the amount of attentional capacity) declines with increasing age (Craik & Byrd, 1982; Salthouse, 1991). On simple tasks, older adults do not experience difficulty because their attentional resources are sufficient. However, the processing resources needed for more complex tasks may exceed older adults' capacity, thus rendering them less efficient and/or less accurate than young adults, who have sufficient resources to handle the demands of complex tasks. The reduced attentional resources/capacity model is related to the age–complexity hypothesis described earlier. The greater the complexity of a task, the more attentional resources will be required. If older adults' attentional resources have limitations, their performance will suffer on complex tasks.

The reduced attentional resources/capacity model has generated a great deal of research, described later in the section on divided attention. However, a criticism of this model has been its lack of clarity about how resources or capacity should be defined and measured (Salthouse, 1991). Some researchers have expressed concern that the reduced attentional resources/capacity explanation of age-related differences in perceptual processing is somewhat circular. Further research is needed to specify the mechanism(s) by which resource limitations affect attention (McDowd, 1997).

The inhibitory deficit model

A second theoretical model is the **inhibitory deficit model** (Hasher & Zacks, 1988), which postulates that aging is associated with a decrease in the ability to ignore irrelevant stimuli (stimuli that are not important for performing a particular task, sometimes called *distractors*) and focus attention on relevant stimuli (stimuli important for performing the task, sometimes called *targets*). If attention to distractors is not suppressed (inhibited), then some portion of attentional capacity will be wasted processing information that is not important and too little will remain for processing important target stimuli. As with the reduced resources/capacity model, the inhibitory deficit model is related to the age–complexity hypothesis because sources of distraction are likely to be more extensive in complex attention tasks than they are in simple ones.

The inhibitory deficit model has generated a great deal of research, described in the section on selective attention. However, this model is not without its critics. One problem has been the lack of clear agreement on how to define inhibitory mechanisms (McDowd, 1997). Also, the model's predictions about age-related differences are not always accurate (Tun & Wingfield, 1997). Nonetheless, this model has been a useful framework for organizing research on aging and cognitive processes, including attention.

The frontal lobe model

Two different neural systems appear to play a role in attentional functioning. One is located in the frontal area of the cortex and the other is in the occipital and parietal areas of the cortex (see Figure 3.5). A third theoretical model to explain age-related decline on attention tasks postulates that the frontal lobes are more susceptible than other regions of the brain to the effects of normal aging (Arbuckle & Gold, 1993; Hartley, 1993; Kramer, Humphrey, Larish, Logan, & Strayer, 1994). The **frontal lobe model** has received support from cognitive neuroscience research that uses neuroimaging techniques such as positron emission tomography (PET) scans, which measure cerebral blood flow and metabolic activity in regions of the brain when individuals are in a resting state and when they are performing various tasks (Madden & Allen, 1996). Reductions in cerebral blood flow seem to occur earlier and be more pronounced in the frontal lobe area than in other regions of the brain. Also, age-related loss of neural tissue is more prominent in the frontal area than it is in other regions of the brain (Arbuckle & Gold, 1993; Kramer et al., 1994).

The frontal lobes are responsible for executive functions such as decision making, planning, and coordinating the processing of multiple streams of stimuli, the initiating and stopping of behaviors, and impulse control. Patients with known frontal lobe damage have difficulty shifting from one type of response to another. For example, if instructed to sort cards on the basis of the color of the object pictured on each card, they have difficulty when they are told to switch to sorting cards on the basis of the shape of the object pictured on each card. Such individuals perseverate, meaning that they revert back to sorting cards based on color.

The frontal lobe model predicts that age-related differences in attention will be most pronounced on tasks that depend heavily on frontal lobe functioning. Kramer et al. (1994) found that older adults had difficulty on two tests (card sorting and stopping) that require the inhibitory functioning that is associated with frontal lobe processing. Older adults made more perseverative errors than young adults when they had to shift to a new criterion for sorting cards. Likewise, older adults were slower than young adults when they were required to react to an occasional signal to abort, or stop, the responses they were making to a visual display. In contrast, age-related differences were much smaller on tests of spatial attention, which do not call for frontal lobe processing – for example, responding quickly to a visual display in which a target letter is surrounded by distractor items.

Arbuckle and Gold (1993) noted that perseveration can take the form of "off-target verbosity," which has been detected more often in the speech patterns of older adults than young adults. Off-target verbosity is characterized by a lack of focus or coherence, and it could be related to difficulty with inhibiting task-irrelevant thoughts, possibly stemming from a decrement in frontal lobe functioning. Table 4.1 gives an example of responses that are low and high in off-target verbosity. Interestingly, however, older adults display more off-target verbosity when answering personal questions than they do when answering factual questions (James, Burke, Austin, & Hulme, 1998).

Such findings are important, but it would be premature to conclude that the frontal lobe model explains all age-related inhibitory difficulties (McDowd & Shaw, 2000). Also, inhibitory mechanisms may not be located exclusively in the frontal lobes of the brain.

Table 4.1 *Examples from Arbuckle and Gold (1993) in answer to the question, "How much education did you get?"*

Low off-target verbosity
"I finished high school and then a bit of college."

High off-target verbosity
"Well, let's see. I went to school in … where, uh, uh, I grew up in … Back in those days, they didn't have the big high schools that they have now. When I went back there a few years ago in … uh, I don't remember exactly when it was. I think it was the summer of 1980 or maybe it was 1981. I went for my brother's 50th wedding anniversary and I didn't recognize the place at all. We went to a small school, the only school in town. It was the only place to go. All the children were in one room. The school only went to grade 9 or uh, uh, I think it was … was it Grade 9? No, it was only grade 8 because … [neighbor's daughter] left to go to nursing school and she had to go to … to finish Grade 9. She never finished nursing anyway. She got married and it didn't last long."

Source: Arbuckle & Gold (1993).

Attention Tasks

Attention tasks fall into three basic categories: sustained attention, divided attention, and selective attention (Kausler, 1994).

Sustained attention

Sustained attention, or **vigilance**, calls for monitoring a situation and remaining ready to detect any change that occurs in a pattern of stimuli that is usually stable and unchanging (Kausler, 1991). On a classic visual vigilance task called the Mackworth Clock Test (Kausler, 1991; Madden & Allen, 1996), individuals monitor the pointer on a clock-like device. The pointer moves in discrete steps much like a second hand on a clock, but individuals must remain ready to detect an occasional two-step jump. In the real world, a quality control manager must be on the lookout to detect a defective product while inspecting a steady stream of that product, or an employee must monitor a piece of equipment for any auditory cue that signals malfunction (Kausler, 1991).

Over extended durations, vigilance tasks can lead to fatigue and ultimately to a decline in accuracy. However, on simple tasks, the accuracy of older adults does not suffer any more than that of younger adults (Kline & Scialfa, 1997). With the Mackworth Clock Test, there is a high level of accuracy in the first 15-minute segment of an hour, with a gradual decline in accuracy over the next three 15-minute time segments. But this decline is no more pronounced for older individuals than for younger ones (Madden & Allen, 1996).

Simple vigilance tasks do not make excessive cognitive demands, and age-related differences are usually small or nonexistent. In fact, older adults are less prone than young adults to having task-unrelated thoughts, or mind wandering, while performing simple vigilance tasks (Giambra, 1989). However, older adults' accuracy suffers more than that of young adults when changes in monitored stimuli occur at a high rate or when vigilance tasks become complex (Kausler, 1991; Rogers & Fisk, 2001). For example, an individual may be required to monitor a screen for a sequence of numbers (for example, 5, 2, 8) as opposed to the simpler task of monitoring the screen for a single number such as 5. Both young and older adults have greater difficulty in monitoring for a three-digit sequence than for a single digit. However, the increased complexity of the three-digit task has a greater negative effect on the performance of older adults than it does on that of young adults, most likely because it requires more attentional resources. Even so, both young and older adults benefit from practice on vigilance tasks (Rogers & Fisk, 2001).

Divided attention

Divided attention is required when attention must be paid to more than one thing at a time, or when two or more stimulus inputs must be processed concurrently. In some dual-task situations, both inputs are presented to the same sense (visual or auditory). In other dual-task situations, one input is presented to one sense (visual) but the other is presented to a different sense (auditory).

In a dual processing task performed in the laboratory, individuals might be required to monitor a screen and respond when a particular geometric form appears. At the same time, they are also required to respond whenever a tone is sounded. The speed and accuracy of their responses when they are required to perform only one of these tasks can be compared with the speed and accuracy of their responses when they must perform both tasks concurrently.

Researchers have used dual attention tasks to determine the extent of age-related decline in processing resources, or capacity. Somberg and Salthouse (1982) demonstrated that young and older adults are equally capable of dividing their attention if tasks are relatively undemanding. As tasks become more demanding, however, the *cost* of dividing attention between more than one of them is greater for older adults than it is for young adults. Cost is measured by comparing how well a task is performed by itself with how well it is performed when a second task

Trying to drive and carry on a cell phone conversation can be hazardous, particularly in heavy traffic and bad weather conditions, because combining these activities could exceed our attentional capacity.

must be performed at the same time. Perhaps young adults have sufficient attentional resources to perform both tasks with little cost. However, dual-task demands may exceed the processing capacity of older adults, whose performance will suffer by becoming slower or less accurate. Again, there are no agreed-upon definitions for capacity and resources, so there is a risk of circularity when these terms are used to explain age-related differences on divided–attention tasks.

Some tasks require a great deal of attention at first, but with practice they require much less attention. Driving is a real-world example. When we first start to drive, we devote considerable attentional resources to learning how to operate the car and follow the rules of the road. With practice, driving requires less effort so it demands fewer attentional resources. In fact, when the weather is good and traffic is light, most of us have little difficulty driving while listening to the radio or carrying on a conversation with a passenger. When weather is inclement or traffic is heavy, we must allocate more attentional resources to our driving. Under demanding conditions, driving while listening to the radio or talking on a cell phone could exceed our attentional capacity. When this happens, the risk of accidents increases. This principle holds true for young and older adults alike, but attentional capacity may be exceeded at an earlier point for older adults. Thus, young drivers might have little difficulty listening to the radio or conversing when it is raining lightly or when traffic conditions are only moderately heavy. Older drivers might find it necessary to turn off the radio or cease talking under these conditions.

McKnight and McKnight (1993) had young, middle-aged, and older participants view videos of traffic situations that called for them to respond by manipulating simulated vehicle controls. At the same time, some study participants engaged in distracting activities such as talking on a cell phone, while others had no distractions. For the oldest group of study participants (ages 50–80), failure to make the appropriate response on the simulated controls was significantly more likely if they were talking on the phone than it was when there were no distractions.

An intriguing study conducted in Finland assessed the strategies used by young (average age 37) and older (average age 68) drivers, mostly men, all of whom owned cars with manual gears (Hakamies-Blomqvist, Mynttinen, Backman, & Mikkonen, 1999). Study participants were allowed to practice driving a 1987 Audi test car that had manual gears and was fitted with seven hidden sensors that recorded the driver's use of the car's controls. After practicing, they drove this car under normal traffic conditions along a previously planned route. The young and older drivers who came to the study with more everyday driving experience tended to use the car's controls in a more parallel manner, meaning that they operated four or more controls simultaneously. Young and older drivers with less prior driving experience did not use as many controls at the same time. Rather, they operated the controls in a more serial manner, favoring the use of no more than three controls at a time. In addition to driving experience, age made a difference. Overall, older drivers used car controls in a more serial manner, while young drivers used car controls in a more parallel manner. In sum, drivers with less prior experience and older drivers were more likely to use the car controls in a serial rather than a parallel manner. Perhaps the serial strategy lowered the demands on their attentional capacity. A serial strategy may work well when traffic conditions are not overly demanding. When driving conditions are complex, however, the serial strategy could increase the risk of accidents because it is more time-consuming than the parallel strategy. This could explain the increased number of traffic accidents involving older adults when driving conditions are demanding.

As with vigilance tasks, practice on divided attention tasks is beneficial for both young and older adults. In the real world, experience can perfect skills. Older adults may be capable of performing several tasks at the same time if they develop expertise in carrying out those tasks (Rybash, Hoyer, & Roodin, 1986). This was illustrated in Hakamies-Blomqvist et al.'s (1999) study, which showed that a greater amount of everyday driving practice was associated with a greater likelihood of the drivers using a parallel strategy to operate the car's controls.

Selective attention

Of all the stimuli that impinge upon us, we must often focus our attention on what is important, or relevant, to the task at hand. We must not allow ourselves to be distracted by unimportant, or irrelevant, information. **Selective attention** is required when we must pay attention to some information while ignoring other information.

Real-world situations often call for selective attention. For instance, a college student trying to study in the library must ignore ongoing conversations taking place nearby despite the posted "Quiet" signs. For the student trying to earn a good grade, the material in the textbook or on the computer is the relevant (target) stimulus. Nearby cell phone conversations represent irrelevant (distracting) stimuli. In this situation, the relevant and irrelevant stimuli are presented to different senses (vision and hearing). The student must attend selectively to the target visual stimuli (the textbook or computer screen), while suppressing attention to the distracting auditory stimuli (other people's cell phone conversations). In other instances, relevant and irrelevant stimuli may impinge upon the same sense. For example, Bernie (described earlier) is trying to focus on a restaurant companion's dinner conversation (target stimulus) but he must "tune out" all sources of background noise (distracting stimuli). The use of the World Wide Web calls for visual selective attention because many web sites place patterned backgrounds behind the text and include unnecessary and distracting graphics and animation (Rogers & Fisk, 2001).

According to the inhibitory deficit model, older adults have particular difficulty selectively focusing on relevant stimuli and ignoring irrelevant distracting stimuli. Inefficient inhibition allows irrelevant stimuli to intrude, which causes errors in processing the relevant stimuli or just slows down processing altogether.

Figure 4.4 *Example of a Stroop color–word test.*

In visual search tasks, the measure of performance is usually the amount of time it takes to locate a target item that is placed among distractor items. The search will take a fair amount of time if individuals must scan all of the distractor items to locate the target item. The search will be quicker if there is spatial precuing in the form of prior information on where the target item will be located among the distractor items. The search will also be quicker if individuals know ahead of time that the target item has certain distinguishing physical characteristics such as color or shape. With precuing about the spatial location or distinctive physical characteristics of a target item, older adults are often no slower than young adults are in locating it (Hartley, 1995). Without precuing, visual search will be slower for both young and older adults, but older adults will be at a greater disadvantage – they will be even slower than young adults. In sum, when visual displays are complex, when distractor stimuli must be scanned and target objects have no outstanding physical characteristics, older adults will have more difficulty than young adults.

The Stroop color–word test (Stroop, 1935) is a well-known visual selective attention task. On this test, the name of a color (for example, "white") is typed in an opposing color of ink (for example, "black") (see Figure 4.4). The task is to name the color of the ink ("black"), while ignoring the fact that the letters typed in black ink spell the word "white." To perform this task, individuals must focus their attention on the color of the letters while suppressing a natural tendency to read the name of the word. What makes the Stroop test especially difficult is the virtual impossibility of completely ignoring the irrelevant stimulus (typed name of the color), which is embedded in the relevant stimulus (the color of the type). This test is difficult for people of all ages, but it is especially challenging for older adults.

To summarize, older adults find it more difficult than young adults do to ignore distracting stimuli, and to focus their attention on target stimuli. One hypothesis is that age-related differences on tests of selective attention stem from inhibitory deficit. We know that older adults are often more susceptible than young adults to interference from distracting stimuli when environments are complex, so distracting stimuli should be kept to a minimum.

Revisiting the Selective Optimization with Compensation and Ecological Models

The Selective Optimization with Compensation (SOC) (Baltes & Baltes, 1990) and Ecological (Lawton, 1989; Lawton & Nahemow, 1973) Models are readily applied to sensory and perceptual processes. With regard to SOC, many older adults make adjustments as they adapt to potential or actual changes in their sensory and perceptual capabilities (Salthouse, 2004). Visual capabilities are optimized if older adults have access to medical screening for diabetes, glaucoma, and cataracts. Prosthetic devices such as reading glasses or bifocals can help older adults compensate for visual changes. Older adults may become selective about the visual conditions under which they function – many limit nighttime driving and drive only when weather conditions are good and traffic conditions light. In many communities, courses are available to train older adults (ages 55+) on how to improve driving skills, and some insurance companies reward the successful completion of such courses with a reduction in auto insurance premiums. With regard to audition, some older adults compensate for hearing loss with hearing aids tailored to their individual needs and many learn to make better use of visual cues.

The Ecological Model would stress the importance of an appropriate match between older adults' sensory and perceptual capabilities and the level of sensory and perceptual challenge in the environment. Individuals with no sensory or perceptual difficulties adapt well in a broad range of environments, but those with limitations adapt best when environments are tailored to their capabilities. Age-related changes in visual functioning call for insuring adequate levels of illumination from light sources that prevent glare. In addition, there should be decreased demand for close visual work. More and more publishers are responding to older adults' need for large print, and many public libraries and bookstores have entire sections of large-print books. Signs posted in areas frequented by older adults should have large letters or numbers printed on a plain and clearly contrasting background. Older adults who give up driving because of visual changes will adapt best in environments that provide transportation such as van service or access to public transportation. Individuals with reduced auditory competence will do well when speakers do not talk too quickly or use too many high-frequency consonants. Ideally, background noise and reverberation should be minimized to insure that auditory challenge is within the adaptation range of the older listener.

? Questions to Consider

1. Do you think talking on the cell phone using a Bluetooth headset will have any effect on how well people in your generation will hear when they get older?
2. Some researchers think that playing video games will sharpen the minds of older adults. Do you agree?
3. Do you think banning handheld cell phones in cars but allowing hands-free devices would greatly reduce the number of accidents among those who talk and drive at the same time? Also, what kinds of driving distraction can be created by having global positioning system (GPS) tracking devices in cars?

Key Points

- Sensory threshold is the minimum amount of stimulation a sensory organ must receive before the presence of a particular stimulus is registered. Sensitivity is the inverse of threshold.
- The signal detection model of determining sensory threshold takes into account sensitivity and decisional response criteria (that is, level of cautiousness). Older adults are often more cautious than young adults.
- Sensation refers to registration of physical stimulation by the sense organs, while perception is the subsequent processing and interpretation of the stimuli at the central (brain) level.
- On reaction time tasks, older adult are usually slower than young adults, and this is more so on complex tasks than on simple ones.
- The nervous system of an older adult takes longer to process information and clear it through the system than the nervous system of a young adult.
- Age-related changes in vision call for greater illumination. There are also changes in color vision and an increasing incidence of presbyopia, although the effects of such visual changes can be minimized. Problems with the retina can result in partial or complete blindness.
- Age-related changes in hearing include presbycusis, which affects high-frequency tones and the ability to understand speech. However, the effects of these auditory changes can be minimized.
- People who communicate with older adults often use elderspeak, some aspects of which are beneficial. However, patronizing speech can result in the older adult's withdrawal from the communication process.
- Older adults may have less attentional resources/capacity compared to young adults. Also, they have greater difficulty inhibiting the effect of distracting stimuli when trying to focus on relevant stimuli.
- Changes in the frontal lobes of the cerebral cortex could be related to deficits on attention tasks that call for inhibiting responses or shifting from one response to another.
- Older adults may have difficulty in complex vigilance tasks and in divided attention tasks that exceed their processing capacity. Also, they have difficulty in selective attention tasks when they must focus on relevant target information and ignore irrelevant distracting information.

Key Terms

absolute threshold   104

age–complexity hypothesis   107

bottom-up and top-down strategies in language processing   119

common cause hypothesis   103

communication predicament of aging model   120

diabetic retinopathy   113

divided attention   125

elderspeak   119

frontal lobe model   123

glaucoma   112

inhibitory deficit model   122

macular degeneration   113

phonemic regression   116

presbycusis   116

presbyopia   112

reaction time   105

reduced attentional resources/capacity model   122

selective attention   127

senile cataracts   113

sensitivity   103

signal detection model   104

stimulus persistence theory   108

threshold   103

useful field of view (UFOV)   114

vigilance   124

5 Memory

Chapter Overview

Close-ups on Adulthood and Aging

Catherine prides herself on remaining mentally active and socially engaged even though she retired from the business world several years back. Her calendar is full, with meetings, fund-raisers, and social gatherings planned months in advance. Catherine just turned 70, and for her birthday her grandson gave her a personal digital assistant (PDA), which he claims is more efficient than writing everything down on a calendar or using Post-It notes. Catherine hopes the high-tech PDA will make it easier for her to keep track of her social agenda. She can also use this device to remind herself to take her medications on schedule, to keep her medical and dental appointments, and to help her stick to her exercise regimen. In addition, it will be handy for keeping track of her children's and grandchildren's birthdays. Catherine is trying to get into the habit of using her PDA, although there have been occasions when she misplaces it or forgets to put it in her purse before she leaves the house.

The Developmental Study of Memory and Age

Memory is essential if we are to make immediate or later use of information in our environment. Being able to function not only in academic settings but in everyday life would be difficult if not impossible without the ability to remember. Memory failures can cause inconvenience (for example, forgetting to buy an item at the grocery store), embarrassment (inability to remember another person's name), and even danger (forgetting to turn off a burner on the stove). Most people are heavily defined by their memories. Perhaps for this reason many individuals, especially older adults, feel threatened when they experience memory lapses.

Concerns About Memory and Aging

Older adults often comment that their memory is not as good as it used to be. Many claim they have increased difficulty finding words, remembering names, recalling where they put things such as glasses or keys, or remembering appointments and birthdays. The term "senior moment" jokingly refers to the often embarrassing memory lapses that are thought to occur more frequently with increasing age.

On a more serious note, older adults and their families often worry that memory failures herald the onset of Alzheimer's disease. Memory impairment is an essential feature of Alzheimer's disease as well as other forms of dementia (see Chapter 11 for a more detailed description). However, memory loss that can occur with aging is not always easy to differentiate from mild dementia (Skoog, Blennow, & Marcusson, 1996). Kral (1962) coined the term "benign senescent forgetfulness" to describe the difficulty some older adults have with remembering nonessential details or parts of past experiences. The terms "age-associated memory impairment" (AAMI) and "age-related memory decline," are terms that refer to mild forms of memory loss that can occur with the aging process (Butler, Lewis, & Sunderland, 1998).

Many normal, healthy older adults experience changes in the accuracy with which they remember things, but changes are not the rule for every aspect of memory. Some types of memory hold up well with age, which suggests that certain memory structures and processes are more vulnerable than others are to the effects of aging.

The Information Processing Model

An early but still influential information processing model (Atkinson & Shiffrin, 1968) conceptualizes memory in terms of stores (see Figure 5.1).

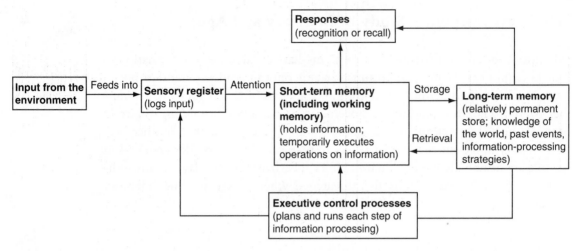

Figure 5.1 *Sensory, short-term, and long-term memory stores.*
Source: Atkinson & Shiffrin (1968).

The Sensory Store

To be processed, information must be registered initially by the sensory store, which holds a momentary perceptual trace – visual (iconic) or auditory (echoic) – for a fraction of a second. The sensory store may be even more fleeting in older adults than it is in young adults. If so, information would dissipate more quickly and be lost more readily from the sensory store for older adults than for young adults.

Because the sensory store holds information so briefly, it has proven difficult to compare young and older adults. There is modest age-related decline, but it is doubtful that such small differences between young and older adults can account for the larger age-related differences on other tests of memory (Botwinick, 1984).

The Short-Term Store

Assuming that the information registered by the sensory store does not fade away too quickly, it enters the **short-term memory store**, where it is held for a longer, though still limited, amount of time (up to 30 seconds). The short-term store has a limited capacity as far as how many items of information can be held at any given time. If this capacity is exceeded, some items of information being held will be displaced as additional items are entered into the short-term store. If items are displaced before being passed on to the long-term store, they will very likely be lost.

The magic number seven

Exactly how much information can be retained in the short-term store? G. A. Miller (1956) referred to the capacity of short-term memory as "the magic number seven plus or minus two." But this limited capacity (five to nine units) can be expanded if individual items of information are "chunked" into meaningful units. For example, a 10-digit telephone number can be reduced to six units if the three-digit area code is chunked into one unit and the three-digit exchange is chunked into another unit.

Some researchers conceptualize short-term memory as consisting of two components, primary memory and working memory. Both have a limited capacity and hold information only temporarily (Cherry & Smith, 1998; Smith, 2006).

Primary memory

Primary memory is a passive receptacle that holds information in the same form in which it was entered. In a test of primary memory, individuals could be instructed to listen to a string of digits (5, 4, 8, 9) and immediately repeat them back in the same order. In general, young and older adults are comparable on short-term memory tasks such as looking up a telephone number and remembering it long enough to punch in the numbers immediately afterward as long as there are no interruptions.

Working memory

Working memory involves both holding information and actively processing and manipulating it (Baddeley, 1986; Smith, 2006). Working memory is like a "mental scratch pad." In a test of working memory, individuals could be instructed to listen to a string of digits (5, 4, 8, 9) and immediately repeat them back in the reverse order (9, 8, 4, 5).

According to Baddeley (1986, 1990), working memory consists of a central executive and two storage/work-space subsystems: the phonological loop and the visuo-spatial sketch pad (see Figure 5.2). The central executive is the decision making mechanism that selects and controls which information will be temporarily held and/or processed by each of the two subsystems (Ellis & Hunt, 1993). Speech-based information, such as a string of spoken numbers, is allocated to the phonological loop, where it is stored or manipulated as necessary. For example, you can rehearse a telephone number in the phonological loop until you can press all the buttons on the phone pad, or until you can code the phone number into smaller meaningful units. Similarly, visual and spatial information (such as remembering the location of objects in a spatial array) are allocated to the visuo-spatial sketch pad, where images are held temporarily and manipulated as necessary. Given the limited capacity of working memory, you can process more information at any given time if

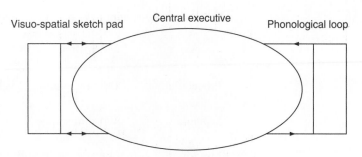

Figure 5.2 *The working memory system.*
Source: Baddeley (1990).

some is speech-based (phonological) and some is visual or spatial (visuo-spatial) than you could if the information were all one or the other.

Some researchers think that the total amount of space in working memory is reduced in older adulthood. Furthermore, the more complex the mental manipulations that must be performed, the more difficulty older adults will experience relative to young adults. For example, a requirement to repeat a string of digits (5, 4, 8, 9) backwards after subtracting 2 from each (7, 6, 2, 3) calls for more complex mental manipulations than simply repeating the digits back in the reverse order (9, 8, 4, 5). Ability for these more complex manipulations shows a greater decrease with age than does ability for simpler manipulations.

To summarize, age-related differences in sensory memory are minimal. Similarly, there is little or no age-related decline in short-term primary memory. However, older adults usually have more difficulty than young adults with working memory, probably because they must actively manipulate information held there (Craik, 1994). The more complex the manipulations required, the greater the age-related decline is likely to be.

The Long-Term Store

Long-term memory is what most people think of when they refer to "memory." According to the information processing model, items of information entered into the **long-term memory store** remain there well beyond 30 seconds. Information can be maintained in this memory store for weeks, months, or years. The capacity of the long-term store appears to be unlimited. Although we are consciously aware of the information in our short-term store, the information in our long-term store is not always in our conscious awareness. Rather, items are retrieved out of the long-term store as needed.

Not all memories in the long-term store are alike. Some researchers (Cherry & Smith, 1998; Smith, 2006) conceptualize long-term memories as falling into three categories: procedural, semantic, and episodic (see Table 5.1).

Table 5.1 *Long-term memory categories, examples, and age-related effects*

Category	Examples	Age-related effects
Procedural	Driving, typing, bicycle riding	Very little or none
Semantic	Word meanings, knowledge	Very little or none
Episodic	Specific events and experiences	Age-related decline

Procedural memory

Procedural memory allows us to acquire skills that we usually demonstrate indirectly by action (Bäckman, Small, & Wahlin, 2001). Examples are knowing how to ride a bicycle, drive a car, play table tennis, play a musical instrument, or type on a keyboard. We acquire these skills gradually with practice over a long time, after which they are readily available without much deliberate recollection. It is almost as if these skills become "automatic" – even if you have not driven a car, played table tennis, or typed for a long time, you will be able to do these things with little conscious effort, although at first you may make some errors.

Some skills stay with us throughout our lives even if we have not used them for a long time.

Not all procedural memories involve motor skills. Being able to read and understand language also calls for procedural memory. Learning a language requires effort and practice, but later we read and engage in conversations without much thought.

Older adults may be somewhat slower than young adults in recovering procedural memories from storage but, given a little additional time, they are just as capable as young adults of doing so. However, skills that call for complex mental manipulations in working memory (such as reading inverted sentences) or very rapid responses do show some age-related decline (Bäckman et al., 2001).

Semantic memory

Semantic memory is akin to general knowledge, or world knowledge. Information in semantic memory has been well learned. Semantic information has been in the long-term store for a considerable time, although no specific time or place can be identified as to when it was placed there. Examples of semantic memory are knowing your mother's maiden name and knowing the name of the first U.S. president. Older adults do not differ from young adults in the content or organization of linguistic knowledge in their semantic store (Light, 1991; Wingfield, 1995). Both know that an apple is a kind of fruit and a cat is a kind of animal. Furthermore, young and older adults associate the same words with one another (for example "up–down" and "baby–cries").

Although linguistic knowledge is preserved with age, word-finding problems are a common complaint among older adults. Compared to young adults, older adults are more likely to report tip-of-the-tongue (TOT) experiences – being temporarily unable to retrieve familiar words (Kemper, 1995). Burke, MacKay,

Worthley, and Wade (1991) had young, middle-aged, and older adults keep a diary over four weeks to record naturally occurring TOTs. Most of their TOTs were for infrequent words in the language and for proper names. Older adults reported more TOTs than young and middle-aged adults, and most of the older adults' TOTs were for names of acquaintances who had not been contacted recently. However, when they are allowed sufficient time and when they make an effort, older adults are usually successful in gaining access to a blocked word or name (Kausler, 1994).

In sum, older adults may be somewhat slower than young adults in retrieving semantic memories from the long-term store, but ultimately, they are usually just as capable as young adults of doing so. There is every reason to assume that semantic memory remains intact in older adulthood (Craik, 1994).

Episodic memory

Episodic memory is memory for events and experiences that occurred at a specific place or time. A good example would be the ability to remember which words were on a list that you saw an hour, a day, or a week ago.

Table 5.2 shows a list of 15 words that individuals might be instructed to study for some period of time such as 60 seconds. Later, they will be asked to say or write down as many as they can remember. This is a test of episodic memory because the words that individuals must remember are those on a list they viewed at a specific time.

Episodic memory will be better for items on the list if individuals use an organizational strategy when they study it. For example, items could be organized according to categories based on semantic knowledge (items on the list are food, trees, clothing, animals, or means of transportation). Thus, semantic memory can be helpful when situations call for episodic memory.

Episodic memory is not limited to word lists. Sometimes we must remember locations, such as where we put our keys or glasses, or where we parked our car at the mall. Older adults often remark that this type of forgetting is bothersome and stressful. Again, however, structure and meaningful organizational cues can help.

Table 5.2 *A sample list of 15 words used to test long-term episodic memory*

Pear	Milk	Apple
Oak	Pine	Birch
Shoe	Hat	Gloves
Cat	Dog	Horse
Train	Car	Bus

Cherry and Jones (1999) asked young and older adults to view 36 small, colorful pieces of dollhouse furniture, which were placed in certain locations on a flat surface. After the items were removed, participants had to reconstruct the arrangement by placing each item back in its original location. Both young and older participants had better memory for spatial location if the items had been arranged in a schematic pattern (clustering living room items such as couch, coffee table, fireplace; clustering nursery items such as high chair, playpen, and hobby horse, and so on) than they did if the items had been placed in random locations on the surface.

In daily life, episodic memory plays an important role in memory for actions and activities. Did you remember to take your medicine, turn off the oven, pay a bill, mail a letter, or lock the door when you left the house? Unlike committing a list of words to memory, we do not usually make a deliberate attempt to remember our actions and activities when we perform them. But even though memory for actions and activities may not be intentional, it would still be considered episodic because actions or activities occur at a specific time and place.

Some older adults report difficulty remembering whether they actually performed actions such as turning off the oven or locking the door, or whether they only thought about performing them. But do older adult actually have more difficulty with this distinction than young adults? In laboratory studies in which the nature and duration of activities can be controlled, individuals of all ages have more accurate memory for motor activities (such as putting rubber bands on a tube) than they do for cognitive activities (such as solving arithmetic problems or word puzzles). Overall, young adults recall about 75% of the activities they performed, whereas older adults recall about 60% (Kausler, 1994).

Applying Research Box 5.1: False Memory

Most research on aging and memory investigates memory accuracy, but are older adults more vulnerable than young adults to false memories? According to Larry Jacoby and Matthew Rhodes (2006), they are. For example, with the Deese–Roediger–McDermott (DRM) paradigm (Roediger & McDermott, 1995), study participants are exposed to a list of semantically related words such as *bed*, *rest*, and *pillow*, all related to a central theme word (*sleep*). The word *sleep* is never presented but is considered to be a critical lure. When tested later, people often falsely recall or recognize the critical lure (*sleep*), even though it was not on the list. However, older adults are more likely than young adults to report false memories for the critical lure. Also, when warned ahead of time about critical lures, young adults' subsequent false recognition is greatly reduced but that of older adults is less so. Older adults' difficulty in suppressing misinformation may make them more susceptible to scams. For example, a scam artist might insist to an older adult that he/she agreed to pay for something when in fact this was not the case. If older adults have greater difficulty recollecting the details of specific events, they could fall prey to a scam artist's insistence and be more easily persuaded that they agreed to something when they actually have not.

Noncontent Attributes of Episodic Memory

Some aspects of episodic memory supplement the content of an event, but there is no conscious intention to remember them. Examples of noncontent attributes are remembering where or from whom an item of information was acquired (**source memory**), remembering when an event occurred or whether one event occurred more recently than another (**temporal memory**), and remembering how frequently a specific event occurred (**frequency-of-occurrence memory**).

Source memory

You heard that a movie playing at local theaters is excellent, but did you acquire this information from a television show, a radio program, the local newspaper, or a magazine you read in the waiting room of a doctor's office? You are introduced to somebody you remember having met before, but you cannot remember where. You heard that an acquaintance is ill, but who told you this? Somebody told you a funny joke, but embarrassment will certainly follow if you repeat the joke to the person who originally told it to you.

Source memory has been investigated in laboratory studies by presenting items of factual information from more than one source. For instance, half of the items may be presented using an overhead projector, while the other half of the items are read aloud. Later, study participants must identify the source by which they were exposed to each item. Another example is having half the items read aloud by one investigator and the other half by a second investigator. On a subsequent test, are young adults more accurate than older adults in identifying which investigator read each item? Older adults are somewhat less proficient in source memory, but the difference between young and older adults is relatively small (Kausler, 1994). Extremely poor source memory may indicate problems with frontal lobe functioning (Kausler et al., 2007). See Chapter 3 for a more detailed discussion of the brain.

Temporal memory

How well do you remember when events occurred or the order in which they occurred? Which day of the week did you do your grocery shopping, put gasoline in your car, get a haircut? Can you remember which event occurred earlier and which happened later? Temporal memory has been investigated in the laboratory by showing study participants a lengthy series of words or having them perform a series of actions (for example, raise your right arm, point to your nose, and so on). Later, they are asked which of two words appeared more recently in the series or which action they performed first. When study participants must reconstruct the order in which words or actions occurred, older adults are usually less accurate than young adults. Patients who suffer from pathology in the frontal lobes exhibit special difficulty on temporal memory tasks (Schacter, 1987). Further investigation is needed, but age-related deficits in temporal memory could be associated with some deterioration in the frontal lobe area of the brain that occurs with the aging process (Kausler, 1994).

Frequency-of-occurrence memory

In the past six months, how many times have you rented movies and how often have you gone to see movies in the theater? In general, individuals are accurate when they make relative frequency judgments (for example, I saw more movies on home video than I did in the theater). They are less accurate when they are required to make absolute frequency judgments (I rented movies exactly 15 times and I went to the movie theater exactly 8 times).

Frequency-of-occurrence memory has been investigated in the laboratory by presenting a long series of word items one at a time. Some words occur only once in the series, while others occur two, three, or more times. Later, study participants are asked which of two word items occurred more frequently (relative judgments) or how many times one particular word occurred (absolute judgments). Some researchers (for example, Hasher & Zacks, 1979) think this type of memory is *automatic* because we do not usually make an intentional effort to remember how often something has happened. The issue of automaticity has been debated (see Kausler, 1991, 1994), but there is little question that people are quite accurate in frequency-of-occurrence memory, and older adults are nearly as accurate as young adults (Kausler et al., 2007).

Stages of Processing in Episodic Memory

Three stages of processing take place in long-term episodic memory: encoding, storage, and retrieval. **Encoding** is related to input, or placing memory traces into the long-term store. **Storage** refers to retaining memory traces in the long-term store. **Retrieval** is related to output, or recovering memory traces from the long-term store when they are needed. Which stages of processing are vulnerable and which may be immune to the effects of aging?

Encoding

As information is prepared for entry into the long-term store, memory traces are established. The quality of these traces depends upon how the information was encoded. Encoding can be *rote* or *elaborative*. With rote encoding, the individual might simply rehearse the items over and over again until they are placed into storage. Traces formed with rote encoding lack the unique characteristics that make items of information memorable because simple repetition does not involve the effort required to process the meaningful characteristics of the information.

In contrast, elaborative encoding entails processing the unique characteristics of the items, which should result in more distinctive traces. Elaborative encoding can be verbal or visual. With verbal encoding, the individual could organize items of information into meaningful categories. For example, the items in Table 5.2

fall into five categories – food, trees, clothing, animals, and means of transportation. The individual making the effort to categorize these items is forced to think about their meaning. With visual encoding, the individual could use imagery. For example, for the items of clothing, one could imagine getting dressed to go out in the morning, putting on shoes, a hat, and gloves. Distinctive memory traces that result from verbal or visual encoding will be easier to retrieve from storage later on compared to the traces formed by simply repeating items over and over again.

Why do older adults usually remember fewer items than young adults do after they study a list like the one in Table 5.2? One hypothesis is that they are less likely than young adults to use elaborative encoding. That is, older adults may simply repeat each item several times ("shoe, shoe, shoe"), and such rote rehearsal will not result in a distinctive memory trace that is easy to access later. But does this mean that older adults are unable to encode information elaboratively?

Inability to encode information elaboratively is **mediation deficiency**. In contrast, being able to encode elaboratively but failing to do so spontaneously is **production deficiency**. Older adults may not take the initiative to encode elaboratively, but when given structure and guidance (for example, specific instructions on how to do so), they are capable of using elaborative encoding strategies and improving their memory scores. Thus, older adults have a production deficiency rather than mediation deficiency.

Young adults may encode information elaboratively because they must in order to do well in school. Most older adults are not students, so they are less accustomed to elaborative encoding and may need to be instructed to do so. Compared to rote encoding, elaborative encoding requires more cognitive effort (uses more cognitive resources). Some have proposed that, with age, cognitive resources are reduced, which could explain why older adults do not expend effort on elaborative encoding unless they are prodded to (see Light, 1991).

Storage

The long-term store can be conceptualized as a bin where memory traces are kept for a long time, often permanently. Presumably, the capacity of this bin is unlimited and the aging process does not affect its sturdiness. Once memory traces are placed into the bin, they should be maintained there. There is little reason to believe that memory traces will be lost from the long-term store with normal aging. However, memory traces will be more accessible if they are placed into the long-term store in an organized fashion, where they can be found easily when there is a need to retrieve them.

Retrieval

After individuals study the list of items on Table 5.2, how many can they retrieve from storage? Several kinds of memory test can be used: recall, cued recall, or recognition. On a **recall** test, individuals study a list of items and afterward are told to say or write down as many as they can remember.

On a **cued recall** test, individuals study a list of items and afterward are told to say or write down as many as they can remember, but they are supplied with hints (cues) to guide their retrieval. For example, they might be asked, "What foods were on the list?" "What trees were on the list?" and so on.

A **recognition** test could consist of multiple-choice questions. Individuals might be presented with two items (milk, juice) and asked to select the item that appeared on the list. Or items could be displayed one at a time, and individuals would be instructed to respond "yes" or "no" to each item, depending on whether or not it was on the list.

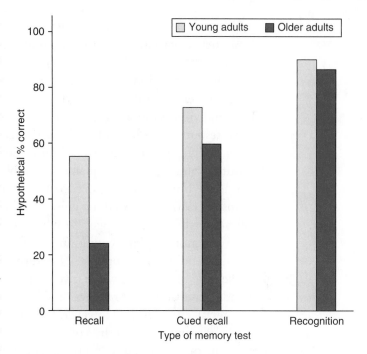

Figure 5.3 *Hypothetical percentage correct for young and older adults on recall, cued recall, and recognition tests.*

Regardless of age, most people retrieve the smallest number of items on recall tests and the largest on recognition tests. Scores on cued recall tests fall in between. But the type of memory test makes a bigger difference for older adults than it does for young adults. The scores of young and older adults show the greatest discrepancy on a recall test (with older adults recalling fewer items), probably because the processing demands of retrieval are greatest on recall tests (Smith, 2006). On a cued recall test, there is less discrepancy in the scores of young and older adults, although older adults may not recall quite as many items as young adults. On a recognition test, there is often very little difference in the scores of young and older adults (see Figure 5.3).

Researchers have long sought to determine whether the source of any age-related decrement in episodic memory is at the stage of encoding or whether it occurs during retrieval. Recent thinking is that encoding and retrieval are not easily differentiated into separate and distinct processes. We need cognitive resources for both and, if the later years bring a reduction in cognitive resources, older adults will be at a disadvantage in both encoding and retrieval.

Craik (1994) proposed that retrieval is the attempt to recreate the original pattern, or context, that was present when information was encoded. According to the *encoding specificity* principle (Tulving & Thomson, 1973), memory will be best if the same information is available at both the time of encoding and the time of retrieval. On recognition tests, the encoding context is reinstated at the time of retrieval because the items present during encoding are reintroduced, resulting in environmental support for retrieval. Individuals of all ages benefit from such environmental support, but it may be especially helpful for older adults.

Unlike recognition tests, recall tests do not reinstate the encoding context, so there is no environmental support to aid in retrieving previously encoded items. Thus, individuals must engage in "self-initiated" processing, which requires cognitive resources. If older adults have reduced cognitive resources, they will experience difficulty on tests that call for extensive effortful self-initiated processing.

But are all older adults equally vulnerable to memory difficulties when there is little environmental support for retrieval? Not necessarily. Craik, Byrd, and Swanson (1987) compared the episodic memory of young adult college students and older adults (average age 74) who varied in their level of verbal ability and social functioning. The young and older adults studied a list of words under varying conditions of support. Not surprisingly, both young and older adults recalled the most words when given support in the form of cues both at time of encoding and at time of retrieval, and both recalled the fewest words when given no cues at either time. However, the higher-functioning older adults recalled almost as many words as the young adults did even when there were no cues at encoding or retrieval. In contrast, older adults low in both verbal ability and level of social functioning recalled fewer words compared not only to the young adults but also to the higher-functioning older adults. Thus, older adults vary considerably with regard to the likelihood of self-initiated processing.

Remote Memory

Although the long-term memory store can hold information for a lengthy time, perhaps permanently, a distinction is sometimes made between long-term memory and very long-term (remote) memory. There are numerous anecdotal reports of older adults' outstanding memory for information from long ago even though their memory for more recent episodic information is less accurate. Older adults themselves often claim that their memory for very dated information is excellent despite difficulties they have remembering what happened yesterday. Ribot's Law, which states that information is forgotten in the reverse order in which it was acquired, has become a stereotype regarding the pattern of age-related memory decline (Ribot, 1882). Researchers have investigated whether very dated information is spared despite age-related decline in memory for more recent information. They have tested **remote memory** for factual information as well as memory for personal, autobiographical information that goes back decades (Erber, 2006).

Factual Information

Remote memory for factual information includes memory for political and sports events from long ago as well as memory for movies, television shows, and songs that were popular decades earlier. It is difficult to assess remote memory for such information because exposure to it took place in the real world and not under strictly controlled laboratory conditions. Not all individuals in a particular age cohort received the same exposure to specific facts earlier in their lives. For example, older adults who were avid moviegoers may have excellent memory for the popular movie stars from earlier times. In contrast, those with little interest or opportunity to see movies did not have direct exposure to them in prior decades. Similarly, it is difficult to determine whether older adults obtained factual knowledge from direct experience when events actually happened, or whether they simply read or heard about these events years later.

Studies on memory for the names and faces of high school classmates (Bahrick, Bahrick, & Wittlinger, 1975) and for the names of streets in a college town that alumni have not visited since graduating (Bahrick, 1979) indicate a fairly rapid rate of forgetting within 4 to 6 years of the information being acquired. Then forgetting levels off, and 20% to 40% of the information is retained. Thus, this type of information is not immune to forgetting, but it is remarkable that a portion of it is retained well into late adulthood without any further loss (Kausler, 1994).

Autobiographical Information

Autobiographical information includes memory for the details of personal events such as proms or weddings. Although such events probably took place decades earlier, older adults often say they remember them very clearly. However, it is not always possible to check the accuracy of these memories. Aunt Alice may remember that the menu at her wedding dinner 50 years earlier included beef tenderloin. But if the information could be checked, it might be discovered that

Understanding Aging Box 5.1: The Reminiscence Bump

Many older adults claim that their strongest and most vivid memories are for events and experiences that occurred between the ages of 10 and 30. This phenomenon, termed the **reminiscence bump** (Jansari & Parkin, 1996), seems to hold for both factual and personal information. The period from ages 10 to 30 is the time during which older adults saw their favorite films, read their favorite books, listened to their favorite music, and considered world events to be most important. Also, older adults are surprisingly accurate in answering multiple-choice questions on Academy Awards, the World Series, and current events that occurred during this period in their lives (Rubin, Rahhal, & Poon, 1998). There are several explanations for the reminiscence bump. One is that the time from late childhood to early adulthood is a period of rapid change as well as peak cognitive functioning, both of which foster elaborative encoding and thus the formation of vivid memories. As well, the period from age 10 to young adulthood may be especially important for developing a sense of identity. Novel and varied social contacts that occur during this time lend themselves to the formation of vivid memories.

her wedding dinner actually was chicken. Each time we retrieve memories of events and experiences that are meaningful to us, we may embellish them. Over time, our memories may represent what we believe rather than what actually happened.

In sum, there is much interest in remote memory, but it is difficult to test the accuracy of personal recollections. Nonetheless, based on what we know and what older adults say, memory for very dated events and experiences is relatively well maintained over a long time.

Memory in Everyday Life

Thus far, we have focused on retrospective memory, which is memory for information that was acquired in the past or for events that occurred in the past. However, sometimes we must remember to do something in the future. Also, sometimes we make a deliberate effort to remember, but under some circumstances past experiences affect our behavior without our conscious awareness. Such memories are implicit rather than explicit. People who experience difficulties with everyday memory can be trained in techniques that help them improve their performance. Finally, everyday functioning depends heavily upon discourse memory, which is the ability to remember language materials that we have either read or heard.

Prospective Memory

Prospective memory is remembering to perform some action at a designated future point. For example, we must remember to pay bills, mail letters and send birthday cards, make phone calls, schedule appointments with doctors and dentists, and make dates with friends. (And of course we must remember to keep those appointments and dates.) The term *absentmindedness* often refers to prospective memory failures (Kausler et al., 2007). Some prospective memory failures, such as forgetting to turn off burners when we finish cooking or forgetting to take medications at the scheduled times, can have serious consequences. Prospective memory plays a crucial role in everyday life. It is important for people of all ages, but it is especially critical in determining older adults' ability to maintain their independence.

Research findings on age and prospective memory have been mixed. Some studies report that older adults' prospective memory is equivalent or even superior to that of young adults, while others find evidence for age-related decline. Ability level, often measured by level of education or scores on a vocabulary test, is an important factor, especially for older adults (Cherry & LeComte, 1999). Educated older adults with high verbal ability perform similarly to young adults on many tests of prospective memory. In contrast, less educated older adults with low verbal ability often perform less well than young adults.

Prospective memory tests vary considerably across studies, which could contribute to the contradictory research findings with regard to age. Prospective memory can be performed in controlled laboratory settings or in naturalistic real-world settings. Also, prospective memory tasks can be event-based or time-based (Einstein & McDaniel, 1990).

Event-based tasks

In event-based prospective memory tasks, individuals must remember to perform a particular action in response to an external cue. In the laboratory, an event-based prospective memory task would be remembering to press a certain computer key when a particular symbol appears on a monitor. A naturalistic event-based prospective memory task would be using a calendar (or a PDA, as in the case of Catherine, who was described at the beginning of this chapter) as an external cue for remembering scheduled activities or appointments or remembering special occasions such as the birthdays of loved ones. Of course, this would assume that detailed reminders have been noted on a calendar (or entered into a PDA) that is readily available. Event-based prospective memory tasks show very little age-related decline as long as such tasks do not have to be performed along with many other activities. In fact, older adults often perform better than young adults.

Time-based tasks

In time-based prospective memory tasks, individuals must remember to perform an action at some point without the aid of any external physical cues. A laboratory-based example would be requiring individuals to note the time when they complete a series of questionnaires. Performance on such tasks generally shows greater age-related decline compared to performance on event-based tasks. In fact, age-related decrement has been noted not only between adults in their 20s and 60s, but also between older adults in their 60s and those in their 80s (Rendell & Thomson, 1999). Time-based tasks provide little environmental support; they require self-initiated processing, which is more difficult for older adults than it is for younger adults.

However, less age-related decline has been noted when time-based prospective memory tasks take place in naturalistic settings. In some studies, participants have been instructed to leave phone messages on a researcher's voice mail at designated times or to mail postcards on certain dates. Although no physical reminders are provided, older adults often perform better on such tasks than young adults, who more often neglect to make phone calls or mail postcards when they are supposed to. Perhaps performance on naturalistic time-based tasks is influenced by motivational factors – older adults may feel more pressure to comply or may conform more to task demands. Also, if daily activities have a more routine pattern for older adults than for young adults, it may be easier for older adults to integrate time-based prospective memory tasks into their everyday schedule (Rendell & Thomson, 1999).

An additional factor to consider is how much delay there is between the moment we remember we have to perform a prospective memory task and the time when we are actually able to execute it. For example, it may occur to you when you get out of bed in the morning that you must remember to take your medication before you eat breakfast, but do you actually do it? In laboratory-based prospective memory studies, there seems to be age-related decline even when delays are brief (Einstein, McDaniel, Manzi, Cochran, & Baker, 2000). However, there is reason to believe that real-world prospective memory holds up quite well over the adult life span. Nonetheless, readily available external cues may be more necessary as prospective memory requirements become more demanding.

Implicit Memory

Up to this point, we have focused on explicit memory, which requires conscious and deliberate recollection of information or events. **Implicit memory** is memory without any deliberate recollection (Howard, 2006; Zacks, Hasher, & Li, 2000). Individuals may be exposed to stimuli or events that they have no conscious intention to remember, and they may remain unaware that any memory traces were encoded. But implicit memory is inferred when such prior exposure affects subsequent test performance or some other kind of behavior or reaction even without the individual's realizing it. A real-life example (Kausler et al., 2007) could be a feeling you have when you are introduced to someone that you have met this person before, but you have no recollection of any such meeting and you do not recall or even recognize the person's name.

How can implicit memory be measured? In a test of implicit memory for words (Howard, 1996), people are shown a series of word fragments, each with a blank space for a missing letter. They are instructed to fill in the blank space with a letter that will make the fragment into an actual word. For example, the word fragment "s ap" would be a word if the letter l, n, or o is inserted. Let's assume that one individual selects o to create the word "soap." On a subsequent task administered later on, this same individual is shown a series of four-letter items and instructed to press a key on the left if the string of letters spells a word and a key on the right if the string of letters does not spell a word. Implicit memory is inferred if the individual reacts more quickly upon seeing the word "soap" than upon seeing the words "slap" or "snap." The quicker reaction to "soap" would suggest implicit memory for "soap," undoubtedly based on the previous word fragment task, even without the individual's conscious awareness of having encoded "soap" on the earlier task.

Especially intriguing is that older adults often perform well on tests of implicit memory even when they show age-related decrements on tests of explicit memory. This means that older adults' behavior can be influenced by stimuli and events in their environment even without their conscious realization. And when age-related decrements in implicit memory are found, they are generally of a smaller magnitude than age-related decrements in explicit memory (Howard, 2006). Such dissociation between implicit and explicit memory is often seen with normal aging, but implicit memory usually holds up better than explicit memory even for older adults with Alzheimer's disease or other types of dementia. Different areas of the brain may be involved with implicit as opposed to explicit memory, and selective preservation of implicit memory could indicate that functioning is maintained better in some parts of the brain than in others.

Another finding that points to a dissociation between these two types of memory is that, for both young and older adults, explicit memory is better when tested at peak (optimal) points in a person's cycle of circadian arousal. In contrast, implicit memory is better when tested at off-peak (nonoptimal) times (May, Hasher, & Foong, 2005). Thus, peak times are important for conscious efforts to process information but not necessarily for unconscious processing.

Memory Training

Older adults often complain that their memory is not as good as it once was. However, they can learn strategies that help them improve everyday memory functioning and at the same time bolster their feelings of competence and self-worth. *Mnemonics* refers to techniques that help improve memory. Mnemonic techniques can be classified into several categories (see Camp et al., 1993; Sugar, 2007), but we will focus on those requiring conscious effort and awareness on the part of the individual using them.

Mnemonic strategies can be external – that is, using physical aids or cues to maintain or improve memory. Examples of **external mnemonics** are cooking timers, bookmarks, calendars, reminder notes, lists, medication organizers, and placing items in a noticeable place. (B. F. Skinner spoke of hanging his umbrella on the front doorknob as a reminder to take it to work.) Many older adults use external mnemonics to insure that they keep appointments, run errands, purchase items, and take medications on the prescribed schedule. Such mnemonics are especially helpful in aiding prospective memory (Lovelace & Twohig, 1990; Sugar, 2007). In the example described at the beginning of the chapter, Catherine's grandson thinks that using a PDA is a good way to remind her of her daily schedule and help her keep appointments and remember important dates.

Internal mnemonics are often taught in memory training classes, where people are instructed to form mental images and verbal associations to help them

This shopper uses a list so that he will not forget to purchase all the items he needs.

remember. To remember names, one can make up rhymes to associate names with faces (for example, "Matt is fat," "Nan is tan"). To remember what items to buy at the store, one could compose a story with all the items in it, or perhaps organize the necessary items into categories (fruits, spices, dairy products). Acronyms used by many organizations are shortcuts that also serve as a verbal mnemonic (for example, CONA stands for the Committee on Aging sponsored by the American Psychological Association, or APA).

Internal mnemonics can also be visual. The *method of loci* was used by Roman orators when they delivered speeches. It requires taking a mental walk through a familiar area such as one's home and mentally placing items that must be remembered in various rooms or locations. Using the method of loci to remember grocery items, one can imagine eggs splattered on the front porch of one's home, loaves of bread stuffed into the front hall closet, and so on. Once at the grocery store, one would simply take a mental walk through one's home to be reminded of which items to purchase.

Older adults show less preference for internal mnemonics than they do for external ones (Lovelace & Twohig, 1990). Using internal mnemonics requires a great deal of cognitive effort, which may be worth expending if external cues cannot be used. For example, when you are introduced to someone, you may not be able to write down that person's name. Perhaps you can use an internal mnemonic to associate the person's name and face until such time as you can write down the name. As described in the earlier discussion of production deficiency, older adults may not make spontaneous use of internal mnemonics. However, they can do so when they are encouraged and given structure and guidance.

A question of practical importance in training older adults to use internal mnemonics is whether immediate positive effects will endure. Here the findings are mixed (see Cherry & Smith, 1998). According to some reports, the benefit of formal memory training lasts for six months or longer. However, other reports are less positive. Conclusive statements about the long-term effectiveness of memory training are difficult to make because studies have varied so widely on

---

Applying Research Box 5.2: Memory Cues and Shopping

A large regional shopping mall in Florida provides both visual and auditory cues to help customers remember where they parked their cars. Each entrance to the mall is identified with a different species (alligator, seahorse, and so on). Placed at the "alligator" entrance is a large figure of an alligator as well as the name ALLIGATOR written in large green letters. As shoppers pass through the "alligator" entrance, a loudspeaker announces, "This is the alligator entrance." These cues promote verbal and visual processing. The shopper can develop an internal mnemonic by repeating "alligator" over and over again, but a more effective way to process these cues might be to imagine oneself being chased into the mall by a hungry alligator. The shopper also has the option of converting the cues to an external mnemonic by writing "alligator entrance" on a notepad to be stored in a wallet or purse or entered into a PDA.

a number of dimensions. The older adult samples in memory training studies have varied considerably in the extent of their memory complaints, their motivation to improve, and their cognitive functioning at the outset. Also, studies have employed a variety of training activities as well as different ways of measuring long-term effectiveness. Memory training interventions should include follow-up to determine whether individuals are continuing to use what they learned earlier. Periodic post-training sessions should be available to encourage older adults to keep using what they have learned (Cherry & Smith, 1998).

In sum, many older adults use external mnemonics effectively. Instructional programs to teach older adults how to use internal mnemonics seem to be helpful, but the long-term effects need further study.

Discourse Memory

After reading an article or listening to a conversation, how much do we remember? Memory for extended language materials, called **discourse memory**, is crucial for everyday functioning. Not surprisingly, memory for spoken language can be impaired when there is age-related loss in peripheral hearing acuity and/or central auditory processing (Wingfield et al., 2005). (See Chapter 4 for a discussion of hearing.) Memory for spoken and written materials may be negatively affected when older adults suffer from dementia or other neurological disorders. But what do we know about discourse memory in older adults who have no serious sensory or cognitive impairments?

Language properties
Wingfield, Tun, and Rosen (1995) had young and older adults listen to tape-recordings of spoken paragraph-length passages. Some passages were interrupted by the speaker at natural syntactic boundaries (after sentences or major clauses). Other passages were interrupted randomly at intervals that were not natural breaks in sentences or clauses. Age-related differences in recall were small for spoken materials that were interrupted at natural boundaries, but older adults made more errors than young adults in recalling passages that were randomly interrupted. Older adults may rely especially heavily on their knowledge of language structure to compensate for age-related decline in the ability to recall spoken discourse. Indeed, conditions that optimize the opportunity to use structural properties of language can lessen or even eliminate age-related deficits in discourse processing (Stine-Morrow, Noh, & Shake, 2006). In contrast, taking away natural language cues prevents older adults from using this knowledge to bolster their recall of spoken discourse.

On-line and off-line measures
Most research on memory for written discourse has employed off-line memory measures, meaning that individuals read or listen to materials and afterward take a memory test on what they just read or heard (Stine, Soederberg, & Morrow, 1996).

In general, older adults do not recall as much information as young adults, although age-related differences are small when the older adults are highly educated and intellectually active (Stine-Morrow et al., 2006).

Fewer studies use on-line techniques, which compare the strategies young and older adults use while they are actually processing discourse materials. For example, eye movements can be tracked as text materials are processed. Even when young and older adults are matched for accuracy of their off-line recall of text materials, Stine-Morrow, Loveless, and Soederberg (1996) found age-related differences in how on-line reading time is allocated. Young adults devoted more time to processing infrequent words and new concepts when these first occur in the passage, whereas older adults allocated their time more evenly as they progressed through the passage.

In the future, more researchers may use neuroimaging techniques (fMRI and PET scans, which were described in Chapter 3) to study brain activation patterns as individuals process discourse materials (Kemper & Mitzner, 2001). This should help us understand how young and older adults use their cognitive resources as they process written text and spoken language.

Memory for gist and memory for details
In general, both young and older adults are better at recalling the gist (themes) of stories and narratives than they are at recalling precise details. In fact, both age groups have a similar level of memory for themes. However, older adults remember fewer details than young adults. Age-related decrement in memory for details becomes more noticeable when materials are less familiar, more grammatically complex, and presented at faster speeds (Stine et al., 1996). Even so, it is interesting to note that older adults often give more detailed reports than young adults when asked to describe personal episodes and events, so some language skills actually increase with age (Kemper, 1995).

In sum, age-related decline has been noted when off-line measures are used to evaluate discourse memory. This decline is more pronounced when older adults are less educated and less intellectually active, and also when they are prevented from using natural language features to help them remember. Further research using on-line measures could help pinpoint the reason for age-related differences. Most people remember themes better than details of discourse materials. Age-related decrements are often found in the recall of details, although older adults tend to give more detailed narratives when describing episodes or events they themselves have experienced.

Knowledge and Beliefs About Memory

What do people believe about memory in general? What do they know about their own memory and what do they think of their memory capabilities? Memory is an important part of self-image, and we often react emotionally to self-evaluations about memory. For example, we may feel proud when we can remember something and embarrassed when we cannot. Complaints about memory are common among older adults, and their beliefs about their own memory capabilities could affect their actual memory performance. Moreover, people in some cultures hold negative stereotypes about memory and age. How do such stereotypes influence the judgments people make about the competence of an older adult who forgets?

Metamemory

If asked, most people would say that multiple-choice tests are easier than essay tests, and they would estimate that a highly associated word pair such as "up–down" would be easier to remember than an unrelated word pair such as "bus–knee." Most people would also agree that making a list helps them remember what they need at the grocery store. **Metamemory** refers to an inherent understanding of memory.

Researchers have questioned whether young and older adults differ in their understanding about how the memory system works. If older adults have a less accurate understanding, they may fail to engage in strategies that would help them remember. If they are deficient in monitoring their own memory processing, they may fail to use their cognitive resources when memory situations call for them.

Older adults are not as adept as young adults in gauging their readiness for taking a memory test (Kausler et al., 2007). Murphy, Sanders, Gabriesheski, and Schmitt (1981) found that older adults did not take all the time allowed for studying materials on which they knew they would be tested later. Even so, their memory scores on such tests were lower than the scores of young adults. When older adults were required to study the materials for additional time, they improved their scores to the level attained by young adults. When left to their own devices, older adults may not realistically assess how much time they would have to study to obtain the best possible memory score (Kausler, 1994). However, despite older adults' lesser ability to gauge their test readiness, they are similar to young adults in their general knowledge of how memory works and their beliefs about which memory tasks would be easy and which ones would be difficult (Light, 1991).

Memory Self-Efficacy

Bandura (1977, p. 191) defined self-efficacy as the conviction that one can successfully execute the behavior required to produce an outcome. **Memory self-efficacy** is the self-evaluative system of beliefs and judgments about one's own memory competence and confidence in one's own memory abilities (Berry, 1999). Berry, West, and Dennehy (1989) devised a Memory Self-Efficacy Questionnaire (MSEQ). For example, individuals rate how confident they would be (10% to 100% in increments of 10) that, if someone were to read them a list of 12 items two times, they would be able to remember a specific number of items (for example, 4, 6, 8, 10, or all 12).

West, Welch, and Thorn (2001) examined whether setting goals would affect memory self-efficacy as well as actual memory performance. Initially, young and older adults studied a 24-item shopping list and then recalled as many items as they could. Then some participants were asked to set a goal that they would consider difficult but not impossible to achieve if they were to view the list a second time. For example, one goal might be, "I will work to remember 7 out of every 10 items, or 70%." The other participants (the control group) were not asked to set a goal before viewing the list a second time. Goal-setting had a positive effect on feelings of self-efficacy and on actual memory performance, although the benefits were somewhat greater for the young adults. In a subsequent study (West, Bagwell, & Dark-Freudeman, 2005), older adults who not only set goals but also received positive feedback on their progress (for example, "You are improving" and "I know you can do it") achieved especially strong performance gains and were even more motivated than young adults. Making older adults aware of their progress toward a goal is beneficial, particularly when they are given encouragement.

But are there individual differences among older adults concerning feelings of personal control and could these be reflected in their actual performance? Riggs, Lachman, and Wingfield (1997) classified older adults into two categories (*internal* and *external*) based on their responses to a questionnaire on beliefs about how much control they had over their own cognitive performance. The internals expressed a strong belief that they could control their performance, whereas the externals expressed only a weak belief that they had any power over their performance. After completing the control questionnaire, participants listened to tape-recorded passages of meaningful spoken prose. They were told to listen to only as many words as they would be able to recall with 100% accuracy. Participants could stop the tape at points of their own choosing, which gave them personal control over the size of the segments they would attempt to recall. The internals chose segments that were well within their capacity for accurate recall, indicating that they were able to gauge their own capabilities and exert the control necessary to achieve the best possible performance outcome. In contrast, the externals chose segments that were longer than their capacity for accurate recall. Likewise, Lachman and Andreoletti (2006) found that older adults' control beliefs were positively related to effective strategy use when they were asked to recall a list of 30 categorizable words such as types of fruit and flowers. Those with a higher sense of control were more likely to categorize the words and in turn had better recall than those with a lower sense of control. It seems that older adults who feel a sense of control are more apt to expend effort to maximize their memory. Consequently, older adults would likely benefit from memory training that devotes some attention to developing a sense of control and feelings of self-efficacy in memory-related situations.

Memory Self-Evaluation

A great deal of information about age-related differences in memory self-evaluation comes from responses to self-report questionnaires on which young and older adults rate their own memory (Cordoni, 1981; Erber, Szuchman, & Rothberg, 1992) or from diaries kept by young and older adults in which they record each time they forget something (Cavanaugh, Grady, & Perlmutter, 1983). With both self-report questionnaires and diaries, older adults typically report experiencing everyday forgetting more frequently than young adults. This substantiates older adults' complaints that their memory is not as good as it once was.

However, it is surprising that older adults' complaints about their memory do not always reflect their actual performance on memory tests. Some older adults report having memory difficulties, yet they perform well on objective memory tests. In longitudinal studies that follow older adults over several years, changes in objective memory performance do not necessarily correlate with self-reports of decline. Perhaps older adults sense decline from an even earlier level of memory functioning even though their objective performance remains within a normal range. It is also possible that older adults' memory complaints reflect depression, sadness, or other emotional difficulties having to do with health problems or general feelings of inadequacy.

Verhaeghen, Geraerts, and Marcoen (2000) conducted a study in Belgium on the relationship between older adults' memory complaints, coping behavior, and feelings of well-being. Older individuals with greater feelings of internal control about their memory ability (who felt that they could act effectively to change it) were more likely to implement coping behaviors in response to perceived memory difficulties than those who felt they had little control. Their coping behaviors included making lists and forming visual imagery. They also made more social comparisons ("At my age, everyone experiences memory troubles from time to time"). Because these coping behaviors seem key to feelings of well-being, Verhaeghen et al. recommend that fostering feelings of internal control should be a basic component of any memory training program for older adults.

Even so, not all studies have found that older adults suffer inordinately when they experience everyday memory failures. Erber et al. (1992) asked young and older adults to rate how frequently they actually experience various types of memory failure and also how much discomfort and annoyance they would feel at experiencing such memory lapses. Compared to young adults, older adults reported a higher frequency of forgetting. Yet, they reported feeling less annoyance and less discomfort with those lapses compared to young adults. Older adults may acknowledge that their memory has deteriorated with age, but often neither they nor their spouses believe this represents any particular handicap in everyday life (Sunderland, Watts, Baddeley, & Harris, 1986).

Stereotypes About Memory and Aging

What do most people believe about memory and aging? They think forgetting increases with age, and they expect older adults to be forgetful (Bieman-Copland & Ryan, 1998; Heckhausen, Dixon, & Baltes, 1989; Ryan, 1992; Ryan & Kwong See, 1993). Relatedly, people think the memory difficulties older adults experience are likely to continue rather than to resolve themselves over time (Erber & Danker, 1995).

Kwong See, Hoffman, and Wood (2001) posed an important question in the real-world context of a courtroom, where juries often make decisions based upon the testimony of eyewitnesses: Are older eyewitnesses perceived through stereotypes about old age? Young adult undergraduates at a Canadian university gave higher honesty ratings to a female witness described as 82 years of age than they did to one 28 years of age. Even so, the older witness was rated as less competent than the young witness, a view that could compromise the believability of older witnesses.

Implicit priming and older adults' memory

Are older adults themselves affected by stereotypes about aging that are either positive or negative? They may well be. Levy (1996) gave older adult study participants 10 minutes of implicit priming that was intended to expose them to stereotypes about aging without their awareness. Specifically, participants were told that their motor and attention skills were being measured and that they should press a key to indicate where on the screen they saw a flash of light. In actuality, the light flashes consisted of words designed to activate either positive stereotypes (wise, alert, sage, learned, advice, creative, insightful) or negative stereotypes (decline, dependent, senile, misplaces, dementia, forgets, confused) of old age. The words were flashed so quickly that participants were not consciously aware of seeing anything other than flashes of light. Participants took a battery of memory tests both before and after this priming, and the astounding finding was that the older participants who were implicitly primed with positive words showed improvement in their memory performance. In contrast, those implicitly primed with negative words did worse. The priming to which older adults were exposed may have activated self-stereotypes, which in turn affected their actual memory performance.

Cross-cultural considerations

Different cultures have different views about aging, and older adults may be debilitated in memory functioning only when they are expected to have poor memory according to a cultural stereotype. Using an attitude-toward-aging measure, Levy and Langer (1994) found that a negative age stereotype was stronger in a sample from mainstream American culture (residents of Boston) than it was in a sample from Chinese culture (residents of Beijing), which has a long tradition of honoring its elderly population. They also found that older adults in the Chinese sample outperformed older adults in the American sample on a series of memory tests. In fact, the Chinese older adults performed just as well on the memory tests as the younger Chinese adults did. Levy and Langer concluded that a negative stereotype about cognitive aging in mainstream American culture contributes to a self-fulfilling prophecy of actual age-related decline in memory. The Chinese culture is less likely to hold negative age stereotypes, so there are fewer negative expectations interfering with older Chinese adults' memory performance.

Levy and Langer's (1994) interpretation is appealing, but the findings of other studies do not all agree. Yoon, Hasher, Feinberg, Rahhal, and Winocur (2000) compared memory test scores of young and older English-speaking Canadian older adults (residents of Toronto, Ontario) with the scores of young and older Cantonese-speaking Chinese adults who had lived in Canada for under 5 years. The English- and Cantonese-speaking individuals were matched for socioeconomic factors and self-rated health. Presumably, the Cantonese-speaking individuals have a more positive view of aging, but the older adults from both cultural groups performed at a similar level, which was lower than that of the young adult comparison groups. These researchers failed to find that memory is maintained better in older Chinese adults than in older Americans. Further investigation is warranted to determine whether and how cultural views about aging may influence the memory capabilities of older members.

Attributions for Memory Failure

In American culture, adults of all ages use an age-based double standard when making causal attributions for another person's forgetful behavior (Erber, 1989; Erber & Rothberg, 1991; Erber, Szuchman, & Rothberg, 1990a, 1990b). Memory failures are considered more serious and are attributed to internal stable factors (poor memory ability, mental difficulty) when the forgetful individual is older. The identical failures are considered less serious and are attributed to internal unstable factors (lack of effort, lack of attention) when the forgetful individual is young.

Internal stable factors are considered less controllable than internal unstable factors, and behaviors considered less controllable usually engender greater sympathy (Weiner, 1993). Thus, it is not surprising that people have greater sympathy for older adults' memory failures than they do for the same failures in young adults (Erber, Szuchman, & Prager, 1997). For example, young and older adults think a store manager is more likely to believe, as well as to have greater sympathy toward, an older shopper than a young shopper who claims she forgot to pay for some merchandise before leaving the store (Erber, Szuchman, & Prager, 2001). Also, people think that company managers would be more forgiving of older employees than of younger employees who forget to do job-related tasks (Erber & Long, 2006).

In sum, people think that older adults forget because of poor memory ability and mental difficulty but young adults forget because of lack of effort and attention. Whether such an age-based double standard would be found in other cultures has yet to be determined.

Individual Differences Among Older Adults

Studies that compare the average performance of young adults as a group versus the average performance of older adults as a group often report that older adults perform more poorly, particularly on episodic memory tasks. But are there individual differences within the older adult age group?

A number of variables are related to older adults' memory performance (Bäckman et al., 2001; Bäckman, Small, Wahlin, & Larsson, 2000). First, specific chronological age plays a role – there is gradual deterioration in memory functioning from the young-old (mid-60s) to the oldest-old (85+) years. Second, while the reasons are not clear, women hold the advantage over men on tests of episodic memory (Bäckman et al., 2001).

Education and Lifestyle

In addition to chronological age and gender, level of education and lifestyle are associated with episodic memory performance. Highly educated older adults perform better on memory tests than older adults with less education. In addition, older adults who lead active lives – visiting friends, attending parties and meetings, and shopping and preparing meals – usually perform better on memory tests than older adults who are less active. (Chapter 6 discusses the cognitive performance/activity level relationship in detail.) However, a causal relationship between activity level and memory has not been clearly established, so no firm conclusions can be drawn about whether high activity causes good memory or whether individuals with good memory functioning are more active (Salthouse, 2006). Educated older adults tend to be economically advantaged and therefore have more opportunities to participate in social and other kinds of activities. To the extent that level of education and lifestyle may differ for various ethnic groups, then memory functioning may differ as well.

Health

Health factors are associated with memory functioning, particularly in very late older adulthood (Bäckman et al., 2000, 2001). Interestingly, for very old individuals who are in optimal physical health, level of education seems to play a less important role in memory functioning (Bäckman et al., 2000). Perhaps those who reach late adulthood with no health difficulties are a highly select group regardless of educational attainment.

Age is associated with increased prevalence of diseases that can affect cognitive functioning, including memory (Bäckman et al., 2000). Older adults with hypertension and coronary heart disease do not perform as well on memory tests as older adults who are free of such health issues. In extreme cases, circulatory problems can result in strokes, which are often associated with cognitive decline. However, even in the absence of diagnosable strokes, less severe abnormalities in circulatory functioning may be associated with deficits in memory functioning.

Diabetes mellitus becomes more prevalent in old age and has been associated with deficits in cognitive functioning, especially when the disease is of long duration. Older adults who are not diagnosed with diabetes but have subclinical problems with glucose tolerance can show lesser cognitive deficits (Bäckman et al., 2000). Memory deficits can also be associated with certain medications and with abnormal thyroid functioning and vitamin deficiencies. To the extent that there is a higher rate of such medical difficulties in some ethnic groups, cognitive deficits may be more prevalent in some subgroups of older adults than in others.

Clearly, pronounced memory difficulties are the hallmark of dementia (see Chapter 11 for a more detailed description of dementia). Researchers who want to study memory in normal aging often attempt to screen study participants for dementia. However, screening does not always eliminate older adults in the earliest stages before dementia has been clinically diagnosed. Thus, some studies may inadvertently include older adults with early dementia and their low memory scores inflate what appear to be age-related differences.

Also associated with memory difficulties is depression (discussed in greater detail in Chapter 11), which is among the most frequent of the emotional, or affective, disorders experienced by the older adult population. Many older adults who are depressed complain about memory difficulties, although there are mixed findings as to whether depression has a uniformly detrimental effect on the actual scores they earn on memory tests (Bäckman et al., 2000).

In sum, individual differences in physical and mental health are an important consideration when it comes to memory functioning in older adulthood. Older individuals who are physically fit and enjoy good mental health are likely to have fewer memory difficulties than older individuals with physical and mental health problems.

Revisiting the Selective Optimization with Compensation and Ecological Models

The Selective Optimization with Compensation (SOC) (Baltes & Baltes, 1990) and Ecological (Lawton, 1989; Lawton & Nahemow, 1973) Models are readily applied to memory and aging. Normal aging does not mean decline in all kinds of memory. Memory for how to do things and for general information remain intact, although there is some degree of age-related decline on tasks involving short-term working memory and episodic long-term memory.

With regard to the SOC Model, well-maintained memory skills can be used to compensate for those maintained less well. For example, semantic memory for word associations and definitions can be helpful for remembering what occurred in specific episodes. Also, older adults can benefit from making effective use of external mnemonics (for example, lists, calendars, pill organizers, and PDAs) as well as from training on how to use internal mnemonics and how to develop a sense of control and self-efficacy in memory-related situations.

With regard to the Ecological Model, environmental factors can play a role in older adults' memory functioning. For older adults whose memory abilities show signs of decline, the memory demands in the environment may need to be reduced. Older adults may need more environmental support to encode and retrieve information. Calendars and activity schedules posted in many older adult living facilities provide such cues. Also, older adults may need more time to retrieve information from their memory store, so situations that call for quick responses to memory demands should be minimized. Even so, environments should not be devoid of memory demands, as too few demands can be detrimental for older adults' cognitive functioning. Opportunities to exercise memory skills as well as physical skills may be especially important for the maintenance of memory functioning.

? Questions to Consider

1. Have you ever experienced anything that could be described as a "senior moment"? If so, what was it? Do you think that your forgetting would be viewed differently depending on your age?
2. What types of things are you good at remembering and what types give you trouble?
3. What kinds of tricks do you use to remember things, including names of people you just met, errands you must do on any given day, or information you need to learn for exams?

Key Points

- In the information processing model, age-related differences are found in working memory and long-term episodic memory. However, long-term procedural and semantic memory are relatively spared.
- Frequency-of-occurrence memory holds up well with age, source memory somewhat less well, and temporal memory shows the greatest age-related deficit.

- Three stages of processing in long-term episodic memory are encoding, storage, and retrieval. Older adults encode less elaboratively than young adults do, but this is related to production deficiency rather than mediation deficiency.

- Recall tests offer the least and recognition tests the most retrieval support. Age-related differences are greatest on recall and smallest on recognition.

- Remote memories are difficult to measure but seem to hold up well with age. Older adults have the most vivid memories for events that happened between the ages of 10 and 30.

- Prospective memory shows little age-related decline if it is event-based. Time-based prospective memory is better in naturally occurring situations than in laboratory situations.

- Implicit memory holds up well with age even when explicit memory shows age-related decline. Explicit and implicit memory processing may occur in different areas of the brain.

- Older adults often use external mnemonics to help them remember. Memory training usually involves internal mnemonics, which require considerable cognitive effort.

- In discourse memory, older adults recall fewer details than young adults, but the age-related difference is smaller when older adults are educated and can make use of natural language characteristics to help them remember.

- Metamemory is the understanding of how the memory system functions. Age-related differences in metamemory may account for some, but not all, age-related differences on memory tests.

- Positive or negative self-stereotypes about old age may affect older adults' actual memory performance. There are cultural differences in stereotypes about age and memory.

- Older adults' memory failures are attributed to poor memory ability and mental difficulty, whereas young adults' memory failures are attributed to lack of effort and attention.

- Memory functioning is higher in the young-old than the oldest-old, and it is higher among older adults with more education, more active lifestyles, and better physical and mental health.

Key Terms

cued recall   145

discourse memory   153

encoding   143

episodic memory   140

external mnemonics   151

frequency-of-occurrence
  memory   142

implicit memory   150

internal mnemonics   151

long-term memory store   138

mediation deficiency   144

memory self-efficacy   155

metamemory   155

primary memory   137

procedural memory   139

production deficiency   144

prospective memory   148

recall   145

recognition   145

reminiscence bump   147

remote memory   146

retrieval   143

semantic memory   139

short–term memory store   136

source memory   142

storage   143

temporal memory   142

working memory   137

6 Intellectual Functioning

Chapter Overview

Close-ups on Adulthood and Aging

John is 61 years old and has been an executive at the same company for more than 20 years. He knows he does not always complete tasks as quickly as some of his young co-workers, but he thinks that his expertise in the operations of the company makes up for the fact that it takes him a little longer to learn some of the new technologies. John is planning to retire from full-time employment within the next several years. After he retires, he intends to keep his mind active by consulting part-time for other companies and participating in intellectually challenging leisure activities such as playing bridge and chess. John hopes that keeping busy with activities that require him to think will ward off the mental slowness that seems to plague some of his former colleagues who lapsed into an unchallenging lifestyle after they retired.

Views of Intelligence

What is intelligence? The term *intelligence* is used frequently, but it is not easy to define. Generally, there is some consensus that individuals with more intelligence learn new things more easily, have better memories, and have a more extensive store of knowledge than individuals with less intelligence (Kausler et al., 2007). In this chapter we'll explore some theories about intelligence and what aspects of intelligence change with aging.

How Many Intelligences Are There?

A long-debated question is whether intelligence is one single ability or whether it consists of multiple abilities. Spearman (1927) defined intelligence as one broad general ability factor referred to as *g*, which was thought to underlie more specific (*s*) factors that represent the abilities needed for particular verbal, mathematical, and logical reasoning tasks. It was assumed that individuals high in *g* would do well, whereas those low in *g* would do poorly on tests of more specific abilities.

A more contemporary view is that intelligence encompasses many different kinds of abilities. According to Thurstone (1938), intelligence is made up of seven separate and distinct components ("primary mental abilities"): verbal meaning, number (arithmetic), word fluency, inductive reasoning, spatial orientation, memory, and perceptual speed. Gardner (1983, 1999) proposed eight distinct intelligences (see Table 6.1). A given individual may be stronger in some intelligences than in others.

Sternberg's Components of Intelligence

Sternberg (1985) emphasizes three components of intelligence, which work together: *contextual*, *experiential*, and *information processing*. With regard to the contextual component, how intelligence is defined can vary from one culture or another, from one period of history to another, and from one stage of the life span to another. What is considered "intelligent" will depend upon the particular culture, the time in history, and the age of the person.

The experiential component of intelligence takes prior experience into account. The way a person approaches a novel task must be evaluated differently from his or her approach to a familiar task, which is probably carried out more efficiently. John, the man described at the beginning of this chapter, is slower than his younger coworkers on tasks involving technology because he has had less experience with it.

The information processing component of intelligence focuses on the cognitive aspects of intelligent behavior. These include being able to identify a problem and deploy a strategy to solve it. It is important to look not only at how

Table 6.1 *Gardner's eight intelligences*

Type of intelligence	Examples
Linguistic intelligence	Reading comprehension, writing, understanding spoken words, vocabulary
Logical-mathematical intelligence	Abstract thinking, reasoning skills, and solving mathematical problems
Spatial intelligence	Ability to understand relationships between objects, to get from one place to another, to read a map
Musical intelligence	Sensitivity to sound patterns, ability to compose or play a musical instrument or to appreciate musical structure
Bodily-kinesthetic intelligence	Skills at dancing, athletics, eye–hand coordination, body control
Interpersonal intelligence	Social skills, sensitivity to other people's behavior, motives, or emotions
Intrapersonal intelligence	Self-understanding, understanding one's own feelings and inner life
Naturalistic intelligence	Understanding patterns in the natural world of plants and animals

efficiently the problem is solved but also at what strategy a person uses to arrive at the correct solution. John is probably superior to his younger and less experienced coworkers in solving company-related problems.

Intelligence and the Aging Process

Many questions can be asked with regard to age and intelligence. Does intellectual functioning decline, stay the same, or improve over the adult life span? If there is age-related decline, which abilities are most vulnerable and which ones are preserved? Do some older adults maintain their intellectual abilities better than others? Can any age-related decline that does occur be reversed? Finally, are there similarities between abilities measured by intelligence tests and abilities needed for functioning in a job or profession, or even for carrying out the tasks of everyday life?

Fluid versus crystallized abilities

Current research shows that biology and culture play an important role in intellectual abilities (Lövdén & Lindenberger, 2007). Some researchers have divided intelligence into two general categories: fluid and crystallized (Cattell, 1963; Horn & Cattell, 1967). **Fluid intelligence (Gf)** is "raw" intelligence, meaning that it is largely a function of the integrity of the central nervous system and is relatively independent of social influences and culturally based learning experiences. It is reflected in abilities such as numerical reasoning, logic, and speed of processing information. Gf is thought to decline from young to older adulthood.

In contrast, **crystallized intelligence (Gc)** is a function of education, experience, and exposure to a specific cultural environment. Gc is reflected in verbal abilities learned in school or information acquired over time from exposure to a particular culture. Gc is thought to be maintained or (as in the case of 61-year-old John described at the beginning of this chapter) to increase from young to older adulthood.

Mechanics versus pragmatics of intelligence

Baltes and his colleagues (Baltes, 1993; Baltes, Dittmann-Kohli, & Dixon, 1984) proposed a dual-process model of intelligence (mechanics and pragmatics). The **mechanics of intelligence** are similar to fluid intelligence (Gf) and include basic operations such as perceptual processing of sensory input, comparing and categorizing information, and carrying out basic memory functions. As with Gf, the mechanics of intelligence are assumed to be genetically and biologically controlled and to depend on basic, physiologically determined brain functioning. The mechanics of intelligence have been likened to the hardware of the mind (Baltes, 1993) and they generally show gradual age-related decline.

The **pragmatics of intelligence** are similar to crystallized intelligence (Gc) and have been likened to the software of the mind (Baltes, 1993). Pragmatics include culturally based factual and procedural knowledge. Specific examples are skills in reading and writing, comprehension of language, and skills in both social and professional domains. With increasing age, there are more opportunities for exposure to sources of pragmatic knowledge. The dual-process model emphasizes the possibilities for age-related cognitive growth in that strong pragmatic abilities can compensate for age-related decline in the mechanics of intelligence.

Figure 6.1 shows the developmental trajectory of fluid abilities (mechanics of intelligence) and crystallized abilities (pragmatics of intelligence). Note that crystallized abilities (pragmatics) are maintained or may increase slightly over the adult life span. In contrast, fluid abilities (mechanics) show gradual decline from a peak reached in early adulthood.

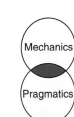
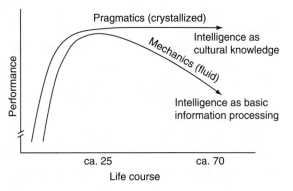

Figure 6.1 *Developmental course (trajectory) of fluid abilities (mechanics of intelligence) and crystallized abilities (pragmatics of intelligence).*
Source: Baltes, Staudinger, & Lindenberger (1999, Fig. 3, p. 487).

The Psychometric Approach to Intelligence

The psychometric approach uses tests to measure intelligence. Such tests include questions and tasks on which test takers earn quantitative scores. When devised, a psychometric test is administered to a large representative sample of individuals drawn from the same population for whom the test is intended. *Test norms* are established based on the scores earned by this *standardization sample*. Later on, an individual test taker's score can be compared to the test norms derived from the standardization sample. In other words, an individual test taker's score is evaluated relative to scores earned by the larger, representative, standardization sample.

Test norms are appropriate for comparison purposes only when the individual test taker is a member of the same population as the standardization sample. For example, norms established on a standardization sample of English-speaking Americans should not be applied to individuals whose native language is not English or to individuals with a different cultural background. Similarly, norms established on young adults should not be applied to people from other age groups.

Brief History of the Test Movement

The test movement, which marked the beginning of psychometric testing, began early in the 20th century and eventually came to play an influential role in the field of psychology. The basic premise was that tests could render a quantitative measure of intelligence.

Early psychometric tests
At the turn of the 20th century, the French government commissioned a psychologist named Binet to develop a test that would distinguish between low-achieving Parisian school children who were lacking in ability as opposed to

simply lacking motivation. In 1905, Binet and Simon constructed the first version of what we now refer to as an intelligence test.

In 1916, Lewis Terman of Stanford University introduced a modified version of Binet and Simon's test to the United States. The Stanford–Binet Test was suitable for children as young as 2 up to adolescents aged 16–18. The items on the Stanford–Binet tapped skills that were expected to be mastered at various stages of children's and adolescents' formal schooling. Thus, it is not surprising that scores on this test were fairly successful in predicting academic performance.

The Army Alpha Test for adults

Interest in extending intelligence testing to adults led to the construction of the Army Alpha Test in 1917. This test could be administered to many individuals at the same time and consisted of items designed to measure abilities in the following eight categories: ability to follow directions, common sense (practical judgment), arithmetic reasoning, number series, knowledge of antonyms and synonyms, sentence rearrangement, verbal analogies, and general information. (See Salthouse, 1991 for a comprehensive discussion of items on the Army Alpha Test.) Scores on this test were used to guide decisions about military job assignments in the U.S. armed forces and to select recruits most likely to succeed in officer training and other military training programs. The Army Alpha Test was suitable for literate adults, but an additional version of the test, the Army Beta, consisted of nonverbal items for those who could not read (Salthouse, 1991).

Scores on the Army Alpha Test earned by approximately 15,000 military officers of various ages indicated a steady decline from the middle 20s through the middle 60s. Also, when Jones and Conrad (1933) administered this test to nonmilitary individuals in New England, they found average scores declined between the ages of 19 and 60. However, this age trend depended upon the type of ability tested. Age-related differences were small on arithmetic reasoning, but agerelated decline was considerable on number series and verbal analogies.

Psychometric Tests and Aging Research

Which psychometric tests do contemporary researchers use to study what happens to intellectual abilities with increasing age? Two frequently used tests are the *Primary Mental Abilities Test* (PMA) and the *Wechsler Adult Intelligence Scale* (WAIS). The PMA can be administered on a group basis, while the WAIS is administered individually.

The Primary Mental Abilities Test

The PMA Test (Thurstone & Thurstone, 1947) is based on Thurstone's (1938) seven components of intelligence (described earlier), each of which represents an independent factor. Five of these factors – verbal meaning, number, word fluency,

Table 6.2   *The five primary mental abilities (PMA factors)*

Verbal meaning (V)	*Ability to recognize and understand words (passive vocabulary).* Test taker must match each test word with another word from a multiple-choice list that has the closest meaning (synonym). V is considered a crystallized ability acquired and maintained by exposure to formal schooling and culturally determined experiences.
Number (N)	*Ability to apply numerical concepts.* Test taker must solve arithmetic problems involving addition and other operations. N is considered a crystallized ability acquired and maintained by exposure to formal schooling and culturally determined experiences.
Word fluency (W)	*Ability to retrieve words from long-term memory using a lexical rule (active vocabulary).* Test taker must write down in a short period of time as many words as he or she can think of that begin with a certain letter. W is considered partly crystallized, but involves an aspect of fluid intelligence as well.
Inductive reasoning (R)	*Ability to identify regularities and infer rules.* Test taker must complete a letter series task by choosing which of several letter sequences does not belong: ABCD, WXYZ, BFLK, JKLM. R is a fluid ability since it involves novel problem solving.
Spatial orientation (S)	*Ability to rotate objects mentally in two-dimensional space.* Test taker is shown a geometric form and must select from several choices how that form would look when rotated. S is a fluid ability because it involves novel problem solving.

Source: Schaie (1989).

inductive reasoning, and spatial orientation – have the greatest importance in measuring intellectual abilities across the adult life span and form the basis of the test that Schaie and his colleagues have used in the Seattle Longitudinal Study (SLS). Table 6.2 lists these factors with a brief description of each one (see Schaie, 1989).

The Wechsler Adult Intelligence Scale

In 1939, Dr. David Wechsler, a psychologist at Bellevue Hospital in New York City, introduced the Wechsler–Bellevue test, which was intended to measure intellectual abilities of adults up to the age of 60. A subsequent version of this test, the Wechsler Adult Intelligence Scale (WAIS), was published in 1955. The WAIS-R, published in 1981, was intended for test takers into their 70s. The WAIS-R consists of 11 subtests that fall into two categories: verbal (6) and performance (5). Unlike the PMA, the WAIS subtests tap a mixture of cognitive abilities rather than separate and distinct cognitive factors (see Schulz & Salthouse, 1999, pp. 139–140). Figure 6.2 lists the 11 subtests from the WAIS-R with an example of a typical item on each.

The WAIS-III, published in 1997, can be used for test takers into their 80s. The WAIS-III includes one additional verbal subtest (letter–number sequencing) and two additional performance subtests (matrix reasoning and symbol search), bringing the total number to 14.

The WAIS-R verbal subtests assess stored information acquired from formal education and cultural exposure (crystallized abilities, or the pragmatics of intelligence) to varying degrees. However, the correspondence is approximate because the digit span subtest taps memory, and the similarities subtest requires reasoning.

The WAIS-R performance subtests tap fluid abilities, or the mechanics of intelligence. In general, these subtests consist of novel problems that often must be solved under timed conditions. Four performance subtests (object assembly, picture completion, picture arrangement, and block design) test spatial abilities. The fifth one, digit symbol, tests perceptual-motor processing speed.

Thanks to psychometric tests such as the WAIS, researchers have gained a greater understanding of which abilities are maintained and which ones may decline over the adult life span. Later in this chapter, we will discuss in greater detail the abilities that are more likely or less likely to hold up well with increasing age.

Intelligence Quotient (IQ)

We often hear or read references to "IQ," but what does it mean? On each WAIS-R subtest, a score is calculated based on the number of points earned and then converted to a scaled score so that each subtest carries equal weight. Scaled scores on the verbal subtests are added together to obtain a total verbal score. Likewise, scaled scores on the performance subtests are added together to obtain a total performance score.

Intelligence quotient (IQ) is related, but not identical, to an individual's score on an intelligence test. The IQ of an individual test taker reflects how the score of an individual test taker compares with the scores earned by people in the standardization sample who were of similar age. Thus, the IQ reflects whether that test taker is average, above average, or below average, compared to his or her age peers. The average score earned by the standardization sample in each age group is set at 100. A higher or lower IQ reflects how much, and in which direction, the individual test taker's score deviates from the average. If the test taker's score is lower than the average score earned by age peers in the standardization

Verbal Subtests

Vocabulary	Test taker must give oral definitions of words.	For example, "What is the meaning of the word 'persistent'?"
Information	Test taker must answer questions about general information and facts about geography, authors, etc.	For example, "How many miles is it from Kansas City to Washington, DC?"
Comprehension	Test taker must answer questions that require common sense judgments and reasoning.	For example, "Why do people put money into banks?"
Similarities	Test taker must explain the way in which two items are alike.	For example, "In what way are a policeman and firefighter alike?"
Arithmetic	Test taker must solve word problems without using paper and pencil.	For example, "If the price of an item is $30, how much will it cost with a 10 percent discount?"
Digit span	Test taker must listen to and repeat back a series of orally presented digits in the same order (digits forward). Then test taker listens to a series of orally presented digits and repeats them in the reverse order (digits backward).	For example, "Repeat these numbers: 64395." For example, "Repeat these numbers backward: 58624."

Performance Subtests

Picture completion	Test taker must identify the element that is missing from each of a series of pictures.	For example, "What is missing from this picture?" 
Digit symbol	Test taker is given a key consisting of digits, each paired with a symbol. The test taker must then write the symbol associated with each digit in a blank box below the digit. Score is based on number of correct digit-symbol substitutions completed within a specific number of seconds.	For example, "Using the key on the left, write the correct symbol below each number without skipping any." 
Block Design	Test taker must arrange a number of one-inch red and white cubes to match a design pictured in a diagram.	
Picture Arrangement	Test taker must arrange series of pictures that are presented in a mixed-up order into a sequence that conveys a meaningful story.	For example, "Arrange these pictures in an order that tells a story."
Object Assembly	Test taker must arrange pieces of a puzzle to make a complete meaningful whole, as in a jigsaw puzzle.	For example, "Put these pieces together to make something."

Figure 6.2 *WAIS subtests with sample item from each one.*

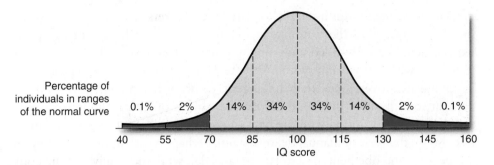

Figure 6.3 *A bell-shaped normal curve with a mean of 100 and a standard deviation of 15.*

sample, then IQ will be less than 100. Alternatively, if the test taker's score is higher than the average score earned by age peers in the standardization sample, then IQ will be greater than 100.

The standard deviation (SD) reflects how much individuals in each age group vary around the average, or mean, test score. The bell-shaped curve in Figure 6.3 shows a normal distribution of test scores. In a normal distribution, approximately 68% of the test scores fall between one SD below the mean and one SD above the mean. If the mean of this distribution is 100 and the SD is 15, then about 68% of the individuals in any given age group will earn scores that fall between 85 and 115.

Cultural Diversity

Psychometric intelligence tests have not been without critics for several reasons. First, such tests are meaningful only if test takers are members of the population on whom the test was standardized in the first place. Test scores are of questionable value when the cultural background and experience of a test taker differs from

---

Applying Research Box 6.1: The Flynn Effect

Test norms must be reestablished periodically because, over time, the abilities of a population can shift. A standardization sample tested today may attain higher (or lower) scores on some tests of intellectual ability in comparison to a standardization sample that was tested 10 or 20 years ago. The possibility that scores attained by a standardization sample tested recently are higher than scores earned by a standardization sample tested at an earlier point in time has been called the **Flynn Effect** (Flynn, 1999). For

example, a standardization sample of 60-year-olds who take an intelligence test in 2010 may earn higher scores than a standardization sample of 60-year-olds who took the same test in 1990. Both samples are the same age, but they differ in cohort membership (born in 1950 and 1930, respectively) and also with regard to the time they took the test (2010 and 1990, respectively). It is important to use updated test norms when comparing a test taker's score with the scores earned by a standardization sample.

that of the standardization sample. Relatedly, test takers who interpret psycho-metric test questions the way in which those who devised the scoring system expect them to are rewarded with more points than test takers whose answers do not agree with the scoring system. Yet a test taker who earns fewer points may be giving an answer considered "intelligent" in his or her culture. Cross-cultural comparisons illustrate this point. In various regions of Africa, children are considered intelligent not only on the basis of cognitive skills such as good memory, but also on the basis of manual dexterity and, perhaps most important, if they are cooperative and obedient in performing tasks that serve the family and the community (Segall, Dasen, Berry, & Poortinga, 1999).

Second, how well do scores on psychometric tests predict a person's ability to function in the real world (see Chapter 2 for further discussion of ecological validity)? Furthermore, what is considered "intelligent" may depend upon a person's generation and age/stage of life (Sternberg, 1985).

Does Intelligence Decline with Age?

The question of whether intelligence declines with age has long been an important concern of aging researchers. Woodruff-Pak (1988, 1989) proposed that, over the decades, there has been an evolution in the perspectives of researchers who study aging and intelligence. Table 6.3 gives a brief summary of the dominant

Table 6.3 *Evolution of perspectives on intelligence over the adult years*

Phase I	Focus is on mapping what is assumed to be a steep and inevitable age-related decline in intelligence beyond the 20s. Most research in this phase is cross-sectional.
Phase II	Focus is on identifying the components of intelligence that remain stable or that decline over the adult life span. There is greater awareness that age is confounded with cohort in cross-sectional studies and that longitudinal studies show later and a lesser degree of age-related decline.
Phase III	Focus is on intraindividual variability in intellectual functioning. There is new interest in how experience, practice, and training can modify intellectual abilities.
Phase IV	Focus is on new ways to define and measure intelligence. Definitions of intelligence are expanded to include qualitative as well as quantitative aspects of functioning.

Source: Adapted from Woodruff-Pak (1988, 1989).

perspective in each of four phases. Entry into a new phase does not mean earlier perspectives are completely abandoned, but rather that the focus of the new phase is the main influence as far as which aspects of intellectual development receive the most attention (Schaie, 1996). This chapter concentrates on the perspectives dominant in Woodruff-Pak's Phases I, II, and III, while Chapter 7 concentrates on the perspective dominant in Phase IV.

Throughout the 1950s (Phase I), the Army Alpha Test and the Wechsler Adult Intelligence Scale (WAIS) were gaining widespread acceptance. Most studies on adult intelligence were cross-sectional and most reported that older adult test takers earned lower scores than young adult test takers. This contributed to the perspective that intellectual functioning reaches a peak in young adulthood, followed by an inevitable decline. Researchers focused mainly on finding the point at which the decline began and determining how steep it was.

By the 1960s (entry into Phase II), some researchers acknowledged that intelligence is not just one entity; rather, it consists of individual abilities that vary in their developmental trajectories. By the 1970s, heated controversy erupted as to the developmental course of intellectual abilities from young to older adulthood. Some (Horn & Donaldson, 1976) argued that there is an age deficit in intellectual abilities (reflecting the Phase I decline perspective). Others (Baltes & Schaie, 1974) argued that the age-deficit view of intelligence could only be described as the "myth of the twilight years" – that intelligence does not decline with age, and in fact may increase. The debate between the proponents of the "age deficit" and the "myth of decline" views resulted in closer scrutiny of the developmental course of specific intellectual abilities. This is described further in the section below on the classic aging pattern.

Phase II also brought increased awareness that the method used to study age and intellectual abilities makes a difference in how much age-related decline is observed. With the cross-sectional method, what is attributed to age could actually be a function of cohort membership. Large-scale studies using the longitudinal method have reported that decline in intellectual abilities is much less extensive and occurs at a later point than was previously thought on the basis of cross-sectional studies (Schaie, 1996). Findings from the Seattle Longitudinal Study (SLS) indicate that community-living older adults show very little decline in fluid abilities until their mid-60s. Decline in crystallized abilities occurs much later, often not becoming apparent until the mid-70s. By age 67, most SLS participants showed some decline on at least one of the primary mental abilities; however, even by age 88, none of the participants had declined on all five of the abilities (Schaie, 1989).

Figure 6.4 shows data from the SLS on the five primary mental abilities (Schaie, 1994). The curves in this figure were constructed from longitudinal gradients, which represent scores earned at 7-year intervals by individuals ranging from 25 to 88 years of age. Note that average scores increase or remain stable until the late 30s or early 40s, and there is stability until the mid-50s or early 60s. In the late 60s, there is some decrement, but it is modest until the mid-70s

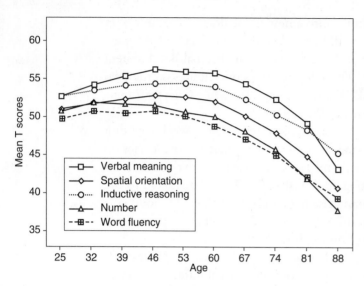

Figure 6.4 *Longitudinal estimates of mean T scores for single markers of the primary mental abilities*
Source: Schaie (1994).

(Schaie, 1996). In short, decline occurs later and is less extensive than would likely be found with a cross-sectional method of research. Not shown in Figure 6.4 are the gender differences in patterns of decline. Schaie and his colleagues found that women decline earlier on fluid abilities, whereas men decline earlier on crystallized abilities (Schaie, 2006; Schaie & Willis, 1996). However, the reason for this gender difference has yet to be determined.

However, the more positive findings of longitudinal studies may be inflated due to selective attrition. Of the initial group, it is often the case that only the most able members return to be retested later, which could result in an overly rosy picture of intellectual functioning. (Chapter 2 discusses selective attrition in longitudinal studies.)

Positive and Negative Cohort Trends

The cross-sectional research method confounds two factors: (a) chronological age and (b) cohort, or generation to which study participants belong. Differences between cohorts, sometimes called *cohort trends*, can affect developmental comparisons. Cohort trends can occur because of shifts in educational emphasis or for reasons that are difficult to determine (Schaie, 1996).

A **positive cohort trend** means that the present-day young adult cohort has a higher level of ability than an older adult cohort had back in their young adult years. The Flynn Effect is an example of this phenomenon. With a positive cohort trend, even if members of an older cohort have not experienced any age-related decline in a particular ability, they still perform at a lower level compared to members of a young adult cohort (Schaie, 1996; Schaie & Willis, 1996). To illustrate, the age-related differences often found on tests of fluid ability are assumed to reflect the integrity of the central nervous system. However, it is conceivable that young adults have an advantage over older adults because of their exposure to newly developed technologies. To the extent that a young cohort's exposure to technology helps on tests of fluid ability, then the young cohort may score higher than the older cohort would have scored even when young. This positive cohort trend could result in an inordinately negative picture of age-related decline on a particular intellectual ability.

A **negative cohort trend** means that the present-day young adult cohort has less ability than an older cohort had when young. To illustrate, when older adults were young, their numerical ability may have been higher than that of young adults today. The reason could be that older adults did not have calculators or computers to help them solve arithmetic problems so they had more practice on this kind of task. If there is such a negative cohort trend, young and older cohorts in a cross-sectional research study might perform at the same level on a test of numerical ability, so it may appear that numerical ability remains stable over the adult life span. However, if the older cohort had started out in young adulthood at a higher level, then there may actually be some age-related decline in numerical ability.

Clearly, a disadvantage of the cross-sectional method for studying age and intellectual abilities is the difficulty in evaluating possible positive or negative cohort trends. Despite this drawback, however, cross-sectional studies are useful for assessing age-related differences in intellectual abilities in the here and now with relative efficiency. Even so, cross-sectional research cannot answer questions about the developmental course of intellectual abilities within individuals. How do intellectual abilities change over time in any given person, and why do some people change more than others? We need longitudinal research to answer these questions, assuming that selective attrition does not result in inordinate positive bias.

In sum, Phase II brought about greater awareness that cross-sectional studies on intellectual abilities can result in a more pessimistic picture than longitudinal studies. Also, there was a heightened appreciation of variation in the developmental trajectories over the adult life span – some abilities decline, some remain stable, and some increase.

The Classic Aging Pattern

Most studies on intellectual functioning over the adult years show age-related decline in some abilities but not in others. Scores on the WAIS subtests often illustrate the **classic aging pattern** (Botwinick, 1984) – scores on the verbal subtests are relatively maintained into older adulthood, so verbal abilities are considered **age-insensitive abilities**. In contrast, scores on the performance subtests usually show age-related decline, so performance abilities are considered **age-sensitive abilities**. Note that *age-insensitivity* and *age-sensitivity* refer to scaled scores and not directly to IQ (which is just an individual's comparison with age peers).

Among the most age-insensitive WAIS verbal subtests are information, vocabulary, and comprehension (Botwinick, 1984). Scores on these subtests hold up well, and in some instances they increase from young to middle to older adulthood. The abilities tapped by these subtests are honed from formal education and cultural exposure, and they fall into the crystallized category (Cattell, 1963; Horn & Cattell, 1967), or the pragmatics of intelligence (Baltes, 1987, 1993).

Among the most age-sensitive WAIS performance subtests are digit symbol, picture arrangement, and block design (Botwinick, 1984). On average, older adults' scores are lower on these subtests compared to the scores of young adults. Each of these subtests calls for the solution of unfamiliar problems in new ways. They tap fluid abilities, or the mechanics of intelligence, which presumably reflect the integrity of central nervous system functioning. The WAIS perform-ance subtests also have time limits or allow bonus points for speed. Because there is some slowing down of responses with increasing age (see Chapter 4 for more discussion of slowing), older adults are at a disadvantage when there are time requirements (Schaie, 1996).

The Life-Span Developmental Perspective

Once again let's review the life-span developmental perspective (Baltes, 1987). This perspective can be applied to many aspects of development, but it is espe-cially relevant to intellectual abilities. Table 2.2 summarizes the key propositions of the life-span developmental perspective, but these are listed below in abbrevi-ated form as they apply to intellectual development.

- Intellectual development occurs over the entire life span.
- Intellectual development is embedded in a historical and sociocultural context unique to each cohort group.
- Intellectual development is multidimensional, multidirectional, and multicausal.
- The study of intellectual development is enhanced by a multidiscipli-nary approach.
- Intellectual development includes both gains and losses over the life span (although the proportion of gains to losses may fluctuate from young to middle to older adulthood).

Understanding Aging Box 6.1: The Dedifferentiation Hypothesis

Many investigators have found evidence for a two-components model of intelligence over the adult life span. Crystallized abilities are age-insensitive from young to older adulthood, meaning that they remain stable, whereas fluid abilities are age-sensitive, meaning that they show age-related decrement over the adult years. However, recent research indicates that in very late old age, the once divergent pat-terns of the crystallized (pragmatics) and fluid (mechanics) components of intelligence become "dedifferentiated," mainly because crystallized abilities are not as well preserved in very late life and show signs of decline (Lövdén & Lindenberger, 2007). With dedifferentiation, there is an increasing degree of association between crystallized and fluid abilities. One interpretation is that in very late old age, a decline in fluid abilities ultimately limits the acquisition, expression, and maintenance of crystallized abilities and drives their decline (Ghisletta & Lindenberger, 2003). Thus, in the very late stage of life, crystallized abilities are increasingly determined by fluid abilities, which include basic functions such as processing speed.

- Intellectual development has plasticity, meaning that it can be modified with practice or training.

The proposition that development is embedded in a historical and sociocultural context unique to each cohort group is evident in Woodruff-Pak's (1988, 1989) Phase II, which brought heightened concern about the method used to study the developmental course of intellectual abilities. Researchers were becoming increasingly aware that intellectual abilities are a function not only of age, but also of cohort membership and time of measurement (see Chapter 2 for further discussion of age, cohort membership, and time of measurement in developmental research). Also, the proposition that development is multidimensional, multidirectional, and multicausal is reflected in the Phase II recognition that abilities can be influenced by different factors and can vary in their developmental course. As illustrated in the classic aging pattern, aging may entail losses, but it may also entail stability and gains.

Maximizing Intellectual Functioning in Older Adulthood

The life-span developmental perspective is apparent not only in Woodruff-Pak's (1988, 1989) Phase II, but it can also be seen in Phase III, when researchers were beginning to entertain the possibility that intellectual abilities are not written in stone. Thus, they were acknowledging there is plasticity, another key proposition of the life-span developmental perspective. Abilities can fluctuate within the same individual over various occasions (**intraindividual variability**) and a person's abilities can be modified through practice and training.

Testing the Limits

Testing the limits is a strategy used to investigate both the range and the limits of a person's cognitive capacity (Kliegl, Smith, & Baltes, 1989). Researchers who recommend this strategy believe that measuring an intellectual ability on a single occasion does not provide a true picture of a person's highest possible level of functioning. Even under normal conditions, there is intraindividual (within-individual) variability in level of performance because an individual's scores can fluctuate. Scores fall within a range, the upper limit of which is the best estimate of that individual's true competence. True competence may be underestimated if a score from only one testing occasion is used. It can be determined only with repeated testing.

Intervention

Not only can intellectual abilities fluctuate across occasions of testing, but they can also be modified by practice and possibly even more so by interventions that entail training. The idea of plasticity, a key premise of the life-span developmental perspective, represents an optimistic stance with regard to intellectual functioning in older adulthood. It is especially appealing with respect to fluid abilities, which show greater age-related decline compared to the better maintained crystallized abilities.

Much of the work on cognitive training has been conducted as part of the Adult Development and Enrichment Project (ADEPT) (Baltes & Willis, 1982; Schaie, 1996) as well as the ongoing Seattle Longitudinal Study (SLS) (Schaie, 1996). Most training studies use pretest/posttest designs. An initial baseline assessment of older adults' abilities is followed by training on test-taking strategies. On the whole, the effects of training are positive. Older adults who receive training improve their scores on tests of inductive reasoning and spatial abilities, both of which ordinarily show age-related decline. The positive effects of training have been replicated by researchers in Germany as well in the United States, and the effects can last for up to seven years (Schaie, 1996). Even so, periodic "booster" training sessions are recommended (Schaie & Willis, 1996). However, replicating training studies on more diverse samples within the United States and in countries other than Germany will allow us to determine whether the benefits of training generalize to a broader segment of the older adult population.

Compensation

The life-span developmental proposition of multidirectionality states that abilities can show both gains and losses over the life span (Baltes, 1987). As was illustrated in Figure 2.1, however, the proportion of gains and losses fluctuates over the life span.

Early in life and through young adulthood, the proportion of gains in intellectual abilities is greater than the proportion of losses. In midlife, the proportion of gains and losses is equivalent. In older adulthood, the proportion of losses outstrips the proportion of gains. Despite the greater proportion of losses in older adulthood, however, gains may be used to offset them. For example, gains in crystallized abilities may compensate for losses in fluid abilities. Similarly, gains in the pragmatics of intelligence may compensate for losses older adults may experience in the mechanics of intelligence. John, the older worker described at the beginning of this chapter, thinks his experience compensates for the longer time it takes him to learn the new technologies.

Unexercised Versus Optimally Exercised Abilities

Denney (1982) proposed that cognitive abilities fall into one of two categories: (a) untrained, unpracticed, or **unexercised abilities** and (b) **optimally exercised abilities**. The developmental course of unexercised abilities reflect a normal, healthy individual's capability, assuming there is no ability-specific training or practice. That is, the level of the unexercised abilities reflects the individual's biological potential under normal environmental conditions. In contrast, the developmental course of optimally exercised abilities reflects the maximum level attainable by normal, healthy individuals who have had opportunities for ability-specific training or practice. At all ages, optimally exercised abilities are superior to unexercised abilities. In American culture, verbal abilities may be more practiced than performance abilities, but Denney's model allows for the possibility that some cultures could call for extensive exercise of performance abilities rather than verbal abilities.

Individual Differences Among Older Adult Test Takers

Thus far, our focus has been on older adults as a group, and on how the intellectual abilities of older adults in general compare to those of young adults. However, members of any age group vary on most dimensions, including intellectual abilities. In fact, the degree of variation among older adults is usually greater than that among young adults. This means that in the older adult age group, there are considerable individual differences in level of intellectual abilities. Some older adults earn low scores on intelligence tests, while others earn high scores. Indeed, the scores of some older adults surpass the scores that average young adults earn.

Factors Related to Maintenance of Intellectual Functioning

Maintenance of intellectual functioning in older adulthood is associated with the absence of severe sensory deficits in vision and hearing (Lindenberger & Baltes, 1994; Wingfield et al., 2005). As described in Chapter 4, the link between sensory and intellectual functioning becomes stronger in older adulthood (Baltes & Lindenberger, 1997).

Longitudinal research has been valuable in pointing to additional variables that are associated with the maintenance, but also with the decline, of intellectual abilities over time. Such information can be useful in determining what can be done to maximize intellectual abilities and minimize the risk of their decline over the adult years. Based on findings from the SLS, Schaie (1994, 1996, 2006) reported that the following factors are associated with reduced risk of age-related decline in intellectual abilities:

- absence of cardiovascular and other chronic diseases
- less than average age-related decline in perceptual processing speed
- above-average level of education and income
- an occupational history of high-complexity jobs that do not simply involve routine tasks
- flexible attitudes and behaviors
- satisfaction with one's accomplishments in midlife and early older adulthood
- membership in an intact family and marriage to a well-educated, intelligent spouse

- having a stimulating and engaged lifestyle
- pursuit of continuing education and participation in clubs and professional associations.

John, the man described at the beginning of this chapter, plans to remain engaged in mentally challenging professional and leisure activities after he retires from full-time employment.

Clearly, the factors listed above overlap. Older adults who held high-level, complex jobs often have relatively high incomes in retirement and are more apt than those with low incomes to live in stimulating environments with opportunities for exposure to cultural and educational resources. Good health may allow individuals to engage in activities that foster intellectual functioning. In sum, it cannot be concluded with certainty that any one factor listed above is a direct cause of high-level intellectual functioning.

Mental Activity and Intellectual Functioning

Do older individuals who engage in cognitively challenging mental activities – for example, reading, attending cultural events, completing crossword puzzles and

playing bridge – actually function at a higher level compared to those who do not? The answer to this question appears to be yes.

According to the **disuse hypothesis of cognitive aging**, skills and abilities get rusty when they are not used on a regular basis (see Kausler et al., 2007; Salthouse, 1991). The cautionary advice "Use it or lose it" is frequently given to older adults who are concerned about keeping up their intellectual abilities (Rowe & Kahn, 1998). The corollary to the disuse hypothesis is that practicing cognitive skills can reverse any decline that has taken place or possibly prevent it from occurring in the first place. According to the **engagement hypothesis**, participation in novel and challenging intellectual tasks will prevent decline in intellectual functioning. Several longitudinal studies have attempted to determine the accuracy of the disuse and engagement hypotheses.

Engaging in mentally challenging activities is associated with maintenance of intellectual abilities in older adulthood.

The Victoria Longitudinal Study (VLS)
Canadian researchers tested the verbal intelligence of 487 healthy, well-educated, professional and semi-professional, community-dwelling men and women between the ages of 55 and 86 (Hultsch,

Hertzog, Small, & Dixon, 1999). At the outset, study participants also completed a self-report questionnaire on their frequency of engaging in cognitive activities (for example, reading, learning a new language, or playing bridge). Not surprisingly, those who reported engaging more frequently in such activities had higher levels of verbal intelligence than those who did so less frequently.

Subsequently, VLS participants were followed for six years and tested several times on a variety of cognitive measures. On each occasion they again reported their level of participation in cognitively challenging activities. Statistical analyses revealed that changes in level of engaging in mentally challenging activities seemed to occur together with changes in level of intellectual functioning. However, Hultsch and his colleagues were not able to determine whether changes in intellectual functioning resulted from reduced engagement in mentally challenging activities or whether the onset of cognitive decline served to limit people's participation in mentally challenging activities. In short, they could not conclude with certainty that engaging in challenging activities actually causes the maintenance of intellectual functioning or, likewise, that failure to engage in such activities causes a decline in intellectual functioning.

The Canadian Veterans Study (CVS)

Other Canadian researchers have made stronger claims about the influence of an engaged lifestyle on intellectual functioning. Pushkar et al. (1999) used archival data from the CVS, which followed a large sample of working-class men longitudinally. These men lived in the community, but their overall health was not as high as that of the VLS participants. On the basis of statistical analyses, Pushkar and her colleagues were able to demonstrate some evidence that decreases in cognitive activity occur prior to any cognitive decline. Thus, they concluded that across the adult life span, a cognitively active lifestyle has a small but significant positive effect on the level of verbal ability, which supports the engagement hypothesis.

Note that not only did the VLS and CVS study samples differ in health and socioeconomic status, but the measures used by the researchers to determine level of cognitive activity were also different. Hultsch et al. (1999) measured engagement in intellectual activity using self-reported participation in specific activities. In contrast, Pushkar et al. (1999) defined an engaged lifestyle more broadly. In addition to measuring participation in intellectual activities, they took socioeconomic status (SES) into account because they contended that SES reflects level of education and complexity of work careers. The contrasting conclusions of these two studies is not surprising given such different participant samples and different ways of defining cognitive activity.

Leisure activities and cognitive functioning

Schooler and Mulatu (2001) investigated the relationship between engaging in complex leisure activities and level of intellectual functioning among a sample consisting mainly of European American men and women (aged 41 to 88) who had participated in a national survey. When these individuals were located again 20 years later, 42% were gainfully employed and the rest were retired. Schooler and Mulatu's index of participation in complex cognitive leisure activities was based on the following:

1. number of books read in past six months;
2. number of magazines read regularly, as well as the magazines' intellectual level;
3. frequency of visits to institutions of fine art, as well as concerts and plays, within the past six months;
4. number of special interests and hobbies and amount of time spent on them per month.

For both workers and retirees, there was moderate evidence that participating in complex leisure activities leads to an increase in intellectual functioning. However, these investigators acknowledge that a high level of intellectual functioning could lead to a high level of environmental complexity, which in turn could raise the level of intellectual functioning. In short, it was not possible to rule out uncontrolled factors that might be influencing both participation in complex leisure activities and level of intellectual functioning.

A longitudinal study in Australia that followed 755 men and women over a 6-year time interval also found that engaging in an active lifestyle was associated with higher cognitive functioning and a smaller degree of cognitive change over time (Newson & Kemps, 2005). Again, however, though the findings suggest that an active lifestyle may promote successful cognitive aging, it was not possible to make cause-and-effect statements that activity prevents decline in cognitive functioning.

In sum, it seems clear that participating in complex and stimulating cognitive activities and maintaining an active lifestyle are positively associated with intellectual functioning. Thus, it is reasonable to recommend that adults of all ages engage in intellectually stimulating activities. They should "take on and solve difficult and challenging problems at work and in their everyday lives" (Hertzog, Hultsch, & Dixon, 1999, p. 533). Schooler and Mulatu (2001) maintain that, even into old age, participating in complex leisure activities could build a capacity to deal with the intellectual challenges inherent in complex environments. Rowe and Kahn (1998) strongly recommend intellectual engagement as an important aspect of successful aging. However, it may be premature to conclude that engaging in challenging intellectual activities will actually prevent cognitive decline in old age (Salthouse, 2007c). At present, there is no guarantee that mental exercise will slow down the rate of age-related decline in mental functioning. However, engaging in mentally stimulating activities certainly has no harmful effects and, to the extent that such activities are enjoyable, they can contribute to a higher quality of life (Salthouse, 2006). Until the whole story is known, Schooler (2007, p. 28) suggests it would be prudent to assume that people are more likely to "lose it" if they do not "use it" and that "using it" could at least delay "losing it."

Everyday Intelligence and Competence

Psychometric tests were devised originally to evaluate the likelihood of a child's success in school. Indeed, such tests have proven useful for decisions about whether to admit children, adolescents, and young adults to special schools, colleges, and universities. For these purposes, the predictive value of psychometric tests, while not perfect, is often significant. Children and young adults spend a good part of their daily lives in school, so psychometric tests represent a measure of their everyday intellectual functioning. But what is the role of psychometric tests beyond young adulthood?

Psychometric Tests and Ecological Validity

For adults, psychometric tests serve two important functions. First, they can be useful for predicting success in jobs that require educationally based knowledge and skills. Employers may use psychometric tests to evaluate whether workers (regardless of their age) are capable of carrying out the tasks required for some jobs (Salthouse & Maurer, 1996). Second, psychometric tests have been useful for clinical assessments of neuropsychological status in the older adult population (Botwinick, 1984; Schaie, 1996; Schaie & Willis, 1996). Tests such as the WAIS tap a broad array of abilities, and a test taker's score can be evaluated in comparison to the scores attained by others of the same age.

Even so, the meaning of psychometric tests for older adults has been called into question. The majority of older adults are not full-time students, and many completed their formal education in the distant past. Thus, the ecological validity of psychometric intelligence tests for older adults has been criticized. Put simply, psychometric intelligence tests may not measure the kinds of intellectual abilities that older adults actually need to function well in the real world.

This criticism has led some to consider that intelligent behavior may not take exactly the same form across the adult years. In other words, intelligence may be *qualitatively* different at different points in the life span, which is the overriding perspective of Woodruff-Pak's (1988, 1989) Phase IV. Clearly, we need to explore new ways of conceptualizing and measuring intelligence. The Phase IV perspective has resulted in some new insights about the purpose, meaning, and function of cognition. This expanded view of intelligence has stimulated interest in wisdom, creativity, and everyday problem solving in a social context. Chapter 7 covers these topics.

Conceptions of Intelligence Across the Adult Life Span

We know something about how psychologists define intelligence. But how is intelligence viewed by people who are not psychologists and are not familiar with psychometric intelligence tests? How do such individuals conceptualize what would be "intelligent" for a young, middle-aged, and older adult? To answer

Table 6.4 *Three factors underlying adults' conceptions of exceptional intelligence, with examples of representative behaviors for each*

Interest in and ability to deal with novelty	Is able to analyze topics in new and original ways Is interested in gaining knowledge and learning new things Is open-minded to new ideas and trends Is able to learn and reason with new kinds of concepts
Everyday competence	Displays good common sense Acts in a mature manner Acts responsibly Is interested in family and home life
Verbal competence	Displays the knowledge to speak intelligently Displays good vocabulary Is able to draw conclusions from information given Is verbally fluent

Source: Berg & Sternberg (1992).

this question, Berg and Sternberg (1992) first asked adults of widely ranging ages (17 to 83) to generate examples of behavior they would consider to be "intelligent." These examples were then categorized on the basis of three factors, which appear in Table 6.4.

Next, Berg and Sternberg asked a new sample of individuals, also of various ages, to describe an "exceptionally intelligent person" aged 30, 50, or 70. Their conception of what would be considered "exceptionally intelligent" differed for the 30-, 50-, and 70-year-olds. "Interest in and ability to deal with novelty" was considered important for the intelligent 30-year-old, but was less important for the intelligent 50-year-old and 70-year-old. In contrast, "everyday competence" and "verbal competence" were considered more important for the intelligent 50-year-old and 70-year-old than they were for the intelligent 30-year-old.

"Interest in and ability to deal with novelty" is closely related to fluid intelligence (mechanics of intelligence), whereas "everyday competence" and "verbal competence" are closely related to crystallized intelligence (pragmatics of intelligence). It is interesting to note that study participants' conception of intelligence over the adult life span is consistent with the classic aging pattern seen on psychometric intelligence tests such as the WAIS.

Berg and Sternberg's participants also believed that intellectual abilities can either increase or decrease over the adult life span and that intellectual functioning can be improved with practice and training. Furthermore, they thought that reading, education, experience, and contact with stimulating people would be associated with increases in intelligence, whereas illness, lack of mental stimulation, or lack of interest in learning would be associated with decreases.

In sum, the opinions these individuals expressed were consistent with the lifespan developmental perspectives of multidirectionality and plasticity. Their belief that participating in stimulating activities and social interactions would be associated with increases in intelligence is consistent with the engagement hypothesis. For the most part, these study participants were middle-class European Americans. Extending this type of research to a more diverse sample in the U.S. population and residents of other countries would test the generality of Berg and Sternberg's findings.

Cognitive Competence and Psychometric Scores

As described earlier, cross-sectional studies on psychometric abilities generally find age-related decrements from the decade of the 20s through the decade of the 70s, particularly on tests of fluid ability. How is it, then, that many older Americans hold responsible and demanding leadership positions?

Salthouse (1990) describes research in which young (21–42) and older (60–79) university faculty members with similar professional specializations took psychometric tests. The scores of the older faculty were lower than those of the younger faculty even though the older faculty members were just as successful as the younger faculty members in their chosen fields. Also, older business executives earned lower scores than young business executives on a battery of complex neuropsychological tests. Yet the older executives held high-level managerial positions that called for complex judgments and decision making.

A key proposition of the life-span developmental perspective is that individuals experience both gains and losses over the life span, although in the later years the proportion of losses may be greater than the proportion of gains (Baltes, 1987). Nonetheless, older adults can use abilities that have improved to compensate for losses. By taking advantage of the cognitive abilities they have honed (see the next section on encapsulation), older adults can maintain, and possibly even increase, their overall level of competence. Such a strategy may account for older adults' high level of success in work-related situations even when their scores on some psychometric tests show loss. Additionally, competence in work-related situations can be a function not only of cognitive abilities, but also of interpersonal abilities. The social and interpersonal aspects of cognitive functioning are covered in greater detail in Chapter 7.

Encapsulation

According to the **encapsulation model** (Rybash et al., 1986), as individuals grow older, their knowledge becomes channeled (encapsulated) within specific areas (domains). In other words, over the adult years, individuals are transformed from

The expertise required for specialized knowledge, skills, and abilities takes years to develop.

generalists into specialists by accumulating, organizing, accessing, and applying their knowledge in specific chosen domains of intellectual functioning. Older adults concentrate on fewer domains of intellectual functioning than young adults, but they become highly efficient at acquiring knowledge related to these domains. At the same time, older adults become less efficient in acquiring knowledge that is unrelated to their specialized, encapsulated, domains.

The encapsulation model provides insight into what would otherwise seem to be contradictory evidence: There is age-related decline in speed and efficiency on fluid psychometric ability tests that require the solution of novel problems; yet, older adults often function at a high level when their thinking and problem-solving abilities are assessed within domains of expertise for which they have learned to utilize their knowledge and experience. John, who was described at the beginning of this chapter, thinks that his years of experience and expertise in the operations of his company compensate for the fact that he may not do certain newer tasks as quickly as some of the younger employees.

Competence in Daily Life

Most of us would probably agree that competence in daily life entails responding effectively to whatever tasks and demands are necessary (Schaie & Willis, 1996). To some extent, the specific tasks and demands depend upon an individual's age or stage of life. In young adulthood, tasks and demands of daily life revolve around school, jobs, and parenting. Older adults' lifestyles are more diverse, so the daily tasks and demands are more variable (Schaie & Willis, 1996). Some enroll in academic programs, although the student role is less normative in older adulthood. Some work full-time or part-time, but many are retired from paid employment. Some are involved in parenting roles, although this too is less normative in older adulthood than it is in young or middle adulthood.

The majority of adults aged 75+ live in the community and often their main concern is to continue living independently. Competence means being able to perform the tasks that allow them to do so. Two domains of competence associated with an independent lifestyle are caring for oneself and managing one's property (Willis, 1996). Clearly, visual and auditory acuity play a role when it comes to competence in these domains. But what other abilities are required for independent living, and are there tests that can measure them? Further, would scores on any such tests have any relationship to scores on psychometric tests of fluid and crystallized abilities?

Activities of daily living and instrumental activities of daily living

A distinction is made between activities of daily living (ADL) and instrumental activities of daily living (IADL), two terms that were introduced in Chapter 3. The ADL category includes the basic personal care tasks necessary for self-maintenance (for example, bathing, dressing, eating, walking, getting to the toilet, transferring from a bed to a chair). ADL assessments are often made to determine disability and need for health-care services.

The IADL category includes the higher-order tasks necessary for carrying out the business of daily life, including management of one's property (Schaie & Willis, 1996, 1999).

The Everyday Problems Test

Willis and her colleagues (Willis & Marsiske, 1993) devised an Everyday Problems Test (EPT) composed of written tasks in each of seven IADL categories (Table 6.5 lists these IADL categories with sample tasks for each). Older adults' scores on the EPT were positively related to their psychometric test scores. However,

Table 6.5 *Instrumental activities of daily living (IADL): categories and sample tasks*

Category	Sample tasks
Managing medications	Read a medicine label and determine how many doses can be taken in a 24–hour period Complete a patient medical history form
Managing finances	Compare Medigap insurance policies Complete an income tax form
Shopping for necessities	Order merchandise from a catalogue Compare brands of a product
Using the telephone	Determine amount to pay for a phone bill Determine emergency phone information
Meal preparation and nutrition	Evaluate nutritional information on a food label Follow recipe directions
Housekeeping	Read instructions for operating a household appliance Comprehend an appliance warrantee
Transportation	Compute taxi rates Read a bus schedule

Adapted from Willis (1996).

the relationship was somewhat stronger for psychometric tests of fluid abilities than for psychometric tests of crystallized abilities (Marsiske & Willis, 1995).

Behavioral measures of competence in daily living

Instead of relying on written materials, Diehl, Willis, and Schaie (1995) used behavioral observations to measure competence in daily living. Older adults were observed in their homes as they performed tasks related to medication adherence (for example, loading a pill reminder device), telephone usage (for example, activating call forwarding on a telephone), and meal preparation (for example, following instructions for use of a microwave oven). Strong positive relationships were found between these behavioral observations and the scores older adults earned on the written EPT described above. As with the written EPT, behavioral observations of everyday tasks were positively related to psychometric test scores. Again, the level of observed behaviors had a stronger positive relationship with scores on psychometric tests of fluid abilities as opposed to crystallized abilities. Diehl et al. (2005) obtained similar results with both European American and African American older adults using a revised version of a behavioral observations test composed of 3 behavioral tasks in each of 3 IADL categories: medication use, telephone use, and financial management. The better the ability to carry out the behavioral tasks, the higher the scores both on a written version of EPT and on psychometric tests, especially those that tap fluid abilities.

The Everyday Cognition Battery (ECB)

Allaire and Marsiske (1999) tested community-living European American and African American older adults ranging from 60 to 92 years of age on traditional psychometric tests of both fluid (reasoning) and crystallized (knowledge) abilities. In addition, they administered a written Everyday Cognition Battery (ECB) that tested both reasoning and knowledge in three categories of daily functioning: food preparation, medication use, and financial management. For example, in the food preparation category, one reasoning item asked test takers to read nutrition labels for two different brands of chili and select the one best suited for a low-fat diet. A knowledge item asked individuals to select the best alternative answer to the following multiple-choice question: "The expiration date, or 'use by' date on a product means: (a) the last date the food should be used; (b) last day the product can be expected to be at its peak quality; (c) the date the food was processed or packaged; (d) none of the above." Study participants' scores on the ECB reasoning and knowledge items were positively correlated with their scores on psychometric tests of reasoning and knowledge, respectively. That is, individuals who scored high on the ECB also scored high on the analogous psychometric test. Furthermore, the classic aging pattern was evident on both the ECB and the psychometric tests: Scores on the everyday and psychometric reasoning tests, both measures of fluid ability, showed age-related decline over the age range of 60 to 92. In contrast, scores on the everyday and psychometric knowledge tests, both measures of crystallized ability, remained stable.

These research findings show that there is overlap between psychometric test scores and everyday competence (see also Marsiske & Margrett, 2006). However, note that the EPT and the ECB measure potential competence on IADL-related tasks. They do not measure how well older adults would actually perform such tasks if these were necessary in their daily lives. Also, keep in mind that everyday competence is defined by the cultural context in which one lives. In some cultures, competence in daily living may not call for the ability to follow a medication regimen or understand the meaning of expiration dates on packaged food.

Finally, most studies that compare psychometric and everyday abilities collect data at only one point in time. However, Willis and her colleagues (Willis et al., 2006) followed older adults who were living independently in six U.S. cities over a period of 5 years. Those who received earlier training sessions on reasoning showed long-lasting benefits with regard to daily functioning and reported less difficulty with IADL tasks. Such longitudinal studies should help us determine what factors could be related to the maintenance of everyday competence.

Legal considerations

Assessment of competence is sometimes necessary for the purpose of legal judgments (Schaie & Willis, 1996, 1999). **Legal guardianship** refers to "care and protection by someone who is empowered to make decisions in the interest of the individual concerning everyday matters such as living arrangements, health care, and provision of other basic needs" (Grisso, 1986, p. 268). Typically, a guardian is a legal representative with the authority to make decisions about health, maintenance and care needs, as well as the use of finances and assets (Eglit, 2004, p. 215). Legal judgments about the need for guardianship are usually made within the context of a specific living environment (Grisso, 1986). Thus, consideration is given to whether a particular living situation fails to meet an older individual's essential needs for survival or whether the older individual is endangering himself or herself or others (Schaie & Willis, 1999).

Legal conservatorship refers to "management of an incompetent person's estate and financial transactions" (Grisso, 1986, p. 268). Thus, a conservator is a legal representative with regard to property (Eglit, 2004, p. 215). Each state within the United States has laws regarding the conditions under which either a guardian or a conservator can be assigned to individuals who are deemed incompetent to care for themselves or to manage their own property or financial affairs, respectively.

Legal definitions of incapacity and incompetence focus on extremes, and the decision to assign a guardian or conservator generally requires indisputable evidence of dysfunctional behavior and inability to solve problems or make decisions (Schaie & Willis, 1999). Sometimes there is little question that older adults are suffering from Alzheimer's disease or some other type of dementia that renders them unable to care for themselves physically or to make decisions (see Chapter 11 for further discussion of dementia). However, the need for legal action, especially conservatorship, is not always clear, as in the following example:

Maria is a middle-aged woman whose 75-year-old widowed father is living independently and seems to be in good health. Maria visits her father one day and discovers he has been writing checks to charities that may or may not be legitimate. She also finds out that her father wrote a check for a sizable amount of money to a very exclusive shop that specializes in fancy cocktail dresses. When Maria asks her father about this, he tells her that the check was for a new dress for a young lady who has worked for several months at the reception desk in his apartment building. This young lady is very pleasant and on several occasions has gotten his groceries when he was unable to get to the store because of bad weather. Maria is beginning to worry that her father is becoming susceptible to scam artists, and she is not sure whether he is still competent to handle his own finances.

In many instances, family members are concerned about the competence of an older relative who makes decisions they do not consider to be financially prudent. However, it is not always a simple matter to determine whether an older adult is incompetent and requires a conservator. The older adult may simply be exercising his or her freedom to spend money as he or she wishes. Often, it is difficult to make an all-or-none determination of an older adult's capacity to make financial and other decisions. Both researchers and clinicians recognize the need for accurate and valid ways to assess older adults' decision making capacity (Moye & Marson, 2007). Clearly, issues surrounding the determination of competence point to the intersect between psychology and the legal system. We need further study to determine what legal strategies are appropriate for protecting older adults while at the same time respecting their autonomy (Kapp, 2007).

Revisiting the Selective Optimization with Compensation and Ecological Models

The Selective Optimization with Compensation (SOC) (Baltes & Baltes, 1990) and Ecological (Lawton, 1989; Lawton & Nahemow, 1973) Models are two theoretical frameworks within which we can view aging and intellectual abilities.

Normal aging is associated with decline in fluid abilities, but crystallized abilities are usually maintained and sometimes they even improve over the adult life span. According to the SOC Model, the pragmatics of intelligence (akin to crystallized abilities) can be used to compensate for any decline in the mechanics of intelligence (akin to fluid abilities). Also, older adults can cope with losses by becoming more selective and concentrating on the domains of intellectual functioning that are most important to them. Even with some loss in fluid abilities, especially those that call for speed of processing, older adults can compensate by making use of their expertise in specific domains of functioning. A recommendation based on the SOC Model would be that older adults not spread themselves too thinly, but rather that they concentrate their efforts on the domains in which they are motivated to maintain a high level of functioning.

From the perspective of the Ecological Model, optimal adaptation will occur if the intellectual press of the environment is tailored to an individual's level of competence. Individuals will experience difficulty in environments with too much press for their level of ability. Older adults in a highly demanding environment that makes too many intellectual demands may become overwhelmed and vulnerable in terms of confusion, mental stress, or even physical peril. Under such circumstances, level of adaptation will improve with the introduction of environmental supports that reduce the level of intellectual press. Supports could include guidance and help with solving problems that are required for optimal daily functioning. At the same time, adaptation is optimal when environments pose some degree of intellectual challenge. An environment with too few demands and with severely limited opportunities for intellectual stimulation could have a detrimental effect on adaptation. All environments should provide opportunities for the exercise of intellectual abilities.

? Questions to Consider

1. Do you think intelligence in an academic setting is the same or different from intelligence in a work setting? Would intelligence differ for a young adult college student as opposed to an older adult who is not in school?
2. What things in your everyday life require crystallized abilities and what things require fluid abilities? Have you developed expertise in some areas of accomplishment?
3. What do you think you can you do to maintain your own level of intellectual functioning?

Key Points

- Many aging researchers conceptualize intellectual abilities as consisting of fluid (Gf) and crystallized abilities (Gc).
- Gf is "raw" intelligence that is largely a function of the integrity of the central nervous system and often shows age-related decline over the adult years.

- Gc is largely a function of education, experience, and cultural exposure and is usually maintained or increases somewhat over the adult years.

- In the dual-process model (mechanics and pragmatics of intelligence), mechanics are analogous to fluid intelligence (Gf), have been likened to the hardware of the mind, and generally show gradual age-related decline.

- Pragmatics are analogous to crystallized intelligence (Gc), have been likened to the software of the mind, and can show age-related cognitive growth.

- Psychometric intelligence is measured by the number of points earned on intelligence tests. To be meaningful, psychometric tests of intelligence must be limited to individuals who are members of the population on whom the test was standardized.

- Psychometric tests that are used frequently to study aging and intellectual abilities are the Primary Mental Abilities (PMA) Test and the Wechsler Adult Intelligence Scale (WAIS).

- In the classic aging pattern, scores on the verbal subtests of the Wechsler Adult Intelligence Scale (WAIS) are maintained with increasing age, whereas scores on the performance subtests decline.

- Longitudinal studies generally find that age-related decline in intellectual abilities occurs later and is smaller than that typically found in cross-sectional studies.

- Intelligence quotient (IQ) on a psychometric test such as the WAIS represents a comparison of an individual test taker's score with the scores of age peers from a standardization sample.

- Despite age-related losses in some abilities, those that are maintained or improved may compensate for those that decline. The idea that gains can be used to offset losses is an important tenet of the SOC Model.

- There is a positive relationship between maintenance of intellectual functioning and good sensory functioning, good health, high educational level, high-level job history, flexibility of personality, membership in an intact family, and engagement in challenging cognitive activities.

- In late adulthood, competence is often measured by how well individuals perform activities of daily living (ADL) and instrumental activities of daily living (IADL). Tests of IADL often correlate with psychometric measures.

- Definitions of incapacity and incompetence are needed when legal decisions must be made about whether to assign a guardian or conservator to an older adult.

Key Terms

age-insensitive abilities   179

age-sensitive abilities   179

classic aging pattern   179

crystallized intelligence (Gc)   169

disuse hypothesis of cognitive aging   184

encapsulation model   189

engagement hypothesis   184

fluid intelligence (Gf)   169

Flynn Effect   175

intelligence quotient (IQ)   173

intraindividual variability   181

legal conservatorship   193

legal guardianship   193

mechanics of intelligence   169

negative cohort trend   179

optimally exercised abilities   182

positive cohort trend   178

pragmatics of intelligence   169

testing the limits   181

unexercised abilities   182

7

Cognition and Problem Solving in the Everyday World

Chapter Overview

Close-ups on Adulthood and Aging

Harold and Hazel turned 65 within a few days of one another and later that month they celebrated their 40th wedding anniversary. At this point in their lives, both of them realize they have reached a crossroads and should make a decision about changes in their lifestyle. Harold wants to sell the large home where they raised their children and move into a condominium with an exercise facility on the premises and access to public transportation, which will come in handy if they give up driving at some point. Hazel is less enthusiastic about this idea. She loves their familiar home, but realizes that she and her husband should have a plan in place for how they will live when they are no longer quite so independent. For starters, she thinks they should install grab bars in the bathrooms and make further physical modifications to their home as needed. At present they do not see eye to eye, but Harold and Hazel are each trying to consider the perspective of the other in the hope that they can create a mutually satisfactory plan. They think it might help to bring their grown sons into the decision making process to see what suggestions they might have.

Stages of Cognitive Development

Many older adults claim their memory is not as good as it once was (Erber et al., 1992). In contrast, however, they feel their ability to think, reason, and solve problems has gotten better over the years (for example, Williams, Denney, & Schadler, 1983). This perception contrasts sharply with the age-related decline found on psychometric tests of fluid abilities that were described in Chapter 6. Perhaps the reason older adults believe that their problem-solving abilities have improved is that the problems they confront in everyday life differ from those found on psychometric tests. Most problems on psychometric tests have only one correct answer, whereas the problems encountered in real life often have more than one solution.

Are there differences in how young and older adults approach and solve everyday problems? At various stages of life, individuals may have different reasons, or motivations, for using their cognitive capabilities. As a first step in approaching cognition and problem solving in the everyday world, we will discuss theories that view cognition as having distinct purposes at each stage of the life span.

Schaie's Stage Model of Cognitive/Intellectual Development

Schaie (1977–1978) contends that we use our cognitive/intellectual capabilities for whatever purposes are most meaningful, or relevant, for our particular stage of life. Initially, Schaie outlined four sequential stages of development, each associated with a different motivation for using cognitive processes (see Table 7.1).

Table 7.1 *Cognitive processes in four sequential stages of the life span*

Age/stage	Description of stage	Motivation for cognitive processes
Childhood/adolescence	Acquisitive	Broad acquisition of knowledge. "What should I know?"
Young adulthood	Achieving	Apply knowledge to achieving long-term goals. "How should I use what I know?"
Middle adulthood	Responsible/executive	Use knowledge to take care of others and/or for leadership roles. "How can I help?"
Older adulthood	Reintegrative	Selective use of knowledge for meaningful purposes. "Why should I know?"

Source: Schaie (1977–1978).

In the **acquisitive stage**, which dominates the childhood and adolescent years, we try to gain as much knowledge and acquire as many skills as possible to prepare ourselves for participation in society. In the **achieving stage** in the young adult years, we shift from acquiring a broad base of knowledge for its own sake to focusing on applying the knowledge we have acquired to establish ourselves as independent, competent members of society and to achieve our long-term goals in the domains of career and marriage. In the **responsible/executive stage**, identified mainly with middle adulthood, we use our knowledge and skills for the purpose of care and concern for others. Many of us are establishing and raising families, thus taking on responsibility for a spouse and possibly offspring. We become homeowners, thereby assuming responsibilities for the community. At work, we are often in charge of directing and supervising others. At some point we might take on executive responsibilities, holding leadership positions in jobs (head of department, president, CEO) or in the community (homeowner, condominium association board member, member of a parent–teacher association). In the **reintegrative stage**, associated with older adulthood, we become more selective about how we expend our cognitive efforts. We are less motivated to acquire large amounts of new information, and we don't want to "waste time" on tasks and pursuits that have little meaning for us. It is not clear whether this selectivity stems from biological and neurological changes that limit cognitive functioning, or whether it is a reaction to reduced responsibility for others and the recognition that the future is less distant.

Schaie and Willis (2000) expanded upon the period of older adulthood by adding a **reorganizational stage** and a **legacy-creating stage** (see Figure 7.1). The reorganizational stage overlaps with the young-old years (ages 65–74), which in American society are associated with retirement from paid work and

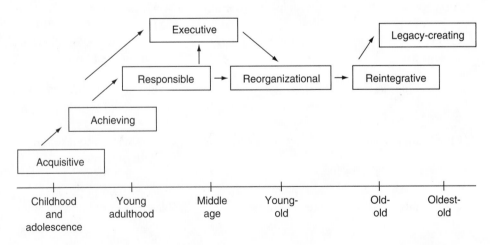

Figure 7.1 *Revised cognitive stage model.*
Source: Schaie & Willis (2000).

an end to responsibilities for offspring, who are now fully grown and independent adults. Young-old individuals apply their cognitive competence to two tasks: (a) restructuring their lives for the years of retirement and (b) planning for a time when they may have to give up some of their independence. Restructuring their lives entails creating a routine of meaningful pursuits to replace the work and family responsibilities of middle adulthood, possibly substituting volunteer and leisure activities. Planning for possible dependence may require contemplating or actually making changes in living situations, as we saw with Harold and Hazel, the couple described at the beginning of the chapter. In terms of financial arrangements, wills and trusts as well as advance medical directives may be written or updated (Chapter 12 describes these documents further).

Note that these reorganizational tasks probably apply best to upper-middle-class European Americans, and that there is diversity even within American culture. For example, some young-old adults take on the role of surrogate parents to their grandchildren because of family crises such as the divorce, illness, or drug addiction of their adult children (Hayslip & Kaminski, 2005). Under such circumstances, there will be little time for leisure pursuits or volunteer work. In some Native American tribes, grandparents rear grandchildren for the first few years of their lives, or at least care for them and impart Native American customs during the summer school holidays (Quadagno, 2008). With regard to planning for future dependence, young-old African American and Hispanic American women are more likely than young-old European American women to live with relatives other than a spouse (Quadagno, 2008), so there may be less need to make plans for change in their living situations.

In a final legacy-creating stage, identified mainly with the old-old (75–84) and oldest-old (85+) years, individuals anticipate the end of life. It is not uncommon for them to reminisce about their past or engage in life review (which Chapter 8 describes in greater detail). Some older adults write autobiographies, but many record oral history, work on a family tree, or leave a legacy by carefully labeling family pictures and heirlooms. Older adults may distribute possessions to relatives or friends or prepare instructions for how such items should be distributed upon their death. Many make final revisions to wills and concrete funeral arrangements.

In sum, Schaie's model is a framework for considering the purpose for which people use their cognitive abilities at various stages of life. The exact chronological age when each stage occurs, and indeed whether every individual experiences all stages, may depend upon factors such as health, socioeconomic status, and cultural background. In any case, cognitive efforts are directed toward meeting challenges and accomplishing goals that are important at a particular stage of life.

Postformal Thought

Jean Piaget, a Swiss physician and psychologist, put forth a theory of cognitive development whereby every member of the human species progresses through a universal set of cognitive stages that occur in a fixed sequence (Piaget, 1952). The *sensorimotor stage* (birth to age 2) culminates in a toddler's becoming capable of cognitive representation of objects and object permanence. Just because an object is out of sight does not mean it is out of mind. In the *preoperational stage* (ages 2 to 7), children acquire spoken language and problem-solving skills that involve objects directly in front of them. In the *concrete operational stage* (ages 7 to 11), children can mentally manipulate objects and sort them into categories. In the final **formal operations** stage (beginning at approximately age 11 and extending into adulthood), individuals can reason logically to solve abstract problems. Through scientific deductive reasoning, they can generate and test hypotheses and systematically eliminate all but the correct solution to a problem.

Piaget's theory has had a major influence on our understanding of human development. However, one criticism has been that not all adolescents, or even all adults for that matter, use a logical scientific approach to solving problems. Furthermore, individuals who use a logical scientific approach to solve one kind of problem do not necessarily use it to solve other kinds of problems. For example, formal logical reasoning is useful for solving a real-world physical problem such as why a car breaks down, and an experienced auto mechanic should be able to eliminate all possible causes except the one actually creating the problem. However, the same individual who uses formal reasoning to solve a car repair problem may not use it to determine why a recipe failed ("Why did that cake I baked come out of the oven only one inch high?"). In short, people often use formal operations in some domains but not in others.

Formal reasoning is beneficial on psychometric tests, especially those that measure fluid abilities (see Chapter 6) because items on such tests call for abstract problem solving and the correct answer is determined through logical deduction. Older adults tend to perform less well than young adults on such tests. However, not all problems that occur in everyday life lend themselves to formal logical solutions – some real-world problems have more than one possible solution (Sinnott, 1996). For example, what is the best way to resolve an argument between two good friends? What is the best way to approach your boss to request a pay increase? Solving these problems is quite different from solving formal logical problems.

Some researchers have extended Piaget's theory by adding a postformal stage of development. In contrast to formal thinking, **postformal thinking** calls for tolerating ambiguity and remaining flexible and open to considering more than one solution to a problem. The relativistic, or dialectical, nature of postformal thinking differs from the formal logical thinking required on tests of psychometric intelligence where each question has only one correct answer.

How do we use postformal thought in real-life situations in which there may be more than one "truth" about an event or a relationship (Sinnott, 1996)? In social situations, we often need to shift perspectives to see things from another person's point of view. Harold and Hazel (the couple described at the beginning of the chapter) will each have to shift perspectives to understand how the other feels as they seek a mutually agreeable solution for how to modify their living situation.

Studying postformal thinking is no simple task. It is difficult to measure with quantitative tests that have been used to measure formal reasoning (Berg & Klaczynski, 1996), and constructing paper-and-pencil tests has met with only limited success (Sinnott, 1996). Postformal thinking is usually assessed by analyzing the verbal responses people give in answer to open-ended questions.

Postformal thinking is now recognized as a legitimate type of cognition that is quite different from that used to solve logical problems. Whether postformal thinking constitutes a stage that emerges more fully in older adulthood, and indeed whether the majority of older adults engage in this type of thinking, remain to be determined. The perspective-taking aspect of postformal thinking is closely linked to the concept of wisdom, which we will now consider.

Wisdom

What is the definition of **wisdom**? More pointedly, what properties of thought, judgment, and advice are considered wise, and what are wise individuals like? Is wisdom related to age, and are older adults more likely to be wise compared to individuals in other age groups?

What Is Wisdom?

Wisdom is not easy to define. The words "wisdom" and "wise" imply elevated forms of behavior – to display wisdom is to behave in admirable, moral ways (Birren & Fisher, 1990; Birren & Schroots, 1996). Baltes and his colleagues (Baltes & Staudinger, 1995; Smith & Baltes, 1990; Smith, Staudinger, & Baltes, 1994) define wisdom as expert knowledge and insight about the fundamental pragmatics of life.

In general, wisdom encompasses cognitive aspects – expert factual and procedural knowledge. Most people think that wisdom is associated with intelligence (Kausler et al., 2007; Sternberg & Lubart, 2001). However, wisdom is not so much how much information you have; rather, it is knowing what you do not have and being able to make good use of what you do have (Birren & Fisher, 1990). An important aspect of wisdom is "problem finding," which means being able to ask appropriate questions when problems are undefined (Arlin, 1990).

The wise individual uses accumulated knowledge to solve life problems and dilemmas that have elements of uncertainty and are often interpersonal (Baltes & Staudinger, 1995). The wise individual also demonstrates exceptional insight and gives good and fair advice about how to deal with important but difficult situations (Smith & Baltes, 1990; Staudinger, Kessler, & Dörner, 2006), while also recognizing that human nature has limitations (Taranto, 1989).

Some professions require expert factual and procedural knowledge and exceptional insight.

Wisdom calls for a balance between reflection and action (Birren & Fisher, 1990). Acting rashly is the antithesis of wisdom. Rather, the wise person weighs what is known and not known, and reflects on the consequences of various actions before carefully choosing which one to take. Wisdom also requires a balance between cognition and emotion. A wise person remains calm and impartial while considering all aspects of a problem. A wise person understands that a reflective state of mind makes it easier to generate alternative solutions when confronting a problem.

Wisdom is similar to postformal thinking in that it calls for an appreciation that truth is not absolute; rather, truth may differ depending upon the perspective one takes (Sternberg & Lubart, 2001). A wise person can integrate opposite points of view and remain objective while considering multiple aspects of complex and uncertain situations. In short, the wise individual thinks before acting and does not allow decisions to be dominated by personal preferences or emotions such as anger or fear.

Age and Wisdom

Wisdom is considered the pinnacle of successful human development (Ardelt, 2000) so it is not surprising that most of us assume that we need time to acquire the necessary experience that makes wisdom attainable (Baltes & Smith, 2008; Birren & Fisher, 1990; Birren & Schroots, 1996). Perhaps for this reason, it is commonly thought that older adults are more likely than young adults to be wise because of their experience from many years of living.

However, not all investigators have found that wisdom is a necessary corollary of age. Even among healthy, educated, financially well-off European American older women who participated in the longitudinal Berkeley Guidance Study, Ardelt (2000) found considerable variation in degree of wisdom. Not surprisingly, those rated higher on cognitive, reflective, and emotional indicators of wisdom by clinically trained interviewers also rated themselves higher in life satisfaction. Clearly, wisdom is desirable, but age does not automatically lead to wisdom.

One way psychologists have investigated wisdom is to present people with a hypothetical dilemma being faced by a fictitious character ("target") and ask what advice they would give to the target on how to resolve it. In most cases, there is no single "correct" solution to the dilemma, but some kinds of advice are considered wiser than others. Smith and Baltes (1990) investigated people's judgments about dilemmas involving work and family. Study participants were young (aged 25–35), middle-aged (40–50), and older (60–81) highly educated adults recruited through advertisements in Berlin newspapers. They read several scenarios (vignettes), each one describing a young or older target who is facing a predicament about future life planning and must come to some decision about what to do. Two examples follow:

> Michael, a 28-year-old mechanic with two preschool-aged children, has just learned that the factory in which he is working will close in 3 months. At present, there is no possibility of further employment in this area. His wife has recently returned to her well-paid nursing career. Michael is considering the following options: He can plan to move to another city to seek employment, or he can plan to take full responsibility for child care and household tasks. Formulate a plan that details what Michael should do and should consider in the next 3 to 5 years. What extra pieces of information are needed?

> Joyce, a 60-year-old widow, recently completed a degree in business management and opened her own business. She has been looking forward to this challenge. She has just heard that her son has been left with two small children to care for. Joyce is considering the following options: She could plan to give up her business and live with her son, or she could plan to arrange for financial assistance for her son to cover child-care costs. Formulate a plan that details what Joyce should do and should consider in the next 3 to 5 years. What extra pieces of information are needed?

Participants were asked to think aloud as they formulated a plan of action for the target, Michael or Joyce. Later, trained raters evaluated the wisdom of the advice each participant would give to the target. To attain a high wisdom rating, the plan of action would have to (a) define and discuss many aspects of the target's problem, (b) offer several alternatives about what the target could do, stating the positive and negative aspects of each one, (c) recognize that all strategies hold some uncertainty and evaluate the risks of each, and (d) suggest that the alternative selected be monitored and revised if necessary.

Only 5% of the study participants' responses received high wisdom ratings, but wise responses were evenly distributed over the young, middle-aged, and older participants. Thus, the older participants' responses were no wiser, but neither was there any age-related decline in this type of cognition. In general, participants' responses seemed to show special insight for the dilemma faced by a similar-aged target. For the dilemma faced by the young target (Michael), the young and middle-aged participants' advice received higher wisdom ratings than the older participants' advice. In contrast, for the dilemma faced by the older target (Joyce), the older participants' advice was rated somewhat higher than the advice given by the young and middle-aged participants. Baltes and Smith (2008) recommend that the set of vignettes used to test wisdom be expanded to determine whether these findings generalize across a broader range of life dilemmas. In addition, they suggest that the responses individuals give be investigated at more than one point in time, especially after they themselves have been exposed to various tasks, events, or advisers.

In sum, there does not seem to be any age-related decline in the cognitive skills necessary to give wise advice. However, there is little support for the assumption that older adults are wiser than young adults. Some older adults are wise, but old age does not guarantee wisdom.

Real-World Intelligence and Problem Solving

In the academic arena, and on most psychometric tests of intelligence, solving problems depends on formal, factual knowledge and the ability to think logically (Sternberg, Wagner, & Okagaki, 1993). When educational level is held constant, young adults usually perform at the highest level on such problems, with a steady decline in performance from middle to older adulthood. But does the ability to solve academic problems go hand in hand with being able to solve problems outside of school? Sternberg and his colleagues (Sternberg, Wagner, Williams, & Horvath, 1995) claim that individuals who do not earn high scores on psychometric tests and do not achieve outstanding grades in school often enjoy great success in their careers.

Practical intelligence

Most of us distinguish between academic intelligence ("book smarts") and practical intelligence ("street smarts"). Unlike academic problems, real-world problems (a) are unformulated and poorly defined, (b) are of personal interest and relevance to everyday experience, (c) lack specific information necessary for solution, (d) have multiple "correct" solutions, each with assets and liabilities, and (e) can be solved using various methods (Sternberg et al., 1995).

A distinction is also made between **formal knowledge** and **tacit knowledge** (Sternberg et al., 1995). Formal knowledge, like academic intelligence, is often measured by psychometric tests and is reflected in the grades earned in school. Tacit knowledge is characterized by the following (Sternberg & Lubart, 2001; Sternberg et al., 1995):

- "Knowing how" rather than just "knowing that." For example, how must an employee behave to get along with superiors or colleagues in the workplace? What must an insurance salesperson do to complete a sale successfully?
- Having a practical use in attaining valued goals. For example, how does a manager make subordinates at work feel valued? Such a goal has practical value for people aspiring to be successful managers, but not for those who do not care.

- Inferred from actions or indirect statements because tacit knowledge is not written or articulated explicitly. For example, to advance in a company, a new employee might have to observe how other employees behave and what rewards they are given.

Sternberg and his colleagues have investigated tacit knowledge by having research participants read vignettes describing problems that could actually arise in the workplace. Afterward, participants select what they perceive as the best solution from a number of possible alternatives (which successful managers have previously ordered by rank). Study participants who choose highly ranked solutions earn more points for tacit knowledge than those who choose lower-ranked solutions. Such studies have found that tacit knowledge scores do not correlate highly with scores on psychometric intelligence tests. Also, unlike the age-related decline frequently noted on psychometric tests of fluid ability, tacit knowledge often increases with both age and experience. When older adults claim their problem-solving abilities have gotten better over time, perhaps (without realizing it) they are referring to improvements in tacit knowledge.

For older adults, tacit knowledge could be especially useful in selecting and adapting to a new living environment. How does an older adult determine the best time to make the transition to a living environment that offers more support (a decision being contemplated by Harold and Hazel at the beginning of the chapter)? How does an older adult who moves into an assisted living facility use tacit knowledge to get along with fellow residents and ensure that his or her needs are met in a timely manner by busy staff members? Tacit knowledge could make an important difference in how well older individuals are able to construct a comfortable niche in such an environment. Tacit knowledge can play a role in successful aging.

Creative Intelligence

Sternberg (1996) distinguishes among three components of intelligence: analytic, practical, and creative (see Figure 7.2). Analytic intelligence is closely related to academic intelligence and is often measured by the psychometric intelligence tests discussed in Chapter 6. However, analytic intelligence can be applied to problems outside the academic arena, such as figuring out what kind of car or house offers the desired features but is still within one's budget. The practical component of intelligence, which includes the tacit knowledge described in the preceding section, is useful for obtaining what one wants in the real world.

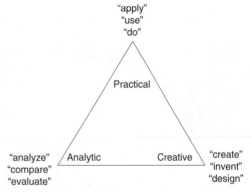

Note: Sternberg (1985, 2004).

Figure 7.2 *Sternberg's triarchic theory of intelligence.*

Source: Sternberg (1985).

The third component, creative intelligence, is somewhat elusive and difficult to measure, but it taps an aspect of intelligence that seems to lie outside the abilities measured by psychometric tests or used in practical situations. In general, creative intelligence connotes divergent thinking, or being able to generate many answers to a question and to find novel, insightful solutions to a problem. One can measure creative intelligence by seeing how many uses a person can think of for an object such as a brick or a ballpoint pen. This differs from the convergent thought typical of analytic intelligence, where the emphasis is on finding the one correct solution to a problem.

Does creativity increase, decrease, or remain stable over the adult years? Some investigators have attempted to chart the work produced over the adult life span of individuals who are recognized as creative geniuses in various fields (Simonton, 1997). Simonton (1990) points out that many creative geniuses have surmounted physical obstacles and continue to be creatively productive. For example, the artist Pierre-Auguste Renoir dealt with rheumatism by painting with a brush tied to his hand. Some creative individuals adapt to altered physical conditions by enlisting help from others. Many older Renaissance artists employed apprentices to perform such tasks as preparing materials. Likewise, illustrious older scientists often have teams of research assistants to facilitate their work.

Lehman (1953) investigated the relationship between age and the rate of producing creative works in various academic fields. Overall, he found that creative output peaks in the decade of the 30s, followed by steady decline. However, Dennis (1966) found that the age of peak productivity in creative output in the arts, sciences, and humanities depends upon the specific field of achievement. In the humanities, productivity tends to remain stable over the adult life span, whereas productivity tends to fall off in the decade of the 60s in the sciences and even earlier in the arts (see Figure 7.3).

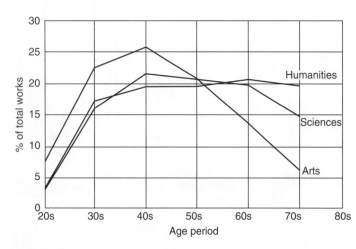

Figure 7.3 *Dennis's research showing productivity over decades for the arts, sciences, and humanities.*
Source: Dennis (1966).

In many academic fields, the specific age at which a peak occurs may depend upon the age when a career is launched (Simonton, 1990, 1997). Individuals who enter a career after mid-life often have a later peak of productivity and a higher rate of output in their older years. Indeed, there are numerous examples of artistic, literary, scientific, and other kinds of creative accomplishments in older adulthood. The classical composer Anton Bruckner did not embark on a creative career as a symphonic composer until mid-life. He composed his first symphony at the age of 42, his first "unquestioned masterpiece" at 50, and his ninth symphony at 70 (Simonton, 1998).

Note that the quantity of output, or productivity, is not necessarily the same as the quality of creative work. However, according to the **constant-probability-of-success model of creativity,** the point of maximum creativity in a career often coincides with the point of maximum productivity (Simonton, 1990, 1998). Thus, individuals who generate the largest number of works (high productivity) have the greatest chance of generating a masterpiece (high creativity). In short, the likelihood of a "creative hit" depends upon how many works are produced during that time, even though some of those works will be less important. If overall productivity falls off with increasing age, the number of creative works may fall off proportionately. However, individuals who are most productive in their early years often continue to be productive in their later years (Simonton, 1990, 1998).

The **swan-song phenomenon** is a resurgence in creative output stemming from a final burst in creative activity in the sixth and seventh decades following a postpeak decline in the rate of creative productivity

Artistic creativity can continue well into the older adult years.

(Simonton, 1990). The peak in the number of last works may not be as high as the peak achieved in mid-life, but often these final works are outstanding in their simplicity and elegance. The swan-song phenomenon "enables the greatest creators to end their career trajectories with a bang, not a whimper" (Simonton, 1998, p. 14). Evidence for the swan-song phenomenon has been demonstrated most pointedly for classical composers such as Beethoven, Brahms, Handel, and Richard Strauss (Simonton, 1990). However, it may hold for visual artists, writers, and scientists as well.

The creative work of musicians, artists, and writers tends to take different forms and to focus on different content over the life span (Lubart & Sternberg, 1998). In general, work produced in older adulthood shows a clarity of style and an integration of ideas. Late-life creative works in basic science, social science, and philosophy often consist of memoirs, historical analyses, or observations made over a period of time, and the content of older adults' creative work often focuses on subjective interpretations of experiences. Not surprisingly, the themes of aging and death are more prominent in the creative works of older adults than in those of younger adults.

Solving Interpersonal Problems

During the course of our daily lives, we often face practical problems such as what to do if we open the refrigerator and find that it is warm inside. Denney and

Palmer (1981) found that the quality of the solutions people suggest for dealing with this type of problem peaks in middle age, with a gradual decline after age 50. Unlike the warm refrigerator problem, however, some problems are more interpersonal. The best solutions to interpersonal problems are often relativistic, which means recognizing that the problem can be approached from more than one perspective and that no single solution will please everyone.

Collins, Luszcz, Lawson, and Keeves (1997) interviewed Australian women ranging from 65 to 90 years of age. Half of them lived independently in the Adelaide community and the other half lived in group nursing hostels (similar to assisted-living facilities) but were screened for physical and cognitive competency. Each woman read a scenario and offered a solution to a problem that was set either in a community-living or a nursing hostel context. The following problem description was adapted from Collins et al.:

> Let's say an elderly couple who moved into the house that adjoins yours watch television and listen to music till late at night. They are both hard of hearing, so the noise is very loud and it keeps you awake. (OR: Let's say you have moved into a new room in the hostel in which you live. The new room is located next to the social lounge, where residents watch TV, play cards, and chat until late at night because they have difficulty sleeping.) You have hesitated to say anything because you get on well with the couple (residents) and you can sympathize with their plight, but you are suffering from loss of sleep. What can you do?

The women in Collins et al.'s study were all older, but the greater their chronological age, the less ideal their solutions. Contrary to what Collins et al. expected, the familiarity of the problem context (community versus nursing hostel) offered neither an advantage nor a disadvantage to the community-living or the nursing hostel groups, respectively. Overall, the community-living women were more relativistic in their problem solutions than the nursing hostel women. However, we cannot conclude that living in the more independent community environment is a direct cause of more relativistic problem solving because the community-living group was somewhat younger chronologically. In any case, the findings of this study provide insight into how older adults say they would approach interpersonal problems that could occur in either living situation.

Decision Making

In the everyday world, we must often make decisions using whatever information is available. What role does age play in the information-seeking and reasoning processes that people use? Do adults of all ages take the same amount of time to make a decision, and is the final decision reached any different for young and older adults?

Decision Making in a Health Context

In general, health-related issues become increasingly important in older adulthood, and as we grow older, we must make important decisions regarding our physical well-being. In selecting a physician, a health-care plan, or a treatment option, we must weigh the potential risks and benefits.

To investigate age-related differences in information acquisition and recall in the realm of health care, Löckenhoff and Carstensen (2007) asked younger and older adults to select a physician and a health plan from four choices. Each of the four physician and health plan alternatives was associated with opportunities to review positive (good), neutral (average), and negative (poor) information. Compared to the younger adults, the older adults reviewed more positive information than negative information before making a choice and also recalled more positive than negative information about the physician or health plan they selected. This age-related **positivity effect** has been noted in a variety of decision making situations (see Kennedy & Mather, 2007), but in this study the positivity effect disappeared when older adults were instructed both before and while reviewing all the choices to "focus on specific facts and details." In short, when older adults are left to their own devices, they focus more on positive than on negative information (Carstensen, Mikels, & Mather, 2006). However, Löckenhoff and Carstensen were able to modify older adults' processing strategy by directing their attention to the total array of facts. In this study, the overall quality of the four options (for both physicians and health plans) was equal, but in the real world that may not be the case. To make optimal decisions, medical and otherwise, it is important to review all aspects of each alternative. Older adults need more structure and guidance that encourages them to take into account not only the positive but also the problematic aspects of each one.

Cancer

Occurrences of cancer are not uncommon in middle and older adulthood and advancing age is a clear risk factor. Cancer of the breast and prostate are the types most frequently diagnosed in women and men, respectively, and for both there is usually more than one treatment alternative. In modern medical practice, it is becoming the norm for patients to play a role in the decision when more than one treatment intervention is available. This sharing of responsibility between physicians and patients contrasts with the older and more traditional practice of treatment decisions being made solely by the physician. Participating in treatment decisions seems to have beneficial effects for patients (Davison, Kirk, Degner, & Hassard, 1999; Zwahr, Park, & Shifren, 1999).

Meyer, Russo, and Talbot (1995) studied women's decision making process when choosing between treatment options for breast cancer. Women (aged 18 to 88) with no personal history of cancer themselves read an authentic case history in which a lump was discovered in a woman's breast. Various treatment options were described, each one justified by some data and expert opinion. In selecting a treatment, these women could use a **bottom-up processing strategy** (collecting and integrating new information) or a **top-down processing strategy** (relying on prior knowledge and experience). The top-down strategy is less cognitively demanding, although it can be effective if the information in storage is accurate and relevant to the decision at hand. However, it is often preferable to collect some new information and integrate it with what is already in the knowledge store. Compared to the older women, the younger women engaged more in bottom-up processing, making more comparisons between treatment options before reaching a final decision. In contrast, the older women relied more on top-down processing, seeking less information and making their final decision more quickly. Many older women said they did not want to delay the decision because it was important to get treatment before the cancer had time to spread. However, reliance on top-down processing could also be a way to compensate for reduced cognitive capacity because cognitive demands are lower if no new information is sought or integrated. This same pattern was found in the decision making strategies of women who had actually been diagnosed with breast cancer themselves within the previous 3 years. As with the older women who only read a case scenario, these older patients sought less information on treatment options and took less time to make a treatment decision than the younger patients.

Meyer, Talbot, and Ranalli (2007) found a similar pattern of decision making among men who had to select a treatment for prostate cancer. They asked men (aged 20 to 87 years) to read a hypothetical scenario about a 60-year-old man with a potential or actual prostate cancer diagnosis. As with women's decisions about breast cancer treatment, the older men made more immediate decisions than the young and middle-aged men. The older men's readiness to reach a decision about prostate cancer was attributed in part to their greater knowledge about the disease. However, Meyer et al. (2007) found that both men and women with more cognitive resources (that is, higher vocabulary and working memory scores) tended to delay their treatment decisions, whereas those with fewer cognitive resources made more immediate decisions.

In sum, older women and men may seek less information before making a treatment decision about breast and prostate cancer, respectively, and they often make decisions more quickly than their younger counterparts. Meyer et al. (1995, 2007) recommend that health-care providers be aware that some older adults may not consider the array of treatments available before they make a final decision.

When people are diagnosed with a disease such as cancer, what sources do they turn to for information about their medical condition? Turk-Charles, Meyerowitz, and Gatz (1997) recruited men and women from an outpatient oncology clinic, most of whom were European Americans aged 18 to 81, and all of whom had been diagnosed and treated for various types of cancer within the past 3 years. There were no age-related differences in these patients' inclination to seek information about their diagnosis. However, the older patients sought a smaller portion of their information from the medical establishment (doctors

Applying Research Box 7.1: Framing Effects in Medical Decisions

Framing effects refer to a phenomenon whereby the decisions people make are influenced by the language used to describe the available options. With regard to cancer treatment, survival statistics associated with various treatments can be framed positively or negatively. Kim, Goldstein, Hasher, and Zacks (2005) asked young and older adults to select which of two cancer treatments they would prefer. The statistics regarding each treatment were presented using a positive frame – for example, "Of 100 people having Treatment A, 90 will survive during treatment, 68 will survive by 1 year and 34 will survive by 5 years"; "Of 100 people having Treatment B, 100 will survive during treatment; 77 will survive by 1 year and 22 will survive by 5 years" –

OR using a negative frame – for example, "Of 100 people having Treatment A, 10 will die during treatment; 32 will have died by 1 year and 66 will have died by 5 years"; "Of 100 people having Treatment B, none will die during treatment; 23 will die by 1 year and 78 will die by 5 years." Older adults were more susceptible than young adults to the framing effect – they focused more on short-term survival with the negative frame but on long-term survival with the positive frame. Interestingly, however, when the older adults were required to justify their selection, they were less vulnerable to framing effects, which indicates that they are capable of basing their decision on objective facts rather than on how the facts are worded.

and nurses) and a larger portion from nonmedical sources (newspapers, television, and friends). Perhaps the older patients had more friends with similar diagnoses with whom they could consult. Also, older adults may feel more deference toward health professionals and consider it impolite to ask for additional information. Health professionals should be aware that older adults may be reluctant to ask for information unless they are encouraged to do so.

Within the past decade, more people have been using the Internet to obtain information on diseases. Further study could determine the extent to which young and older adults use this source, and also how well they discriminate between information that is objective and information that is not.

Long-term care

As discussed earlier, many older adults plan for a time when they may experience some loss of independence. Harold and Hazel, the couple described at the beginning of the chapter, are contemplating this possibility. In the oldest-old group (85+ years), some people may require care that can be offered only in assisted-living facilities or nursing homes. Many older adults and their families seek the advice of health professionals when making decisions about long-term care. However, the judgments and recommendations of such experts may not be completely unbiased and can be influenced by their professional background (Kane, Bershadksy, & Bershadsky, 2006).

To fill the potential need for services and care, many insurance companies are offering long-term care (LTC) policies. In exchange for a yearly premium, such policies provide financial benefits for nursing home stays. Some policies also cover the expense of assisted-living facilities, or even home health-care benefits if older adults want to remain in their own homes but need help. LTC policies vary widely in price and specific benefits offered. Whether to purchase such a policy, and if so which one, is a complex decision many middle-aged and older Americans face. A decision about whether to purchase an LTC policy should be based on a variety of factors. Each individual or couple must consider personal health risks and projected financial situation. Social factors also enter into the decision. For example, will family members be available if care and assistance become necessary? Furthermore, the decision to purchase an LTC policy should take into account the financial soundness of the company selling it. As such, some aspects of the decision to purchase long-term care insurance fall into the consumer category, which the following section discusses further.

Decision Making in a Consumer Context

Many of our decisions involve which items to buy. The discerning consumer decides about large purchases only after considerable thought about cost, quality, and potential satisfaction with a product that will be used for a long time. Are decision processes any different for young and older adults?

Johnson (1990) examined how young adult college students and older retirees would make a decision about which car to purchase. Using a computer, study participants could access comparative information (fuel economy, riding comfort, maintenance cost, safety record, styling, purchase price, resale value) on six cars, so Johnson was able to trace the search strategies they used as they tried to make a decision. Overall, the young and older adults took approximately the same amount of time to reach a final decision about which car to purchase. However, the older retirees viewed fewer pieces of information about the cars and spent more time than young students on each one. In contrast, the young college students viewed more pieces of information but spent less time than the older retirees on each one. Johnson concluded that the older retirees had a greater tendency to use **noncompensatory decision rules**, meaning that they eliminated alternatives after an incomplete search. In contrast, the young students used **compensatory decision rules**, which entail summing, weighing, and averaging all possible alternatives prior to making a decision. Compensatory decision rules pose heavier cognitive processing demands than noncompensatory decision rules. Johnson hypothesized that decisions such as what car to purchase may be only moderately difficult for young adults but could present a cognitive challenge for older adults. However, it is also possible that greater experience with purchasing cars led the older adults to focus on a smaller array of facts prior to making a selection. Further study is certainly warranted to clarify how young and older adults reach important consumer decisions.

Decision Making in a Legal Context

In civil trials, the lawyer for the plaintiff and the lawyer for the defendant present evidence to a panel of jurors. Afterward, jurors must make a decision about the liability of the defendant that is consistent with the evidence and also with legal principles. If the defendant is found liable, a further decision must be made about how the defendant will compensate the plaintiff.

Fitzgerald (2000) compared the decision making processes of young adult (aged 19 to 35) and older adult (aged 55 to 75) mock jurors who were similar in level of education, ethnic background, and socioeconomic status. These mock jurors viewed one of two versions of a two-hour video of a civil trial in which four plaintiffs were claiming that a large corporation (the defendant) had allowed a chemical to leach into the local groundwater. Information in the video favored the plaintiffs, who varied in the extent of the injuries they were claiming (exposure to illnesses and economic damages from tainted farm property and polluted water supply). The two versions of the video were identical except for the timing of the judge's instructions to the jurors explaining legal concepts such as "liability" and "compensatory damages." Half the mock jurors in each age group heard a version in which the judge's instructions were at the standard time, right after the opening arguments and liability evidence were presented. The other half in each age group heard a version in which jurors were "preinstructed" – that is, the judge gave instructions before the opening arguments and liability evidence were presented.

Mock jurors in both age groups benefited from preinstruction – after viewing the video, they gave more detailed and more cohesive accounts of the evidence that was presented. However, the older mock jurors benefited especially from the preinstruction: When asked to explain how they reached their liability decision, they gave more probative statements than evaluative statements. Probative statements are based on evidence and thus considered more appropriate in jury decision making than evaluative statements. In contrast, older jurors instructed at the standard time gave more evaluative statements (expressions of opinion about witnesses, attorneys, or plaintiffs). Moreover, the older mock jurors who were preinstructed made more appropriate distinctions between the most injured and least injured plaintiffs with regard to compensation awards.

Why did older mock jurors benefit more from preinstruction? Older adults depend more than young adults on using knowledge structures as a scaffold upon which to organize incoming information (Bransford & Johnson, 1972). With instructions given before incoming information, a scaffolding structure is in place to guide processing and thus minimize cognitive demands.

In sum, structure is especially helpful to older adults who are engaged in decision making. Also, older adults may need some encouragement to consider the full array of alternatives before making a final decision.

Social Cognition

Social cognition has to do with how we process social information. Such processing is influenced by our cognitive representations, or **schemas.** We all have schemas about ourselves (Chapter 8 covers self-concept – how schemas about the self are formed, maintained, and revised). But schemas also influence how we form impressions of other people, interpret their behavior, and appraise social dilemmas (Blanchard-Fields, 1999; Blanchard-Fields & Abeles, 1996). Do young and older adults have different preexisting schemas, and can their schemas be modified?

Impression Formation

Individuals ("perceivers") form impressions of other people ("targets") whom they encounter in everyday life. Such impressions guide how individuals interact with others and ultimately how they adapt to the social world.

Perceivers use two types of cognitive operations when forming impressions about targets (Cuddy & Fiske, 2002; Hess, 1999). **Category-based operations** rely on previously formed schemas. Thus, once a target is identified as a member of a certain category (for example, college professor), perceivers base their impression of that target on the schema they already have about the characteristics of college professors (for example, scholarly, absentminded, and so on). Category-based operations are similar to top-down processing, which was described earlier. An advantage of category-based operations is that they are efficient and place minimal demand on the perceiver's cognitive resources. A possible disadvantage is that a schema that might have been useful in the past may not be appropriate in a new situation. When perceivers rely exclusively on category-based operations, they do not pay full attention to detailed information about a specific target or situation.

In contrast to category-based operations, perceivers also use **piecemeal operations**, which are akin to bottom-up processing. With piecemeal operations, perceivers construct a unique and possibly a more accurate representation of a target by integrating individual items of information (such as physical characteristics, specific behaviors, stated likes and dislikes, motivations, and goals). Piecemeal operations require active processing of detailed information, so they consume more cognitive resources than category-based operations.

If there are age-related limitations in cognitive resources, then older perceivers may make less use of piecemeal operations when forming impressions of others and rely more on category-based operations. However, older adults may have less need for piecemeal operations because they come to social situations with extensive knowledge and experience that they can use when making judgments about others.

Causal Attributions

How do people interpret what caused the social events they encounter in everyday life? Do young and older perceivers make similar causal attributions for why

Understanding Aging Box 7.1: Trait Diagnosticity

When we form impressions of other people, which of their behaviors are especially telling when we are trying to determine whether they possess a particular personal characteristic, or trait? According to Hess and his colleagues (Hess, 1999; Hess & Auman, 2001; Hess, Bolstad, Woodburn, & Auman, 1999), behaviors that are especially informative about a particular trait are high in **trait diagnosticity**, but behaviors that carry less information about a particular trait are low in trait diagnosticity. For example, in the United States, getting good grades (a positive behavior) is high in diagnosticity for the trait of competence; perceivers think targets who make high grades in a calculus course are high in mathematical ability. On the other hand, a poor grade in calculus (a negative behavior) is not high in diagnosticity for inferring poor mathematical competence because perceivers may think a target earned the poor grade because he or she did not study enough. For the trait of morality, negative behaviors are more diagnostic than positive ones. Targets who steal money (a negative behavior) are considered dis-

honest, so stealing is high in diagnosticity for inferring low morality. In contrast, honest acts are not high in trait diagnosticity for morality, possibly because a target's motivation for performing such acts is not always clear (a target may behave in an honest way simply because he or she fears the consequences of stealing).

With increasing age, perceivers place greater emphasis on the diagnostic value of a target's behaviors. After reading a brief description of a target that includes information about behaviors high in trait diagnosticity, older perceivers are more likely than young perceivers to maintain the impression they form about the target's traits even when, later, they are given additional information that is low in trait diagnosticity. Older perceivers' greater reliance on information high in trait diagnosticity may signify an age-related increase in social expertise – the ability to focus on aspects of behavior that are more informative as opposed to less informative when making inferences about a target's traits. This ability could represent adaptive functioning in the society or culture in which older perceivers live.

these events occurred? These questions are significant because perceivers' causal attributions give us clues about how they view social reality and how they might deal with real-life social dilemmas.

One factor that influences a perceiver's appraisal of a social dilemma is the schema he or she brings to the situation. Such a schema is probably shaped by prior encounters in similar situations, and the nature of prior experience could be a function of a perceiver's chronological age or cohort membership. In addition, a schema is influenced by the culture, or society, in which a perceiver lives.

A popular approach to investigating social reasoning is to present perceivers with a brief sketch, or vignette, about a target who faces a dilemma or has experienced a particular social outcome. Perceivers are instructed to make attributions for what caused the dilemma or outcome. Blanchard-Fields (1996) offers the following example:

> Allen had been dating Barbara for over a year. At Barbara's suggestion, they moved in together. Everyone kept asking when they were going to get married. Allen

found it extremely uncomfortable to live with Barbara and not be married to her. Even though Barbara disagreed, Allen kept bringing up the issue of marriage. Eventually, they broke up.

Perceivers' causal attributions could be dispositional, situational, or interactive. **Dispositional attributions** put responsibility for the breakup entirely on the personal characteristics of the individuals involved (for example, Allen was impatient or rigid, or Barbara was immature or lacked commitment to Allen). Alternatively, **situational attributions** place the responsibility for the breakup on external extenuating circumstances (for example, the reaction of families, friends, or society in general to Allen and Barbara's living together without marriage). **Interactive attributions** take both dispositional and situational factors into account rather than attributing the outcome entirely to one or the other. Interactive attributions represent a more compromising view and seem to be more common in Asian than in Western cultures (Peng & Nisbett, 1999). Even within Western culture, however, age or cohort membership could make a difference in the attributions people make. For example, today's older adult cohort is less likely than today's young adult cohort to have lived as couples without marriage, and the different experiences of these cohort groups might influence their attributions for Allen and Barbara's breakup.

One hypothesis is that, compared to young perceivers, older perceivers will make more interactive attributions because their maturity and years of experience render them more open to considering multiple perspectives (similar to the perspective-taking aspect of postformal thinking or perhaps wisdom). But do older adults actually make more interactive attributions than young adults? In one study (Blanchard-Fields, 1994), older adults made more interactive attributions (thinking an outcome is caused by both the main character and the situation) than young adults when the vignettes they read described dilemmas about relationships but not when dilemmas were related to achievement (such as a college student's receiving a failing grade in a course). Apparently, there is no set rule that older adults make more interactive attributions than young adults – it all depends on what they are evaluating. In addition, the age of the character in the vignette, as well as how closely the character's dilemma is related to the perceiver's life, could influence the attributions made (Blanchard-Fields, Baldi, & Stein, 1999).

When making attributions for the social outcomes of others, perceivers often overemphasize dispositional factors (such as the target's characteristics) and underemphasize the possible influence of situational factors. For example, when told that a target earned a poor grade in a course, perceivers attribute this negative outcome to the target's poor ability rather than to the possibility that the exam was unfair. This bias, called the **fundamental attribution error** (Gilbert & Malone, 1995; Jones, 1979; Ross, 1977), is especially apparent when perceivers have minimal specific information and when the outcome of an event is negative rather than positive (Blanchard-Fields, 1994). Evidence for the fundamental attribution error has been found mainly in individualistic cultures in North America and Europe. It is less frequent in the more collectivist East Asian cultures, many of which foster a strong belief that individuals should always be considered within the context of their particular situation (Choi, Nisbett, & Norenzayan, 1999).

Most research on the fundamental attribution error has been conducted with young adult perceivers, but do middle-aged and older perceivers also show this bias? In one study (Blanchard-Fields, 1994), young, middle-aged, and older adult perceivers read brief vignettes, each describing a scenario in which a target experiences either a negative or a positive social outcome in a relationship situation or an achievement situation. In all of the vignettes, the factors that actually caused the event were ambiguous. When the outcome was negative, the older perceivers had an even greater tendency than the young and middle-aged perceivers to commit the fundamental attribution error, overattributing the target's negative outcome to dispositional factors. However, the age of the target described in the vignette made a difference – perceivers of all ages made higher dispositional attributions for young targets but higher situational attributions for old targets. Also, dispositional attributions were higher if the event took place in a work context, whereas situational attributions were higher if the event took place in a family context (Blanchard-Fields et al., 1999).

In sum, conclusions about age-related differences in causal attributions and the fundamental attribution error must be qualified by the context in which attributions are made (relationship, family, achievement, work), by whether the outcome is positive or negative, and by the age of the target in the vignette.

Moral Reasoning

In many instances, we find ourselves making judgments about the "rightness" or "wrongness" of the choices made or actions taken by others (Pratt & Norris, 1994). For example, if a person is caught stealing, most of us would consider it wrong and we would have a low opinion of that individual's morality. But are there some circumstances under which we might consider stealing to be morally acceptable? Consider the following scenario, which was one of several hypothetical dilemmas Kohlberg (1969) used to study moral reasoning:

> A druggist insists on charging a premium amount for a medication that will save a woman's life. The woman's husband is unable to borrow enough money to purchase the medication, so he breaks into the pharmacy and steals the medicine.

What reasoning do people use to determine whether it was right or wrong for the husband to behave the way he did? Kohlberg (1969) proposed a three-level cognitive-developmental framework for evaluating moral reasoning, or moral maturity. On the basis of their responses to hypothetical moral dilemmas (like the one described above), individuals are assigned scores that indicate their level of moral maturity.

Level 1   *Preconventional morality* (typical of children ages 4–10): Moral judgments are made with an eye to obtaining a reward or avoiding punishment.

Level 2   *Conventional morality* (commencing some time after the age of 10): Moral judgments are made on the basis of pleasing others, being "nice," "good," doing one's duty and what is expected, and maintaining the social order.

Level 3   *Postconventional morality* (commencing in adolescence or young adulthood, but not necessarily reached by everyone): Morality is fully internalized. Moral judgments are based on abstract ethical principles as opposed to concrete rules, with the recognition that conflict may exist between the laws and expectations of society and universal ethical principles such as justice, compassion, and equality.

Kohlberg's ideas are widely respected, but his levels were devised within Western culture and may not address culturally based differences in moral values. Also, Kohlberg conducted his studies chiefly with boys and men, and Gilligan (1982) questioned whether Kohlberg's framework is applicable to women. For example, men might think in terms of justice, whereas women might focus more on preserving and enhancing relationships (Pratt & Norris, 1994).

Chap (1986) asked younger (aged 30–49) and older (aged 63–85) men and woman from the metropolitan Washington, DC area to give open-ended responses to several moral dilemmas. The content of some of the dilemmas was age-appropriate for the younger group, while that of other dilemmas was age-appropriate for the older group. The following are examples:

Age-appropriate dilemma for the young/early-middle-aged group: A woman considers lying in a child custody hearing about her husband's suitability as a parent to ensure that she will gain custody.

Age-appropriate dilemma for the older group: A 70-year-old man living on a fixed income occasionally shoplifts a few dollars' worth of food to make ends meet.

Based on their responses, participants got a score for their level of moral maturity that was based on Kohlberg's framework. When scores were adjusted for level of education, no gender or age differences were found. However, the age appropriateness of the dilemma was significant – participants received higher moral maturity scores for their responses to dilemmas that were relevant to their own age group.

In addition to level of moral maturity, Chap (1986) investigated **moral perspective taking**, which is the inclination to consider a moral dilemma from various perspectives. Table 7.2 describes four levels of moral perspective taking. At the lowest level, responses focus on one point of view and discount all others. At the highest level, responses show recognition that there can be several points of view.

Table 7.2 *Four levels of moral perspective taking*

Level 1	Only a single point of view is considered, with no acknowledgment that other points of view could or do exist.
Level 2	Several points of view are acknowledged, but no attempt is made to reconcile them, or to recommend that one character in the dilemma try to understand another character's point of view.
Level 3	Two or more points of view are considered, and it is recommended that one character in the dilemma try to understand another's point of view (but not vice versa).
Level 4	Two or more points of view are considered, as in Level 3, but there is acknowledgment of reciprocity between the competing points of view.

Adapted from Chap (1986).

The young and older adults in Chap's study differed in their level of moral perspective taking. The older group was less likely than the younger group to consider the perspective of all the characters involved in the dilemma; instead, they tended to voice the opinion that there was only one correct point of view.

To determine whether the level of moral maturity and moral perspective taking remain constant over time, or whether there is a regression to a lower level, Pratt, Diessner, Pratt, Hunsberger, and Pancer (1996) followed middle-aged (35–54) and older (64–80) adults over 4 years. At the outset, and again 4 years later, participants responded to descriptions of moral dilemmas. These researchers used the same measures as Chap (1986) did to assess participants' level of moral maturity and moral perspective taking.

Pratt et al.'s longitudinal results reflect Chap's cross-sectional findings. Over the 4-year period, the level of moral maturity did not change for either age group. However, there were small changes in the older group's level of perspective taking. Both age groups started out with an average of 2.5 on the 4-level perspective-taking scale. By the end of the study, the middle-aged group's perspective-taking level remained unchanged, whereas the older group's level declined to an average of 2.0.

Because Pratt et al.'s participants were relatively well-educated residents of a moderate-sized metropolitan area in eastern Canada, they were not broadly representative of the general population of North American adults. However, even within this relatively select sample, Pratt et al. found that "resource" variables (level of education, self-reported health at the study's start, and perceived social support from others) seemed to protect against decline in levels of moral maturity and moral perspective taking. In both age groups, participants who had the highest level of education, considered themselves most healthy, and reported the greatest access to social support were the ones most likely to maintain their level of moral maturity over the 4-year interval. The resource variables also served a protective function with regard to perspective taking, although there was still some decline in the older group over the 4 years. Perhaps the decline in perspective taking reflects a strategic attempt on the part of the older adults to minimize cognitive overload as they deliberate about moral issues.

Collaboration in Reasoning and Problem Solving

In **collaborative cognitive activities**, more than one individual performs a common task with a common goal (Dixon, 1999). Researchers have a great deal of interest in the utility of collaboration when real-life decisions are necessary (Dixon & Gould, 1996, 1998). By its very nature, collaborative cognition has a social element.

Just as scientists may collaborate to find a solution to an abstract problem in a research laboratory, so individuals may collaborate to find optimal solutions to the logistical problems of everyday life. Consider a married couple, Martha and Jack. Martha has been a homemaker throughout her 40-year marriage to Jack. She has had complete charge of shopping, cooking, and other household chores, while Jack held a full-time job. Their collaboration has been based on a strict division of labor. Recently, Jack retired and now he wants to become involved in the shopping and household tasks. Martha and Jack will need to restructure their daily lives, forging a mutually agreeable solution as to who will do what. Likewise, Harold and Hazel (the couple described at the beginning of the chapter) must collaborate to forge a plan for changing their lifestyle. In these examples, the collaborators are married couples. However, collaborative problem solving is not limited to marital relationships or to just two people working together.

When solving a real-life problem, how extensively do older adults consult with others? The problems they face could range from selecting a new shade of paint for a room in the house to deciding how to distribute possessions to relatives or friends when downsizing from a large home to an apartment or assisted-living facility. Clearly, some decisions have more social and emotional implications than others, but all decisions involve choices. Ideally, collaborative decisions are reached with input from all involved. However, in interactions between older mothers and their adult children regarding caregiving decisions, the adult child (particularly sons) often dominates and the older mother plays a subordinate role, deferring to the adult child's suggestions (Cicirelli, 2006). When interactions are not balanced, the outcome is less likely to be satisfactory (Chapter 9 discusses the importance of balance in social interactions).

In general, individuals who consult with others before making final decisions tend to think about problems in more complex ways, possibly because consulting with others encourages them to consider a situation from more than one perspective. Harold and Hazel, described earlier, think their sons might offer suggestions that will help them come to a decision. Those who seek out advice, support, and validation from others whom they trust are likely to enjoy greater satisfaction once a solution has been reached. True collaboration is associated with increased quality of reasoning about everyday problems and dilemmas and ultimately with a more positive outcome. Perhaps collaboration can compensate for any age-related decline in reasoning abilities experienced by the individuals involved.

Emotion and Cognition

Historically, aging researchers viewed emotion and cognition as two separate domains (Carstensen et al., 2006), but more recently, emotion and cognition are considered to be interrelated (Labouvie-Vief, 2003; Labouvie-Vief & Diehl, 2000). Thus, they affect one another in ways that depend upon cultural background, age, and cohort factors. The relationship between emotion and cognition has special relevance when social information is processed.

Blanchard-Fields and her colleagues (Blanchard-Fields, Jahnke, & Camp, 1995; Blanchard-Fields, Mienaltowski, & Seay, 2007; Blanchard-Fields & Norris, 1994) investigated the strategies that individuals of various ages say they would use to resolve dilemmas that were either low or high in emotional significance. Dilemmas low in emotional significance described instrumental problems that occur in everyday life. For example, what would you do if you found that some merchandise you had purchased was defective? Dilemmas high in emotional significance described problems that occur in interpersonal situations. For example, how would you handle conflicts with coworkers, friends, or family members? Solutions that the study participants gave for dealing with the dilemmas fell into the following categories:

Problem-focused strategies	Taking direct action to control, or "fix," the problem
Cognitive-analytic strategies	Trying to solve the problem by thinking it through logically
Passive-dependent strategies	Attempting to withdraw from the situation or relying on others to solve it
Avoidant strategies	Denying the problem or attempting to reinterpret its meaning, suppressing any emotions evoked

For dilemmas low in emotional significance, participants of all ages most frequently endorsed problem-focused strategies. However, middle-aged and older adults were even more likely than adolescents and young adults to say they would use problem-focused strategies such as taking defective merchandise back to the store. Also, middle-aged and older adults engaged in extensive cognitive-analytical analyses of the dilemmas, indicating that they are capable of using complex strategies most likely honed by years of experience.

For dilemmas high in emotional significance, problem-focused strategies were less likely to be endorsed by participants of all ages, but this was especially true for older adults: Older adults were even less likely than younger adults to say they would confront an interpersonal situation directly. Instead, older adults tended to endorse passive-dependent and avoidant strategies, indicating they are less willing to confront such dilemmas head-on. The fact that older adults are more willing to avoid, or passively accept, an interpersonal dilemma could mean that they are more accepting of ambiguity and uncertainty in emotionally laden situations (Blanchard-Fields, 1997). It could also mean that they use greater emotional control, avoiding conflict, stressors, and negativity when relating to others (Magai & Passman, 1997). In some sense, older people seem to be better at picking their battles than younger people (Birditt, Fingerman, & Almeida, 2005). When there is interpersonal conflict, young adults are more likely than older adults to argue and yell. In contrast, older adults often elect to do nothing and to wait and see if things improve. Either older adults feel less negative emotion or they are better able to regulate their behavioral reactions when there is tension. In a recent study on electrophysiological responses to emotionally valenced images (Kisley, Wood, & Burrows, 2007), older adults were less reactive than younger adults to negative images but no different from younger adults in their reactions to positive images. This suggests there may be an age-related reduction in responsiveness to negative information.

Labouvie-Vief (1997, 1999) contends that older adults are less likely than young adults to engage in impulsive behavior such as hostile acting out or turning against others. Rather, they tend to reinterpret negative situations, avoid conflict, and accept negative events. These strategies may screen out negative experiences, thereby reducing the complexity of any emotional conflict. It is possible that when there is interpersonal conflict, older adults adapt to restrictions in cognitive and emotional resources by becoming less confrontational and more self-protective. Their well-regulated behavior may allow them to maintain a tolerable level of emotional arousal (Blanchard-Fields, 2007).

Most research on emotion and aging has been cross-sectional, so older adults' tendency to avoid negative conflicts in interpersonal relationships could reflect how their generation was socialized (Labouvie-Vief, 1999). Clearly, we need longitudinal studies following the same people over time to determine whether there are age-related changes in emotional regulation.

Revisiting the Selective Optimization with Compensation and Ecological Models

The Selective Optimization with Compensation (SOC) (Baltes & Baltes, 1990) and Ecological (Lawton, 1989; Lawton & Nahemow, 1973) Models are two theoretical frameworks within which we can consider how older adults engage in everyday problem solving.

The SOC Model is useful for considering how older adults use cognitive processes in the everyday world and what strategies they employ when solving problems, making creative contributions, making decisions, and forming impressions. Older adults may direct their cognitive efforts toward concerns that are most meaningful for their particular stage of life. They may rely more heavily than young adults on top-down, or category-based, processing as opposed to bottom-up, or piecemeal, processing. This could reflect a way of compensating for limitations in cognitive capability. However, with their accumulated wealth of experience, older adults may be less dependent than young adults on piecemeal processing of details. Given their expertise in some areas of decision making and impression formation, top-down strategies may serve them well, limiting their need to reinvent the wheel each time a new problem must be resolved or a new decision made. In their creative endeavors, older adults may place greater value on the simplification and synthesis of ideas as opposed to making complex, novel contributions.

The Ecological Model is a framework for determining which environments are likely to foster the highest level of adaptive functioning for older adults. If older adults make final decisions without considering all the alternatives, they may benefit from having an array of alternatives introduced in a structured and organized manner. To adapt to new environments, older adults may need to make use of tacit knowledge gathered from the actions and indirect statements of others. If older adults are hesitant to confront highly emotional situations, they may adapt best in environments where they are not forced to do so.

? Questions to Consider

1. If you wanted to seek advice about a career or a personal relationship, who would you be most likely to consult?
2. If you were asked by two friends who disagree to determine which of them is right, how would you proceed?
3. If you heard that someone you knew lost his or her job but you knew very little about the details of the situation, what attribution would you make for why this happened?

Key Points

- Motivations for using cognitive capabilities differ across the life span. In older adulthood, motivations are reorganizational, reintegrative, and legacy-creating.
- Postformal reasoning calls for perspective taking and is well suited for real-life interpersonal problems that have more than one correct solution. Many older adults think postformally but there are mixed findings as to whether older adults use this type of thinking more than young adults.

- Wisdom is associated with perspective taking. It involves knowing what one does not know, and maintaining a balance between reflection and action. Some older adults are wise, but old age does not guarantee wisdom.

- Practical intelligence is "knowing how" rather than "knowing what." Relatedly, tacit knowledge, which must be inferred from actions and indirect statements, could help older adults adapt to new environments.

- Some creative contributions peak in mid-life, but there can be a resurgence later on. Creative works of older musicians, artists, and writers show simplicity of style and integration of ideas, and often there is an emphasis on subjective experience.

- Real-world decisions are made in many contexts, including health, consumer, and legal. Older adults weigh fewer alternatives than young adults before reaching a decision. Also, older adults use top-down strategies more, while young adults use bottom-up strategies more. In addition older adults focus disproportionately on positive information.

- When forming impressions of other people, older adults rely more than young adults on behaviors high in trait diagnosticity. Older adults seem to have a heightened ability to detect aspects of behavior that are most informative.

- Causal attributions for a social outcome can be dispositional, situational, or interactive. Whether there are age-related differences in a particular type of causal attribution depends upon a number of factors, including the context in which the outcome occurs.

- For dilemmas that are not emotional, adults of all ages prefer a problem-focused strategy, confronting the situation directly. For interpersonal emotional dilemmas, older adults tend to avoid, reinterpret, or passively accept the situation.

Key Terms

8 Personality and Coping

Chapter Overview

Close-ups on Adulthood and Aging

Ever since she turned 75, Bernice has found herself thinking back over her life and reviewing the choices she made that determined what path it would take. Even as a teenager, she was more interested in fashion than she was in book learning. At a very young age, she married a man with strong business skills and, for many years, the two of them operated a highly successful women's clothing store. She handled the customers, helping them select outfits that would be flattering, and her husband kept the books. So it seems fitting that, even though she is now retired, her friends and neighbors constantly seek out her fashion advice. Bernice does her best to keep abreast of clothing styles that will enhance her appearance. She realizes some changes that come with age are inevitable and her appearance is not the same as it was 25 years ago. Overall, however, she thinks she is faring better than most women her age. Bernice is certain that she will maintain her interest in fashion although modified to fit her age and stage of life.

Studying Personality in Aging and Older Adulthood

Most of us make judgments about what other people are like by how they behave. For example, a person who is friendly and approachable would be viewed as outgoing, or extraverted, whereas a person who is quiet and shy would not. Ideally, our inferences about someone's personality are based on observations of that person's behavior on a number of occasions and not behavior that occurs only once.

Another aspect of personality is how we view ourselves. What is important to us? What is distasteful? What opinions do we have about various issues? In short, what is our own theory about who we are? In some instances, the way others view us corresponds with how we view our inner self. However, there are exceptions. For example, a person who is viewed as hard-nosed by others because of his or her behavior as a manager at work may perceive him- or herself as tender-hearted and showing concern for employees by being strict.

In sum, personality is a complex construct (Hall, Lindzey, & Campbell, 1998). It has to do with how we view others, how they view us, and how we view ourselves. The way people act conveys information about what they are like. However, personality also has an inner aspect because it relates to how we see ourselves, and our inner thoughts and feelings are not always reflected in our immediate behavior.

Approaches to Investigating Personality

What approaches are used to investigate personality development in the field of adult development and aging? As discussed in Chapter 2, the developmental aspects of personality can be studied using a cross-sectional research design, comparing the personality characteristics of individuals in two or more age groups. To illustrate, if we compare 20-year-olds with 70-year-olds at the same point in time, we may find that these two age groups differ in some aspects of personality. This difference could be associated with differing chronological ages, but it could also be a function of the fact that the two age groups come from different cohorts.

Another way to study the developmental aspects of personality is to follow the same individuals over time. This longitudinal design can detect changes within each person. However, there may be selective attrition – participants who drop out of the study may have different personality characteristics compared with those who remain. For example, those who drop out may not be as dependable or as well adjusted as those willing to be retested.

Personality Over the Adult Years

Does personality undergo change with increasing age, and are some aspects of personality more dominant at one stage of life than at another? Fleeson and

Heckhausen (1997) contend that early adulthood is a time of exploration, striving for growth, self-actualization, and mastery of new roles. Middle adulthood is a time of productivity and gains in the ability to deal competently and confidently with the world through experience. In older adulthood, there is less striving for competency and a greater tendency to reflect, hopefully with satisfaction and contentment, on what has been accomplished in life.

Some personality characteristics may be more common in a particular age group, but no two people are exactly alike. Within any age group, there are individual differences. For example, some people are more contemplative and thoughtful while others are more impatient, daring, and willing to take risks. However, a fundamental question is: "What personality characteristics are typical of individuals who age successfully?" How individuals cope with challenges encountered over the course of adulthood, and individual differences in the ability to maintain a positive outlook and achieve happiness, are of great interest to aging researchers.

How Is Personality Measured?

How do we measure personality? One way would be to ask individuals to describe themselves. A less direct approach would be to ask them to respond to ambiguous visual or verbal stimuli in the hope that what they say will tell us something about what they are like. Yet another approach would be to observe how individuals behave either in completely naturalistic settings or under more carefully controlled conditions. Regardless, personality measures should be both reliable and valid (see Chapter 2 for detailed explanation of these concepts). Now let's take a closer look at these three ways of measuring personality.

Self-Report Questionnaires

Personality inventories are self-report measures consisting of questions test takers answer about themselves. On some questionnaires, test takers are instructed to agree or disagree with a series of statements. For example, "I always want to be with other people and I never want to be alone" would be a statement with which an outgoing person would agree but a shy person may not. On some self-report questionnaires, test takers are given a list of traits (for example, "talkative" or "quiet") and told to check the ones that describe them or rate how much each trait describes them (such as "not at all," "a little," or "very much"). Some personality inventories have norms based on the responses of a large sample of individuals who completed the inventory previously. Responses of an individual test taker can be compared with those of the larger standardization sample.

Self-report questionnaires can be written or oral, but an advantage of written inventories is that they can be given to large numbers of people. However, self-disclosure is required even on a written questionnaire, so a test taker's responses may not be totally candid. Unbeknown to test takers, some personality inventories include "lie scales" and "social desirability scales." If a test taker receives a high score on a lie scale (giving responses that are untrue for most people) or on a social desirability scale (giving responses he or she thinks are expected or that appear socially acceptable), a red flag is raised indicating that the test may not be a valid measure for that individual.

Self-report information can also be gathered using open-ended interviews. With this technique, information may come to light that would not be revealed by a person's answers to a predetermined set of questions. However, responses to open-ended interviews can be difficult to quantify, and they must be interpreted by more than one objective rater.

Projective Techniques

With projective techniques, inferences are made about personality based on a test taker's responses to ambiguous stimuli. The Thematic Apperception Test (TAT), a projective measure used in some studies on aging and personality, consists of pictures of characters that appear to be involved in ambiguous social interactions. Test takers tell a brief story about what has gone on and what will happen to these characters. Other examples of projective techniques are word association tests and sentence completion tests. Asking a test taker to say the first word that comes to mind in response to another word or to complete the last few words of a phrase may uncover something about his or her personality. Responses to ambiguous stimuli may reveal feelings and thoughts that test takers might be unwilling or unable to express directly on personality inventories or in open-ended interviews. Again, however, these responses may be difficult to interpret.

Behavioral Observation

Another way to evaluate personality is to observe how people behave. We can rate the behavior of others on various scales or use behavior checklists to record how many times specific behaviors actually occur. For example, if we want to determine whether residents of an assisted-living facility are friendly (see Chapter 10 for a discussion of assisted-living facilities), we could arrange for observers to visit them several times during the day for a week. Residents who smile, make eye contact, and talk to others would probably be considered friendlier than those who do not display these behaviors. These observations are made in a real-life naturalistic setting, but a disadvantage is that we cannot hold all aspects of the environment constant so that we can observe every resident under the same conditions. Also, there is no guarantee that residents will exhibit the behaviors of interest at the times they are observed.

Behavior can also be observed under more controlled conditions. For example, after signing a consent form (see Chapter 2 for a discussion of ethics), individuals can sit in a room equipped with a one-way mirror so that they can be observed, though they cannot see who is watching them. A stooge (that is, a person trained by a researcher to follow a specific script) could enter the room and ask these individuals a series of questions in a set tone of voice. The verbal responses and body language of each individual can be recorded on videotape and later evaluated by raters, who must agree on what they observe. A possible drawback is that individuals' behavior may be affected by the knowledge that they are being observed.

In sum, we can measure personality in a number of different ways, each having advantages and disadvantages. Those who study personality over the adult life span must take into consideration which approach is best suited to their goals.

Normative Models of Personality

Are there universal (called *normative*) changes in personality as we progress through adulthood, or do personalities remain stable over time? There is more than one school of thought on this issue. Initially, we will focus on stage theories of personality, which emphasize changes that occur over the course of adulthood. Then we will turn to theories that emphasize that personality traits are stable over the adult life span. Finally, we will look at how personality development is viewed by nonprofessional (lay) people who do not conduct scientific studies but are natural observers of others as well as of themselves.

Stage Models

Stage models view personality as something that unfolds over time and takes on different forms as people progress through their adult years. Stages of personality development are linked to a chronological age range, with each one qualitatively different from the others. At each stage, certain qualities, or traits, are thought to predominate, or there may be a focus on coping with specific personal concerns.

Sigmund Freud (1856–1939) was a prominent stage theorist who lived most of his life in Vienna, where he attended medical school and specialized in neurology and nervous disorders (Hall et al., 1998). Based chiefly on case histories, Freud's psychoanalytic theory emphasized the role of unconscious biological instincts in motivating behavior. According to Freud's theory, personality development proceeds in a series of psychosexual stages that begin in infancy and extend through adolescence. However, Freud emphasized the importance of early childhood experiences in the formation of the basic personality structure. Carl Jung and Erik Erikson were both trained in the Freudian tradition and, like Freud, both are stage theorists. But later, each one developed his own theory which extended beyond adolescence and throughout the adult years. Jung and Erikson acknowledged the importance of biological factors, but both placed more emphasis than Freud did on the influences of the environment and society.

Carl Jung

Carl Jung (1875–1961) was a Swiss psychiatrist who studied with Freud, but by 1916 Jung developed his own theory of personality. Jung believed that, throughout adulthood, we continue to grow toward the realization of our potential by balancing various aspects of our personality in response to both our inner needs and the demands of society (Hall et al., 1998). At different points in the adult life span, the balance can shift, with some aspects receding into the background and others coming to the forefront. Jung believed that biological and social needs are primary in the first half of life, but cultural and spiritual needs become more important in the second half (Stevens, 1994).

Among other concepts, Jung described personality development in terms of two personality dimensions: introversion/extraversion and masculinity/femininity. He believed that a person's position on each of these dimensions could shift at different stages of development. With regard to introversion/extraversion, the emphasis in young adulthood is on meeting the demands of the external world and expanding the social environment. Important tasks at this stage of life include finding a mate and a vocation, both of which are more attainable if the outgoing (extravertive) aspects of personality predominate and the inner (introverted) aspects are suppressed. By middle adulthood, there is less pressure to meet the demands of the external world and more time to devote to the inner self. Accordingly, there is a greater balance between the external and internal aspects of the personality. In older adulthood, the demands of the external social world are reduced further, leaving more time for reflection on the inner self, so the balance shifts further toward the introversion pole of the dimension.

Jung also contended that every individual's personality has both masculine and feminine aspects. These can coexist and even complement one another. However, in young adulthood, same-sex tendencies predominate – that is, the masculine aspects predominate in young men and the feminine aspects predominate in young women. Beginning in middle age and more so in older adulthood, there is less pressure to fulfill culturally prescribed sex roles, so opposite-sex tendencies are no longer suppressed. Accordingly, older men become more accepting of their feminine side and thus are more receptive to their nurturing and sensual feelings, whereas older women are more accepting of their

In older adulthood, men are freer to express their nurturing side than they were when they were younger.

aggressive and self-centered impulses. This pattern has been found in various geographical areas and subcultures within the United States (in the Midwest and in rural Florida among both European American and African American ethnic groups) as well as in Israel, Asia, and Africa. Regardless of ethnic background, older men seem to be more tolerant than younger men of their domestic interests and focus less on competitiveness. In contrast, older women are more domineering and less submissive compared to their younger counterparts (Gutmann, 1977). The fact that these sex differences are similar cross-culturally suggests that they may be truly developmental.

Erik Erikson

Erik Erikson (1902–1994) is the most prominent stage theorist in the field of adult development and aging. He acknowledged the contribution of biological factors and inner psychological processes to personality development, but he also emphasized cultural and social forces. He thought that society had an expansive influence on development and that social institutions such as school and marriage play a positive role in psychosocial development.

According to Erikson's theory, development unfolds in a sequence of eight psychosocial stages that span from infancy to old age. Each stage revolves around a different crisis, or challenge, that represents the central concern for that developmental period. The challenge of each developmental stage can be resolved

Table 8.1 *Erikson's eight stages of psychosocial development*

	Stage (age range)	Psychosocial challenge
I.	Infancy (birth to age 1)	Trust versus mistrust
II.	Early childhood (ages 1–3)	Autonomy versus shame and doubt
III.	Childhood (ages 3–6)	Initiative versus guilt
IV.	School age (ages 6–12)	Industry versus inferiority
V.	Adolescence (teens)	Identity versus role confusion
VI.	Young adulthood (20–40)	Intimacy versus isolation
VII.	Middle adulthood (40–65)	Generativity versus stagnation
VIII.	Late adulthood (65+)	Ego integrity versus despair

Source: Erikson (1950).

positively or negatively. If it is resolved positively, the self is strengthened, the social world expands, and the individual has a good chance of resolving the next stage positively. If the challenge is resolved negatively, the individual's development suffers because it will be more difficult to achieve a positive resolution in the stages that follow. Thus, there is sequential interdependence of the stages – how the challenge of an earlier stage is resolved will affect how positively or negatively subsequent stages are resolved.

Erikson's last three stages cover young, middle, and older adulthood, respectively. In the sixth stage, the main challenge is **intimacy versus isolation**. Young adults who resolve this challenge positively are successful in developing close give-and-take relationships with others. Intimate relationships are important well into older adulthood, but the ability to form a close relationship with another person may develop in young adulthood. Young adults who resolve this challenge positively are graced with the *virtue of love*.

In the seventh stage, the main challenge is **generativity versus stagnation**. Middle-aged adults who resolve this challenge positively are able to take responsibility for others and feel they are making a contribution to the next generation. They are graced with the *virtue of care*. In middle age, many adults lose their parents and in some sense become the barrier to death for the next generation. They become protectors rather than protectees. Those who fail to resolve this challenge positively feel that life has little meaning, which can lead to a sense of boredom and a tendency toward self-indulgence. Stagnated middle-aged adults often take on youthful habits to defend against thoughts of aging and death. This behavior fits what has been popularly referred to as the *mid-life crisis* (Levinson, 1978), which we often identify with middle-aged men who are dissatisfied, feel they are running out of time to accomplish anything worthwhile, and yearn to return to the freedom of their adolescent years and start over again making different choices.

In the eighth and final stage, the main challenge is **ego integrity versus despair**. Older adults who resolve this challenge positively feel their lives have consistency, coherence, and purpose. Ego integrity is associated with contentment and satisfaction with the life one has led despite its imperfections. Older adults with ego integrity are graced with the *virtue of wisdom*. If this challenge is not resolved positively, older individuals will feel despair and disappointment with their lives. They may dwell on all the roads not taken.

Erikson's theory was not based on empirical data from large numbers of individuals and for this reason there has been criticism of it. In recent years, however, several researchers have tested Erikson's assumptions. For example, Hannah, Domino, Figueredo, and Hendrickson (1996) interviewed 520 healthy, relatively well-educated men and women between the ages of 55 and 84. For these individuals, a positive resolution in the final stage (ego integrity) was tied to a positive resolution in the preceding stage (generativity), which supports Erikson's assumption of sequential interdependence of the stages.

Erikson also proposed that each stage is characterized by a unique, central challenge. If so, concern with a particular challenge should reach a peak in the designated stage. In keeping with this assumption, McAdams, de St. Aubin, and Logan (1993) found that middle-aged adults had more generative concerns than young adults, as indicated by middle-aged individuals' frequently expressed desire to be a positive role model for younger people, to help their children work through difficult situations, and to provide for others to the best of their ability.

Peck's necessary adjustments in old age

Robert Peck (1968) described three adjustments that must occur in older adulthood. Success in each will result in positive growth, leading to what Erikson called ego integrity. In contrast, failure to make these adjustments could result in what Erikson called despair.

The first of Peck's necessary adjustments is **ego differentiation versus work-role preoccupation**. In late adulthood, retirement from work is approaching or has already occurred, so older individuals must learn to define their self-worth outside the workplace. They must ask themselves, "Am I a worthwhile person only if I can perform a full-time job, or can I be worthwhile in other ways?" A well-adjusted older adult (one with ego differentiation) will have a varied set of roles and a complex sense of identity and self-worth that does not depend completely upon work.

The second of Peck's necessary adjustments is **body transcendence versus body preoccupation**. Late adulthood often brings some physical decline, and aches and pains may prevent older adults from engaging in the same activities they did in their younger years. In addition, there may be cosmetic changes such as wrinkles. To adjust positively, older adults must rise above physical discomfort and avoid placing too much importance on appearance. They must find ways to enjoy life with reduced physical capabilities and less physical perfection.

Peck's third necessary adjustment, **ego transcendence versus ego preoccupation**, has to do with adapting to the prospect that life is finite and that the focus must be on future generations and not on one's own needs. The older adult who makes this adjustment feels that he or she has achieved something of lasting meaning. This meaning could come from the knowledge that children have been raised, strong personal relationships have been formed, and meaningful contributions have been made to society. This adjustment bears some similarity to Erikson's idea of generativity, although Peck emphasizes achievements that have already been attained rather than achievements that are occurring on an ongoing basis. Ultimately, the individual with ego transcendence is likely to have what Erikson called ego integrity.

Life review

Many people believe that older adults "live in the past" (Cohen & Taylor, 1998). Indeed, older adults often claim they remember things that happened a long time ago with a clarity that eludes them when they try to remember what happened a day or week ago (Erber, 2006). Reminiscence involves evoking personal memories from the past, possibly in a somewhat reconstructed form that is not completely objective. Reminiscence is not necessarily confined to the older adult age group, but older adults seem to engage in it more than younger age groups. Young adults may be less concerned with life review because they do not feel they have a limited time left to live.

Some years ago such reminiscence, or **life review**, was considered an idle pursuit, best discouraged in the elderly. However, Butler (1963) was one of the first to contend that life review is an active and important part of the aging process, and older adults (like Bernice, described at the beginning of this chapter) use it to integrate who they are now (present) and who they were before (past). If older adults' life review is positive, they come to accept their lives as meaningful. Thus, life review enables older adults to achieve what Erikson called ego integrity. However, if life review does not result in an adequate integration of the present and past, older adults may wish they could do things over again. This could lead to feelings of despair because older adults realize time is running out.

That life review can play a significant role in successful aging has been acknowledged by professionals who work with older adults. Life story discussion groups are popular with community-living older adults, and reminiscence therapy is often recommended for nursing home residents. In one study (Haight, Michel, & Hendrix, 1998), older adults who had been recently admitted to nursing homes were randomly assigned to one of two different interventions. Half of the nursing home residents met individually for six weeks with a trained therapeutic listener who encouraged them to reminisce about various facets of their lives. The other half received friendly visits from the same listeners. However, residents assigned to this friendly visit group were discouraged from reminiscing, and the topics of conversation during the visits focused on health, weather, television shows, and current events. Compared with residents who got friendly visits, residents who were encouraged to reminisce derived greater benefit both immediately and one year later, as indicated by their lower degree of depression, hopelessness, and despair, and their higher degree of life satisfaction and psychological well-being. Life review, or reminiscence therapy, may be an effective preventive intervention for elderly individuals who are at risk for depression.

However, reminiscence can take different forms, some more beneficial than others. Wong and Watt (1991) interviewed older adults who lived in the community and in retirement and nursing homes. Through careful screening, these older adults were categorized as either "successful agers" (meaning they were superior in physical and mental well-being) or "unsuccessful agers" (meaning they were less healthy and had a low sense of well-being). The successful and unsuccessful agers were asked to review their past and identify one or two events that had shaped their lives significantly. When the content of these reviews was analyzed, the reviews of the successful agers had more integrative and instrumental themes. Integrative reminiscences indicate that the individual feels at peace about the way past conflicts were resolved. For example, "I resented my parents' divorce when I was a young adult but in time I came to understand why they did not get along and I was able to maintain a relationship with both of them." Instrumental reminiscences show that the individual has drawn on past experience to reach a positive resolution of more recent problems. For example, "During the Great Depression, life was very hard and we had very little money. We learned to survive by budgeting and doing without many things. That experience helped me when I retired and had to adapt to living on a pension." In contrast, reviews of the unsuccessful agers had more obsessive themes that indicated persistent unresolved feelings such as guilt. For example, "My husband died while I was out shopping. He fell and I was not there to help him and I still cannot forgive myself." The fact that certain types of reminiscence seem to be associated more with successful aging suggests it may be best to encourage integrative and instrumental reminiscences but discourage those that stir up feelings of guilt.

McAdams's life story model

According to McAdams (1996), individuals construct a personal myth to make sense of their lives. This myth is a **life story** that integrates a reconstructed past with a perceived present and an anticipated future. As such, it allows people to feel that their lives have unity and purpose. The stories people construct are actually ongoing narratives that shape their behavior and establish their identity (McAdams & Pals, 2006).

Life stories reflect the values of the culture in which individuals live. In Western cultures, young adults enter the workplace, begin raising families, establish themselves in the community, and commit themselves to roles such as worker, spouse, parent, and so on. Over time, they refine the plot of their life story, and by middle adulthood they become concerned with integrating and balancing its various themes. Middle-aged individuals are often considered to be in the prime of their lives, but the themes of their life stories indicate increasing concern with mortality and what will survive them after death. Thus, middle-aged individuals start to fashion a generativity script, which guides what gifts they want to leave for the generations that follow. In the decades of the 40s, 50s, and 60s, individuals concentrate on integrating the beginning and middle of the life story narrative, but also on creating an appropriate and satisfying ending. Ideally, this ending will have continuity and purpose and will tie together the various threads of the story. A "good" ending makes it possible for individuals to attain a kind of symbolic immortality, or legacy of the self, which will live on after their death (McAdams, 1996). McAdams's idea of a good ending bears some similarity to Erikson's conception of ego integrity.

Personality Dimensions and Traits

Rather than emphasizing that personality evolves in stages over the adult life span, some theorists focus on whether personality is consistent over time (Berry & Jobe, 2002). For example, Bernice (described at the beginning of this chapter) has had a lifelong interest in fashion. Personality dimensions can be broad categories of personality such as neuroticism and extraversion, each consisting of a constellation of personality traits. For example, someone high on a neuroticism dimension would probably be anxious and hostile, while someone high on an extraversion dimension would probably be warm and sociable. Are personality dimensions stable across adulthood, and do personality traits stay the same?

The Baltimore Longitudinal Study

An ideal way to examine personality over the adult life span would be to follow the same individuals over time. Researchers Costa and McCrae did just that as part of the Baltimore Longitudinal Study (BLS), in which a large initial sample of individuals ranging from their 20s to their 80s completed two well-established self-report personality inventories, the Cattell 16PF and the Guilford–Zimmerman Temperament Survey.

By analyzing study participants' responses, these researchers proposed a personality structure consisting of five dimensions, or factors: neuroticism, extraversion, openness to experience, agreeableness, and conscientiousness (NEO-AC). Based on this **Five-Factor Model (FFM) of Personality**, Costa and McCrae (1991, 1992) developed a self-report questionnaire, the Revised NEO Personality Inventory (NEO-PI-R), which consists of 240 items, or statements that are intended to measure six traits that make up each of the five factors. (An abbreviated version, the NEO-FFI, has only 60 items.) Test takers rate each statement on a 5-point scale from "strongly disagree" to "strongly agree." High agreement with the statements results in a high score on that personality factor. The factors, as well as the six traits within each one, are listed in Table 8.2.

As BLS participants were followed longitudinally, the same five personality factors continued to emerge in their self-report responses, indicating a consistency over time in the personality factors. Furthermore, when BLS participants were tested repeatedly, they retained their approximate rank order on the factors compared to others their age. In other words, individuals who scored high on the neuroticism, extraversion, or other factors at one point in time compared to others of the same age tended to score high on these factors at subsequent points in time compared to others of the same age. In addition, evidence from numerous longitudinal studies also found a high level of consistency as to which traits are associated with each factor, particularly when late middle-aged and older adults were followed over 6-year periods (Roberts & DelVecchio, 2000).

What does being high on the various personality factors mean? High scores on some are associated with positive affect and feelings of well-being, while high

Table 8.2 *The big five personality factors and six specific traits within each factor*

Personality factor	Traits
Neuroticism (N)	Anxiety, angry hostility, depression, self-consciousness, impulsiveness, vulnerability
Extraversion (E)	Warmth, gregariousness, assertiveness, activity, excitement seeking, positive emotions
Openness to experience (O)	Fantasy, aesthetics, feelings, actions, ideas, values
Agreeableness (A)	Trust, straightforwardness, altruism, compliance, modesty, tender-mindedness
Conscientiousness (C)	Competence, order, dutifulness, achievement-striving, self-discipline, deliberation

Adapted from McCrae and Costa (1997).

scores on others are not (McCrae & Costa, 1991). Most notably, being high on the extraversion factor is associated with positive affect and feelings of well-being, while being high on the neuroticism factor is associated with negative affect and a lower degree of well-being. Being high on the openness to experience factor is associated with both positive and negative affect, with no overall effect on level of well-being. Being high on the agreeableness and conscientiousness factors is associated more with positive than with negative affect but there is only a weak positive association with feelings of well-being.

McCrae and Costa (1982) contend that the choices we make at various transition points are influenced by where we fall on the five personality factors, and that personality functions jointly with age to influence whether outcomes are positive at various stages of development. They pose the following questions, which are quite different from the questions that stage model theorists might ask:

- How do lives of those high in extraversion differ from the lives of those low in extraversion?
- What aspects of life are influenced by openness to experience?
- What role does personality play in adapting to stressful life events?

Theorists working within this continuity framework are not likely to use the term *mid-life crisis*. Rather, they would consider some individuals, notably those high in neuroticism, to be crisis-prone. Moreover, they might speculate that an individual who experiences a crisis in middle adulthood most likely experienced

Understanding Aging Box 8.1: Personality and Mortality

Can personality influence mortality, especially in older adulthood? According to Mroczek, Spiro, and Griffin (2006), being low in conscientiousness is associated with earlier mortality, possibly because such individuals are less likely to adhere to healthy behaviors and more likely to engage in risky behaviors. Being high on neuroticism has also been associated with poor health and earlier mortality. Silver, Bubrick, Jilinskaia, and Perls (1998) studied 23 New England centenarians aged 100 to 110, mostly females. When these centenarians completed the 60-item Five-Factor Inventory (NEO-FFI), they were relatively low on the neuroticism factor. Neuroticism is associated with sensitivity to stress, so being low on this factor suggests better ability to manage stress. Although neuroticism may be negatively associated with longevity, however, it would be premature to conclude there is a cause-and-effect relationship. Mroczek et al. emphasize the need for additional study on what might underlie this association. For example, those high in neuroticism may be more emotionally reactive to daily stressors, and over a lifetime of reactivity there could be physical damage that contributes to mortality.

crises earlier in life as well, although the exact nature of a particular crisis might depend upon the individual's age and stage of life.

Cross-cultural comparisons

McCrae and Costa (1991) acknowledge the importance of biological, historical, and cultural influences on personality, so it is particularly noteworthy that the five-factor model seems to generalize across cultures (McCrae, 2002). When translated versions of the NEO-PI-R questionnaire were administered to over 7,000 individuals from diverse cultures, the five-factor structure already demonstrated in English-speaking samples was also found in Germany, Portugal, Israel, China, and Japan (McCrae & Costa, 1997). Furthermore, the traits that made up each of the five personality factors were very much the same in American, German, Italian, Portuguese, Croatian, and Korean study samples (McCrae et al., 1999). Thus, not only is there a common overall personality structure across cultures in terms of factors, but there is also cross-cultural similarity in the specific traits that define the factors.

Cross-sectional studies

The dimensional continuity model just described emphasizes stability in personality factors over time. But does this mean that personality is written in stone and people do not change at all throughout adulthood? Much of our information on personality is based on cross-sectional studies, with people of various ages all tested at the same time. McCrae et al. (1999) found that between young and middle adulthood, there is a decrease in the neuroticism, extraversion, and openness-to-experience factors but an increase in the agreeableness and conscientiousness factors. Similar decreases and increases have been reported when translated versions of the NEO-PI-R questionnaire are given to German, Italian, Portuguese, Croatian, and Korean samples. Also, in cross-sectional studies conducted not only in the United States but also in countries such as Turkey, South Korea, and Poland, older adults have higher scores than younger adults on traits related to conscientiousness and agreeableness, whereas older adults have lower scores than younger adults on traits related to neuroticism, extraversion, and openness to experience (Helson, Kwan, John, & Jones, 2002). Such cross-cultural similarity is interpreted as evidence for universal maturational differences in personality.

Age and cohort cannot be separated in cross-sectional studies, so it will be important to conduct further longitudinal studies following the same individuals over time and plotting small changes in personality traits. As described earlier, a person who falls on the high end of the extraversion factor at one age will likely fall at the high end later on. However, average scores on the extraversion factor may decline with age. Thus, an individual could decline in extraversion with increasing age but still remain high on this factor compared to others of the same age. To illustrate, a young adult high in extraversion may feel the need to socialize with other people on a daily basis, but an older adult high in extraversion may feel the need to socialize with other people a few times a week. In terms of absolute need to socialize, the older adult is lower than the young adult, but the older adult may still retain a high need to socialize compared to his or her age peers. In sum, a person's absolute score on the extraversion factor may decline over time, but that person could still remain high in extraversion compared to others the same age.

Questions of stability and change in personality will probably continue to be prominent on the agendas of developmental researchers (Ryff, Kwan, & Singer, 2001). A recent perspective emphasizes individual differences in change (Mroczek et al., 2006). That is, do some people remain stable and others change? The issue of individual differences in intraindividual change is studied using sophisticated statistical techniques whereby day-to-day variation within the individual can be tracked. Over long periods of time, some people may change more than others. The rate and extent of change within the individual most likely depends on the environment, genetic makeup, and health, as well as on his or her motivation to change (McAdams & Pals, 2006).

Lay Views of Personality

How do ordinary individuals who are not research scientists conceptualize personality? Do these lay individuals view themselves as having stayed the same or having changed over time? In their opinion, do the personalities of other people stay the same or do they change with age?

People's views of their own personality

Many older adults feel a strong sense of continuity. For example, when Troll and Skaff (1997) interviewed 150 individuals aged 85 and older, the majority felt that they were basically the same as they had always been.

Most of us have perceptions about what we were like in the past and what we are like at the present time, but what do we think we will be like in the future? Fleeson and Heckhausen (1997) tested adults ranging from 26 to 64 years of age using a short self-report inventory that measured Costa and McCrae's five dimensions of personality (NEO-AC). Participants rated how much they thought each item on the inventory would describe what they were like when they were aged 20–25 (past), what they are like now (present), and what they anticipate they will be like when they reach the age of 65–70 (future). There was a moderate degree of stability across the three time periods regarding how participants viewed themselves – those who rated themselves high in present level of extraversion and agreeableness tended to rate themselves high on these dimensions both retrospectively (in the past) and prospectively (in the future).

Perceptions of the personality traits of others

Despite evidence for stability in self-reported personality dimensions and traits over the adult life span (McCrae & Costa, 1982), do lay individuals associate certain personality traits with older adulthood? Are some traits viewed as either increasing with age or decreasing with age?

Heckhausen et al. (1989) asked young, middle-aged, and older adult residents of Berlin, Germany to rate the desirability of 358 traits and to estimate the rise and fall of each trait over the adult years. Participants from all three age groups showed considerable agreement in their beliefs. In general, they viewed development as multidirectional, with both gains and losses over the adult life span. Gains were defined as an increase over the adult life span in desirable traits such as wise, responsible, and level-headed. Losses were defined as an increase in undesirable traits such as weak, dependent, and stubborn. Overall, expected gains outnumbered expected losses. However, the proportion of expected gains decreased somewhat with increasing age.

Heckhausen and Krueger (1993) asked young, middle-aged, and older adults (also residents of Berlin, Germany) to rate desirable traits (for example, assertive, affectionate, dependable, self-controlled, knowledgeable) and undesirable traits (for example, inhibited, quarrelsome, irresponsible, nervous, naive) as to whether each one (a) increases over the seven decades of adulthood (20s, 30s, 40s, 50s, 60s, 70s, 80s), (b) decreases over the seven decades of adulthood, and (c) can be modified, or controlled. In one session participants rated themselves, and in another they rated what they thought was true for most other people. Heckhausen and Krueger's study participants were optimistic about adult development – they expected that gains (increases in desirable traits and decreases in undesirable traits) would outnumber losses (decreases in desirable traits and increases in undesirable traits). However, the predominance of expected gains was greater for early adulthood than it was for late adulthood. Even so, most participants thought that it would be possible to control, or modify, undesirable traits.

There was considerable agreement between what individuals thought would be true for themselves and what would be true for other people. For instance, if they thought they themselves would become more dependable with increasing age, they believed the same would be true for other people. Even so, there was some evidence for self-enhancement among the middle-aged and older adults – they expected that increases in desirable attributes would be greater for themselves than for other people, and they anticipated that increases in undesirable attributes would be smaller for themselves than for others. In short, individuals are even more optimistic about their own future personality traits than they are about how their age peers will fare.

Hummert et al. (1994) asked young, middle-aged, and older adults about traits they would consider typical of older adults. Table 8.3 lists 20 traits that were named by at least 20% of the adults in at least one age group or at least 10% of the adults in all three age groups. There was considerable overlap in the traits generated by the three age groups. Some were positive (for example, trustworthy), while others were negative (for example, depressed).

Slotterback (1996) posed an important question: Are the perceptions young adults have about older adults' personality traits related to older adults' chronological age or are they related to older adults' generation, or cohort? Young adult college students rated a hypothetical individual (target) on scales that were based on Costa and McCrae's five personality dimensions. They were told the target was 21, 41, or 69 years old and also that the target lived in the past, present, or future. The students thought that openness to experience would decrease with increasing age. However, they thought the present generation of older adults had always been less open to experience even when they were young adults. Also, they believed that conscientiousness decreases with age, but they thought that the present generation of older adults is more conscientious compared to the present generation of young adults. Slotterback's findings serve to remind us that our perceptions of personality characteristics can be influenced not only by people's chronological age but also by their cohort.

Stereotypes about older adults

Stereotypes are ideas we hold in our heads about categories of people. With age stereotypes, we make assumptions about people based on their chronological age. Using age stereotypes can lighten the load of processing a great deal of complex information about older adults. However, a potentially negative consequence is that age stereotypes interfere with our ability to make judgments about a specific older adult as a unique individual (Hummert, 1999).

Sometimes age stereotypes are not in our conscious awareness. However, when unconscious stereotypes are activated, or primed, they can influence our behavior even without our realizing it. Perdue and Gurtman (1990) demonstrated that young adult college students were more efficient at remembering the trait "forgetful" after it was presented along with the word "old" rather than along with the word "young." Bargh, Chen, and Burrows (1996) asked young adult

Table 8.3 *Traits descriptive of a typical elderly adult named most frequently by young, middle-aged, and elderly adults*

Age group trait	Young (n = 40)	Middle-aged (n = 40)	Elderly (n = 40)	Trait valence
Conservative	7.5	20.0	2.5	Positive
Depressed	12.5	20.0	7.5	Negative
Determined	2.5	20.0	17.5	Positive
Eager to learn and experience	0.0	17.5	25.0	Positive
Sense of humor	12.5	15.0	12.5	Positive
Health-conscious	15.0	45.0	30.0	Positive
Independent	5.0	25.0	22.5	Positive
Likes social activities	25.0	20.0	17.5	Positive
Move after retirement	22.5	10.0	2.5	Positive
Politically aware and active	22.5	17.5	17.5	Positive
Pursues a hobby	30.0	30.0	27.5	Positive
Religious	12.5	32.5	20.0	Positive
Scared of becoming sick and incompetent	0.0	35.0	52.5	Negative
Successful	12.5	25.0	5.0	Positive
Timid	5.0	27.5	7.5	Negative
Tired	25.0	17.5	2.5	Negative
Travels often	10.0	20.0	32.5	Positive
Trustworthy	2.5	20.0	5.0	Positive
Well-groomed	5.0	17.5	20.0	Positive
Worried about finances	7.5	5.0	35.0	Negative

Source: Hummert et al. (1994).

college students to unscramble five-word sets by constructing grammatically correct sentences using four of the words. The sets unscrambled by half the students were intended to prime age stereotypes and contained words stereotypically associated with older adults (for example, forgetful, conservative, withdrawn, dependent). The sets unscrambled by the other half of the students (control group) contained neutral words that were unrelated to an elderly stereotype (for example, thirsty, clean, private). After they completed the unscrambling task, Bargh et al. timed how long it took the students to walk down a corridor from the laboratory to the elevator. Students in the elderly-prime condition walked more slowly than students in the neutral-prime condition did. As is typical with implicit priming, the students were unaware that the prime words had affected them in any way, or even that the words they had unscrambled were related to an elderly stereotype. Yet, the slower walking of the students exposed to elderly-stereotypic words indicated that they had an unconscious age stereotype, which when primed without their awareness influenced their behavior.

Stereotypes about older adults are often negative. Traits such as absentminded, forgetful, obstinate, and depressed are thought to have their onset in late middle age (Heckhausen & Baltes, 1991). Furthermore, older adults are often viewed as overcautious and dependent (Heckhausen et al., 1989). Such negative views are even harbored by older adults themselves, which could explain why many older adults insist that they feel younger than they are and think they compare favorably with others the same age. Surprisingly, evidence for negative age stereotypes has even been found among young adults in Thailand, a country known for its tradition of respect for the elderly (Sharps, Price-Sharps, & Hanson, 1998).

However, the idea that stereotypes of older adults are uniformly negative may be overly simplistic. When Lichtenstein et al. (2005) asked middle-school children to draw a picture of a "typical" older person and then describe it in a few words, no cohesive stereotypes of elders emerged from their diverse images. This suggests that young adolescents do not have a built-in bias toward older adults or uniformly negative views of age-associated changes. As mentioned earlier, Heckhausen et al. (1989) asked young, middle-aged, and older adults to estimate the expected age of onset for 358 traits. Of the traits thought to have a late onset (age 55 or later) and believed to remain stable into very late old age, some were undesirable (bitter, forgetful), but others were desirable (dignified, wise). Hummert (1990) found that young adult college students hold multiple stereotypes about older adults. The students did not view negative stereotypes such as "inflexible senior citizen" (including traits such as "set in ways" and "old-fashioned") as any more typical of the elderly than they did positive stereotypes such as "perfect grandparent" (including traits such as "generous" and "loving"). Cuddy, Norton, and Fiske (2005) found that college students express an evaluatively mixed stereotype – they judge older adults with cognitive difficulties as being low in competence but high in warmth. In short, stereotypes about older adults are not all negative. Furthermore, stereotypes may be applied to older adults as an abstract group, but they are less likely to be assumed in the case of individual older adults, especially when detailed information about them is available (Kite, Stockdale, Whitley, & Johnson, 2005).

In sum, the stereotypes people have about older adults as a group are not uniformly negative. Even so, not all older adults are the same, so let's now turn our attention to individual differences among older adults rather than what they have in common.

Individual Differences in Coping and Adjustment

Rather than trying to determine what might be typical of older adults in general, some investigators focus on how they differ. The study of individual differences in personality is often coupled with an interest in which older adults experience high levels of life satisfaction and psychological well-being (Ryff et al., 2001). Life satisfaction and well-being are usually associated with self-acceptance, positive relations with others, autonomy, and feelings of environmental mastery, purpose in life, and personal growth (Ryff, 1989). How can we distinguish between these older adults and those who are unhappy and dissatisfied?

Closely tied to the idea of well-being is the concept of coping. How do individuals handle events and challenges that take place over the life course? Effective coping strategies become increasingly important in dealing with changes and losses that occur in late adulthood. Are some coping strategies more likely than others to maximize the chance of successful aging? We will approach these questions first by introducing the idea of self-concept. Then we will proceed to a discussion about feelings of personal control.

Self-Concept

All of us have ideas about who we are, and researchers often refer to these ideas as *schemas*. Our schemas play a part in how we define ourselves. They also determine what information we attend to most and also how we process that information (Hooker, 1992). **Self-concept** is the image we have of ourselves (McCrae, 2006). Rather than being one general image, however, our self-concept consists of a collection of schemas that are related to different domains. For example, an individual might have a schema about his or her physical appearance (physical domain), intellectual capability (intellectual domain), or social skills (social domain). The domains most important for a particular individual's self-concept dictate what he or she considers meaningful (Markus & Herzog, 1991). As described at the beginning of this chapter, Bernice's interest in the physical domain, particularly in fashion, has been a theme throughout her adult years. Recent views of the self are that it is not just a passive reactive agent, but rather it is active and creative and can undergo change and revision (Ruth, 2007).

Self-esteem is the affective, or evaluative, aspect of the self-concept. A person with high self-esteem perceives himself or herself as having worth, whereas a person with low self-esteem does not. As with self-concept, self-esteem can occur in different domains. A person may have high self-esteem in one domain ("I feel good about my appearance") but low self-esteem in another ("I feel bad that I cannot understand computers"). In light of some of the negative age stereotypes that exist, it is surprising that self-esteem does not decline significantly in late life (George, 2006). However, people often evaluate themselves in comparison with others, so self-esteem can be high or low depending upon the group with which one compares oneself (Baron & Byrne, 2000).

Theorists have emphasized the importance of self-concept for the aging process because the schemas that make up our self-concept are important in regulating our behavior and guiding the decisions we make (see Figure 8.1). The content, organization, and functioning of these schemas may hold the key to how we negotiate life events and successfully navigate changes that occur as we move from young to middle to older adulthood (Cross & Markus, 1991; Markus & Herzog, 1991).

As individuals grow older, some aspects of their past self-concept continue to define who they are. For example, retired teachers may continue to identify with

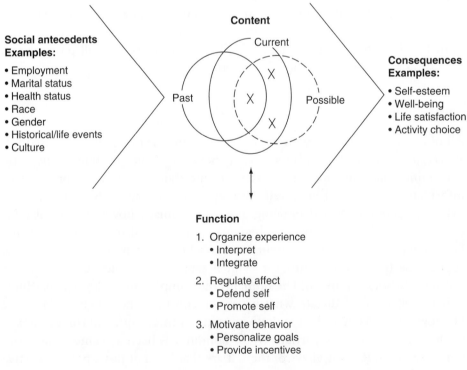

Figure 8.1 *The dynamic self-concept.*
Source: Markus & Herzog (1991).

their profession even after they formally retire from the classroom. Seventy-five-year-old Bernice, described at the beginning of the chapter, no longer owns a retail clothing store but she is still interested in fashion and it is an important part of her self-concept.

Possible selves

Not only do we have schemas about our past and present (current) selves, but also we have schemas about what we may be like in the future. **Possible selves** include schemas about what we would like to become (hoped-for selves) as well as what we are afraid of

Even after they officially retire, some teachers continue to identify with their profession, which is an important part of their self-concept.

becoming (feared selves) (Cross & Markus, 1991; Markus & Herzog, 1991). Examples of hoped-for possible selves might be the rich self, the attractive self, the independent self, or the healthy self. Examples of feared possible selves might be the poor self, the unattractive self, the dependent self, or the unhealthy self.

Possible selves of adults over age 60 often have less to do with occupation and career and more to do with establishing leisure pursuits and physical functioning (Cross & Markus, 1991). In comparison with hoped-for selves of young adult college students, hoped-for selves of older adults are more invested in health (Hooker, 1992). Concern with attaining healthy selves actually begins to gain importance in mid-life, with middle-aged adults reporting more feared selves than hoped-for selves regarding health (Hooker & Kaus, 1994).

Possible selves, both hoped for and feared, continue into very old age. Smith and Freund (2002) studied transcripts of interviews conducted over 4 years in which individuals aged 70 to 103 years expressed their personal hopes and fears for the future. Even the oldest members in their sample showed evidence of dynamic possible selves, with images added and deleted over time.

The assimilation, accommodation, and immunization (AAI) model

The AAI model (Brandtstädter, 1999; Brandtstädter & Greve, 1994) outlines three self-protective coping strategies, or processes, that individuals use to maintain personal continuity and integrity of the self. These are not unique to older adulthood, but they are useful for understanding how older adults cope with age-related discrepancies between actual and desired selves.

Assimilation, often termed *tenacious goal pursuit* (Brandtstädter, 1999; Brandtstädter & Renner, 1990), is usually the first process activated when individuals detect a gap between hoped-for goals and actual circumstances.

Applying Research Box 8.1: Possible Selves and Daily Activities

Possible selves are not just idle fantasies. They motivate us to set and achieve goals and they can regulate our behavior. As part of the Berlin Aging Study, Hoppmann, Gerstorf, Smith, and Klumb (2007) investigated the association between possible selves in three domains (health, cognition, and social relations) and the daily activities related to each one (for example, taking a walk, doing a crossword puzzle, and having a phone conversation, respectively) in 83 older men and women (mean age 81 years). Those with hoped-for selves in two of the domains (health and social relations but not cognition) tended to perform more daily activities in those domains, and this linkage between the hoped-for possible self and activity was associated with feelings of well-being and also with a higher probability of survival over a 10-year period. There was no linkage between feared possible selves and activities in any of the domains, which suggests that hopes are more likely than fears to translate into engaging in domain-specific activities.

Assimilative processes typically involve intentional actions or efforts. In early adulthood, assimilative efforts focus on goals that extend well into the future. For example, many young adults work at a succession of jobs with a long-term goal of establishing their identity in a career. Assimilative efforts can also be preventive, corrective, or compensatory. In late adulthood, such efforts are often directed toward maintaining resources and avoiding mismatches between skills and demands. An especially important goal in later life is minimizing health risks (Hooker, 1992), and assimilative efforts could include modification of eating and exercise habits. Another goal for older adults is maintaining a competent and independent level of functioning. Many cope with changes in physical capabilities by assimilative actions such as installing grab bars in the bathroom, strobe lights on telephones, and emergency call buttons in each room.

Brandtstädter (1999) argues that continued use of assimilative strategies when goals are clearly unattainable can lead to frustration and negative emotions. At this point, accommodative processes may be activated. **Accommodation**, often characterized as *flexible goal adjustment* (Brandtstädter & Renner, 1990), is usually unintentional. Accommodative processes entail reevaluating, adjusting, or even redefining personal goals and preferences in accordance with situational and personal limitations. In late adulthood this may become necessary when ambitions and preferences must be adjusted in accordance with situational constraints (Brandtstädter, 1999; Brandtstädter, Wentura, & Greve, 1993; Heckhausen & Schulz, 1995). Accommodative processes include revising one's goals and aspirations and changing one's standards of self-evaluation. For example, Bernice (described at the beginning of this chapter) thinks she has fared well compared to others her age. Accommodative processes can buffer older adults against losses, allowing them to maintain the integrity of their self-concepts and thus their feelings of life satisfaction (Brandtstädter & Greve, 1994; Brandtstädter & Renner, 1990).

Immunization shields individuals against threats to aspects of the self-concept that are central to their identity (Brandtstädter, 1999). Like accommodative processes, immunizing processes are usually unintentional and they protect people from information that conflicts with the definitions they have of themselves. To illustrate, Peter prides himself on being an excellent golfer and this plays an important role in his self-concept. Until recently, he has won almost every golf tournament he enters and these successes are easily assimilated into his identity as an excellent golfer. Lately, however, Peter's scores have been disappointing and this season he has not won any tournaments. Immunizing processes offer a line of defense against information that conflicts with this crucial aspect of Peter's self-concept. Peter could attribute his poor scores to substandard maintenance of the golf course, to his recent sleeping problems, or to the loud conversations of the other members of the foursome that distract him from his game. In some sense, immunizing processes are rationalizations, but they help Peter preserve the continuity of his self-concept and prevent his self-esteem from plummeting. Immunizing processes cannot serve a protective purpose forever, but they allow Peter some time to take stock of the situation. He may decide to engage in further assimilative actions to improve his golf game (for example, taking lessons from a new golf pro). If these do not help, Peter may eventually lower his standards or possibly focus on other aspects of his self-concept.

Personal Control

Feelings of personal control relate to the perception that one governs what happens in one's own life. Personal control can be considered on a general level or within more specific domains. For example, one can feel a sense of personal control physically, socially, cognitively, and so on.

Internal versus external control

Rotter (1966) defined personal control along an internal–external dimension. Individuals with an **internal locus of control** feel they have a great deal of personal control over what happens to them. They believe that experiencing positive outcomes and avoiding negative outcomes are contingent upon their own efforts, actions, and behavior. In contrast, individuals with an **external locus of control** feel that their own efforts, actions, and behavior have little to do with what happens to them. They believe positive and negative outcomes are determined by chance or other outside forces.

Rotter devised an internal–external locus of control scale consisting of pairs of statements. One statement in each pair indicates feelings of internal control ("When I make plans, I am almost certain that I can make them work"), while the other statement in the pair indicates feelings of external control ("It is not always wise to plan too far ahead because many things turn out to be a matter of good or bad fortune anyhow"). Individuals select the statement from each pair that best describes their personality.

A central question in the study of aging and older adulthood is whether the sense of personal control changes over the adult life span. A common belief is that as individuals move from young to older adulthood, they become less internal and more external in their locus of control (Pratt & Norris, 1994). This assumption is based on the fact that many events that occur in older adulthood (for example, loss of loved ones, loss of the work role, illness) do not seem to be within the realm of personal control. However, the idea that older adults have decreased feelings of control compared to young adults has been called into question.

Gatz and Karel (1993) analyzed the responses of individuals from four generations (grandchildren, children, parents, grandparents) who participated in a study on locus of control that was conducted over 20 years, from 1971 to 1991. Participants were given several pairs of statements from Rotter's locus of control scale and asked to select the statement that would best describe them. Of the 1,267 participants, 560 participated at all four times of measurement, so the study yielded both cross-sectional and longitudinal information.

In the cross-sectional analysis of the responses of the 1,267 individuals tested only once, those from all four generations were similar in their feelings of internal control. In the longitudinal analysis on the responses of the 560 individuals tested at four different times, there was a small but significant trend toward increased internal control over the 20-year period. However, Gatz and Karel speculate that increased feelings of internal control in individuals followed longitudinally could represent a time-of-measurement effect – sociocultural changes over 20 years might have encouraged autonomy and fostered a spirit of self-improvement, resulting in greater feelings of internal control. In any case, there was no evidence that internal control declines with age either in the cross-sectional or longitudinal part of the study.

Rhee and Gatz (1993) asked young adult college students and older adult university alumni to rate themselves on an adapted version of Rotter's locus of control scale. Compared to the young students, the older alumni expressed a higher degree of internal control, so again, the assumption that older adults have a lower sense of personal control was not borne out. Even so, the young students perceived the older alumni as being more external than older adults' self-ratings actually reflected. Likewise, the older alumni perceived the young students as more internal than the young students' self-ratings actually reflected. In sum, the beliefs individuals held about their own personal control did not agree with how they were viewed by those from a different age group. Young adults may assume older adults are externally controlled, but older adults do not actually feel this way.

Ultimately, however, older adults' feelings of internal control could be influenced by how others view them (Rodin & Langer, 1980). Labeling older adults as "helpless" could have a negative effect on their feelings of personal control. This can be a vicious circle – if older adults feel that they have little or no control, they may lose their motivation to engage in behaviors that could actually affect what happens to them.

It is generally believed that older adults who live in nursing homes have little control over their environment. If so, then what would happen if nursing home residents were given an opportunity to exert some control? In a classic study (Schulz, 1976), older adult nursing home residents were visited by college students. Half of the residents were allowed to control the frequency and duration of the visits. The other half received visits from the same college students but they had no choice about the frequency or duration of the visits. Even when Schulz controlled for the number, duration, and quality of the visits received by the nursing home residents in the two groups, he found that the positive impact of the visits on the residents' well-being was greater when the residents were allowed to control them.

In another classic study (Langer & Rodin, 1976), one group of nursing home residents received a communication that emphasized they were responsible for themselves. In addition, they were given a plant and told they were in charge of its care. A second group of nursing home residents received a communication that emphasized the staff was responsible for them. They too were given a plant, but they were told the staff would care for it. Compared to the nursing home residents in the cared-for group, residents in the responsible group were more alert, participated more in activities, and had a higher general sense of well-being. In sum, even when individuals have little control over their environment, allowing them to determine even a small aspect of it can benefit their psychological well-being.

Compared to older adults who reside in nursing homes, older adults who live in the community probably have more control over their environment. Nonetheless, even community-living older adults can experience some decrease in feelings of control over what happens to them, especially with health-related life events and losses. Thus, it is reasonable to speculate that with increasing age, individuals will experience some drop in their level of life satisfaction and psychological well-being. Yet, studies with large international samples have found little evidence for any overall decline in life satisfaction with increasing age (Diener & Suh, 1997). Level of life satisfaction seems to be stable across the adult years and well into older adulthood.

If life events that older adults confront – for example, illness, widowhood and loss of other close relationships, or loss of income through retirement – permit little personal control, how do older adults manage to maintain their level of life satisfaction? Feelings of personal control are probably more complex than was previously thought. They may be derived not only from how much objective control individuals can actually exert but also from their expectations about personal control. Schulz and Hanusa (1980) argue that feelings of well-being decline only when actual level of control differs drastically from the level of control that is expected. A large discrepancy between actual and expected levels of control is most likely to occur when a change in actual amount of control is sudden and individuals do not have time to adjust their expectations.

Primary and secondary control

In addition to the concepts of internal and external locus of control, a related model refers to primary control and secondary control. **Primary control processes** are actions and behaviors that influence, shape, or change the environment (Heckhausen & Schulz, 1995; Schulz & Heckhausen, 1996). Individuals use these processes to influence, shape, and change the environment to fit their needs and desires (Schulz & Heckhausen, 1996). As such, primary control processes are similar to the assimilative processes discussed earlier.

Behaviors and actions aimed at primary control may be applied to specific areas of functioning. For example, people may make efforts to exert primary control in the area of cognitive competence, social competence, or physical competence. One person might concentrate on mastering cognitive skills, while another might devote efforts to mastering social skills, and yet another to maintaining physical functioning. Bernice, described at the beginning of the chapter, plans to maintain a physical aspect – her stylish appearance.

If too many attempts to achieve primary control meet with limited success or outright failure, the individual may become frustrated and discouraged and could begin to feel helpless and depressed. At this point, **secondary control processes** come into play. Unlike primary control processes, which are characterized by actions and behaviors directed at the external world, secondary control processes are related to internal resources (Heckhausen & Schulz, 1993). They are similar to accommodative processes in that they involve altering goals and expectations and accepting existing realities that cannot be changed. For example, a person who tries to become an expert in computer skills on his or her own may become frustrated if these attempts fail. A form of secondary control would be for this individual to lower the expectation of being able to learn these skills without help. Bernice, described at the beginning of the chapter, modifies her style in line with her age and stage of life. Secondary control processes buffer the individual against the negative effects of failure at achieving primary control. This buffering protects emotional well-being and self-esteem and enables the individual to remain motivated, perhaps making further attempts at primary control in areas where efforts have a good chance of being successful (Heckhausen & Schulz, 1995).

According to the **optimization of primary and secondary control (OPS)** model (Heckhausen, 1997), physical and cognitive losses may reduce the likelihood of achieving primary control in advanced old age, so older adults must become increasingly selective about where they place their efforts. Being selective is adaptive because efforts at primary control can be directed toward areas where success is most attainable. In late adulthood, primary control may include compensatory strategies that require technical aids such as hearing aids and assistance from other people (Heckhausen & Schulz, 1993).

Over the life span, primary and secondary control processes operate jointly. But with the approach of middle age and especially older adulthood, biological and social challenges may limit the broad use of primary control, and secondary control may take on greater importance. "As the ratio of gains to losses in primary control becomes less and less favorable, the individual increasingly resorts to secondary control processes" (Schulz & Heckhausen, 1996, p. 709). Lachman (2006) contends that the older adults who maintain a strong sense of control may be those who are most adept at using secondary control strategies to cope with events that are uncontrollable and goals that are unattainable.

In sum, life satisfaction does not significantly decline in older adulthood and this may well reflect older adults' success in achieving a balance between primary and secondary control processes. Perhaps older adults cannot or do not wish to pursue the same goals, or as many goals, as they did in their younger years. Accordingly, they adjust their expectations and concentrate their primary control efforts on goals that are age-appropriate and attainable.

Revisiting the Selective Optimization with Compensation and Ecological Models

The Selective Optimization with Compensation (SOC) (Baltes & Baltes, 1990) and Ecological (Lawton, 1989; Lawton & Nahemow, 1973) Models are readily applied to personality and coping over the adult life span.

According to the SOC model, selection, optimization, and compensation are necessary processes for realizing developmental goals. Stage theories imply that certain aspects of personality and personal issues are more dominant at some ages and stages of adulthood than at others. Individuals function optimally when they meet challenges that are most compelling at their particular stage of life rather than facing too many challenges at the same time. With regard to the view that personality dimensions and traits are stable over time, it is possible that some individuals are better equipped to meet challenges than others, but those who struggle at one age and stage of life may have an easier time at other stages. Even so, it may be possible to compensate for being low on some dimensions of personality by being high on others. Further research is needed to identify older adults who are best able to profit from using SOC strategies to achieve subjective well-being (Jopp & Smith, 2006).

Also in keeping with the SOC Model, when irreversible and uncontrollable losses occur, older adults may find it necessary to concentrate their efforts on the goals most important to them. They may give up some aspects of their self-concept and focus on a more select set of possible selves. Compared with young adults, older adults report having fewer possible selves, but they remain highly directed toward achieving the goals of their hoped-for possible selves and preventing their feared possible selves (Markus & Herzog, 1991).

With regard to the Ecological Model, older adults adapt best in environments that permit them to realize their ideals of who they are and wish to become and also allow them sufficient opportunities to exert some level of personal control. Older adults may engage in assimilative actions to reduce the challenge of the environment so that it matches their level of competence more closely. The closer the match is between their coping abilities and the demands of the environment, the more likely older adults are to enjoy a maximum level of adaptation.

? Questions to Consider

1. Where do you think you would fall on the dimensions of the FFM (NEO-AC)?
2. What would you do if you experienced a disappointment in attaining a goal that was very important to you?
3. Over which aspects of your own life do you feel you have the most control and over which aspects of your life do you feel you have the least control?

Key Points

- Cross-sectional and longitudinal research can be used to study the developmental aspects of personality.
- Personality can be measured using self-reports, projective techniques, or behavioral observation.
- According to stage theorists such as Erikson, personality unfolds over time, taking on different forms or revolving around different challenges as people progress through the adult years.
- Some theorists focus on whether the dimensions of personality remain stable or change over time. Longitudinal studies indicate relative continuity over time in personality dimensions, but cross-sectional studies find some age-related differences in the absolute level of personality dimensions and traits.
- People associate various personality characteristics, or traits, with older adulthood. Some of these traits are negative, but some are positive.
- Self-concept is the image we have about ourselves and consists of multiple schemas in any number of domains. Self-concept has past, present, and future aspects. Much of our behavior is influenced by our future hoped-for and feared possible selves.
- Self-esteem is the affective, or evaluative, aspect of the self-concept.

- Assimilation, accommodation, and immunization are three coping processes individuals use to maintain personal continuity and integrity of the self.
- Feelings of personal control are related to the perception that one governs what happens in one's own life. There are mixed findings as to whether internal control declines and external control increases in older adulthood.
- If efforts at primary control are not successful, secondary control processes come into play. Secondary control processes involve alterations in goals and expectations about things that cannot be changed by using primary control processes.
- Maintaining life satisfaction in older adulthood may reflect older adults' achieving a balance between primary and secondary control processes.

Key Terms

accommodation   254
assimilation   253
body transcendence versus body
   preoccupation   240
ego differentiation versus work-role
   preoccupation   240
ego integrity versus despair   239
ego transcendence versus ego
   preoccupation   240
external locus of control   255
Five-Factor Model (FFM) of Personality   243
generativity versus stagnation   239

immunization   255
internal locus of control   255
intimacy versus isolation   239
life review   241
life story   242
optimization of primary and secondary
   control (OPS)   258
possible selves   253
primary control processes   258
secondary control processes   258
self-concept   251
self-esteem   252

9 Social Interaction and Social Ties

Chapter Overview

Close-ups on Adulthood and Aging

Maxine became a widow last year at the age of 76, and she recently moved into a senior citizen apartment building located 5 miles from her daughter and son and their families. Maxine sees her adult children and grandchildren about once a week, and she speaks to at least one of them on the phone almost every day. Maxine chose her new apartment because several close friends moved into the building after they lost their husbands, and they persuaded her to follow suit. She enjoys spending time with these longtime friends – playing cards, going to movies, or just chatting over lunch or coffee in each other's apartments. So far, Maxine has not felt the need to strike up new friendships in the building because she would just as soon stick with old, familiar friends. Maxine misses her husband, but between her adult children (especially her daughter), her grandchildren, and her small circle of friends, there is always someone to talk to. Maxine realizes she will have to ask her children for help if she ever becomes seriously ill. Nevertheless, she feels fortunate to have friends in the building she can count on for small favors and she is more than happy to reciprocate.

Social Interaction in Older Adulthood

Social interactions are an essential part of life, but do they differ in older adulthood from other points in adult life? How are social interactions related to older adults' level of well-being, and what kinds of interactions buffer them against feelings of depression? Investigators have been very interested in the patterns of social interactions and social ties that are most likely to be associated with successful aging.

Early research focused primarily on the quantity of social interactions in older adulthood, and the emphasis was on the positive aspects of social interactions. More recently, there is greater recognition that social interactions are complex – they have rewarding aspects, but they can also be stressful. In short, it is important to evaluate not only the number of social interactions but also their quality because social interactions play a role in determining life satisfaction, well-being, and adaptation to stressful situations.

It is generally recognized that the level of social interaction declines somewhat in older adulthood. Factors such as loss of a partner through widowhood, loss of the work role through retirement, loss of income through both widowhood and retirement, loss of a familiar environment because of relocation, and in some cases loss of health are all associated with reduced opportunities for social interaction. Several theories, described below, offer a perspective on the meaning and implications of the apparent age-related decrease in social interactions.

Activity Theory and Disengagement Theory

According to **activity theory**, older adults strive to maintain their level of social interaction by substituting new roles when old roles are lost. For example, a man who retires from paid employment might become involved in volunteer work, or a woman who loses her husband might join a new social group. To the extent that older adults are successful in replacing social roles, they will enjoy high life satisfaction, or high morale and feelings of well-being (Passuth & Bengston, 1988). Most contemporary researchers do not subscribe to activity theory in its original form. Yet elements of this theory are evident in popular media communications urging retired older adults to remain engaged by doing volunteer work and participating in social groups.

According to **disengagement theory**, social and psychological withdrawal is a necessary component of successful aging. Older adults withdraw voluntarily from roles they played in middle age. At the same time, society withdraws from older adults, expecting them to step aside to make room for the upcoming younger generation. This mutual withdrawal of older individuals and society from each other benefits them both (Passuth & Bengston, 1988). Older adults who disengage meet with society's approval and experience a high level of life satisfaction (Cumming & Henry, 1961).

The suggestion that older adults are willing to withdraw from society and are happy and satisfied when allowed to do so most certainly conflicted with the activity theory premise that older adults disengage only because of circumstances beyond their control. Over time, it became evident that neither theory by itself could explain all of the variations in older adults' level of social interaction or life satisfaction. However, these two theories laid the groundwork for more sophisticated ideas about the nature and role of social interactions in older adulthood.

Socioemotional Selectivity Theory

Socioemotional selectivity theory (SEST) is a life-span model which proposes that the reduced social activity often seen in old age reflects a lifelong selection process (Carstensen, 1991, 1995). The number of individuals in a person's social network may be smaller in older adulthood than it was in young adulthood. However, close social relationships are maintained in older adulthood, while more superficial ones are filtered out, and age-related reductions in social interactions can be adaptive.

Carstensen and her colleagues (Carstensen, Gross, & Fung, 1997; Carstensen, Isaacowitz, & Charles, 1999) emphasize that there are two goals, or motives, when it comes to social interactions: information seeking and emotion regulation. Figure 9.1 illustrates their importance over the life span.

Information seeking
Acquiring information is a prominent motive for social interactions early in life when we are reaching out to meet new people from whom we will ultimately select a spouse or life partner or form long-term friendships. Also, early in life we gather information about potential careers and interests we want to pursue in the future. Acquiring such information calls for interactions with new people, or novel partners. In later adulthood, there is less need to acquire new information for future use. Social interactions also help us mold how we perceive ourselves. An important goal in adolescence and young adulthood is identity formation, which is best served by interacting with novel partners. In later adulthood, there is less motivation to develop identity, so we may prefer spending time with familiar partners on whom we can rely to affirm who we are.

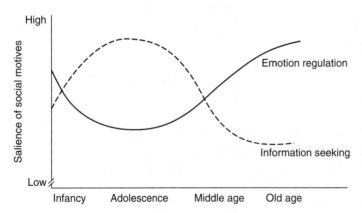

Figure 9.1 *Socioemotional selectivity theory (SEST) conception of the importance of two social motives across the life span.*
Source: Carstensen et al. (1997).

Emotional regulation
Social interactions, especially pleasant ones, fulfill emotional needs.

According to SEST, emotional fulfillment (or emotional regulation) becomes more important in older adulthood. Older adults prefer to socialize with familiar partners because they place great importance on the positive feelings that come from intimate and gratifying social interactions. There is less guarantee of experiencing positive affect in interactions with novel partners. Maxine, the 76-year-old widow described at the beginning of the chapter, prefers to mingle with family members and old friends.

The choice of social partners may be influenced not only by chronological age, but also by the perception of time (Carstensen et al., 1999). When time is perceived as open-ended, or unlimited, our main motivation for engaging in social interactions is acquiring information and we tend to seek out new (novel) social partners. In contrast, when time is perceived as limited, emotional regulation becomes the primary motive. Older adults may prefer interactions with emotionally meaningful and familiar social partners because they feel that the amount of time they have left is limited.

To test the importance of time as it relates to preference for social partners, Fredrickson and Carstensen (1990) manipulated "anticipated endings." Young and older adults were told to imagine having 30 minutes of leisure time with no pressing commitments, and they were instructed to select whether they would prefer to spend that time with a family member (familiar partner) or a recent acquaintance (novel partner). Not surprisingly, 65% of the older adults chose the familiar partner, whereas only 35% of the young adults did. But when the young adults were told to imagine they were preparing for a cross-country move, leaving family and friends behind, 80% selected the familiar partner. Thus, when time limitations are explicitly stated, the young adults' preference for the familiar social partner is similar to that of the older adults. This finding was replicated in a parallel study conducted in Hong Kong (Fung, Carstensen, & Lutz, 1999) in which some participants were told to imagine they would be emigrating in the near future and others were not. Older Asians selected a familiar social partner whether or not they were told emigration was imminent. When told they would be emigrating soon, young Asians were more likely to select the familiar social partner.

In sum, SEST predicts that social preferences are related to the perception of time. Information-seeking motives and novel social partners take precedence when time is unlimited. In contrast, emotional goals and familiar social partners are more important when time is limited. In general, time is likely perceived as more limited in older adulthood than in young adulthood (Carstensen & Fredrickson, 1998).

Social Exchange Theory

According to **social exchange theory** (Dowd, 1975), social interactions can have both rewards and costs. Rewards entail positive feelings, but costs may include unpleasantness experienced during the course of a social exchange.

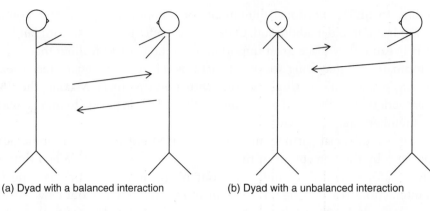

(a) Dyad with a balanced interaction

(arrows indicate that the
two individuals have equal
desire of reward from the other.)

(b) Dyad with a unbalanced interaction

(arrows indicate that the individual
on the right values the reward from the interaction
more than the individual on the left does.)

Figure 9.2 *Social exchange theory.*

There is a greater risk of incurring costs if the interaction is with someone who is not a close family member or friend.

A social interaction between two partners (a dyad) is balanced if both partners have an equal desire for the reward offered by the other. However, one partner may value the reward from the exchange more than the other partner. The concept of power enters in when there is imbalance in a social exchange. The less powerful partner values the exchange more and thus feels obliged to comply with the demands of the more powerful partner. Over time, such compliance becomes increasingly costly to the less powerful partner; if the costs of the interaction continue to outweigh the benefits, the less powerful partner may withdraw from the interaction. The more powerful partner may be another individual but could also be an institution in the broader social environment.

Dowd (1975) contended that in American society, power increases from young adulthood through late middle age, only to be followed by a sharp decrease in old age. However, he predicted that in the future, older adults would be more educated and more independent financially; therefore, they would experience less decline in power. As the baby boomers enter older adulthood, there is good reason to believe that Dowd's earlier prediction will come true.

Nonetheless, social exchange theory is useful for understanding social interactions in some contexts. For example, older residents of long-term care facilities such as nursing homes often experience difficulties negotiating with administrators and staff members to get what they need. To combat this imbalance in power, many states in the United States have laws that require long-term care facilities to post a list of "Nursing Home Residents' Rights." The statements in Table 9.1 are adapted from Florida Statute 400.022 concerning nursing home residents' rights in the state of Florida.

In addition, most states have ombudsman programs. Ombudsmen are usually volunteers trained in how to resolve complaints about quality of care that are

Table 9.1 *Nursing Home Residents' Rights*

Nursing home residents enter their new home losing none of the civil rights they were entitled to in the community. Additionally, state regulation requires nursing homes to assure residents special rights, including the following:

Civil and religious liberties, including independent personal decisions.

Private and uncensored communication, including mail, phone access, and visitation.

Reasonable access to health, social, and legal providers, and immediate access to any representative of federal and state government, including the Department of Children and Families, Agency for Health Care Administration, law enforcement, ombudsman, and the resident's personal physician.

Present grievances as well as organize and participate in resident groups.

Participate in social, religious, and community activities.

Manage their own financial affairs.

Be fully informed of the charges and services not covered by per diem rate.

Be adequately informed of their medical condition and proposed treatment.

Refuse medication or treatment and be informed of the consequences.

Receive adequate and appropriate health care and protective and support services.

Be given privacy in treatment and in caring for personal needs.

Be given courteous, fair, and dignified treatment.

Be assured freedom from mental and physical abuse, punishment, and seclusion.

Be transferred or discharged only for medical reasons or for the welfare of other residents, and only with advance notice of no less than 30 days.

Be given freedom of choice in selecting a personal physician, pharmaceutical supplier, and services.

Be allowed to retain and use personal clothing and possessions as space permits.

Be given copies of facility rules and regulations.

Receive notice before any room change is made.

Be fully informed of the nursing home's bed reservation policy in case of hospitalization.

Adapted from Florida Statutes 400.022.

made by or on behalf of older adults who reside in nursing homes and assisted-living facilities. Ombudsmen work to insure that the older adults who reside in such facilities receive the legal, financial, social, and rehabilitative services to which they are entitled. In some sense, their role is to maintain a balance in the exchange between residents and facility administrators.

Positive and Negative Aspects of Social Relationships

Research on social relationships in older adulthood has concentrated largely on the benefits of social interactions. Less attention has been paid to the negative aspects of social interactions (Lachman, 2003; Rook, 1997) even though most of us have experienced interactions with people who are unsympathetic, demanding, or even antagonistic.

Rook (1984) asked relatively healthy, independent widowed older women (aged 60 to 89) to identify people to whom they could turn for socializing and confiding their personal problems, and for help when they are ill (positive relationships). The same women also identified people who cause them problems such as invading their privacy, breaking promises of help, and provoking conflicts or feelings of anger (negative relationships). Women who reported many negative relationships did not necessarily have few positive ones; likewise, women who reported very few negative relationships did not necessarily have many positive ones. In short, older women who have problematic relationships do not lack social skills because they have good relationships as well.

Not surprisingly, positive social exchanges (for example, interacting with others who give reassurance or care in times of upset or illness) are associated with feelings of well-being. In contrast, negative social exchanges (for example, interacting with others who are too demanding) are associated with feelings of loneliness and depression, which not only detract from psychological well-being in later life (Sorkin & Rook, 2006) but also can have adverse affects on physical health (Krause, 2006). The connection between negative social interactions and negative feelings is especially strong when older adults are already experiencing multiple stressors – losing a spouse or friend, experiencing illness, moving to a new residence, retiring from work, and so on (Ingersoll-Dayton, Morgan, & Antonucci, 1997).

As individuals age, they become more selective in their social relationships, maintaining ties with social partners who enhance their emotional well-being. Older adults report fewer negative social exchanges with a spouse, children, relatives, and friends. In general, they express less ambivalence about close social relationships (Fingerman, Hay, & Birditt, 2004). Older adults seem to choose social partners who provide them with uniformly positive social experiences. Indeed, older adults who strive to maintain harmony and goodwill in a relationship seem to experience fewer and less intense stressful interactions with others (Sorkin & Rook, 2006).

Understanding Aging Box 9.1: Emotional Intensity and Interpersonal Exchanges

Interpersonal exchanges can have positive aspects that are gratifying as well as negative aspects that are unpleasant. Emotional reactions to positive exchanges include feelings of happiness and pride, whereas emotional reactions to negative exchanges include feelings of annoyance and fear. Charles and Piazza (2007) asked younger and older adults to list 10 individuals (social partners, including family members, established friends, and new acquaintances) with whom they had interacted during the past week for at least 10 minutes. Then they rated the intensity of positive emotions and negative emotions they felt during each interaction. Compared to younger adults, older adults reported a lower intensity of positive emotions when interacting with new acquaintances, a similar level of positive emotions when interacting with established friends, and a higher intensity of positive emotions when interacting with family members. Compared to younger adults, older adults reported a lower intensity of negative emotions when interacting with all three types of social partners, but the difference between the younger and older adults was most pronounced for interactions with new acquaintances. These findings are consistent with the SEST proposition that older adults have considerable positive emotional investment in ties with family members (with close friends coming in a close second) but much less interest in forming ties with new acquaintances.

Social Ties in Older Adulthood

Social ties are an important factor in older adults' physical and psychological well-being (Fees et al., 1999), and some relationships are closer and longer-lasting than others. Many ties are with family members but some are with individuals outside the family.

Social Convoys, Social Networks, and Reciprocity

According to the **convoy model** (Antonucci, Sherman, & Akiyama, 1996), individuals move through life both affecting and being affected by a constellation of other people who play a central role in their network of social relationships and influence their well-being. The people in the social convoy are often family members, but there may also be friends with whom there is close contact on a regular basis. For Maxine, the 76-year-old widow described at the beginning of this chapter, the social convoy consists of her adult children and grandchildren and some longtime close friends.

The term **social network** refers to the structural characteristics of an individual's social ties, including the number, age, sex, relationship, and frequency of contact with people who are part of it (Antonucci et al., 1996). Some researchers study social networks by asking individuals to map their social ties onto a three-tier concentric-circle diagram (see Figure 9.3). Individuals place the people who are closest

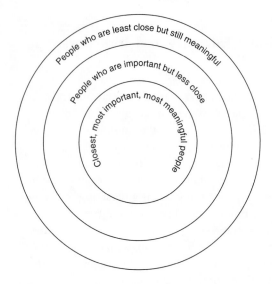

Figure 9.3 *Three concentric circles used to demonstrate a person's social network.*

and most important to them in the innermost circle, those somewhat less close in the middle circle, and those who are least close but still somewhat important in the outermost circle (Antonucci, 1986).

Members of our social network provide social support in various forms (Antonucci et al., 1996; Levitt, Weber, & Guacci, 1993). Some offer assistance when we are ill or help when we encounter financial difficulties. Others are individuals in whom we can confide when we are upset or worried and who can replenish our feelings of control and self-worth (Krause & Borawski-Clark, 1994). Still others are just people with whom we want to spend time (Antonucci & Akiyama, 1987; Levitt et al., 1993). Social support in all of these forms can buffer individuals against the negative effects of stress (Antonucci et al., 1996).

Reciprocity

Social exchanges that are balanced in terms of support both provided and received have **reciprocity**. In reciprocal social exchanges, each individual gives as much support as he or she receives. In nonreciprocal exchanges, an individual gives more support than he or she receives, or conversely, receives more support than he or she gives. One suggestion is that we make deposits into a **support bank** by giving more support than we receive as long as we are able to do so. Later, we may need more support than we can give, at which point we feel it is legitimate to make withdrawals from the support bank (Antonucci et al., 1996).

Levitt et al. (1993) asked triads of women – young adult daughters (university students), their mothers, and their grandmothers – to map their social networks onto a concentric three-circle diagram, placing those individuals to whom they were most attached in the inner circle. Each woman also indicated the extent to which members of her network provide support of various types (giving reassurance, advice, care if she is ill, and so on). As predicted, the women in the older generation (grandmothers) reported giving less support than the young women and their middle-aged mothers did. The grandmothers may have provided more support in the past, but they are now receiving more support than they are giving. Family members were an important source of support for all three generations, but the proportion of friends in the network declined from the young to middle to older generation. Levitt et al. speculate that the young adults' more extensive friendship networks help them attain independence from their families so that they can establish intimate relationships that lead to new family structures through marriage and the birth of children. Later, family members are likely to become the primary source of support.

In Levitt et al.'s (1993) study, the triads were bicultural (English-speaking or Spanish-speaking). There was considerable similarity in network structure and type of support across the two cultural groups – both English-speaking and Spanish-speaking participants placed close family members in the inner circle. However, the Spanish-speaking triads were more family-focused, with a greater proportion of family members in their support networks.

Size of older adults' social network

Both chronological age and individual differences in personality play a role in the size of older adults' social network. In a study conducted in Berlin, Germany, the size of the social networks reported by individuals between the ages of 70 and 104 was negatively related to chronological age (Lang & Carstensen, 1994). That is, the older the person, the smaller the social network. Even into very late older adulthood, individuals maintain meaningful emotional ties with others, but they become more exclusive. The oldest members of the sample reported a decline in the number of social interactions, but this decline was due mainly to the more limited interactions with people who were not considered to be particularly close.

With regard to personality, extraverts have larger social networks than introverts even into the ninth decade of life (Lang, Staudinger, & Carstensen, 1998). Similarly, individuals who are more open to experience have larger social networks than those who are less open. In short, older adults who are outgoing, sociable, and seek new experiences tend to maintain larger social networks than older adults who are less outgoing, less sociable, and less open to new experiences. Still, it is important to emphasize that older adults with smaller social networks are emotionally close to those who are in it.

Older adults with family members available to them tend to have larger social networks and seem to enjoy greater feelings of social belonging. When a spouse and adult offspring are available, emotional closeness with other social partners may be less important. However, when a spouse and adult children are not available, older adults may seek support from other relatives or friends.

Family Relationships

Family is sometimes defined in terms of household members. The **nuclear family household** is common in urban American society and consists of parents and their children who live under the same roof. For the parents, the nuclear family represents the **family of procreation**. For the children, the nuclear family represents the **family of origin**. Eventually, children grow up and many move out to form their own family of procreation.

The **extended family household**, which was common in rural areas in earlier decades, consists of members from more than two generations (grandparents, parents, children), all living under the same roof or in very close proximity. The extended family household could also include aunts, uncles, and cousins.

Some extended families formed an economic unit, such as running the family farm. In the United States today, there are fewer multigenerational extended families living under the same roof or working together. This has given rise to a common myth that older adults are isolated from and abandoned by their families (Bengston, Rosenthal, & Burton, 1996).

In an extensive survey of older adults, Shanas (1979) found that, contrary to this myth, older adults do not yearn to live under the same roof as adult children and grandchildren. Rather, many express a preference for **intimacy at a distance**, which means that they welcome contact and involvement with family members but prefer to maintain their own households as long as they are physically and financially capable. Over half lived within 10 minutes of at least one adult child and many had visited with an adult child in the week prior to the survey. In addition, many older adults had frequent contact with siblings and other relatives in the form of either face-to-face visits or telephone conversations. Thus, older adults are not alienated or uninvolved with their families just because they do not live under the same roof. In fact, Shanas concluded that the dominant family structure in the United States is the **modified extended family**, which consists of a broad kinship network including grandparents, parents, grandchildren, siblings, and even nephews, nieces and other relatives by blood or marriage. Members of this family network have frequent contact and provide support for one another even though they do not live under the same roof or work together. Maxine, the 76-year-old widow described at the beginning of this chapter, lives within 5 miles of all her children and their families and has regular contact with them. Even so, she enjoys having her own apartment and spending time with same-aged friends.

Another common belief is that because of the increase in geographic mobility in the U.S. population, ties with elderly family members are weakening. However, based on data from the U.S. Current Population Survey, geographic mobility has actually declined from the 1950s for young and older adults and has remained stable for middle-aged adults (Wolf & Longino, 2005).

The **beanpole family structure** describes what families will be like in the future. Thanks to the increase in life expectancy, more families will have four or even five living generations. However, each generation will have fewer members because the birth rate is lower today than it was in earlier decades.

The **blended family** is a term for families in which some members are unrelated by blood but nonetheless live together and share family responsibilities. Such families are usually the result of divorce and remarriage. One or both members of a remarried couple may bring children from a prior marriage into a newly formed (reconstituted) family.

Marital satisfaction

The marital relationship is central to the lives of many adults, and among older married couples feelings of closeness are associated with high self-esteem and reduced depression and anxiety, even when one or both members of the pair face some degree of disability (Mancini & Bonanno, 2006).

In general, though, what is the course of marital satisfaction over the adult life span? The **upswing hypothesis of marital satisfaction** refers to a phenomenon that characterizes some marriages over time (Anderson, Russell, & Schumm, 1983). The level of marital satisfaction is high in the early years of marriage before the arrival of children, followed by a dip in the ensuing years when the focus is on rearing children and estab-

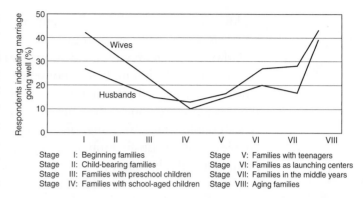

Stage   I: Beginning families   Stage   V: Families with teenagers
Stage   II: Child-bearing families   Stage   VI: Families as launching centers
Stage III: Families with preschool children   Stage VII: Families in the middle years
Stage IV: Families with school-aged children   Stage VIII: Aging families

Figure 9.4 *The upswing hypothesis of marital satisfaction.*
Source: Rollins & Feldman (1970).

lishing careers. Later, marital satisfaction shows an increase, or upswing, although perhaps not to quite as high a level as in the early years. This upswing occurs around the time children are launched, at which point many couples are in good health and can enjoy more personal freedom.

The upswing hypothesis was based on cross-sectional research in which couples of various ages and number of years married were interviewed at the same time. Note that individuals who remain in a marital relationship for a long time may represent a select subgroup whose relationships have withstood stresses that caused other couples to separate or divorce.

Interactions between married couples

Even when couples have been married a long time, they do not necessarily agree on everything. Carstensen, Gottman, and Levenson (1995) and Levenson, Carstensen, and Gottman (1993) studied middle-aged couples (aged 40–50 and married at least 15 years) and older couples (aged 60–70 and married at least 35 years). Most of the couples were in first marriages, had been married at about the same age, and had children. All of the couples resided in Berkeley, California, were predominantly European American (85%), upper middle class, well educated, and similar in level of education and income. When these couples were asked to rate how much disagreement they had experienced in 10 areas of potential conflict, the greatest difference between the middle-aged and older couples was in the area of children, which ranked highest as a source of conflict for the middle-aged couples but only fourth in importance for the older couples. Middle-aged couples had children who were still living at home or had left home recently, which could explain why children were a more immediate source of conflict. The older couples' children were grown and no longer living with them, which could explain why children were a more enjoyable topic of conversation.

Overall, the older couples reported having fewer disagreements than the middle-aged couples. This finding bodes well for long-term marriages, although it is conceivable that couples who experience significant conflict in middle age may simply not remain married. If so, the older couples may represent a positively selected group.

Although all the couples had been married for years or decades, there was considerable variation in their responses to a self-report questionnaire on marital satisfaction, which all of them completed at the beginning of the study. Based on the self-report responses, these investigators divided middle-aged couples and older couples into two subgroups: satisfied and dissatisfied. Not surprisingly, couples in the dissatisfied subgroup reported greater disagreement than couples in the satisfied subgroup in almost all areas of potential conflict (children, money, communication, sex, friends, and so on).

Among the dissatisfied couples, the wives reported more physical and psychological symptoms than the husbands did. In general, being married seems to have a more uniformly positive influence on happiness and well-being for men than it does for women (Mroczek & Kolarz, 1998). As such, men as a group are better off when married, but women are better off only when happily married. Perhaps women have a greater need to feel emotionally important to their spouses and are more likely to derive their feelings of self-worth from an interpersonal connection to a spouse (Tower & Kasl, 1996). When the spousal relationship is not fulfilling, women suffer more, whereas men tend to buffer themselves against health problems by withdrawing from conflict (Levenson et al., 1993).

In addition to collecting self-report data on marital satisfaction, Carstensen et al. (1995) made video recordings as each couple interacted during the course of a 15-minute conversation about a problem that they claimed was causing continuing disagreement in their marriage. The feelings, or emotional affect, shown by members of the pair were rated by objective observers for verbal content, voice tone, facial expression, gestures, and body movement. Compared with the older couples, the middle-aged couples displayed more emotion, both positive (interest, humor, joy) and negative (anger, disgust, belligerence, defensiveness, whining). The older couples seemed to show greater emotional regulation, or control (Gross et al., 1997), including greater effort to maintain harmony in an already committed relationship (Sorkin & Rook, 2004).

In addition to age-related differences, gender differences were noted in both the middle-aged and older couples. The wives' facial expressions showed more emotion, both positive and negative, and they also expressed more emotion verbally. In contrast, the husbands' facial expressions were more neutral, and their verbal expression of emotion was more restrained. Husbands in the dissatisfied couples were especially careful to avoid conflict.

Overall, these findings illustrate that even after many years of marriage, some couples are happy and satisfied, and this is reflected in their expressions of humor and affection, even when they are discussing topics that arouse marital conflict. On the other hand, even in long-term marriages there can be dissatisfaction and negative emotions. However, when they do disagree, older couples show less negative affect, less emotional intensity, and greater affection than the middle-aged couples. In short, older couples who are dissatisfied show more restraint in expressing negative emotions.

Even when interactions do not involve married couples, older adults are more likely than younger adults to control their feelings and reactions (Diehl, Coyle, & Labouvie-Vief, 1996) and to express emotion less intensely (Lawton, Kleban, Rajagopal, & Dean, 1992). In a study of community-living adults ranging from 19 to 96 years of age, Gross et al. (1997) found a consistent pattern of age-related increase in emotional regulation in European American, African American, and Asian American groups. Based on phone interviews with 666 individuals aged 25 to 74, Birditt et al. (2005) found that, compared to younger adults, older adults report fewer interpersonal tensions in their day-to-day lives, fewer stressful experiences, and less likelihood of arguing.

In sum, with increasing age, negative emotions tend to decline and there is greater control over emotional expression and reactions to problems. Carstensen et al. (2006) contend that "decreases in negative affect and increases in positive affect and emotional control indicate that the emotional lives of older adults are more pleasant and manageable relative to their younger counterparts" (p. 346).

Same-sex couples

Studies on older couples have focused mainly on heterosexual married couples. Less is known about older gay (men) and lesbian (women) couples. Yet, a number of such couples have long-term partnerships that last for decades (Hooyman & Kiyak, 2008; Kimmel, 1992), and it is not uncommon to see the word "companion" in published obituaries (Kimmel, 1992). Compared to younger cohorts of gay and lesbian adults, older gay and lesbian adults probably experienced more

---

Applying Research Box 9.1: Cohabitation Among Older Couples

The prevalence of heterosexual cohabitation in the United States has grown dramatically in recent decades among all age groups (Brown, Lee, & Bulanda, 2006). Most of the attention surrounding cohabitation has focused on younger adults, some of whom live together prior to marriage. However, figures from the 2000 U.S. Census indicate that more than one million individuals ages 51 and older were cohabiting. The majority (71%) of older cohabiters are separated or divorced, 18% are widowed, but only 11% have never been married. How do cohabiting older couples compare to remarried older couples? Older cohabiters appear to be at a disadvantage compared those who are remarried: They have lower incomes, are less likely to own a house or have health insurance, and less likely to have social ties with friends and relatives who live nearby. The disadvantage associated with later life cohabitation is especially pronounced among women, who seem to derive fewer benefits from this arrangement compared to men. We need further information on the benefits and costs of cohabitation among older adults because this arrangement is expected to become more common as baby boomers move into their older years.

discrimination because American society was less accepting in the past of same-sex relationships. Even so, many older gay and lesbian couples express satisfaction with their lives (Kausler et al., 2007). Some have built "surrogate families" from a self-created network of friends who provide strong social support (Hooyman & Kiyak, 2008; Kimmel, 1992; Quadagno, 2008). Older gay men are especially likely to derive social support from friends (Dorfman et al., 1995). Even so, some have close relationships with their biological families, and family members often count on them for material and emotional support in times of emergency (Kimmel, 1992). Some serve as caretakers of aging parents, perhaps because they have more disposable income and fewer child rearing responsibilities (Quadagno, 2008).

Intergenerational relationships

What is the nature of the relationships between older adults and their adult children? In both European American and African American families, adult children maintain greater contact with their older mothers than they do with their older fathers (Spitze & Miner, 1992). Moreover, the bond seems to be strongest between mothers and daughters (Fingerman, 1996). Most often, women are the kin-keepers, meaning that they work harder than men do to keep the family in touch and they provide more social support to family members (Bengston et al., 1996). Even though contact is less frequent between mothers and sons than between mothers and daughters, the bond between older parents and their adult sons may be underrated (Bengston et al., 1996), possibly because questionnaires that assess older parent/adult child social support consist disproportionately of items that deal with relationships between women (for example, serving a comforting role). There is a clear need for more research on men's role in intergenerational family relationships.

Close relationships generally imply family solidarity, which includes affection, contact, and mutual support. Even so, few relationships are without some interpersonal tension. However, investigators have found that older adults are more reluctant than their adult children to admit that any tension exists in their relationships (Mancini & Bleiszner, 1989). This discrepancy between older parents' and adult children's tendency to report conflict has been attributed to the **intergenerational stake hypothesis** (Bengston & Kuypers, 1971). Older parents are invested in perceiving their offspring in a favorable light – they view their relationships with adult children through rose-colored glasses. In contrast, adult offspring wish to make their own mark on the world, so they are motivated to perceive their parents as less compatible.

Fingerman (1996) interviewed 48 pairs (dyads) of healthy, active, independent, educated European American older mothers (average age 76) and their adult daughters (average age 44). The older mothers and their daughters each considered the other to be an important part of their lives, and both expressed generally positive feelings about their relationship. In keeping with the intergenerational stake hypothesis, however, the older mothers tended to praise their daughters even when discussing their faults and many named the daughter as a preferred confidante and the person with whom they most enjoy spending time. In contrast, the daughters were more likely to find their mothers' need for closeness to be intrusive. Also, the older mothers felt they were an integral part of their daughter's family of procreation, but the daughters felt that their relationship with their mothers was separate and distinct from the relationship they had with their spouse and offspring. Most of the middle-aged daughters were married, but fewer than half of the older mothers were, so perhaps older mothers needed to feel part of their daughters' family of procreation.

In another study, Clarke, Preston, Raksin, and Bengston (1999) conducted a mail survey asking older parents (average age 62) and adult children (average age 39) to respond to the following open-ended question:

> No matter how well two people get along, there are times they disagree or get annoyed about something. In the last few years, what are some things on which you have differed, disagreed, or been disappointed about (even if not openly discussed) with your child (or parent)? (Clarke et al., 1999, p. 262)

Survey participants were not at all reluctant to acknowledge that tension existed – over two-thirds of both older parents and adult children willingly supplied examples of conflict. But what, specifically, were the sources of tension between older parents and their adult children? The most common area of conflict older adults reported had to do with lifestyle choices (for example, disapproval of style of dress, hair style, educational or occupational choices, or use of alcohol), whereas the most common area of conflict adult children reported revolved around communication issues (for example, strained or nonexistent communication, yelling, or criticism). However, the fact that the older parents were just as likely as the adult children to acknowledge tension would seem to contradict the intergenerational stake hypothesis, which predicts that the parent generation has a more positive view of their children than the children have of their parents. Perhaps the older adults were more comfortable airing complaints about adult children in a mail survey than they would have been in face-to-face interviews. Also, note that the average age of Clarke et al.'s older survey respondents was 62 as opposed to the average age of 76 in Fingerman's study. The intergenerational stake hypothesis may be less applicable in the early older adult years than it is later on in older adulthood. Despite conflict in some areas, however, many older parents and their children maintain close relationships (Bengston et al., 1996).

Caregiving

Relationships between older parents and adult children can be reciprocal, with older parents providing support to their adult children and vice versa. By some measures, older parents are more likely to give help than they are to receive it (Norris & Tindale, 1994; Spitze & Logan, 1992). For example, many older adults provide financial assistance to adult children and their families, and if they are in good health they may help care for grandchildren when parents are working. In China, it is quite common for older adults to act as surrogate parents when their adult children migrate to find work in urban areas (Silverstein, 2006).

However, as people live into the old-old (75–84) and oldest-old (85+) years, they may need help from family members to continue living in the community. For example, older adults who give up driving because of a decline in sensory or perceptual capabilities need help with transportation for shopping, doctors' appointments, and so on. Such help is often provided by adult children. Widowed older adults may need help with tasks a spouse used to perform (for example, managing finances or food preparation). Those who lose a spouse may need emotional support, especially if close friends are no longer available because of death or relocation to places too distant to visit. Also, older family members with failing health may need assistance with personal care such as bathing and dressing.

When older adults do need care, who gives it? Men often help with tasks such as finances, whereas women help more with day-to-day tasks such as shopping, transporting to doctors' appointments, and providing emotional support. Middle-aged women have been labeled the **sandwich generation** because many are caught between competing intergenerational demands (Bengston et al., 1996). Not only do they provide care for their older parents, but many also have obligations to a spouse and children still living at home. On the positive side, many middle-aged married women who are caregivers for older parents get emotional support from their spouses, and this may buffer them against some of the negative effects of caregiving stress (Franks & Stephens, 1996). In contrast, single or divorced middle-aged daughters often bear responsibility for older parents by themselves, with little support from anyone else (Brody, Litvin, Albert, & Hoffman, 1994). Currently, less is known about unmarried middle-aged sons, but with the increasing beanpole family structure, adult sons may take a more active role in caring for older parents in the future. However, widowed older women may feel more comfortable having personal care provided by adult daughters than by adult sons (Bengston et al., 1996).

It is commonly assumed that caregiving for elderly parents places a burden on adult children, but adult children often derive satisfaction from helping their elderly parents. Walker, Acock, Bowman, and Li (1996) followed 128 predominantly European American mother–daughter pairs over two years to determine the daughters' level of satisfaction with caregiving. The older mothers were at least age 65, single (widowed or divorced), and living within 45 miles of their middle-aged daughters. The support the daughters gave to their mothers was mostly help with shopping, indoor maintenance, and food preparation. The length of time the mothers needed care was not a significant factor in the daughters' satisfaction. However, if the amount of care the mothers needed increased over time, the daughters' positive feelings declined. Even so, the daughters' satisfaction remained relatively high over the two-year period, which suggests that any costs the daughters incurred were largely offset by the rewarding aspects of their caregiving role.

The older mothers in this study had some physical problems, but most were cognitively intact and did not require extensive care. It is not clear whether the rewards of caregiving would still offset the costs if these mothers had suffered from cognitive impairment or needed extensive personal care such as help getting dressed rather than help with errands and household chores.

When older adults experience a decline in health, it is often daughters who provide social support, especially for their mothers (Silverstein, Gans, & Yang, 2006). However, the quality of a mother–daughter relationship can moderate the middle-aged daughter's feelings about caregiving. Compared with daughters who are not close to their mothers, daughters with positive relationships and strong feelings of attachment feel less subjective burden even if they provide extensive care for their mothers (Cicirelli, 1993; Walker, Martin, & Jones, 1992).

In well-functioning mother–daughter relationships, there is a balance between connection and autonomy (McGraw & Walker, 2004). To the extent possible, caregiving daughters must support the independence of their older mothers, but even frail older mothers must be responsive to their caregiving children's needs.

Dilworth-Anderson, Williams, and Cooper (1999) studied how families provided care to 42 male and 160 female widowed African Americans (average age 74), most of whom had physical limitations and some degree of cognitive impairment. In some of the families, caregiving fell to only one family member; in others, responsibilities were shared by two or more caregivers. Not surprisingly, shared caregiving was more common when the older family member had greater needs and also when several adult children lived close by. However, Dilworth-Anderson et al. theorize that the shared caregiving may stem from an African American cultural legacy. Roff et al. (2004) investigated how family caregivers of community-dwelling older adults with dementia felt about their caregiving role. Compared with the European American caregivers, the African American caregivers were less anxious and perceived caregiving more favorably (for example, caregiving made them feel useful and appreciated). The African American caregivers also expressed greater religiosity, and their higher commitment to religious practice and belief was also associated with more favorable appraisals of caregiving. Hopefully, researchers will continue to search for factors associated with satisfaction among family caregivers.

With increasing life expectancy, people are spending more time as grandparents and many will become great-grandparents as well.

Grandparenthood

With the increase in life expectancy, many older adults will become grandparents and could spend four or more decades in this role (Kivnick & Sinclair, 1996).

However, with the beanpole family structure, grandparents in the future will probably have fewer grandchildren than grandparents had in the past. Even so, not only will they become grandparents, but they also stand a good chance of becoming great-grandparents.

The nature of the grandparent role can vary depending upon gender, socio-economic status, marital status, ethnicity, age of the grandchildren, and the age and stage of life when grandparenthood actually begins. Grandparents who are chronologically younger may still have children living at home and many still work full-time, so competing roles can limit the amount of time spent with grandchildren. Older grandparents are more likely to be retired and have more time to spend with grandchildren, but the nature of their activities with their grandchildren may depend upon their health. For example, grandparents must be in good health to take their grandchildren to places such as Disney World. Relationships with grandchildren may also depend on how close they live. Grandparents who live closer to their grandchildren have more chances to see them than grandparents who live hundreds of miles away.

Kivnick and Sinclair (1996) identified three grandparenting styles: remote, companionate, and involved. *Remote grandparents* are emotionally distant and formal. Many live far from their grandchildren or are busy with work or other interests. *Companionate grandparents*, probably the most common style in contemporary American society, engage in entertaining and pleasurable leisure activities with grandchildren (for example, playing games and baking cookies). In general, however, they avoid interfering in the discipline of grandchildren, leaving it to the parents. Perhaps this is a wise strategy, given the negative attitudes, particularly of middle-class European American mothers, toward grandparents who give unsolicited advice about child rearing (Norris & Tindale, 1994; Thomas, 1990). Advice from grandparents may be more acceptable in African American and Asian American families, especially when the grandparents live in the same household (Norris & Tindale, 1994). *Involved grandparents* spend a great deal of time with grandchildren, in some instances caring for them while their parents work outside the home. With the increasing divorce rate, more parents of young children must work, and sometimes they turn to grandparents to assist with child care. Involved grandparents may function as surrogate parents if their adult children are deceased or otherwise unable to fulfill the parental role because of substance abuse or problems with mental or physical health. Under such circumstances, grandparents assume the role of authority in bringing up their grandchildren. In urban African American families, grandmothers are often responsible for rearing grandchildren, especially if the grandchildren's mother is a single parent. However, across all ethnic and economic groups, custodial grandparents who care for grandchildren on a full-time basis are becoming more prevalent. From 1990 to 2001 there was a 30% increase in the number of children living in households headed by grandparents (Hayslip & Kaminski, 2005).

When grandparents and grandchildren do not live in the same household, their relationship is often influenced by the middle generation (Giarrusso &

Silverstein, 1995). If parents (that is, adult children and/or their spouses) are close to grandparents, then grandchildren are likely to spend time with grandparents. Grandchildren tend to have a closer relationship with maternal grandparents simply because they see them more often than they do paternal grandparents.

Disruption of nuclear families through divorce can affect grandparents' involvement with their grandchildren. Grandparents on the familial side of the custodial parent usually see more of their grandchildren and often become closer than they were before the parents divorced. Sometimes divorced adult children move in with their older adult parents on a temporary or permanent basis, both for economic reasons and to provide additional family support for the grandchildren. In contrast, grandparents on the familial side of the noncustodial parent may see less of the grandchildren and may even lose contact with them altogether. In some states in the United States, grandparents' rights legislation allows grandparents to go to court to secure the right to visit their grandchildren (Giarrusso & Silverstein, 1995). Even so, such litigious conditions could compromise relationships with grandchildren. With divorce and remarriage becoming so common, there is much to be learned about how grandparents successfully negotiate attachments and relationships not only with grandchildren, but also with step-grandchildren.

A grandparent's marital status may have some bearing on time spent with grandchildren. Widowed grandparents, particularly grandmothers, tend to spend more time with grandchildren than do married grandparents, who may have busier social lives that compete with the grandparent role. Divorce of a grandparent couple can affect relationships with adult children and grandchildren because one or both members of the grandparent couple may spend less time with the grandchildren, especially if they remarry.

Sibling relationships

Sibling attachments and sibling rivalry exert strong socializing influences when children are growing up in the family of origin. However, as children grow into young adulthood, they usually establish their own households, and with marriage and the birth of children, the family of procreation becomes more dominant (Bengston et al., 1996). Rivalry between brothers and sisters in the family of origin may die down, but at the same time, young adult and middle-aged siblings become less close as each becomes absorbed in raising children and establishing a career.

Geographical proximity is an important factor in the closeness of sibling ties (Connidis, 1994). Opportunities for career advancement may necessitate geographical relocation and physical separation from siblings. Those who relocate often have less contact with the family of origin. Many develop a surrogate family by forming a network of friends who live close by and share common interests.

However, there is an **hourglass effect in sibling relationships** over the life span (Norris & Tindale, 1994). Ties that were strong when siblings lived under the same roof tend to weaken in young and middle adulthood, but often they are

Sibling attachments often become closer in older adulthood, and usually the bond between sisters is the strongest.

reactivated in the later years. The reestablishment of sibling ties in later adulthood can be attributed to several factors, one of which is more free time once children in the nuclear family of procreation leave home. Also, the friendship networks adults establish during their young and middle adult years may shrink due to geographical migration, divorce, and death. One further factor contributing to increased closeness in later adulthood is that siblings who were scattered across geographical regions may return to the location of their family of origin when they retire. Sometimes sibling ties are revitalized in older adulthood simply because sources of conflict that interfered with their relationship earlier in life no longer exist or become less important (Bedford, 1989). For example, a spouse who interfered with a strong sibling relationship may cease to be an obstacle due to divorce or death. Conflicts between siblings sometimes arise over the need to share caregiving responsibilities for an elderly parent. This source of tension may be lessened when the elderly parent moves into a nursing home or is deceased. Finally, as people grow older, many place greater value on memories of a common past, which they can share only with siblings who grew up in the same family of origin (Cicirelli, 1995).

Compared to interactions with spouses and children, interactions with siblings are generally considered to be more voluntary (Bengston et al., 1996). But what kinds of support do siblings provide for one another in times of need? According to the **hierarchical-compensatory model** (Cantor, 1979), individuals have a hierarchy of relationships that they call upon when they need support. When a spouse or adult children are not available because of divorce, death, or geographical distance, older adults compensate by turning to siblings, who are lower down in the hierarchy. The hierarchical-compensatory model could explain why sibling support is stronger among older adults who are single or widowed, and childless, than among older adults who are married and have adult children (Cicirelli, Coward, & Dwyer,1992). In a Canadian survey of individuals aged 55 and over (Connidis, 1994), marital status was a significant predictor of sibling support. Compared with married respondents, those who were widowed were more likely to receive sibling support during an illness and to expect they would receive long-term support from siblings if needed. Furthermore, widowed and divorced respondents were more likely than married ones to say that a sibling could live with them if circumstances made it necessary. However, unless siblings have a reciprocal relationship whereby they help one another, support from a sibling is usually temporary (Cicirelli, 1995).

Does number of siblings make a difference in the support a brother or sister will receive in a time of need? Compared to older adults with two or more siblings, those with only one sibling were less likely to receive support in a time of need and less likely to expect sibling support would be available (Connidis, 1994).

It is not clear why having only one sibling should represent a disadvantage because actual support is usually supplied by only one individual. Perhaps one sibling's efforts result from active negotiation among all of the siblings, who reach an agreement over who will be responsible for helping a brother or sister in need.

In addition to number of siblings, sibling gender is a significant factor. Of Connidis' (1994) study respondents with two or more siblings, those with sisters were more likely to think they would receive support during a crisis than those who had only brothers. Respondents with only one sibling were less likely to think they would receive sibling support during a crisis than those with two or more siblings. However, they felt that their chances of receiving support were greater if that sibling was a sister rather than a brother. This reinforces the common belief that women maintain stronger ties to their family of origin than men. Men may have a closer attachment to their wives' family of origin, including her siblings, than to their own family of origin (Bengston et al., 1996). Longitudinal research studies that follow sibling attachments over time would be of great value in aiding our understanding of how family dynamics influence sibling support.

The hierarchical-compensatory model does not take into account the many variations in sibling relationships. Based on interviews of 89 European American late-life sibling dyads, Gold (1989) identified five categories of sibling relationships, which fall on a continuum from a greater to a lesser degree of emotional closeness:

- *Intimate siblings* are highly devoted, share a relationship of mutual love and understanding, confide their personal thoughts and feelings, and consider each other "best friends." Contact is frequent, including visits and telephone calls.
- *Congenial siblings* feel strong friendship and caring, but their emotional ties are not as deep except in times of crisis or stress. There may be weekly or monthly contact, but congenial siblings would name a spouse or child as the person to whom they feel closest.
- *Loyal siblings* have a bond based on shared family background and a strong sense of family obligation. There is little contact, but they appear upon request at important family occasions like weddings, funerals, and holiday celebrations. They rarely exchange emotional support, but they would help in times of illness or financial difficulties.
- *Apathetic siblings* are not close and are not interested in taking any responsibility for one another. They do not attend family occasions, and contact is rare even if they live nearby. They may go for years without talking to each other out of indifference rather than anger or disagreement.
- *Hostile siblings* go out of their way to avoid one another. They feel disdain and anger and claim they would reject any requests for support. They are emotionally involved, but in a negative way. Sometimes hostility stems from a dispute over an inheritance or envy from past sibling rivalry or parental favoritism.

Table 9.2 *Categories of closeness in European American and African American sibling dyads*

Category of closeness	European American sibling dyads (%)	African American sibling dyads (%)
Intimate	14	20
Congenial	30	20
Loyal	34	55
Apathetic	11	2
Hostile	11	3

Source: Gold (1989, 1990).

Sibling dyads that included a woman (either woman–woman or woman–man) clustered in the more positive categories, whereas male–male dyads had less involvement. In a further study, Gold (1990) compared information from interviews with 64 African American dyads with information obtained previously from the 89 European American sibling dyads. The two groups were similar in age (average age mid-70s) and level of education (at least some college), and those in both groups were healthy and considered themselves middle or upper middle class.

Compared to the European American dyads, the African American dyads were closer and more interested in providing support for each other (see Table 9.2). However, we cannot conclude that race causes closer sibling relationships because factors associated with race (such as religion) could be the basis for the difference between the two groups.

The numbers of dyads in Gold's studies were small, so her findings may not generalize to broader groups of older European American and African American siblings. Further research on late-life sibling relationships is especially important because the rate of divorce is higher today than in decades past, and married couples are having fewer children. In the near future, siblings may be an even more important source of support for older adults than they are now.

Gold's categorical scheme affords some insight into sibling relationships, but it may not capture the complexities resulting from a history of interactions between family members. Family dynamics do not necessarily cease when children grow up and physically leave the family of origin. For many siblings, getting together in late middle age over shared concerns for aging parents may strengthen feelings of closeness. However, if siblings harbor resentment over earlier conflicts that were never resolved, then negative feelings may flare up when they are forced to reunite later in life over caregiving for aging parents (Bengston et al., 1996; Connidis, 1994). The sibling who lives closest often shoulders the responsibility for the aging parent. This sibling may resent brothers and sisters who live far away and make no effort to help out with regular visits or financial contributions when these are needed. The resentment felt by the sibling with the caregiving responsibility can be especially intense if he or she feels that a brother or sister was always favored by the parent.

Nonfamilial Relationships

Not all close social ties are with family members. Older adults have friends who are important to them and to whom they feel attached. Also, older adults who have lived in the same place for a long time maintain social ties in the community, where friends and acquaintances are a meaningful part of their daily lives.

Friends

When family members are available, friends make up a smaller proportion of older adults' social networks than they do in the social networks of young or even middle-aged adults (Levitt et al., 1993). In the old–old years and beyond (age 75 and over), social involvement outside the family tends to decline (Field & Minkler, 1988). Nonetheless, friends who are familiar and close are likely to remain in the inner circle of an older adult's social network, as in the case of Maxine (described at the beginning of the chapter).

Close friends are a significant source of emotional support even in late older adulthood. When family members are unavailable, friends are particularly important (Lang et al., 1998). However, even when family members are available, friends can be a source of enjoyment, emotional fulfillment, and moral support in times of need. Being able to converse with friends of similar age about common problems can help to ease stress. Often, friends serve as confidantes to whom we can entrust our worries and on whom we can count for emotional support.

Unlike family members, friends are not bound to each other by duty or formal rules. Perhaps because friendship is voluntary, reciprocity in giving and receiving support is especially important (Rook, 1987). Many older adults enjoy spending time with friends (Connidis, 1989), and thinking that they can reciprocate friends' favors helps older adults maintain a feeling of independence. Maxine, the widow described earlier, feels fortunate to have a circle of friends living in the same apartment building. However, older adults hesitate to ask for help from friends if they do not think they will be able to return the favor within a reasonable amount of time. If they cannot reciprocate, they may not be able to maintain an equitable social exchange relationship with their friends (Connidis, 1989). In critical situations such as serious illness, especially when help will be needed on a long-term basis, older adults often turn to adult children or other family members.

Friendship may be based on common interests or on a deep, long-term, emotionally meaningful bond (Kausler et al., 2007). Interest-related friendships that revolve around hobbies such as playing bridge or golf may decline in older adulthood when health problems or transportation difficulties limit opportunities for getting together. In contrast, deep, long-term friendships involve a close bond based on familiarity because of a common background such as living in the same neighborhood for many years or raising children who went to the same school. Such friendships are likely to be maintained in older adulthood (Fredrickson & Carstensen, 1990).

When older adults develop limitations in physical mobility or when they no longer have access to transportation, they often maintain emotionally intimate relationships with close friends via telephone (Fees et al., 1999). As mentioned earlier, older adults prefer to engage in social interactions with friends who are emotionally meaningful, and their interest in making new friends or initiating social exchanges with new acquaintances seems to decline (Carstensen, 1992). Particularly in the old-old and oldest-old years, many individuals prefer to spend time alone rather than participating in social interactions that are not deeply meaningful (Lang & Baltes, 1997).

Women are usually the main instigators and perpetuators of friendship, and among married couples, men often rely on their wives for planning social activities and cultivating a social network (Norris & Tindale, 1994). It remains to be seen whether married women's entry into the workplace on a full-time basis means they will have a less dominant role in organizing the social life in couple relationships. Of course, in older adulthood women are more likely than men to be widowed and less likely to remarry, so older women have more opportunities to spend time with friends.

Peripheral social relationships

Older adults may focus on social interchanges with individuals with whom they feel emotionally close, but they still maintain peripheral ties with people who are not intimate members of their social circle. Such ties are with individuals seen regularly but from whom extensive social support is not expected. For example, older adults have regular contact with individuals working in the local pharmacy, grocery store, department store, hair salon, barber shop, restaurant, or doctor and dental offices. There are the passing "hellos" of neighbors out walking their dogs or working in their yards. Such contacts are not intimate but often have significance in older adults' daily lives.

Fingerman and Griffiths (1999) investigated peripheral ties represented by the exchange of greeting cards during the holiday season. They surveyed young, middle-aged and older individuals and found that the older group both sent and received the greatest number of greeting cards and older women sent and received more greeting cards than older men did. Some cards were exchanged with people that had close emotional ties, but individuals in all three age groups also exchanged cards with those who were not central to their day-to-day social network. The older adults considered greeting card exchanges a link to their personal past, whereas the young adults considered them an opportunity to build future relationships.

In sum, older adults have social ties within and outside the family. Many have relationships with a spouse or partner, adult children, grandchildren, and siblings. In addition, they have social relationships with close, long-term friends. In the periphery of their social networks are people with whom older adults are familiar in their daily commerce or with whom they maintain contact on a yearly basis.

Elder Abuse and Neglect

Elder abuse is the darker side of social interactions. It refers to harmful behavior directed toward older adults by formal or informal caregivers whom the older adult loves or trusts, or on whom the older person depends for assistance (McDonald, 2007). Formal caregivers can be professionals and semi-professionals (for example, social workers, physicians, lawyers, home care providers, nurses, financial advisers); informal caregivers include family members or close family associates who are responsible for the older person's care.

Elder abuse occurs among all racial, ethnic, and socioeconomic groups (Lantz, 2006), and it can take several forms. *Physical abuse* involves the infliction of physical discomfort, pain, or injury. *Sexual abuse* includes any kind of nonconsensual sexual contact. *Psychological/emotional abuse* involves intentional infliction of mental anguish or provocation of fear of violence or isolation in the older person. *Material/financial abuse* refers to the intentional, illegal, or improper exploitation of the older adult's property.

Neglect refers to intended or unintended failure of a caregiver to fulfill the older adult's needs (McDonald, 2007). Examples are failing to provide an older person who cannot properly care for himself or herself with necessities such as food, water, clothing, shelter, medicine, or comfort. Table 9.3 lists some of the warning signs for each type of abuse and for neglect.

Abuse and neglect are generally committed by others on the elderly victim, but in some instances there is *self-neglect*. For example, consider an elderly man who lives across the street from you in a large house that is in obvious need of repair. You catch sight of him in his yard and notice he looks disheveled and undernourished. He never responds when you try to greet him, and the neighbors say he is not willing to seek or accept any help. Not everyone agrees that self-neglect is in the same category as neglect committed by someone an older adult trusts, and not all states in the United States include self-neglect in their definition of abuse (see Eglit, 2004).

Abuse in Domestic Settings

Elder abuse and neglect have undoubtedly been occurring for many decades, but official recognition of the problem began in the late 1970s. The rate of occurrence is difficult to determine and therefore it is probably underestimated. Abused or neglected older adults are often isolated; many come to the attention

Table 9.3 *Warning signs and symptoms of elder abuse and neglect*

Physical abuse	Bruises around arms, neck, or legs Wounds, burns, and repeated unexplained injuries Pain or wincing when touched Inappropriate use of physical restraints
Sexual abuse	Unexplained vaginal or anal injuries Bruises on breasts or genitals Sexually transmitted diseases
Psychological/emotional abuse	Symptoms of fear, anxiety, agitation, withdrawal Hesitation to talk openly, evasiveness, ambivalence Fear of leaving room or home Contradictory statements about condition or well-being
Material/financial abuse	Large or frequent withdrawals from bank account New unexplainable debt and failure to pay bills Caregiver's name added to bank accounts, credit cards, checks Large or expensive "gifts" from older adult to caregiver
Neglect	Malnutrition or dehydration with no explainable cause Lack of follow-up with medical treatment Soiled clothing and unkempt appearance Forced isolation due to lack of assistance

Adapted from Lantz (2006, Table 1, p. 353).

of professionals when they visit hospital emergency rooms (Lantz, 2006). Approximately 90% of abuse cases that occur in the community are perpetrated by family members, and in two-thirds of these cases, the abusers are spouses or adult children (Lantz, 2006; McDonald, 2007). Spousal abusers often suffer from poor health themselves, which creates additional stress in marital situations that are already less than ideal (Wolf, 1996). Abusive adult children may be overburdened with multiple responsibilities (Lantz, 2006), but adult children or in-laws who abuse elderly family members often have a history of mental instability and problems with substance abuse (McDonald, 2007; Schiamberg & Gans, 2000). Many live in the same household with the older victim and are dependent on the victim for financial and/or emotional support.

The typical victim of abuse is a woman aged 75 or over and in frail health, although elderly men have been victims of abuse as well (McDonald, 2007; Pillemer & Suitor, 1992). In domestic settings, the most common types of elderly abuse in order of prevalence are as follows: financial exploitation, neglect, emotional abuse, physical abuse, and sexual abuse (Lachs & Pillemer, 2004). Many victims of elder abuse suffer from cognitive difficulties so they have limited capacity to report it. Victims who are cognitively capable of reporting abuse may hesitate to do so out of family loyalty, feelings of shame, or fear that nursing home placement will be the only alternative. Based on the limited statistics available, the incidence of elder abuse in domestic settings seems to be increasing in the United States. However, greater sensitivity to the problem of elder abuse and more stringent rules about reporting it could make increases appear greater than they really are. Each state in the United States now has laws mandating that physicians, nurses, social workers and law enforcement workers report any instances of suspected elder abuse and neglect (Quinn, 1995).

Pillemer and Suitor (1992) conducted interviews with educated, European American caregivers (mainly adult children and some spouses) who were caring for elderly relatives diagnosed with Alzheimer's disease or other forms of dementia. Caregivers answered questions on their feelings of violence and also violent acts they had committed. Three factors associated with caregivers' feelings and fears that they would become violent were (a) living in the same household with the elderly care recipient, (b) low self-esteem, and (c) caring for an elderly relative who is physically aggressive. Two factors associated with caregivers' admitting to actually engaging in violent acts toward an elderly care recipient were (a) violent behavior on the part of the elderly care recipient and (b) being a spousal caregiver (which would of course be associated with living with the care recipient). Pillemer and Suitor stress the need for longitudinal studies that track the relationship between feelings of violence and acts of violence. Such studies could reveal what factors cause caregivers to cross the line from thoughts of violence to actually committing it.

Understanding why elder abuse occurs is essential if abusive situations are to be prevented. One perspective, the **situational model of elder abuse**, views elder abuse as a caregiver's response to a stressful situation (McDonald, 2007). The total dependency of an older adult on a single caregiver creates an especially heavy burden. Long hours caring for a frail older adult with no relief can lead to exhaustion, frustration, and social isolation, and ultimately to abuse. However, this perspective does not account for caregivers under equal or greater stress who do not mistreat older adults. Even so, there is little question that caregiving can be associated with stress (Zarit, Johansson, & Jarrott, 1998), and it is important to develop ways to alleviate it. Availability of adult day-care services has proven helpful in reducing the stress and increasing the psychological well-being of family caregivers (Zarit, Stephens, Townsend, & Greene, 1998). Family caregivers can take elderly relatives to such day-care centers while they themselves work at outside jobs or tend to personal matters.

Abuse in Institutional Settings

Compared to abuse in domestic settings, less is known about abuse and neglect in institutional settings such as hospitals, nursing homes, assisted-living facilities, and board and care homes. Yet physical abuse (for instance, a staff member's rough treatment or excessive use of restraints on a nursing home resident), verbal abuse (for instance, a staff member's yelling at a nursing home resident), and neglect (disinterested staff, lack of activities) do occur in institutional environments (Lantz, 2006; Pillemer & Moore, 1989). The Nursing Home Residents' Rights (see Table 9.1) together with ombudsman advocacy programs provide some protection for elderly individuals.

Caregiver stress can occur in institutional settings when the demands of the elderly residents' care are placed upon too few staff members. In a telephone survey of nurses and nursing aids, Pillemer and Bachman-Prehn (1991) found that two factors were significant predictors of reported incidences of physical and verbal abuse in institutional settings: level of staff–patient conflict and degree of staff "burnout." Providing staff members with educational and morale-building workshops, together with increased pay so that nursing home staff members do not need to hold a second job, could help reduce institutional abuse.

Clearly, a number of factors contribute to elder abuse and neglect. We need better methods of detection, improvement in enforcing laws that require reporting suspected abuse and neglect, and more services to relieve caregiver burden.

Revisiting the Selective Optimization with Compensation and Ecological Models

The Selective Optimization with Compensation (SOC) (Baltes & Baltes, 1990) and Ecological (Lawton, 1989; Lawton & Nahemow, 1973) Models are readily applied to social interaction and social ties in older adulthood.

The socioemotional selectivity theory (SEST) complements the SOC Model by specifying the goals of social interactions that older adults select and the strategies they use to insure that social interactions will optimize their needs (Baltes & Carstensen, 1996). A core of close others follow us throughout a large part of our lives. Over time, the social convoy becomes smaller, but those who remain in it (largely family members but close friends as well) provide social support, feelings of social embeddedness, and chances for positive social exchanges, all essential in optimizing older adults' feelings of life satisfaction and well-being.

With regard to the Ecological Model, social interaction and social ties represent one aspect of environmental press. Older adults adapt best when environments offer access to social ties and sufficient opportunities for social interaction, especially with individuals who hold significance for them. However, older adults prefer to weed out relationships that have less importance, so the chances for positive adaptation are enhanced when the level of social press does not exceed their wishes and needs. Adaptive functioning is maximized when older adults have opportunities for meaningful social interactions and when the likelihood of negative social exchange is minimized.

1. Who is in your inner circle (convoy) of social relationships? How many are relatives and how many are friends?
2. What kinds of things do you do for close family members and friends and what do you expect them to do for you?
3. Does the latest technology affect how you communicate with those in your convoy? Does it change the way you keep in touch with old friends and relatives who live far away or even the way you form new social relationships?

Key Points

- Activity theory, disengagement theory, socioemotional selectivity theory, and social exchange theory offer hypotheses about the quantity and quality of social interactions in older adulthood.
- Social interactions can have negative and positive aspects, and older adults can experience both.
- Individuals move through life with a social convoy of others who play a central role in their network of social relationships. This convey consists of family members and long-term friends.
- The marital relationship is central to many adults, and when discussing topics on which they disagree, older married couples tend to show more control of negative emotions than do middle-aged married couples.
- Older adults may not live under the same roof with adult children or other family members, but their relationships can still be close. Older mothers and their daughters are especially close, even though they may have areas of conflict.
- Many older adults are grandparents, but there is wide variability in how they play this role. Some see grandchildren occasionally, while others actually bring them up.
- Older adults are often closer to siblings than they were in young adulthood. Siblings, especially sisters, provide support for one another when help is needed.
- Older adults enjoy spending time with friends, with whom they have reciprocal relationships, but they turn to family members for long-term help.
- Elder abuse can be physical, sexual, psychological, or material, and it can occur in both domestic and institutional settings. Abuse and neglect are difficult to study, but many factors are related to its occurrence.

Key Terms

activity theory   265
beanpole family structure   274
blended family   274
convoy model   271
disengagement theory   265
extended family household   273
family of origin   273
family of procreation   273
hierarchical-compensatory model   284
hourglass effect in sibling relationships   283
intergenerational stake hypothesis   278
intimacy at a distance   274

modified extended family   274
nuclear family household   273
reciprocity   272
sandwich generation   280
situational model of elder abuse   291
social exchange theory   267
social network   271
socioemotional selectivity theory
    (SEST)   266
support bank   272
upswing hypothesis of marital
    satisfaction   275

10 Employment, Retirement, and Living Arrangements

Chapter Overview

Close-ups on Adulthood and Aging

Jerome has worked at the same company for 30 years and always planned to retire from his job at the age of 65. However, he just learned that because of changes in the U.S. Social Security program, he will not be eligible for his full Social Security benefits until he turns 66, so he will postpone his retirement until that time. Jerome's wife Priscilla will retire from her job at the same time, after 20 years of working for a different company. Jerome and Priscilla feel fortunate that not only will they receive pension benefits from Social Security but, because Priscilla decided to work full-time outside the home once their daughter was in high school, both she and Jerome will receive monthly checks from their respective company pension plans. This guarantees that they will have a comfortable retirement without having to work part-time to make ends meet. Jerome always assumed retirement was a time for kicking back and leading a life of leisure. Now he thinks that after some period of time spent traveling and enjoying recreational pursuits, he and Priscilla will probably want to shape a more structured routine that includes leisure activities, household tasks, and volunteer work in the community.

Employment

This chapter highlights aspects of living that hold special significance for older adults: employment, retirement, and living arrangements. Some older adults continue to work full-time or part-time, but others retire from paid employment. Those who retire have greater freedom to relocate for reasons such as better climate, but the majority of older adults continue to live in the same geographical location (Uhlenberg, 2006; Wolf & Longino, 2005), and many remain in the same house where they have always lived.

Riley (1994) contends that the social structure of present-day American society is "age-differentiated," meaning that education is for youth and young adults, work is for the middle-age years, and leisure is confined to older adulthood (see Figure 10.1). Riley proposed that the ideal structure would be age-integrated, with a balance between education, work, and leisure over the entire adult life span.

The Older Worker

The term *older worker* generally refers to individuals aged 45 and older (Cleveland & Shore, 2007). By 2010, half of the U.S. workforce will likely be aged 45 or older (Moyers, 2006). However, age 55 and older has also been used to delineate the category of older workers (Hardy, 2006). The 55+ age group represented 15% of the U.S. labor force in 2000 but this is expected to increase to 25% by 2020 (Sterns & Sterns, 2006).

To what age do most Americans continue to work at paid jobs? The median age of retirement is the chronological age by which half of the population have left the paid labor force but half still remain. A younger median age indicates that individuals are leaving the paid workforce early, whereas an older median age indicates that they are working longer. Most of our information is based on European American men. We know less about women, and we have little information about African American, Asian American, Native American, or Hispanic American workers because, until recently, fewer records have been kept for these groups (Gendell & Siegel, 1996).

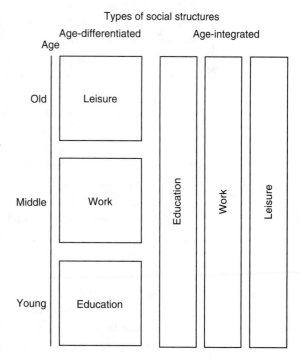

Figure 10.1 *An age-differentiated and age-integrated social structure.*
Source: Riley (1994).

It is expected that more and more older adults will continue to participate in the paid labor force. Many older workers express great satisfaction with their jobs.

What we do know is that the median age of retirement in the United States dropped from approximately 67 in 1950–1955 to 63 in 1985–1990, indicating a trend for workers to leave the paid labor force at younger ages. This decline in the median age of retirement was similar for European American and African American men, although at various points of comparison, the absolute age of exit from the labor force was somewhat lower for African American men compared to European American men.

However, the median age of retirement began to level off in the early 1990s (Gendell & Siegel, 1996), and by the mid-1990s, experts were debating about future trends. Some predicted that in the early 21st century, median retirement age would drop further, possibly falling below 62, because workers would leave positions of paid employment at even younger ages than previously. Others predicted the opposite – that the median age of retirement would increase in the early 21st century because workers would remain in the paid labor force longer than in prior years. Recent statistics indicate that the number of men and women aged 65–69 still in the labor force has in fact been increasing (Sterns & Sterns, 2006). The following arguments bolster the prediction that in the future people will work for more rather than fewer years:

- Americans are healthier now and physically able to work longer (Crimmins, Reynolds, & Saito, 1999). Also, jobs are less physically demanding today than they were in the past.
- Average life expectancy has been increasing (see Chapter 3), so workers who retire in their early 60s could live 30 years or more after leaving the paid labor force. If they cannot accumulate enough economic resources during their working years to last for three decades, they will have to continue working out of financial need.
- Mandatory retirement has been eliminated for most jobs, so individuals cannot be forced to retire at a certain chronological age.
- As Jerome (the man described at the beginning of this chapter) just learned, the age at which workers are eligible for their full Social Security pension benefits is increasing in a phased-in process. It has

gone from age 65 to 66 and eventually will reach 67. Also, thanks to recent legislation, people who reach retirement age are no longer restricted as to the amount of money they can earn without losing Social Security benefits.

In sum, improved health, easing of physical requirements in the workplace, increased life expectancy, elimination of mandatory retirement, and economic incentives all point to the distinct possibility that more, rather than fewer, older adults will participate in the paid labor force. Thus, there is good reason to learn more about older employees.

Job Performance

How well do older employees perform their jobs? Some common stereotypes are that, compared to younger workers, older workers are less productive, less motivated, less receptive to innovations, and less able to learn, especially when it comes to new technologies (Czaja, 2001; Panek, 1997). Other stereotypes are that older workers are physically unable to do their jobs and have a high rate of accidents and absenteeism.

In fact, the information we have paints a very different picture. Older workers are dependable, productive, and have lower accident rates than younger workers (Sterns & Sterns, 2006). When injury or illness occur, older workers may need more time than younger workers to recover, but for male workers especially, avoidable absenteeism (being absent without prior approval) tends to decrease with age (Panek, 1997), and age is a weak predictor of attendance (Cleveland & Shore, 2007). Older workers are highly committed to their jobs and have a great deal of emotional investment in the work role (Ekerdt, 1986). Older workers often express greater satisfaction with their jobs than younger workers (Ekerdt & DeViney, 1993). However, a strong relationship between age and job satisfaction seems to be concentrated mainly in human service and white collar jobs as opposed to factory and clerical jobs (Cleveland & Shore, 2007).

There are relatively few well-controlled studies on age and job proficiency, probably due to the difficulty in making accurate or meaningful comparisons between young and older workers (Salthouse & Maurer, 1996). Only a limited number of occupations have been investigated, and most studies have included small samples and therefore lack the sensitivity to detect whether any differences exist between young and older employees. Also, the test instruments used to measure job performance have not always been reliable or valid (Chapter 2 discusses the importance of reliability and validity). In addition, jobs held by a young and an older worker may have the same title but may not actually call for identical responsibilities so may not really be equivalent. Finally, younger employees are often new to the job. In contrast, older employees have usually worked in the job for a longer time; they have demonstrated competency and therefore been retained in the occupation. Given these considerations, conflicting reports regarding age and job performance should come as no surprise. Overall, there seems to be little relationship between age and job performance (McEvoy & Cascio, 1989; Waldman & Avolio, 1986).

Job performance is a function of both ability and experience (Salthouse & Maurer, 1996). Older employees may use accumulated knowledge and expertise to compensate for any age-related decline, particularly when it comes to speed of response (Cleveland & Shore, 2007). In a classic study illustrating this point, Salthouse (1984) demonstrated that experienced older typists maintained the same level of speed and accuracy as younger typists by placing greater reliance on anticipating forthcoming keystrokes. The same principle could apply to strokes on computer keyboards.

In recent years, computers have become more important in occupational settings, and the effect of technology on older workers is being examined (Czaja, 2001). In one study (Czaja & Sharit, 1993), women ranging from 25 to 70 years of age performed three computer-based tasks: data entry, file maintenance, and inventory management. On all three tasks, the older women were slower than the younger ones. However, none of the study participants had much prior experience with computers, so the older participants did not have time to gain experience that they could use to compensate for declines in speed. In a subsequent study, Czaja and Sharit (1998) demonstrated that prior experience with computers was an important factor in how well older adults performed a data entry task. Sharit et al. (2004) trained "younger" older adults (50–65 years) and "older" older adults (66–80 years) on how to use e-mail to respond to customer queries. Both age groups improved over four consecutive days, but the improvement was especially marked for the "older" older adults. It is clear that older adults are receptive to learning and capable of acquiring technological skills, although they may need more training and practice than young adults. It is important to design technology that is age-friendly based on the findings of human factors research on aging (Burdick, 2005).

In general, job experience is a positive factor in the workplace, but with rapid changes in technology, some skills that employees have sharpened over the years become obsolete. Therefore, workers of all ages must be open to regular training and education to update their skills (Sterns & Sterns, 2006). A common myth is that older workers are less flexible and less willing than young workers to change their ways. In other words, you can't teach an old dog new tricks. However, older workers have probably been following a certain procedure for longer than younger workers, so they will need to put greater effort into switching to new procedures. Even so, there is little reason to assume that older workers cannot be trained, although they benefit more when there is less pressure and more time to learn (Panek, 1997). Training older workers is a good investment because they are often committed to their jobs and less likely than younger workers to switch companies.

Table 10.1 *Sample statements from Abraham and Hansson's selection, optimization, and compensation (SOC) work strategy survey questionnaire*

Type of strategy	Sample survey questionnaire statements
Selection	"I now try to avoid spreading myself too thin." "I now delegate low-priority responsibilities to others."
Optimization	"I am now more likely to participate in training to polish rusty skills and abilities." "I now pay more attention to keeping up my work skills and abilities."
Compensation	"I now try to perform my job in such a way that my weaker points are less visible." "I now try to make my accomplishments visible to my boss and co-workers."

Source: Abraham & Hansson (1995).

What strategies do older workers use to maintain their performance on the job? Abraham and Hansson (1995) developed a survey questionnaire based on Baltes and Baltes's (1990) Selective Optimization with Compensation (SOC) Model. A selection strategy would include efforts to restrict or narrow one's range of work activities. An optimization strategy would require efforts to maximize one's work capabilities. A compensation strategy would entail efforts to create a positive impression by downplaying deficiencies and presenting oneself in a positive light. Table 10.1 shows examples of survey statements with which test takers may or may not agree.

Abraham and Hansson administered their questionnaire to 224 workers, mostly European American men and women aged 40 to 69, who worked in a broad range of jobs (professional, managerial, administrative/clerical). Overall, the selection strategies were endorsed more by men, many of whom held managerial positions that might allow them to adopt such strategies. In contrast, the optimization and compensation strategies were endorsed more by women, many of whom worked in administrative/clerical positions that would probably allow them less flexibility to control which aspects of the job they would select. With regard to age, the older respondents were more likely than the younger ones to say they would use all three types of strategy (selection, optimization, and compensation), although there was no way to check whether they actually did so.

Evaluating Older Employees

Do supervisors use the same standards to evaluate older employees as they do younger employees? Evaluations of older workers may be positively influenced by the perception that they are loyal and reliable, and older workers may be given credit for past achievements, experience, and their low rate of avoidable absenteeism.

Erber and Szuchman (2002) found that older volunteer workers were considered more disciplined, reliable, dependable, knowledgeable, and cheerful than younger volunteer workers. Such positive perceptions regarding their personal qualities could make up for the possibility that older workers take longer to complete a task. Overall, older workers may be judged to be just as valuable as young workers. On the other hand, supervisors' appraisals of younger workers might be positively influenced by a belief that they will devote more years to the company and thus are better candidates for promotion than older workers.

Age of coworkers in the same company or office can influence how older workers are evaluated. One or two older workers among a majority of younger coworkers will likely be evaluated more negatively than older workers who have additional coworkers in the same age range. Also, the age difference between a supervisor and an employee can influence how an older employee is evaluated (Cleveland & Shore, 1992). When they have limited information about employees who work for them, young supervisors rate older employees less favorably than they do young employees (Finkelstein, Burke, & Raju, 1995; Lee & Clemons, 1985). On a more optimistic note, as the proportion of older workers increases, chronological age may become less important for decision makers, and evaluations of job performance may be more heavily based on skills and productivity, as well they should.

Age Discrimination in Employment

Some years ago, mandatory retirement was the rule and most workers had to retire at a specific age, typically 65. Also, employers could refuse to hire anyone above a certain age, and they were permitted to demote or reduce the salaries of older workers. The **Age Discrimination in Employment Act (ADEA)**, first enacted in the United States in 1967 and revised in 1978 and 1986, applies to companies with more than 20 employees. ADEA prohibits discrimination against workers aged 40 and older by making it illegal to use age in hiring decisions, or to terminate, demote, or reduce the salaries of older workers without showing good cause.

One exception to the ADEA is that employment decisions can be based on age if it can be demonstrated that older employees are not capable of performing the job in a way that is reasonably necessary for the normal operation of the business (McCann & Giles, 2002). Presently, commercial airline pilots and some highly paid executives in major leadership positions can be required to retire at a certain age (Sterns & Sterns, 2006). Not surprisingly, many employers attempt (successfully or unsuccessfully) to use this exception as the basis of their defense when older employees file charges of age discrimination (McCann & Giles, 2002).

A further amendment to the ADEA in 1990 prohibited employers from treating older workers any differently from young workers when companies reduce their workforce, or downsize. In principle, the ADEA deems it illegal for employers to make work-related decisions on the basis of age stereotypes concerning abilities, physical status, or performance. Thus, employers need to keep accurate performance evaluation records of their employees. In turn, employees are well advised to keep copies of their performance evaluations in the event they must show that they have been the subject of age discrimination.

Thanks to the ADEA, today there are fewer flagrant examples of age discrimination such as publishing job advertisements that specify age, telling job applicants that they are too old, or informing employees that they are being terminated because of age. However, subtle forms of age discrimination persist, as evidenced by the large number of age discrimination cases that have been filed. Between 1990 and 1993 there was a 26% increase in the number of age discrimination charges filed with federal and state agencies; as of 1996, 30,600 cases had been filed (Sterns & Sterns, 1997). Some plaintiffs lose their cases in court, but these figures suggest that not all older workers are leaving their jobs voluntarily and many may be subject to subtle forms of age discrimination. The majority of discrimination complaints have been filed by men, especially senior European American professionals and managers. Fewer cases are filed by women, though women are more likely than men to win their cases (Cleveland & Shore, 2007). However, the courts have ruled it legal to terminate long-time (often older) workers if employers can show that there are budgetary constraints or that the jobs performed by the older workers have become obsolete.

Unfortunately, the ADEA has not been highly effective in insuring that older adults will be hired or in unconditionally guaranteeing that older workers will be treated fairly in the workplace (Quadagno & Hardy, 1996). In many instances, young job applicants are selected over older applicants with equivalent credentials (Cleveland & Shore, 2007). Sometimes older job applicants try to increase their chances of being hired by attempting to hide their age. Interestingly, it is considered poor strategy for older job applicants to emphasize their experience, stability, loyalty, and maturity. These qualities are positive, but they are stereotypically associated with age (Lavelle, 1997).

Perry, Kulik, and Bourhis (1996) investigated how undergraduate business administration students evaluate young versus older job applicants, all of whom had average qualifications and were applying for either a young-type job (selling CDs and tapes) or an old-type job (selling stamps and coins). Student evaluators who harbored a preexisting bias against older workers (as indicated by their responses to a survey administered one month earlier) gave the older job applicant lower evaluations than did student evaluators who were not biased to begin with. Also, the students gave higher evaluations to older applicants who were applying for an old-type job – the older applicant for the job of selling stamps and coins was evaluated more favorably than the older applicant for the job of selling CDs and tapes. Apparently, young adult business majors, our future business leaders, show age discrimination in some situations.

With regard to how employees are treated on the job, age discrimination can take the form of giving older employees fewer opportunities for training and fewer rewards for updating their skills, which could ultimately lead to their obsolescence (Avolio & Waldman, 1990). Erber and Danker (1995) asked employees of a large corporation to imagine themselves as managers in a hypothetical company that is under pressure to downsize, and in that role to evaluate a younger or older employee who is experiencing performance problems related to poor memory. Study participants thought that the older worker's performance problems would continue to occur and they were less likely to recommend training opportunities when the employee was older rather than younger. Given the importance of job training, this represents an indirect form of age discrimination in the workplace, which is not confined to the United States. In a study conducted in Britain (Fuller, 2007), human resource (HR) managers were asked to allocate a training budget across young and older employees and to justify their decisions. HR managers favored employees under the age of 30, and they thought older workers offered a lower return on investment in training.

In sum, age discrimination is less glaring now than previously. However, if workers are to remain in the paid labor force to older ages out of economic necessity or desire, we must remain alert to the conditions under which it can occur.

Retirement

Some people continue to work full-time into late old age, but there is an increasing trend for older workers to be employed in *bridge jobs* that are usually part-time as opposed to full-time career jobs (Cahill, Giandrea, & Quinn, 2006). Others, like Jerome and Priscilla described at the beginning of the chapter, have plans to exit from the paid labor force completely. What does it mean to be retired and what makes people decide to stop working?

What Is Retirement?

Retirement is a social institution with rules about when it is permissible for workers to leave the paid labor force. Also, it "designates a social status that has become established as a historically new stage in the life course" (Ekerdt & Sergeant, 2006, p. 1032). For the individual, retirement represents a transition to a stage of life that does not require paid employment (Atchley, 1996, 2007). But when are individuals actually considered "retired"? Definitions vary, but factors that define retirement include reduced labor force participation, cessation of a career, receipt of income from pensions (periodic financial payments made to formerly employed individuals, to be discussed later), willingness to identify themselves as retired, or some combination of these factors (Ekerdt & Sergeant, 2006).

For people with a steady work history over their adult years, it is easy to identify the transition to retirement. Such individuals often choose to retire and have little difficulty considering themselves retired as soon as they stop working (Szinovacz & DeViney, 1999). Most likely, Jerome and Priscilla will fall into this category. However, retirement is not always voluntary. For many workers, their retirement is forced due to health limitations, job displacement, or the obligation to care for others (Szinovacz & Davey, 2005).

When there are interruptions in a person's job history, it is not easy to ascertain whether a specific exit from the labor force is the final one to be counted as retirement, or whether it simply represents a time gap between leaving an old job and starting a new one (Gendell & Siegel, 1996). In today's cohort of older adults, a work career with few disruptions is more typical for men than for women. Many of today's older women did not participate in the labor force; if they did, they probably experienced periods of interruption to rear children or care for elderly parents. With regard to race and ethnic background, it is more common for African American workers than it is for European American workers to exit the labor force for health reasons, although some prefer to identify themselves as retired rather than disabled (Szinovacz & DeViney, 1999). Also, compared to European American older workers, African American and Hispanic American older workers are more vulnerable to involuntary job loss. Once jobs are lost, it may be difficult to find new employment, especially with limited education and few job qualifications. After a prolonged period of joblessness, many individuals eventually refer to themselves as "retired." In sum, retirement can be ambiguous, particularly for women and minorities, because of movement into and out of the labor force (Flippen & Tienda, 2000).

Effects of Retirement

It is difficult to study the effects of retirement because we cannot control who remains in the workforce and who leaves. For individuals who retire due to poor health or job loss through downsizing, retirement is not voluntary and could well be associated with negative outcomes in the physical or psychological domains. However, there is little evidence that voluntary retirement causes poor physical or mental health. When individuals choose to leave the workforce and when their departure is "on time," meaning that they discontinue paid employment at a stage of life that is typical in their culture, then retirement does not seem to have detrimental physical or psychological effects.

To explore the social and psychological consequences of retirement, Reitzes, Mutran, and Fernandez (1996) conducted a two-year longitudinal study, testing levels of self-esteem and depression in 757 male and female workers (83% European American, aged 58–64) every six months. During the two-year interval, 299 of the workers made the transition to retirement but the rest continued to work full-time. For both groups, the level of self-esteem remained relatively stable over time, but depression scores actually declined in the group that retired. Perhaps the retired individuals enjoyed some relief from work-related stress.

Herzog, House, and Morgan (1991) interviewed 1,339 individuals aged 55 and older and found that the extent of their labor force participation had little relationship to health and well-being in and of itself. What was important for study participants' health and well-being was whether the level of labor force participation (that is, full-time work, part-time work, or no work) reflected personal preference as opposed to constraints imposed by forces outside their own control. Those who chose whether to work and how much to work reported having better health and well-being compared to those with little control over whether and how much they worked.

When they retire, older adults lose a role that once held a prominent place in their lives. For those with a strong commitment to the work role, does retirement trigger a "crisis" in identity, with negative effects on physical and mental well-being (Atchley, 1971)? Some individuals experience anxiety surrounding the anticipation or actual event of retirement (Fletcher & Hansson, 1991), but loss of the work role does not usually result in an identity crisis. Most people replace the work role and social contacts they had at work. For the majority of older adults, the years before and after retirement are characterized by continuity (Atchley, 1971). Even so, retirement does involve adjustment that entails both social and psychological detachment from work (van Solinge & Henkens, 2008). The transition to retirement may be smoother if individuals can still identify with their former occupations. For example, teachers may continue to identify themselves as members of that profession even when they no longer have a formal classroom.

How does retirement affect the marital relationship? Vinick and Ekerdt (1991) interviewed couples (aged 55 and over) in which the women did not work and the men had been retired for 6–22 months. The majority of the men reported greater participation in household tasks, and most of the couples had increased the number of leisure activities they did together. Approximately half the women admitted some feelings of impingement on their sphere of personal activity now that their husbands were retired, but most claimed they had adjusted to the situation. Today, more married women are participating in the paid workforce and wives are more likely to have full-time career paths similar to those of their husbands. Dual-earner couples who time their retirements to coincide and who share household chores seem to have a high level of well-being (Quadagno, 2008).

Economics of Retirement

Retirement is a legitimate right earned through years of work. Even so, leaving the paid labor force means giving up a regular paycheck, so how do retired

Understanding Aging Box 10.1: Couples and Retirement

Researchers with a life course perspective view the transition from work to retirement in the context of many factors, an important one being the marital relationship. Using data from the longitudinal U.S. Health and Retirement Survey (HRS) that was launched in 1992, Szinovacz and Davey (2004) selected a subsample of married respondents (aged 51–61) who were employed at Time 1. When they were followed up at Time 2, each member of a couple was either still working or fully retired. Recently retired husbands reported more depressive symptoms if their wives were still working. The wives' continued employment may conflict with traditional gender-role expectations, which could undermine the retired husbands' perceived status in the

marriage. Interestingly, when both members of a married couple are employed, wives usually perform more than half of the household tasks, but many wives accept this inequity in the division of labor. However, once husbands exit from the labor force, there can be marital conflict over division of household labor if wives continue to work. Fortunately, the negative effect of wives' continued employment on retired husbands' well-being seems to weaken over time, possibly because husbands get involved in postretirement activities and/or the couple resolve conflicts over household tasks. But when their wives join them in retirement, husbands are especially happy, particularly if the couple participate in and enjoy joint activities.

individuals pay their living expenses? Access to financial resources is an important factor in determining postretirement lifestyle (van Solinge & Henkens, 2008). Other than savings and investments accumulated during the working years, pensions are an important source of income for most retirees. Pensions are regular payments that produce a steady income based on the retired worker's former participation in the paid labor force. Pension payments (that is, benefits) can come from a public source such as the federal government or from private employers or corporations.

Social Security

In the United States, a federally sponsored public pension plan was established with the passing of the Social Security Act in 1935, during the years of the Great Depression. Older adults who had worked at paid jobs for a certain minimum number of three-month periods (quarters) were eligible to receive monthly benefits from the government. These benefits made it possible for older workers to retire, thus making room for younger workers during a time of extreme job scarcity.

The **Social Security** system in the United States was modeled after the German retirement system devised by Otto von Bismarck in 1871, which designated 65 as the age when retired workers could begin receiving pension benefits. Similarly, American workers were eligible for monthly benefits from Social Security at the age of 65, with a dollar amount based on the salary they earned prior to retirement. Currently, those who have worked for the required number of quarters are eligible for full Social Security benefits when they turn 66 or 67 depending on their year of birth. Retired workers are eligible for reduced benefits at 62, with a dollar amount less a percentage of what they would receive if they waited until their full retirement age. On the other hand, monthly payments increase by a set percentage for those who delay taking benefits beyond their full retirement age.

Decline in the rate of poverty for older adults can be traced at least in part to Social Security benefits, which include yearly cost-of-living increases. Another factor contributing to their improved economic well-being is the introduction of Medicare, the federally sponsored health insurance program (described in Chapter 3). Even so, a considerable portion of retired older adults are not financially "comfortable" (Hess & Markson, 1995). On average, African American and Hispanic American workers earned lower salaries than European American workers. Lower salaries are reflected in lower Social Security benefits after they retire.

Social Security benefits were actually intended as a financial cushion and not as the sole source of income in retirement. A likely reason for the greater economic disadvantage of the old-old group compared to the young-old group is that savings accumulated during their working years to supplement Social Security payments are depleted after a decade of retirement. In addition, there is more poverty among older women than among older men. Sixty percent of Social Security beneficiaries are women, and more women than men rely on Social Security benefits as their sole source of income. Three out of every four poor older adults are women, especially women who are single and live alone (Smeeding, Estes, & Glasse, 1999).

With regard to married couples, if one member of a couple is eligible for Social Security benefits, the spouse is eligible for an additional 50% of that amount even if he or she never worked outside the home. For example, if Tomas receives a monthly benefit of $1,000, his wife Elena, always a homemaker, will receive $500. Together, they will receive a total of $1,500. If either Tomas or Elena dies, the benefit paid to the living member of the couple will be the higher of these two amounts – Tomas or Elena will receive only $1,000 per month rather than the $1,500 they received as a couple. This reduction can cause financial hardship for a widowed older adult who relies solely on Social Security benefits for retirement income.

Today, more women are entering the workforce and in the future there will be more dual-earner couples. As is likely with Priscilla (described at the beginning of the chapter), married women may qualify for higher Social Security benefits based on their own work history than they would based on their status as a spouse. Even so, individuals and couples will need to supplement Social Security benefits with other sources of income.

The rules and regulations for government pensions vary considerably even among developed nations. In the United States, workers and employers both contribute a percentage of the worker's wages to the Social Security system, whereas this may not be the case in all industrialized countries. Also, a person's eligibility for retirement benefits from Social Security is tied to age and prior work history but not to financial need (although income taxes may have to be paid on part of Social Security benefits, depending upon total income). In some countries, any benefits received from the government are means tested – older adults are eligible for payments only if they fall below a certain income level. For example, the pension program sponsored by the Australian government (described by Quadagno, 2008) is not linked to prior employment but rather is based on age, residency, and financial need. Older Australian residents can receive pension benefits if their income and assets fall below a certain level, so eligibility is determined on a case-by-case basis. Each year, the criteria for eligibility are raised to a higher level, so fewer people qualify for payments.

Private pensions

In addition to federally sponsored Social Security benefits, some retired employees (like Jerome and Priscilla) will receive benefits from pensions sponsored by the companies for which they worked. The specific details of private pensions vary, but most fall into two basic categories: **defined benefit pension plans** (DB) and **defined contribution pension plans** (DC).

In general, DB plans require that individuals work for a certain number of years for the company in order to be *vested* (that is, eligible to receive benefits when they retire), and employees must reach a specific age before they begin receiving benefits. The dollar amount of the monthly benefit from a DB pension is usually based on an employee's salary in the latter years on the job. DB plans generally pay benefits to retirees for the rest of their lives and some offer periodic cost-of-living increases. With DB plans, the burden of paying benefits to retired employees falls squarely on the employer (or in the case of Social Security, on the federal government). (Social Security is a DB pension plan, but the federal government, rather than a private employer, sponsors it.)

In recent years, companies have been moving away from DB pension plans and switching to DC plans (Cutler, 1996). DC pension plans place the burden of pension income on the employee. With each paycheck, employers make contributions, usually a percentage of the employee's salary, into the employee's retirement account. Depending on the specific rules of the plan, the employee may or may not be required to match the employer's contribution. Regardless, contributions into the employee's retirement account accumulate and are taxed only when the employee begins to make withdrawals at any time after the age of 59½. Withdrawals prior to 59½ incur a 10% penalty over and above the taxes paid. However, withdrawals from a DC pension plan must begin by the time a retired individual reaches the age of 70½. Many DC plans give employees some choice about how their own contributions, or even those of their employers, are invested. Thus, during their working years, employees make investment decisions that will determine their standard of living in retirement. The earlier in their work careers they contribute and make wise investment decisions, the better their chances of accumulating sufficient funds to finance their retirement years (Cutler, 1996). Employees with DC pension plans are not required to remain with the same employer for a long time to receive the accumulated benefits in retirement, so DC pension plans are more *portable* than DB pension plans.

Because they earned lower salaries during their working years, retired older women receive lower benefits than retired men not only from Social Security but also from employer-sponsored DB and DC pension plans. In a study of full-time middle-aged employees enrolled in employer-sponsored (private) pension plans, anticipated pension wealth (an important factor in retirement income) was 76% greater for men than it was for women (Johnson, Sambamoorthi, & Crystal, 1999). Less than one-third of this gender gap could be explained by differences in level of education, demographics, or even by variation in the men and women's job characteristics. Rather, the gender gap in anticipated pension wealth was attributed to women's less advantaged employment situations in terms of wages, years on the job, and types of industries that employ women. Whether the gender gap in pension benefits will narrow in the future remains to be seen.

As discussed earlier, median retirement age declined from the 1950s to the 1990s, most likely because employees were confident that they would receive adequate pension benefits once they left the paid workforce (Fronstin, 1999). However, the era of early retirement may be drawing to a close. The age of eligibility for full Social Security benefits is increasing to 67. Financial incentives that large corporations offered to encourage employees to retire in their 50s or early 60s are becoming less common. Furthermore, some companies are hiring workers on an hourly basis with no pension benefits at all, which leaves workers to make financial plans for retirement on their own. These factors, combined with today's middle-aged workers' low level of savings and high level of debt, lead to a forecast that retirement age will increase and people will spend more years in the paid labor force.

In sum, income from public and private pensions, together with savings and assets, determines older adults' standard of living once they retire. In the United States, Social Security provides a base for living expenses, but older adults will need to supplement Social Security benefits with income from private pensions, assets, or continued part-time or full-time work.

Retirement as a Process

Is retirement from paid employment a sudden event or is it just the end point in a process that ultimately leads to a decision to leave the workforce? Ekerdt (2004) contends that concern about retirement is no longer concentrated in the second half of life because young adults and even adolescents are being reminded to start planning for retirement, at least economically.

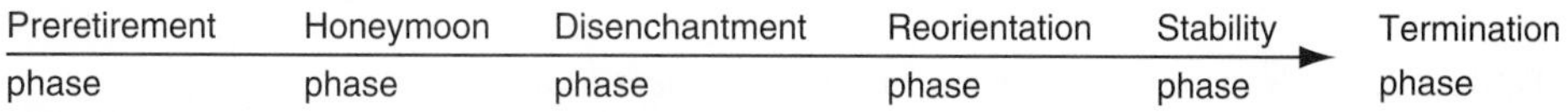

Preretirement phase	Honeymoon phase	Disenchantment phase	Reorientation phase	Stability phase	Termination phase

Figure 10.2 *Phases of retirement.*
Based on Atchley (1994).

Atchley (1994) proposed that retirement takes place in a series of phases (see Figure 10.2). Not every individual goes through every phase, but this framework is a way to consider retirement as a process rather than a single event that occurs only when a paid employee stops working.

In the preretirement phase, workers make remote and then more immediate plans for retirement. Once retirement actually occurs, some individuals experience a honeymoon phase, a period of euphoria and enthusiasm typified by a high level of activity. New retirees try to do everything they did not have time for when they were working. They try to fulfill preretirement fantasies, a common example being travel. This phase could be brief or it could continue for a year or more, but it does not usually last indefinitely. Its duration may depend upon the health of the retiree and/or the retiree's spouse or upon financial resources. However, even with good health and sufficient finances, most retirees cannot keep up the pace of the honeymoon phase. Some experience a period of disenchantment, with feelings of emotional let-down, boredom, or even depression. After some time, however, they enter a reorientation phase, taking stock and beginning to fashion a realistic structure for their daily lives. They develop new interests, pursue hobbies, visit family and friends, or do volunteer work. Once they establish a satisfactory and comfortable routine, retirees enter the stability phase.

Some, but not all, retirees enter a final termination phase, which can occur when the retirement role no longer suits their needs. Some miss working and decide to reenter the labor force, as in the case of a 91-year-old man who was restless and bored in retirement and applied for a job selling luggage at a local department store, giving his age as 66 to secure the job. Within two years, he had won the honor of "Sales Star of the Month" several times even though he worked only 16–20 hours per week (Greenberg, 1998). For this man, work was the key to feeling happy and productive. Other individuals relinquish the retirement role because frailty prevents them from taking part in an active retirement lifestyle.

Many workers entertain thoughts about what their lives will be like in retirement for some period of time before they actually exit the paid labor force. Ekerdt, DeViney, and Kosloski (1996) developed a profile of intended retirement plans based on the responses of 5,072 predominantly European American workers (aged 51–61) to questions from the 1992 Health and Retirement Survey. These individuals were working at least 35 hours per week when interviewed, and their plans fell into five categories, as Table 10.2 shows.

The older individuals were less likely than the younger ones to plan a job change, and they were also less likely than the younger ones to have no plans at all.

Table 10.2 *Categories of survey respondents' retirement plans*

Retire completely	20% of the respondents said that by a certain age or date, they planned to stop working altogether.
Retire partially	20% of the respondents said that by a certain age or date, they planned to reduce their work efforts.
Change jobs	9% of the respondents said that by a certain age or date, they planned to continue working full-time, either in a new job or in a self-employment context.
Never retire	7% of the respondents said that they would never stop working.
No plans	40% or more of the respondents stated that they had no plans for retirement.

Source: Ekerdt, DeViney, & Kosloski (1996).

Of the 20% of the respondents who planned to stop working altogether by a certain age or date, there were more men than women, and many worked for companies that would pay them private pensions. Women were more likely than men to say they would reduce their hours of employment or change jobs rather than stop working altogether, and more women than men had no set plans. It is probable that because more men than women had jobs that guaranteed a private pension, men were in a better position to make concrete plans. Also, married respondents were more likely than unmarried ones to have plans to retire completely, presumably because they anticipated retirement would give them more time for companionship. Other investigators (Reitzes, Mutran, & Fernandez, 1998) have also reported that married workers are more likely than unmarried ones to engage in retirement planning and to retire earlier, especially if their level of marital satisfaction is high.

Ekerdt and DeViney (1993) studied job attitudes over three years in a sample of 900 men from the Veterans Administration Normative Aging Longitudinal Study. These men ranged in age from 50 to 69. They worked full-time, but all of them had a definite target date by which they planned to retire from their jobs. Regardless of their exact chronological ages, the closer these workers were to their retirement target date, the more likely they were to report their jobs were causing tension and fatigue. The inclination to view a job as more burdensome as the retirement target date draws near suggests that workers engage in a preretirement "role-exit" process. That is, they gradually disengage psychologically from the work role in preparation for actual retirement. Ekerdt and DeViney's study is correlational so no firm conclusions can be drawn about cause-and-effect relationship between job attitudes and the proximity of planned retirement. Nonetheless, the suggestion that older workers engage in a psychological role-exit process is intriguing because older workers often express positive attitudes and high levels of satisfaction with their jobs.

Ekerdt and DeViney were the first to study variation in job attitudes along a temporal dimension of time left to work. Their sample consisted entirely of men, so their findings may not generalize to women. Women experience more work career interruptions, so their attitudes toward work and anticipation of retirement could well differ from those of men. Regardless of gender, it is doubtful that workers with less stable jobs would engage in the same role-exit process as employees with continuous work careers over many decades.

Life After Retirement

Today, many consider retirement to be "an active stage of life that occurs between the cessation of employment and the onset of frailties that can come with old age" (Atchley, 2007, p. 453). But how do people shape their lives once they leave positions of paid employment?

The busy ethic

When relatives, friends, and former coworkers ask new retirees how they manage to keep busy, the retirees often remark, "I am busier now than when I was working!" The **busy ethic** (Ekerdt, 1986) is most applicable to retirees in the young-old age category (ages 65 to 74), many of whom are in good health.

Retirees keep busy with educational pursuits, projects such as quilting, playing cards, or taking up a musical instrument, maintenance activities (household tasks, shopping, going to the doctor), socializing with family members and friends, and volunteer work. Ekerdt stresses that specific activities are not important. What is important is that retirees feel busy and other people think they are busy. Keeping a list of activities may help retirees feel busy regardless of whether they actually do everything on the list.

Ekerdt suggests several reasons retirees have a busy ethic. First, an active lifestyle is socially desirable in American society – leisure unbalanced by work is considered self-indulgent. The busy ethic stems from a work ethic philosophy, wherein work is considered virtuous and individuals are viewed positively if they are diligent and industrious. Relaxation is guilt-free only when it is balanced by work, so retirees may strive to feel busy to legitimize their leisure time. Second, the busy ethic may allow people to feel that their activities in retirement are not that different from those they performed at work. As such, the busy ethic narrows the psychological gap between work and retirement, making the transition to retirement less drastic. Also, feeling busy may alleviate retirees' fears of becoming useless or obsolescent.

However, retirees' claims that they are busy may not be wholly attributable to a need to feel socially desirable or a fear of being seen as obsolescent. Conceivably, age-related slowing, even for those in good health, could influence older retirees' perceptions of how busy they are. A trip to the grocery store that young or middle-aged adults tack on at the end of an eight-hour workday may be perceived by the older retiree as a great deal of activity. In any case, keeping active and busy in retirement is touted by the popular media as a necessary strategy for holding at bay the possibility of stagnation and decline. Articles in newspapers and magazines feature retired older adults with active and engaged lives.

Education in retirement

Many retirees take advantage of educational opportunities that are increasingly available for older adults. Some have dreamed of completing an education interrupted because of family responsibilities. The author has had several women in their mid-70s enroll in undergraduate psychology courses. They raised families and worked at paying jobs throughout their adult lives, and some cared for aging parents or spouses with debilitating illnesses. Now they were free to fulfill a long-held wish of obtaining a college degree.

Some universities permit older adults to audit courses free of charge, so older retirees can pursue knowledge without the specific intention of obtaining a course grade or official degree. They enjoy mingling with young students and taking part in campus life. Some universities have formed institutes for retired older adults, which for a nominal fee provide opportunities for intellectual and social stimulation. Older adults can attend lectures and enjoy library privileges and cultural events on campus.

Elderhostel is a program offering an extensive network of noncredit short courses and seminars held on college campuses in various locations. Older adults can live in dormitories for a week or two while they take these courses. Elderhostel provides intellectual stimulation, socialization with age peers, and a chance to spend time in a new place.

The recent growth of technology has altered many aspects of everyday life and created a need for education for people of all ages. Adolescents and young adults learn computer skills in high school and college. But today's older adults were not exposed to computers during their years of formal education and most of them did not use computers at work. However, many retired older adults want to learn basic computer skills. A popular use of computers is electronic mail (e-mail), which makes it easy to keep in touch with loved ones who live at great distances. Older adults also use computers to access the Internet for information about government agencies, health issues, or consumer products such as the ratings and prices of new and used cars. They use it to shop "online" for all manner of goods, from purchasing stocks and bonds to ordering books and clothing. Online shopping is especially advantageous if older adults no longer drive. Older adults can combat loneliness and isolation by visiting chat rooms. Chen and Persson (2002) found that older Internet users express a higher level of psychological well-being compared with older adults who do not use the Internet. There are many opportunities for computer training. Courses are sponsored by continuing education programs at community colleges, short courses are available in local public libraries and community centers, and training may be available right on the premises of apartment buildings where older adults live.

Some older adults take up volunteer work for the first time after they retire from paid employment. They volunteer for religious organizations, schools, community centers, hospitals, nursing homes, and advocacy and political groups. Some retired executives volunteer as consultants to business entrepreneurs both within and outside the United States. Approximately 25% of those aged 65 and older volunteer, but it is estimated that up to 50% of baby boomers will contribute to the community through volunteering (Morrow-Howell, 2006). Not only does volunteering benefit others, but those who volunteer report high self-rated health and feelings of well-being and having a meaningful purpose in life (Greenfield & Marks, 2004; Quadagno, 2008).

In sum, avenues for structuring a meaningful life in retirement are numerous and varied. An important decision older adults make at around the time they retire is where they will live. As we will see, there are many options, and some provide more physical and social support than others.

Living Arrangements

There is a common belief that as soon as older adults retire, they pack up and move to distant locations to live out their "golden years" in the sun. In fact, the majority of older adults do not relocate across state lines, but those who do are often seeking milder climates and opportunities for year-round outdoor recreation. Such migration has stimulated economic expansion in states such as Florida and North Carolina, where booms in the construction of retirement communities have had a significant impact on local communities.

Stages in Long-Distance Migration

Litwak and Longino (1987) separate long-distance migration into three stages. In the first stage, usually immediately following retirement, older adults who migrate are usually in the young-old (65–74) age category. Most are in good health, have intact marriages and adequate financial resources, and are eager to join with age peers in taking full advantage of the swimming pools, golf courses, and tennis courts available in many retirement communities. Such moves have been termed *amenity migration*.

In the second stage, older adults in their mid- or late 70s are beginning to experience moderate physical or cognitive difficulties. A number of them have had spouses die and some have seen their financial resources dwindle. At this point, migration tends to occur in the reverse direction − from the sun belt back to the frost belt – because older adults return to hometowns or places where they can count on informal care and support from family members, most often adult children (Stoller & Longino, 2001). This type of move has been characterized as one of *independence maintenance* because older adults often continue to live on their own but need some help to do so (Rowles & Ravdal, 2002).

Not all older adults reach a third stage, but those who do have more severe disabilities. They usually require more help than informal caregivers such as family members can give. These older adults need a more supportive environment, such as an assisted-living facility or nursing home (discussed below). For older adults who reach the third stage, such *dependency moves* are typically local and often involuntary (Rowles & Ravdal, 2002).

Although a proportion of older adults make long-distance moves when they retire, the majority of older adults remain in their native geographical areas after they retire. Some continue to live in the very same dwelling units where they have lived for years or decades.

Aging in Place

Individuals who remain in the same locale and continue to live in the same housing unit are said to be **aging in place**. Older adults who remain in homes where they have lived for many years may need to make physical modifications to insure ease and safety of bathing, cooking, climbing steps, and performing household chores. Such modifications include installing improved lighting and safety features in bathrooms and kitchens, mounting railings in stairwells, and placing ramps in entryways. In addition to physical modifications, another key to aging in place successfully is willingness to enlist assistance with tasks such as transportation, shopping, housekeeping, and meal preparation.

In many cases, older couples manage to age in place if the capabilities of one member of the pair complement those of the other. For example, one member may still drive, while the other is perfectly capable of cooking and doing household chores. Together, the couple can fulfill their everyday needs, but either member alone would experience difficulties. The single older adult who ages in place may count on neighbors or friends to help with transportation or shopping. However, these sources of support are not always reliable and become less available if familiar people move away and the older adult is left behind in a deteriorating neighborhood (Thompson & Krause, 1998). Often, family members who live in the vicinity, particularly adult daughters, help with transportation, shopping, and social outings. Older adults who never married or have no adult children may get help from siblings, nieces, nephews, or longtime friends.

One option for older adults who live alone and have no family members nearby is to share their homes with unrelated individuals. Such sharing can be a source of additional income or could be provided in exchange for household repairs, assistance with personal care, or just for company and companionship. Some public agencies sponsor match-up programs where older adults receive monetary subsidies for taking in unrelated housemates. However, this type of arrangement is not common and only a small proportion of match-ups seem to be successful on a long-term basis (Pynoos & Golant, 1996). Communal living is another option, particularly for single, unrelated older women who would otherwise live alone. However, living with unrelated individuals does not appear to be widespread among community-living older adults.

When individuals want to age in place but have little access to informal help from relatives, neighbors, or friends, they may need to pay for supportive services. However, knowing how and where to purchase such services can be an overwhelming task. Medicare, the federally sponsored health insurance program, pays for some in-home health-care services for older adults, but only for a limited time following a hospitalization or certain medical procedures (Pynoos & Golant, 1996). In recent years, there has been an increase in the number of private agencies that offer not only home health care but also assistance with transportation and housekeeping tasks such as meal preparation and laundry. Workers from such agencies transport older adults or accompany them on shopping trips or visits to doctors and dentists. However, these services are costly – many agencies charge by the hour and require a minimum number of hours.

Recent years have also brought an expansion of community-based day-care services for older adults. Some day-care centers are targeted to private-paying individuals or their families, while others are subsidized by local and state agencies and charge fees based on the older adult's financial means. With the support of day-care centers during part of the week, older adults may be able to continue living in their own homes or apartments. Day-care services can also be vital for employed relatives who provide informal care for older adults. They can be assured that their older family members are being served a nutritious meal, are receiving medication on schedule, and are enjoying opportunities to socialize throughout the day. Some day-care centers even provide door-to-door transportation.

Some older adults want to continue living in their own homes but utilities, repairs, renovations, or property taxes and insurance are becoming too costly for their retirement budgets. Those who qualify financially may be eligible for federal programs that subsidize the cost of utilities, and some states and counties make allowances for property taxes. For homeowners over the age of 62 who have little or no mortgage debt remaining on their homes, lenders have started offering reverse mortgages whereby homeowners sell the equity in the house in exchange for a lump sum payment or a monthly payment while they are still living in it. This concept is relatively new, and older adults are only beginning to be aware of it.

Age–Segregated Living Arrangements

Some older adults remain in the same locale but move to another residence that is more functional for their stage of life. They can select housing that is either age-integrated or age-segregated.

Age-integrated housing includes apartments and condominiums that have no specific age requirements. Compared to single-family housing, age-integrated apartments and condominiums require less maintenance, frequently supply greater security, and often are more conveniently located in relation to public transportation. Even so, these are essentially independent living arrangements because residents are responsible for their own transportation needs, housekeeping tasks, meal preparation, and social life. Some older adults move to small apartments ("granny flats" or "echo housing") that are attached or semi-attached to their relatives' main living quarters (Kendig & Pynoos, 1996). They have access to support close by, but they also enjoy some privacy and independence.

Some older adults move to **age-segregated housing** that is intended for individuals over a particular age, usually 62. Such living arrangements often include services such as group meals in a common dining room, planned in-house social activities or group social outings, and transportation (Silverstein & Zablotsky, 1996). These arrangements are well suited for older adults with health problems, physical disabilities, or sensory losses that make living in a single-family home or other type of age-integrated housing difficult or unsafe. Older adults may choose these more supportive living environments because they are unable or unwilling to rely on adult children or other relatives, but they want to feel secure in knowing that immediate assistance is available in case of emergencies or perhaps on a regular basis (Pynoos & Golant, 1996).

In exchange for the services provided in age-segregated environments, older adults must be willing to make whatever compromises are necessary for living in a group situation with others their age. It is especially important that the characteristics of the living environment match the individual's personal preferences (Kahana, 1982). Older adults who are extravertive and enjoy being with other people are likely to adapt well to age-segregated living environments where residents eat one or more meals in a common dining area. While outgoing older adults may look forward to such meals as pleasurable social events, older adults who prefer time alone in a quiet environment may dread what they perceive as the social pressure of group dining. Such individuals might be happier if they remain in a private residence and pay for supportive services from an agency.

In general, age-segregated environments offer more services on the premises than age-integrated environments, but they vary in the extent of support provided. Table 10.3 lists housing arrangements that range from totally independent (very little support) to highly dependent (extensive support). The sections that follow describe age-segregated living arrangements on a continuum from least to most supportive.

Table 10.3 *Types of housing on a continuum ranging from independence to dependence*

Housing type	Independent	Semi-independent	Dependent	
Single-family home	X			
Apartment/condominium	X	X		
Granny flat, echo housing		X	X	
Retirement hotel		X	X	
Retirement community		X	X	
Adult congregate living facility			X	X
Board and care home			X	X
Assisted-living facility				X	X
Nursing home				X	X

Adapted from Kendig & Pynoos (1996).

Retirement hotels

Often located in urban areas, **retirement hotels** are occupied primarily by single residents, most typically men from lower income groups. There are housekeeping services such as vacuuming and changing linens but meals are not usually served on the premises. Residents may have hot plates, microwaves, or coffeemakers in their rooms, but they eat most meals in nearby restaurants and cafeterias. With urban renewal and gentrification, many old retirement hotels have been torn down to make way for luxury hotels or

Low-cost retirement hotels such as this one on Ocean Drive in South Beach, Florida (ca. 1991) have been replaced by upscale hotels and gourmet restaurants.

high-priced condominiums that are beyond the means of lower income older adults. Inexpensive coffee shops and cafeterias have been replaced by upscale cafes and gourmet dining spots. South Beach in Miami Beach, Florida is an example of such a transformation. Twenty years ago, South Beach was lined with retirement hotels populated by older adults of limited means. These hotels have been renovated and are affordable now only to affluent vacationers, as are the high-priced restaurants and shops in the surrounding area.

Retirement communities

Unlike retirement hotels, **retirement communities** attract more affluent older adults. Some are subsidized by government agencies or religious organizations, but many are not. Unsubsidized retirement communities attract the most affluent older adults because residents bear the total cost of living in them. Large retirement communities such as Sun City in Arizona resemble towns or villages. Many retirement communities are enclosed complexes accessible only through secured entry gates. They feature a centrally located clubhouse, which is used for social activities and programs, as well as recreational facilities such as swimming pools, tennis courts, and sometimes even golf courses. Many retirement communities operate vans for transporting residents within the community if it is large or to points outside the community such as grocery stores and shopping malls. In most instances, residents are responsible for their own housekeeping, meal preparation, and health care. However, retirement communities provide a relatively secure environment in which older adults can lead active lives with their age peers.

Despite the potential advantages, moving from a single-family home to smaller but more functional living quarters can be stressful. Not only are older adults leaving their old familiar environment, but many have accumulated a large stock of possessions and must make difficult decisions about what to dispose of or give away (Ekerdt, Sergeant, Dingel, & Bowen, 2004; Marx, Solomon, & Miller, 2004). Some older adults become "trapped" by their belongings and unable to move to a more manageable living environment. Those who do make a move may require some time to adapt to a new living situation. Adjusting to a retirement community or other age-segregated living environment is usually easier if older adults themselves, and not their adult children, make the decision about such a move.

Adult congregate living facilities

Adult congregate living facilities require residents to meet a minimum age requirement (often 62) but to be capable of living with relative independence. Apartments in congregate facilities are equipped with safety features such as grab bars in bathrooms and call buttons in case emergency assistance is needed. Many congregate living facilities serve at least one meal a day in a common dining area, the cost of which may be included in the monthly rent. In one such facility visited by the author, residents must notify the director if they plan to skip a group meal. This notification policy serves as a check on each resident's well-being.

Many congregate facilities provide housekeeping services and most have office staff. Residents' committees make plans or suggestions to the staff about social programs. Some residents still drive, but many facilities provide van service for transporting residents to grocery stores, shopping malls, medical appointments, or for scheduled group outings.

Constant and accommodating housing

Lawton, Greenbaum, and Liebowitz (1980) describe two different models for older adult housing: **constant housing and accommodating housing**. Constant housing aims to preserve the original character of the tenants. Tenants may be relatively independent when they move in. Later, if they need more services, they are forced to find alternative housing and a new cohort of relatively independent tenants moves in to take their place. In contrast, accommodating housing is more flexible in providing additional services to meet the needs of an aging tenant population. For example, arrangements might be made to deliver meal trays to residents' apartments if they are unable to eat in a common dining area because of temporary illness or disability. Or a facility that serves only dinner in the common dining area may begin to offer breakfast and lunch as tenants become less capable of preparing meals in their own kitchens. Such flexibility may necessitate physical modifications to the facility because space may have to be added or existing space remodeled.

Board and care homes

Board and care homes are small, privately run homes, often converted from single-family structures. They serve three or four individuals who are unable to live independently in the community. Many board and care residents are widowed European American women with no children or other close kin (Quadagno, 2008). The proprietors of board and care homes provide meals, supervision, and limited assistance with daily activities (Pynoos & Golant, 1996). Board and care residents tend to be somewhat older and have lower incomes than residents of adult congregate living facilities. They share a living room, dining room, kitchen, and bathroom, and in some cases even bedrooms. Board and care homes are subject to the licensing regulations of the state in which they are located, but many smaller ones slip through the cracks and remain uninspected and unlicensed (Kendig & Pynoos, 1996; Quadagno, 2008).

Assisted-living facilities

In the United States, **assisted-living facilities** (ALFs) are a rapidly growing type of age-segregated living environment (Kendig & Pynoos, 1996). ALFs offer more services than board and care homes do, and they are usually more upscale, mainly serving middle- and upper-income older adults (Pynoos & Golant, 1996). Most ALFs have common dining and lounge areas, but individual residents or couples have private rooms with an adjoining bath or in some cases efficiency apartments with limited kitchen facilities. ALFs combine the privacy of private living space with provision of all three meals in a common dining area. Residents receive housekeeping and laundry service, help with personal care such as bathing and dressing, and staff members to monitor their medication on a 24-hour basis. Many ALFs offer social programs and exercise classes on the premises, as well as transportation to medical appointments, and occasional social outings.

Nursing homes

Of all the age-segregated living environments, **nursing homes** provide the most support and are also the most costly and closely regulated in terms of licensing requirements. Many nursing homes have a hospital-like atmosphere. In addition to meals and personal care, residents have access to skilled nursing services around the clock. Although some nursing homes offer several levels of care, nursing home residents tend to be physically frail and many suffer from mental disorders, most commonly Alzheimer's disease and depression (described in Chapter 11). Most need help with activities of daily living (ADLs) such as eating, walking, transferring from a bed to a chair, dressing, bathing, and using a toilet.

In the United States today, nursing homes are an integral part of the managed health-care system. Some older adults spend time in a nursing home immediately following a hospital stay but eventually they return to less supportive environments such as assisted-living facilities, congregate living facilities, or even private homes or apartments. Those who reside in nursing homes on a long-term basis usually do so out of necessity – they need the intensive services provided in such an environment.

Continuing care retirement communities

Continuing care retirement communities (CCRCs) are living environments with support levels ranging from independent living to assisted living to

---

Applying Research Box 10.1: Innovative Models for Long-Term Care

In the 1990s, William Thomas, MD, the physician-director of a nursing home, originated a long-term care concept called "Eden alternative" (Hill, 2005). Eden alternative facilities are designed to resemble home environments rather than medical establishments. There are special efforts to enhance residents' quality of life by providing social stimulation and opportunities for residents to both give and receive care. To the extent they are able, residents care for plants and pets in the home, and in some cases they volunteer to help in child-care centers located in the home or nearby. In short,

residents are encouraged to control some part of their environment so that they do not feel helpless. The Green House movement is an offshoot of Eden that includes small, private, community-based homes of 5 or 6 residents who are afflicted with dementia (dementia is discussed in Chapter 11) (Mitty, 2006). Residents play a role in the day-to-day running of the home by helping the staff with cooking and housekeeping. These innovative models for long-term care are intended to optimize residents' quality of life by giving them a say in their living situation.

nursing home care. Older adults who move into CCRCs must initially qualify for the independent level, and usually they pay an entrance fee that guarantees access to higher levels of care if necessary. CCRCs are a good option for couples because one member of the pair can get a higher level of care if necessary but still remain within close range of the other.

In sum, there are a variety of living arrangements for older adults. A proper match between older adults' needs and preferences and the support available will result in the best outcome for their level of functioning and satisfaction with life.

Revisiting the Selective Optimization with Compensation and Ecological Models

Employment, retirement, and living arrangements can all be viewed from the perspective of the Selective Optimization (SOC) (Baltes and Baltes, 1990) and Ecological (Lawton, 1989; Lawton & Nahemow, 1973) Models.

With regard to work, older employees optimize their job performance when they compensate for age-related slowing by selecting and concentrating on aspects of their jobs for which they have expertise. In terms of optimal perform-ance and satisfaction, older workers adapt best if their skills and ability levels match the demands of the work environment (Panek, 1997). The challenge of retirement lies in the older adult's success at shaping a life with an appropriate level of challenge.

No single living arrangement is ideal for all older adults, but an environment that matches an older adult's physical capabilities and social needs will maxi-mize the likelihood of positive adaptation. Environments should not be so demanding that accidents are likely or that the older adult's ability to be as independent as possible is compromised. For example, a multistory single-fam-ily home may present an overwhelming challenge for the older adult with severe arthritis. For such an individual, a one-story residence or an apartment building with an elevator would be more appropriate. Some living environ-ments may be too challenging, but environments should offer sufficient chal-lenge. Older adults who are physically fit and able to participate in community-based activities may not adapt well if they live in environments with on-site social programming. Similarly, older adults who enjoy cooking and other housekeeping tasks might find too little challenge in facilities where meals and cleaning services are provided. A close match between the older adult's competence and the demands of the living environment contributes to older adults' adaptation and sense of well-being.

> **?** Questions to Consider

1. If forced to make a choice, do you think an employer would hire a young adult or an older adult?
2. When will you start to make plans for retirement and how much do you think you will be able to depend on Social Security for retirement income when you finally stop working?
3. Where do you think you will live when you reach older adulthood? Where do your older relatives live?

Key Points

- In general, the median age of retirement decreased from the 1950s to the 1990s, but in the near future, people will remain in the paid labor force to later ages.
- In general, older workers have a high level of job commitment and many have developed expertise from years of experience.
- Overall, there is little connection between age and job performance, although older workers benefit more from training when there is less pressure and more time to learn.
- It is illegal to use age in hiring decisions, or to terminate, demote, or reduce the salaries of older workers without showing good cause. Even so, subtle forms of age discrimination still exist in the workplace.
- When workers retire voluntarily, there are few if any adverse effects on their physical or mental health. Most people adapt well to retirement, keeping busy with hobbies, educational pursuits, volunteer work, and other activities.
- Most retired Americans receive monthly Social Security benefits from the federal government. Some also receive benefits from private defined benefit or defined contribution pension plans. The latter are becoming more popular but require financial planning on the part of the worker.
- Some older adults relocate to warm climates, but most stay in the same area where they have always lived. Some age in place, meaning they continue to live in the same housing unit. Others move into more functional living environments.
- Supportive living environments are usually age-segregated (for people over a certain age) rather than age-integrated (for people of all ages).

- On a continuum from the least to the most supportive age-segregated living environments are retirement communities and retirement hotels, adult congregate living facilities, board and care homes and assisted-living facilities, and nursing homes.

Key Terms

adult congregate living facilities   320
Age Discrimination in Employment Act (ADEA)   302
age-integrated housing   318
age-segregated housing   318
aging in place   316
assisted-living facilities   321
board and care homes   321
busy ethic   313
constant housing and accommodating housing   321

continuing care retirement communities (CCRCs)   322
defined benefit pension plans   309
defined contribution pension plans   309
Elderhostel   314
nursing homes   322
retirement   304
retirement communities   320
retirement hotels   319
Social Security   307

11

Mental Health, Psychopathology, and Therapy

Chapter Overview

Close-ups on Adulthood and Aging

Lately, Sam has become concerned about his wife Ruth, who just turned 67. Until six months ago, Ruth was at the helm of the small retail business that she started 20 years ago. But over the past several months, she seems to have lost interest in the operations of her store. She prefers staying home, and she has been handing over important responsibilities to some of her newer employees. Sometimes her employees call her at home and she forgets whether they are at the store or on a business buying trip. Also, Ruth has always been an avid bridge player. But when she and Sam are invited to be in a foursome, she has made excuses such as feeling fatigued or no longer enjoying the game. Sam realizes that the two of them are getting older, but he is worried that something besides age is behind these changes. Recently, Ruth lost her younger sister, who died suddenly of an aneurysm, and her longtime best friend moved to Florida. Sam does not know whether Ruth's behavior indicates she is suffering from depression because of these losses, or whether it signals the onset of Alzheimer's disease, which he has heard so much about in the news.

Mental Health in the Older Adult Population

A high proportion of older adults report being happy and satisfied with their lives (Hinrichsen & Dick-Siskin, 2000). Many have close relationships with family members and friends, and most older adults cope effectively with illnesses, physical limitations, and loss of loved ones. In a national survey of Americans aged 65+, only 2% reported that they had experienced psychological stress during the past 30 days (*A Profile of Older Americans*, 2007). That the majority of older adults are so successful at adapting to these age-related challenges is a testament to their mental health. At the same time, some older adults need mental health services and a minority have diagnosable psychiatric disorders.

Rate of Mental Disorders Among Older Adults

What percentage of older Americans suffer from mental disorders? Several decades ago, the estimated rate ranged from 12% to 22% (Dye, 1978). More recent estimates range from 18% to 28% (Gatz, 1995; Gatz & Finkel, 1995; Qualls & Smyer, 2006). One estimate for a combination of community-living and institutional older adults aged 65 and older is that approximately 22% meet the criteria for some type of mental disorder if both emotional dysfunction and cognitive impairment are included (Gatz & Smyer, 2001). This figure is close to that reported for individuals aged 18 and over, so the proportion of the population that meets the criteria for mental disorders does not vary greatly with age. However, different disorders predominate at different points in the lifespan. Also, mental disorders can be longstanding for some older adults but could occur for the first time in the later years for others (Gatz, Kasl-Godley, & Karel, 1996).

Epidemiological research on mental disorders in the population has been largely cross-sectional (Gatz et al., 1996), so studies estimating the prevalence of mental disorders experienced by young, middle-aged, and older adults have been conducted at one specific time. (Chapter 2 discusses cross-sectional studies.) Each cross-sectional study is guided by the version of the American Psychiatric Association's *Diagnostic and Statistical Manual of Mental Disorders* (DSM) that was in use at the time it was conducted. Since 1980, the *Diagnostic and Statistical Manual* has been revised three times (DSM-III in 1980; DSM-III-R in 1987; and DSM-IV in 1994), with a new revision expected by 2012. Because the nomenclature and diagnostic criteria for mental disorders vary across DSM versions, it is difficult to compare the findings of cross-sectional studies conducted at different times.

By any measure, however, the number of older adults with mental health problems will increase in the 21st century (Knight, Kaskie, Shurgot, & Dave, 2006). By 2030, one in five Americans will be over the age of 65, which translates into a greater number of older adults who will experience mental health difficulties. Also, members of the baby boom generation have already shown relatively high rates of depression, anxiety, and substance abuse, and these problems may well follow them into old age (Gatz & Smyer, 2001; Knight, 2004; Parmelee, 2007). In addition, more people are living into the oldest-old (85+) age range. As we will see later in this chapter, the incidence of dementia, one of the most prevalent mental disorders in the older population, escalates with increasing age. If no effective cure or preventive measures become available in the near future, the number of individuals with dementia will be higher than it is today.

Older Adults and Mental Health Services

Numerous studies have found that a comprehensive mental health system for older Americans is lacking, and that mental health services are fragmented, unco-ordinated, and highly variable in quality (Lebowitz, 2006). On the whole, how-ever, today's older cohort does not make full use of the mental health services that are available. Some older adults still believe that mental health problems entail long-term stays in locked hospital wards, and that such problems are best kept to oneself. However, Knight (2004) contends that upcoming generations of older adults are more attuned to psychology and will be more open to psycho-therapy.

Therapists who work with older clients must have a firm understanding of developmental processes. Not only must they be well informed about normal aging, but they must also be trained regarding clinical issues unique to the older adult population (Packard, 2007). The American Psychological Association (1998) has published guidelines for psychological practice with older adults. Among the issues addressed are the likely need for interdisciplinary collaboration when therapists work with older adults and also the special concern therapists must have with legal competency (discussed in Chapter 6) as well as with main-taining confidentiality.

When older adults need psychological services, how do they pay for them? Financial issues have plagued the delivery of mental health services to the older population. There have been improvements, but the level of health insurance reimbursement to providers who treat mental disorders is still considerably lower than it is for those who treat physical disorders (Lebowitz, 2006). The managed care model in the United States relies to a large extent on primary care and general health-care practitioners, which means that older adults with mental disorders may not see a mental health provider. On the positive side, there have been concerted efforts to train health-care professionals in clinical geropsychol-ogy. Hopefully, this will increase the chances that older adults who require eval-uation, treatment, and follow-up will be referred to a trained mental health professional (Lebowitz, 2006).

Karlin and Humphreys (2007) point out that meeting the psychological needs of older Americans will depend heavily on Medicare (the federal health insur-ance program for Americans age 65+, which is described in Chapter 3). At present, Medicare reimbursement guidelines limit older Americans' access to psychological services, and there is an urgent need to expand coverage for psychological services aimed at prevention, screening, and early intervention.

Psychopathology

The current version of DSM (**DSM-IV**) consists of a classification system with five axes: (I) a list of clinical syndromes, (II) a list of developmental (mental retardation) and personality disorders, (III) a list of physical disorders/general medical conditions, (IV) a checklist of psychosocial stressors, and (V) a Global Assessment of Functioning Scale. On Axis I, the focus here, there is no distinction between functional and organic disorders as was made in earlier versions of the DSM (Butler et al., 1998). A number of the mental disorders listed on Axis I have been diagnosed in adults of all ages, but the following sections describe those of greatest concern for the older age group.

Depression

Depression is not a normal part of aging, but it is one of the most common disorders older adults experience. Depression is an affective, or mood, disturbance. The psychological symptoms include painful sadness, feelings of emptiness, irritability, generalized withdrawal of interest and decreased pleasure in activities that were enjoyed previously, pessimism, diminished self-esteem, and feelings of guilt, worthlessness, hopelessness, and helplessness. Depression can also be associated with bodily, or somatic, symptoms, such as feelings of fatigue and loss of energy, sleep difficulties, changes in appetite and weight, and bowel disturbance. Furthermore, depression can be accompanied by cognitive difficulties such as problems with attention, concentration, and memory, as well as a slowing down of speech, thought, and decision making.

The symptoms of major depressive disorders are more severe and last longer than the less severe and more transient symptoms of milder depressive disorders. Also, depression has been differentiated into primary and secondary categories (Cohen, 1990). Primary depression occurs in the absence of physical disorders or drug side effects, whereas secondary depression either accompanies or can be traced to bodily illness or adverse reactions to medication. In individuals over the age of 65, unipolar depressive disorder is more common than bipolar disorder, which is characterized by manic–depressive mood swings (Gatz et al., 1996).

The diathesis–stress model

Why do some individuals suffer from depression while others do not? Some psychologists use the **diathesis–stress model** as a framework for understanding why disorders such as depression occur (Monroe & Simons, 1991). Diathesis refers to an individual's level of vulnerability (for example, genetic propensities,

Table 11.1 *The diathesis–stress model*

	Moderate stress	**Extreme stress**
High diathesis	Mild disorder	Severe disorder
Low diathesis	No disorder	Mild disorder

Adapted from Monroe & Simons, 1991.

acquired biological vulnerability, or psychological factors). Stress refers to negative events (for example, loss of a loved one, loss of a job, illness, or difficulties related to a particular living situation). Individuals with high diathesis are especially sensitive to stressful conditions and may succumb to a disorder even if the stress level is not very high. Those with low diathesis can withstand moderate levels of stress without succumbing; if they do succumb with higher stress, the disorder will be relatively mild and short-lived (see Table 11.1). Careful consideration of age-related and/or cohort-related differences in diathesis, as well as level of exposure to stress at different stages of development, could help us understand why mental disorders such as depression could occur more (or less) frequently at different stages of life (Gatz et al., 1996).

Prevalence
Depression can take many forms (Knight, 2004), but just how prevalent is it in the older adult years? A common assumption is that the incidence of depression is higher in older adults than it is in younger ones. Contrary to this belief, however, a number of large-scale surveys report a lower incidence of major depressive disorders among community-living older adults than among younger adults, with as little as 2.5% of the older population meeting the DSM-IV diagnostic criteria for depression (Gatz et al., 1996; Parmelee, 2007). Thus, the rate of major depression does not seem to be higher in older adults than it is in younger adults, and indeed it may be lower (Knight, 2004; Parmelee, 2007).

However, surveys that ask participants to complete brief symptom checklists usually report a higher incidence of depression. Up to 27% of older adult respondents have acknowledged having some symptoms of depression (Koenig & Blazer, 1996). A National Institutes of Health panel on the diagnosis and treatment of depression estimated that symptoms of depression occur in approximately 15% of community-living residents over the age of 65 but in 25% of older adult nursing home residents (Friedhoff, 1994).

Gatz and Hurwicz (1990) analyzed responses from a cross-sectional survey that used the Center for Epidemiological Studies Depression Scale (CES-D), which is a self-report questionnaire used in many large-scale studies on depression.

Depression scores declined from early adulthood to late middle age but increased after the age of 75. However, the reasons for depressive symptoms probably differ for young adults and adults over the age of 75, who are more likely to be suffering from physical illness and the loss of loved ones.

Risk factors

What are the risk factors for depression in older adulthood? Overall, a higher proportion of women than men report symptoms of depression. However, this trend is reversed after the age of 80, at which point men report more symptoms (La Rue, Dessonville, & Jarvik, 1985). Also, with their relatively high incidence of physical illness and frequent use of medication, older adults are more at risk than other age groups for secondary depression (Cohen, 1990). Depression can coexist with heart disease, stroke, cancer, diabetes, and painful conditions such as arthritis. However, it is not always clear whether depression is an outcome of physical illness or whether it increases an older adult's vulnerability to physical illness (Parmelee, 2007).

Stressful life events involving loss also place older adults at risk for depression. Aging may bring loss of the work role, loss of income, loss of community because of relocation, and loss of loved ones (Parmelee, 2007). Ruth, who was described at the beginning of this chapter, may be suffering from depression because of the recent loss of her sister and best friend. It is also possible that when social contacts are reduced, older adults become hesitant to express feelings of anger for fear of alienating the few people left in their lives. Their angry feelings may be turned inward, which could be a risk factor for depression (Cohen, 1990).

Another risk factor for depression is being the sole caregiver for a chronically ill family member (Hinrichsen & Dick-Siskin, 2000). Many older adults, particularly women, care for spouses or other relatives with physical illnesses or cognitive disorders such as dementia (described later in this chapter). Caregiver burden involving heavy responsibility and accompanying social isolation is a potential source of depression. Thus far, research on caregiver burden has been conducted largely on European Americans who are taking care of family members diagnosed with dementia. However, Roth, Haley, Owen, Clay, and Goode (2001) followed African American and European American caregivers over a two-year period. All had a family member with dementia, and caregivers from both ethnic groups reported an increase in their own physical symptoms over time. Even so, the African American caregivers experienced fewer psychological symptoms of depression. Perhaps the African American caregivers' psychological resiliency is attributable to family role expectations, prior experience with stress, or stronger spiritual beliefs.

Caregivers from different ethnic groups may minister to family members with varying disabilities. For example, many Hispanic American caregivers are responsible for family members with diabetes-related complications, which tend to occur earlier in the adult life span than disorders such as Alzheimer's disease (Aranda & Knight, 1997). Also, family support systems may be more readily available for African American and Hispanic American caregivers than they are for European American caregivers. Even so, socioeconomic factors may limit ethnic minority groups' access to services that could alleviate any caregiving burden they experience.

Recent research is evaluating how cerebrovascular factors could be related to depression in later life. Studies using imaging techniques have found that some older adults with depressive disorders have decreased blood flow to the hypothalamic area of the brain, which is associated with mood (Blazer, 2006). Furthermore, vascular lesions in subcortical brain structures that are not dramatic enough to cause stroke or even hypertension could actually impede cerebral blood flow, resulting in the apathy and slowness sometimes seen in late-life depression. Research on late-life vascular depression is in its early stages, but it could clarify an important risk factor for late-life depression (Parmelee, 2007).

Diagnosis

Because the symptoms of depression are varied, it can be confused with other conditions and it may remain unidentified by older adults, their families, and even health-care workers (Blazer, 2006). Also, in older adults, depression can coexist or be confused with physical illness (Schneider, 1995). Indeed, symptoms of depression are often difficult to differentiate from those of illnesses such as cancer and heart disease, or from the side effects of medications used to treat those illnesses.

In some cases, older adults who seem to be in a state of vague physical decline may actually be suffering from depression (Cohen, 1990). Some investigators have identified a "depletion syndrome" that is characterized by loss of interest and lethargy rather than by an intense depressed mood (Blazer, 2006; Knight, 2004). In some instances, fatigue and sleep problems are assumed to be a normal consequence of aging when such symptoms actually signify depression (La Rue et al., 1985). Additionally, it can be difficult to determine when older adults' grief reactions are a normal response to loss and when they are a sign of depression. For all these reasons, depression may be *underdiagnosed* and thus remain untreated.

Just as depression can be underdiagnosed in older adults, it may also be overdiagnosed. *Overdiagnosis* is a readiness to diagnose depression when symptoms actually stem from another source. Changes in appetite and in bowel and sleep habits can be part of the normal aging process, but items on many self-report depression scales ask about somatic complaints. If a diagnosis of depression is based on the number of such items older adults endorse, then depression may be overdiagnosed.

The Geriatric Depression Screening (GDS) scale, developed specifically for older adult populations, consists of 30 items that deemphasize bodily questions and focus on test takers' feelings (Yesavage, 1982–1983). Two examples of yes/no questions on the GDS are as follows (a "yes" answer to the first question and a "no" answer to the second one would be counted toward an overall depression score):

- Do you feel your situation is hopeless?
- Are you in good spirits most of the time?

With regard to cognitive symptoms as well, depression may be either over-diagnosed or underdiagnosed. Normal aging may be associated with some decline in memory functioning, and older adults often complain about it. With overdiagnosis, older adults' memory complaints are interpreted as a sign of depression when they actually stem from something else. On the other hand, health-care workers untrained to work with older adults may assume that older adults who complain about memory are suffering from dementia, in which case depression is underdiagnosed (Knight, 2004). If cognitive symptoms are automatically considered a sign of dementia when they are actually a sign of depression, then appropriate treatment intervention may not occur. In short, cognitive symptoms can signify more than one potential problem, so **differential diagnosis** (that is, determining the exact basis for a particular constellation of symptoms) can be challenging. Ruth, who was described at the beginning of the chapter, will need to be carefully evaluated to determine the reason for her recent forgetting and fatigue.

Treatment

Once diagnosed, can depression be treated? Treatment interventions include drug therapy (often antidepressant medications) and electroconvulsive therapy (ECT). ECT ("shock therapy") is reserved for severe episodes of depression or for cases in which drug therapy is not effective or cannot be administered because of coexisting medical conditions (Blazer, 2006; King & Markus, 2000).

For long-term maintenance of functioning, psychological therapies are useful, either alone or in combination with drug therapy. **Cognitive-behavioral therapy** (CBT) has shown promise for older adults suffering from depression (Dick, Gallagher-Thompson, & Thompson, 1999; King & Markus, 2000). With CBT, clients are encouraged to identify aspects of their lives they think can be changed. They are told to keep track of the relationship between their behavior and mood and trained to avoid self-defeating thoughts and behavior. In this way, older adults learn to take an active role in monitoring negative patterns of thinking and making plans for how to handle future stressful events.

Suicide

Suicide is the voluntary termination of one's life. It is a behavior rather than a mental disorder, but suicidal ideas and/or actions are often associated with mental illness, particularly severe depression (Duberstein & Conwell, 2000; Kastenbaum, 2006). Some view suicide as a final act driven by intolerable psychological pain and feelings of hopelessness (Blazer & Koenig, 1996). There is evidence that suicide is less likely in older adults who practice religion, attend church frequently, and take an active role in church-related activities (Duberstein, Evinger, & Conwell, 2002).

Attempts to commit suicide may be direct – in mainstream American society, firearms have become the most common means of suicide for both older men and older women (Kastenbaum, 2006). Even so, a larger proportion of older men

(79%) than older women (33%) use firearms as a means of suicide (Canetto, 2007). The use of firearms may reflect their availability in the United States. In developing countries, the most common method of suicide is poison (Canetto, 2007). Less direct methods of suicide include refusal to eat, refusal to seek medical care, or failure to follow a prescribed medical regimen for a serious medical condition (Blazer & Koenig, 1996; Canetto, 2007; Cohen, 1990).

Older adults who set out to commit suicide are more likely than younger adults to complete the act. Death is the outcome for 1 suicide attempt in 25 for younger adults but for 1 attempt in 4 for adults ages 65+ (Kastenbaum, 2006). In the United States, suicide rates increase with advancing age, but gender is a factor – men aged 65+ account for 80% of the suicides among those aged 65+ (Canetto, 2007). Furthermore, suicide rates are highest among older European American men (Duberstein & Conwell, 2000) – there are 51.1 suicides per 100,000 among European American men aged 85+, compared to the U.S. national rate of 11 suicides per 100,000 (Kastenbaum, 2006).

Individuals who take their own lives were probably suffering from depression, but their symptoms went unrecognized and untreated. Older adults, especially men, may not report sadness or other symptoms, which makes it difficult for health-care providers to detect depression (Duberstein & Conwell, 2000; Allen-Burge, Storandt, Kinscherf, & Rubin, 1994). Older women's lower rate of suicide could be related to the likelihood that they have a wider social network outside the marital relationship (Bengston et al., 1996). Women may find it easier to get emotional support from others if they feel downhearted and this may prevent them from reaching the point of hopelessness. There is little question that some physical illnesses older adults experience can cause extreme pain and accompanying feelings of helplessness and hopelessness. Under such circumstances, older adults may view suicide as a rational alternative to extreme suffering or to a life of complete dependence upon others for physical care (Knight, 2004).

Understanding Aging Box 11.1: Suicide and the Gender Paradox

In older adulthood, experiencing loss is a risk factor for depression and potentially for suicide. That is why Canetto (2007) contends it is a paradox that European American men, who by many measures are more protected from adversity and less impacted by loss than any other group of older Americans, have the highest rate of suicide. Older women (as well as older members of ethnic minority groups) have a lower suicide rate than European American older men even though they are generally less well-off financially. Furthermore, older women more frequently experience widowhood and afterward are less likely than older men to remarry and more likely to live alone. Finally, even though older women are more likely than older men to suffer from physical disabilities, older women still have a lower rate of suicide. Canetto (2007) hypothesizes that in Western culture, completed suicide may be viewed as a masculine act that is more acceptable among older men. Particularly among European Americans, suicide "attempts" may be viewed as feminine behavior that indicates lack of courage and determination.

In sum, depression is one of the most frequent emotional disorders experienced by the older adult population, and suicide is an extreme consequence. On the positive side, depression, when diagnosed properly, is one of the most treatable mental health problems experienced by older adults (Butler et al., 1998; Gatz & Hurwicz, 1990).

Anxiety Disorders

Compared to depression, anxiety has received less attention in the older adult population, but it can result in impairment in concentration, attention, and memory, and in dizziness, severe insomnia, and disabling fear (Schneider, 1995). **Anxiety disorders** include generalized anxiety disorder, phobic disorders, obsessive-compulsive disorder, and posttraumatic stress disorder (Schneider, 1995). Anxiety disorders often begin early in life – Gatz et al. (1996) estimated that only 3% of anxiety disorders have their initial onset after age 65. Older adults may suffer from anxiety because of situational factors, but anxiety can also occur for no apparent reason. When it does, it can severely disable older adults who might otherwise function adequately (Schneider, 1995).

Diagnosing anxiety disorders in older adults can be challenging. First, anxiety can coexist with depression (Gatz et al., 1996; Knight, 2004), and the symptoms of these two disorders often overlap. As with depression, anxiety reactions are associated with changes in cognitive functioning such as inability to concentrate, remember, or make decisions. Second, the symptoms of both anxiety and depression can mimic those of cardiovascular disease (heart attacks) and endocrine disorders (Schneider, 1995). Furthermore, symptoms of anxiety such as rapid heartbeat and intestinal cramps can be side effects of some medications older adults take for chronic health problems.

Therapists unaccustomed to working with older adults might assume that behavioral manifestations of anxiety such as rambling speech and disorganized thinking are signs of dementia. Indeed, anxiety can occur with dementia, but a reduction in symptoms following relaxation exercises is one indication that an older adult's main problem is anxiety (Knight, 2004). For those with anxiety symptoms, psychosocial therapy and relaxation training seem preferable to total reliance on prescriptions for tranquilizers. In some instances, individuals who suffered from anxiety earlier in life actually show improvement in older adulthood, possibly because there is less pressure in their lives.

Hypochondriasis

Hypochondriasis is a somatoform disorder, meaning that its symptoms suggest a physical problem. However, a diagnosis of hypochondriasis is usually made when physical findings are negative despite a patient's preoccupation with illness and anxious concern with bodily functions that seem to intensify in the presence of medical personnel. Individuals with hypochondriasis often resist any suggestion that their symptoms are related to emotional stress. It is difficult to determine whether hypochondriasis reflects a longstanding personality dimension (Costa & McCrae, 1985) or whether it increases with age.

The symptoms of hypochondriasis and depression can overlap – some depressed individuals show signs of bodily preoccupation. In general, however, the depressed individual will not seek out help actively, whereas the individual with hypochondriasis will make frequent trips to the doctor (Butler et al., 1998).

There are several interpretations of the underlying basis for hypochondriasis in older adulthood. One is that older adults' anxiety about loss of social prestige and/or financial security is shifted to heightened concern with bodily functioning. Another is that in American society, physical illness is an acceptable excuse for failure to perform, so those who claim physical illness are exempt from normal social responsibilities. Hypochondriasis could also stem from social isolation – the energy that older adults previously invested in social interactions is turned inward, resulting in an exaggerated focus on bodily processes (Cohen, 1990).

Because hypochondriasis can be a psychological defense against anxiety, it is not generally recommended that doctors reassure older patients that their medical condition is perfectly normal. A familiar physician who is willing to acknowledge and understand a patient's worry can be helpful in reducing the patient's anxiety. With the spread of managed care, however, older patients are less likely to visit medical personnel who are familiar and they are less likely to be given kindly reassurance and emotional support from physicians who have severe constraints on their time.

When today's young and middle-aged adults enter older adulthood, they may be more willing than the present-day older cohort to attribute any distress they feel to emotional causes and to seek the help they need. Perhaps the incidence of hypochondriasis will be lower in future older adult cohorts. Keep in mind, however, that physical health problems do increase with age, and there is always a chance that older adults' complaints are based on undiagnosed medical conditions.

Paranoid Disorders

In DSM-IV, schizophrenia is categorized as a severe psychiatric disorder marked by disturbances in thought, perception, and attention. Most often, schizophrenia has its onset in early adulthood, although in some cases it can occur for the first time in later life (Knight, 2004). The paranoid type of schizophrenia is characterized by delusions, hallucinations, and disorganization in speech and behavior (Meeks, 2000).

However, **paranoid disorders** can occur in milder form, in which case they are classified in the category of personality disorder (Axis II of DSM-IV). Mild paranoia may represent a lifelong pattern or it may occur for the first time in older adulthood (Butler et al., 1998). Individuals with paranoid disorders tend to construct faulty explanations or interpretations of events. They are highly suspicious and distrustful of others when there does not seem to be a realistic basis for suspicion or distrust.

Paranoia can occur in connection with a mood disorder such as depression or a cognitive disorder such as dementia. Paranoid thinking that occurs for the first time in older adulthood is often associated with sensory impairment (Knight, 2004), particularly in vision and hearing (discussed in Chapter 4). For example, an older woman attempts to follow a conversation among some acquaintances, but with all the background noise she is unable to decipher what they are saying. She may assume they are purposely excluding her and perhaps even gossiping about her. In this instance, paranoid thinking may be the woman's attempt to fill in the blanks as she tries to interpret inaccurately perceived information. Paranoid thinking can also be associated with a decline in cognitive functioning. For example, an older adult who misplaces a pair of glasses or a wallet may accuse others of stealing those items. This accusation may be a defense against acknowledging problems with memory. Paranoid reactions may also be a defense against social isolation. For example, the older woman who does not receive any Mother's Day cards from her adult children may find it less threatening to conclude that someone is stealing her mail rather than admit to herself or others that her adult children have forgotten about her.

In some sense, paranoid reactions are adaptive – they protect the older adult from feelings of decline or failure. Unfortunately, though, paranoid reactions can alienate important members of an older adult's social support system. For example, a longtime live-in housekeeper might quit if accused of stealing. An adult daughter might become estranged from an older mother who accuses her of stealing money from the checking account that she has been helping her mother to balance.

Treating older adults who express paranoid ideas entails correcting sensory or cognitive deficits to the extent possible and providing a friendly and familiar but structured environment. Small doses of tranquilizers are sometimes prescribed to reduce anxiety. Even so, Knight (2004) cautions that an older adult's suspicions should always be checked before they are written off as paranoid thinking. What may appear to be paranoid thinking could actually have some basis in reality. For example, an elderly woman confined temporarily to a nursing home complains that her nephew is stealing from her unoccupied home. A thorough investigation may reveal that he has indeed been helping himself to her belongings. Unfortunately, it is not uncommon for older adults who live alone or are dependent upon others to care for them to become victims of thieves or scam artists. Thus, it is imperative to follow up an older adult's complaint that a housekeeper is stealing silverware, jewelry, or money to determine whether this has actually been occurring. In such situations, perpetrators may be counting on the likelihood that nobody will believe the older adult who makes such accusations.

Some older adults have a longstanding drinking problem, but others turn to alcohol late in life to alleviate feelings of loneliness and depression.

Alcoholism

Alcohol-related disorders (which fall under the category of substance-related disorders on Axis I of DSM-IV) are not always readily apparent in the older population, but chronic and acute alcoholism are not uncommon in this age group. Epidemiological surveys estimate between 1% and 15% of community-living older adults have problems with alcohol, with the incidence at the higher end of this range for older outpatients in primary health-care settings (Knight et al., 2006). Another estimate is that 21% of hospitalized adults aged 60 and over have a diagnosis of alcoholism and 14% of older adults treated in hospital emergency rooms have a drinking problem (Dupree & Schonfeld, 1999). Alcohol consumption can be particularly detrimental when older adults have coexisting physical disorders such as heart problems or when they take medications that exaggerate the effect of alcohol. It may take less alcohol for older adults to become intoxicated than it would for young adults (Zarit & Haynie, 2000).

Older adults may not readily admit either to themselves or to others that they have a problem with alcohol. Compared to younger adults with alcohol problems, older adults are less likely to get into fights or to have work-related problems because many are retired. However, the older drinker is more vulnerable to health problems and accidents such as falls (Gomberg, 2007). Alcoholism may be discovered only when the older adult is hospitalized after a fall or is being treated for other health problems. Even so, physicians are more likely to misdiagnose alcoholism as depression in female patients than in male patients (Tasker, 2003), which may be one reason the information available about female alcoholics is so sparse (Gomberg, 2007). Another reason is that older women tend to drink at home, whereas older men are more likely to drink in public places (Gomberg, 2007).

Some older adults have a longstanding problem with alcohol, while others turn to alcohol late in life to alleviate depression or anxiety. Interestingly, there is a gender difference in the age of onset of alcohol problems – more than one-third of older female alcoholics developed the problem within the last ten years as opposed to only 4% of male alcoholics (Gomberg, 2007). Thus, men's problems with alcohol are more longstanding.

What is the appropriate treatment for older drinkers? Programs that are supportive rather than confrontational have had a high rate of success (Dupree & Schonfeld, 1999; Knight et al., 2006). In an emotionally supportive atmosphere, counselors can assist older clients in identifying high-risk situations for drinking and teach them how to rehearse coping skills that control their drinking behavior. Treatment programs seem to be most effective for late-onset drinkers who are highly motivated to recover (Woods, 1999). Many professionals view group therapy as preferable to individual treatment because many older adults have experienced loss and feel isolated. There is some debate about whether group programs should cater specifically to older clients as opposed to clients of mixed ages (Knight, 2004; Lisansky-Gomberg, 2000). Gomberg (2007) contends that elder-specific programs may be advantageous because they can have a slower tempo and counselors can encourage reminiscence as well as discussion of current problems.

Delirium

Delirium falls into the category of cognitive disorders on Axis I of DSM-IV. It is an acute physiological brain dysfunction of sudden onset that is characterized by confusion, disorganized thinking, incoherent speech, and an altered and fluctuating level of consciousness. Those in a state of delirium have difficulty focusing attention and may suffer from hallucinations, disturbances of the sleep–wake cycle, disorientation, and memory impairment (Flaherty, 2007; Freter, 2006; Zarit and Haynie, 2000). Individuals in a state of delirium are generally not in contact with the immediate environment (Knight, 2004). For example, they may believe they are in a foreign country rather than in a hospital room.

Delirium often occurs in older hospitalized patients following surgical procedures (Freter, 2006). However, it is also associated with sensory impairment (not having glasses or hearing aid in place), intoxication from alcohol as well as from sedative-hypnotic and antidepressant medications, anti-inflammatory medications, analgesics, antibiotics, anticonvulsants, antihypertensive and cardiovascular drugs, ulcer drugs, anticancer medications, or even over-the-counter medications. Delirium can also result from malnutrition as well as electrolyte imbalance and toxins produced by the body in response to renal, endocrine, metabolic, and infectious disorders.

Recent evidence indicates that delirium falls into two categories, hyperactive and hypoactive (Freter, 2006), although some patients have a combination (Flaherty, 2007). Hyperactive delirium is associated with agitation and disruptive behavior and therefore is easier to detect. Hypoactive delirium is characterized by lethargy. It is more common, but often it is overlooked by nurses and physicians. A patient with hypoactive delirium may be misdiagnosed as being depressed or as having dementia if caretakers are not familiar with that individual's preexisting level of cognitive functioning.

Understanding Aging Box 11.2: The Sundown Syndrome

Although a clear and consistent definition is still lacking, **sundown syndrome** is "the appearance or exacerbation of symptoms of confusion or agitation associated with the late afternoon, evening, or nighttime hours – that is, after sunset" (Hazelton, 2006, p. 1157). With sundowning, older adults show signs of confusion, disruptive vocalization, restlessness, agitation, and pacing or wandering. Such symptoms are similar to those seen with hyperactive delirium, which health professionals must rule out as the basis for the behavior. Risk factors for sundowning include cognitive impairment (dementia), physical problems such as dehydration and incontinence, and disturbance of the sleep–wake cycle. Sundowning can also be precipitated by environmental conditions such as social isolation, recent institutional admission or room transfer, low environmental light, and use of physical restraints. Maintaining the older adult's safety and comfort are essential when sundowning occurs. Nonpharmacologic interventions used to treat sundowning include aromatherapy, pet therapy, bright-light therapy and insuring sufficient light levels, especially in institutional environments. Other recommendations are implementing a daytime routine of physical activity, reducing daytime napping, and making sure a close family member is present during the sunset hours. Pharmacologic treatments are available for delirium and sleep disturbance, but those that specifically treat sundowning are still being investigated.

Before delirium can be treated, its cause must be identified. A stable environment and appropriate medication may be helpful. Some patients are briefly restrained to prevent harm to themselves and others (Schneider, 1995), but there is a risk of increased confusion when physical restraints are used (Freter, 2006; Sullivan-Marx, 1995). If the condition underlying delirium is identified and treated, the symptoms are often reversed and the individual has an excellent chance of returning to a normal level of cognitive functioning. However, if no efforts are made to determine the cause, delirium could persist for months and dysfunction may become permanent (Knight, 2004).

Dementia

Dementia (listed under cognitive disorders on Axis I of DSM-IV) is a syndrome of global cognitive decline that typically occurs for the first time in older adulthood (Corey-Bloom, 2000; Skoog et al., 1996). One estimate is that dementia affects 6% to 8% of adults aged 65+, but 25% to 30% of those 85+ (Gatz, 2007; Knight et al., 2006). However, approximately 58% of institutionalized older adults have some form of dementia, possibly because dementia is a major factor in decisions to place older adults in institutions (Skoog et al., 1996).

Individuals with dementia have deficits in memory, language, orientation, abstract thinking and reasoning, decision making, and problem solving. These

Table 11.2 *A brief Mental Status Questionnaire (MSQ) used to screen for dementia*

1. Where are we now?
2. Where is this place (located)?
3. What is today's date/day of month?
4. What month is it?
5. What year is it?
6. How old are you?
7. What is your birthday?
8. What year were you born?
9. Who is the President of the United States?
10. Who was President before him?

Number of errors and presumed mental status: 0–2 errors (dementia absent/mild); 3–8 errors (moderate dementia); 9–10 errors (severe dementia).
Source: Kahn, Goldfarb, & Pollack (1964).

deficits represent a significant decline from a prior level and are sufficiently severe to affect functioning in occupational and/or social domains. For a diagnosis of dementia to be made, cognitive deficits cannot occur exclusively during the course of delirium, which is a temporary condition. Unlike patients with delirium, patients with dementia maintain a normal level of consciousness until late in the disorder, although there can be changes in personality and emotional responsiveness (Corey-Bloom, 2000).

Health professionals often use brief mental status exams to screen for dementia. Table 11.2 shows an early form, the **Mental Status Questionnaire (MSQ)**, with suggested cut-off scores that identify the extent of the dementia (Kahn, Goldfarb, & Pollack, 1964).

The **Mini-Mental State Examination (MMSE)** (Folstein, Folstein, & McHugh, 1975) is a widely used and somewhat lengthier test that includes orientation questions similar to those in the MSQ. In addition, the MMSE tests whether the individual can recall three unrelated words right after the tester says them and again later on in the testing session. Attention and calculation abilities are assessed by asking the individual to count backwards from 100 by sevens or to spell a word backwards. Language ability is assessed by asking the individual to repeat a sentence spoken by the tester, to read and follow an instruction, and to write a sentence. As a test of spatial ability, the individual is asked to copy a geometric figure. However, more extensive testing is needed to make a clear diagnosis of dementia and to determine the reason for the cognitive decline (Butler et al., 1998). A complete assessment involves further cognitive testing as well as medical tests to rule out other possible causes of a person's symptoms.

No two patients diagnosed with dementia are exactly alike. Some show signs of anxiety and depression, others of paranoia and violent and angry behavior, while still others may simply withdraw. The behavioral manifestations vary with the extent of the brain impairment, the rapidity of onset of the illness, the personality of the individual, and the nature of the living environment. In determining whether symptoms indicate dementia, clinicians usually take the individual's history into account. They may interview a spouse, close family member, or friend to learn about the individual's past interests, abilities, and prior level of functioning. A clinician assessing Ruth (who was described at the beginning of the chapter) would most likely take into consideration her spouse Sam's account of her history as a competent businesswoman and avid bridge player. That information, together with a relatively low score on a test of mental status, would suggest dementia as a possible diagnosis.

According to a report of the Alzheimer's Disease Education & Referral Center (ADEAR) (2006), the two most common forms of dementia in adults aged 60+ are Alzheimer's disease (AD) and vascular dementia (VaD), sometimes called multi-infarct dementia (MID). However, adults aged 85+ often have a mixture of AD and VaD (Corey-Bloom, 2000; Rockwood, 2006; Whitehouse, 2007a). One suggestion is that dementia can result from a combination of AD and VaD, with neither sufficient by itself to produce dementia-like symptoms (Skoog et al., 1996).

Alzheimer's disease

Alzheimer's disease (AD) is an irreversible brain disorder that develops over a period of years. It has an insidious onset – the initial symptoms of memory loss are often mistaken for age-related memory change (National Institute on Aging (NIA), 2005–2006; Whitehouse, 2007b). Early in the course of the disorder, memory and intellectual problems may be difficult to differentiate from those that occur with normal aging. Ruth's husband Sam (described at the beginning of the chapter) is not sure whether his wife's behavior is just related to growing older. Individuals may complain about misplacing items, forgetting appointments, and forgetting names, and there might be slight impairment in language, concentration, and judgment. Table 11.3 lists seven warning signs that may be indicative of AD.

With AD, interpersonal skills are often preserved until much later, and some individuals continue to function at work and in social situations (Corey-Bloom, 2000; Skoog et al., 1996). However, a prospective longitudinal study following older adults who did not have dementia at the outset found that even before any memory difficulties became apparent, changes in personality (increases in rigidity, self-centeredness, and emotional lability) were noticed by those familiar with study participants who were ultimately diagnosed with AD (Storandt, 2008).

The gradual and slow progression of decline in cognitive functioning typical of AD eventually affects language (finding words), problem solving, and decision

Table 11.3   *Seven warning signs of Alzheimer's disease*

- Asking the same question over and over again
- Repeating the same story, word for word, again and again
- Forgetting how to cook, how to make repairs, or how to play cards – activities that were previously done with ease and regularity
- Losing the ability to pay bills or balance a checkbook
- Getting lost in familiar surroundings, or misplacing household objects
- Neglecting to bathe, or wearing the same clothes over and over again, while insisting they have taken a bath or that their clothes are still clean
- Relying on someone else, such as a spouse, to make decisions or answer questions they previously would have handled themselves

Source: ADEAR (2006).

making. However, the first time family members suspect something is seriously wrong often occurs with an episode such as the older adult's getting lost while traveling to a location that ordinarily would have been reached with no difficulty. Also, the older adult may be unable to remember entire recent events or experiences. For example, a woman complains to her husband that it has been months since they saw a movie when in fact the two of them had gone to a movie the day before. This scenario is quite different from one in which the woman remembers attending a movie the day before but just forgets the title of the movie, the actor who played the main character, or the details of the story plot. Difficulties generally develop at work if the older adult has not yet retired, and there may be withdrawal from demanding social interactions. At this point, the older adult often denies any difficulties. For example, the individual who gets lost insists, "I got lost because of the construction on the roads." Anxiety and anger can break through if the individual is confronted with too great a challenge. At the same time, there may be a decline in emotional responsiveness and the individual may appear to be depressed. As mentioned previously, astute clinical skills are needed to make a differential diagnosis of depression versus dementia. However, individuals with depression tend to complain about difficulty with concentration, poor appetite, or sleep disturbance, whereas those with AD usually deny having such problems.

In the late phases of AD, cognitive functions are severely impaired. There is extreme confusion and disorientation. In some cases the individual can mistake a spouse for a parent or a daughter for a sister (Schneck, Reisberg, & Ferris, 1982), and there may be severe agitation and psychotic symptoms such as delusions, hallucinations, and paranoid reactions. The older adult may not recognize himself or herself in the mirror and may be afraid of the reflection or talk to it as if it were another person. Physical functions are also impaired – the afflicted individual will need assistance with activities of daily living such as bathing, dressing, eating, and toileting. When incontinence of urine and feces develop, many families decide to place the older adult in a nursing home.

How long can people with AD live? The precise onset of the disease is difficult to pinpoint. The individual with AD often lives for 8 to 10 years after the symptoms first appear, but the disease can last up to 20 years (Alzheimer's Disease Education & Referral Center (ADEAR), 2006). The immediate cause of death is often pneumonia or some other infection brought on by the patient's lack of mobility in the final stages of the illness (Whitehouse, 2007b).

AD is not part of normal aging, but symptoms usually appear after the age of 65 and the risk increases with age (NIA, 2005–2006). About 5% of individuals between ages 65 and 74 have AD, and up to half of those 85 and older may have it (ADEAR, 2006). In terms of numbers, approximately 4.5 million Americans have the disease. With increased life expectancy, more people are living into the oldest-old years, so 13.2 million Americans could have AD by 2050 if no effective means of treatment or prevention is discovered.

At any one point in time, it can be difficult to differentiate AD from other types of dementia. Laboratory tests can rule out secondary causes of dementia such as thyroid disorders, vitamin deficiency, or chronic infections. Visual imaging can identify treatable structural diseases such as hematomas and tumors (Skoog et al., 1996). Diagnosis of AD is becoming more accurate with techniques such as magnetic resonance imagery (MRI) and positron emission tomography (PET). Strictly speaking, however, AD remains a diagnosis of exclusion substantiated with certainty only when pathologists examine the brain upon autopsy (NIA, 2005–2006; Whitehouse, 2007b).

The cognitive losses AD victims experience have been traced to the death of brain cells (neurons) and breakdown of connections between them (NIA, 2005–2006). In certain areas of the brain there is extensive formation of neuritic plaques and neurofibrillary tangles that interfere with neuron functioning and survival. Plaques and tangles are also seen in the brains of very old individuals with no behavioral evidence of dementia prior to death (Snowdon, 1997), but usually these are less extensive than they are in the brains of AD victims (Skoog, et al., 1996). Also, there are large spaces (vacuoles) in the brains of patients with advanced AD.

What are the risk factors for AD? One is gender – women are more susceptible than men, even when women's greater longevity is taken into account (Corey-Bloom, 2000). Also, there is speculation that highly educated people are more protected against dementia because they have more "brain reserve" (that is, brain volume or quantity of dendritic connections between neurons) than people with less education. Some studies suggest that engaging in cognitively stimulating activities (for example, reading and doing crossword puzzles) may lower the risk of AD, so those who are not cognitively active may be more at risk. Researchers have also investigated the association of lifestyle factors (physical exercise and diet) with the risk of AD or other dementias (NIA, 2005–2006). It appears that physical exercise may be beneficial not only for

Understanding Aging Box 11.3: The Puzzle of Mild Cognitive Impairment (MCI)

Scientists have been trying to differentiate between normal age-related memory loss and memory loss that foreshadows Alzheimer's disease (AD). Individuals with more than the normal age-related memory problems have **mild cognitive impairment (MCI)**, meaning they are more forgetful than most people their age. Older adults with *amnestic* MCI (a subcategory of MCI with memory impairment as the most prominent cognitive symptom) have lower scores on memory tests than their age peers. However, they do not meet the criteria for Alzheimer's disease (AD) because they do not experience confusion or difficulty with language and they are still able to carry on with normal activities of daily living (ADEAR, 2006).

However, brain imaging studies have found that during the completion of certain cognitive tasks, different brain regions are activated in cognitively healthy older adults compared to those with MCI. Are older adults with *amnestic* MCI at a greater than average risk for eventually developing AD? Thus far, the answer appears to be "yes." A higher percentage of them will go on to develop AD compared to older adults with only a normal degree of age-related memory loss. Individuals with *amnestic* MCI are playing an important role in research on the precursors of AD (NIA, 2005–2006). Some studies have reported that a brief smell identification test can differentiate people who are cognitively healthy from those with MCI and AD.

the body but also for the brain. Likewise, there seems to be an association between a nutritious diet (rich in fruits, vegetables, and whole grains), as well as moderate alcohol consumption, and maintained cognitive functioning. Lifestyle habits of exercise and diet are effective in reducing the risk of high blood pressure, heart disease, and diabetes (see Chapter 3). At present, scientists are conducting further research to determine whether controlling high blood pressure and diabetes reduces the risk of AD. Even though epidemiological studies on large numbers of people show associations between lifestyle factors and risk of AD, we cannot yet make definitive statements about cause-and-effect relationships.

Scientists are also investigating the role of genetics in AD. A rare type of early-onset (prior to age 60) AD does seem to be associated with specific genetic mutations. For the more common type of late-onset (after age 60) AD, there is no obvious family history or inheritance pattern (ADEAR, 2006; Skoog et al., 1996). However, there may be genes that predispose rather than cause this type of AD (Gatz, 2007). Thus far, a certain form of genetic material (the APOE epsilon4 allele) has been associated with increased risk of late-onset AD in individuals with no family history of the disease (ADEAR, 2006).

At present, scientists think that AD results from a complex series of events in the brain that interact to trigger the disease. AD may result from a series of pathological processes associated with age, possibly combined with a reduced reserve capacity (Skoog et al., 1996). Finding reliable biological markers that increase the risk of AD is important for understanding why the disease occurs, but also because it is best to diagnose the disease in its early stages. As medications become available, they are likely to be most effective when given earlier rather than later in the course of the disease. Also, individuals who are diagnosed early have time to plan for their future care while they are still able to.

Thus far, approaches to treating AD consist of efforts to slow down the progression of cognitive deterioration. Several medications can reduce AD symptoms for a relatively short time, but there are no long-term effects, and as yet there is no cure. Antidepressant medications can be helpful for mood disturbances associated with AD, as are medications for treating behavioral disturbances such as agitation and hallucinations that can occur in the late stage.

With regard to prevention, some studies have found there is a reduced incidence of AD among individuals who regularly take anti-inflammatory drugs such as ibuprofen (for example, Advil or Motrin) and that vitamin E or ginkgo biloba extracted from the leaves of the ginkgo tree slows down the progression of AD. But high doses of these substances can have undesirable side effects, and it is not yet proven that any of them directly prevents AD or slows down its progression. Likewise, postmenopausal women who took high doses (120 mg/day) of raloxifene (Evista, which is a drug used to treat osteoporosis) over a three-year period of time had a significantly lower risk of developing MCI and a somewhat lower risk of developing AD compared to women on lower doses of Evista or a placebo control group. In some studies, many with animal models, there are hints that substances such as turmeric (used in yellow curry), omega-3 fatty acid (found in some kinds of fish), vitamin E, and soy isoflavones may have cognitive benefits, but it is still not clear whether they can prevent cognitive decline of the type seen with AD. Preliminary findings are hopeful, but the search continues for ways to reduce the risk of developing AD and to moderate its symptoms.

Over the past two decades, AD has received a great deal of publicity, which has been important in raising the level of research funding that will improve the chances that effective treatments will be developed or preventive measures discovered. Publicity has also increased people's awareness of the devastating effects AD can have on both the victims and their families – AD is now one of the most feared diseases among Americans aged 55+ (Gatz, 2007). However, there is a danger that those who have not had experience with AD will conclude prematurely that an older adult's memory difficulties certainly stem from AD when in fact the individual may be suffering from a more treatable and possibly reversible disorder (Knight, 2004). Knight cautions that heightened awareness of AD must be balanced with a concern for accurate differential diagnosis. But there is little question that AD is a major health problem, and as more people live into the oldest-old years, there will be increasing numbers of AD victims unless scientists find a way to cure or prevent the disease.

Vascular dementia

Vascular dementia (VaD), the second most common form of dementia in older adults, is associated with disorders of the cerebrovascular system such as blockage of cerebral blood vessels that can lead to focal destruction of brain tissue (Gatz et al., 1996) or affect how areas of the brain areas interact with each other (Rockwood, 2006). The term *VaD* is sometimes used interchangeably with the term **multi-infarct dementia (MID)**, which stems from multiple small or large brain infarcts, or strokes. However, VaD includes a broader category of dementias associated with a variety of vascular problems or with lesions in the subcortical white matter (Skoog et al., 1996). Thus, MID is one type of VaD.

Patients with MID often have a history of stroke or hypertension (Skoog et al., 1996). Risk factors are advanced age, being male, being a smoker, and having hypertension, heart disease, or diabetes. Ethnic groups with higher rates of diabetes are more vulnerable to this type of dementia. Prevention of and treatment for VaD are similar to those used to prevent and treat cerebrovascular disease (Rockwood, 2006).

Computed tomography (CT) and magnetic resonance imaging (MRI) scans are sometimes used to differentiate MID from AD. CT scans can detect areas of cerebral degeneration (or atrophy) in the structure of the brain. MRI scans use magnetic fields to detect abnormalities in soft tissue. These scanning techniques can often detect small focal lesions in the brain, which suggest a diagnosis of MID. However, there is not always a strict one-to-one relationship between such lesions and behavioral symptoms.

In contrast to the gradual and insidious onset of AD, VaD comes on more abruptly. Also, in contrast to AD's slow but steady downhill progression, deterioration can be stepwise and fluctuating (Skoog et al., 1996), possibly stemming from a series of strokes, each of which may be followed by partial but not complete recovery over a period weeks or months (Knight, 2004). Usually, the course of VaD is not as lengthy as is that of AD – approximately 50% of those diagnosed with VaD survive fewer than three years (Rockwood, 2006).

Differential diagnosis of AD and VaD is not always straightforward. First, the symptoms of the two types of dementia can overlap. Second, a number of individuals in the age 85+ group have a mixture of AD and VaD. Finally, scientists now think that vascular risk might be a common factor in both VaD and AD (Gatz, 2007). Even so, there may be somewhat greater preservation of personality with VaD than with AD. In addition, individuals with VaD may have difficulties with motor functioning earlier than those with AD (Rockwood, 2006).

In sum, most scientists believe that dementia is not an inevitable consequence of old age. However, its prevalence does increase with age. AD and other types of dementia have had an enormous impact on the cost of health care in the United States as well as on the need for social services. Family caregivers for victims of AD and other dementias are themselves vulnerable to physical symptoms and mental health problems such as depression. Counseling, support groups, and relief in the form of day-care services are essential for caregivers. Strategies that alleviate caregiver burden not only minimize caregiver stress, but hopefully prolong the time that patients with dementia can remain in a home environment as opposed to needing institutionalization.

Therapeutic Interventions With Older Adults

A number of therapeutic interventions are effective in treating older adults with mental disorders. Some are employed with young and middle-aged adults as well, while others are uniquely tailored to problems experienced in older adulthood. The sampling of therapeutic techniques described below is not all-inclusive but represents an array of psychosocial approaches for treating older adults.

Environmental Design and Sensory Retraining

Modifying an older adult's physical environment can be therapeutic, particularly when physical and/or cognitive competence has declined to the point where opportunities for physical, cognitive, or social stimulation are limited (Erber, 1979). In particular, older adults with dementia may benefit if they live in properly designed environments (Gladwell, 1997). Cues such as distinctive floor coverings in different corridors can prevent disorientation. Enclosed outdoor spaces should offer accessible garden areas that older adults can visit when they want to, but trees and shrubs can cast shadows that are often misperceived by patients with dementia. With appropriate environmental design, older adults with dementia can remain physically active and experience slower deterioration in functioning. An added benefit is that family members and friends will feel more comfortable visiting older adults who live in pleasant environments that encourage their independence to the extent possible.

Sensory retraining therapy (Richman, 1969) consists of activities and exercises that stimulate kinesthetic, proprioceptive, tactile, visual, auditory, and olfactory receptors (for example, recognizing odors such as cinnamon). In addition to encouraging older adults to recognize stimuli, some exercises have a perceptual-motor component (for example, catching a ball). The origins of sensory retraining derive from the field of early childhood education, where sensory contact and stimulation are considered essential for development. Sensory retraining therapy is well suited for older adults with limited physical and cognitive capabilities, and it is often carried out in small groups of geriatric patients in institutional settings.

Behavioral Interventions

Therapists can use interventions to modify behaviors that can have a negative effect on the quality of an older adult's life (Newton & Lazarus, 1992). Some behaviors frustrate caregivers and lead to institutional placement. But even for older adults who already reside in institutional settings, unacceptable behavior can affect the way they are treated – they may be excluded by fellow residents and responded to negatively by staff members. Unacceptable behavior may drive away family members who would otherwise visit

With **behavior therapy**, attempts are made to manipulate environmental cues that prompt negative behaviors or change the environmental consequences that reinforce unwanted behaviors. Prior to designing an intervention intended to shape new and more appropriate behaviors, it is important to gather information about the older adult's reinforcement history and analyze the reinforcement contingencies that already exist. However, such intervention techniques are appropriate only when there is reason to believe that the older adult is capable of benefiting from them.

Behavioral training has been successful in helping nursing home residents to gradually reacquire and maintain self-feeding skills (Baltes & Zerbe, 1976). Incontinence has also improved when older adults are trained in techniques such as self-monitoring and self-scheduled toileting (Burgio & Engel, 1990). In some instances, older adults with insomnia can learn to regulate their sleep habits by eliminating daytime naps, going to sleep and getting up at the same time each day, and controlling cues in their sleep environment by eliminating sleep-incompatible behaviors such as reading in bed (Puder, Lacks, Bertelson, & Storandt, 1983). Behavioral interventions hold great promise for boosting older adults' feelings of personal control and self-esteem.

Reality Orientation and Reminiscence Therapy

Reality orientation (RO) therapy has been used to treat older adults with moderate to severe memory loss, confusion, and disorientation. It is often beneficial when living environments would otherwise lack cues that help older adults stay oriented to time and place. Many institutional settings have bulletin boards that post information such as the day and date and list scheduled activities, the menu of the next meal to be served, the next holiday to be celebrated, and so on. In some instances, staff members hold classroom sessions with several older adults who are encouraged to discuss topics relevant to the here and now. There are some reports that these sessions lower older adults' level of confusion, but one criticism is that residents in institutional settings may not want to be reminded of the here and now, and such reminding may not improve their emotional outlook (Schwenk, 1979).

Reminiscence therapy encourages older adults to think and talk about the past. Life review (see Chapter 8) is considered a naturally occurring healthy phenomenon (Butler, 1963). Reminiscence therapy helps older adults reevaluate and integrate their life experiences, which could alleviate feelings of depression and sadness and give them a sense of continuity and self-worth. If conducted in a group, reminiscence therapy could also reduce older adults' feelings of loneliness, particularly if they have a common past. However, this type of therapy may not be appropriate for older people who focus on the past to avoid resolving issues that exist in the present (Newton & Lazarus, 1992). One study (Baines, Saxby, & Ehlert, 1987) found that a combination of reminiscence therapy and reality orientation resulted in greater improvement in the cognitive and behavioral functioning of nursing home residents compared with either technique by itself. Nursing home residents derived the greatest benefit when they participated in reality orientation therapy first, followed by reminiscence therapy. Although further research is needed, an effective strategy may be to conduct reality orientation sessions to orient people to the present before involving them in remembering the past.

Pet Therapy

Having a person in whom one can confide one's deepest thoughts and fears has long been recognized as a buffer against the risk of depression. Unfortunately, opportunities for social interaction with a confidante may diminish in older adulthood. But can interactions with pets make up for this?

The beneficial effect of pets is not confined to older adults, but pets may be an important source of support for individuals in this age group. Research on pet therapy includes studies of naturally occurring pet ownership as well as studies in which pets are introduced into the environment as a therapeutic intervention. With naturally occurring pet ownership, participants usually live in the community and take care of the pet themselves. There is some evidence that mental or physical benefits are associated with pet ownership (Siegel, 1993), although this has not been found in every study (Tucker, Friedman, Tsai, & Martin, 1995). In an early study on community-living older women (Goldmeier, 1986), pet ownership was associated with higher morale, but only if the women lived alone. Attachment to pets seems to moderate some of the psychological stress experienced by men and women who are caring for a cognitively impaired older adult (Fritz, Farver, Hart, & Kass, 1996).

It is difficult to evaluate the validity of studies on pet ownership (see Chapter 2 for a discussion of validity) because there may be a self-selection effect – people who are physically and mentally healthy may be more likely to own pets. It seems advisable to assess the effect of pet ownership within the context of an individual older adult's larger environment and lifestyle.

Most studies on **pet-facilitated therapy (PFT)** with older adults have been conducted in institutional environments such as nursing homes or assisted-living

Introducing friendly pets into nursing homes or assisted-living facilities can lift the spirits of residents and staff alike.

facilities. In some instances, a dog or cat becomes a permanent resident of the facility, but more often, an animal is introduced into the environment for a limited time, during which residents can make whatever contact they wish (for example, petting the animal, talking to the animal, or just observing).

Allegations about the effectiveness of PFT are frequently based on clinical impressions, and it is not always certain that the pet is the direct cause of improvements in older adults' morale or level of social interaction. Pets may elicit positive responses not only from the nursing home residents, but also from the nursing home staff, many of whom believe fervently in the benefit of PFT (Siegel, 1993). Introducing pets into an institutional environment may increase the morale of the staff, which could benefit the residents indirectly. Moreover, family members may find their visits more enjoyable when pets are present, and visitor enjoyment may have a positive effect on the residents themselves.

In sum, glowing anecdotal reports of improved morale and social interaction among nursing home residents following the introduction of pets cannot be ignored. PFT may not be the first line of therapy in the case of serious mental disorders, but it may be beneficial for treating feelings of loneliness when older adults experience loss. Also, pets can make institutional environments more stimulating, which could provide an incentive for family members to visit. As such, PFT could help to prevent more serious psychological problems.

Individual Psychotherapy

In the past, many therapists assumed that older adults only needed emotional support. With supportive therapy, a therapist would simply encourage the older adult to maintain self-esteem in the face of losses and physical impairments. However, other types of individual therapy have been useful for older adults. Insight-oriented therapy can be effective with psychologically healthier and more vigorous older adults who have the cognitive resources, the capacity for introspection, and the motivation for establishing a relationship with the therapist (Newton & Lazarus, 1992).

With psychodynamic approaches, older adults are helped to develop a fuller understanding of psychological issues in relation to their individual personality structure, self-image, and earlier development. Brief psychodynamic approaches can be effective when older adults are dealing with retirement, widowhood, or physical losses (Newton & Lazarus, 1992).

Cognitive-behavioral therapy (CBT), described earlier in the section on depression, helps older adults modify maladaptive thinking habits. This approach can be effective when depression or anxiety stem from feelings of incompetence and uselessness (Gallagher & Thompson, 1983). However, to benefit from CBT, older adults must be capable of comprehending and remembering. Positive results have been reported mainly with middle-class and upper-class European Americans, but we need more information on the effectiveness for older adults from racial and ethnic minority groups (Dick et al., 1999).

Family Issues

Even when older adults live alone, they are typically members of a broader family system. In some situations, it can be effective for therapists to meet with older adults and other family members as well (Herr & Weakland, 1979; Knight, 2004).

A common source of conflict among families is an older relative's apparent or actual need for assistance. For example, a late middle-aged or young-old married couple may disagree about care for an older relative. Conflict can arise when one member of the couple feels that an older relative's needs are interfering with time available for the rest of the family, or that the older relative's demands for assistance are excessive. Care of an older parent often falls to one adult child, who may resent siblings that are perceived as shirking their responsibilities. In some cases, however, an adult child feels driven to over-serve an elderly parent because of a longstanding need for that parent's approval.

In other situations, conflict can occur when adult children detect signs of physical and/or cognitive decline in an older relative, but the older relative is adamant about maintaining his or her independence. Another situation that can lead to conflict occurs when a middle-aged child returns to the nest. Adult children who leave their parents' home but come back some years later are referred to as **boomerang kids**. This scenario is becoming more common given the realities of divorce and economic hardship. An older couple may disagree about whether to allow an adult child to move back in. If the adult child does move back, conflict can arise over expectations about daily responsibilities and financial contributions to the household or even how long this living arrangement should last. In some cases, family therapy serves as a forum where the concerns of all parties can be addressed in a fair and equitable manner.

In sum, many older adults and their families face problems that could benefit from therapeutic intervention. To be effective, the intervention should be matched to the specific problem and to the needs and capabilities of the older adult.

Revisiting the Selective Optimization with Compensation and Ecological Models

The Selective Optimization with Compensation (SOC) (Baltes & Baltes, 1990) and Ecological (Lawton, 1989; Lawton & Nahemow, 1973) Models are two theoretical frameworks that we can use to consider how older adults can attain a high level of mental health and emotional well-being. When mental difficulties are experienced, how can they be understood and hopefully minimized?

According to the SOC Model, maintaining an optimal level of mental health requires focusing selectively on aspects of life that are most fulfilling and minimizing those that are least fulfilling. The most and least fulfilling aspects might vary depending upon the individual. For one person, being near family members might have priority, but for another, being near a religious congregation or having access to cultural events might take precedence. Focusing selectively on the aspects of life that are most important can compensate for giving up less important ones.

With regard to the Ecological Model, mental health can be conceptualized in terms of the older adult's competence (which is related to the concept diathesis, or vulnerability, which was discussed earlier) and the press of the environment (which is related to the degree of stress). Adaptation can be viewed as maintaining mental health or minimizing any disabling effects of mental disorder. Adaptation is most likely when there is a match between an individual's competence and the degree of environmental press. The Ecological Model can guide the design of environments for older adults with Alzheimer's disease (AD), who will likely enjoy an optimal level of functioning when there is some but not too much press.

? Questions to Consider

1. Do you think people your own age would be resistant to seeking psychological help if they were feeling sad and blue?
2. Have you ever had difficulty concentrating on your studies or work after you have experienced a social disappointment such as a break-up of a relationship with a significant other?
3. If you have a pet, how does that pet make you feel when you come home after a stressful day at school or work?

Key Points

- Most older adults enjoy an adequate level of emotional well-being and have satisfying relationships, but a proportion of them suffer from mental disorders.
- The overall rate of mental disorders is no greater in older adults than it is in young adults, although the types of disorder may differ.
- The number and proportion of older adults who need mental health services will increase in the future mainly because of increased life expectancy and cohort factors.
- Older adults are underserved by the mental health system partly because of their attitudes but also because of the nature of the health-care system and the level of reimbursement for mental health service.

- Among the mental disorders in older adulthood are depression, anxiety disorder, hypochondriasis, paranoid disorders, alcoholism, delirium, and dementia. Of these disorders, depression is one of the most common but also the most treatable.
- Delirium and dementia are disorders with cognitive symptoms, but it is important to distinguish between them.
- Delirium is an acute physiological brain dysfunction that develops suddenly but subsides when its cause is treated.
- Dementia is a syndrome of global cognitive decline that most typically occurs in old age, with increasing likelihood from the young-old to the oldest-old years. Dementia involves deficits in cognitive functioning, including memory.
- Among older adults, Alzheimer's disease (AD) is the most common form of dementia, while vascular dementia (VaD) comes second. The symptoms of AD and VaD can overlap, but the two types of dementia have different patterns of onset and course. Some older adults have a combination of AD and VaD.
- AD is more common among women and comes on gradually, whereas VaD is more common among men and comes on more abruptly. AD has a steady downhill course, whereas the progression of VaD is often stepwise and fluctuating.
- Therapy serves a useful purpose for older adults with mental disorders, but therapeutic interventions must be matched to the problem and the older adult's level of functioning.
- Compared with young and middle-aged adults, older adults are more likely to have coexisting physical and/or cognitive difficulties that have a bearing on the effectiveness of therapeutic interventions.

Key Terms

12 Coping with Death, Dying, and Bereavement

Chapter Overview

Close-ups on Adulthood and Aging

Vincent is 73 years old and six months ago he became a widower after being married for almost 50 years. His wife Theresa was ill for several years, but shortly after she was diagnosed she made her wishes known in writing that she did not want any heroic measures used to keep her alive if things got to the point where she was in great pain or in a comatose state. As Theresa's illness progressed, Vincent gradually took over all the household tasks. He had always been in charge of paying bills, making household repairs, and mowing the lawn. However, he was a novice at doing the laundry, cooking meals, and cleaning the house. Vincent was astounded at the day-to-day effort involved in taking care of the things his wife always did. Recently, one of Theresa's female acquaintances, a widow, invited Vincent to her home for dinner. Although he is flattered, he is not at all certain he is ready to become involved in a relationship. He misses the daily companionship he had with his wife, but among other things, he is concerned about what his adult children will think if he starts dating. For now, Vincent thinks he should try to form new social connections by volunteering at a school or hospital.

Death and Dying

Human development cannot be fully understood without attention to death and bereavement (Kastenbaum, 1999), and in older adulthood many people spend time anticipating the end of their own lives (Lawton, 2001). We will discuss death and dying first, followed by bereavement, which often follows the loss of a loved one.

When does death occur? Death is the irreversible cessation of biological functioning. In the past, the moment of death was determined by signs such as lack of respiration, pulse, or response to stimulation as well as lowered body temperature. However, partly because of modern life-support technology that maintains respiration and other vital functions, it is now more difficult to detect when the exact moment of death occurs (Corr, Nabe, & Corr, 2009).

Dying is the process of physical decline that ends in death (Kastenbaum, 2007). However, with modern medical advances, people with life-threatening illnesses can sometimes live for months or years. Surgery, new medications, and improved organ donation techniques have extended the interval between the onset of some illnesses and the actual event of death. Indeed, it is often not clear whether or not a person has entered the dying process.

Thanks to improvements in public health and sanitation, relatively few young people in the United States and other developed countries die from acute infectious diseases, and we take it for granted that most of us will live long lives. Table 12.1 shows death rates in the United States per 100,000 population in

Table 12.1 *Death rate per 100,000 population by age range in the United States (2004)*

Age range (years)	Death rate
25–34	102.1
35–44	193.5
45–54	427.0
55–64	910.3
65–74	2,164.6
75–84	5,275.1
85+	13,823.5

Source: cdc/nchs/data/statab/mortfinal2004_worktable23r.pdf

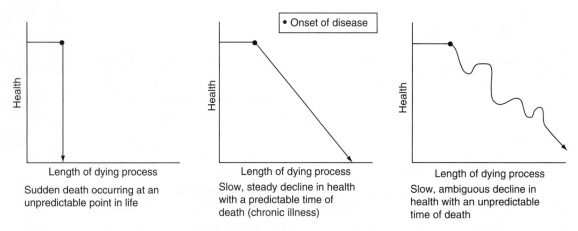

Figure 12.1 *Contrasting dying trajectories.*
Source: Corr et al. (2009, Fig. 2.2, p. 33).

various adult age groups. Note that the rate goes up from the younger to the later years. However, the increase in death rates is dramatic in the old-old (75–84) and especially the oldest-old (85+) years, illustrating that death is most likely to occur in old age. As discussed in Chapter 3, the leading causes of death among older adults in the United States are chronic illnesses such as heart disease, cancer, and stroke.

The Dying Trajectory

The rate of decline in functioning that precedes death can vary considerably (see Figure 12.1). With a sudden **dying trajectory**, death of a healthy individual occurs instantaneously, as in a fatal car accident or after a brief acute illness. At the opposite extreme is the gradual trajectory – death is certain to occur eventually but not immediately. For example, a person could be diagnosed with an illness or condition with no known cure, but medical treatments could extend life for weeks, months, or years. Gradual dying trajectories are common in modern technologically advanced societies. Vincent's wife Theresa (described at the beginning of the chapter) had a gradual dying trajectory – she was ill for several years before her life ended.

A gradual trajectory allows the dying individual time to resolve personal issues such as rifts with family members and to make decisions about the distribution of property to family members, friends, and charities. Additionally, as with Theresa, the individual can make choices about medical care (Lawton, 2001). In the case of Alzheimer's disease (AD), discussed in Chapter 11, the dying trajectory is gradual because individuals often live for more than a decade after the diagnosis is made. Tragically, however, individuals with AD lose the cognitive capability that would enable them to prepare for death.

End-of-Life Decisions

Given the likelihood of a gradual dying trajectory, what kinds of decisions can people make ahead of time?

Wills

A **will** is a formal document that states how individuals want their property distributed to heirs upon their death. At the time a will is drawn up, a person must be of sound mind and not subject to undue influence. A will can be changed at any point before death as long as the person remains of sound mind. The most recent version is used to determine the disposition of the deceased individual's property.

The signing of a will must be witnessed by the specific number of people required by state law, and witnesses cannot have any personal interest in the will. Depending on the laws of the state in which a deceased person has lived, handwritten, or unwitnessed ("holographic"), wills may be accepted. However, it is highly advisable to seek professional legal assistance when making a will. A will usually names a personal representative, or executor, who will carry out the business of collecting the property of the deceased individual and notifying those who will receive it. If no executor is named, the court appoints an administrator.

Unfortunately, people often put off drawing up a will, and individuals who die without a valid will are said to have died *intestate*, or without a testament stating their wishes (Corr et al., 2009). Each state has laws governing how the property of an intestate individual will be distributed. Sadly, this may not correspond with what the deceased individual would have wanted, which is why it is important to have a will. Also, a will often specifies the type of funeral or memorial service the individual wishes to have and whether there is a preference for burial or cremation.

The living will

In addition to specifying how property should be distributed upon their death, individuals can specify what type of medical care they would choose in the event they lack the capacity to express their wishes at some time in the future. With a **living will**, a person diagnosed with a terminal illness can have a say in what, if any, medical intervention should be used to prolong life in the event he or she becomes unable to express a preference later. Living wills are also important if there is a tragic accident that results in severe injuries.

The living will is an advance directive that first appeared in 1968, opening the way for public dialogue on end-of-life issues that previously were not usually discussed (Kastenbaum, 1999). The term *advance directive* commonly refers to the individual's wishes for his or her own end-of-life care. The living will instructs physicians and family members about a patient's wishes regarding the use of medical treatments that would artificially prolong the dying process if death is determined to be inevitable (Mishkin, Mezey, & Ramsey, 1995). Theoretically, a living will could request that life-prolonging measures be administered even if death is inevitable, but consent to withhold life-prolonging treatments is more typical. In most living wills, the preference is to withhold certain kinds of interventions ("artificial means" or "heroic measures") so that the dying process can take its own natural course. Also, a living will may give permission for medical personnel to administer "palliative" (pain-reducing) treatments even if such treatments hasten the actual moment of death. Vincent's wife Theresa made her wishes known that no heroic measures be used to prolong her life.

Initially, the living will had no basis in law and many physicians and hospitals were hesitant to honor a living will, partly out of fear of malpractice lawsuits. Recent years have brought greater acceptance of the idea that a competent adult has the right to refuse medical treatment. Today, each state in the United States has procedures for creating a legally valid living will (Mishkin et al., 1995).

In 1991, federal legislation known as the **Patient Self-Determination Act (PSDA)** was enacted. The PSDA requires that all health-care facilities (hospitals, nursing homes, health-maintenance organizations) that receive funds from Medicare and Medicaid (two government health-care programs, discussed in Chapter 3) provide patients with information on advance directives that could be used should a critical situation arise. Individuals who do not already have an advance directive must be informed about it so they can express their preference for accepting or refusing specific treatments. However, Kastenbaum (1999) points out that health-care facilities vary as to how extensively they explain a patient's options. Some simply ask patients to endorse one of two statements such as "I want my life to be prolonged as long as possible, no matter what my quality of life" or "I do not want my life prolonged if I will be permanently unconscious." Unfortunately, not all people are competent to make this decision at the time they enter a hospital or nursing home. It is preferable for people to execute advance directives when they are of sound mind and before they are facing a medical crisis.

Efforts to educate community-living older adults about advance directives have not been very effective in boosting the number who actually execute them. Older adults often express a preference that a family member, close friend, or even a physician, be the one to make treatment decisions for them should they become incapacitated. Cicirelli (1997) asked 388 European American and African American adults ranging from 60 to 100 years of age about the end-of-life decision they would make if they faced a situation in which their quality of life was poor. Interestingly, the majority of these older adults stated they would want to continue living, undergoing whatever treatments that might extend their lives. However, those who favored maintaining life were more likely to be African American, to have lower socioeconomic status (less education and lower occupational level), and to have stronger religious feelings. These individuals had less fear of dying but greater fear of destruction of the body. In contrast, those who favored ending their lives tended to be European American and to have higher

Understanding Aging Box 12.1: Desired Length of Life and End-of-Life Desires

In a survey conducted in Germany, Lang, Baltes, and Wagner (2007) asked men and women between the ages of 20 and 90 how long they would prefer to live (desired lifetime duration, or DLT). For the majority of the respondents, the DLT was in the mid-80s, although a small number of participants (mostly those older than 80 years of age) wanted to live into their 90s. In addition, when asked how much control they wanted to have over when and how they would die, approximately three-quarters of the respondents expressed a desire for self-determination. Surprisingly, however, only 11% of the respondents had actually completed a living will. Perhaps the recent and internationally polarizing case of Terri Schiavo, a young woman who did not have a written living will and remained in a vegetative state for 15 years before her husband won a battle with her family to have her feeding tube removed, will serve to boost people's awareness of how important a living will can be.

socioeconomic status and weaker religious feelings. These individuals had more fear of the dying process but less fear of destruction of the body.

The durable power of attorney in health-care matters

The **durable power of attorney in health-care matters** is an advance directive that is separate from the living will. With this document, the individual designates a trusted relative or friend who can make health-care decisions on his or her behalf in the event of serious incapacitating physical illness or mental incapacity. Without this document, the medical system generally relies on relatives to make such decisions. However, a person can use this document to specify in advance which of several family members should be the final decision maker. This can be crucial when relatives disagree about what medical decision should be made (Mishkin et al., 1995), or when the individual prefers that a friend or companion rather than a relative make health-care decisions.

In sum, the will, living will, and durable power of attorney in health-care matters are all documents individuals can use to plan for a time when they themselves are unable to make important decisions about their property or medical care. It is best to give a relative or close companion the name of the lawyer who has a copy of the will. Also, a relative or good friend as well as a health-care provider should have copies of the living will and durable power of attorney in health-care matters because these documents serve no purpose if nobody knows where they are.

Anxiety About Death

It may seem paradoxical that older adults are closest to death but they express less fear of, or anxiety about, death compared to middle-aged adults (Kastenbaum, 1999; Fortner, Neimeyer, & Rybarczyk, 2000). One reason for the higher anxiety

California Medical Association
DURABLE POWER OF ATTORNEY FOR HEALTH CARE DECISIONS
(California Probate Code Sections 4600–4753)

WARNING TO PERSON EXECUTING THIS DOCUMENT

This is an important legal document. Before executing this document, you should know these Important facts:

This document gives the person you designate as your agent (the attorney-in-fact) the power to make health care decisions for you. Your agent must act consistently with your desires as stated in this document or otherwise made known.

Except as you otherwise specify in this document, this document gives your agent power to consent to your doctor not giving treatment or stopping treatment necessary to keep you alive.

Notwithstanding this document, you have the right to make medical and other health care decisions for yourself so long as you can give informed consent with respect to the particular decision. In addition, no treatment may be given to you over your objection, and health care necessary to keep you alive may not be stopped or withheld if you object at the time.

This document gives your agent authority to consent, to refuse to consent, or to withdraw consent to any care, treatment, service, or procedure to maintain, diagnose, or treat a physical or mental condition. This power is subject to any statement of your desires and any limitations that you include in this document. You may state in this document any types of treatment that you do not desire. In addition, a court can take away the power of your agent to make health care decisions for you if your agent (1) authorizes anything that is illegal, (2) acts contrary to your known desires or (3) where your desires are not known, does anything that is clearly contrary to your best interests.

This power will exist for an indefinite period of time unless you limit its duration in this document.

You have the right to revoke the authority of your agent by notifying your agent or your treating doctor, hospital, or other health care provider orally or in writing of the revocation.

Your agent has the right to examine your medical records and to consent to their disclosure unless you limit this right in this document.

Unless you otherwise specify in this document, this document gives your agent the power after you die to (1) authorize an autopsy, (2) donate your body or parts thereof for transplant or therapeutic or educational or scientific purposes, and (3) direct the disposition of your remains.

If there is anything in this document that you do not understand, you should ask a lawyer to explain it to you.

---

1. CREATION OF DURABLE POWER OF ATTORNEY FOR HEALTH CARE

By this document I intend to create a durable power of attorney by appointing the person designated below to make health care decisions for me as allowed by Sections 4600 to 4753, inclusive, of the California Probate Code. This power of attorney shall not be affected by my subsequent incapacity. I hereby revoke any prior durable power of attorney for health care. I am a California resident who is at least 18 years old, of sound mind, and acting of my own free will.

2. APPOINTMENT OF HEALTH CARE AGENT

(Fill in below the names, address and telephone number of the person you wish to make health care decisions for you if you become incapacitated. You should make sure that this person agrees to accept this responsibility. The following may not serve as your agent: (1) your treating health care provider; (2) an operator of a community care facility or residential care facility for the elderly; or (3) an employee of your treating health care provider, a community care facility, or a residential care facility for the elderly, unless that employee is related to you by blood, marriage or adoption, or unless you are also an employee of the same treating provider or facility. If you are a conservatee under the Lanterman-Paris-Short Act (the law governing Involuntary commitment to a mental health facility) and you wish to appoint your conservator as your agent, you must consult a lawyer, who must sign and attack a special declaration for this document to be valid.)

I _____hereby appoint:
(insert your name)

Name _____

Address _____

Work Telephone (_____) _____ Home Telephone (_____) _____

as my agent (attorney-in-fact) to make health care decisions for me as authorized in this document. I understand that this power of attorney will be effective for an indefinite period of time unless I revoke it or limit its duration below.

(Optional) This power of attorney shall expire on the following date: _____

Figure 12.2 *Example of a durable power of attorney for health-care decisions.*
Source: California Medical Association, 1996.

Individuals can use this advance directive to designate a trusted friend or relative to make health care decisions on their behalf if they are unable to do so themselves.

among middle-aged adults may be that many have children who are not fully launched into independent lives and they may also be helping elderly parents. Their anxiety about death could stem from concern about the well-being of those who would be left behind. In contrast, older adults probably have children who are fully grown, independent adults, so they may worry less about leaving their children to fend for themselves. Also, many older adults feel that they have had time to carry out whatever they planned to do in their lives and hopefully they consider their lives to have had purpose and meaning.

According to Thorson and Powell (2000), young adults find it difficult to imagine there might not be a long future stretching out in front of them. In contrast, older adults are more aware that death is inevitable and some feel that the future does not hold as many possibilities as it did earlier in life. Also, older adults may express less anxiety about death because they have experienced the death of friends and loved ones with increasing frequency with the passing of time. In some sense, they are socialized to the possibility of death. It is not uncommon for older adults to read the obituaries in local newspapers on a daily basis. Many older adults are not so much afraid of death as they are about the circumstances of dying. They wish to die with dignity.

Clearly, however, any conclusion that older adults are less anxious than middle-aged adults about death must be qualified by their individual coping styles and social supports as well as the ethnic and religious groups to which they belong (Neimeyer & Fortner, 2006). Fortner et al. (2000) contend that older adults with strong religious beliefs (that is, intrinsic belief in God and belief in the afterlife, though not necessarily frequent church attendance) have less death anxiety than those without strong religious beliefs. However, Wink and Scott (2005) found that among educated older European American men and women (the majority of whom were raised in Protestant families), those who considered themselves moderately religious feared death more than did those either high or low in religiousness (Wink & Scott, 2005). Further study is needed to clarify which aspects of religious belief or practice, or lack thereof, may buffer people against the fear of death.

In comparing European American and African American adults over the age of 60, Cicirelli (2002) found no differences in the fear of death these two groups expressed. However, older adults with more physical problems and those living in institutional settings such as nursing homes expressed higher anxiety about death compared to those in better health who were living in the community. Perhaps older adults who are dependent upon others feel less in control of their environment and therefore have more anxiety about the circumstances surrounding their death.

Stages of Death and Dying

In spite of its inevitability, death has been, and to some extent still is, a taboo topic in American society. In the 1960s, Elisabeth Kübler-Ross, a Swiss psychiatrist

Applying Research Box 12.1: Coping With Thoughts of Death

Nathan DeWall and Roy Baumeister (2007) investigated how young adults cope with thoughts about their eventual death. They asked young adult participants questions that were intended to induce thoughts either about their own eventual death or about an unpleasant but not fatal experience (a painful visit to the dentist). Thinking about death did not produce any increase in conscious negative emotions, but it did activate what these researchers consider to be unconscious emotional coping responses: Compared to the young adults induced to think about dental pain, those induced to think about mortality subsequently completed ambiguous word stems with more emotionally positive words and also favored more positive emotional word associations. This suggests that when forced to contemplate the psychological threat of death, young adults may have an automatic psychological immune system that is outside their awareness but that searches for happy thoughts. Relatedly, researchers on aging and cognitive processes have found evidence for an automatic shift in older adulthood toward emphasizing positive, pleasant information (see Chapter 7 for discussion of the positivity effect). This may help explain how older adults cope with the imminent threat of death.

practicing at the University of Chicago Hospital, was approached by theology students who wanted to learn more about terminally ill patients. To humanize the dying process and counteract the tendency she saw in America to depersonalize dying persons, Kübler-Ross invited dying patients to share their thoughts and feelings with these students. Based on interviews with over 200 patients, many of whom were diagnosed with terminal cancer, Kübler-Ross (1969, 1974) noted five stages in the dying process (shown in Table 12.2).

The first of **Kübler-Ross's five stages of death and dying**, denial, often occurs when the individual is initially diagnosed with a terminal illness. The individual's initial reaction is often disbelief and a feeling that the diagnosis could not possibly be correct. According to Kübler-Ross, denial serves as a short-term buffer that allows time for the individual to take in the shocking news. As the realization begins to sink in that there is no mistake about the diagnosis, the individual may express anger and resentment that other people are healthy. Later on, some individuals may attempt to strike a bargain for more time or a second chance by promising to be on their best behavior (for example, by strictly following the doctor's orders or by praying). Possibly related to this stage are some reports of a dip in deaths prior to birthdays and major holidays that is followed by an increase afterward. In the next stage, depression, the individual feels a great sense of loss and sadness that life is coming to an end. There is a tendency to withdraw from emotional attachments to all but a few people with whom the dying individual has the most meaningful relationships. In the final stage, acceptance, the individual reaches a state of peace that the end is near.

Kübler-Ross's stages captured the attention of professionals who deal with death and dying and many adopted her ideas wholeheartedly. Eventually, however, some people leveled criticism at her ideas, contending that dying patients

Table 12.2 *Five stages of death and dying*

Stage	Example of a dying patient's response
Denial	No, not me, it cannot be true.
Anger	Why me?
Bargaining	Maybe I will have more time if I pray and ask God nicely.
Depression	I am going to die and that is sad.
Acceptance	I am at peace and ready for death.

Adapted from Kübler-Ross (1969).

do not necessarily progress through the stages in an orderly manner and furthermore, that not every dying individual goes through all of the stages Kübler-Ross described. For example, not all dying patients bargain for more time, nor do all of them reach the final stage of acceptance. Such criticism was not entirely fair because Kübler-Ross never insisted on hard and fast rules for the stages. In fact, she had pointed out that some individuals remain in the stage of denial right up to the end and that reactions to dying vary considerably depending upon age, specific illness, cultural background, and the dying individual's social network. Also, there may be a series of overlapping reactions during the dying process (Wortman & Silver, 1990). In any case, Kübler-Ross's stages have been a major cornerstone in our thinking about the dying process, and it would be a mistake to underestimate her contribution to lifting some of society's taboos about death and dying.

Not only do Kübler-Ross's stages apply to dying, but they are also helpful for understanding how people deal with the loss of a loved one. An individual with a sudden dying trajectory obviously has not had time to work through the stages, but Kübler-Ross contended that loved ones left behind may go through these stages as they deal with their loss. With a lengthier trajectory, however, close friends and relatives as well as the dying individual himself or herself may experience aspects of Kübler-Ross's stages. In some instances, Kübler-Ross's stages have also been applied to loss through circumstances other than death of a loved one. For example, individuals who separate or divorce may experience feelings similar to those of someone who has lost a loved one through death.

Care of the Dying Patient

In American society, more than 46% of people who die do so in hospitals or medical centers (Corr et al., 2009). Even so, the focus of traditional hospital care is on diagnostic testing and interventions aimed to extend life (Kastenbaum, 1999). Unfortunately, not all dying patients can benefit from the acute care provided in traditional hospital settings. Even when they cannot be cured, however, they may need pain-reducing (palliative) care.

Hospice

Hospice care is an alternative to the acute medical intervention provided in traditional hospital settings. It is administered by a team of professionals including physicians, nurses, social workers, and counselors, but highly trained volunteers also play an important role. The aim of hospice care is to enhance the terminally ill patient's quality of life. Medication is administered as needed to control the patient's pain. In addition to palliative treatment, spiritual, psychological, and social support are provided not only for dying patients but also for their families.

The modern hospice movement is attributed to Dr. Cicely Saunders, who founded St. Christopher's Hospice in London in 1967 as a place to care for incurably ill patients. Initially, hospice care was provided on an in-patient basis in units located within a traditional hospital or in nearby buildings. The atmosphere of hospice settings conveys a sense of warmth and comfort for patients and family members, who are encouraged to visit at any hour of the day or night. Later, hospice care was extended to terminally ill outpatients who wish to remain in their own homes.

The first hospital-based hospice in North America was established in 1975 as a palliative care unit in Royal Victoria Hospital in Montreal. In the United States, the first hospice program was established in 1974 in New Haven, Connecticut, as a community-based home care program. Across North America today, there are approximately 3,300 hospice programs (Hayslip & Hansson, 2007).

As of 1983, hospice care became a recognized benefit under Medicare (the federally sponsored health insurance program for 65+ adults in the United States), which now pays for more than 85% of hospice services (Corr et al., 2009; Hayslip & Hansson, 2007). Three years later hospice care became an allowable benefit under Medicaid (the federal program administered by individual states for individuals below a certain income level). Some private health insurance companies are moving toward providing hospice care coverage (Hayslip & Hansson, 2007). To be eligible for hospice care, Medicare patients cannot be seeking cure-oriented treatment for a terminal illness. However, they have the right to withdraw from hospice care if they change their minds and decide to pursue life-prolonging measures.

In sum, hospice care for terminally ill patients and their families emphasizes quality over quantity of life. Dying individuals are encouraged to make their own decisions until they are unable or unwilling to do so, and they are made as comfortable as possible on either an in-patient or a home care basis. After the patient's death, hospice workers provide emotional support to family members.

Euthanasia

A topic that has sparked heated controversy is euthanasia, a term that refers to a gentle and easy death, or more specifically to the action of inducing, or bringing about, a gentle and easy end to another person's life (Jecker, 2006). **Passive euthanasia** involves withholding action that would sustain a patient's life, such as failing to apply cardiopulmonary resuscitation after a heart attack or not using (or even withdrawing) life-sustaining medical treatment. **Active euthanasia** involves taking action to induce a patient's death, such as administering a lethal injection. Euthanasia is usually distinguished from **assisted suicide**, whereby the patient is provided with the means (for example, prescribing lethal medications but not administering them) to end his or her own life (Jecker, 2006).

Some have argued that euthanasia and assisted suicide are compassionate when mentally competent and informed patients are experiencing severe pain and make repeated requests that something be done to end their suffering. However, opponents of these practices argue that they violate the sanctity of human life and it is not always possible to determine whether patients are mentally competent when they ask for help to end their lives. Because patients' true wishes may not be known, critics claim that helping them end their lives may not be what they really want. Other arguments against euthanasia and assisted suicide are that it is difficult to decide how great a patient's pain and suffering should be before such practices are applied, and it is not usually known how soon death would occur naturally.

How are euthanasia and assisted suicide viewed from a legal standpoint? In some nations (for example, the Netherlands), euthanasia is legal. In 2002, the Dutch parliament formally exempted physicians from criminal liability for euthanasia and assisted suicide, but only under the following circumstances: The patient must request it voluntarily, must be informed about his or her situation and prospects, must be experiencing lasting and unbearable suffering, and both patient and physician must believe there is no other reasonable solution. Finally, the physician must consult with another independent physician to insure all the above conditions are met (Jecker, 2006).

In the United States, euthanasia is illegal. At the age of 79, Dr. Jack Kevorkian was released on parole after serving eight years in prison for second degree murder. Kevorkian helped more than 100 people commit suicide, including one man who was a victim of amyotrophic lateral sclerosis (ALS), a debilitating and incurable neurological disease. In 1997 the Supreme Court ruled that patients did not have the right to assisted suicide, although it allowed that in some cases, individual states could legalize its use (Quadagno, 2008). So far, Oregon is the only state to have done so, passing the Death with Dignity Act in 1997, which makes it possible for terminally ill patients to obtain prescriptions for lethal medications from their physicians if they make two oral requests and one written request. These medications cannot be directly administered by a physician or by anyone other than the patient himself or herself (Jecker, 2006). Even so, there have been attempts on the federal level to invalidate the Oregon Death with Dignity Act. There is little doubt that legal and ethical issues concerning euthanasia and assisted suicide will continue to be debated.

Bereavement and Loss

During the course of our lives, most of us will experience the loss of meaningful relationships. Such loss may occur in early childhood when a best friend moves to another neighborhood or city, or it may occur in adolescence or adulthood when a love relationship ends. Loss also occurs when someone we know dies.

Bereavement refers to both the situation and the long-term process of adjusting to the death of someone to whom a person feels close. **Grief** is the affective, or emotional, response to bereavement, whereas **mourning** refers to culturally patterned ways of behaving and rituals followed when there is a loss (Lund, 2007). Aspects of mourning include participating in funeral or memorial services as well as burials, abstaining from everyday routines for a specified time, dressing in certain kinds of clothing, and behaving in ways that are culturally acceptable for someone who has lost a loved one, especially a family member.

Bereavement due to the loss of a close family member or friend is not unique to older adulthood, but in modern societies it occurs more frequently in the later years. However, children and young adults may also go through a bereavement process when they lose an older family member. With the increase in life expectancy, it will not be unusual for children to experience bereavement with the death of a great-grandparent.

Attitudes Toward Death

Most of us experience feelings of sadness and grief over the death of loved ones regardless of their age. However, our attitude toward family members and close friends may not be the same as our attitude toward death in general, or death of people we do not know well (Tomer, 2000). Is there any difference in the responses people have to the death of a child or young adult compared to the death of an older adult?

According to Jecker and Schneiderman (1996), people view the death of a child or young adult as a catastrophic event, but they tend to think the death of an older adult is sad but acceptable. For example, there may be feelings of sorrow, anger, despair, and even a sense of injustice when a child dies because the family could not obtain a bone marrow transplant. In contrast, there may be a sense of loss over an adult aged 70 or 80 who dies because of age-based rationing of kidney dialysis, but people are less likely to consider this a tragic event. When asked to respond to a story about either a 19-year-old or a 79-year-old victim of a fatal car accident, both young and older adults felt that the younger person's death was more tragic and unjust than the older person's death (Chasteen & Madey,

2003). Also, there is some evidence that even when medical intervention has little chance of success, medical teams treat young persons more aggressively than they do older persons. Why is this so, and is this way of thinking typical in all societies?

Jecker and Schneiderman (1996) contend that one justification for the attitude that death is unfair when people are young is that young people have not yet had a chance to experience events such as falling in love, becoming a parent, or fulfilling life ambitions. Also, a common view in contemporary American society is that the younger generation represents society's future and young people have more potential contributions to make. In contrast, older adults have already had opportunities to experience meaningful life events and have already made whatever contributions to society they are going to make. In some sense, older adults symbolize the past, and upcoming younger generations are expected to improve upon what older generations have done. However, not all societies hold this view. In ancient Greek society and among some groups living in Africa today, the death of a small child is considered less tragic than the death of a mature adult who has built a network of meaningful relationships and earned respect and honor in the community.

Even so, if all human beings are considered equally worthy, shouldn't medical technology and treatments that could prolong life be available regardless of age? There is little doubt that ethical questions about access to both basic and specialized health care will become increasingly important in modern societies with aging populations but only a limited supply of sophisticated and expensive medical technology. Under such conditions, a society's attitude can influence the way health resources and life-prolonging techniques are allocated among different age groups (Kane, Priester, & Neumann, 2007).

Loss of a Spouse

The marital relationship is often longstanding, so the death of a spouse has a clear impact on the one left behind. More research has been conducted on the effects of losing a spouse than on losing others who hold meaningful places in our lives. However, much of what is known about the loss of a spouse can be applied to the loss of any close relationship. Losing a spouse, partner, significant other, sibling, or close friend becomes more and more probable as people progress through the adult years.

The term **widowhood** refers to the status of a person (like Vincent at the beginning of the chapter) who has lost a spouse through death and has not remarried. Becoming a widow or widower (the respective terms for a woman or man who loses a spouse) involves the event of a spouse's death, followed by a funeral and then a period of bereavement. But when a spouse suffers from a long-term illness with a lengthy dying trajectory, the process of becoming a widow or widower may actually start before the actual event of the spouse's death (Lopata, 1995).

The bereavement process

How do people cope with the loss of a spouse or any close relationship? Early in the bereavement process, there are often strong feelings of grief, including disbelief, confusion, numbness, sadness, and in some cases anger and guilt. According to Lund (2007), the widowed individual (or for that matter any person who loses a close companion) may feel abandoned, lonely, depressed, and preoccupied with thoughts of the events surrounding the loved one's death. However, there are no set rules about the exact nature or intensity of a person's reaction to losing a spouse. Some feel anger or guilt, while others feel a sense of relief, especially if the spouse had a long and painful dying trajectory. Some suffer from overwhelming sadness and depression, while others view their situation as an opportunity for growth.

There is also considerable variation in the time course of people's reactions to the loss of a loved one (Wortman & Silver, 1990). For some, feelings of grief are intense but subside quickly. For others, feelings of grief are less intense but resurface months or years later (Lund, 2007). A common view is that people who do not show signs of distress within the first weeks or months following the loss of a loved one will not be successful in "working through" to a resolution of the bereavement process because feelings of distress will "leak out" at some later time, possibly causing physical and mental health problems. However, Wortman and Silver (1990) point out that a minority of individuals do not express intense distress either shortly after a loss or later on, but their long-term adjustment does not seem to differ from that of individuals who do express intense distress.

Feelings of psychological and physical distress often taper off after 12 months, but never to a level as low as that of individuals who are not bereaved (Gallagher-Thompson, 1995). Most bereaved individuals manage to get through one day at a time but for many, the bereavement process can take up to two years (Martin-Matthews, 1996). Eventually, life may become enjoyable once again. Even so, widowed individuals often report, "You never get over it – you learn to live with it" (Lund, 2007).

Successful mastery of the bereavement process is thought to involve three tasks: (a) accepting the loss intellectually (being able to make sense of why the loss occurred), (b) accepting the loss emotionally (no longer feeling the need to avoid reminders of the loss), and (c) recovering to a normal level of functioning (Wortman & Silver, 1990).

For the most part, the nature and length of the bereavement process is related to the bereaved individual's personality traits, the social support available from close friends and family members after the loss, the circumstances surrounding a spouse's death, and the bereaved individual's competence in handling the tasks of daily living on his or her own (Lund, 2007). Sudden death of a spouse who seemed to be perfectly healthy would be particularly difficult for the widow or widower who was highly dependent on the deceased spouse or did everything in the company of the deceased spouse and had no close social relationships outside the marriage. Also, loss of a spouse or significant other can occur in the context of other stressors (Wortman & Silver, 1990). For example, a spouse's long illness may result in financial hardship for the surviving member of the pair, and the surviving spouse may suffer physically or psychologically from a long stretch of unrelieved intensive care for the deceased spouse. Furthermore, losing a spouse can be more stressful if the surviving spouse is also responsible for the care of dependent children or older parents (Martin-Matthews, 1996).

We still have much to learn about the bereavement processes of young and older individuals who lose spouses (Gallagher-Thompson, 1995). Comparisons of widowed younger and older adults are complicated by many factors. Younger widowed adults have probably been married fewer years than older widowed adults, and they probably have greater responsibilities for dependent children and jobs. These responsibilities can be stressful, but on the positive side, children and coworkers may provide comfort and emotional support. In contrast, widowed older adults may have fewer responsibilities, but at the same time they may not have as many opportunities for emotional support and social involvement. The loneliness bereaved older adults feel may be especially intense because, like Vincent (described at the beginning of the chapter), many are left to live on their own for the first time in decades.

The experience of widowhood can vary across ethnic groups as well as in individual families. In some groups, it is assumed that if a spouse dies, the widowed older adult will move into the same house with adult children and be taken care of by them. A widowed older woman may be expected to turn all of her attention to her grandchildren. In other groups, widowed older adults are expected to carry on alone, developing new interests and social networks. Also, in some groups, family members live close by and are available to offer emotional support. In other groups, adult children and other family members are scattered across the country and remain in the vicinity for only a short time following the funeral. This was the case in the poignant American film directed by Alexander Payne, *About Schmidt* (2002), in which Jack Nicholson plays a man in his 60s who is suddenly widowed and whose daughter comes back to town only long enough to attend her mother's funeral.

Comparing widows and widowers

Is loss of a spouse experienced any differently by women and men? Sheer numbers could play a role in this regard. In the United States, older widows (women) greatly outnumber older widowers (men). Reasons for this gender imbalance are that women tend to marry men older than they are, women have a longer life expectancy than men, and women are less likely than men to remarry once they are widowed. Not only are older widowers more likely to remarry, but many pick younger women. This is one reason older men are more likely than older women to live in the community with a spouse until the end of their days and wives will probably care for older husbands at some point (Moen, 1996).

But do all older adults who are widowed yearn to remarry? Davidson (2001) interviewed 25 widows and 26 widowers over the age of 65 who lived in the United

Often, widowed older men who depended on their wives throughout the years they were married to take care of household tasks must learn how to cook for the first time

Kingdom and had been alone for at least two years. More women than men stated that they were hesitant to consider remarriage because they were reluctant to give up their new-found freedom to do whatever they wanted. Older women are more likely than older men to live alone once they become widowed. Unfortunately, when they begin to suffer from health problems, they may find it difficult to continue living on their own. The fact that more nursing home residents are women is undoubtedly related to the longer life expectancy of women and the lower likelihood that older women have a living spouse to serve in a care-giving role if necessary.

Many of today's generation of widowed older women depended on their husbands to take care of taxes, insurance, and other financial arrangements. When widowed, they face the daunting task of handling these things by themselves. Older widowers depended on their wives to cook, do the laundry, and run the household. As with Vincent, described at the beginning of the chapter, they must learn how to prepare nutritious meals and perform household tasks that they formerly took for granted. To the extent there is less gender-based division of labor among today's young and middle-aged couples, future generations of older widows are likely to have greater financial know-how and older widowers may have more expertise in the kitchen.

With regard to social interactions, widowed older women often find that as time passes, they see less and less of married couples with whom they had socialized before (Norris & Tindale, 1994). This can be especially difficult for a woman who is the first in her circle of married friends to lose a spouse. Eventually, however, many widowed women form a social network with other widows. Widows who keep active and see friends seem to adjust best (Quadagno, 2008).

Widowed men often find social connections through remarriage. Even so, remarriage for widowed older adults can meet with resistance from adult children, who are unable to conceive of an older parent becoming romantically involved with someone new. Vincent, described earlier, has this very concern. Children may also fear that a widowed older parent's remarriage will jeopardize a possible inheritance. One further barrier to remarriage is a common reaction of grieving spouses to idealize the deceased mate to the point of sanctification (Lopata, 1995). For example, a widower may remember his late wife as being

Understanding Aging Box 12.2: Widowers and Bereavement

Widows and widowers both go through a period of bereavement, but the process seems to have a more negative emotional impact on men. Men who lose a spouse are more likely than women to suffer from depression (Umberson, Wortman, & Kessler, 1992), and in the first six months to a year after the death of a spouse, the mortality rate is higher for widowed men than it is for widowed women (Wortman & Silver, 1990). Kate Bennett (2007) contends that conventional views of masculinity include the themes "no sissy stuff" and "sturdy oak," which convey an image of strength, self-reliance, and control (both behavioral and emotional). Accordingly, some widowed men feel social pressure to maintain a stiff upper lip at a time when they have lost a life partner and are most in need of an emotional outlet. However, widowed men seek ways to express feelings that will not conflict with masculine expectations. For example, many feel that emotional expression is acceptable in private but not in public and that it is suitable to share their feelings with friends but not with strangers. When widowed men do express their emotions, they often use rhetorical devices that convey masculinity, such as insisting they are doing their best to remain strong for the sake of other people (for example, adult children).

perfect and having no irritating habits. It would be difficult for a living woman to meet these unrealistically high standards.

Older widows are usually at a greater economic disadvantage compared to older widowers. Some widowed women face financial difficulties immediately, especially if a spouse suffered from a lingering illness and left many medical expenses. Losing a spouse is associated with a significant drop in income more often for women than for men. The majority of women aged 65 and over may not be poor, but many are "within poverty's reach" (Moen, 1996). Reduced economic resources can limit a widow's social life if she does not have sufficient funds for travel, eating in restaurants, or even entertaining friends at home. Advance financial planning is the key to minimizing the negative economic impact of widowhood. Future generations of women who are financially savvy may not suffer negative economic consequences with widowhood to the same extent that the present generation does.

Loss of Other Meaningful Relationships

Losses experienced in older adulthood are not limited to widowhood. With regard to the marital relationship, loss can occur through divorce. As described in Chapter 1, the proportion of divorced older women and men has increased over the last decade. The increase can be attributed mainly to a higher rate of divorce occurring in young and middle adulthood. However, a small but growing number of people are divorcing in older adulthood after long-term marriages. Such individuals probably go through a bereavement process as they adjust to the single life after decades of couplehood. After a divorce, older adults (especially older women) experience a drop in financial status that can severely limit their daily activities and living situation. Even so, after an initial period of adjustment, there may be improved physical health, especially among divorced older women, possibly because there is a stronger relationship between degree of marital satisfaction and health for women (Kausler et al., 2007). Divorce often affects relationships between older adults and their adult children. Especially for older divorced men, there are fewer exchanges with adult children and grandchildren in terms of cash and informal care (Miller, 2006).

Finally, cohabiting couples in both heterosexual and homosexual relationships can experience loss of a partner. There is less recognition by society that such losses are significant, and often there is little emotional support for those who grieve (Corr et al., 2009).

In addition to losing a marital or other partner, older adults can experience loss of siblings. Sibling relationships (discussed in Chapter 9) are based on a common family history, and many siblings find renewed closeness in later life. Relationships between older adult sisters are especially close and often involve social and emotional support. With the death of a sibling, the surviving brother or sister may feel intense grief and a sense of incompleteness. Because a deceased sibling's spouse and children are usually considered to be the primary mourners, the bereaved sibling may not be given as much emotional support from family members as might be needed (Cicirelli, 1995).

Some older adults experience the loss of adult children. This is especially devastating because it goes against the natural order whereby members of the oldest generation are expected to predecease their children. However, we know less about older parents' bereavement following the death of an adult child than we do about their reactions to the death of a spouse. Also, some people reach their older adult years before they experience the loss of their parents. In the future, it may become more common for adults in their 60s and 70s to experience the loss of parents in their 80s, 90s, or older.

Finally, older adults lose friends. Longstanding friendships are based on a common history over an extended time and are difficult to replace with newer friendships. Depending on how long the friendship has endured, it may be just as close as a sibling relationship. Loss of close friends will most certainly be followed by bereavement not unlike that found with loss of siblings.

In sum, nobody is immune to the experience of bereavement. Over the course of a lifetime, one can suffer the loss of family members and close friends. With the loss of loved ones, especially spouses and companions, older adults must restructure their lives. The surviving member of a couple may be forced to learn new skills, as with Vincent who was described at the beginning of the chapter. After a period of bereavement, older adults must build or strengthen new social ties, perhaps by substituting new activities and goals. Vincent has plans to volunteer his time in a school or hospital. New relationships may not replace those lost, but taking steps to form them can be important in determining an older adult's success in adapting to a changed environment.

Revisiting the Selective Optimization with Compensation and Ecological Models

Throughout this book, we have used the Selective Optimization with Compensation (SOC) Model (Baltes & Baltes, 1990) and the Ecological Model (Lawton, 1989; Lawton & Nahemow, 1973) to conceptualize aging as a process of adaptation. Perhaps in no other aspect of the aging process is the SOC framework more valuable than when considering loss because this model would emphasize the strategies aging individuals can use to compensate for it. For example, the older adult approaching the end of life may selectively concentrate on aspects of life and relationships that are most meaningful. After a period of bereavement, the older adult who suffered the loss of a spouse or other loved one must recreate an optimal life by selecting goals that compensate for those that are no longer possible.

The Ecological Model would focus somewhat more heavily on environmental characteristics. For example, the older adult who experiences a decline in health is likely to achieve the highest level of adaptation in an environment with greater physical and possibly emotional support than was needed previously. The older adult who suffers the loss of a loved one may adapt best in an environment that offers an increased level of social support.

As people travel through life, they experience loss. This may be loss of physical or cognitive capabilities or loss of close relationships. It is remarkable that the majority of older adults are able to adjust and derive a sense of life satisfaction in the face of loss.

? Questions to Consider

1. Do you have any of the advance directives mentioned in this chapter (a will, a living will, or durable power of attorney for health-care matters)?
2. Have you discussed with older family members what their wishes would be if they were unable to make medical decisions for themselves?

Key Points

- In the United States and other developed countries, death occurs most frequently in older adulthood. However, an individual's dying trajectory can be sudden or gradual.
- Individuals can make plans about their property by drawing wills, and they can have advance directives about their medical care by signing living wills and designating a durable power of attorney for health-care matters.

- As a group, older adults tend to express less anxiety, or fear of death, compared to middle-aged adults. Within the older age group, however, religiousness, living situation, and health are often related to degree of anxiety about death.

- Kübler-Ross noted five stages in the dying process: denial, anger, bargaining, depression, and acceptance. These stages can be experienced by the dying individual and by family members and close friends.

- Hospice refers to a humane approach to providing palliative (pain-reducing) care for dying patients and addressing the needs of terminally ill people and their families.

- Euthanasia (both passive and active) and assisted suicide are ways of ending life that continue to be hotly debated from both an ethical and a legal standpoint.

- Bereavement is the long-term process of adjusting to the death of someone to whom a person feels close. Grief is the affective response to bereavement. Mourning refers to culturally patterned ways of behaving and the rituals followed when there is a loss.

- In comparisons of men and women who lose a spouse, men (widowers) are less likely than women (widows) to suffer economically, more likely than widows to remarry, and less likely than widows to have a social network outside a marital relationship. Widowers are more likely to suffer from depression and are more at risk for mortality.

Key Terms

active euthanasia   369
assisted suicide   369
bereavement   370
durable power of attorney in health-care
   matters   363
dying trajectory   360
grief   370
hospice care   368

Kübler-Ross's five stages of death and
   dying   366
living will   361
mourning   370
passive euthanasia   369
Patient Self-Determination Act (PSDA)   362
widowhood   371
will   361

13 Looking Ahead: Aging in the Future

Chapter Overview

Aging in the Future

Questions to Consider

Key Points

Key Terms

Close-ups on Adulthood and Aging

Ellen just turned 50, but at her birthday celebration all her friends toasted her by saying "50 is the new 30." Even so, she wonders what things will be like when she reaches older adulthood, however that might be defined nowadays. With her healthy lifestyle, she thinks she could easily live another 35 years. After several decades as a homemaker, Ellen returned to the university to earn a law degree, and she is just beginning to realize her dream of a professional career. Now that they are empty-nesters, Ellen and her husband Ralph want to sell their large two-story home and move to a smaller house, which they can adapt to their physical needs in the years ahead. Ralph is several years older than Ellen and will retire soon from his company. But as soon as he exits the corporate world, he plans to start a small business as a second career. Ellen's parents are in their late 70s, and they live independently in the community. When they eventually need assistance with shopping, transportation, or cooking, Ellen and Ralph will help out on weekends. But because she and Ralph will both be working during the week, Ellen intends to hire someone from an agency to assist her parents so that they can remain in their own home for as long as possible.

Aging in the Future

You have reached the end of this book and now you have a great deal of current knowledge about older adulthood. But in the future, what will the later stages of life be like? First, let's speculate in terms of two phases: the **third age** and the **fourth age** (Baltes, 1997; Weiss & Bass, 2002). There are no strict chronological boundaries, but the third age typically refers to the period between 65 to 74 years of age (the young-old years, as described initially in Chapter 1), whereas the fourth age coincides with advanced old age. After contemplating the future for people in the third and fourth ages, we will make a final visit to the Selective Optimization with Compensation (SOC) Model (Baltes & Baltes, 1990) and the Ecological Model (Lawton, 1989; Lawton & Nahemow, 1973), particularly as these models relate to *positive aging*, which was described initially in Chapter 1 (see Understanding Aging Box 1.1).

The Third Age

According to Weiss and Bass (2002), the first age (youth) is a phase of life during which individuals prepare for the activities of maturity, namely employment and child rearing. In the second age (maturity), individuals devote themselves almost exclusively to those activities. The third age occurs between retirement from the paid workforce and the start of age-imposed limitations. The third age can last for a short time, but it could extend for several decades.

In some sense, the third age is an extension of middle age, but without the work or child rearing responsibilities. Typically, third agers have sufficient health and vitality, so there are no major limitations in their activities. Many have raised children to adulthood and are retired from the paid labor force. Ideally, third agers have pensions and accumulated savings that enable them to maintain a standard of living close to what they had when they were working.

What are the lives of today's third agers like? Their choices appear to be unlimited and include traveling, playing golf, visiting children and grandchildren, or just staying home and occasionally getting together with family and friends. Many pay strict attention to physical fitness by walking, swimming, or participating in other sports, and to cognitive fitness by exercising their memory and attending lectures, movies, or plays that stimulate their thinking (see Chapters 5 and 6 for discussion of factors related to memory functioning and the benefits of engaging in cognitive and physical activities). Occasionally, there may be a crisis such as a family illness or the divorce of an adult child that requires their help. In general, however, third agers enjoy great freedom. Some do volunteer work in the community or pursue interests put off earlier in life. Others realize their dream of returning to college, auditing courses or taking them for credit toward a degree, as we saw with Marge, who was described at the beginning of Chapter 1. Many universities have institutes for lifelong learning that offer noncredit courses for older adults. However, some (like Ralph, described at the beginning of this chapter) launch new careers.

Weiss and Bass (2002) contend that the third age as just described is now available to a larger number of Americans for two main reasons. First, a sizable portion of middle-class retired older adults have a high standard of living thanks to generous company pensions, carefully accumulated savings and investments, and substantial financial gains from homes bought years earlier for low prices and sold years later for extremely high ones. Second, increases in life expectancy due to medical advances in treating and preventing diseases that used to afflict individuals in their young-old years have made it possible for many third agers to remain in good health. This illustrates a phenomenon known as *compression of morbidity* (discussed in Chapter 3) – illness and physical limitations have been pushed to a much later point in the life course. Clearly, however, this description of third agers does not apply to older adults whose work careers were less steady, who worked at low-paying jobs throughout their lives and now have difficulty making ends meet, who suffer from poor health, or who cannot afford the medical care they need to maintain an adequate quality of life.

What is the future outlook for the third age? Nobody knows for sure, but further advances in medical care mean that an even larger proportion of third agers may be able to enjoy good health and vitality. However, retirement in the early or mid-60s may be a thing of the past (see Chapter 10 for further discussion of work and retirement). The chronological age to qualify for full Social Security pension benefits from the federal government is now 66 and will increase further to 67. Furthermore, fewer private companies will offer the generous pension plans that so many of today's third agers enjoy (see Chapter 10 for discussion of pensions). Middle-class wage earners in today's young adult and middle-aged cohorts are less accustomed to saving money and more comfortable with incurring debt. In addition, the cost of health care is soaring at the same time as companies are cutting back on health insurance benefits for both workers and retirees. In short, it is becoming increasingly difficult to stay ahead financially let alone save enough money to live for two or three decades in retirement. According to the U.S. Health and Retirement Survey (HRS) conducted in 2004, 33% of workers aged 51 to 56 reported that they would work past the age of 65. This represents a sharp increase from the 27% of workers aged 51 to 56 who stated they planned to work past the age of 65 when they were interviewed in 1992 (Mermin, Johnson, & Murphy, 2007). Mermin et al. contend that in the future, there will be less demarcation between work and retirement because many third agers will work in part-time jobs that serve as bridges to retirement.

Although future third agers will probably have lengthier work careers, fewer will be steadily employed by a single company that eventually rewards them with a guaranteed lifetime pension. There will be greater job mobility, and more people will embark on new careers in midlife or later (like Ralph, described at the beginning of the chapter). People will have to update their skills to keep abreast with technical and other advances in the workplace, so many more will seek opportunities for higher education.

In the future, a greater number of women will participate in the labor force. Ellen (described at the beginning of the chapter) attended law school in midlife and in her 50s she is just getting established in a professional career. In the future, women may enter the workforce earlier than Ellen did, and their work careers may be more similar to those of men. This should result in a stronger financial situation in their later years and, hopefully, in feelings of accomplishment both within and outside the home. With regard to couples, women's steadier participation in the labor force may allow men greater freedom to cut back on their working hours or (as in the case of Ralph) to embark on a new career.

Future third agers could have greater responsibility for the younger generation. With the high divorce rate among young and middle-aged adults, members of the older generation may be called upon more frequently to help with rearing grandchildren. Third agers themselves are more likely to be divorced, or to have been married more than once, so more families will have complex social networks consisting of stepchildren and step-grandchildren.

Another responsibility likely to fall more heavily on the shoulders of future third agers is care of the older generation. The term *sandwich generation* (described in Chapter 9) generally refers to middle-aged women who care for both children and older parents. However, more women (like Ellen, described at the beginning of the chapter) will be working well into the third age. When older family members live in the community but need assistance, perhaps there will be a greater degree of gender crossover, with caregiving more evenly distributed across young-old men and women (Moen, 1996). But, as Ellen contemplates, there will be a demand for professionals to provide home services for the oldest-old generation when family members are not available.

The *beanpole family structure* (described in Chapter 9) means that families will have more living generations but there will be fewer members in each one. Thus, fewer third agers will be available to share the caregiving responsibilities for elderly parents. Perhaps grandchildren and great-grandchildren will play a more important caregiving role.

Given the possibility of further increases in life expectancy, people in the third age, or perhaps earlier, will need to plan ahead for their living arrangements. Ellen and Ralph are moving to a home that they can modify to suit their physical needs as they grow older. Such planning is critical for people who want to live independently in the community into late old age.

In sum, future third agers will have less leisure time. However, there could be a silver lining. Weiss and Bass (2002) claim that many present-day third agers find life enjoyable but some do not feel that they are fully engaged or contributing to society. In the coming years, many will still be working (at least part-time), and they will be called upon more to help both younger and older generations. In short, they will have more responsibilities, but their lives will have more purpose.

The Fourth Age

Entry into the fourth age is often marked by the 80th birthday (Baltes, 1997), but in general, this phase of life overlaps with the latter part of the old-old (75–84) age category and with the oldest-old (85+) age category, which is the fastest-growing segment of the population in the United States and other technologically advanced countries (see Chapter 1 for further description of demographic trends). Those who celebrate their 80th birthday have an excellent chance of living an additional seven years or longer.

The fourth age commonly brings some decline in independence for all but the most fortunate. Many fourth agers face health challenges. Studies conducted in the United States and Germany have found that a sizable proportion experience some degree of dysfunction that forces them to limit their level of activity (Baltes, 1997). Thus, there is good reason for concern about the quality of life in this phase of older adulthood (Baltes, 2006; Kane, 2005; Lawton, 2001).

In the fourth age, dysfunction may be not only physical but also cognitive. For example, the risk of dementia such as Alzheimer's disease (see Chapter 11 for more discussion) increases dramatically from the decade of the 60s to that of the 90s. The majority of fourth agers will be spared, but more people will reach the phase of life when the risk of dementia is very real. It is crucial that researchers have sufficient resources to investigate ways to prevent or treat the symptoms of dementia. With regard to mental health, future fourth agers will probably be more willing to seek help when necessary (see Chapter 11), and hopefully they will have access to services that enable them to experience pleasure and satisfaction in this final phase of life.

What other factors play a role in determining the quality of life in the fourth age? An important aspect is a living environment that provides support but also fosters independence to the extent possible. For example, improved visual cues can make it safer for individuals in their 80s and older to continue driving. Large signs that clearly mark danger zones should be posted far in advance of any hazard and devices could be installed in cars to assist older drivers who have hearing difficulties. For example, a sound sensor that responds to sirens could be programmed to trigger a flashing light on the dashboard to insure that older drivers pull over in time. For older adults who choose not to or who should not drive, other forms of transportation must be available. In this regard, older adults who live in urban areas with efficient public transportation systems will fare better than those in distant suburbs or rural areas. There will be a greater need for reasonably priced door-to-door car or van service. For older pedestrians, "walk" signs must allow sufficient time for crossing the street, and benches should be strategically placed in shopping districts and malls.

Fourth agers who live in their own houses or apartments can often benefit from in-home services, especially if family members are not available on a regular basis (as with Ellen and Ralph). They may need groceries and other items delivered to their homes, particularly when the weather limits their mobility.

Some grocery chains have implemented on-line shopping and home-delivery service for a set charge and minimum order. The demand is not always sufficient to make such a venture cost-effective. However, an increasing number of fourth agers willing to pay for this type of service could make it a worthwhile business venture in the future. If not, fourth agers will need personal shoppers to deliver groceries or other items to their homes or to accompany them on shopping trips, medical appointments, or other activities. In addition, there will be increased demand for day-care or daytime activities and programs in community centers that provide both social and cognitive stimulation. As well, there will be a need for door-to-door transportation to these centers so that older adults who no longer drive do not become housebound.

The majority of fourth agers will probably live in the community, although a substantial number will live in institutional settings such as nursing homes and assisted-living facilities, or in independent adult congregate living facilities (see Chapter 10 for a description of these living environments). Such living arrangements usually include some services on the premises and van transportation may be available. The challenge for older adults who reside in these facilities is to remain integrated in the outside community. Ideally, such housing could be located within safe walking distance of grocery stores, enclosed bus stops, shaded parks with adequate benches, and schools or community centers where older adults can play a volunteer role if they so choose.

The growth of technology will be a boon for individuals in the fourth age, and the personal computer will be an essential part of their daily lives. At present, approximately 70% of Americans in their 30s and 40s live in a home where a computer is available, and level of education is an important predictor of computer use (Cutler, Hendricks, & Guyer, 2003). Future cohorts of older adults will have a higher level of education compared to the present cohort, and older adults should not differ from middle-aged adults in their use of computers and related technology. E-mail keeps family members in touch even if they live at a distance, and it enables older adults to keep up with friends whom they cannot visit in person. In addition, new computer applications (for example, Skype) with video conferencing capabilities make it possible for older adults both to see and to chat with family members and friends in faraway cities and countries. Some forms of health care may be delivered via such technology – at present, efforts are under-way to use computer technology to keep track of older adults who live in rural areas, but computers could be an efficient means of reaching older adults in urban areas as well. In addition, computers allow pharmacists to keep a record of patients' medications, thereby minimizing the chances of unwanted or dangerous drug interactions. In short, technology will play an ever more important role in keeping fourth agers safe and in touch with family, friends, and health-care providers.

With regard to health care, Medicare (the federal health insurance program) is available to most older Americans once they reach the age of 65 (see Chapter 3), although there are deductibles and co-payments. With the recent implementation of Medicare Part D, a larger proportion of older adults stand to benefit from prescription medications that control chronic health conditions. Preventive medicine will contribute to the quality of life for older Americans.

In the future, advance planning and decision making will be important for living arrangements. Many middle-aged adults (such as Ellen and Ralph, described earlier) are thinking in terms of future housing needs. Some are modifying their residences, while others are designing new homes that will accommodate the physical needs they anticipate in the later years. Less attention has been paid to the delivery of in-home services, which may be necessary if fourth agers want to continue living in these carefully designed homes.

Positive Aging

Scientists have yet to discover how to extend the maximum human life span beyond approximately 120 years (see Chapter 3), but there is no question that there have been marked improvements in the health and vitality of individuals in their older years. In a large-scale survey conducted by the National Center for Health Statistics (NCHS) between 1982 and 2003, the proportion of people aged 70 and older who reported having a disability declined at the rate of 1.38% per year, and the proportion of people aged 70 and older who reported their health was only fair or poor declined at the rate of 1.85% per year (Martin, Schoeni, Freedman, & Andreski, 2007). In short, more individuals are approaching the fourth age with a reasonable level of health and vitality.

Even so, the experience of loss becomes more likely as people travel through life (Kane, 2005). Particularly in the fourth age, there may be loss of physical and/or cognitive capabilities (Baltes, 2006) and loss of close relationships. How, then, can individuals manage to enjoy *positive aging*, experiencing feelings of happiness and well-being even in the face of objective adversity (Seligman & Csikszentmihalyi, 2000)?

Earlier in this book (Chapter 8), we looked at the concept of *life story* – an ongoing narrative whereby we integrate a reconstructed past with a perceived present and an anticipated future, which allows us to establish our identity and feel our lives have unity and purpose (McAdams & Pals, 2006). We also explored the role of *accommodative processes* in modifying self-concept and redefining goals in accordance with situational and personal limitations (Brandtstädter & Renner, 1990). Finally, *hoped-for possible selves* (Cross & Markus, 1991; Markus & Herzog, 1991) are the ideas and goals about what we would like to become. King and Hicks (2007) contend that over the years, our life story undergoes change as we revise what we might have been. Through accommodative processes, we adjust our self-concept so it conforms to our circumstances, and in some instances we modify or give up hoped-for goals that do not seem attainable. Reflecting on goals we have had to revise and disengaging from lost possible selves may not be pleasant, but it is not a negative aspect of development. Rather, thinking about losses (and the regret we feel over them), but recognizing that challenging life events can disrupt some of our goals, is an important step in positive personality development. Acknowledging loss (but not being consumed by it) can spur us on to develop goals for our future possible selves. In sum, the ability to accommodate the self-concept and adjust future goals is consistent with subjective feelings of well-being that are a key element in positive aging.

Throughout this book, two theoretical models have provided a framework for considering how individuals can best achieve positive aging: Selective Optimization with Compensation (SOC) Model (Baltes & Baltes, 1990) and the Ecological Model (Lawton, 1989; Lawton & Nahemow, 1973). Both conceptualize aging in terms of adaptation. The SOC Model emphasizes strategies individuals can use when they experience loss, with the premise that adaptation will be optimal if older adults focus on aspects of life that are most meaningful and select goals that compensate for those no longer relevant or attainable. Hill (2005) contends that positive aging is intimately tied to how effectively individuals employ SOC strategies to buffer themselves against loss. Clearly, mindset is important – an older adult must think there is quality of life even when there are physical, psychological, or social limitations. With regard to the Ecological Model, older adults adapt best in environments that provide an appropriate level of physical and social support but at the same time offer a sufficient degree of challenge and allow for as much independence as possible. To that end, early planning should maximize the chances of finding an environment that will match the needs we have in our later years.

Robert Kane (2005) maintains that older adults are truly remarkable in their ability to derive life satisfaction and a sense of well-being given the adjustments they must make. He recommends that we acknowledge the effects the aging process can have, but that we recognize and try to emulate those who have been successful in rising to its challenges and making the best of their additional years.

? Questions to Consider

1. When you reach the third age, do you think your lifestyle will be similar to or different from those of your parents or grandparents?
2. What would be your suggestions if someone asked for your advice on how to age positively?

Key Points

- The third age is the phase of life that coincides with the young-old years. Many of today's third agers are in good health, are free from work and child rearing responsibilities, and are able to do what they please.
- Future third agers will probably continue to work at least part-time, and they will also have greater responsibilities for others.
- The fourth age is the phase of advanced old age marked by the 80th birthday onward. It overlaps with the late old-old and oldest-old age categories. This rapidly growing segment of the U.S. population often experiences some decline in health and some loss of independence.
- Positive aging is most likely when older adults make effective use of SOC strategies, when they live in environments that offer challenge but at the same time match their level of competence, and when they are flexible in adapting their goals when there is objective loss.

Key Terms

fourth age   381   third age   381

Glossary

absolute threshold the intensity of stimulation that a person needs to detect a stimulus 50% of the time when it is present.

accommodation unintentional processes activated when individuals must reevaluate and adjust personal goals and preferences in accordance with situational and personal limitations.

achieving stage the second of Schaie's (1977–1978) four stages of cognitive development, which occurs in the young adult years when individuals apply the knowledge they have gained.

acquisitive stage the first of Schaie's (1977–1978) four stages of cognitive development, which occurs in childhood and adolescence when individuals are motivated to gain as much information and knowledge as they possibly can.

active euthanasia taking action to induce a patient's death, such as administering a lethal injection.

activities of daily living (ADL) activities related to basic personal care that are necessary for self-maintenance (for example, bathing, dressing, eating, getting to the toilet, transferring from a bed to a chair).

activity theory the perspective that older adults have the same social wants and needs as young and middle-aged adults and they strive to maintain their level of social interaction (and feelings of well-being) by substituting new roles when old roles are lost.

adult congregate living facilities buildings that require residents to meet a minimum age requirement (often 62) and to live with relative independence, although some services may be provided on the premises.

age–complexity hypothesis the theory that older adults are at a greater disadvantage relative to young adults as the complexity of a task increases. For example, the gap between young and older adults' speed of response increases as tasks go from simple to choice to complex.

Age Discrimination in Employment Act (ADEA) legislation initially enacted in 1967 to protect workers aged 40 and older from discrimination in both hiring and employment practices.

age-insensitive abilities intellectual abilities that do not show age-related decline.

age-integrated housing houses, apartments, and condominiums that are independent living arrangements with no specific age requirements.

age-segregated housing residences for individuals over a particular age, usually 62, that typically provide some services and support.

age-sensitive abilities intellectual abilities that show age-related decline.

ageism discriminatory attitudes directed toward older adults that involve low expectations and negative beliefs, or stereotypes, about older adults as a group.

aging in place a term used to describe older adults who remain in the same locale and live in the same housing unit where they have lived for many years.

Alzheimer's disease (AD) the most common type of dementia in older adulthood, this gradually progressive brain disorder results in memory loss and changes in personality and behavior because of the death of brain cells (neurons), breakdown of connections between them, and extensive neuritic plaques and neurofibrillary tangles in certain areas of the brain.

anxiety disorders disorders characterized by impairment in concentration, attention, and memory, as well as insomnia, fear, and phobias that can be disabling.

assimilation intentional processes that individuals use to maintain continuity and integrity of the self. These call for efforts to transform actual situations into situations that are closer to ideal.

assisted-living facilities supportive living environments (private rooms or small apartments) that offer meals, personal care, medication monitoring, and activity programs.

assisted suicide providing a patient with the means (for example, supplying lethal medications) to end his or her own life.

avoidant strategies when faced with a dilemma, the individual denies the problem, often by reinterpreting its meaning.

baby boom years the years between 1946 and 1964 when the U.S. birthrate was very high.

beanpole family structure families with four or more living generations, but only a small number of members in each one.

behavior therapy manipulating environmental cues that prompt negative behaviors or environmental consequences that reinforce unwanted behaviors and designing interventions to shape more appropriate behaviors.

bereavement the situation and the long-term process of adjusting to the death of someone to whom a person feels close.

biological age where people stand relative to the number of years that they will live, or how a person's organ systems and physical appearance compare with others in the same chronological age group.

blended family families in which some members are unrelated by blood but nonetheless live together and share family responsibilities. Such families can result from divorce and remarriage when members of the remarried couple bring children from a prior marriage into a newly formed (reconstituted) family.

board and care homes small, privately run homes converted from single-family structures to house three or four individuals that are unable to live independently in the community.

body transcendence versus body preoccupation one of Peck's (1968) necessary adjustments, whereby older adults must rise above physical changes and discomfort and find ways to enjoy life with reduced physical capabilities and less physical perfection.

boomerang kids adult children who leave their parents' home but then return, sometimes many years later.

bottom-up and top-down strategies of language processing in processing spoken language, a bottom-up strategy calls for registering the details of the sensory-perceptual input, whereas a top-down strategy uses contextual information about the semantic (word meaning) and syntactic (grammatical) structure of language as well as its prosodic features (intonation, stress, and timing).

bottom-up processing strategy gathering and integrating new information when trying to make a decision.

busy ethic a term that stems from the work ethic philosophy, wherein work is considered virtuous and individuals who are diligent and industrious are viewed positively. Older adults often claim to be busier in retirement than they were when working.

category-based operations a way of thinking whereby people rely on previously formed cognitive representations (schemas) when they form impressions about others, thus reducing the demand on their own cognitive resources.

centenarians people who live to the age of 100 or beyond.

chronological age maturational level, defined by the number of units of time (months or years) that have elapsed since birth.

classic aging pattern the developmental course of different types of intellectual abilities, whereby verbal ability test scores are relatively maintained into older adulthood, whereas performance ability test scores show age-related decline.

cognitive-analytic strategies when faced with a dilemma, the individual makes an effort to resolve the problem by thinking it through.

cognitive-behavioral therapy a way to help individuals modify maladaptive thinking habits, which is often effective when depression or anxiety stems from feelings of incompetence and uselessness.

cohort a generation of individuals born at the same point in time, either in a particular year or during a circumscribed period such as five years. Members of a cohort often have certain common experiences during the course of their development.

collaborative cognitive activities activities in which more than one individual performs a common cognitive task with a common goal.

common cause hypothesis the theory that the link between sensory processes and cognitive functioning becomes stronger in older adulthood than it was earlier in life.

communication predicament of aging model a theory that people hold stereotyped expectations of older adults as lacking cognitive competence, so they modify their speech patterns too extremely when communicating with older adults. The result is that the speaker and the older adult listener have an unsatisfactory communication experience and avoid communicating on future occasions.

compensatory decision rules summing, weighing, and averaging all possible alternatives prior to making a decision.

compression of morbidity a term referring to a situation in which illness and extreme disability are delayed and compressed into a short interval of time very late in life.

compression of mortality a term referring to a situation in which a high proportion of deaths occur during a very narrow period toward the upper limit of the human life span.

constant housing and accommodating housing two different models for older adult housing that are inflexible or flexible, respectively, with regard to making changes and accommodations to meet the needs of an aging tenant population.

constant-probability-of-success model of creativity the premise that, during the course of a career, the point of maximum creativity coincides with the point of maximum productivity. Thus, individuals who generate the largest number of works (high productivity) have the greatest chance of generating a masterpiece.

contextual metamodel a view of development as a series of bidirectional transactions between the organism and the environment, resulting in a dialectical process whereby a constantly changing organism develops within a constantly changing environment.

continuing care retirement communities (CCRCs) living environments with various levels of support, ranging from independent (often congregate) living to assisted living to nursing home care.

convoy model the theory that individuals move through life both affecting and being affected by a constellation of others (family members or close friends) who play a central role in their social network and influence their feelings of well-being.

cross-sectional research design a commonly used developmental design that compares individuals from two or more age groups at the same point in time and that confounds the factors of age and cohort.

crystallized intelligence (Gc) intelligence that is a function of education, experience, and exposure to a specific cultural environment and is usually reflected in verbal and informational abilities.

cued recall studying a list of items or other pieces of information and afterward saying or writing down as many items or pieces of information as possible when supplied with hints, or cues, to guide retrieval.

defined benefit pension plans retirement plans that require individuals to work for a certain number of years to be vested, or eligible to receive financial benefits when they reach the age of retirement. These plans guarantee lifetime monthly benefits to retirees, with the burden of paying pension benefits falling squarely on the employer.

defined contribution pension plans retirement plans in which employers contribute a percentage of the employee's salary to a tax-deferred account over which employees usually have some control. Upon retirement, employees are entitled to the money accumulated even if they have changed employers.

delirium an acute and often reversible physiological brain dysfunction characterized by confusion, disorientation, disorganized thinking, memory impairment, disturbance of consciousness, and perceptual disturbances.

dementia a syndrome of global cognitive decline that typically occurs for the first time in old age.

demography the scientific study of populations that investigates past, present, and future trends and characteristics of broad groups within a specific population or across different populations.

depression an affective, or mood, disturbance, with symptoms that include painful sadness, pessimism, diminished self-esteem and feelings of guilt, worthlessness, and hopelessness. It can also be associated with bodily symptoms such as fatigue, sleep difficulties, changes in appetite and weight, and bowel disturbance. In addition, there may be problems with attention, concentration, and memory, as well as slowing down of speech, thought, and decision making.

descriptive approach research in which variables are not manipulated and are neither independent nor dependent, but the relationships between them are studied.

diabetic retinopathy a complication of long-term diabetes in which changes in the structure and function of blood vessels cause damage to receptor cells in the retina, often leading to blindness.

diathesis–stress model a theoretical model whereby an individual's diathesis (level of vulnerability in terms of genetic propensities, acquired biological vulnerability, or psychological factors), in combination with stressful events, determines whether that individual will succumb to a mental disorder such as depression.

differential diagnosis determining the exact basis for a particular constellation of symptoms that could signify more than one possible disorder.

discourse memory memory for extended language materials, both spoken and written.

disengagement theory the theory that older adults voluntarily withdraw from roles they played in middle age, and at the same time society withdraws from older adults by expecting them to step aside voluntarily to make room for the upcoming younger generation. When older adults are allowed to disengage, they experience a high level of life satisfaction.

dispositional attributions in causal reasoning as to why an event or social dilemma has occurred, perceivers place the responsibility for the event or dilemma on the personal characteristics of the individual involved rather than on any external extenuating circumstances.

disuse hypothesis of cognitive aging the idea that intellectual skills and abilities get rusty and thus decline when they are not used on a regular basis.

divided attention the attention required when we must focus on more than one thing at a time, or when two or more stimulus inputs must be processed concurrently.

DSM-IV a diagnostic classification system for categorizing mental disorders (American Psychiatric Association, 1994).

durable power of attorney in health-care matters an advance directive whereby the individual designates a trusted relative or friend to make health-care decisions on his or her behalf in the event of serious incapacitating physical illness or mental incapacity.

dying trajectory the speed, or rate, of decline in functioning that precedes death.

Ecological Model of Aging a framework for conceptualizing the aging process that focuses on adaptation as a function of the interaction between an individual's level of competence and the level of challenge (press) in the environment.

ecological validity one type of external validity that refers to whether results obtained with a particular test instrument are an accurate reflection of real-world functioning or behavior.

ego differentiation versus work-role preoccupation one of Peck's (1968) necessary adjustments, whereby older adults must learn to define self-worth outside the work role.

ego integrity versus despair Erikson's eighth and final stage of development, in which older adults face the challenge of feeling their lives have consistency, coherence, and purpose as opposed to feeling disappointed with the outcome.

ego transcendence versus ego preoccupation one of Peck's (1968) necessary adjustments, whereby older adults must adapt to the prospect that life is finite and must focus on future generations rather than being preoccupied with their own needs.

Elderhostel a program for older adults that offers an extensive network of noncredit short courses and seminars, which are held on campuses in various locations. Elderhostel provides intellectual stimulation, socialization with age peers, and a chance to spend time in a new geographical location.

elderspeak a style of speaking often used by those who communicate with older adults, which is characterized by short sentences, simplified grammar, repetition and elaboration, and exaggerated pitch and intonation.

encapsulation model the theory that, as individuals grow older, their knowledge becomes channeled into specific domains and they are transformed from generalists into specialists who concentrate on fewer domains of intellectual functioning but become highly efficient at acquiring knowledge related to those domains.

encoding establishing and preparing memory traces for entry into the long-term memory store.

engagement hypothesis the idea that participation in novel and challenging intellectual tasks is a way to prevent decline in intellectual functioning.

episodic memory memory for events and experiences that occurred at a specific place or time.

experimental approach research with independent and dependent variables, with the treatment levels of a categorical independent variable manipulated by the researcher, who randomly assigns research participants to each level. Dependent variables measure the outcome of the manipulated independent variable, and cause-and-effect statements can be made.

extended family household an arrangement whereby family members from more than two generations (grandparents, parents, children, and possibly other relatives) live under the same roof or in very close proximity.

external locus of control feeling that one's own efforts, actions, and behavior have little to do with what happens and that positive and negative outcomes are determined by chance or other outside forces.

external mnemonics strategies that make use of physical aids or cues (such as calendars, notes, and PDAs) to maintain or improve memory.

external validity being able to generalize findings obtained from a sample of study participants to the population of interest.

family of origin the family into which children are born.

family of procreation the family that individuals form when they marry and have children. For parents, the nuclear family represents the family of procreation.

Five-Factor Model (FFM) of Personality Costa and McCrae's (1991) theory that the structure of personality consists of five dimensions, or factors: neuroticism, extraversion, openness to experience, agreeableness, and conscientiousness (NEO-AC).

fluid intelligence (Gf) "Raw" intelligence that is largely dependent on the integrity of the central nervous system and relatively independent of social influences and culturally based learning experiences.

Flynn Effect a phenomenon whereby scores on tests of intellectual ability attained by members of a recent standardization sample are higher than scores attained by a standardization sample tested at an earlier time.

formal knowledge according to Sternberg et al. (1995), knowledge that is measured by psychometric intelligence tests and reflected in the grades earned in academic courses.

formal operations Piaget's fourth and final stage of cognitive development, beginning in early adolescence and extending into adulthood, in which individuals become capable of using scientific deductive reasoning to reach logical solutions to abstract problems.

fourth age the phase of advanced old age, often marked by the 80th birthday onward, that brings declining independence and, for all but the most fortunate, the need to face deteriorating health.

frequency-of-occurrence memory remembering how many times you have heard, seen, done, or otherwise experienced a particular event.

frontal lobe model the theory that the frontal lobes are more susceptible than other regions of the brain to the effects of normal aging.

functional age a person's competence in carrying out specific tasks in comparison with the competence of chronological age peers.

fundamental attribution error when making attributions for negative social outcomes involving others (targets), perceivers show bias by over-emphasizing dispositional factors (the target's characteristics) and underemphasizing the possible influence of situational factors.

generativity versus stagnation Erikson's seventh stage of development, in which the main challenge middle-aged adults face is taking responsibility for others and feeling they are contributing to the next generation as opposed to feeling stagnated.

geriatrics the branch of medicine specializing in the medical care and treatment of the diseases and health problems of older adults.

gerontology the study of the biological, behavioral, and social phenomena that occur from the point of maturity to old age.

glaucoma a disease of the eye associated with elevated pressure in the aqueous humor that, if left untreated, can cause irreversible damage to the nerve cells in the retina.

grief the affective, or emotional, response to bereavement.

heterotypic continuity whether a measure used to assess an underlying quality, or characteristic, has the same degree of internal validity for different age groups in a cross-sectional study, or for the same people as they are followed over time in a longitudinal study.

hierarchical-compensatory model a theoretical perspective about late-life sibling ties whereby individuals are thought to have a hierarchy of relationships to call upon when they need support. At the top of the hierarchy are a spouse and adult children, but when these are not available, older adults turn to siblings or others lower down in the hierarchy.

hospice care an alternative to the acute medical intervention provided in traditional hospital settings whereby a terminally ill patient's quality of life is enhanced through palliative treatment, and spiritual, psychological, and social support is provided for patients and their families.

hourglass effect in sibling relationships a description of sibling ties over the life span. Ties that were strong earlier in life when siblings lived under the same roof tend to weaken in young and middle adulthood but are often reactivated in the later years.

hypochondriasis a somatoform disorder with symptoms that suggest a physical disorder, but upon closer examination appear to be psychologically caused. A diagnosis of hypochondriasis is made when physical findings are negative despite a patient's preoccupation with illness and anxious concern with bodily functions.

immunization unintentional processes that individuals use to protect against threats to their self-concept, which involve tactics that temporarily shield them from information that conflicts with the definitions they have of themselves.

implicit memory memory without awareness that memory traces were encoded and without any deliberate recollection or conscious intention to remember.

inhibitory deficit model the theory that with increasing age there is a decreased ability to ignore irrelevant stimuli (distractors) and focus attention on relevant stimuli (targets).

instrumental activities of daily living (IADL) activities required to carry out the business of daily life, such as taking medication, preparing meals, managing personal finances, doing housework, using the telephone, and shopping.

Intelligence Quotient (IQ) how much, and in which direction, an individual test taker's score on a psychometric test of intellectual ability differs (deviates) from the average score of age peers in the standardization sample.

interactive attributions in causal reasoning for why a social dilemma occurred, perceivers take both dispositional and situational factors into account rather than attributing the outcome entirely to one or the other.

intergenerational stake hypothesis the discrepancy between older parents' and adult children's tendency to report conflict, attributed to the fact that older parents perceive their offspring in a favorable light and view their relationships with adult children as highly compatible, whereas adult offspring perceive their parents as less compatible.

internal locus of control feeling that one's personal efforts, actions, and behavior have a great deal to do with determining whether positive outcomes are experienced and negative outcomes are avoided.

internal mnemonics strategies that use mental images and verbal associations to aid memory. These techniques, often taught in memory training classes, require a great deal of cognitive effort but are helpful when external mnemonics cannot be used.

internal validity the accurate identification and interpretation of the factor(s), or effect(s), responsible for an observation in a research study.

intimacy at a distance the preference expressed by many older adults that they welcome contact and involvement with adult children and their families, but they prefer to maintain their own households as long as they are able to do so.

intimacy versus isolation Erikson's sixth stage of development, in which the main challenge young adults face is developing close give-and-take relationships with others as opposed to remaining isolated.

intraindividual variability change within the same individual.

Kübler-Ross's five stages of death and dying five stages – denial, anger, bargaining, depression, and acceptance – often seen when a person's trajectory of dying allows time.

legacy-creating stage in Schaie and Willis's (2000) model of cognitive development, a stage identified with the old-old (75–84) and oldest-old (85+) years, when individuals expend cognitive effort anticipating the end of life and deciding how their property and possessions should be distributed.

legal conservatorship management of an incompetent person's estate and financial transactions.

legal guardianship care and protection given by someone empowered to make decisions in the interest of the individual concerning everyday matters such as living arrangements, health care, and provision of other basic needs.

life expectancy the average number of years that individuals in a particular birth cohort can be expected to live.

life review once considered an idle pursuit best discouraged in the elderly, life review is now viewed as an important part of the aging process whereby older adults integrate who they are now (present) and who they were before (past).

life span the maximum longevity, or extreme upper limit of time, that members of a species can live.

life-span developmental perspective a set of theoretical propositions that development occurs across the entire life span and is a multifaceted, multidirectional process, with behavior a product of a dynamically changing organism as well as a dynamically changing environment. There is plasticity in development, meaning that individuals can change and learn throughout their lives.

life story the personal myth individuals construct to make sense of their lives in which they integrate a reconstructed past with a perceived present and an anticipated future. As such, it allows them to feel their lives have unity and purpose.

living will an advance directive that instructs physicians and family members about a patient's wishes regarding the use of medical treatments that would artificially prolong the dying process if death is determined to be inevitable.

longevity the length and duration of life.

longitudinal research design a developmental research design in which the same individuals are followed over time and tested on two or more occasions, but in which the factors of age and time of measurement are confounded.

long-term memory store in the information processing model, the store with an unlimited capacity that maintains information for weeks, months, or years.

macular degeneration a disease associated with an irreversible loss of receptor cells in the macula located near the fovea in the central retina, which results in visual distortion or loss of vision for fine detail.

mechanics of intelligence in the dual-process model, intelligence analogous to the hardware of the mind. As with fluid intelligence, the mechanics of intelligence are assumed to be genetically and biologically controlled and dependent upon basic, physiologically determined, brain functioning.

mechanistic metamodel a machine metaphor that views development in terms of external environmental forces as input and the organism's behavior as output, that breaks down complex phenomena into parts and studies each one separately, and that focuses on quantitative indexes of behavior.

mediation deficiency inability to encode information elaboratively by processing the unique, meaningful, characteristics of items so that their traces are more distinctive.

Medicaid a federal health-care program administered by individual states that is means tested. To qualify for coverage, individuals must fall below a certain income level and can own only limited assets.

Medicare the federal government-sponsored health insurance program initiated in 1965 that covers a large proportion of adults aged 65 and over in the United States.

memory self-efficacy a self-evaluative system of beliefs and judgments regarding one's own memory competence and confidence in one's own memory abilities

Mental Status Questionnaire (MSQ) a brief test with suggested cut-off scores used to screen for dementia.

metamemory an inherent understanding about how the memory system works.

mild cognitive impairment (MCI) memory difficulty that is greater than typical for the older age group but not severe enough to meet the criteria for Alzheimer's disease (AD).

Mini-Mental State Examination (MMSE) a widely used test designed to determine the existence and extent of dementia. The MMSE is more detailed than the Mental Status Questionnaire (MSQ).

modified extended family the dominant family structure in the United States consisting of a broad kinship network of grandparents, parents, grandchildren, siblings, nephews, nieces and other relatives by blood or marriage. Members of this network have frequent contact and provide support for one another even though they do not live under the same roof.

moral perspective taking the inclination to consider a moral dilemma from various perspectives.

morbidity illness and disease.

mortality death.

mourning culturally patterned ways of behaving and rituals followed when there is a loss, including participation in funeral or memorial services and burials as well as abstaining from everyday routines for a specified time.

multifactor research design studies with more than one categorical variable, one of which is often age.

multi-infarct dementia (MID) one type of vascular dementia that stems from multiple small or large brain infarcts, or strokes, and is associated with a history of hypertension, heart disease, or diabetes.

nature and nurture two influences on development. *Nature* refers to hereditary, genetic, and biological factors; *nurture* refers to environmental factors and life experience.

negative cohort trend a phenomenon that occurs when a present-day young adult cohort has a lower level of ability than an older cohort had back in their young adult years.

negative correlation a measure of the relationship between two variables indicating that a high value on one variable is associated with a low value on the other.

neuroimaging techniques such as functional magnetic resonance imaging (fMRI) and positron emission tomography (PET), which measure brain activation and show which parts of the brain are most active while individuals are performing cognitive tasks.

neuropsychology the study of brain–behavior relationships, and the evaluation of how impairments in various areas of the brain affect memory functioning.

noncompensatory decision rules in making a decision, eliminating alternatives after an incomplete search, thereby reducing the cognitive processing demands of the task.

nonnormative life events influences on the development of an individual that do not affect all, or even most, members of a particular cohort.

normative age-graded influences biological or environmental events and occurrences that are associated with chronological age and influence development.

normative history-graded influences influences on development that result from events such as wars or from a gradual evolution of societal structure that affect all members of a population.

nuclear family household parents and their children who live under the same roof.

nursing homes institutions that provide a high level of support (personal care as well as skilled nursing services around the clock) and are closely regulated in terms of licensing requirements.

oldest-old individuals aged 85+, who have the highest rate of health problems and greatest need for services and are also the fastest-growing age group in the United States.

old-old individuals in the 75–84-year age range, who experience more age-related changes in sensory, perceptual, and cognitive functioning compared to those in the young-old age group.

optimally exercised abilities abilities that reflect the maximum level of functioning attainable by a normal, healthy individual who has had opportunities for ability-specific training or practice.

optimization of primary and secondary control (OPS) a theoretical model that proposes that, with increasing age, biological and social challenges limit the broad use of primary control. Older adults must apply their efforts at primary control selectively where success is most attainable. Otherwise, secondary control takes on greater importance.

organismic metamodel a biological metaphor that views development as a series of complex, constantly changing phenomena originating from within the organism. The organism acts upon rather than reacting to the environment and progresses through a series of qualitatively different stages that are directed toward a goal.

organismic variable a variable such as age, gender, ethnicity, and socioeconomic status that is inherent within the individual and therefore cannot be controlled or manipulated.

paranoid disorders mental disorders characterized by the construction of faulty explanations or interpretations of events and suspicion and distrust of others even when there is no apparent basis for suspicion or distrust.

passive-dependent strategies when faced with a dilemma, the individual attempts to withdraw from the situation.

passive euthanasia withholding action that would sustain a patient's life, such as failing to apply cardiopulmonary resuscitation after a heart attack.

Patient Self-Determination Act (PSDA) federal legislation that requires all health-care facilities receiving funds from Medicare and Medicaid to provide patients with information on advance directives.

pet-facilitated therapy (PFT) a therapeutic intervention whereby an animal is introduced into the environment for a limited time and individuals are allowed to make whatever contact they want (petting the animal, talking to the animal, or just observing).

phonemic regression a phenomenon whereby individuals' understanding of speech or other complex signals is poorer than it should be based solely on their sensitivity to pure tones.

piecemeal operations a way of thinking that is demanding of cognitive resources because it requires individuals to actively process detailed information.

population pyramid a bar graph that illustrates how a population is distributed in terms of both age and gender.

positive cohort trend a phenomenon that occurs when a present-day young adult cohort has a higher level of ability than an older adult cohort had back in their young adult years.

positive correlation a measure of the relationship between two variables indicating that a high value on one variable is associated with a high value on the other.

positivity effect a phenomenon reported to occur in a variety of decision making situations whereby older adults focus more on positive information than on negative information.

possible selves cognitive schemas we have about what we may be like in the future, including what we would like to become (hoped-for selves) as well as what we do not want to become (feared selves).

postformal thinking a type of thinking proposed by some researchers to come after Piaget's stage of formal operations which entails flexible, relativistic thinking and tolerance for ambiguity when problems have more than one correct solution.

pragmatics of intelligence in the dual-process model, intelligence analogous to the software of the mind. As with crystallized intelligence, the pragmatics of intelligence are based on exposure to culturally based factual and procedural knowledge. Pragmatics of intelligence can compensate for age-related declines in mechanics of intelligence.

presbycusis a pattern of hearing loss associated with aging that is characterized by an increased threshold (decreased sensitivity) to high-frequency tones and difficulty discriminating between words with high-frequency consonants as well as difficulty understanding speech in noisy conditions.

presbyopia far-sightedness (difficulty focusing on near objects) resulting from an increase in the size and thickness of the lens of the eye and a decrease in its flexibility.

primary aging unavoidable (inevitable) biological processes that are intrinsic to the organism and affect all members of a species.

primary control processes actions and behaviors that individuals direct at the external world with the intention of influencing, shaping, or changing the environment so that it fits more closely with their needs and desires.

primary memory the component of the limited-capacity short-term memory store that holds information in the same form in which it was entered.

problem-focused strategies when faced with a dilemma, the individual takes direct action to control, or fix, the problem.

procedural memory memory for skills that were learned with practice over a long period of time and later are readily available without much deliberate recollection.

production deficiency possessing the ability to encode information elaboratively by processing unique, meaningful characteristics that make memory traces distinctive, but failing to do so spontaneously.

programmed theories of biological aging theories that postulate aging is a function of a genetically based program that directs the aging process.

prospective memory remembering to perform some action at a designated future point.

psychological age how well a person is able to use cognitive, personal, or social skills to adapt to changing conditions or adjust to new circumstances. Being flexible is associated with being psychologically young.

quantitative or qualitative differences developmental measures used to compare young and older adults can be quantitative (how much?) or qualitative (what kind?).

quasi-experimental approach studies that have the same form as a true experiment, but research participants are not randomly assigned to levels of a categorical factor, thus eliminating the possibility of cause-and-effect statements.

reaction time the interval elapsing between the onset of a stimulus (a light, a tone) and the completion of a motor response.

reality orientation (RO) a therapy for treating older adults with moderate to severe memory loss, confusion, and disorientation that involves providing cues that help them stay oriented to time and place.

recall studying a list of items or other pieces information and afterward being able to say or write down as many as possible.

reciprocity social exchanges between two or more individuals that are balanced in terms of support given and received.

recognition after studying a list of items or other pieces of information, being able to pick them out from a larger set of items.

rectangular survival curve a graph indicating that more and more people will live closer to the maximum human life span.

reduced attentional resources/capacity model the theory that the quantity of processing resources, or the amount of attentional capacity, declines with increasing age.

reintegrative stage the fourth of Schaie's (1977–1978) stages of cognitive development, associated with older adulthood, whereby individuals are more selective, expending their cognitive efforts on tasks that are most meaningful to them.

reliability the dependability, or consistency, of instruments used to measure variables or phenomena of interest. Reliability applies to specific test instruments but it also applies to the findings of research studies.

reminiscence bump a phenomenon whereby older adults have the strongest and most vivid memories for events and personal experiences that occurred when they were between the ages of 10 and 30.

reminiscence therapy encouraging older adults to think and talk about the past so they can reevaluate and integrate their life experiences and, ideally, derive a sense of self-worth and alleviate feelings of depression.

remote memory memory for facts as well as personal, autobiographical information that goes back decades.

reorganizational stage in Schaie and Willis's (2000) model of cognitive development, a stage in which young-old adults (aged 65–74) expend cognitive effort restructuring their lives for the years of retirement and making plans for a time when they may have to give up some of their independence.

reserve capacity the extra capacity needed when stressful or demanding situations require more than the normal capacity. Reserve capacity is thought to decline with increasing age.

responsible/executive stage the third of Schaie's (1977–1978) stages of cognitive development identified with middle adulthood, when individuals apply their knowledge and skills to care and concern for others and in some cases hold leadership positions in jobs or the community.

retirement a social institution with rules about when it is permissible for workers to leave the paid labor force, and also a transition to a stage of life in which there is an end to paid employment.

retirement communities independent living communities inhabited by older adults that resemble villages or enclosed subdivisions and usually feature a centrally located clubhouse and recreational facilities.

retirement hotels buildings with individual rooms rented primarily by single residents, most typically men from lower income groups, that usually provide housekeeping services but not meals.

retrieval recovering memory traces from the long-term episodic memory store when they are needed.

sandwich generation a label for middle-aged adults, often women, who are caught between competing intergenerational demands because they provide care for their older parents but also have obligations to a spouse and children still living at home.

schemas cognitive representations that individuals have about themselves, others, or everyday situations and events. Schemas influence how people view themselves, how they interpret the behavior of others, and how they evaluate social dilemmas.

secondary aging biological processes that accelerate aging and are experienced by most, but not necessarily all, members of a species and are the result of disease, disuse, and abuse.

secondary control processes when primary control is not possible or successful, individuals use internal processes to alter goals and expectations and accept existing realities that cannot be changed.

selective attention the kind of attention required when we must focus on some information in the environment while ignoring other information.

selective attrition fluctuation in the composition of a longitudinal study sample whereby, over time, the individuals who remain in the study become more selective and less representative of the population.

Selective Optimization with Compensation (SOC) Model of Aging a framework for conceptualizing successful aging that focuses on the strategies used to compensate for losses by capitalizing on selected areas of maintained functioning.

self-concept how we think about and define ourselves, or our self-image, which is composed of a collection of schemas about who we are and what is important to us.

self-esteem the affective, or evaluative, aspect of the self-concept that determines whether we perceive ourselves as having worth.

semantic memory generic memory, general knowledge, or world knowledge that is well learned, has been in the long-term store for a considerable period of time, and is remembered without regard to when or where it was learned.

senile cataracts areas of cloudiness or opacity in the lens of the eye that are found in a large proportion of older adults and often cause them to experience glare.

sensitivity the capability of the biological system to respond to stimulation, which is the inverse of *threshold*.

sensory retraining therapy a type of therapy suited for older adults with limited physical and cognitive capabilities that involves activities and exercises that stimulate their kinesthetic and proprioceptive, tactile, olfactory, auditory, and visual receptors.

sequential research designs complex research designs involving some combination of cross-sectional, longitudinal, or time-lag comparisons, which are intended to disentangle the factors of age, cohort, and time of measurement.

short-term memory store in the information processing model, the short-term store holds information for a relatively brief period of time and has a limited capacity (approximately 5 to 9 units of information). Unless items enter the long-term store, they will be displaced and lost as new items are added.

signal detection model a model for determining threshold that takes into account not only biological sensitivity but also the individual's decisional response criteria.

single-factor research design a study with one categorical variable that can be independent or organismic and, in the simplest case, having only one dependent variable.

situational attributions causal reasoning for why an event or social dilemma occurred whereby perceivers place the responsibility for the event or dilemma on external extenuating circumstances rather than on the personal characteristics of the individual involved.

situational model of elder abuse the view that elder abuse is the abuser's response to a stressful situation that stems from being overburdened with the care of an older adult who has extreme physical and/or cognitive incapacities.

social age views held by most members of a society about what individuals in a particular chronological age group should do and how they should behave.

social exchange theory the theory that social interactions between two people have both rewards and costs, and the individuals continue to interact only as long as the rewards are greater than the costs. Interactions are balanced only if both partners have an equal desire for the reward offered by the other.

social network the structural characteristics of an individual's social ties, including the number, age, sex, relationship, and frequency of contact with people who are part of it.

Social Security enacted in 1935, federal legislation makes it possible for older adults who have worked in paid jobs for a certain minimum number of quarters to be eligible for monthly benefit payments from the government for the rest of their lives.

socioemotional selectivity theory (SEST) a life-span model which proposes that the reduced social activity often seen in old age reflects a life-long selection process whereby the number of individuals in an older adult's social network becomes smaller because close social relationships are maintained while superficial ones are filtered out.

source memory remembering where, when, or from whom an item of information was acquired.

stimulus persistence theory the theory that, once a stimulus is registered by a sensory organ, it takes longer to be processed and cleared through the older nervous system than it does through the young nervous system.

stochastic theories of biological aging theories of biological aging that postulate factors both internal and external to the organism result in random damage, which determines the rate of biological aging.

storage retaining memory traces in the long-term episodic memory store.

suicide the voluntary termination of one's own life, which is usually viewed as a behavior rather than a mental disorder but is considered a final act driven by intolerable psychological pain and feelings of hopelessness.

sundown syndrome the label for symptoms of confusion or agitation that some older adults experience in the late afternoon, evening, or nighttime hours.

support bank the idea that individuals give more support than they receive as long as they are able to do so. Later, they feel it is legitimate to get more support than they can give.

swan-song phenomenon a resurgence in creative output in the sixth and seventh decades following a postpeak decline in the rate of creative contributions, thus allowing creative individuals to end their career with a bang rather than a whimper.

tacit knowledge practical knowledge gleaned with little help from others that is used to attain valued goals. It includes "knowing how" rather than just "knowing that."

telomeres the protective caps at the tail ends of the chromosomes located in each cell. Each time a cell divides, the telomeres lose some length until they become so short that division is no longer possible.

temporal memory remembering when events occurred or the order in which they occurred.

terminal drop the steep decline on tests of intellectual ability often shown by individuals prior to their death.

testing the limits a strategy for investigating cognitive capacity that calls for measuring intellectual abilities on more than one occasion to determine the highest possible level of functioning.

third age the phase in life that usually occurs during the young-old years before illness limits activity and during which most individuals are able to live life as they please.

threshold the minimum amount of stimulation a sensory organ must receive before it registers the presence of a particular stimulus.

time-lag research design a research design that tests individuals of a particular chronological age at two or more different points in time, usually some number of years or decades apart, so that the factors of cohort and time of measurement are confounded.

time of measurement a factor referring to the conditions that prevail during the time when a research study is conducted.

top-down processing strategy when making a decision, individuals rely on prior experience and knowledge that is already in storage rather than acquiring and integrating new information.

trait diagnosticity the degree to which behaviors are informative when perceivers make inferences about another person's traits, or characteristics. Behaviors high in trait diagnosticity are associated exclusively with a specific characteristic, whereas those low in trait diagnosticity carry less information about a particular characteristic.

unexercised abilities abilities that are untrained and unpracticed and reflect the individual's biological potential under normal environmental conditions.

upswing hypothesis of marital satisfaction a phenomenon found to characterize marriages over the course of adulthood whereby level of satisfaction is highest in the early years, followed by a dip when children are reared, but then an increase (upswing) after children are launched.

useful field of view (UFOV) an index of visual functioning defined by the visual area over which target stimuli can be recognized and localized during a brief glance, without the person's making any eye or head movements.

validity various types of validity all have to do with whether we are measuring what we think we are measuring. The concept of validity applies both to specific measurement instruments and to the findings of research studies.

vascular dementia (VaD) the second most common form of dementia in older adults, which includes a broad array of dementias associated with a variety of vascular problems or focal destruction of brain tissue.

vigilance sustained attention that requires the ability to monitor a situation and remain ready to detect any change that may occur in a pattern of stimuli that is usually stable and unchanging.

widowhood the status of a person who has lost a spouse through death and has not remarried.

will a formal document that states how individuals wish their property to be distributed to heirs upon their death.

wisdom a concept that implies admirable and moral behavior, exceptional insight into life's problems, and the ability to consider multiple aspects of complex situations while maintaining some level of objectivity.

working memory the component of the limited-capacity short-term memory store analogous to a mental scratch pad – information is not only held, but also worked on, or processed.

young-old individuals in the 65–74-year age range, whose physical vigor is often very similar to that of people in their late middle adult years.

References

Abraham, J. D., & Hansson, R. O. (1995). Successful aging at work: An applied study of selection, optimization, and compensation through impression management. *Journal of Gerontology: Psychological Sciences, 50B*, P94–P103.

Allaire, J. C., & Marsiske, M. (1999). Everyday cognition: Age and intellectual ability correlates. *Psychology and Aging, 14*, 627–644.

Allen-Burge, R., Storandt, M., Kinscherf, D. A., & Rubin, E. H. (1994). Sex differences in the sensitivity of two self-report depression scales in older depressed inpatients. *Psychology and Aging, 9*, 443–445.

Alzheimer's Disease Education & Referral Center (ADEAR) (2006). Diagnosis, symptoms, general information, causes, and treatment. Retrieved May 5, 2007, from http://www.nia.nih.gov/Alzheimers/AlzheimersInformation/Diagnosis/

American Psychiatric Association (1994). *Diagnostic and statistical manual of mental disorders* (4th ed.). Washington, DC: American Psychiatric Association.

American Psychological Association (1998). *What practitioners should know about working with older adults.* Retrieved March 18, 2009, from http://www.apa.org/pi/aging/practitioners.pdf

Anderson, S. A., Russell, C. S., & Schumm, W. R. (1983). Perceived marital quality and family life-cycle categories: A further analysis. *Journal of Marriage and the Family, 45*, 127–139.

Anstey, K. J., Luszcz, M. A., & Sanchez, L. (2001). A reevaluation of the common factor theory of shared variance among age, sensory function, and cognitive function in older adults. *Journal of Gerontology: Psychological Sciences, 56B*, P3–P11.

Antonucci, T. C. (1986). Hierarchical mapping technique. *Generations, 10*(4), 10–12.

Antonucci, T. C., & Akiyama, H. (1987). Social networks in adult life and a preliminary examination of the convoy model. *Journal of Gerontology, 42*, 519–527.

Antonucci, T. C., Sherman, A. M., & Akiyama, H. (1996). Social networks, support, and integration. In J. E. Birren (Ed.), *Encyclopedia of gerontology: Age, aging, and the aged* (Vol. 2, pp. 505–515). San Diego: Academic Press.

Aranda, M. P., & Knight, B. G. (1997). The influence of ethnicity and culture on the caregiver stress and coping process: A sociocultural review and analysis. *Gerontologist, 37*, 342–354.

Arbuckle, T. Y., & Gold, D. P. (1993). Aging, inhibition, and verbosity. *Journal of Gerontology: Psychological Sciences, 48*, P225–P232.

Ardelt, M. (2000). Antecedents and effects of wisdom in old age. *Research on Aging, 22*, 360–394.

Arlin, P. K. (1990). Wisdom: The art of problem finding. In R. J. Sternberg (Ed.), *Wisdom: Its nature, origins, and development* (pp. 230–243). New York: Cambridge University Press.

Atchley, R. C. (1971). Retirement and leisure participation: Continuity or crisis? *Gerontologist, 11*, 13–17.

Atchley, R. C. (1994). *Social forces and aging* (7th ed.). Belmont, CA: Wadsworth.

Atchley, R. C. (1996). Retirement. In J. E. Birren (Ed.), *Encyclopedia of gerontology: Age, aging, and the aged* (Vol. 2, pp. 437–449). San Diego: Academic Press.

Atchley, R. C. (2007). Retirement. In J. E. Birren (Ed.), *Encyclopedia of gerontology: Age, aging, and the aged* (2nd ed., Vol. 2, pp. 449–460). Boston: Elsevier Academic Press.

Atkinson, R. C., & Shiffrin, R. M. (1968). Human memory: A proposed system and its control processes. In K. W. Spence & J. T. Spence (Eds.), *The psychology of learning and motivation* (Vol. 2, pp. 89–105). New York: Academic Press.

Avolio, B. J., & Waldman, D. A. (1990). An examination of age and cognitive test performance across job complexity and occupational types. *Journal of Applied Psychology, 75,* 43–50.

Bäckman, L., Small, B. J., & Wahlin, A. (2001). Aging and memory: Cognitive and biological perspectives. In J. E. Birren & K. W. Schaie (Eds.), *Handbook of the psychology of aging* (5th ed., pp. 349–377). San Diego: Academic Press.

Bäckman, L., Small, B. J., Wahlin, A., & Larsson, M. (2000). Cognitive functioning in very old age. In F. I. M. Craik & T. A. Salthouse (Eds.), *The handbook of aging and cognition* (2nd ed., pp. 499–558). Mahwah, NJ: Erlbaum.

Baddeley, A. D. (1986). *Working memory*. Oxford: Oxford University Press.

Baddeley, A. D. (1990). *Human memory: Theory and practice*. Boston: Allyn & Bacon.

Bahrick, H. P. (1979). Maintenance of knowledge: Questions about memory we forgot to ask. *Journal of Experimental Psychology: General, 108,* 296–308.

Bahrick, H. P., Bahrick, P. O., & Wittlinger, R. P. (1975). Fifty years of memory for names and faces: A cross-sectional approach. *Journal of Experimental Psychology: General, 104,* 54–75.

Baines, S., Saxby, P., & Ehlert, K. (1987). Reality orientation and reminiscence therapy: A controlled crossover study of elderly confused people. *British Journal of Psychiatry, 151,* 222–231.

Ball, K., Beard, B., Roenker, D., Miller, R., & Griggs, D. (1988). Age and visual search: Expanding the useful field of view. *Journal of the Optical Society of America, 5,* 2210–2219.

Ball, K., & Owsley, C. (1991). Identifying correlates of accident involvement for the older driver. *Human Factors, 33,* 583–595.

Ball, K., & Rebok, G. W. (1994). Evaluating the driving ability of older adults. *Journal of Applied Gerontology, 13,* 20–38.

Baltes, M. M., & Carstensen, L. L. (1996). The process of successful ageing. *Aging and Society, 16,* 397–422.

Baltes, M. M., & Zerbe, M. B. (1976). Independence training in nursing home residents. *Gerontologist, 16,* 428–432.

Baltes, P. B. (1987). Theoretical propositions of life-span developmental psychology: On the dynamics between growth and decline. *Developmental Psychology, 23,* 611–626.

Baltes, P. B. (1993). The aging mind: Potential and limits. *Gerontologist, 33,* 580–594.

Baltes, P. B. (1997). On the incomplete architecture of human ontogeny. *American Psychologist, 52,* 366–380.

Baltes, P. B. (2005). *A psychological model of successful aging*. Keynote Lecture, 2005 World Congress of Gerontology, Brazil. Retrieved June 6, 2008, from http://www.baltes-paul.de/Baltes_Rio_Gerontology.pdf

Baltes, P. B. (2006). Facing our limits: Human dignity in the very old. *Daedalus, 135,* 32–39.

Baltes, P. B., & Baltes, M. M. (1990). Psychological perspectives on successful aging: The model of selective optimization with compensation. In P. B. Baltes & M. M. Baltes (Eds.), *Successful aging: Perspectives from the behavioral sciences* (pp. 1–34). Cambridge: Cambridge University Press.

Baltes, P. B., Dittmann-Kohli, F., & Dixon, R. A. (1984). New perspectives on the development of intelligence in adulthood: Toward a dual process conception and a model of selective optimization with compensation. In P. B. Baltes & O. G. Brim, Jr. (Eds.), *Life-span development and behavior* (Vol. 6, pp. 33–76). New York: Academic Press.

Baltes, P. B., & Lindenberger, U. (1997). Emergence of a powerful connection between sensory and cognitive functions across the adult life span: A new window to the study of cognitive aging? *Psychology and Aging, 12,* 12–21.

Baltes, P. B., & Schaie, K. W. (1974). Aging and IQ: The myth of the twilight years. *Psychology Today, 7,* 35–40.

Baltes, P. B., & Smith, J. (1995). Developmental psychology. In G. L. Maddox (Ed.), *The encyclopedia of aging* (2nd ed., pp. 267–270). New York: Springer.

Baltes, P. B., & Smith, J. (2008). The fascination of wisdom: Its nature, ontogeny, and function. *Perspectives on Psychological Science, 3*, 56–64.

Baltes, P. B., & Staudinger, U. M. (1995). Wisdom. In G. L. Maddox (Ed.), *The encyclopedia of aging* (2nd ed., pp. 971–974). New York: Springer.

Baltes, P. B., Staudinger, U. M., & Lindenberger, U. (1999). Lifespan psychology: Theory and application to intellectual functioning. *Annual Review of Psychology, 50*, 471–507.

Baltes, P. B., & Willis, S. L. (1982). Enhancement (plasticity) of intellectual functioning in old age: Penn State's Adult Development and Enrichment Project (ADEPT). In F. I. M. Craik & S. Trehub (Eds.), *Aging and cognitive processes* (pp. 353–389). New York: Plenum Press.

Bandura, A. (1977). Self-efficacy: Toward a unifying theory of behavioral change. *Psychological Review, 84*, 191–215.

Bargh, J. A., Chen, M., & Burrows, L. (1996). Automaticity of social behavior: Direct effects of trait construct and stereotype activation on action. *Journal of Personality and Social Psychology, 71*, 230–244.

Baron, R. A., & Byrne, D. (2000). *Social psychology* (9th ed.). Boston: Allyn & Bacon.

Bedford, V. H. (1989). Understanding the value of siblings in old age. *American Behavioral Scientist, 33*, 33–44.

Beller, S., & Palmore, E. (1974). Longevity in Turkey. *Gerontologist, 14, Part 1*, 373–376.

Bengston, V. L., & Kuypers, J. A. (1971). Generational differences and the developmental stake. *Aging and Human Development, 2*, 249–260.

Bengston, V., Rosenthal, C., & Burton, L. (1996). Paradoxes of families and aging. In R. H. Binstock & L. K. George (Eds.), *Handbook of aging and the social sciences* (4th ed., pp. 253–282). San Diego: Academic Press.

Bennett, K. M. (2007). "No sissy stuff": Towards a theory of masculinity and emotional expression in older widowed men. *Journal of Aging Studies, 21*, 347–356.

Berg, C. A., & Klaczynski, P. A. (1996). Practical intelligence and problem-solving: Searching for perspectives. In F. Blanchard-Fields & T. M. Hess (Eds.), *Perspectives on cognitive change in adulthood and aging* (pp. 323–357). New York: McGraw-Hill.

Berg, C. A., & Sternberg, R. J. (1992). Adults' conceptions of intelligence across the adult life span. *Psychology and Aging, 7*, 221–231.

Bergeman, C. S., & Ong, A. D. (2007). Behavioral genetics. In J. E. Birren (Ed.), *Encyclopedia of gerontology: Age, aging, and the aged* (2nd ed., Vol. 1, pp. 149–160). Boston: Elsevier Academic Press.

Berry, J. M. (1999). Memory self-efficacy in its social cognitive context. In T. M. Hess & F. Blanchard-Fields (Eds.), *Social cognition and aging* (pp. 69–96). San Diego: Academic Press.

Berry, J. M., & Jobe, J. B. (2002). At the intersection of personality and adult development. *Journal of Research in Personality, 36*, 283–286.

Berry, J. M., West, R. L., & Dennehy, D. (1989). Reliability and validity of the Memory Self-Efficacy Questionnaire (MSEQ). *Developmental Psychology, 25*, 701–713.

Bieman-Copland, S., & Ryan, E. B. (1998). Age-biased interpretation of memory successes and failures in adulthood. *Journal of Gerontology: Psychological Sciences, 53B*, P105–P111.

Binstock, R. H. (2002). In memoriam: Bernice L. Neugarten. *Gerontologist, 42*, 149–151.

Birditt, K. S., Fingerman, K. L., & Almeida, D. M. (2005). Age differences in exposure and reactions to interpersonal tensions: A daily diary study. *Psychology and Aging, 20*, 330–340.

Birren, B. A., & Stine-Morrow, E. A. L. (1999). A history of Division 20 (Adult Development and Aging): Analysis and reminiscences. In D. A. Dewsbury (Ed.), *Unification through division: Histories of the divisions of the American Psychological Association* (Vol. 4, pp. 35–64). Washington, DC: American Psychological Association.

Birren, J. E. (1974). Translations in gerontology – from lab to life: Psychophysiology and speed of response. *American Psychologist, 29*, 808–815.

Birren, J. E. (1996). History of gerontology. In J. E. Birren (Ed.), *Encyclopedia of gerontology: Age, aging, and the aged* (Vol. 1, pp. 655–665). San Diego: Academic Press.

Birren, J. E., & Fisher, L. M. (1990). The elements of wisdom: Overview and integration. In R. J. Sternberg (Ed.), *Wisdom: Its nature, origins, and development* (pp. 317–332). New York: Cambridge University Press.

Birren, J. E., & Schroots, J. J. F. (1996). History, concepts, and theory in the psychology of aging. In J. E. Birren & K. W. Schaie (Eds.), *Handbook of the psychology of aging* (4th ed., pp. 3–23). San Diego: Academic Press.

Birren, J. E., & Schroots, J. J. F. (2001). The history of geropsychology. In J. E. Birren & K. W. Schaie (Eds.), *Handbook of the psychology of aging* (5th ed., pp. 3–28). San Diego: Academic Press.

Black, J. E., Greenough, W. T., Anderson, B. J., & Isaacs, K. R. (1987). Environment and the aging brain. *Canadian Journal of Psychology, 41,* 111–130.

Blanchard-Fields, F. (1994). Age differences in causal attributions from an adult developmental perspective. *Journal of Gerontology: Psychological Sciences, 49,* P43–P51.

Blanchard-Fields, F. (1996). Causal attributions across the adult life span: The influence of social schemas, life context, and domain specificity [Special issue]. *Applied Cognitive Psychology, 10,* 5137–5146.

Blanchard-Fields, F. (1997). The role of emotion in social cognition across the adult life span. In K. W. Schaie & M. P. Lawton (Eds.), *Annual review of gerontology and geriatrics* (Vol. 17, pp. 238–265). New York: Springer.

Blanchard-Fields, F. (1999). Social schematicity and causal attribution. In T. M. Hess & F. Blanchard-Fields (Eds.), *Social cognition and aging* (pp. 219–236). San Diego: Academic Press.

Blanchard-Fields, F. (2007). Everyday problem solving and emotion: An adult developmental perspective. *Current Directions in Psychological Science, 16,* 26–31.

Blanchard-Fields, F. & Abeles, R. P. (1996). Social cognition and aging. In J. E. Birren & K. W. Schaie (Eds.), *Handbook of the psychology of aging* (4th ed., pp. 150–161). San Diego: Academic Press.

Blanchard-Fields, F., Baldi, R., & Stein, R. (1999). Age relevance and context effects on attributions across the adult lifespan. *International Journal of Behavioral Development, 23,* 665–683.

Blanchard-Fields, F., Jahnke, H., & Camp, C. J. (1995). Age differences in problem solving style: The role of emotional salience. *Psychology and Aging, 10,* 173–180.

Blanchard-Fields, F., Mienaltowski, A., & Seay, R. B. (2007). Age differences in everyday problem-solving effectiveness: Older adults select more effective strategies for interpersonal problems. *Journal of Gerontology: Psychological Sciences, 62B,* P61–P64.

Blanchard-Fields, F., & Norris, L. (1994). Causal attributions from adolescence through adulthood: Age differences, ego level, and generalized response style. *Aging and Cognition, 1,* 67–86.

Blazer, D. G. (2006). Depression. In R. Schulz (Ed.), *The encyclopedia of aging* (4th ed., pp. 303–306). New York: Springer.

Blazer, D. G., & Koenig, H. G. (1996). Suicide. In J. E. Birren (Ed.), *Encyclopedia of gerontology: Age, aging, and the aged* (Vol. 2, pp. 529–538). San Diego: Academic Press.

Blumenthal, J. A., & Madden, D. J. (1988). Effects of aerobic exercise training, age, and physical fitness on memory-search performance. *Psychology and Aging, 3,* 280–285.

Bondareff, W. (2007). Brain and central nervous system. In J. E. Birren (Ed.), *Encyclopedia of gerontology: Age, aging, and the aged* (2nd ed., Vol. 1, pp. 187–190). Boston: Elsevier Academic Press.

Botwinick, J. (1984). *Aging and behavior* (3rd ed.). New York: Springer.

Brandtstädter, J. (1999). Sources of resilience in the aging self: Toward integrating perspectives. In T. M. Hess & F. Blanchard-Fields (Eds.), *Social cognition and aging* (pp. 123–141). San Diego: Academic Press.

Brandtstädter, J., & Greve, W. (1994). The aging self: Stabilizing and protective processes. *Developmental Review, 14,* 52–80.

Brandtstädter, J. & Renner, G. (1990). Tenacious goal pursuit and flexible goal adjustment: Explication and age-related analysis of assimilative and accommodative strategies and coping. *Psychology and Aging, 5,* 58–67.

Brandtstädter, J., Wentura, D., & Greve, W. (1993). Adaptive resources of the aging self: Outlines of an emergent perspective. *International Journal of Behavioral Development, 16,* 323–349.

Bransford, J. D., & Johnson, M. K. (1972). Contextual prerequisites for understanding: Some investigations of comprehension and recall. *Journal of Verbal Learning and Verbal Behavior, 11,* 717–726.

Brody, E. M., Litvin, S. J., Albert, S. M., & Hoffman, C. J. (1994). Marital status of daughters and patterns of parent care. *Journal of Gerontology: Social Sciences, 49,* S95–S103.

Brody, H. (2006). Central and peripheral nervous systems morphology. In R. Schulz (Ed.), *The encyclopedia of aging* (4th ed., pp. 198–206). New York: Springer.

Brown, S. L., Lee, G. R., & Bulanda, J. R. (2006). Cohabitation among older adults: A national portrait. *Journal of Gerontology: Social Sciences, 61B,* S71–S79.

Burdick, D. C. (2005). Technology and aging: Not an oxymoron. *AGHE Exchange, 28*(4), 1, 8–9.

Burgio, K. L., & Burgio, L. D. (1991). The problem of urinary incontinence. In P. A. Wisocki (Ed.), *Handbook of clinical behavior therapy with the elderly client* (pp. 317–336). New York: Plenum Press.

Burgio, L. D., & Engel, B. T. (1990). Biofeedback-assisted training for elderly men and women. *Journal of the American Geriatrics Society, 38,* 338–340.

Burke, D. M., MacKay, D. G., Worthley, J. S., & Wade, E. (1991). On the tip of the tongue: What causes word finding failures in young and older adults? *Journal of Memory and Language, 30,* 542–579.

Busse, E. W. (1995). Primary and secondary aging. In G. L. Maddox (Ed.), *The encyclopedia of aging* (2nd ed., p. 754). New York: Springer.

Butler, R. N. (1963). The life review: An interpretation of reminiscence in the aged. *Psychiatry, 26,* 65–76.

Butler, R. N., Lewis, M. I., & Sunderland, T. (1998). *Aging and mental health: Positive psychosocial and biomedical approaches* (5th ed.). Boston: Allyn & Bacon.

Cahill, K. E, Giandrea, M. D., & Quinn, J. F. (2006). Retirement patterns from career employment. *Gerontologist, 46,* 514–523.

Camp, C. J., Foss, J. W., Stevens, A. B., Reichard, C. C., McKitrick, L. A., & O'Hanlon, A. M. (1993). Memory training in normal and demented populations: The E-I-E-I-O model. *Experimental Aging Research, 19,* 277–290.

Canetto, S. S. (2007). Suicide. In J. E. Birren (Ed.), *Encyclopedia of gerontology: Age, aging, and the aged* (2nd ed., Vol. 2, pp. 575–581). Boston: Elsevier Academic Press.

Cantor, M. (1979). Neighbors and friends: An overlooked resource in the informal support system. *Research on Aging, 1,* 434–463.

Carr, C., Jackson, T. W., Madden, D. J., & Cohen, H. J. (1992). The effect of age on driving skills. *Journal of the American Geriatrics Society, 40,* 567–573.

Carstensen, L. L. (1991). Socioemotional selectivity theory: Social activity in life-span context. In K. W. Schaie & M. P. Lawton (Eds.), *Annual review of gerontology and geriatrics* (Vol. 11, pp. 195–217). New York: Springer.

Carstensen, L. L. (1992). Social and emotional patterns in adulthood: Support for socioemotional selectivity theory. *Psychology and Aging, 7,* 331–338.

Carstensen, L. L. (1995). Evidence for a life-span theory of socioemotional selectivity. *Current Directions in Psychological Science, 4,* 151–156.

Carstensen, L. L., & Fredrickson, B. L. (1998). Influence of HIV status and age on cognitive representations of others. *Health Psychology, 17,* 494–503.

Carstensen, L. L., Gottman, J. M., & Levenson, R. W. (1995). Emotional behavior in long-term marriage. *Psychology and Aging, 10,* 140–149.

Carstensen, L. L., Gross, J. J., & Fung, H. H. (1997). The social context of emotional experience. In K. W. Schaie & M. P. Lawton (Eds.), *Annual review of gerontology and geriatrics* (Vol. 17, pp. 325–352). New York: Springer.

Carstensen, L. L., Isaacowitz, D. M., & Charles, S. T. (1999). Taking time seriously: A theory of socioemotional selectivity. *American Psychologist, 54,* 165–181.

Carstensen, L. L., Mikels, J. A., & Mather, M. (2006). Aging and the intersecton of cognition, motivation, and emotion. In J. E. Birren & K. W. Schaie (Eds.), *Handbook of the psychology of aging* (6th ed., pp. 343–362). Boston: Elsevier Academic Press.

Cattell, R. B. (1963). Theory of fluid and crystallized intelligence: A critical experiment. *Journal of Educational Psychology, 54*, 1–22.

Cavanaugh, J. C., Grady, J. G., & Perlmutter, M. (1983). Forgetting and use of memory aids in 20- to 70-year-olds' everyday life. *International Journal of Aging and Human Development, 17*, 113–122.

Cerella, J. (1994). Generalized slowing and Brinley plots. *Journal of Gerontology: Psychological Sciences, 49*, P65–P71.

Cerella, J. (1995). Reaction time. In G. L. Maddox (Ed.), *The encyclopedia of aging* (2nd ed., pp. 792–795). New York: Springer.

Chap, J. B. (1986). Moral judgment in middle and late adulthood: The effects of age-appropriate moral dilemmas and spontaneous role taking. *International Journal of Aging and Human Development, 22*, 161–172.

Charles, S. T., & Piazza, J. R. (2007). Memories of social interactions: Age differences in emotional intensity. *Psychology and Aging, 22*, 300–309.

Chasteen, A. L., & Madey, S. F. (2003). Belief in a just world and the perceived injustice of dying young or old. *Omega, 47*, 313–326.

Chen, Y., & Persson, A. (2002). Internet use among young and older adults: Relation to psychological well-being. *Educational Gerontology, 28*, 731–744.

Cherniack, N. S., & Cherniack, E. P. (2007). Respiratory system. In J. E. Birren (Ed.), *Encyclopedia of gerontology: Age, aging, and the aged* (2nd ed., Vol. 2, pp. 443–449). Boston: Elsevier Academic Press.

Cherry, K. E., & Jones, M. W. (1999). Age-related differences in spatial memory: Effects of structural and organizational context. *Journal of General Psychology, 126*, 53–73.

Cherry, K. E., & LeCompte, D. C. (1999). Age and individual differences influence prospective memory. *Psychology and Aging, 14*, 60–76.

Cherry, K. E., & Smith, A. D. (1998). Normal memory aging. In M. Hersen & V. B. Van Hasselt (Eds.), *Handbook of clinical geropsychology* (pp. 87–110). New York: Plenum Press.

Choi, I., Nisbett, R. E., & Norenzayan, A. (1999). Causal attributions across cultures: Variation and universality. *Psychological Bulletin, 125*, 47–63.

Cicirelli, V. G. (1993). Attachment and obligation as daughters' motives for caregiving behavior and subsequent effect on subjective burden. *Psychology and Aging, 8*, 144–155.

Cicirelli, V. G. (1995). Siblings. In G. L. Maddox (Ed.), *The encyclopedia of aging* (2nd ed., pp. 857–859). New York: Springer.

Cicirelli. V. G. (1997). Relationship of psychosocial and background variables to older adults' end-of-life decisions. *Psychology and Aging, 12*, 72–83.

Cicirelli, V. G. (2002). Fear of death in older adults: Predictions from terror management theory. *Journal of Gerontology: Psychological Sciences, 57B*, P358–P366.

Cicirelli. V. (2006). Caregiving decision making by older mothers and adult children: Process and expected outcome. *Psychology and Aging, 21*, 209–221.

Cicirelli, V. G., Coward, R. G., & Dwyer, J. W. (1992). Siblings as caregivers for impaired elders. *Research on Aging, 14*, 331–350.

Clark, R. L. (2006). Economics. In R. Schulz (Ed.), *The encyclopedia of aging* (4th ed., pp. 348–351). New York: Springer.

Clarke, E. J., Preston, M., Raksin, J., & Bengston, V. L. (1999). Types of conflicts and tensions between older parents and adult children. *Gerontologist, 39*, 261–270.

Cleveland, J. N., & Shore, L. M. (1992). Self- and supervisory perspectives on age and work attitudes and performance. *Journal of Applied Psychology, 77*, 469–484.

Cleveland, J. N., & Shore, L. M. (2007). Work and employment: Individual. In J. E. Birren (Ed.), *Encyclopedia of gerontology: Age, aging, and the aged* (2nd ed., Vol. 2, pp. 683–694). Boston: Elsevier Academic Press.

Cohen, G., & Taylor, S. (1998). Reminiscence and ageing. *Ageing and Society, 18*, 601–610.

Cohen, G. D. (1990). Psychopathology and mental health in the mature and elderly adult. In J. E. Birren and K. W. Schaie (Eds.), *Handbook of the psychology of aging* (3rd ed., pp. 359–371). San Diego: Academic Press.

Collins, K., Luszcz, M., Lawson, M., & Keeves, J. (1997). Everyday problem solving in elderly women: Contributions of residence, perceived control, and age. *Gerontologist, 37*, 293–302.

Collins, L. M. (1996). Research design and methods. In J. E. Birren (Ed.), *Encyclopedia of gerontology: Age, aging, and the aged* (Vol. 2, pp. 419–429). San Diego: Academic Press.

Connidis, I. A. (1989). *Family ties and aging*. Toronto: Butterworths.

Connidis, I. A. (1994). Sibling support in older age. *Journal of Gerontology: Social Sciences, 49*, S309–S317.

Cordoni, C. N. (1981). Subjective perceptions of everyday memory failure. *Dissertation Abstracts International, 42*, 2047B.

Corey-Bloom, J. (2000). Dementia. In S. K. Whitbourne (Ed.), *Psychopathology in later adulthood* (pp. 217–243). New York: John Wiley.

Corr, C. A., Nabe, C. M., & Corr, D. M. (2009). *Death and dying, life and living* (6th ed.). Belmont, CA: Wadsworth Cengage Learning.

Costa, P. T., Jr., & McCrae, R. R. (1985). Hypochrondriasis, neuroticism, and aging. *American Psychologist, 40*, 19–28.

Costa, P. T., Jr., & McCrae, R. R. (1991). *NEO Five-Factor Inventory*. Odessa, FL: Psychological Assessment Resources.

Costa, P. T., Jr., & McCrae, R. R. (1992). *Revised NEO Personality Inventory (NEO-PI-R) and NEO Five-Factor Inventory (NEO-FFI) professional manual*. Odessa, FL: Psychological Assessment Resources.

Cousins, S. O. (2000). "My heart couldn't take it": Older women's beliefs about exercise benefits and risks. *Journal of Gerontology: Psychological Sciences, 55B*, P283–P294.

Craik, F. I. M. (1994). Memory changes in normal aging. *Current Directions in Psychological Science, 3*, 155–158.

Craik, F. I. M., & Byrd, M. (1982). Aging and cognitive deficits: The role of attentional resources. In F. I. M. Craik & S. Trehub (Eds.), *Aging and cognitive processes* (pp. 191–211). New York: Plenum Press.

Craik, F. I. M., Byrd, M., & Swanson, J. M. (1987). Patterns of memory loss in three elderly samples. *Psychology and Aging, 2*, 79–86.

Crimmins, E. M., Reynolds, S. L., & Saito, Y. (1999). Trends in health and ability to work among the older working-age population. *Journal of Gerontology: Social Sciences, 54B*, S31–S40.

Cristofalo, V. J., Tresini, M., Francis, M. K., & Volker, C. (1999). Biological theories of senescence. In V. L. Bengston & K. W. Schaie (Eds.), *Handbook of theories of aging* (pp. 98–112). New York: Springer.

Cross, S., & Markus, H. (1991). Possible selves across the life span. *Human Development, 32*, 230–255.

Cuddy, A. J. C., & Fiske, S. T. (2002). Doddering but dear: Process, content, and function of stereotyping older persons. In T. D. Nelson (Ed.), *Ageism: Stereotyping and prejudice against older persons* (pp. 3–26). Cambridge, MA: MIT Press.

Cuddy, A. J. C., Norton, M. I., & Fiske, S. T. (2005). This old stereotype: The pervasiveness and persistence of the elderly stereotype. *Journal of Social Issues, 61*, 267–285.

Cumming, E. M., & Henry, W. (1961). *Growing old: The process of disengagement*. New York: Basic Books.

Cutler, N. E. (1996). Pensions. In J. E. Birren (Ed.), *Encyclopedia of gerontology: Age, aging, and the aged* (Vol. 2, pp. 261–269). San Diego: Academic Press.

Cutler, S. J., Hendricks, J., & Guyer, A. (2003). Age differences in home computer availability and use. *Journal of Gerontology: Social Sciences, 58B*, S271–S280.

Czaja, S. J. (2001). Technological change and the older worker. In J. E. Birren and K. W. Schaie (Eds.), *Handbook of the psychology of aging* (5th ed., pp. 547–568). San Diego: Academic Press.

Czaja, S. J., & Sharit, J. (1993). Age differences in the performance of computer based work as a function of pacing and task complexity. *Psychology and Aging, 8*, 59–67.

Czaja, S. J., & Sharit, J. (1998). Ability–performance relationships as a function of age and task experience for a data entry task. *Journal of Experimental Psychology: Applied, 4,* 332–351.

Danner, D. D., Snowdon, D. A., & Friesen, W. V. (2001). Positive emotions in early life and longevity: Findings from the Nun Study. *Journal of Personality and Social Psychology, 80,* 804–813.

Davidson, K. (2001). Late life widowhood, selfishness, and new partnership choices: A gendered perspective. *Aging and Society, 21,* 297–317.

Davison, B. J., Kirk, P., Degner, L. F., & Hassard, T. H. (1999). Information and patient participation in screening for prostate cancer. *Patient Education and Counseling, 37,* 255–263.

Deary, I. J., & Der, G. (2005). Reaction time explains IQ's association with death. *Psychological Science, 16,* 64–69.

Denney, N. W. (1982). Aging and cognitive changes. In B. B. Wolman (Ed.), *Handbook of developmental psychology* (pp. 807–827). Englewood Cliffs, NJ: Prentice Hall.

Denney, N. W., & Palmer, A. N. (1981). Adult age differences on traditional and practical problem-solving. *Journal of Gerontology, 36,* 323–328.

Dennis, W. (1966). Creative productivity between the ages of 20 and 80 years. *Journal of Gerontology, 21,* 1–8.

DeWall, C. N., & Baumeister, R. F. (2007). From terror to joy: Automatic tuning to positive affective information following mortality salience. *Psychological Science, 18,* 984–990.

Dick, L. P., Gallagher-Thompson, D., & Thompson, L. W. (1999). Cognitive-behavioral therapy. In R. T. Woods (Ed.), *Psychological problems of ageing: Assessment, treatment, and care* (pp. 253–291). Chichester, England: John Wiley.

Diehl, M., Coyle, N., & Labouvie-Vief, G. (1996). Age and sex differences in strategies of coping and defense across the life span. *Psychology and Aging, 11,* 127–139.

Diehl, M., Marsiske, M., Horgas, A. L., Rosenberg, A., Saczynski, J. S., & Willis, S. L. (2005). Revised observed tasks of daily living: A performance-based assessment of everyday problem-solving in older adults. *Journal of Applied Gerontology, 24,* 211–230.

Diehl, M., Willis, S. L., & Schaie, K. W. (1995). Everyday problem solving in older adults: Observational assessment and cognitive correlates. *Psychology and Aging, 10,* 478–491.

Diener, E., & Suh, M. E. (1997). Subjective well-being and age: An international analysis. In K. W. Schaie & M. P. Lawton (Eds.), *Annual review of gerontology and geriatrics* (Vol. 17, pp. 304–324). New York: Springer.

Dilworth-Anderson, P., Williams, S. W., & Cooper, T. (1999). Family caregiving to elderly African Americans: Caregiver types and structures. *Journal of Gerontology: Social Sciences, 54B,* S237–S241.

Dixon, R. A. (1999). Exploring cognition in interactive situations: The aging of N + 1 minds. In T. M. Hess & F. Blanchard-Fields (Eds.), *Social cognition and aging* (pp. 267–290). San Diego: Academic Press.

Dixon, R. A., & Gould, O. N. (1996). Adults telling and retelling stories collaboratively. In P. B. Baltes & U. M. Staudinger (Eds.), *Interactive minds: Life-span perspectives on the social foundation of cognition* (pp. 221–241). New York: Cambridge University Press.

Dixon, R. A., & Gould, O. N. (1998). Younger and older adults collaborating on retelling everyday stories. *Applied Developmental Science, 2,* 160–171.

Dorfman, R., Walters, K., Burke, P., Harden, L., Karanik, T., Raphael, J., et al. (1995). Old, sad, and alone: The myth of the aging homosexual. *Journal of Gerontological Social Work, 24,* 29–44.

Dowd, J. J. (1975). Aging as exchange: A preface to theory. *Journal of Gerontology, 30,* 584–594.

Duberstein, P. R., & Conwell, Y. (2000). Suicide. In S. K. Whitbourne (Ed.), *Psychopathology in later adulthood* (pp. 245–275). New York: John Wiley.

Duberstein, P. R., Evinger, J. S., & Conwell, Y. (2002). *Religion and completed suicide.* Paper presented at the American Psychological Association Convention, Chicago.

Dupree, L. W., & Schonfeld, L. (1999). Management of alcohol abuse in older adults. In M. Duffy (Ed.), *Handbook of counseling and psychotherapy with older adults* (pp. 632–649). New York: John Wiley.

Dye, C. J. (1978). Psychologists' role in the provision of mental health care for the elderly. *Professional Psychology, 9*, 38–49.

Ebersole, P., & Hess, P. (1998). *Toward Healthy Aging* (5th ed.). St. Louis: Mosby.

Effros, R. B. (2006). Immune system. In R. Schulz (Ed.), *The encyclopedia of aging* (4th ed., pp. 565–569). New York: Springer.

Eglit, H. (2004). *Elders on trial: Age and ageism in the American legal system.* Gainesville: University Press of Florida.

Einstein, G. O., & McDaniel, M. A. (1990). Normal aging and prospective memory. *Journal of Experimental Psychology: Learning, Memory, and Cognition, 16*, 717–726.

Einstein, G. O., McDaniel, M. A., Manzi, J., Cochran, B., & Baker, M. (2000). Prospective memory and aging: Forgetting intentions over short delays. *Psychology and Aging, 15*, 671–683.

Ekerdt, D. J. (1986). The busy ethic: Moral continuity between work and retirement. *Gerontologist, 26*, 239–244.

Ekerdt, D. J. (2004). Born to retire: The foreshortened life course. *Gerontologist, 44*, 3–9.

Ekerdt, D. J., & DeViney, S. (1993). Evidence for a preretirement process among older male workers. *Journal of Gerontology: Social Sciences, 48*, S35–S43.

Ekerdt, D. J., DeViney, S., & Kosloski, K. (1996). Profiling plans for retirement. *Journal of Gerontology: Social Sciences, 51B*, S140–S149.

Ekerdt, D. J., & Sergeant, J. F. (2006). Retirement. In R. Schulz (Ed.), *The encyclopedia of aging* (4th ed., pp. 1032–1037). New York: Springer.

Ekerdt, D. J., Sergeant, J. F., Dingel, M., & Bowen, M. E. (2004). Household disbandment in later life. *Journal of Gerontology: Social Sciences, 59B*, S265–S273.

Elias, M. F., Elias, P. K., & Elias, J. W. (1977). *Basic processes in adult developmental psychology.* St. Louis: Mosby.

Ellis, H. C., & Hunt, R. R. (1993). *Fundamentals of cognitive psychology* (5th ed.). Madison, WI: Brown & Benchmark.

Engel, B. T. (1995). Incontinence. In G. L. Maddox (Ed.), *The encyclopedia of aging* (2nd ed., pp. 501–502). New York: Springer.

Erber, J. T. (1979). The institutionalized geriatric patient considered in a framework of developmental deprivation. *Human Development, 22*, 165–179.

Erber, J. T. (1989). Young and older adults' appraisal of memory failures in young and older adult target persons. *Journal of Gerontology: Psychological Sciences, 44*, P170–P175.

Erber, J. T. (2006). Memory, remote. In R. Schulz (Ed.), *The encyclopedia of aging* (4th ed., pp. 749–752). New York: Springer.

Erber, J. T., & Danker, D. C. (1995). Forgetting in the workplace: Attributions and recommendations for young and older employees. *Psychology and Aging, 10*, 565–569.

Erber, J. T., & Long, B. A. (2006). Perceptions of forgetful and slow employees: Does age matter? *Journal of Gerontology: Psychological Sciences, 61B*, P333–P339.

Erber, J. T., & Rothberg, S. T. (1991). Here's looking at you: The relative effect of age and attractiveness on judgments about memory failure. *Journal of Gerontology: Psychological Sciences, 46*, P116–P123.

Erber, J. T., & Szuchman, L. T. (2002). Age and capability: The role of forgetting and personal traits. *International Journal of Aging and Human Development, 54*, 173–189.

Erber, J. T., Szuchman, L. T., & Prager, I. G. (1997). Forgetful but forgiven: How age and life style affect perceptions of memory failure. *Journal of Gerontology: Psychological Sciences, 52B*, P303–P307.

Erber, J. T., Szuchman, L. T., & Prager, I. G. (2001). Ain't misbehavin': The effects of aging and intentionality on judgments about misconduct. *Psychology and Aging, 16*, 85–95.

Erber, J. T., Szuchman, L. T., & Rothberg, S. T. (1990a). Age, gender, and individual differences in memory failure appraisal. *Psychology and Aging, 5*, 600–603.

Erber, J. T., Szuchman, L. T., & Rothberg, S. T. (1990b). Everyday memory failure: Age differences in appraisal and attribution. *Psychology and Aging, 5*, 236–241.

Erber, J. T., Szuchman, L. T., & Rothberg, S. T. (1992). Dimensions of self-report about everyday memory in young and older adults.

International Journal of Aging and Human Development, 34, 311–323.

Erikson, E. H. (1950). *Childhood and society.* New York: Norton.

Fees, B. S., Martin, P., & Poon, L. W. (1999). A model of loneliness in older adults. *Journals of Gerontology Series B: Psychological Sciences, 54B*, P231–P239.

Field, D., & Minkler, M. (1988). Continuity and change in social support between young-old and old-old or very-old age. *Journal of Gerontology: Psychological Sciences, 43*, P100–P106.

Fillenbaum, G. G. (1995). Activities of daily living. In G. L. Maddox (Ed.), *The encyclopedia of aging* (2nd ed., pp. 7–9). New York: Springer.

Finch, C. E., & Seeman, T. E. (1999). Stress theories of aging. In V. L. Bengston & K. W. Schaie (Eds.), *Handbook of theories of aging* (pp. 81–97). New York: Springer.

Fingerman, K. L. (1996). Sources of tension in the aging mother and adult daughter relationship. *Psychology and Aging, 11*, 591–606.

Fingerman, K. L. & Griffiths, P. C. (1999). Season's greetings: Adults' social contacts at the holiday season. *Psychology and Aging, 14*, 192–205.

Fingerman, K. L., Hay, E. L., & Birditt, K. S. (2004). The best of ties, the worst of ties: Close, problematic, and ambivalent social relationships. *Journal of Marriage and the Family, 66*, 792–808.

Finkelstein, L. M., Burke, M. J., & Raju, N. S. (1995). Age discrimination in simulated employment contexts. *Journal of Applied Psychology, 80*, 652–663.

Fisk, A. D., & Fisher, D. L. (1994). Brinley plots and theories of aging: The explicit, middled, and implicit debates. *Journal of Gerontology: Psychological Sciences, 49*, P81–P89.

Fitzgerald, J. M. (2000). Younger and older jurors: The influence of environmental supports on memory performance and decision-making in complex trials. *Journal of Gerontology: Psychological Sciences, 55B*, P323–P331.

Flaherty, J. H. (2007). Delirium. In J. E. Birren (Ed.), *Encyclopedia of gerontology: Age, aging, and the aged* (2nd ed., Vol. 1, pp. 359–368). Boston: Elsevier Academic Press.

Fleeson, W., & Heckhausen, J. (1997). More or less "me" in past, present, and future: Perceived lifetime personality during adulthood. *Psychology and Aging, 12*, 125–136.

Fletcher, W. L., & Hansson, R. O. (1991). Assessing the social components of retirement anxiety. *Psychology and Aging, 6*, 76–85.

Flippen, C., & Tienda, M. (2000). Pathways to retirement: Patterns of labor force participation and labor market exit among pre-retirement population by race, Hispanic origin, and sex. *Journal of Gerontology: Social Sciences, 55B*, S14–S27.

Flynn, J. R. (1999). Searching for justice: The discovery of IQ gains over time. *American Psychologist, 54*, 5–20.

Folstein, M. F., Folstein, S. E., & McHugh, P. R. (1975). Mini-Mental State: A practical method for grading the cognitive state of patients for the clinician. *Journal of Psychiatric Research, 12*, 189–198.

Fortner, B. V., Neimeyer, R. A., & Rybarczyk, B. (2000). Correlates of death anxiety in older adults: A comprehensive review. In A. Tomer (Ed.), *Death attitudes and the older adult: Theories, concepts, and applications* (pp. 95–108). Philadelphia: Brunner-Routledge.

Franks, M. M., & Stephens, M. A. P. (1996). Social support in the context of caregiving: Husbands' provision of support to wives involved in parent care. *Journal of Gerontology: Psychological Sciences, 51B*, P43–P52.

Fredrickson, B. L., & Carstensen, L. L. (1990). Choosing social partners: How old age and anticipated endings make us more selective. *Psychology and Aging, 5*, 335–357.

Freter, S. (2006). Delirium. In R. Schulz (Ed.), *The encyclopedia of aging* (4th ed., pp. 285–288). New York: Springer.

Friedhoff, A. J. (1994). Consensus panel report. In L. S. Schneider, C. F. Reynolds, B. D. Lebowitz, & A. J. Friedhoff (Eds.), *Diagnosis and treatment of depression in late life: Results of the NIH consensus development conference.* Washington, DC: American Psychiatric Press.

Fries, J. F. (1995). Compression of morbidity/disease postponement. In G. L. Maddox (Ed.), *The encyclopedia of aging* (2nd ed., pp. 213–216). New York: Springer.

Fries, J. F. (1997). Will future elderly persons experience more years of disability? Yes. In A. E. Scharlach & L. W. Kaye (Eds.), *Controversial issues in aging* (pp. 214–218). Boston: Allyn & Bacon.

Fritz, C. L., Farver, T. B., Hart, L. A., & Kass, P. H. (1996). Companion animals and the psychological health of Alzheimer patients' caregivers. *Psychological Reports, 78,* 467–481.

Fronstin, P. (1999). Retirement patterns and employee benefits: Do benefits matter? *Gerontologist, 39,* 37–47.

Fuller, G. (2007). *HR believes older staff offer "lower return on investment" in training.* Retrieved February 25, 2009, from http://www.person neltoday.com/Articles/2007/01/16/38880/ hr-believes-older-staff-offer-lower-return-on-investment-in.html

Fung, H. H., Carstensen, L. L., & Lutz, A. (1999). The influence of time on social preferences: Implications for life-span development. *Psychology and Aging, 14,* 595–604.

Gallagher, D. E., & Thompson, L. W. (1983). Treatment of major depressive disorder in older adult outpatients with brief psychotherapies. *Psychotherapy: Theory, research, and practice, 19,* 482–490.

Gallagher-Thompson, D. (1995). Bereavement. In G. L. Maddox (Ed.), *The encyclopedia of aging* (2nd ed., pp. 105–108). New York: Springer.

Gardner, H. (1983). *Frames of mind: The theory of multiple intelligences.* New York: Basic Books.

Gardner, H. (1999). Are there additional intelligences? The case for naturalistic, spiritual, and existential intelligences. In J. Kane (Ed.), *Education, information, and transformation* (pp. 111–131). Upper Saddle River, NJ: Prentice Hall.

Gatz, M. (Ed.) (1995). *Emerging issues in mental health and aging.* Washington, DC: American Psychological Association.

Gatz, M. (2007). Genetics, dementia, and the elderly. *Current Directions in Psychological Science, 16,* 123–127.

Gatz, M., & Finkel, S. I. (1995). Education and training of mental health service providers. In

M. Gatz (Ed.), *Emerging issues in mental health and aging* (pp. 282–302). Washington, DC: American Psychological Association.

Gatz, M., & Hurwicz, M. L. (1990). Are old people more depressed? Cross-sectional data on Center for Epidemiological Studies Depression Scale factors. *Psychology and Aging, 5,* 284–290.

Gatz, M., & Karel, M. J. (1993). Individual change in perceived control over 20 years. *International Journal of Behavioral Development, 16,* 305–322.

Gatz, M., Kasl-Godley, J. E., & Karel, J. J. (1996). Aging and mental disorders. In J. E. Birren & K. W. Schaie (Eds.), *Handbook of the psychology of aging* (4th ed., pp. 365–382). San Diego: Academic Press.

Gatz, M., & Smyer, M. A. (2001). Mental health and aging at the outset of the twenty-first century. In J. E. Birren & K. W. Schaie (Eds.), *Handbook of the psychology of aging* (5th ed., pp. 523–544). San Diego: Academic Press.

Gendell, M., & Siegel, J. S. (1996). Trends in retirement age in the United States, 1955–1993, by sex and race. *Journal of Gerontology: Social Sciences, 51B,* S132–S139.

George, L. K. (2006). Self-esteem. In R. Schulz (Ed.), *The encyclopedia of aging* (4th ed., pp. 1055–1056). New York: Springer.

Ghisletta, P., & Lindenberger, U. (2003). Age-based structural dynamics between perceptual speed and knowledge in the Berlin Aging Study: Direct evidence for ability dedifferentiation in old age. *Psychology and Aging, 18,* 696–713.

Giambra, L. M. (1989). Task-unrelated thought frequency as a function of age: A laboratory study. *Psychology and Aging, 4,* 136–143.

Giarrusso, R., & Silverstein, M. (1995). Grandparent–grandchild relationships. In G. L. Maddox (Ed.), *The encyclopedia of aging* (2nd ed., pp. 421–422). New York: Springer.

Gilbert, D. T., & Malone, P. S. (1995). The correspondence bias. *Psychological Bulletin, 117,* 21–38.

Gilligan, C. (1982). *In a different voice: Psychological theory and women's development.* Cambridge, MA: Harvard University Press.

Gilmore, G. C. (1996). Perception. In J. E. Birren (Ed.), *Encyclopedia of gerontology: Age, aging, and the aged* (Vol. 2, pp. 271–279). San Diego: Academic Press.

Gladwell, M. (1997, October 20 & 27). The Alzheimer's strain. *New Yorker*, pp. 122–139.

Gold, D. T. (1989). Sibling relationships in old age: A typology. *International Journal of Aging and Human Development, 28*, 37–51.

Gold, D. T. (1990). Late-life sibling relationships: Does race affect typological distribution? *Gerontologist, 30*, 741–748.

Goldmeier, J. (1986). Pets or people: Another research note. *Gerontologist, 26*, 203–206.

Goldsmith, R. E., & Heiens, R. A. (1992). Subjective age: A test of five hypotheses. *Gerontologist, 32*, 312–317.

Gomberg, E. S. W. (2007). Alcohol and drugs. In J. E. Birren (Ed.), *Encyclopedia of gerontology: Age, aging, and the aged* (2nd ed., Vol. 1, pp. 64–71). Boston: Elsevier Academic Press.

Gordon-Salant, S. (1996). Hearing. In J. E. Birren (Ed.), *Encyclopedia of gerontology: Age, aging, and the aged* (Vol. 1, pp. 643–653). San Diego: Academic Press.

Green, D. M., & Swets, J. A. (1966). *A signal detection theory and psychophysics*. New York: John Wiley.

Greenberg, B. (1998, March 11). 93-year-old Macy's worker charms customers, rings up sale. *Miami Herald*, 14A.

Greenfield, E. A., & Marks, N. F. (2004). Formal volunteering as a protective factor for older adults' psychological well-being. *Journal of Gerontology: Social Sciences, 59B*, S258–S264.

Greenwood, P. M. (2007). Functional plasticity in cognitive aging: Review and hypothesis. *Neuropsychology, 21*, 657–673.

Grisso, T. (1986). *Evaluating competencies: Forensic assessments and instruments*. New York: Plenum Press.

Gross, J. J., Carstensen, L. L., Pasupathi, M., Tsai, J., Skorpen, C. G., & Hsu, A. Y. (1997). Emotion and aging: Experience, expression, and control. *Psychology and Aging, 12*, 590–599.

Gruenewald, T. L., Karlamangla, A. S., Greendale, G. A., Singer, B. H., & Seeman, T. E. (2007). Feelings of usefulness to others, disability, and mortality in older adults: The MacArthur Study of Successful Aging. *Journal of Gerontology: Psychological Sciences, 62B*, P28–P37.

Gueldner, S. H., Grabo, T. N., Britton, G., Pierce, C., & Lombardi, B. (2007). Osteoporosis and aging related bone disorders. In J. E. Birren (Ed.), *Encyclopedia of gerontology: Age, aging, and the aged* (2nd ed., Vol. 2, pp. 293–303). Boston: Elsevier Academic Press.

Gutmann, D. (1977). The cross-cultural perspective: Notes toward a comparative psychology of aging. In J. E. Birren & K. W. Schaie (Eds.), *The handbook of the psychology of aging* (pp. 302–326). New York: Van Nostrand.

Haight, B. K., Michel, Y., & Hendrix, S. (1998). Life review: Preventing despair in newly relocated nursing home residents: Short- and long-term effects. *International Journal of Aging and Human Development, 47*, 119–143.

Hakamies-Blomqvist, L., Mynttinen, S., Backman, M., & Mikkonen, V. (1999). Age-related differences in driving: Are older drivers more serial? *International Journal of Behavioral Development, 23*, 575–589.

Hall, C. S., Lindzey, G., & Campbell, J. B. (1998). *Theories of Personality* (4th ed.). New York: John Wiley.

Hannah, M. T., Domino, G., Figueredo, A. J., & Hendrickson, R. (1996). The prediction of ego integrity in older persons. *Educational and Psychological Measurement, 56*, 930–950.

Hardy, M. (2006). Older workers. In R. H. Binstock & L. K. George (Eds.), *Handbook of aging and the social sciences* (6th ed., pp. 201–218). Boston: Elsevier Academic Press.

Harkins, S. W., & Scott, R. B. (1996). Pain and presbyalgos. In J. E. Birren (Ed.), *Encyclopedia of gerontology: Age, aging, and the aged* (Vol. 2, pp. 247–260). San Diego: Academic Press.

Harley, C. B. (2006). Telomeres and cellular senescence. In R. Schulz (Ed.), *The encyclopedia of aging* (4th ed., pp. 1179–1182). New York: Springer.

Harris, M. B. (1994). Growing old gracefully: Age concealment and gender. *Journal of Gerontology: Psychological Sciences, 49*, P149–P158.

Hartley, A. A. (1995). Attention. In G. L. Maddox (Ed.), *The encyclopedia of aging* (2nd ed., pp. 91–93). New York: Springer.

Hasher, L., & Zacks, R. T. (1979). Automatic and effortful processes in memory. *Journal of Experimental Psychology: General, 108*, 356–388.

Hasher, L., & Zacks, R. T. (1988). Working memory, comprehension and aging: A review and a new view. In G. H. Bower (Ed.), *The psychology of learning and motivation*: Vol. 22 (pp. 193–225). New York: Academic Press.

Hawkins, H., Kramer, A., & Capaldi, D. (1992). Aging, exercise, and attention. *Psychology and Aging, 7*, 643–663.

Hawkley, L. C., & Cacioppo, J. T. (2007). Aging and loneliness: Downhill quickly? *Current Directions in Psychological Science, 16*, 187–191.

Hayflick, L. (1994). *How and why we age*. New York: Ballantine Books.

Hayflick, L. (1995). Biological aging theories. In G. L. Maddox (Ed.), *The encyclopedia of aging* (2nd ed., pp. 113–118). New York: Springer.

Hayslip, B., Jr., & Hansson, R. O. (2007). Hospice. In J. E. Birren (Ed.), *Encyclopedia of gerontology: Age, aging, and the aged* (2nd ed., Vol. 1, pp. 700–709). Boston: Elsevier Academic Press.

Hayslip, B., Jr., & Kaminski, P. L. (2005). Grandparents raising their grandchildren: A review of the literature and suggestions for practice. *Gerontologist, 45*, 262–269.

Hazelton, L. (2006). Sundown syndrome. In R. Schulz (Ed.), *The encyclopedia of aging* (4th ed., pp. 1156–1158). New York: Springer.

Heckhausen, J. (1997). Developmental regulation across adulthood: Primary and secondary control of age-related changes. *Developmental Psychology, 33*, 176–187.

Heckhausen, J., & Baltes, P. B. (1991). Perceived controllability of expected psychological change across adulthood and old age. *Journal of Gerontology, 46*, P165–P173.

Heckhausen, J., Dixon, R. A., & Baltes, P. B. (1989). Gains and losses in development throughout adulthood as perceived by different adult age groups. *Developmental Psychology, 25*, 109–121.

Heckhausen, J., & Krueger, J. (1993). Developmental expectations for the self and most other people: Age grading in three functions of social comparison. *Developmental Psychology, 29*, 539–548.

Heckhausen, J., & Schulz, R. (1993). Optimisation by selection and compensation: Balancing primary and secondary control in life span development.

International Journal of Behavioral Development, 16, 287–303.

Heckhausen, J., & Schulz, R. (1995). A life-span theory of control. *Psychological Review, 102*, 284–304.

Helson, R., Kwan, V. S. Y., John, O. P., & Jones, C. (2002). The growing evidence for personality change in adulthood: Findings from research with personality inventories. *Journal of Research in Personality, 36*, 287–306.

Herr, J. J., & Weakland, J. H. (1979). *Counseling elders and their families*. New York: Springer.

Hertzog, C. (1990). *Methodological issues in cognitive aging research*. Invited address to the 3rd Cognitive Aging Conference, Atlanta, GA.

Hertzog, C., Hultsch, D. F., & Dixon, R. A. (1999). On the problem of detecting effects of lifestyle on cognitive change in adulthood: Reply to Pushkar et al. (1999). *Psychology and Aging, 14*, 528–534.

Herzog, A. R., House, J. S., & Morgan, J. N. (1991). Relation of work and retirement to health and well-being in older age. *Psychology and Aging, 6*, 202–211.

Hess, B. B., & Markson, E. W. (1995). Poverty. In G. L. Maddox (Ed.), *The encyclopedia of aging* (2nd ed., pp. 748–751). New York: Springer.

Hess, T. M. (1999). Cognitive and knowledge-based influences on social representations. In T. M. Hess & F. Blanchard-Fields (Eds.), *Social cognition and aging* (pp. 239–263). San Diego: Academic Press.

Hess, T. M., & Auman, C. (2001). Aging and social expertise: The impact of trait-diagnostic information on impressions of others. *Psychology and Aging, 16*, 497–510.

Hess, T. M., Bolstad, C. A., Woodburn, S. M., & Auman, C. (1999). Trait-diagnosticity versus behavioral consistency as determinants of impression change in adulthood. *Psychology and Aging, 14*, 77–89.

Hill, R. D. (2005). *Positive aging: A guide for mental health professionals and consumers*. New York: W. W. Norton.

Hinrichsen, G. A., & Dick-Siskin, L. P. (2000). General principles of therapy. In S. K. Whitbourne (Ed.), *Psychopathology in later adulthood* (pp. 323–350). New York: John Wiley.

Hooker, K. (1992). Possible selves and perceived health in older adults and college students.

Journal of Gerontology: Psychological Sciences, 47, P85–P95.

Hooker, K., & Kaus, C. R. (1994). Health-related possible selves in young and middle adulthood. *Psychology and Aging, 9,* 126–133.

Hooyman, N., & Kiyak, H. A. (2008). *Social gerontology: A multidisciplinary perspective* (8th ed.). Boston: Allyn & Bacon.

Hoppmann, C. A., Gerstorf, D., Smith, J., & Klumb, P. L. (2007). Linking possible selves and behavior: Do domain-specific hopes and fears translate into activities in very old age? *Journal of Gerontology: Psychological Sciences, 62B,* P104–P111.

Horn, J. L., & Cattell, R. B. (1967). Age difference in fluid and crystallized intelligence. *Acta Psychologica, 26,* 107–129.

Horn, J. L., & Donaldson, G. (1976). On the myth of intellectual decline in adulthood. *American Psychologist, 31,* 701–719.

Howard, D. V. (1996). The aging of implicit and explicit memory. In F. Blanchard-Fields and T. M. Hess (Eds.), *Perspective on cognitive change in adulthood and aging* (pp. 221–254). New York: McGraw-Hill.

Howard, D. V. (2006). Implicit memory and learning. In R. Schulz (Ed.), *The encyclopedia of aging* (4th ed., pp. 573–576). New York: Springer.

Hoyer, W. J., & Rybash, J. M. (1996). Life span theory. In J. E. Birren (Ed.), *Encyclopedia of Gerontology: Age, aging, and the aged* (Vol. 2, pp. 65–71). San Diego: Academic Press.

Hultsch, D. F., Hertzog, C., Small, B. J., & Dixon, R. A. (1999). Use it or lose it: Engaged lifestyle as a buffer of cognitive decline in aging? *Psychology and Aging, 14,* 245–263.

Hummert, M. L. (1990). Multiple stereotypes of elderly and young adults: A comparison of structure and evaluations. *Psychology and Aging, 5,* 182–193.

Hummert, M. L. (1999). A social cognitive perspective on age stereotypes. In T. M. Hess & F. Blanchard-Fields (Eds.), *Social cognition and aging* (pp. 175–196). San Diego: Academic Press.

Hummert, M. L., Garstka, T. A., Shaner, J. L., & Strahm, S. (1994). Stereotypes of the elderly held by young, middle-aged, and elderly adults.

Journal of Gerontology: Psychological Sciences, 49, P240–P249.

Ingersoll-Dayton, B., Morgan, D., and Antonucci, T. (1997). The effects of positive and negative social exchanges on aging adults. *Journal of Gerontology: Social Sciences, 52B,* S190–S199.

Jacoby, L. L., & Rhodes, M. G. (2006). False remembering in the aged. *Current Directions in Psychological Science, 15,* 49–53.

James, L. E., Burke, D. M., Austin, A., & Hulme, E. (1998). Production and perception of "verbosity" in younger and older adults. *Psychology and Aging, 13,* 355–367.

Jansari, A., & Parkin, A. J. (1996). Things that go bump in your life: Explaining the reminiscence bump in autobiographical memory. *Psychology and Aging, 11,* 85–91.

Jecker, N. S. (2006). Euthanasia. In R. Schulz (Ed.), *The encyclopedia of aging* (4th ed., pp. 392–394). New York: Springer.

Jecker, N. S., & Schneiderman, L. J. (1996). Is dying young worse than dying old? In J. Guadagno & D. Street (Eds.), *Aging for the twenty-first century: Readings in social gerontology* (pp. 514–524). New York: St. Martin's Press.

Johnson, M. M. S. (1990). Age differences in decision making: A process methodology for examining strategic information processing. *Journal of Gerontology: Psychological Sciences, 45,* P75–P78.

Johnson, R. W., Sambamoorthi, U., & Crystal, S. (1999). Gender differences in pension wealth: Estimates using provider data. *Gerontologist, 39,* 320–333.

Jones, E. E. (1979). The rocky road from acts to dispositions. *American Psychologist, 34,* 107–117.

Jones, H. E., & Conrad, H. (1933). The growth and decline of intelligence: A study of a homogeneous group between the ages of ten and sixty. *Genetic Psychological Monographs, 13,* 223–298.

Jones, J. H. (1993). *Bad blood: The Tuskegee syphilis experiment.* New York: Free Press.

Jopp, D., & Smith, J. (2006). Resources and life-management strategies as determinants of successful aging: On the protective effect of selection, optimization, and compensation. *Psychology and Aging, 21,* 253–265.

Kahana, E. (1982). A congruence model of person–environment interaction. In M. P. Lawton, P. G. Windley, & T. O. Byerts (Eds.), *Aging and the environment: Theoretical approaches* (pp. 97–121). New York: Springer.

Kahn, R. L., Goldfarb, A. I., & Pollack, M. (1964). The evaluation of geriatric patients following treatment. In P. H. Hoch & J. Zubin (Eds.), *Evaluation of geriatric treatment.* New York: Grune & Stratton.

Kane, R. L. (2005). What's so good about aging? *Research in Human Development, 2,* 103–114.

Kane, R. L., Bershadsky, B., & Bershadsky, J. (2006). Who recommends long-term care matters. *Gerontologist, 46,* 474–482.

Kane, R. L., Priester, R., & Neumann, D. (2007). Does disparity in the way older adults are treated imply ageism? *Gerontologist, 47,* 271–279.

Kapp, M. B. (2007). Assessing assessments of decision-making capacity: A few legal queries and commentary on "Assessment of decision-making capacity in older adults." *Journal of Gerontology: Psychological Sciences, 62B,* P12–P13.

Karlin, B. E., & Humphreys, K. (2007). Improving Medicare coverage of psychological services for older Americans. *American Psychologist, 62,* 637–649.

Kastenbaum, R. (1999). Dying and bereavement. In J. C. Cavanaugh & S. K. Whitbourne (Eds.), *Gerontology: An interdisciplinary perspective* (pp. 155–186). New York: Oxford University Press.

Kastenbaum, R. (2006). Suicide. In R. Schulz (Ed.), *The encyclopedia of aging* (4th ed., pp. 1155–1156). New York: Springer.

Kastenbaum, R. (2007). Death and dying. In J. E. Birren (Ed.), *Encyclopedia of gerontology: Age, aging, and the aged* (2nd ed., Vol. 1, pp. 345–350). Boston: Elsevier Academic Press.

Katchadourian, H. (1987). *Fifty: Midlife in perspective.* New York: W. H. Freeman.

Kausler, D. H. (1982). *Experimental psychology and human aging.* New York: John Wiley.

Kausler, D. H. (1991). *Experimental psychology, cognition, and human aging* (2nd ed.). New York: Springer.

Kausler, D. H. (1994). *Learning and memory in normal aging.* San Diego: Academic Press.

Kausler, D. H., Kausler, B. C., & Krupshaw, J. A. (2007). *The essential guide to aging in the twenty-first century.* Columbia: University of Missouri Press.

Kemper, S. (1994). Elderspeak: Speech accommodations to older adults. *Aging and Cognition, 1,* 17–28.

Kemper, S. (1995). Language production. In G. L. Maddox (Ed.), *The encyclopedia of aging* (2nd ed., pp. 538–540). New York: Springer.

Kemper, S., & Harden, T. (1999). Experimentally disentangling what's beneficial about elderspeak from what's not. *Psychology and Aging, 14,* 656–670.

Kemper, S., & Mitzner, T. L. (2001). Language production and comprehension. In J. E. Birren & K. W. Schaie (Eds.), *Handbook of the psychology of aging* (5th ed., pp. 378–398). San Diego: Academic Press.

Kendig, H., & Pynoos, J. (1996). Housing. In J. E. Birren (Ed.), *Encyclopedia of gerontology: Age, aging, and the aged* (Vol. 1, pp. 703–713). San Diego: Academic Press.

Kennedy, Q., & Mather, M. (2007). Aging, affect, and decision making. In K. D. Vohs, R. F. Baumeister, & G. Loewenstein (Eds.), *Do emotions help or hurt decision making? A Hedgefoxian perspective* (pp. 245–267). New York: Russell Sage Foundation.

Kim, S., Goldstein, D., Hasher, L., & Zacks, R. T. (2005). Framing effects in younger and older adults. *Journal of Gerontology: Psychological Sciences, 60B,* P215–P218.

Kimmel, D. (1992). The families of older gay men and lesbians. *Generations, 16,* 37–38.

Kimmel, D. C. (2006). Homosexuality. In R. Schulz (Ed.), *The encyclopedia of aging* (4th ed., pp. 537–539). New York: Springer.

King, D. A., & Markus, H. E. (2000). Mood disorders in older adults. In S. K. Whitbourne (Ed.), *Psychopathology in later adulthood* (pp. 141–172). New York: John Wiley.

King, L. A. & Hicks, J. A. (2007). Whatever happened to "what might have been"? *American Psychologist, 62,* 625–636.

Kisley, M. A., Wood, S., & Burrows, C. L. (2007). Looking at the sunny side of life: Age-related change in an event-related potential measure of the negativity bias. *Psychological Science, 18,* 838–843.

Kite, M. E., Stockdale, G. D., Whitley, B. E., Jr., & Johnson, B. T. (2005). Attitudes toward younger and older adults: An updated meta-analytic review. *Journal of Social Issues, 61,* 241–266.

Kite, M. E., & Wagner, L. S. (2002). Attitudes toward older adults. In T. D. Nelson (Ed.), *Ageism: Stereotyping and prejudice against older persons* (pp. 129–161). Cambridge, MA: MIT Press.

Kivnick, H. Q., & Sinclair, H. M. (1996). Grandparenthood. In J. E. Birren (Ed.), *Encyclopedia of gerontology: Age, aging, and the aged* (Vol. 1, pp. 611–623). San Diego: Academic Press.

Kleemeier, R. W. (1962). Intellectual change in the senium. In *Proceedings of the Social Statistics Section of the American Statistical Association, 1,* 290–295.

Kliegl, R., Smith, J., & Baltes, P. B. (1989). Testing-the-limits and the study of adult age differences in cognitive plasticity of a mnemonic skill. *Developmental Psychology, 25,* 247–256.

Kline, D. W. (2006). Vision: System, function, and loss. In R. Schulz (Ed.), *The encyclopedia of aging* (4th ed., pp. 1212–1215). New York: Springer.

Kline, D. W., & Scialfa, C. T. (1996). Visual and auditory aging. In J. E. Birren & K. W. Schaie (Eds.), *Handbook of the psychology of aging* (4th ed., pp. 181–203). San Diego: Academic Press.

Kline, D. W., & Scialfa, C. T. (1997). Sensory and perceptual functioning: Basic research and human factors implications. In A. D. Fisk & W. A. Rogers (Eds.), *Handbook of human factors and the older adult* (pp. 27–54). San Diego: Academic Press.

Knight, B. G. (2004). *Psychotherapy with older adults* (3rd ed.). Thousand Oaks, CA: Sage.

Knight, B. G., Kaskie, B., Shurgot, G. R., & Dave, J. (2006). Improving the mental health of older adults. In J. E. Birren & K. W. Schaie (Eds.), *Handbook of the psychology of aging* (6th ed., pp. 407–424). Boston: Elsevier Academic Press.

Koenig, H. G., & Blazer, D. G., II (1996). Depression. In J. E. Birren (Ed.), *Encyclopedia of gerontology: Age, aging, and the aged* (Vol. 1, pp. 415–428). San Diego: Academic Press.

Kogan, N., & Mills, M. (1992). Gender influences on age cognitions and preferences: Sociocultural or sociobiological? *Psychology and Aging, 7,* 98–106.

Kohlberg, L. (1969). Stage and sequence: The cognitive-developmental approach to socialization. In D. A. Goslin (Ed.), *Handbook of socialization theory and research* (pp. 347–480). Chicago: Rand McNally.

Kral, V. A. (1962). Senescent forgetfulness: Benign and malignant. *Canadian Medical Association Journal, 86,* 257–260.

Kramer, A. F., Fabiani, M., & Colcombe, S. J. (2006). Contributions of cognitive neuroscience to the understanding of behavior and aging. In J. E. Birren & K. W. Schaie (Eds.), *Handbook of the pychology of aging* (6th ed., pp. 57–83). Boston: Elsevier Academic Press.

Kramer, A. F., Humphrey, D. G., Larish, J. F., Logan, G. D., & Strayer, D. L. (1994). Aging and inhibition: Beyond a unitary view of inhibitory processing in attention. *Psychology and Aging, 9,* 491–512.

Krause, N. (2006). Social relationships in late life. In R. H. Binstock & L. K. George (Eds.), *Handbook of aging and the social sciences* (6th ed., pp. 181–200). Boston: Elsevier Academic Press.

Krause, N., & Borawski-Clark, E. (1994). Clarifying the functions of social support in later life. *Research on Aging, 16,* 251–279.

Krueger, J., Heckhausen, J., & Hundertmark, J. (1995). Perceiving middle-aged adults: Effects of stereotype-congruent and incongruent information. *Journal of Gerontology: Psychological Sciences, 50B,* P82–P93.

Kübler-Ross, E. (1969). *On death and dying.* New York: Macmillan.

Kübler-Ross, E. (1974). *Questions and answers on death and dying.* New York: Macmillan.

Kwong See, S. T., Hoffman, H. G., & Wood, T. L. (2001). Perceptions of an old female eyewitness: Is the older eyewitness believable? *Psychology and Aging, 16,* 346–350.

Kyucharyants, V. (1974). Will the human life-span reach 100? *Gerontologist, 14, Part 1,* 377–380.

Labouvie-Vief, G. (1997). Cognitive-emotional integration in adulthood. In K. W. Schaie & M. P. Lawton (Eds.), *Annual review of gerontology and geriatrics* (Vol. 17, pp. 206–237). New York: Springer.

Labouvie-Vief, G. (1999). Emotions in adulthood. In V. L. Bengston & K. W. Schaie (Eds.), *Handbook of theories of aging* (pp. 253–267). New York: Springer.

Labouvie-Vief, G. (2003). Dynamic integration: Affect, cognition, and the self in adulthood. *Current Directions in Psychological Science, 12,* 201–206.

Labouvie-Vief, G., & Diehl, M. (2000). Cognitive complexity and cognitive-affective integration: Related or separate domains of adult development? *Psychology and Aging, 15,* 490–504.

Lachman, M. E. (2003). Negative interactions in close relationships: Introduction to a special section. *Journal of Gerontology: Psychological Sciences, 58B,* P69.

Lachman, M. E. (2006). Perceived control over age-related declines: Adaptive beliefs and behaviors. *Current Directions in Psychological Science, 15,* 282–286.

Lachman, M. E., & Andreoletti, C. (2006). Strategy use mediates the relationship between control beliefs and memory performance for middle-aged and older adults. *Journal of Gerontology: Psychological Sciences, 61B,* P88–P94.

Lachs, M. S., & Pillemer, K. (2004). Elder abuse. *Lancet, 364,* No. 9441, 1263–1272.

Lang, F. R., & Baltes, M. M. (1997). Being with people and being alone in late life: Costs and benefits for everyday functioning. *International Journal of Behavioral Development, 21,* 729–746.

Lang, F. R., Baltes, P. B., & Wagner, G. G. (2007). Desired lifetime and end-of-life desires across adulthood from 20 to 90: A dual-source information model. *Journal of Gerontology: Psychological Sciences, 62B,* P268–P276.

Lang, F. R., & Carstensen, L. L. (1994). Close emotional relationships in late life: Further support for proactive aging in the social domain. *Psychology and Aging, 9,* 315–324.

Lang, F. R., Staudinger, U. M., & Carstensen, L. L. (1998). Perspectives on socioemotional selectivity in late life: How personality and social context do (and do not) make a difference. *Journal of Gerontology: Psychological Sciences, 53B,* P21–P30.

Langer, E. J., & Rodin, J. (1976). The effects of choice and enhanced personal responsibility for the aged: A field experiment in an institutional setting. *Journal of Personality and Social Psychology, 34,* 191–198.

Lantz, M. S. (2006). Elder abuse and neglect. In R. Schulz (Ed.), *The encyclopedia of aging* (4th ed., pp. 352–354). New York: Springer.

La Rue, A., Dessonville, C., & Jarvik, L. F. (1985). Aging and mental disorders. In J. E. Birren and K. W. Schaie (Eds.), *Handbook of the psychology of aging* (2nd ed., pp. 664–702). New York: Van Nostrand Reinhold.

Lavelle, M. (1997, March 9) On the edge of age discrimination. *New York Times Magazine,* 66–69.

Lawton, M. P. (1989). Environmental proactivity in older people. In V. L. Bengston & K. W. Schaie (Eds.), *The course of later life: Research and reflections* (pp. 15–23). New York: Springer.

Lawton, M. P. (1999). Environmental design features and the well-being of older persons. In M. Duffy (Ed.), *Handbook of counseling and psychotherapy with older adults* (pp. 350–363). New York: John Wiley.

Lawton, M. P. (2001). Quality of life and the end of life. In J. E. Birren & K. W. Schaie (Eds.), *Handbook of the psychology of aging* (5th ed., pp. 592–616). San Diego: Academic Press.

Lawton, M. P., & Brody, E. M. (1969). Assessment of older people: Self-maintaining and instrumental activities of daily living. *Gerontologist, 9,* 179–186.

Lawton, M. P., Greenbaum, M., & Liebowitz, B. (1980). The lifespan of housing environments for the aging. *Gerontologist, 20,* 56–64.

Lawton, M. P., Kleban, M. H., Rajagopal, D., & Dean, J. (1992). Dimensions of affective experience in three age groups. *Psychology and Aging, 7,* 171–184.

Lawton, M. P., & Nahemow, L. (1973). Ecology and the aging process. In C. Eisdorfer and M. P. Lawton (Eds.), *The psychology of adult development and aging* (pp. 619–674). Washington, DC: American Psychological Association.

Lebowitz, B. D. (2006). Mental health services. In R. Schulz (Ed.), *The encyclopedia of aging* (4th ed., pp. 770–771). New York: Springer.

Lee, J. A., & Clemons, T. (1985). Factors affecting employment decisions about older workers. *Journal of Applied Psychology, 70,* 785–788.

Lehman, H. C. (1953). *Age and achievement.* Princeton, NJ: Princeton University Press.

Levenson, R. W., Carstensen, L. L., & Gottman, J. M. (1993). Long-term marriage: Age, gender, and satisfaction. *Psychology and Aging, 8,* 301–313.

Levinson, D. (1978). *The seasons of a man's life.* New York: Knopf.

Levitt, M. J., Weber, R. A., & Guacci, N. (1993). Convoys of social support: An intergenerational analysis. *Psychology and Aging, 8,* 323–326.

Levy, B. (1996). Improving memory in old age through implicit self-stereotyping. *Journal of Personality and Social Psychology, 71,* 1092–1107.

Levy, B., & Langer, E. (1994). Aging free from negative stereotypes: Successful memory in China and among the American deaf. *Journal of Personality and Social Psychology, 66,* 989–997.

Lichtenstein, M. J., Pruski, L. A., Marshall, C. E., Blalock, C. L., Liu, Y., & Plaetke, R. (2005). Do middle school students really have fixed images of elders? *Journal of Gerontology: Social Sciences, 60B,* S37–S47.

Light, L. L. (1991). Memory and aging: Four hypotheses in search of data. *Annual Review of Psychology, 42,* 333–376.

Lindenberger, U., & Baltes, P. B. (1994). Sensory functioning and intelligence in old age: A strong connection. *Psychology and Aging, 9,* 339–355.

Lindenberger, U., Scherer, H., & Baltes, P. B. (2001). The strong connection between sensory and cognitive performance in old age: Not due to sensory acuity reductions operating during cognitive assessment. *Psychology and Aging, 16,* 196–205.

Lisansky-Gomberg, E. S. (2000). Substance abuse disorders. In S. K. Whitbourne (Ed.), *Psychopathology in later adulthood* (pp. 277–298). New York: John Wiley.

Litwak, E., & Longino, C. F., Jr. (1987). Migration patterns among the elderly: A developmental perspective. *Gerontologist, 27,* 266–272.

Liu, L. L., & Park, D. C. (2004). Aging and medical adherence: The use of automatic processes to achieve effortful things. *Psychology and Aging, 19,* 318–325.

Löckenhoff, C. E., & Carstensen, L. L. (2007). Age, emotion, and health-related decision strategies: Motivational manipulations can reduce age differences. *Psychology and Aging, 22,* 134–146.

Longino, C. F., Jr. (2003). Socio-physical environments at the macro level: The impact of population migration. In H. W. Wahl, R. J. Scheidt, and P. G. Windley (Eds.), *Annual review of gerontology and geriatrics* (Vol. 23, pp. 110–129). New York: Springer.

Lopata, H. Z. (1995). Widowhood. In G. L. Maddox (Ed.), *The encyclopedia of aging* (2nd ed., pp. 969–971). New York: Springer.

Lövdén, M., & Lindenberger, U. (2007). Intelligence. In J. E. Birren (Ed.), *Encyclopedia of gerontology: Age, aging, and the aged* (2nd ed., Vol. 1, pp. 763–770). Boston: Elsevier Academic Press.

Lovelace, E. A., & Twohig, P. T. (1990). Healthy older adults' perceptions of their memory functioning and use of mnemonics. *Bulletin of the Psychonomic Society, 28,* 115–118.

Lubart, T. I. & Sternberg, R. J. (1998). Life span creativity: An investment theory approach. In C. E. Adams-Price (Ed.), *Creativity and successful aging: Theoretical and empirical approaches* (pp. 21–41). New York: Springer.

Lund, D. A. (2007). Bereavement and loss. In J. E. Birren (Ed.), *Encyclopedia of gerontology: Age, aging, and the aged* (2nd ed., Vol. 1, pp. 160–170). Boston: Elsevier Academic Press.

Madden, D. J., & Allen, P. A. (1996). Attention. In J. E. Birren (Ed.), *Encyclopedia of gerontology: Age, aging, and the aged* (Vol. 1, pp. 131–140). San Diego: Academic Press.

Madden, D. J., Blumenthal, J. A., Allen, P. A., & Emery, C. F. (1989). Improving aerobic capacity in healthy older adults does not necessarily lead to improved cognitive performance. *Psychology and Aging, 4,* 307–320.

Magai, C., & Passman, V. (1997). The interpersonal basis of emotional behavior and emotion regulation in adulthood. In K. W. Schaie & M. P. Lawton (Eds.), *Annual review of gerontology and geriatrics* (Vol. 17, pp. 104–137). New York: Springer.

Maier, H., & Smith, J. (1999). Psychological predictors of mortality in old age. *Journal of Gerontology: Psychological Sciences, 54B*, P44–P54.

Mancini, A. D., & Bonanno, G. A. (2006). Marital closeness, functional disability, and adjustment in late life. *Psychology and Aging, 21*, 600–610.

Mancini, J. A., & Bleiszner, R. (1989). Aging parents and adult children: Research themes in intergenerational relations. *Journal of Marriage and the Family, 51*, 275–290.

Markus, H. R., & Herzog, A. R. (1991). The role of the self-concept in aging. In K. W. Schaie & M. P. Lawton (Eds.), *Annual review of gerontology and geriatrics* (Vol. 11, pp. 110–143). New York: Springer.

Marsiske, M., Klumb, P., & Baltes, M. M. (1997). Everyday activity patterns and sensory functioning in old age. *Psychology and Aging, 12*, 444–457.

Marsiske, M., & Margrett, J. A. (2006). Everyday problem solving and decision making. In J. E. Birren (Ed.), *Handbook of the psychology of aging* (6th ed., pp. 315–342). Boston: Elsevier Academic Press.

Marsiske, M., & Willis, S. L. (1995). Dimensionality of everyday problem solving in older adults. *Psychology and Aging, 10*, 269–283.

Martin, G. M. (2007). Premature aging. In J. E. Birren (Ed.), *Encyclopedia of gerontology: Age, aging, and the aged* (2nd ed., Vol. 2, pp. 379–384). Boston: Elsevier Academic Press.

Martin, L. G., Schoeni, R. F., Freedman, V. A., & Andreski, P. (2007). Feeling better? Trends in general health status. *Journal of Gerontology: Social Sciences, 62B*, S11–S21.

Martin, P., Bishop, A., Poon, L., & Johnson, M. A. (2006). Influence of personality and health behaviors on fatigue in late and very late life. *Journals of Gerontology: Psychological Sciences, 61B*, P161–P166.

Martin-Matthews, A. (1996). Widowhood and widowerhood. In J. E. Birren (Ed.), *Encyclopedia of gerontology: Age, aging, and the aged* (Vol. 2, pp. 621–625). San Diego: Academic Press.

Marx, J. I., Solomon, J. C., & Miller, L. Q. (2004). Gift wrapping ourselves: The final gift exchange. *Journal of Gerontology: Social Sciences, 59B*, S274–S280.

Masoro, E. J. (2006a). Are age-associated diseases an integral part of aging? In E. J. Masoro & S. N. Austad (Eds.), *Handbook of the biology of aging* (6th ed., pp. 43–62). Boston: Elsevier Academic Press.

Masoro, E. J. (2006b). Body composition. In R. Schulz (Ed.), *The encyclopedia of aging* (4th ed., pp. 142–144). New York: Springer.

May, C. P., Hasher, L., & Foong, N. (2005). Implicit memory, age, and time of day. *Psychological Science, 16*, 96–100.

McAdams, D. P. (1996). Narrating the self in adulthood. In J. E. Birren, G. M. Kenyon, J. E. Ruth, J. J. F. Schroots, & T. Svensson (Eds.), *Aging and biography: Explorations in adult development* (pp. 131–148). New York: Springer.

McAdams, D. P., de St. Aubin, E., & Logan, R. L. (1993). Generativity among young, midlife, and older adults. *Psychology and Aging, 8*, 221–230.

McAdams, D. P., & Pals, J. L. (2006). A new big five. *American Psychologist, 61*, 204–217.

McAuley, E., Konopack, J. F., Morris, K. S., Motl, R. W., Hu, L., Doerksen, S. E., et al. (2007). Physical activity and functional limitations in older women: Influence of self-efficacy. *Journal of Gerontology: Psychological Sciences, 61B*, P270–P277.

McCann, R., & Giles, H. (2002). Ageism in the workplace: A communication perspective. In T. D. Nelson (Ed.), *Ageism: Stereotyping and prejudice against older persons* (pp. 163–199). Cambridge, MA: MIT Press.

McCay, C. M., Crowell, M. F., & Maynard, L. A. (1935). The effect of retarded growth upon the length of life span and upon the ultimate body size. *Journal of Nutrition, 10*, 63–79.

McCrae, R. R. (2002). The maturation of personality psychology: Adult personality development and psychological well-being. *Journal of Research in Personality, 36*, 307–317.

McCrae, R. R. (2006). Self-concept. In R. Schulz (Ed.), *The encyclopedia of aging* (4th ed., pp. 1054–1055). New York: Springer.

McCrae, R. R., & Costa, P. T., Jr. (1982). Aging, the life course, and models of personality. In T. M. Field, A. Huston, H. C. Quay, L. Troll, & G. E. Finley (Eds.), *Review of Human Development* (pp. 602–613). New York: John Wiley.

McCrae, R. R., & Costa, P. T., Jr. (1991). Adding Liebe und Arbeit: The full five-factor model and well-being. *Personality and Social Psychology Bulletin, 17,* 227–232.

McCrae, R. R., & Costa, P. T., Jr. (1997). Personality trait structure as a human universal. *American Psychologist, 52,* 509–516.

McCrae, R. R., Costa, P. T., Jr., de Lima, M. P., Simoes, A., Ostendorf, F., Angleitner, A., et al. (1999). Age differences in personality across the adult life span: Parallels in five cultures. *Developmental Psychology, 35,* 466–477.

McDonald, L. (2007). Abuse and neglect of elders. In J. E. Birren (Ed.), *Encyclopedia of gerontology: Age, aging, and the aged* (2nd ed., Vol. 1, pp. 1–9). Boston: Elsevier Academic Press.

McDowd, J. M. (1997). Inhibition in attention and aging. *Journal of Gerontology: Psychological Sciences, 52B,* P265–P273.

McDowd, J. M., & Shaw, R. J. (2000). Attention and aging: A functional perspective. In F. I. M. Craik & T. A. Salthouse (Eds.), *The handbook of aging and cognition* (2nd ed., pp. 221–292). Mahwah, NJ: Erlbaum.

McEvoy, G. M., & Cascio, W. F. (1989). Cumulative evidence of the relationship between employee age and job performance. *Journal of Applied Psychology, 74,* 11–17.

McGraw, L. A., & Walker, A. J. (2004). Negotiating care: Ties between aging mothers and their caregiving daughters. *Journal of Gerontology: Social Sciences, 59B,* S324–S332.

McKnight, A. J., & McKnight, A. S. (1993). The effect of cellular phone use upon driver attention. *Accident Analysis and Prevention, 25,* 259–265.

McNamara, C. (2006). Diabetes. In R. Schulz (Ed.), *The encyclopedia of aging* (4th ed., pp. 312–316). New York: Springer.

Medvedev, Z. A. (1974). Caucasus and Altay longevity: A biological or social problem? *Gerontologist, 14, Part 1,* 381–387.

Meeks, S. (2000). Schizophrenia and related disorders. In S. K. Whitbourne (Ed.), *Psychopathology in later adulthood* (pp. 189–215). New York: John Wiley.

Menec, V. H., Chipperfield, J. G., & Perry, R. P. (1999). Self-perceptions of health: A prospective analysis of mortality, control, and health. *Journal of Gerontology: Psychological Sciences, 54B,* P85–P93.

Mermin, G. B. T., Johnson, R. W., & Murphy, D. P. (2007). Why do boomers plan to work longer? *Journal of Gerontology: Social Sciences, 62B,* S286–S294.

Meyer, B. J. F., Russo, C., & Talbot, A. (1995). Discourse comprehension and problem solving: Decisions about the treatment of breast cancer by women across the life-span. *Psychology and Aging, 10,* 84–103.

Meyer, B. J. F., Talbot, A. P., & Ranalli, C. (2007). Why older adults make more immediate treatment decisions about cancer than younger adults. *Psychology and Aging, 22,* 505–524.

Miller, G. A. (1956). The magic number seven plus or minus two: Some limits on our capacity for processing information. *Psychological Review, 63,* 81–97.

Miller, R. B. (2006). Divorce. In R. Schulz (Ed.), *The encyclopedia of aging* (4th ed., pp. 327–329). New York: Springer.

Mishkin, B., Mezey, M., & Ramsey, G. (1995). Advance directives in health care: Living wills and durable power of attorney. In G. L. Maddox (Ed.), *The encyclopedia of aging* (2nd ed., pp. 26–28). New York: Springer.

Mitty, E. L. (2006). Nursing Homes. In R. Schulz (Ed.), *The encyclopedia of aging* (4th ed., pp. 842–853). New York: Springer.

Moen, P. (1996). Gender, age, and the life course. In R. H. Binstock & L. K. George (Eds.), *Handbook of aging and the social sciences* (4th ed., pp. 171–187). San Diego: Academic Press.

Monroe, S. M., & Simons, A. D. (1991). Diathesis–stress theories in the context of life stress research: Implications for depressive disorders. *Psychological Bulletin, 110,* 406–425.

Montepare, J. M., & Lachman, M. E. (1989). "You're only as old as you feel": Self-perceptions of age, fears of aging, and life satisfaction from adolescence to old age. *Psychology and Aging, 4,* 73–78.

Morrell, R. W., Park, D. C., Kidder, D. P., & Martin, M. (1997). Adherence to antihypertensive medications across the life span. *Gerontologist, 37,* 609–619.

Morrow-Howell, N. (2006). Volunteerism. In R. Schulz (Ed.), *The encyclopedia of aging* (4th ed., pp. 1217–1219). New York: Springer.

Moye, J., & Marson, D. C. (2007). Assessment of decision-making capacity in older adults: An emerging area of practice and research. *Journal of Gerontology: Psychological Sciences, 62B,* P3–P11.

Moyers, P. A. (2006). Older workers. In R. Schulz (Ed.), *The encyclopedia of aging* (4th ed., pp. 870–872). New York: Springer.

Mroczek, D. K., Hurt, S. W., & Berman, W. H. (1999). Conceptual and methodological issues in the assessment of personality disorders in older adults. In E. Rosowsky, R. C. Abrams, & R. A. Zweig (Eds.), *Personality disorders in older adults: Emerging issues in diagnosis and treatment* (pp. 135–150). Mahwah, NJ: Erlbaum.

Mroczek, D. K., & Kolarz, C. M. (1998). The effect of age on positive and negative affect: A developmental perspective on happiness. *Journal of Personality and Social Psychology, 75,* 1333–1349.

Mroczek, D. K., Spiro, A., III, & Griffin, P. W. (2006). Personality and aging. In J. E. Birren & K. W. Schaie (Eds.), *Handbook of the psychology of aging* (6th ed., pp. 363–377). Boston: Elsevier Academic Press.

Murphy, M. D., Sanders, R. E., Gabriesheski, A. A., & Schmitt, F. A. (1981). Metamemory in the aged. *Journal of Gerontology, 25,* 268–274.

Myers, G. C. (1990). Demography of aging. In R. H. Binstock & L. K. George (Eds.), *Handbook of aging and the social sciences* (3rd ed., pp. 19–44). San Diego: Academic Press.

Myers, G. C., & Eggers, M. L. (1996). Demography. In J. E. Birren (Ed.), *Encyclopedia of gerontology: Age, aging, and the aged* (Vol. 1, pp. 405–413). San Diego: Academic Press.

National Academy on an Aging Society (1999, December). *Hearing Loss.* No. 2.

National Academy on an Aging Society (2000, April). *Diabetes.* No. 6.

National Center for Health Statistics (2007, November 20). *National Vital Statistics Report,* Vol. 56, No. 5. Retrieved from http://www.cdc.gov/nchs/data

National Institute on Aging (NIA) (2005–2006). *Progress report on Alzheimer's disease.* Retrieved November 14, 2007, from http://www/nia.nih.gov/Alzheimers/Publications/ADProgress2005_2006

National Institutes of Health (2005, March 16). Obesity threatens to cut U.S. life expectancy. *NIH News.* Retrieved September 20, 2007, from http://www.nih.gov/news/pr/mar2005/nia-16.htm

Neimeyer, R. A., & Fortner, B. (2006). Death anxiety. In R. Schulz (Ed.), *The encyclopedia of aging* (4th ed., pp. 283–284). New York: Springer.

Neugarten, B. L. (1977). Personality and aging. In J. E. Birren & K. W. Schaie (Eds.), *Handbook of the psychology of aging* (pp. 626–649). New York: Van Nostrand Reinhold.

Newson, R. S., & Kemps, E. B. (2005). General lifestyle activities as a predictor of current cognition and cognitive change in older adults: A cross-sectional and longitudinal examination. *Journal of Gerontology: Psychological Sciences, 60B,* P113–P120.

Newton, N. A., & Lazarus, L. W. (1992). Behavioral and psychotherapeutic interventions. In J. E. Birren, R. B. Sloane, & G. D. Cohen (Eds.), *Handbook of mental health and aging* (2nd ed., pp. 699–719). San Diego: Academic Press.

Nichols, N. R. (2006). Stress theory of aging. In R. Schulz (Ed.), *The encyclopedia of aging* (4th ed., pp. 1142–1145). New York: Springer.

Norris, J. E., & Tindale, J. A. (1994). *Among generations: The cycle of adult relationships.* New York: W. H. Freeman.

O'Connor, B. P., & Rigby, H. (1996). Perceptions of baby talk, frequency of receiving baby talk, and self-esteem among community and nursing home residents. *Psychology and Aging, 11,* 147–154.

Olshansky, S. J., Carnes, B. A., & Grahn, D. (1998). Confronting the boundaries of human longevity. *American Scientist, 86,* 52–61.

Olshansky, S. J., Hayflick, L., & Carnes, B. A. (2002). No truth to the fountain of youth. *Scientific American, 286,* 92–95.

Olshansky, S. J., Hayflick, L., & Perls, T. T. (2004). Anti-aging medicine: The hype and the reality – Part II. *Journal of Gerontology: Biological Sciences, 59A,* 649–651.

Packard, E. (2007). Polishing those golden years. *Monitor on Psychology, 38,* 34–35.

Palloni, A., & Arias, E. (2004). Paradox lost: Explaining the Hispanic adult mortality advantage. *Demography, 41,* 385–415.

Palmore, E. (2001). The ageism survey: First findings. *Gerontologist, 41,* 572–575.

Panek, P. E. (1997). The older worker. In A. D. Fisk & W. A. Rogers (Eds.), *The handbook of human factors and the older adult* (pp. 363–394). San Diego: Academic Press.

Parmelee, P. A. (2007). Depression. In J. E. Birren (Ed.), *Encyclopedia of gerontology: Age, aging, and the aged* (2nd ed., Vol. 1, pp. 400–409). Boston: Elsevier Academic Press.

Passuth, P. M., & Bengston, V. L. (1988). Sociological theories of aging: Current perspectives and future directions. In J. E. Birren & V. L. Bengston (Eds.), *Emergent theories of aging* (pp. 333–355). New York: Springer.

Peck, R. C. (1968). Psychological developments in the second half of life. In B. L. Neugarten (Ed.), *Middle age and aging* (pp. 88–92). Chicago: University of Chicago Press.

Peng, K., & Nisbett, R. E. (1999). Culture, dialectics, and reasoning about contradiction. *American Psychologist, 54,* 741–755.

Perdue, C. W., & Gurtman, M. B. (1990). Evidence for the automaticity of ageism. *Journal of Experimental Social Psychology, 11,* 177–186.

Perls, T. T. (2004a). Anti-aging quackery: Human growth hormone and tricks of the trade – more dangerous than ever. *Journal of Gerontology: Biological Sciences, 59A,* 682–691.

Perls, T. T. (2004b). The oldest old. *Scientific American: The science of staying young* [special edition], *14,* 6–11.

Perls, T., & Silver, M. H. (1999, November/December). Will you live to be 100? *Modern Maturity.*

Perry, E. L., Kulik, C. T., & Bourhis, A. C. (1996). Moderating effects of personal and contextual factors in age discrimination. *Journal of Applied Psychology, 81,* 628–647.

Phelan, J. T. (2006). Evolutionary theory. In R. Schulz (Ed.), *The encyclopedia of aging* (4th ed., pp. 394–396). New York: Springer.

Piaget, J. (1952). *The origins of intelligence in children.* New York: International Universities Press.

Pillemer, K., & Bachman-Prehn, R. (1991). Helping and hurting: Predictors of maltreatment of patients in nursing homes. *Research on Aging, 13,* 74–95.

Pillemer, K., & Moore, D. (1989). Abuse of patients in nursing homes: Findings from a survey of the staff. *Gerontologist, 29,* 314–320.

Pillemer, K., & Suitor, J. J. (1992). Violence and violent feelings: What causes them among family caregivers? *Journal of Gerontology: Social Sciences, 47,* S165–S172.

Poon, L. W., Sweaney, A. L., Clayton, G. M., & Merriam, S. B. (1992). The Georgia Centenarian Study. *International Journal of Aging and Human Development, 34,* 1–17.

Population Reference Bureau (2007). *World population data sheet.* Retrieved October 30, 2007 from http://www.prb.org/pdf07/07wpds-Eng.pdf

Pratt, M. W., Diessner, R., Pratt, A., Hunsberger, B., & Pancer, S. M. (1996). Moral and social reasoning and perspective taking in later life: A longitudinal study. *Psychology and Aging, 11,* 66–73.

Pratt, M. W., & Norris, J. E. (1994). *The social psychology of aging: A cognitive perspective.* Cambridge, MA: Blackwell.

A Profile of Older Americans (1996). Document PF3049 (1296). Washington, DC: American Association of Retired Persons.

A Profile of Older Americans (2007). Administration on Aging (AoA), U.S. Department of Health and Human Services. Retrieved February 25, 2009, from http://www.aoa.gov/prof/Statistics/profile/2007/2007profile.pdf

Puder, R., Lacks, P., Bertelson, A. D., & Storandt, M. (1983). Short-term stimulus control treatment of insomnia in older adults. *Behavior Therapy, 14,* 424–429.

Pushkar, D., Etezadi, J., Andres, D., Arbuckle, T., Schwartzman, A. E., & Chaikelson, J. (1999). Models of intelligence in late life: Comment on Hultsch et al. (1999). *Psychology and Aging, 14,* 520–527.

Pynoos, J., & Golant, S. (1996). Housing and living arrangements for the elderly. In R. H. Binstock & L. K. George (Eds.), *Handbook of aging and the social sciences* (4th ed., pp. 303–324). San Diego: Academic Press.

Quadagno, J. (2008). *Aging and the life course: An introduction to social gerontology* (4th ed.). Boston: McGraw-Hill.

Quadagno, J., & Hardy, J. (1996). Work and retirement. In R. H. Binstock & L. K. George (Eds.), *Handbook of aging and the social sciences* (4th ed., pp. 325–345). San Diego: Academic Press.

Qualls, S. H., & Smyer, M. A. (2006). Mental health. In R. Schulz (Ed.), *The encyclopedia of aging* (4th ed., pp. 767–770). New York: Springer.

Quinn, M. J. (1995). Elder abuse and neglect. In G. L. Maddox (Ed.), *The Encyclopedia of Aging* (2nd ed., pp. 304–306). New York: Springer.

Raz, N. (2007). Comment on Greenwood (2007): Which side of plasticity? *Neuropsychology, 21*, 676–677.

Raz, N., & Rodrigue, K. M. (2006). Differential aging of the brain: Patterns, cognitive correlates and modifiers. *Neuroscience and Behavioral Reviews, 30*, 730–748.

Reitzes, D. C., Mutran, E. J., & Fernandez, M. E. (1996). Does retirement hurt well-being? Factors influencing self-esteem and depression among retirees and workers. *Gerontologist, 36*, 649–656.

Reitzes, D. C., Mutran, E. J., and Fernandez, M. E. (1998). The decision to retire: A career perspective. *Social Science Quarterly, 79*, 607–619.

Rendell, P. G., & Thomson, D. M. (1999). Aging and prospective memory: Differences between naturalistic and laboratory tasks. *Journal of Gerontology: Psychological Sciences, 54B*, P256–P269.

Reuter-Lorenz, P. A., & Cappell, K. A. (2008). Neurocognitive aging and the compensation hypothesis. *Current Directions in Psychological Science, 17*, 177–182.

Revenson, T. A. (1989). Compassionate stereotyping of elderly patients by physicians: Revisiting the social contact hypothesis. *Psychology and Aging, 4*, 230–234.

Rhee, C., & Gatz, M. (1993). Cross-generational attributions concerning locus of control beliefs. *International Journal of Aging and Human Development, 37*, 153–161.

Ribot, T. (1882). *Diseases of memory*. New York: Appleton.

Richman, L. (1969). Sensory training for geriatric patients. *American Journal of Occupational Therapy, 23*, 254–257.

Riggs, K. M., Lachman, M. E., & Wingfield, A. (1997). Taking charge of remembering: Locus of control and older adults' memory for speech. *Experimental Aging Research, 23*, 237–256.

Riley, M. W. (1994). Aging and society: Past, present, and future. *Gerontologist, 34*, 436–446.

Roberts, B. W., & DelVecchio, W. F. (2000). The rank-order consistency of personality traits from childhood to old age: A quantitative review of longitudinal studies. *Psychological Bulletin, 126*, 3–25.

Roberts, J. C. (1995). Eye: Structure and function. In G. L. Maddox (Ed.), *The encyclopedia of aging* (2nd ed., pp. 354–359). New York: Springer.

Rockwood, K. (2006). Vascular cognitive impairment. In R. Schulz (Ed.), *The encyclopedia of aging* (4th ed., pp. 1208–1210). New York: Springer.

Rodin, J., & Langer, E. (1980). Aging labels: The decline of control and the fall of self-esteem. *Journal of Social Issues, 36*, 12–29.

Roediger, H. L., & McDermott, K. B. (1995). Creating false memories: Remembering words not presented in lists. *Journal of Experimental Psychology: Learning, Memory, and Cognition, 21*, 803–814.

Roff, L. L., Burgio, L. D., Gitlin, L., Nichols, L., Chaplin, W., & Hardin, J. M. (2004). Positive aspects of Alzheimer's caregiving: The role of race. *Journal of Gerontology: Psychological Sciences, 59B*, P185–P190.

Rogers, W. A. (1997). Individual differences, aging, and human factors: An overview. In F. D. Fisk and W. A. Rogers (Eds.), *Handbook of human factors and the older adult* (pp. 151–170). San Diego: Academic Press.

Rogers, W. A., & Fisk, A. D. (2001). Understanding the role of attention in cognitive aging research.

In J. E. Birren & K. W. Schaie (Eds.), *Handbook of the psychology of aging* (5th ed., pp. 267–287). San Diego: Academic Press.

Rollins, B. C., & Feldman, H. (1970). Marital satisfaction over the family life cycle. *Journal of Marriage and the Family, 32*, 20–28.

Rook, K. S. (1984). The negative side of social interaction: Impact on psychological well-being. *Journal of Personality and Social Psychology, 46*, 1097–1108.

Rook, K. S. (1987). Reciprocity of social exchange and social satisfaction among older women. *Journal of Personality and Social Psychology, 52*, 145–154.

Rook, K. S. (1997). Positive and negative social exchanges: Weighing their effects in later life. *Journal of Gerontology: Social Sciences, 52B*, S167–S169.

Ross, L. (1977). The intuitive psychologist and his shortcomings: Distortions in the attribution process. In L. Berkowitz (Ed.), *Advances in experimental social psychology* (Vol. 10, pp. 173–220). New York: Academic Press.

Roth, D. L., Haley, W. E., Owen, J. E., Clay, O. J., & Goode, K. T. (2001). Latent growth models of the longitudinal effects of dementia caregiving: A comparison of African American and White family caregivers. *Psychology and Aging, 16*, 427–436.

Rotter, J. B. (1966). Generalized expectancies for internal versus external control of reinforcement. *Psychological Monographs, 80* (Whole No. 609).

Rowe, J. W., & Kahn, R. L. (1998). *Successful aging*. New York: Pantheon Books.

Rowles, G. D., & Ravdal, H. (2002). Aging, place, and meaning in the face of changing circumstances. In R. S. Weiss & S. A. Bass (Eds.), *Challenges of the third age: Meaning and purpose in later life* (pp. 81–114). New York: Oxford University Press.

Rubin, D. C., Rahhal, T. A., & Poon, L. W. (1998). Things learned in early adulthood are remembered best. *Memory and Cognition, 26*, 3–19.

Ruth, J.-E. (2007). Personality. In J. E. Birren (Ed.), *Encyclopedia of gerontology: Age, aging, and the aged* (2nd ed., Vol. 2, pp. 342–354). Boston: Elsevier Academic Press.

Ryan, E. B. (1992). Beliefs about memory changes across the adult life span. *Journal of Gerontology: Psychological Sciences, 47*, P41–P46.

Ryan, E. B., Anas, A. P., & Gruneir, A. J. S. (2006). Evaluations of overhelping and underhelping communication. *Journal of Language and Social Psychology, 25*, 97–107.

Ryan, E. B., Bourhis, R. Y., & Knops, U. (1991). Evaluative perceptions of patronizing speech addressed to elders. *Psychology and Aging, 6*, 442–450.

Ryan, E. B., Hamilton, J. M., & Kwong See, S. (1994). Patronizing the old: How do younger and older adults respond to baby talk in the nursing home? *International Journal of Aging and Human Development, 39*, 21–32.

Ryan, E. B., Hummert, M. L., & Anas, A. P. (1997, November). *The impact of old age and hearing impairment on first impressions*. Paper presented at the Gerontological Society of America Convention, Cincinnati, Ohio.

Ryan, E. B., Hummert, M. L., & Boich, L. H. (1995) Communication predicaments of aging: Patronizing behavior toward older adults. *Journal of Language and Social Psychology, 14*, 144–166.

Ryan, E. B., & Kwong See, S. (1993). Age-based beliefs about memory changes for self and others across adulthood. *Journal of Gerontology: Psychological Sciences, 48*, P199–P201.

Rybash, J. M., Hoyer, W. J., & Roodin, P. A. (1986). *Adult cognition and aging: Developmental changes in processing, knowing, and thinking*. New York: Pergamon Press.

Ryff, C. D. (1989). Happiness is everything, or is it? Explorations on the meaning of psychological well-being. *Journal of Personality and Social Psychology, 57*, 1069–1081.

Ryff, C. D., Kwan, D. M. L., & Singer, B. H. (2001). Personality and aging: Flourishing agendas and future challenges. In J. E. Birren & K. W. Schaie (Eds.), *Handbook of the psychology of aging* (5th ed., pp. 477–499). San Diego: Academic Press.

Salthouse, T. A. (1982). *Adult cognition: An experimental psychology of human aging*. New York: Springer.

Salthouse, T. A. (1984). Effects of age and skill in typing. *Journal of Experimental Psychology: General, 113*, 345–371.

Salthouse, T. A. (1990). Cognitive competence and expertise in aging. In J. E. Birren, & K. W. Schaie (Eds.), *Handbook of the psychology of aging* (3rd ed., pp. 310–319). San Diego: Academic Press.

Salthouse, T. A. (1991). *Theoretical perspectives on cognitive aging.* Hillsdale, NJ: Erlbaum.

Salthouse, T. A. (1996). The processing-speed theory of adult age differences in cognition. *Psychological Review, 103,* 403–428.

Salthouse, T. A. (2004). What and when of cognitive aging. *Current Directions in Psychological Science, 13,* 140–144.

Salthouse, T. A. (2006). Mental exercise and mental aging. *Perspectives on Psychological Science, 1,* 68–87.

Salthouse, T. A. (2007a). Comment on Greenwood (2007): Functional plasticity in cognitive aging. *Neuropsychology, 21,* 678–679.

Salthouse, T. A. (2007b). Reaction time. In J. E. Birren (Ed.), *Encyclopedia of gerontology: Age, aging, and the aged* (2nd ed., Vol. 2, pp. 407–410). Boston: Elsevier Academic Press.

Salthouse, T. A. (2007c). Reply to Schooler: Consistent is not conclusive. *Perspectives on Psychological Science, 2,* 30–32.

Salthouse, T. A., & Maurer, T. J. (1996). Aging, job performance, and career development. In J. E. Birren, & K. W. Schaie (Eds.), *Handbook of the psychology of aging* (4th ed., pp. 353–364). San Diego: Academic Press.

Schacter, D. L. (1987). Memory, amnesia, and frontal lobe dysfunction. *Psychobiology, 15,* 21–36.

Schaie, K. W. (1965). A general model for the study of developmental problems. *Psychological Bulletin, 64,* 92–107.

Schaie, K. W. (1977–1978). Toward a stage theory of adult cognitive development. *Aging and Human Development, 8,* 129–138.

Schaie, K. W. (1989). The hazards of cognitive aging. *Gerontologist, 29,* 484–493.

Schaie, K. W. (1994). The course of adult intellectual development. *American Psychologist, 49,* 304–313.

Schaie, K. W. (1995). Research methods in gerontology. In G. L. Maddox (Ed.), *The encyclopedia of aging* (2nd ed., pp. 812–815). New York: Springer.

Schaie, K. W. (1996). Intellectual development in adulthood. In J. E. Birren, & K. W. Schaie (Eds.), *Handbook of the psychology of aging* (4th ed., pp. 266–286). San Diego: Academic Press.

Schaie, K. W. (2006). Intelligence. In R. Schulz (Ed.), *The encyclopedia of aging* (4th ed., pp. 600–602). New York: Springer.

Schaie, K. W., & Willis, S. L. (1996). Psychometric intelligence. In F. Blancard-Fields & T. M. Hess (Eds.), *Perspectives on cognitive change in adulthood and aging* (pp. 293–322). New York: McGraw-Hill.

Schaie, K. W., & Willis, S. L. (1999). Theories of everyday competence and aging. In V. L. Bengston & K. W. Schaie (Eds.), *Handbook of theories of aging* (pp. 174–195). New York: Springer.

Schaie, K. W., & Willis, S. L. (2000). A stage theory model of adult cognitive development revisited. In R. L. Rubinstein, M. Moss, & M. H. Kleban (Eds.), *The many dimensions of aging* (pp. 175–193). New York: Springer.

Schiamberg, L. B., & Gans, D. (2000). Elder abuse by adult children: An applied ecological framework for understanding contextual risk factors and the intergenerational character of quality of life. *International Journal of Aging and Human Development, 50,* 329–359.

Schiffman, S. (1996). Smell and taste. In J. E. Birren (Ed.), *Encyclopedia of gerontology: Age, aging, and the aged* (Vol. 2, pp. 497–504). San Diego: Academic Press.

Schneck, M. K., Reisberg, B., & Ferris, S. H. (1982). An overview of current concepts of Alzheimer's disease. *American Journal of Psychiatry, 139,* 165–173.

Schneider, B. A., & Pichora-Fuller, M. K. (2000). Implications of perceptual deterioration for cognitive aging research. In F. I. M. Craik & T. A. Salthouse (Eds.), *The handbook of aging and cognition* (2nd ed., pp. 155–219). Mahwah, NJ: Erlbaum.

Schneider, E. L. (1997). Will future elderly persons experience more years of disability? Yes. In A. E. Scharlach & L. W. Kaye (Eds.), *Controversial issues in aging* (pp. 210–212). Boston: Allyn & Bacon.

Schneider, L. S. (1995). Efficacy of clinical treatment for mental disorders among older persons. In M. Gatz (Ed.), *Emerging issues in mental health and aging* (pp. 19–71). Washington, DC: American Psychological Association.

Schone, B. S., & Weinick, R. M. (1998). Health-related behaviors and the benefits of marriage for elderly persons. *Gerontologist, 38*, 618–627.

Schooler, C. (2007). Use it – and keep it, longer, probably. *Perspectives on Psychological Science, 2*, 24–29.

Schooler, C., & Mulatu, M. S. (2001). The reciprocal effects of leisure time activities and intellectual functioning in older people: A longitudinal analysis. *Psychology and Aging, 16*, 466–482.

Schroots, J. J. F. (1996). Theories of aging: Psychological. In J. E. Birren (Ed.), *Encyclopedia of gerontology: Age, aging and the aged* (Vol. 2, pp. 557–567). San Diego: Academic Press.

Schulz, R. (1976). The effects of control and predictability on the psychological and physical well-being of the institutionalized aged. *Journal of Personality and Social Psychology, 33*, 563–573.

Schulz, R. (1994). Introduction: Debate on generalized theories of slowing. *Journal of Gerontology: Psychological Sciences, 49*, P59.

Schulz, R., & Hanusa, B. H. (1980). Experimental social gerontology: A social psychological perspective. *Journal of Social Issues, 36*, 30–46.

Schulz, R., & Heckhausen, J. (1996). A life span model of successful aging. *American Psychologist, 51*, 702–714.

Schulz, R., & Salthouse, T. (1999). *Adult development and aging: Myths and emerging realities* (3rd ed.). Upper Saddle River, NJ: Prentice Hall.

Schwenk, M. A. (1979). Reality orientation for institutionalized aged: Does it help? *Gerontologist, 19*, 373–377.

Segall, M. H., Dasen, P. R., Berry, J. W., & Poortinga, Y. H. (1999). *Human behavior in global perspective: An introduction to cross-cultural psychology* (2nd ed.). Boston: Allyn & Bacon.

Seligman, M. E. P., & Csikszentmihalyi, M. (2000). Positive psychology: An introduction. *American Psychologist, 55*, 5–14.

Shanas, E. (1979). Social myth as hypothesis: The case of the family relations of old people. *Gerontologist, 19*, 3–9.

Sharit, J., Czaja, S. J., Hernandez, M., Yang, Y., Perdomo, D., Lewis, J. E., et al. (2004). An evaluation of performance by older persons on a simulated telecommunicating task. *Journal of Gerontology: Psychological Sciences, 59B*, P305–P316.

Sharps, M. J., Price-Sharps, J. L., & Hanson, J. (1998). Attitudes of young adults toward older adults: Evidence from the United States and Thailand. *Educational Gerontology, 24*, 655–660.

Siegel, J. M. (1993). Companion animals: In sickness and in health. *Journal of Social Issues, 49*, 157–167.

Siegler, I. C. (1995). Functional age. In G. L. Maddox (Ed.), *The encyclopedia of aging* (2nd ed., p. 385). New York: Springer.

Siegler, I. C., & Botwinick, J. (1979). A long-term longitudinal study of intellectual ability of older adults: The matter of selective subject attrition. *Journal of Gerontology, 34*, 242–245.

Sigelman, C. K., & Rider, E. A. (2003). Life-span human development: An integrated topical/chronological approach (4th ed.). Belmont, CA: Wadsworth/Thomson Learning.

Silver, J. H., Bubrick, E., Jilinskaia, E., & Perls, T. T. (1998). *Is there a centenarian personality?* Paper presented at the 106th Annual Convention of the American Psychological Association, San Francisco, CA.

Silverstein, M. (2006). Intergenerational family transfers in social context. In R. H. Binstock & L. K. George (Eds.), *Handbook of aging and the social sciences* (6th ed., pp. 165–180). Boston: Elsevier Academic Press.

Silverstein, M., Gans, D., & Yang, F. M. (2006). Intergenerational support to aging parents: The role of norms and needs. *Journal of Family Issues, 27*, 1068–1084.

Silverstein, M., & Zablotsky, D. L. (1996). Health and social precursors of later life retirement-community migration. *Journal of Gerontology: Social Sciences, 51B*, S150–S156.

Simon, H. B. (2004). Longevity: The ultimate gender gap [special edition]. *Scientific American, 14*(3), 19–23.

Simonton, D. K. (1990). Creativity in the later years: Optimistic prospects for achievement. *Gerontologist, 30*, 626–631.

Simonton, D. K. (1997). Creative productivity: A predictive and explanatory model of career trajectories and landmarks. *Psychological Review, 104,* 66–89.

Simonton, D. K. (1998). Career paths and creative lives: A theoretical perspective on late life potential. In C. E. Adams-Price (Ed.), *Creativity and successful aging: Theoretical and empirical approaches* (pp. 3–18). New York: Springer.

Sinnott, J. (1996). The developmental approach: Postformal thought as adaptive intelligence. In F. Blanchard-Fields & T. M. Hess (Eds.), *Perspectives on cognitive change in adulthood and aging* (pp. 358–383). New York: McGraw-Hill.

Skoog, I., Blennow, K., & Marcusson, J. (1996). Dementia. In J. E. Birren (Ed.), *Encyclopedia of gerontology: Age, aging, and the aged* (Vol. 1, pp. 383–403). San Diego: Academic Press.

Slawinski, E. B., Hartel, D. M., & Kline, D. W. (1993). Self-reported hearing problems in daily life throughout adulthood. *Psychology and Aging, 8,* 552–561.

Slotterback, C. S. (1996). Projections of aging: Impact of generational differences and the aging process on perceptions of adults. *Psychology and Aging, 11,* 552–559.

Smeeding, T. M., Estes, C. L., & Glasse, L. (1999, August). Social Security in the 21st century. More than deficits: Strengthening Security for women. *Gerontology News.*

Smith, A. D. (2006). Memory and memory theory. In R. Schulz (Ed.), *The encyclopedia of aging* (4th ed., pp. 755–759). New York: Springer.

Smith, J., & Baltes, P. B. (1990). Wisdom-related knowledge: Age/cohort differences in response to life-planning problems. *Developmental Psychology, 26,* 494–505.

Smith, J., & Freund, A. M. (2002). The dynamics of possible selves in old age. *Journal of Gerontology: Psychological Sciences, 57B,* P492–P500.

Smith, J., Staudinger, U. M., & Baltes, P. B. (1994). Occupational settings facilitating wisdom-related knowledge: The sample case of clinical psychologists. *Journal of Consulting and Clinical Psychology, 62,* 989–999.

Snowdon, D. A. (1997). Aging and Alzheimer's disease: Lessons from the Nun Study. *Gerontologist, 37,* 150–156.

Solomon, D. H. (1999). The role of aging processes in aging-dependent diseases. In V. L. Bengston & K. W. Schaie (Eds.), *Handbook of theories of aging* (pp. 133–150). New York: Springer.

Somberg, B. L., & Salthouse, T. A. (1982). Divided attention abilities in young and old adults. *Journal of Experimental Psychology: Human Perception and Performance, 8,* 651–663.

Sontag, S. (1972, September 23). The double standard of aging. *Saturday Review,* 29–38.

Sorkin, D. H., & Rook, K. S. (2004). Interpersonal control strivings and vulnerability to negative social exchanges in later life. *Psychology and Aging, 19,* 555–564.

Sorkin, D. H., & Rook, K. S. (2006). Dealing with negative social exchanges in later life: Coping responses, goals, and effectiveness. *Psychology and Aging, 21,* 715–725.

Spearman, C. E. (1927). *The abilities of man.* New York: Macmillan.

Spitze, G., & Logan, J. (1992). Helping as a component of parent–adult child relations. *Research on Aging, 14,* 291–312.

Spitze, G., & Miner, S. (1992). Gender differences in adult child contact among Black elderly parents. *Gerontologist, 32,* 213–218.

Starr, B. D. (2006). Sexuality. In R. Schulz (Ed.), *The encyclopedia of aging* (4th ed., pp. 1067–1072). New York: Springer.

Staudinger, U. M., Kessler, E., & Dörner, J. (2006). Wisdom in social context. In K. W. Schaie & L. L. Carstensen (Eds.), *Social structures, aging, and self-regulation in the elderly* (pp. 33–53). New York: Springer.

Sternberg, R. J. (1985). *Beyond IQ: A triarchic theory of human intelligence.* New York: Cambridge University Press.

Sternberg, R. J. (1996). *Successful intelligence: How practical and creative intelligence determine success in life.* New York: Simon & Schuster.

Sternberg, R. J. (2004). *Psychology* (4th ed.). Belmont, CA: Wadsworth/Thomson Learning.

Sternberg, R. J., & Lubart, T. I. (2001). Wisdom and creativity. In J. E. Birren & K. W. Schaie (Eds.), *Handbook of the psychology of aging* (5th ed., pp. 500–522). San Diego: Academic Press.

Sternberg, R. J., Wagner, R. K., & Okagaki, L. (1993). Practical intelligence: The nature and role of tacit knowledge in work and at school. In J. M. Puckett & H. W. Reese (Eds.), *Mechanisms of everyday cognition* (pp. 205–227). Hillsdale, NJ: Erlbaum.

Sternberg, R. J., Wagner, R. K., Williams, W. M., & Horvath, J. A. (1995). Testing common sense. *American Psychologist, 50*, 912–927.

Sterns, A. A., & Sterns, H. L. (1997). Should there be an affirmative action policy for hiring older persons? Yes. In A. E. Scharlach & L. W. Kaye (Eds.), *Controversial issues in aging* (pp. 35–39). Boston: Allyn & Bacon.

Sterns, H. L., & Sterns., A. A. (2006). Industrial gerontology. In R. Schulz (Ed.), *The encyclopedia of aging* (4th ed., pp. 580–581). New York: Springer.

Stevens, A. (1994). *Jung.* New York: Oxford University Press.

Stine, E. A. L., Soederberg, L. M., & Morrow, D. G. (1996). Language and discourse processing through adulthood. In F. Blanchard-Fields & T. M. Hess (Eds.), *Perspectives on cognitive change in adulthood and aging* (pp. 255–290). New York: McGraw-Hill.

Stine-Morrow, E. A. L., Loveless, M. K., & Soederberg, L. M. (1996). Resource allocation in on-line reading by younger and older adults. *Psychology and Aging, 11*, 475–486.

Stine-Morrow, E. A. L., Noh, S. R., & Shake, M. C. (2006). Memory: Discourse. In R. Schulz (Ed.), *The encyclopedia of aging* (4th ed., pp. 741–744). New York: Springer.

Stoller, E. P., & Longino, C. F., Jr. (2001). "Going home" or "leaving home"? The impact of person and place ties on anticipated counterstream migration. *Gerontologist, 41*, 96–102.

Stone, L. O. (2006). Demography. In R. Schulz (Ed.), *The encyclopedia of aging* (4th ed., pp. 299–302). New York: Springer.

Stones, M., & Stones, L. (2007). Sexuality, sensuality, and intimacy. In J. E. Birren (Ed.), *Encyclopedia of gerontology: Age, aging, and the aged* (2nd ed., Vol. 2, pp. 482–489). Boston: Elsevier Academic Press.

Storandt, M. (2008). Cognitive deficits in the early stages of Alzheimer's disease. *Current Directions in Psychological Science, 17*, 198–202.

Strawbridge, W. J., Wallhagen, M. I., Shema, S. J., & Kaplan, G. A. (2000). Negative consequences of hearing impairment in old age: A longitudinal analysis. *Gerontologist, 40*, 320–326.

Stroop, J. R. (1935). Studies of interference in serial verbal reactions. *Journal of Experimental Psychology, 18*, 643–662.

Sugar, J. A. (2007). Memory, Strategies. In J. E. Birren (Ed.), *Encyclopedia of gerontology: Age, aging, and the aged* (2nd ed., Vol. 2, pp. 145–151). Boston: Elsevier Academic Press.

Sullivan, R. J. (1995). Cardiovascular system. In G. L. Maddox (Ed.), *The encyclopedia of aging* (2nd ed., pp. 133–138). New York: Springer.

Sullivan-Marx, E. M. (1995). Delirium. In G. L. Maddox (Ed.), *The encyclopedia of aging* (2nd ed., pp. 256–259). New York: Springer.

Sunderland, A., Watts, K., Baddeley, A. D., & Harris, J. E. (1986). Subjective memory assessment and test performance in elderly adults. *Journal of Gerontology, 41*, 376–384.

Szinovacz, M. E., & Davey, A. (2004). Honeymoons and joint lunches: Effects of retirement and spouse's employment on depressive symptoms. *Journal of Gerontology: Psychological Sciences, 59B*, P233–P245.

Szinovacz, M. E., & Davey, A. (2005). Predictors of perceptions of involuntary retirement. *Gerontologist, 45*, 36–47.

Szinovacz, M. E., & DeViney, S. (1999). The retiree identity: Gender and race differences. *Journal of Gerontology: Social Sciences, 54B*, S207–S218.

Taranto, M. A. (1989). Facets of wisdom: A theoretical synthesis. *International Journal of Aging and Human Development, 29*, 1–21.

Tasker, G. (2003, October 14). My grandfather (or grandmother) the alcoholic. *Miami Herald*, 10E–12E.

Thomas, J. L. (1990). The grandparent role: A double bind. *International Journal of Aging and Human Development, 31*, 169–177.

Thompson, E. E., & Krause, N. (1998). Living alone and neighborhood characteristics as predictors of social support in late life. *Journal of Gerontology: Social Sciences, 53B*, S354–S364.

Thorson, J. A., & Powell, F. C. (2000). Death anxiety in young and older adults. In A. Tomer (Ed.),

Death attitudes and the older adult: Theories, concepts, and applications (pp. 123–136). Philadelphia: Brunner-Routledge.

Thurstone, L. L. (1938). *Primary Mental Abilities*. Psychometric Monographs (Whole No. 1) Chicago: University of Chicago Press.

Thurstone, L. L., & Thurstone, T. G. (1947). *Primary Mental Abilities Test*. Chicago: Science Research Associates.

Tobin, A. J. (2003). *Asking about life* (2nd ed.). Belmont, CA: Brooks/Cole.

Tomer, A. (2000). Death-related attitudes: Conceptual distinctions. In A. Tomer (Ed.), *Death attitudes and the older adult: Theories, concepts, and applications* (pp. 87–94). Philadelphia: Brunner-Routledge.

Tonna, E. A. (1995). Musculoskeletal system. In G. L. Maddox (Ed.), *The encyclopedia of aging* (2nd ed., pp. 656–658). New York: Springer.

Tower, R. B., & Kasl, S. V. (1996). Gender, marital closeness, and depressive symptoms in elderly couples. *Journal of Gerontology: Psychological Sciences, 51B*, P115–P129.

Troll, L. E., & Skaff, M. M. (1997). Perceived continuity of self in very old age. *Psychology and Aging, 12*, 162–169.

Tucker, J. S., Friedman, H. S., Tsai, C. M., & Martin, L. R. (1995). Playing with pets and longevity among older people. *Psychology and Aging, 10*, 3–7.

Tucker, J. S., Wingard, D. L., Friedman, H. S., & Schwartz, J. W. (1996). Marital history at midlife as a predictor of longevity: Alternative explanations to the protective effect of marriage. *Health Psychology, 15*, 94–101.

Tulving, E., & Thomson, D. M. (1973). Encoding specificity and retrieval processes in episodic memory. *Psychological Review, 80*, 352–373.

Tun, P. A. (1998). Fast noisy speech: Age differences in processing rapid speech with background noise. *Psychology and Aging, 13*, 424–434.

Tun, P. A., & Wingfield, A. (1997). Language and communication: Fundamentals of speech communication and language processing in old age. In A. D. Fisk & W. A. Rogers (Eds.), *Handbook of human factors and the older adult* (pp. 125–149). San Diego: Academic Press.

Tun, P. A., & Wingfield, A. (1999). One voice too many: Adult age differences in language processing with different types of distracting sounds. *Journal of Gerontology: Psychological Sciences, 54B*, P317–P327.

Turk-Charles, S., Meyerowitz, B. E., & Gatz, M. (1997). Age differences in information-seeking among cancer patients. *International Journal of Aging and Human Development, 45*, 85–98.

Turker, J. (1996). Premature aging. In J. E. Birren (Ed.), *Encyclopedia of gerontology: Age, aging, and the aged* (Vol. 2, pp. 341–354). San Diego: Academic Press.

Turra, C. M., & Goldman, N. (2007). Socioeconomic differences in mortality among U.S. adults: Insights into the Hispanic paradox. *Journal of Gerontology: Social Sciences, 62B*, S184–S192.

Uchino, B. N., Berg, C. A., Smith, T. W., Pearce, G., & Skinner, M. (2006). Age-related differences in ambulatory blood pressure during daily stress: Evidence for greater blood pressure reactivity with age. *Psychology and Aging, 21*, 231–239.

Uhlenberg, P. (2006). Migration. In R. Schulz (Ed.), *The encyclopedia of aging* (4th ed., pp. 777–780). New York: Springer.

Umberson, D., Wortman, C. B., & Kessler, R. C. (1992). Widowhood and depression: Explaining long-term gender differences in vulnerability. *Journal of Health and Social Behavior, 33*, 10–24.

U.S. Census Bureau (2002). *Statistical Abstract of the United States, 2002*. Washington, DC: US Government Printing Office.

van Solinge, H., & Henkens, K. (2008). Adjustment to and satisfaction with retirement: Two of a kind? *Psychology and Aging, 23*, 422–434.

Vasselli, J. R., Weindruch, R., Heymsfield, S. B., Pi-Sunyer, F., Boozer, C. N., Yi, N., et al. (2005). Intentional weight loss reduces mortality rate in a rodent model of dietary obesity. *Obesity Research, 13*, 693–702.

Vercruyssen, M. (1997). Movement control and speed of behavior. In A. D. Fisk & W. A. Rogers (Eds.), *Handbook of human factors and the older adult* (pp. 55–86). San Diego: Academic Press.

Verhaeghen, P. (2006). Reaction time. In R. Schulz (Ed.), *The encyclopedia of aging* (4th ed., pp. 1006–1009). New York: Springer.

Verhaeghen, P., Cerella, J., & Basak, C. (2006). Aging, task complexity, and efficiency modes: The influence of working memory involvement in age differences in response times for verbal and visuospatial tasks. *Aging, Neuropsychology, and Cognition, 13*, 254–280.

Verhaeghen, P., Geraerts, N., & Marcoen, A. (2000). Memory complaints, coping, and well-being in old age: A systemic approach. *Gerontologist, 40*, 540–548.

Vinick, B. H., & Ekerdt, D. J. (1991). Retirement: What happens to husband–wife relationships? *Journal of Geriatric Psychiatry, 24*, 23–40.

VonDras, D. D., & Blumenthal, H. T. (2000). Biological, social-environmental, and psychological dialecticism: An integrated model of aging. *Basic and Applied Social Psychology, 22*, 199–212.

Waldman, D. A., & Avolio, B. J. (1986). A meta-analysis of age differences in job performance. *Journal of Applied Psychology, 71*, 33–38.

Walji, S., & Badley, E. M. (2007). Arthritis and rheumatic diseases. In J. E. Birren (Ed.), *Encyclopedia of gerontology: Age, aging, and the aged* (2nd ed., Vol. 1, pp. 90–99). Boston: Elsevier Academic Press.

Walker, A. J., Acock, A. C., Bowman, S. R., & Li, F. (1996). Amount of care given and caregiving satisfaction: A latent growth curve analysis. *Journal of Gerontology: Psychological Sciences, 51B*, P130–P142.

Walker, A. J., Martin, S. S., & Jones, L. L. (1992). The benefits and costs of caregiving and care receiving for daughters and mothers. *Journal of Gerontology: Social Sciences, 47*, S130–S139.

WCCO (2008, July 22). New clue to Alzheimer's found in protein. Retrieved March 9, 2009, from http://wcco.com/national/Alzheimer's.disease.clue.2.754115.html

Weg, R. B. (1996). Sexuality, sensuality, and intimacy. In J. E. Birren (Ed.), *Encyclopedia of gerontology: Age, aging, and the aged* (Vol. 2, pp. 479–488). San Diego: Academic Press.

Weindruch, R. (1996, January). Caloric restriction and aging. *Scientific American*, 46–52.

Weiner, B. (1993). On sin versus sickness: A theory of perceived responsibility and social motivation. *American Psychologist, 48*, 957–965.

Weisenberger, J. M. (2007). Touch and proprioception. In J. E. Birren (Ed.), *Encyclopedia of gerontology: Age, aging, and the aged* (2nd ed., Vol. 2, pp. 641–652). Boston: Elsevier Academic Press.

Weiss, R. (1997, November). Aging: New answers to old questions. *National Geographic, 192*, 10–31.

Weiss, R. S., & Bass, S. A. (2002). Introduction. In R. S. Weiss & S. A. Bass (Eds.), *Challenges of the third age: Meaning and purpose in later life* (pp. 3–12). New York: Oxford University Press.

West, R. L. (1996). An application of prefrontal cortex function theory to cognitive aging. *Psychological Bulletin, 120*, 272–292.

West, R. L., Bagwell, D. K., & Dark-Freudeman, A. (2005). Memory and goal setting: The response of older and younger adult to positive and objective feedback. *Psychology and Aging, 20*, 195–201.

West, R. L., Welch, D. C., & Thorn, R. M. (2001). Effects of goal-setting and feedback on memory performance and beliefs among older and younger adults. *Psychology and Aging, 16*, 240–250.

Whitehouse, P. J. (2007a). Dementia. In J. E. Birren (Ed.), *Encyclopedia of gerontology: Age, aging, and the aged* (2nd ed., Vol. 1, pp. 368–374). Boston: Elsevier Academic Press.

Whitehouse, P. J. (2007b). Dementia: Alzheimer's. In J. E. Birren (Ed.), *Encyclopedia of gerontology: Age, aging, and the aged* (2nd ed., Vol. 1, pp. 374–379). Boston: Elsevier Academic Press.

Williams, S. A., Denney, N. W., & Schadler, M. (1983). Elderly adults' perception of their own cognitive development during the adult years. *International Journal of Aging and Human Development, 16*, 147–158.

Willis, S. L. (1996). Everyday cognitive competence in elderly persons: Conceptual issues and empirical findings. *Gerontologist, 36*, 595–601.

Willis, S. L., & Marsiske, M. (1993). *Manual for the Everyday Problems Test*. University Park, PA: Pennsylvania State University Press.

Willis, S. L., Tennstedt, S. L., Marsiske, M., Ball, K., Elias, J., Koepke, K. M., et al. (2006). Long-term effects of cognitive training on everyday functional outcomes in older adults. *Journal of the American Medical Association, 296*, 2805–2814.

Wingfield, A. (1995). Language comprehension. In G. L. Maddox (Ed.), *The encyclopedia of aging* (2nd ed., p. 538). New York: Springer.

Wingfield, A. (1996). Cognitive factors in auditory performance: Context, speed of processing, and constraints of memory. *Journal of the American Academy of Audiology, 7,* 175–182.

Wingfield, A., Prentice, K., Koh, C. K., & Little, D. (2000). Neural change, cognitive reserve, and behavioral compensation in rapid encoding and memory for spoken language in adult aging. In L. T. Connor & L. K. Obler (Eds.), *Neurobehavior of language and cognition: Studies of normal aging and brain damage* (pp. 3–21). Boston: Kluwer Academic.

Wingfield, A., & Stine-Morrow, E. A. L. (2000). Language and speech. In F. I. M. Craik & T. A. Salthouse (Eds.), *Handbook of aging and cognition* (2nd ed., pp. 359–416). Mahwah, NJ: Erlbaum.

Wingfield, A., Tun, P. A., & McCoy, S. L. (2005). Hearing loss in older adulthood: What it is and how it interacts with cognitive performance. *Current Directions in Psychological Science, 14,* 144–148.

Wingfield, A., Tun, P. A., & Rosen, M. J. (1995). Age differences in veridical and reconstructive recall of syntactically and randomly segmented speech. *Journal of Gerontology: Psychological Sciences, 50B,* P257–P266.

Wink, P., & Scott, J. (2005). Does religiousness buffer against the fear of death and dying in late adulthood? Findings from a longitudinal study. *Journal of Gerontology: Psychological Sciences, 60B,* P207–P214.

Wolf, D. A., & Longino, C. F., Jr. (2005). Our "increasingly mobile society"? The curious persistence of a false belief. *Gerontologist, 45,* 5–11.

Wolf, R. S. (1996). Understanding elder abuse and neglect. *Aging, 367,* 4–13. Administration on Aging, U.S. Department of Health and Human Services.

Wong, P. T., & Watt, L. M. (1991). What types of reminiscence are associated with successful aging? *Psychology and Aging, 6,* 272–279.

Woodruff-Pak, D. S. (1988). *Psychology and aging.* Englewood Cliffs, NJ: Prentice Hall.

Woodruff-Pak, D. S. (1989). Aging and intelligence: Changing perspectives in the twentieth century. *Journal of Aging Studies, 3,* 91–118.

Woodruff-Pak, D. S., & Papka, M. (1999). Theories of neuropsychology and aging. In V. L. Bengston & K. W. Schaie (Eds.), *Handbook of theories of aging* (pp. 113–132). New York: Springer.

Woods, R. T. (1999). Mental health problems in late life. In R. T. Woods (Ed.), *Psychological problems of ageing* (pp. 73–110). Chichester, England: John Wiley.

Wortman, C. B., & Silver, R. C. (1990). Successful mastery of bereavement and widowhood: A life-course perspective. In P. B. Baltes & M. M. Baltes (Eds.), *Successful aging: Perspectives from the behavioral sciences* (pp. 225–264). Cambridge: Cambridge University Press.

Yardley, L., Bishop, F., Beyer, N., Hauser, K., Kempen, G., Piot-Ziegler, C., et al. (2006). Older people's views of falls-prevention interventions in six European countries. *Gerontologist, 46,* 650–660.

Yardley, L., Donovan-Hall, M., Francis, K., & Todd, C. (2007). Attitudes and beliefs that predict older people's intention to undertake strength and balance training. *Journal of Gerontology: Psychological Sciences, 62B,* P119–P125.

Yesavage, J. A. (1982–1983). Development and validation of a geriatric depression screening scale: A preliminary report. *Journal of Psychiatric Research, 17,* 37–49.

Yoon, C., Hasher, L., Feinberg, F., Rahhal, T. A., & Winocur, G. (2000). Cross-cultural differences in memory: The role of culture-based stereotypes about aging. *Psychology and Aging, 15,* 694–704.

Zacks, R. T., Hasher, L., & Li, K. Z. H. (2000). Human memory. In F. I. M. Craik & T. A. Salthouse (Eds.), *The handbook of aging and cognition* (2nd ed., pp. 293–357). Mahwah, NJ: Erlbaum.

Zarit, S. H., & Haynie, D. A. (2000). Introduction to clinical issues. In S. K. Whitbourne (Ed.), *Psychopathology in later adulthood* (pp. 1–26). New York: John Wiley.

Zarit, S. H., Johansson, L., & Jarrott, S. E. (1998). Family caregiving: Stresses, social programs, and clinical interventions. In I. H. Nordhus, G. R. VandenBos, S. Berg, & P. Fromholt (Eds.), *Clinical geropsychology* (pp.345–360).Washington, DC: American Psychological Association.

Zarit, S. H., Stephens, M. A. P., Townsend, A., & Greene, R. (1998). Stress reduction for family caregivers: Effects of adult day care use. *Journal of Gerontology: Social Sciences, 53B,* S267–S277.

Zwahr, M. D., Park, D. C., & Shifren, K. (1999). Judgments about estrogen replacement therapy: The role of age, cognitive abilities, and beliefs. *Psychology and Aging, 14,* 179–191.

Credits and Sources

The editors and publisher gratefully acknowledge the permission granted to reproduce the copyright material in this book.

Figures

4.2 C. K. Sigelman & E. A. Rider, *Life-Span Human Development: An Integrated Topical/Chronological Approach* (4th ed.), Belmont, CA: Wadsworth/Thomson Learning © 2003 by Wadsworth, a part of Cengage Learning, Inc. Reproduced by permission, http://www.cengage.com/permissions   111

4.3 Adapted from A. J. Tobin, *Asking About Life* (2nd ed.), Belmont, CA: Brooks/Cole © 2003 by Brooks/Cole, a part of Cengage Learning, Inc. Reproduced by permission, http://www.cengage.com/permissions   115

5.1 R. C. Atkinson & R. M. Shiffrin, "Human Memory: A Proposed System and Its Control Processes," in K. W. Spence & J. T. Spence (Eds.), *The Psychology of Learning and Motivation*, Vol. 2, New York: Academic Press, pp. 89–105 © 1968   136

5.2 A. D. Baddeley, *Human Memory: Theory and Practice*, Boston: Allyn & Bacon © 1990 by Taylor & Francis Group LLC – Books. Reproduced with permission of Taylor & Francis Group LLC – Books in the format Textbook via Copyright Clearance Center. Reprinted by permission   137

6.1 P. B. Baltes, U. M. Staudinger, & U. Lindenberger, "Lifespan Psychology: Theory and Application to Intellectual Functioning," *Annual Review of Psychology, 50* © 1999 by Annual Reviews. Reprinted by permission of the authors and Annual Reviews, http://www.Annualreviews.org   170

6.4 K. W. Schaie (1994), "The Course of Adult Intellectual Development," *American Psychologist, 49*, 304–313 © 1994 by the American Psychological Association. Reprinted by permission of the publisher   178

7.1 K. W. Schaie & S. L. Willis, "A Stage Theory Model of Adult Cognitive Development Revisited," in R. L. Rubinstein, M. Moss, & M. H. Kleban (Eds.), *The Many Dimensions of Aging*, New York: Springer, pp. 175–193 © 2000 by K. W. Schaie and S. L. Willis. Reprinted by kind permission of the authors   202

7.3 From W. Dennis, "Creative Productivity Between the Ages of 20 and 80 Years," *Journal of Gerontology, 21*, 1–8 © 1966 by The Gerontological Society of America. Reproduced with permission of The Gerontological Society of America in the format Textbook via Copyright Clearance Center   210

8.1 H. R. Markus & A. R. Herzog, "The Role of the Self-Concept in Aging," in K. W. Schaie & M. P. Lawton (Eds.), *Annual Review of Gerontology and Geriatrics*, Vol. 11, New York: Springer, pp. 110–143 © 1991 by Springer Publishing Company, Inc. Reproduced with the permission of Springer Publishing Company, LLC, New York, NY 10036   252

9.1 L. L. Carstensen, J. J. Gross, & H. H. Fung, "The Social Context of Emotional Experience," in K. W. Schaie & M. P. Lawton (Eds.), *Annual Review of Gerontology and Geriatrics*, Vol. 17, New York: Springer, pp. 325–352 © 1997 by Springer Publishing Company, Inc. Reproduced with the permission of Springer Publishing Company, LLC, New York, NY 10036   266

9.4 B. C. Rollins & H. Feldman, "Marital Satisfaction Over the Family Life Cycle," *Journal of Marriage and the Family, 32*, 20–28 © 1970 by the National Council on Family Relations. Reprinted by permission of Blackwell Publishing Ltd   275

10.1 M. W. Riley, "Aging and Society: Past, Present, and Future," *Gerontologist, 34*, 436–446 © 1994 by The Gerontological Society of America. Reproduced with permission of The Gerontological Society of America in the format Textbook via Copyright Clearance Center   297

12.1 C. A. Corr, C. M. Nabe, & D. M. Corr (2009), *Death and Dying, Life and Living* (6th ed.), Belmont, CA: Wadsworth Cengage Learning © 2009 by Wadsworth, a part of Cengage Learning, Inc. Reproduced by permission, www.cengage.com/permissions   360

Tables

1.1 Population Reference Bureau, *World Population Data Sheet* © 2007. Reprinted by permission of the Population Reference Bureau   14

2.2 Adapted from P. B. Baltes, "Theoretical Propositions of Life-Span Developmental Psychology: On the Dynamics Between Growth and Decline," *Developmental Psychology, 23*, 611–626 © 1987 by the American Psychological Association. Reprinted by permission of the publisher   38

3.5 T. Perls & M. H. Silver, "Will You Live to be 100?" *Modern Maturity* (November/December) © 1999 by the American Association of Retired Persons (AARP). Reprinted with permission   78

4.1 T. Y. Arbuckle & D. P. Gold, "Aging, Inhibition, and Verbosity," *Journal of Gerontology: Psychological Sciences, 48*, P225–P232 © 1993 by The Gerontological Society of America. Reproduced with permission of The Gerontological Society of America in the format Textbook via Copyright Clearance Center   124

6.3 Adapted from D. S. Woodruff-Pak, *Psychology and Aging*, Englewood Cliffs, NJ: Prentice Hall, 1988, and D. S. Woodruff-Pak, "Aging and Intelligence: Changing Perspectives in the Twentieth Century," *Journal of Aging Studies, 3* (1989), 91–118 © 1989 by Elsevier Science, Inc. All rights reserved. Reprinted with permission from Elsevier   176

6.4 C. A. Berg & R. J. Sternberg, "Adults' Conceptions of Intelligence Across the Adult Life Span," *Psychology and Aging, 7*, 221–231 © 1992 by the American Psychological Association. Reprinted by permission of the publisher   188

6.5 Adapted from S. L. Willis, "Everyday Cognitive Competence in Elderly Persons: Conceptual Issues and Empirical Findings," *Gerontologist, 36*, 595–601 © 1996 by The Gerontological Society of America. Reproduced with permission of The Gerontological

Society of America in the format Textbook via Copyright
Clearance Center 191

7.1 K. W. Schaie, "Toward a Stage Theory of Adult Cognitive
Development," *Aging and Human Development, 8*, 129–138 © 1977
by Baywood Publishing Company, Inc. Reproduced with permission
of Baywood Publishing Company, Inc., in the format Textbook via
Copyright Clearance Center 201

7.2 Adapted from J. B. Chap, "Moral Judgment in Middle and
Late Adulthood: The Effects of Age-Appropriate Moral Dilemmas
and Spontaneous Role Taking," *International Journal of Aging and
Human Development, 22*, 161–172 © 1986 by Baywood Publishing
Company, Inc. Reproduced with permission of Baywood
Publishing Company, Inc., in the format Textbook via Copyright
Clearance Center 223

8.2 Adapted from R. R. McCrae & P. T. Costa, Jr., "Personality
Trait Structure as a Human Universal," *American Psychologist, 52*,
509–516 © 1997 by the American Psychological Association.
Reprinted by permission of the publisher 244

8.3 M. L. Hummert, T. A. Garstka, J. L. Shaner, & S. Strahm (1994),
"Stereotypes of the Elderly Held by Young, Middle-Aged, and
Elderly Adults," *Journal of Gerontology: Psychological Sciences, 49*,
P240–P249 © 1994 by The Gerontological Society of America.
Reproduced with permission of The Gerontological Society of
America in the format Textbook via Copyright Clearance Center 249

9.2 D. T. Gold, "Sibling Relationships in Old Age: A Typology,"
International Journal of Aging and Human Development, 28, 37–51
© 1989 by Baywood Publishing Company, Inc. Reproduced with
permission of Baywood Publishing Company, Inc., in the format
Textbook via Copyright Clearance Center. And from D. T. Gold,
"Late-Life Sibling Relationships: Does Race Affect Typological
Distribution?" *Gerontologist, 30*, 741–748 © 1990 by The
Gerontological Society of America. Reproduced with permission of
The Gerontological Society of America in the format Textbook
via Copyright Clearance Center 286

9.3 Adapted from M. S. Lantz, " Elder Abuse and Neglect," in
R. Schulz (Ed.), *The Encyclopedia of Aging* (4th ed.), New York:
Springer, pp. 352–354 © 2006 by Springer Publishing Company,
Inc. Reproduced with permission of Springer Publishing Company,
LLC, New York, NY 10036 290

10.2 D. J. Ekerdt, S. DeViney, & K. Kosloski, "Profiling Plans for
Retirement," *Journal of Gerontology: Social Sciences, 51B*, S140–S149
© 1996 by The Gerontological Society of America. Reproduced
with permission of The Gerontological Society of America in the
format Textbook via Copyright Clearance Center 312

10.3 Adapted from H. Kendig & J. Pynoos, "Housing," in J. E. Birren
(Ed.), *Encyclopedia of Gerontology: Age, Aging, and the Aged*, Vol. 1,
San Diego: Academic Press, pp. 703–713 © 1996 by Elsevier.
Reprinted by permission of the publisher 319

11.1   Adapted from S. M. Monroe & A. D. Simons, "Diathesis–Stress
        Theories in the Context of Life Stress Research: Implications
        for Depressive Disorders," *Psychological Bulletin, 110,* 406–425 ©
        1991 by the American Psychological Association. Reprinted by
        permission of the publisher   332

Photographs

© Bettmann/Corbis   8
© Monkey Business Images/Shutterstock   11
© Lisa F. Young/Shutterstock   11
© Larry Williams/Corbis   19
© Hulton Archive/Getty Images   45
© Monkey Business Images/Shutterstock   45
Courteney Arciaga, San Diego, 1997. Photo © Karen Kasmauski/Corbis   72
© Eduardo Jose Bernadino/istockphoto   87
© Robert Essel/Surf/Corbis   112
© Paul Barton/Corbis   125
© Glenda Powers/istockphoto   139
© iofoto/Shutterstock   151
© Pali Rao/istockphoto   184
© Chuck Savage/Corbis   190
© Guy Cali/Corbis   206
© Christopher Jones/istockphoto   211
© Gary Sludden/istockphoto   237
Photograph supplied by Chris Cardone. Courtesy of Elaine Norelli.   253
© Joan T. Erber   281
© Joan T. Erber   284
Anderson Ross/Stockbyte/Getty Images   298
© Stephanie L. Erber   319
© Andrew Murphy/Alamy   340
Photograph supplied by Chris Cardone   352
© Carme Balcells/Shutterstock   374

Name Index

Subject Index

Note: Page numbers in **bold** type refer to the Glossary